Great
Musicals
of the
American Theatre

Also by Stanley Richards

BOOKS:

Ten Great Musicals of the American Theatre
The Best Short Plays 1976
The Best Short Plays 1975
The Best Short Plays 1974
The Best Short Plays 1973
The Best Short Plays 1972
The Best Short Plays 1971
The Best Short Plays 1970
The Best Short Plays 1969
The Best Short Plays 1968
America on Stage: Ten Great Plays of American History
Best Mystery and Suspense Plays of the Modern Theatre
10 Classic Mystery and Suspense Plays of the Modern Theatre
Best Plays of the Sixties
Best Short Plays of the World Theatre: 1968–1973
Best Short Plays of the World Theatre: 1958–1967
Modern Short Comedies from Broadway and London
Canada on Stage

PLAYS:

Through a Glass, Darkly
August Heat
Sun Deck
Tunnel of Love
Journey to Bahia
O Distant Land
Mood Piece

Mr. Bell's Creation
The Proud Age
Once to Every Boy
Half-Hour, Please
Know Your Neighbor
Gin and Bitterness
The Hills of Bataan

District of Columbia

Great Musicals of the American Theatre

VOLUME TWO

Edited, with an introduction
and notes on the
plays, authors and composers, by

STANLEY RICHARDS

Chilton Book Company
Radnor, Pennsylvania

Copyright © 1976 by Stanley Richards
First Edition   *All Rights Reserved*

Published in Radnor, Pa., by Chilton Book Company
and simultaneously in Don Mills, Ontario, Canada
by Nelson Canada Limited

Designed by Carole L. De Crescenzo

Manufactured in the United States of America

Library of Congress Cataloging in Publication Data

Main entry under title:

Great musicals of the American theatre, volume two.

   Includes the librettos of Leave it to me, Lady in the
dark, Lost in the stars, Wonderful town, Fiorello, Camelot,
Man of La Mancha, Cabaret, Applause, and A little night
music.
   I. Musical revues, comedies, etc.—Librettos.
I. Richards, Stanley—
ML48.T37   782.8′1′2   75–29441
ISBN 0–8019–6177–1

2 3 4 5 6 7 8   7 6 5 4 3 2 1

for
Bella Spewack
and
John D. Kelly

CONTENTS

ix *&*   *Introduction*

1 *&*   *LEAVE IT TO ME!*

> *Book:* Bella and Samuel Spewack
> *Music and Lyrics:* Cole Porter

55 *&*   *LADY IN THE DARK*

> *Book:* Moss Hart
> *Lyrics:* Ira Gershwin
> *Music:* Kurt Weill

125 *&*   *LOST IN THE STARS*

> *Book and Lyrics:* Maxwell Anderson
> *Music:* Kurt Weill

177 *&*   *WONDERFUL TOWN*

> *Book:* Joseph Fields and Jerome Chodorov
> *Lyrics:* Betty Comden and Adolph Green
> *Music:* Leonard Bernstein

239 *&*   *FIORELLO!*

> *Book:* Jerome Weidman and George Abbott
> *Lyrics:* Sheldon Harnick
> *Music:* Jerry Bock

307 *&*   *CAMELOT*

> *Book and Lyrics:* Alan Jay Lerner
> *Music:* Frederick Loewe

365 *&*   *MAN OF LA MANCHA*

> *Book:* Dale Wasserman
> *Lyrics:* Joe Darion
> *Music:* Mitch Leigh

411 *&*   *CABARET*

> *Book:* Joe Masteroff
> *Lyrics:* Fred Ebb
> *Music:* John Kander

461 & *APPLAUSE*

       Book: Betty Comden and Adolph Green
       Lyrics: Lee Adams
       Music: Charles Strouse

527 & *A LITTLE NIGHT MUSIC*

       Book: Hugh Wheeler
       Music and Lyrics: Stephen Sondheim

INTRODUCTION

The success of this editor's earlier collection of musicals (published in 1973) prompted the compilation of this second volume, and while working on the manuscript of this book, once again I joyously relived some of the American musical theatre's most cherished moments. Songs, dances and production numbers sprung to immediate recall, great musical performances passed before my eyes, laughter in the theatre repeatedly came to mind, emotional reactions were just as spontaneous as ever while going over the texts and lyrics. In short, these ten musicals proved to be as gloriously entertaining and absorbing on the typewritten and/or printed page as they had been on the Broadway stage where I initially became acquainted with them.

The American musical has brought enchantment to millions of theatregoers. For the statistically minded, since 1900 to mid-1975, 1,663 major musicals were mounted on Broadway. This figure does not include the myriad off-Broadway presentations that have dominated that area in the past two decades or more. Nor does it represent those ambitious productions that unfortunately capsized on the road between their various tryout centers and the New York stage.

Indisputably, not all of them were successful, for the musical theatre can be as capricious as the dramatic stage. Indeed, to cite one recent example, there is the currently running *The Wiz*. A black, soul version of L. Frank Baum's 1900 classic, *The Wonderful Wizard of Oz*, it encountered countless difficulties during its pre-Broadway tryout tour as well as an operating loss estimated at about $300,000. It had no stars, no theatre parties and a minimal advance sale. But the powers in charge had faith and persisted, making many alterations on its somewhat tenuous journey to Manhattan. Then a miracle happened. Through word-of-mouth (and a clever advertising campaign), *The Wiz*, after its rather uncertain opening, started to steadily climb in audience attendance and, as of this writing, is in its twenty-fourth week, playing to capacity audiences and record-breaking grosses. To further justify the faith of its creators, *The Wiz* won seven Antoinette Perry (Tony) Awards including one for best musical of the season.

On the other hand, there have been some highly-touted musicals (with established stars and noted contributors of material) that could not sustain a run after their pre-booked theatre parties were ended. It is difficult to determine in advance just what will strike a successful chord or a sour note, but one factor is fairly evident: audience acceptance is the final arbiter.

The American musical today represents bigger "business" than any other form of theatre, and is served by the most eminent librettists, lyricists, composers, directors, choreographers and designers. If a musical is a success, its original cast albums and recordings of its songs sell in vast quantities; a film generally is made; touring companies are organized; it is produced in London and other foreign countries; and it may well be taken into the repertory alongside the classical operettas in European houses that normally are geared for opera.

With a few rare exceptions, successful musicals have a greater durability and longevity than straight plays. In addition to providing the major portion of Broadway's annual grosses (as well as those of other national theatre centers), they are performed by touring road companies, at dinner theatres, mammoth outdoor playhouses and indoor arenas, on the summer stock circuit and finally, by community, educational and amateur companies. And then, of course, there are the frequent first-class professional revivals of the most successful works which bring them to full circle. There is scarcely an area in the United States (and in most parts of the world) that has not been exposed to the best of our musical theatre.

In the 1930's and even into the 1940's, it was still possible to purchase an orchestra seat for a musical for the sum of $4.40. Today, those same seats may go for as high as $17.50, yet they still manage to attract and entice audiences which illustrates the vital, vibrant and magnetic art of our musical theatre.

The ten musicals contained within these pages tallied 8,265 performances in their original New York engagements. What went beyond—with countless revivals, road, stock and amateur performances and foreign productions—only God and the musicals' copyright holders can determine. (For critical approbation and listings of various awards, please see Editor's Notes at the beginning of each play.)

Ever since 1932, when the Pulitzer Prize was awarded to *Of Thee I Sing*, the American musical has been regarded as serious dramatic literature worthy of endurance, not only on the stage but also on the printed page.

It is therefore the hope of this editor to once again perpetuate in print and entertain readers with ten of the finest examples of the American musical theatre, which continues to command the admiration and respect of the entire world.

Stanley Richards

LEAVE IT TO ME!

Book by Bella *and* Samuel Spewack
Music and Lyrics by Cole Porter

Editor's Notes

A jubilant musical, *Leave It to Me!* made history in a number of ways: it was the first musical written by Bella and Samuel Spewack (and their initial association with Cole Porter); it reunited the team of William Gaxton and Victor Moore who scored in the 1932 Pulitzer Prize musical, *Of Thee I Sing* (published in this editor's earlier collection); it converted the indomitable and spirited Sophie Tucker from a vaudeville and nightclub single into a musical comedy star; and it rocketed an unknown singer, Mary Martin, to instant stardom. Her delivery of "My Heart Belongs to Daddy," while shedding her furs and other raiment in a simulated striptease at a wayside Siberian railroad station is still regarded as one of the most sensational debuts in American musical comedy history. And to add to the event, there was a young dancer in the show who also was making his debut: Gene Kelly.

Although the original playbill does not state the fact, many critics described *Leave It to Me!* as a musical version of the Spewacks' earlier comedy, *Clear All Wires.* Bella Spewack asserts that this is not quite so, "the musical just *took off* from *Clear All Wires.*" Actually, it all began aboard a French ocean liner. The Spewacks and William Gaxton and his wife were fellow passengers and during the course of the voyage, Gaxton approached the noted writing team with "What about doing a musical?" Mrs. Spewack recalls that "Sam reacted as if he couldn't hear. I said, 'we'll pick it up later.' " Pick it up they did and it became one of the biggest and most delightful musical hits of the 1930's.

The drama critics, in the main, greeted the arrival of *Leave It to Me!* with almost rapturous approval. Brooks Atkinson of *The New York Times* described it as "a handsome carnival that adds merriment to the season." John Mason Brown noted in the *New York Post* that: "*Leave It to Me!* comes as a rewarding example of professional Broadway at its best . . . Its spirit is gay, topical, likable and irreverent. It contains many amusing lines and convulsing situations. Then, too, it is punctuated by some admirable Cole Porter lyrics, and by some of the same Mr. Porter's gayer melodies."

John Anderson (New York *Evening Journal*) termed it "A musical madhouse— a winner by a laugh-slide. Producer Vinton Freedley has added another to his list of blue ribbon musicals, a large and lavish show, light-hearted and light-footed, built around the Spewacks' hilarious farce of some seasons back called *Clear All Wires* . . . In gaiety and inventiveness Cole Porter's score goes back to the upper brackets expected of our most urbane music-maker, and sets off some deftly amusing tunes . . . Broadway has a new ambassador of good will in a handsome and amusing show that at last makes diplomats as funny as they look."

Leave It to Me! was in every way an opulent production, studded with comedy, witty songs and beauty, and swiftly paced. (Indeed, Brooks Atkinson commented that: "As the director, Samuel Spewack has developed speed-mania and will doubtlessly get his summons from the police!")

The musical (published here for the first time) ran in New York for 307 performances, then embarked on a lengthy road tour.

In 1948, the Spewacks and Cole Porter joined forces once again, this time to create the now legendary musical *Kiss Me, Kate*, which ran for more than 1,000 performances in New York, garnered dozens of awards and is still being performed in many foreign countries. (NOTE: *Kiss Me, Kate* is included in this editor's previous volume.)

After three previous attempts, *The Solitaire Man* (1926), *Poppa* (1928), and *The War Song* (1928), the writing team of Bella and Samuel Spewack was firmly established in 1932 with the successful production of *Clear All Wires.* Then in

1934, they wrote a drama, *Spring Song.* According to Mrs. Spewack, "When people came out of the theatre in tears, I would say, 'don't cry, it's only a play.' " Thereafter, the Spewacks stuck to comedy.

How did their collaboration start? As Mrs. Spewack wrote in a moving remembrance to her husband published in the *Dramatists Guild Quarterly* after his death in 1971: "I suggested after a series of long walks that we be partners. We were then nineteen. For some reason, you misconstrued that and proposed marriage. All I had in mind was to start a magazine for the Pullman people to distribute free to its riders. We had railroads then.

"You had a steady job on the *New York World*, and I an unsteady and frequently payless job on the *New York Call.* I wrote short stories, all tragic or fantasy which sold from time to time but not enough to support my mother and half-brother. You always accused me of being stage-struck, Sam. I never wanted to act, but writing for the theatre was something else. I started writing one-act plays, and then three-acters later in Berlin.

"Our actual play collaboration didn't really take hold until after our return to the United States after four years of Moscow and Berlin. (NOTE: Mrs. Spewack was assistant to her husband who represented the *New York World* as foreign correspondent in Russia and Germany from 1922 to 1926.) We were broke. That's when you collaborated and took over with your brand of philosophical and political comedy, but it met with the same reaction as my unmitigated tragedies: not commercial, not box-office. So the various agents told us. That's when I picked up our plays and tackled theatrical offices myself."

Once Mrs. Spewack handled the reins, things began to happen and during the course of their collaboration they turned out a dozen plays. Among them were: *Boy Meets Girl* (which opened in November, 1935, and ran for 669 performances), *Miss Swan Expects* (1939), *Woman Bites Dog* (1946), and *My Three Angels* (from the French of Albert Husson, 1953).

The Spewacks also collaborated on a number of screenplays, including, *My Favorite Wife, Three Loves Has Nancy, The Cat and the Fiddle, Weekend at the Waldorf,* as well as doing the screen versions of several of their plays.

On his own, Mr. Spewack contributed to the theatre *Two Blind Mice* (1949), *The Golden State* (1950), *Under the Sycamore Tree* (1952), and *Once There Was a Russian* (1961). He also published novels and short stories; and during World War II, he wrote and produced for the government the highly acclaimed, full-length documentary, *The World at War.*

One of the twentieth century's outstanding creators of words and music, Cole Porter (1891–1964) was born in Peru, Indiana. His grandfather was a wealthy lumber merchant and the young Cole grew up in an ambience of luxury. His mother, Kate, supervised his early musical training, having him study the violin and, later, the piano.

In 1909, he entered Yale and during his tenure there wrote a number of football songs, two of which were to become famous: "Bingo Eli Yale" and "Bull Dog." He also was president of the Yale Glee Club and created several successful campus shows. Following his graduation in 1913, he attended Harvard Law School but after a year he abandoned the idea of pursuing law and transferred to the School of Music at Harvard.

His first Broadway musical was *See America First* which had a fleeting engagement in 1916. After an absence of several years, he was represented again on the New York stage with songs for the revue *Hitchy-Koo of 1919.* He next contributed material to the *Greenwich Village Follies of 1924.* But it was the 1928 musical, *Paris,* that firmly established him as the grand sophisticate of songwriters.

The Porter touch highlighted many shows after that significant year. In addition to *Leave It to Me* and *Kiss Me, Kate*, there were: *Fifty Million Frenchmen* (1929), *The New Yorkers* (1930), *Gay Divorce* (1932), *Nymph Errant* (1933), *Anything Goes* (1934), *Jubilee* (1935), *Red, Hot and Blue!* (1936), *You Never Know* (1938), *Panama Hattie* (1940), *Let's Face It* (1941), *Something for the Boys* (1943), *Mexican Hayride* (1944), *Seven Lively Arts* (1944), *Around the World in Eighty Days* (1946), *Can-Can* (1953), and *Silk Stockings* (1955).

Cole Porter also had the distinction of closing two successive decades with his musicals. *Wake Up and Dream* opened on December 30, 1929, and *Du Barry Was a Lady* was the final musical to be presented in the thirties (December 6, 1939).

He also contributed the scores to many films, notably, *Born to Dance, Rosalie, Broadway Melody of 1940, The Pirate, High Society*, and *Les Girls*.

Production Notes

Leave It to Me! was first presented by Vinton Freedley at the Imperial Theatre, New York, on November 9, 1938. The cast was as follows:

First Secretary, *Ruth Bond*
Second Secretary, *Beverly Hosier*
Buckley Joyce Thomas, *William Gaxton*
First Reporter, *William Lilling*
Second Reporter, *Walter Monroe*
Dolly Winslow, *Mary Martin*
J. H. Brody, *Edward H. Robins*
Mrs. Goodhue, *Sophie Tucker*
Mrs. Goodhue's Daughters, *April, Mildred Chenaval, Ruth Daye, Audrey Palmer, Kay Picture*
Reporter, *Chett Bree*
Photographer, *George E. Mack*
French Conductor, *Walter Armin*
Chauffeur, *James W. Carr*
Alonzo P. Goodhue, *Victor Moore*
Secretaries to Mr. Goodhue, *Gene Kelly, Maurice Kelly, Roy Ross, Jack Seymour, Jack Stanton, Walter B. Long, Jr.*
Prince Alexander Tomofsky, *Eugene Sigaloff*
Jerry Grainger, *Dean Carlton*
Colette, *Tamara*
Kostya, *Joseph Kallini*

Peasant, *Peter Lopoubin*
Sozanoff, *Alexander Asro*
Military Attaché, *John Eliot*
Naval Attaché, *John Panter*
Secretaries, *Roy Ross, Jack Seymour*
Decorators, *Michael Forbes, Thomas Jafolla*
Waiter, *Don Cortez*
German Ambassador, *Hans Hansen*
French Ambassador, *Walter Armin*
Latvian Minister, *Peter Lopoubin*
British Ambassador, *J. Colville Dunn*
Italian Ambassador, *Thomas Jafolla*
Japanese Ambassador, *George E. Mack*
Mackenzie, *Charles Campbell*
Graustein, *Matthew Vodnoy*
Golkin, *Ivan Izmailov*
Secretary, *Stanton Bier*
Foreign Minister, *Alexis Bolan*
Stalin, *Walter Armin*
The Buccaneers, *Don Cortez, John Eliot, Michael Forbes, Eddie Heisler, Tom Jafolla, William Lilling, Walter Munroe, John Panter*

Guests, *Monica Bannister, Adele Jergens, Ruth Joseph, Evelyn Kelly, Viva Selwood, Frances Tannehill, Evelyn Bonefine.*
Les Girls, *Vickie Belling, Dorothy Benson, Ruth Bond, Pearl Harris, Beverly Hosier, Dorothea Jackson, Nancy Lee, June LeRoy, Evelyn Moser, Mary Ann Parker, Barbara Pond, Jean Scott, Lawrie Shevlin, Zynaid Spencer, Marie Vanneman, Marie Vaughan.*

Staged by *Samuel Spewack*
Dances and Ensembles by *Robert Alton*
Settings by *Albert Johnson*
Costumes Designed by *Raoul Pene du Bois*
Musical Direction: *Robert Emmett Dolan*
Orchestral Arrangements by *Donald J. Walker*

Act One

Scene 1: City Room of the Paris and Chicago *World-Tribune.*
Scene 2: Gare de l'Est, Paris.
Scene 3: A Park in Moscow.
Scene 4: Anteroom in the American Embassy, Moscow.
Scene 5: Goodhue's Bedroom in the Embassy.
Scene 6: The Park.
Scene 7: Thomas' Hotel Suite in Moscow.
Scene 8: Red Square.

Act Two

Scene 1: Red Square, two weeks later.
Scene 2: A Droshky.
Scene 3: Goodhue's Bedroom in the Embassy.
Scene 4: A Steppe.
Scene 5: Anteroom in the American Embassy, Moscow.
Scene 6: Embassy Reception Room.
Scene 7: The Park.
Scene 8: Railroad Station. Moscow.

Musical Numbers

Act One

How Do You Spell Ambassador	Reporters
We Drink to You, J.H. Brody	Thomas and Guests
Vite, Vite, Vite	Porters and Girls
Taking the Steps to Russia	Mrs. Goodhue, Daughters, Secretaries and Les Girls
Get Out of Town	Colette
Most Gentlemen Don't Like Love	Mrs. Goodhue, Daughters and Secretaries
When All's Said and Done	Thomas, Dolly and Les Girls
Comrade Alonzo	Ensemble

Act Two

Opening	Ensemble
From Now On	Thomas and Colette
I Want to Go Home	Goodhue
My Heart Belongs to Daddy	Dolly
Tomorrow	Mrs. Goodhue and Ensemble
Far Away	Thomas and Colette
From the U.S.A. to the U.S.S.R.	Goodhue, Mrs. Goodhue and Daughters
Finale	Entire Company

ACT ONE

SCENE:

Screen. Reproduction of Page One of the Paris and Chicago World-Tribune: We see a huge reproduction of photograph of BUCKLEY JOYCE THOMAS *and his publisher. Caption:* "World's Greatest Correspondent Greets World's Greatest Publisher."

Page One turns on screen to Page Two. Headline: "J. H. Brody Rumored New U. S. Ambassador to Moscow."

Now the second page turns on screen and we see Page Three. Another photograph, this time alone, of THOMAS. *Caption:* "World's Greatest Correspondent Says World's Greatest Publisher Will Be World's Greatest Ambassador."

SCENE 1

Paris, France. City Room of the Paris and Chicago World-Tribune.

There are six desks, each with typewriters and telephones. Three desks are downstage and three upstage directly in front of each other. At stage right there is a teletype machine. In upper corner of stage left there is a large world globe. Darts are placed on framework.

There are two entrances on stage left, lower and upper. Also same on stage right. Upstage right of center is one double swinging door, leading from THOMAS' *private office. Printed on door:* "Buckley Joyce Thomas, Private". *There is one cushion bench upstage.*

At Rise: Presses are rolling, eight REPORTERS *at their desks, working and typing. There are also four girl* SECRETARIES. *Two are* THOMAS' *private secretaries.*

REPORTERS: *(Sing "How Do You Spell Ambassador")*
FIRST REPORTER:
How do you spell ambassador?

OTHERS:
Can't say.

SECOND REPORTER:
How do you spell Moscow, men?

OTHERS:
Too tough, by far.

THIRD REPORTER:
How do you spell contributor?

OTHERS:
Won't play.

FOURTH REPORTER:
How do you spell administration, then?

OTHERS:
Just put F.D.R.

FIFTH REPORTER:
How do you spell Soviet?

OTHERS:
Taint fair.

SIXTH REPORTER:
How do you spell Stalin, *I forget?*

OTHERS:
Don't care.

SIX REPORTERS: (Together)
Why bother to spell those tricky names
And add years to your age
When the paper is only read by dames
Who make the Society Page.
Why bother, therefore?
They only care for
The Society Page.

(During song, REPORTERS *answer telephones. "Bombing in Rome?" . . . "Earthquake in Vienna?" . . . "Sextuplets in Prague," etc . . . A* GIRL *with a stenographic notebook crosses directly to the* FIRST REPORTER*)*

GIRL: *(Reading quickly)* "Among the other guests at Mr. Buckley Joyce Thomas' reception for the distinguished publisher and diplomat *were!. . . .*"

SECOND GIRL: *(To* SECOND REPORTER*)* By Buckley Joyce Thomas . . . quote "not since the days of Benjamin Franklin has—"

FIRST GIRL: "The Prince and Princess . . . The Duke and Duchess . . . The Count and Countess. . . ."

SECOND GIRL: "William Hinkleshinkel, president of Rotary—"
(Telephone shrill)

FIRST GIRL: "Paris *World-Tribune.* Exalted Ruler . . . His Eminence . . . Her Lordship . . . His Ladyship . . . His Excellency. . . ."

SECOND GIRL: "The Elks, the Masons, the American Legion. . . ."

FIRST GIRL: *(Concluding)* "*And* Buckley Joyce Thomas."

SECOND GIRL: *(Concluding) And* Buckley Joyce Thomas!

FIRST GIRL: *(Picking up phone)* Who's calling Mr. Thomas? The Duke of Windsor? Just a moment, please . . . *(She runs to the door)* Mr. Thomas. . . . Mr . . . Thomas . . . The Duke of Windsor is on the wire.

*(*THOMAS *emerges from his office, formally dressed for the afternoon. He is fixing his tie)*

THOMAS: Who's calling?

FIRST GIRL: The Duke of Windsor.

THOMAS: Tell him I'm tied up—All right, I'll talk to him. *(Snatching phone)* Hello, David . . . *(Another telephone rings. Vehemently)* No! No!. . . . When I put J.H. on, you say: *(With English accent)* "At long last America has an Ambassador worthy of the name . . ." And don't call from Harry's Bar, you mug, or the story'll be all over town. *(Hangs up)*

FIRST GIRL: *(At telephone)* Butch Oleson is calling.

THOMAS: *(Snatching phone)* Listen, Butch, when the boss comes, you ring up.

You're Mussolini. Get it? You say, "I shall watch your career with great interest . . . Any friend of Buckley Joyce Thomas is a friend of mine . . ." and keep it clean, Butch. *(Hangs up)*

SECOND REPORTER: *(Shouting at teletype)* Oh, Buck! Bulletin! German troops mobilized on Swiss border!

THOMAS: Probably aren't German troops anyway. Just a German peace mission traveling in tanks.

(THOMAS strides to wall, where there's the revolving globe of huge proportions, with feathered pins. FIRST GIRL follows him)

THOMAS: *(To GIRL)* Send a wire to Jenkins in Warsaw to fly to Geneva. *(He takes out pin and moves it)*

GIRL: But you sent Mr. Jenkins to Riga to arrange a reception for J. H.

THOMAS: *(Studying map)* So I did . . . Corcoran in Brussels! That's the man . . . Take a wire . . . Corcoran to Geneva . . .

GIRL: *(Before he can reach the pin)* Mr. Corcoran's in Prague arranging a reception for J. H.

THOMAS: My God! I've got it! *(He takes out pin and jabs it)* Wire our man in Geneva to go to Geneva.

GIRL: Yes, sir.

REPORTER: *(Showing him story)* This what you want, Mr. Thomas?

THOMAS: *(Studying it)* That's it! . . . "From the far corners of the world congratulations poured in—" A brilliant lead, my boy.

REPORTER: You wrote it.

THOMAS: Brilliant! *(Turns to copy boy)* Let her roll! *(As REPORTERS and SECRETARIES move out, DOLLY WINSLOW enters)*

THOMAS: *(Going to her quickly)* Yes, what can I do for you, Miss?

DOLLY: I'd like to renew my subscription.

THOMAS: Why, certainly, miss.

(As soon as they're alone, THOMAS takes her in his arms, kisses her. They're locked in embrace)

DOLLY: Oh, Buckie, this is such a nice reception.

THOMAS: *(Looking about furtively)* Gad, we ought to be more careful. We're not free souls, you know.

DOLLY: We'll be free souls as soon as the old job's gone to Moscow.

THOMAS: Don't call him an old job . . . After all, he's my publisher . . . He's been good to me, Dolly, after his fashion.

DOLLY: Sorry?

THOMAS: About last night? It was wonderful . . . But I have a conscience. I hate deception.

DOLLY: So do I . . . But you don't expect a girl to concentrate on an old job, just because he gives her an apartment and a singing teacher.

THOMAS: *(Ardently)* You innocent, adorable child!

DOLLY: After all, I gave up a lovely friendship with a Belgian for J. H.

THOMAS: Don't! Don't rake up the dead past!

DOLLY: And I stopped corresponding with a boy in Harvard—

THOMAS: *(Hurt)* Please, Dolly—

DOLLY: We were saving stamps together.

THOMAS: Don't!

DOLLY: That's how I got interested in J.H . . . He came into the Paradise one night with a Bolivian stamp 1884 . . . I didn't know who he was . . . But I had to have a Bolivian '84 . . .

THOMAS: *(Taking her in his arms)* I know I shouldn't . . . I mustn't . . . But God, you're lovely!

DOLLY: Well, I try to keep myself nice and dainty. *(She kisses him)* Love me?

THOMAS: I'm nuts about you. But you can't come here. I'll lose my job.

DOLLY: And you don't love anybody else, Buckie, do you?

THOMAS: I never did—not really—

DOLLY: How about that French girl who used to work here? Colette! Colette something or other.

THOMAS: *(Laughs)* Why, she's a newspaper woman!

DOLLY: Well, aren't newspaper women girls?

THOMAS: No.

DOLLY: *(Relieved. Snuggles up to him)* Oh Buckie, tell me again what we're going to do when the old job goes to Moscow—

THOMAS: *(Taking her in his arms)* Gad, you're lovely—when you don't talk . . .

(The REPORTERS *and* GUESTS *enter formally dressed in afternoon attire.* DOLLY *exits.* WAITERS *bring in two trays with ice cream sodas for everyone.* BOY *warns* THOMAS *of* BRODY'S *arrival.* BRODY *enters from office with a smile. He is dressed in a cutaway)*

THOMAS: Just a moment, folks. His Excellency, The United States Ambassador to Moscow. *(Begins to sing "We Drink to You, J. H. Brody")*

(Verse)

THOMAS:

Your Excellency,
On behalf
Of the members of your numerous publications,
And particularly
Of this staff,
I offer you congratulations.
Your official appointment's due, any moment now.

BOYS:

Good luck.

THOMAS:

But till Washington sends it through, here's how!

BOYS:

You said it, Buck.

(Refrain)

THOMAS:

We drink to you, J. H. Brody!

BOYS:

Our next Ambassador to Russia, hey, hey!

THOMAS:

We drink to you in ice cream sody,

BOYS:

The vodka of the U.S.A.

THOMAS:
> *Our glasses clink to you, J. H. Brody*
> *Because we know you're sure*
> *To come through.*
> *The Russian flag is red*
> *But you've got over your head*
> *Forever the Red, White and Blue.*

BOYS:
> *With Cordie Hull to back you, Mister Brody,*
> *To the Kremlin you will never have to toady,*

THOMAS:
> *The Russian flag is red*
> *But you've got over your head*

THOMAS AND THE BOYS:
> *Forever the Red, White and Blue.*

(REPORTERS pick up glasses, and respond. DOLLY re-enters, crosses to J. H.)
DOLLY: Hello, daddy . . . Am I late?
(Telephone rings)
J. H.: No . . . you're very prompt . . . Very prompt . . . And how did the music lesson go?
DOLLY: It was wonderful . . . I knocked off *Boheme.*
J. H.: *(Correcting her)* You mean you finished *Boheme.*
DOLLY: That's what my teacher said. He said I shouldn't wait for my debut. He said we ought to get it over with now.
REPORTER: Mr. Thomas, Rome calling. Il Duce?
THOMAS: Chief, have you a moment to spare for Mussolini?
J. H.: On the wire?
THOMAS: Right here . . .
J. H.: *(Delighted)* Well—Hello, Your Excellency. Yes. I can't hear you. What? Oh, yes. Yes. Why, thank you very much . . . Thank you very much . . . Why, yes, indeed . . . Thank you . . . *(He hangs up)* That's strange.
THOMAS: What's strange?
J. H.: While Mussolini was talking—
THOMAS: Yes?
J. H.: An orchestra was playing *Bei Mir Bist Du Schoen.*
THOMAS: Well, that's just reached Rome. *(Lifts his hand)* Ladies and gentlemen: I don't know whether I can persuade my chief and my friend to say a few words on this historic occasion, but I'm going to try . . . Your Excellency, will you honor us?
MAN: *(At teletype. Excitedly)* Oh, Mr. Thomas—
THOMAS: Shh . . . *(MAN waves to him)*
MAN: Bulletin from Washington!
THOMAS: Ah, the official announcement, your Excellency!
MAN: *(Reading)* "Secretary of State Hull announced today that the New American envoy to Russia would be Alonzo P. Goodhue, of Topeka, Kansas."
J. H.: What's that? Goodhue?

THOMAS: *(Striding over)* That's impossible! *(Looks at the bulletin, snatches phone)* Get me Associated Press.

(The GUESTS *buzz meanwhile)*

J. H.: I'm sure it's an error . . .

THOMAS: This is Buckley Joyce Thomas . . . Listen, what the devil do you mean by putting fake news on the wire? Alonzo P. Goodhue, the new Ambassador to Moscow . . . *(Weakly)* He is? It's official?

J. H.: *(Almost crying)* It can't be! Why, Farley told me to wait in Paris!

FIRST REPORTER: Well, I guess the reception is over.

SECOND REPORTER: Might as well give back the suits. They charge by the hour.

*(*GUESTS *and* REPORTERS *exit.* J. H. *pays no attention. He strides up and down the room)*

DOLLY: Does this mean you're not going to Moscow?

J. H.: No.

DOLLY: Oh, dear.

THOMAS: *(Looking at* DOLLY*)* I'm sorry, boss . . . deeply, deeply sorry.

J. H.: Goodhue! . . . The last man in the world to send to Russia. Why, he manufactures bathtubs!

THOMAS: I never even heard of him! The rat!

J. H.: Just because he gave a hundred thousand to the Democratic campaign, they make Goodhue ambassador . . . I only gave ninety-five . . . That's what happened . . . He nosed me out.

THOMAS: Maybe they learned you contributed to the Republicans, too.

J. H.: They couldn't. The check was anonymous.

THOMAS: When I think of the editorial support you've given the administration.

J. H.: I don't expect gratitude.

THOMAS: Why, we've supported every New Deal measure except the AAA, the Wagner Act, the Court Bill, the PWA, the WPA and the income tax.

DOLLY: *(Who's been thinking)* Why don't you go to Moscow anyway?

J. H.: Quiet, child, I'm thinking.

DOLLY: You don't have to go as an Ambassador. Just go!

J. H.: Quiet, child.

DOLLY: And they'll see what they're missing.

J. H.: *(Suddenly)* Buckley—

THOMAS: Yes, chief—

J. H.: I consider Goodhue's appointment a disgrace to the diplomatic service.

THOMAS: You took the very words out of my editorial tomorrow.

J. H.: I want him recalled!

THOMAS: What do you suggest, chief?

J. H.: *(Thinking aloud)* Goodhue can't last . . . He's an absurdity. He's bound to say the wrong thing, do the wrong thing . . . *We've got to help him!*

THOMAS: I get it, Chief . . . Masterly! . . . I'll send three men into Moscow. They'll put his foot in his mouth and keep it there.

J. H.: That's it . . . that's it . . .

THOMAS: Consider it done!

J. H.: I have only one suggestion. I don't want three men. I don't trust three men. I want one man—you.

THOMAS: Me?

J. H.: How soon can you leave for Moscow?

THOMAS: *(Aghast)* Me?

J. H.: Yes, Buckley—you.

THOMAS: Chief, I can't leave Paris. *(Looking at DOLLY)* The paper— *(She nods)* the bureau— *(She nods)* news is breaking— *(She nods)* It's hot!

DOLLY: I'll say.

THOMAS: Besides, is it ethical?

J. H.: *(Coldly)* You've never questioned my ethics before, Buckley—nor have I ever questioned yours. Your contract expires next month. I'd like to renew it, Buckley. Come along, Dolly—Say goodbye to Mr. Thomas . . .

THOMAS: *(Brokenly)* Chief, you don't know what you're making me give up.

DOLLY: Goodbye— *(Her voice breaks)*

J. H.: Why my child, what's wrong?

DOLLY: I—I—always cry when I say goodbye . . . Goodbye, Mr. Thomas . . . *(Wailing)* I think it's a lousy break!

J. H.: Come along, child. *(He takes her out. Sadly, THOMAS goes to globe, takes out pin)*

THOMAS: Thomas—to Moscow! *(He jabs pin viciously)*

> Blackout

SCENE:

Screen. Screen is lowered. Paris and Chicago World-Tribune Editorial Page: A cartoon showing A. P. Goodhue in bathtub rowing. Heading: "The Vulgar Boatman." Editorial Caption: "Recall Goodhue, etc."

SCENE 2

> *Railroad Station—Gare de l'Est, Paris.*
> *A grill fence leading to station with gate in center.*
> *At Rise: Some of the* SHOWGIRLS *and* SINGING BOYS *are discovered on stage. On music cue,* PORTERS *and additional* SHOWGIRLS *enter carrying bags.* PORTERS *continue this action during number.*

PORTERS, GIRLS and BOYS: *(Sing "Vite, Vite, Vite")*

PORTERS:
> *Vite, vite, vite,* (Pronounced Veet)
> *For the Moscow Express.*
> *Vite, vite, vite,*
> *You give a tip to me, no, yes?*
> *Vite, vite, vite,*
> *Hurry and get your seat*
> *If you want to go to Moscow,*
> *Madame, you better be* vite!

FIRST GIRL:
> *Oh! I've lost my hat box,*

SECOND GIRL:
> *I've lost my sables,*

THIRD GIRL:
> *I've lost my suitcase*
> *The one with the beautiful labels!*

FOURTH GIRL:
I lost my trav'lers checks
Only this afternoon,

FIFTH GIRL:
I've still got my
Virginity (Pronounced to rhyme with *my*)
But I'm hoping to lose it soon.

FIVE BOYS:
Farewell, my sweetheart,
Don't fail to write,
I'm going to miss you
More and more ev'ry night.
While you're away, dear,
From me so far
I shall be waiting for you at the Ritz, in the bar.

FIVE GIRLS:
Farewell, my lover,
Daily I'll write,
I'm going to miss you
More and more ev'ry night.

FIVE BOYS:
While you're away, dear,
From me so far
I shall be waiting for you at the Ritz, in the bar.

(At the same time)

PORTERS:
Vite, vite, vite,
Hurry and get your seat,
If you want to go to Moscow,
Madame, you better be vite!

(PRINCE ALEXANDER TOMOFSKY enters from left stage. He is dressed in morning suit, derby, and cane. This is his only suit and he uses it throughout the play. JERRY GRAINGER *also enters on same cue stage right. He is dressed in top coat. They meet at center stage)*
GRAINGER: Pardon me, can you tell me when the Moscow Express leaves?
PRINCE: In exactly fifteen minutes.
GRAINGER: Thank you. *(About to move off when the* PRINCE *stops him)*
PRINCE: Pardon me, could you change a hundred-franc note?
GRAINGER: Why certainly. *(He takes the note and looks at it)* I'm sorry but I think this is counterfeit!
PRINCE: You're perfectly right.
(GRAINGER and PRINCE go off through gate. CONDUCTOR and DOLLY enter)
CONDUCTOR: But Mademoiselle, there is no more room on the Moscow Express, the American Ambassador has taken everything.
DOLLY: Hasn't Mr. Buckley Joyce Thomas a compartment?
CONDUCTOR: Why, yes.

DOLLY: Well, put my bags in with his . . .

CONDUCTOR: But where will we put you?

DOLLY: With my bags.

(Exits through gate followed by CONDUCTOR. PORTERS *enter with* MRS. GOODHUE)

MRS. GOODHUE: *(To* PORTERS*)* Boys! Boys! Be careful of that caviar. *(Indicating huge packing case)* They're just fish eggs, you know.

REPORTERS: But Mrs. Goodhue, you're not taking caviar to Russia?

MRS. GOODHUE: I thought it'd be a nice gesture.

REPORTER: By the way, where is the Ambassador?

MRS. GOODHUE: I'm offering a reward for him myself . . . *(She looks about as if missing something)* Children!

DAUGHTERS' VOICES: *(Offstage)* Yes, mother.

MRS. GOODHUE: Keep away from that poster! *(Five* DAUGHTERS *enter, dressed alike)* Children, meet the reporters. *(One wobbles a little)* Mind your knee, honey . . . *(Now the* GIRLS *back away à la Buckingham Palace presentation)* *(Bitterly)* Farley promised us England. Huh! *(Now one of the* GIRLS *does a pinwheel. Ends in split)* Double-jointed!

PHOTOGRAPHER: Can we have a family picture?

MRS. GOODHUE: By all means— *(*DAUGHTERS *group themselves back of her)*

REPORTER: But where is the Ambassador?

MRS. GOODHUE: Is he necessary?

(Flashlights pop. FRENCH OFFICIAL *comes on, perspiring, through gate)*

OFFICIAL: Madame, we have added forty special cars for your luggage.

MRS. GOODHUE: That's nice. We don't like to be cramped.

DAUGHTERS: Mother, where is the Prince?

MRS. GOODHUE: *(Calls)* Here Prince! Prince! Here Prince! *(*PRINCE *re-enters through gate)* Prince, meet the reporters. He's a real prince, the last of the Romanoffs. The children found him in the catacombs.

(Troupe of DANCING GIRLS *enter.* PRINCE *exits through gate)*

REPORTER: *(To* PHOTOGRAPHER*)* Keep your eye open for the Ambassador.

MRS. GOODHUE: My entourage. *(They step. To* REPORTERS*)* Les Girls!

REPORTER: You're not taking dancers to Russia?

MRS. GOODHUE: Why not? For years I've been sitting in Topeka, paying out good money to English lecturers, feeding 'em, flattering 'em, and what did I get? *(Mockingly)* "America has no culture." I resented that. So when I was appointed Her Excellency, the wife of the United States Ambassador to Moscow, I said to myself: I'm going to bring my culture with me.

MRS. GOODHUE, DAUGHTERS, SECRETARIES and LES GIRLS: *(Sing "Taking the Steps to Russia")*

(Verse)
From what I hear
I greatly fear
For the mujik and his mate.
For the Soviet
Hasn't learned as yet
How to make 'em syncopate.

The Moscovites
Complain that their nights
Are so long they never end,
And so to get 'em in the groove
And prove
That I'm a friend

(Refrain)
I'm taking the steps to Russia,
I'm showing 'em how to dance,
I'm starting the shag in Moscow,
I'm putting red ants in their pants.
The way they still love Tschaikowsky
I'm sure is not quite the right thing,
I know what's the matter with 'em,
What they need is Harlem rhythm,
So I'm making Communithm
Thwing!

(Patter)
The gypsies in the bars,
All over the place,
No more will strum guitars
But slappa the bass. (Pronounced *base*)
Each Volga boatman and
Each mountain woodman,
Will start to beat the band
Like Benny Goodman
Those proletari-ats
And agitators,
Will all be alley-cats
And alley-gators,
The thing to cheer 'em up is jam and jive,
A Yank attack
Is what they lack
So, to bring 'em back
Alive
So I'm taking my flock of chickies
To show 'em some brand new trickies
And we'll make the Bolshevikies
Swing!

(Trumpets are heard, marching feet . . . LEGIONNAIRES, FRENCH VETERANS, BUGLERS *and* GUARD OF HONOR *come on.* THOMAS *appears, followed by* J. H. BRODY*)*

THOMAS: Thanks, thanks very much for this touching and unexpected demonstration.

MRS. GOODHUE: *(Sotto voce)* Who the hell is that?

J. H.: Buckley, you certainly have a following. *(Enter* CHAUFFEUR. J.H. *crosses to* MRS. GOODHUE*)* Why, Leora Goodhue. This is a pleasure. Buckley, I want you to meet Mrs. Goodhue.

MRS. GOODHUE: *(Stiffly)* You have the advantage over her Excellency.

J. H.: Why, Leora—

MRS. GOODHUE: I read that smelly editorial in that smelly rag of yours—"Recall Goodhue!" And that cartoon! Alonzo in a bathtub rowing to Moscow.

THOMAS: Didn't you like it? It showed the simplicity of the man, and in simplicity, Mrs. Goodhue, we find greatness!

MRS. GOODHUE: Her Excellency thinks you're a cock-eyed liar! Come along, children . . . By the way, how's Mrs. Brody? Still weaning her Pomeranian? *(Exits with DAUGHTERS through gate)*

CHAUFFEUR: Pardon me, Mr. Brody, but it's almost time for your boat train.

THOMAS: *(Stares)* Chief, are you sailing home?

J. H.: On the Queen Mary at five. I'm going to work the Washington end while you're busy in Moscow, Buckley.

THOMAS: *(Clearing his throat)* Is Miss Winslow going—with you?

J. H.: No, I thought it best to put Dolly in a retreat—to guard her voice. Well, Buckley, goodbye—and good luck.

THOMAS: Chief, this is going to be the toughest assignment of my career.

J. H.: Buckley, I have every confidence in you.

(J. H. pushes through with CHAUFFEUR. GRAINGER re-enters)

GRAINGER: Hello! Buck.

THOMAS: Hello, Grainger. Coming to see me off?

GRAINGER: As a matter of fact, I came to see the Ambassador off but I can't find him. Buck, will you do me a favor?

THOMAS: I'll do anything for a rising young diplomat.

GRAINGER: Will you give this to Colette—when you see her. It's just a little thing but it's something she admired.

THOMAS: Colette? Is Colette in Moscow?

GRAINGER: Yes. She has been there some time for the *Herald.*

THOMAS: Sure I'll do it. *(Sticks present in his pocket)* Take this wire . . . *(Gives him pencil)* Where's she stopping?

GRAINGER: Hotel Savoy.

THOMAS: Hotel Savoy. Moscow . . . Meet me without fail arriving Wednesday afternoon four. Love. Buck.

GRAINGER: And another thing, Buck. Will you see a lot of Colette, please? . . . Take her out . . . spend a lot of time with her. She won't marry me until she gets you out of her system. And she's bound to find out you're devious, tricky, superficial, in short, a heel.

THOMAS: I am amazed!

GRAINGER: *(Moving off quickly)* Good-bye! You will rush her, won't you?

THOMAS: My boy, I'm big enough to forgive you. In fact, I'll be best man at your wedding.

GRAINGER: If she'll have me, you can be bridesmaid.

(He exits. The REPORTERS re-enter and come up to THOMAS through the gate)

REPORTER: No sign of Goodhue, Buck . . .

SECOND REPORTER: We couldn't find him. We looked in the locomotive . . . in the freight cars . . . under the cars . . .

THOMAS: I'll show you School of Journalism whelps how to find an American in Paris.

(He goes to BUGLERS and whispers in their ear. They strike up several bars of "Columbia, the Gem of the Ocean". A. P. GOODHUE, laden with parcels, appears.

He is dressed in a misfit business suit and hat. As he hears the music he stops. He drops his parcels. A PORTER *follows and picks up parcels. He takes his hat off.* THOMAS, *with a flourish, takes his off. Music stops.* THOMAS *eases* REPORTERS *and* BUGLERS *away)*

THOMAS: Your Excellency, I'm Buckley Joyce Thomas of the Paris and Chicago *World-Tribune.*

GOODHUE: Oh, are you an American? I'm an American, too.

THOMAS: Briefly, your Excellency, to what do you attribute your success?

GOODHUE: My father left me a very good business. *(Peers about)* I seem to have lost my party . . .

*(*CONDUCTOR *enters and crosses stage)*

CONDUCTOR: ALL aboard, all aboard! *(He exits. People exit right and left)*

GOODHUE: *(Peers some more)* You haven't seen a woman with five children? They're Americans, too.

THOMAS: Your family's on the train. Safe and sound. And a mighty nice family it is, too.

GOODHUE: I think so, but of course I'm prejudiced.

THOMAS: You've kept in touch with the general European situation in our papers, of course.

GOODHUE: I only read the funnies . . . The children always save them for me.

THOMAS: You're familiar with the Russian experiment?

GOODHUE: Oh, is it an experiment? I thought they had people living there.

THOMAS: In all my experience, I've never met a man more fitted for a key diplomatic post.

GOODHUE: That's what the Russian consul in New York said . . . Nice fellow, for a foreigner. He gave me this stamp. *(He opens coat, and we see visa stamps hanging from vest pockets)* See? Visa stamps . . . I got all kinds. I called on all the consuls . . . Lithuanian . . . Latvian . . . Belgian . . . I guess that's my job, isn't it? Putting stamps on passports.

THOMAS: Good God, man, no! You're an Ambassador! Vice consuls do that. Underlings!

GOODHUE: Don't I have any fun? . . . *(Peers at him)* Did you say you were a reporter? You fellows have a lot of fun . . . When I was Mayor of Topeka, the newspaper boys let me go with them to the fires. *(Sighs)* Those were the good old days. *(There's a suspicion of a sob in his voice)*

THOMAS: What's wrong, your Excellency? Aren't you feeling well?

GOODHUE: How would you feel if you hadn't done anything and the State Department tore you away from your home, your friends and everything you hold dear and sent you away to a strange country?

THOMAS: Don't you *want* to be an Ambassador?

GOODHUE: No . . . Somebody in Washington doesn't like me.

THOMAS: Do you mean to tell me you contributed to the Democratic Campaign Committee and you didn't *know* you were going to be an Ambassador?

GOODHUE: I didn't contribute. Mrs. Goodhue did . . . while I was pitching horseshoes with some of the boys back of the plant.

THOMAS: Why, this is simple. You don't have to go to Moscow. I don't have to go to Moscow. All you've got to do is resign!

GOODHUE: Mrs. Goodhue won't let me.

THOMAS: She won't?

GOODHUE: No, I asked her. . . . Is there a Western Union boy here? I've got to send a cable to Mr. Hull . . . That's another thing. They won't let you send cables in English . . . Only in secret code . . . *(He takes out book and gives it to him)* See?

THOMAS: Want me to write it for you? What do you want to say?

GOODHUE: This is going to be very difficult. I want to say I went to the French Foreign Office—the Fifi D'Orsay.

THOMAS: The Quai. D'Orsai.

GOODHUE: And a man there—I think he was French—

THOMAS: I'm pretty sure he was.

GOODHUE: He said France will never forget.

THOMAS: Forget what?

GOODHUE: He didn't tell me.

THOMAS: Anything else?

GOODHUE: Then we went to the Louvre, and Mrs. Goodhue bought a corset.

THOMAS: You sure you want Hull to know?

GOODHUE: I'm supposed to tell him everything. Then we parked the kids and had a drink.

THOMAS: *(Crumpling copy paper)* I can't take candy from a child . . . Look, Mr. Goodhue—

GOODHUE: The boys call me Stinky—because I never can stop the barber from putting things on my hair. Can you?

THOMAS: I shouldn't like you, but I do . . . You may not realize it, but your appointment has taken me from the arms of the woman I love.

GOODHUE: It's a small world, isn't it?

THOMAS: Stinky—are you *sure* you don't want to be an Ambassador?

GOODHUE: Oh, I wouldn't mind being an Ambassador if I didn't have to go abroad.

THOMAS: *(Insistently)* You don't want Moscow!

GOODHUE: Oh, no . . . But what's the use of butting my head against a stone wall.

THOMAS: Look, Stinky—how would you like to be recalled?

GOODHUE: Recalled?

THOMAS: Not all Ambassadors resign. Some are recalled!

GOODHUE: What do you have to do to get recalled? Do I have to contribute?

THOMAS: Not one single penny.

GOODHUE: I don't mind paying ransom.

THOMAS: Can you be indiscreet? Can you say the wrong thing? Do the wrong thing?

GOODHUE: I don't know. I don't even know what the *right* thing is. Mrs. Goodhue is studying all that up.

THOMAS: Stinky, a man to be recalled, must be discredited.

GOODHUE: Do you think I could do that?

THOMAS: Will you put yourself in my hands? Will you give me your whole-hearted cooperation? Will you do as I tell you, when I tell you?

GOODHUE: Oh, certainly, if you promise to get me discredited.

THOMAS: *(Extending his hand)* I promise—Leave it to me!

GOODHUE: Shake. *(A shrill French train whistle is heard)*

GOODHUE: Mrs. Goodhue is calling me.

Blackout

SCENE 3

A Park in Moscow. Sign: "Park of Culture and Rest".
There is a park bench left of center.
At rise: SINGING BOYS *and* SHOWGIRLS *are discovered on, dressed as peasants and Russian characters.* COLETTE *is seated at bench reading telegram.* KOSTYA *enters. He is dressed in business suit and Russian blouse. He goes to bench.*

KOSTYA: Oh, Miss Arnaud . . . I have just left Mr. Thomas at the Foreign Office. He says he must see you, immediately.

COLETTE: Tell Mr. Thomas you couldn't find me. Tell him I'm not in Moscow.

KOSTYA: I cannot tell a lie.

COLETTE: If you're going to work for him, you'd better learn.

KOSTYA: But what shall I tell him?

COLETTE: Tell him anything you please. Tell him to get out of town!

KOSTYA: Very well, I shall tell a lie. *(Exits)*

*(*COLETTE *sings "Get Out of Town" assisted by* SINGING BOYS*)*
(Verse)
The farce was ended,
The curtain drawn,
And, I at least pretended
That love was dead and gone.
But now from nowhere
You come to me as before,
To take my heart
And break my heart
Once more.

(Refrain)
Get out of town,
Before it's too late, my love.
Get out of town,
Be good to me, please
Why wish me harm?
Why not retire to a farm
And be contented to charm
The birds off the trees?
Just disappear,
I care for you much too much,
And when you are near,
Close to me, dear,
We touch too much.
The thrill when we meet
Is so bitter-sweet
That, darling, it's getting me down,
So on your mark, get set,
Get out of town.

Curtain

SCENE 4

Anteroom in the American Embassy, Moscow.

This is part of the Embassy Reception Room. A settee is direct center. At right, there is a single armless chair. Stage left: a small desk and chair. On the desk, a portable typewriter and telephone, newspapers and desk equipment. The only entrances are at stage left and right.

At Rise: GRAINGER, *in dark suit, and* MILITARY ATTACHÉ *in uniform, a* NAVAL ATTACHÉ, *and two* SECRETARIES *are grouped about the desk.*

GOODHUE *enters, reading a speech to himself. He is dressed in silk knicker-bockers.*

MILITARY ATTACHÉ: Ready, sir.

NAVAL ATTACHÉ: Ready, sir.

SECRETARIES: We're ready, sir.

GOODHUE: Who are you boys?

GRAINGER: Why—That is Captain Holmsby, military attaché.

GOODHUE: What does he do?

GRAINGER: Why, he collects military information and sends it to the War Department. Lieutenant Commander Green here, as naval attaché, collects naval information and sends it to the Navy Department.

GOODHUE: Oh! Spies!

GRAINGER: Certainly not.

GOODHUE: Who are you?

GRAINGER: I'm your first secretary. I just flew in from Paris. I'm Grainger.

GOODHUE: I'm Goodhue. Are you an American? I'm an American, too.

(MRS. GOODHUE enters, followed by TWO MALE DECORATORS)

MRS. GOODHUE: I want that wall out . . . I want a fireplace there . . . I'd like something Victorian in that corner. A fountain would be nice. And rip out that monstrosity. *(Points to GOODHUE)*

MAN: But Madame, that is the Ambassador.

MRS. GOODHUE: A.P., pull up your stockings!

GOODHUE: Yes, dear.

MRS. GOODHUE: I go to all that trouble to make you look nice and neat. Your knickerbockers clean?

GOODHUE: Yes, dear.

MRS. GOODHUE: It's a wonder they can't give you two pair with that suit. *(Calls)* Children! . . . Children! Your father's a mess again! *(DAUGHTERS enter. They brush him off)* Five Snow Whites and one dwarf! *(She exits. DECORATORS follow)*

GRAINGER: We're due at the Foreign Office in exactly ten minutes. If you're ready, sir—

(DAUGHTERS go to settee and read, knit, etc.)

GOODHUE: You may be ready—but I'm not. I haven't got my speech down pat yet . . . *(He crosses downstage and reads speech aloud)* "Mr. Foreign Minister, Mr. Stalin, and all you other fellows whose names I can't pronounce. In presenting my credentials as Ambassador of the United States, I wish to make this plain: Something's got to be done, and pretty darn quick about the brokerage situation in Moscow. It is a fact, is it not, that not one Wall Street house maintains a branch office here. Why? No ticker service. Why? . . . No Dow Jones averages. Why? Are you going to deprive the citizenry the privilege of sharing the wealth with our hard-working financiers? You've got another guess coming!"

GRAINGER: Mr. Ambassador—

GOODHUE: Buck Thomas wrote this for me. He can think of the darnedest things.

GRAINGER: Mr. Ambassador, you can't possibly say that to the Foreign Minister. He'll be annoyed.

GOODHUE: Won't I be discredited?

GRAINGER: Of course you will.

GOODHUE: That's all right then. Let's go. *(He exits with staff)*

(GRAINGER goes to the telephone)

GRAINGER: Get me the Foreign Office . . . Mr. Izvolsky . . . Izvolsky? Listen . . . Tell the Foreign Minister to pay no attention to Mr. Goodhue's speech . . . He's a great practical joker. You know how we Americans are. Certainly . . . The costume alone will tip you off.

(Laughs, hangs up, and is perplexed. He exits as MRS. GOODHUE *returns)*

MRS. GOODHUE: Time for your story hour, children. *(They group themselves about her)* Children, when we go to Buckingham Palace—and we are going to Buckingham Palace—I want you to do everything the English expect from well-bred Americans.

(FIRST GIRL chews gum. SECOND GIRL *slaps the third girl on the back, and says:* "Hi ya, Kid, skiddoo, twenty-three." FOURTH GIRL *does Indian call.* FIFTH GIRL *does jitterbug. Then they do the Buckingham Palace bow)*

MRS. GOODHUE: You'll be the most popular girls in England. You see, children, England is the mother country and is civilized. And now, as a mother and a woman, a word of advice.

MRS. GOODHUE: *(Sings "Most Gentlemen Don't Like Love")*
(Verse)
When Mummy in her sixteenth year
Was dreaming of romance a lot,
She thought that she was Guinevere
And ev'ry boy Sir Launcelot,
But now that Mummy's more mature
And knows her way about,
She doesn't b'lieve in "Vive l'amour"
For Mummy's found out—

(1st Refrain)
Most gentlemen don't like love, they just like to kick it around,
Most gentlemen can't take love, 'cause most gentlemen ain't that profound.
As Madam Sappho in some sonnet said
"A slap and a tickle
Is all that the fickle
Male
Ever has in his head,"
For most gentlemen don't like love.
I've been in love,

So I know what I'm talking of
And, oh, to my woe I have found
They just like to kick it around.

(MRS. GOODHUE *exits, and* FIVE DAUGHTERS *and* FIVE SECRETARIES *dance one refrain.* MRS. GOODHUE *calls "Children" offstage. They reply "Yes, Mother."* MRS. GOODHUE *re-enters, says "I told you". Then resumes song)*

(2nd Refrain)
Most gentlemen don't like love, they just like to kick it around,
Most gentlemen can't take love, 'cause most gentlemen ain't that profound.
So just remember when you get that glance,
A romp and a quickie
Is all little Dickie
Means when he mentions romance.
For most gentlemen don't like love
I've been in love,
So I know what I'm talking of
And, oh, to my woe I have found
They just like to kick it around.

(MRS. GOODHUE *remains on, after* FIVE DAUGHTERS *exit, and sings)*

Now if some fine day your boy friend should say
He loves you forever and part from you never
Just push 'em out of the bay—way
'Cause most gentlemen don't like love
They just like to kick it around.

(As she exits, two WAITERS *enter left carrying a large platter with a huge fish and cross stage and off right.* THOMAS *enters and sits at desk, picks up phone)*
THOMAS: This is Buckley Joyce Thomas. Get me two tickets for Paris. I know I just arrived. I work fast.
(KOSTYA *enters)*
Kostya, did you get me a worker and a peasant?
KOSTYA: Sir?
THOMAS: *(Rises)* I told you I wanted to interview a worker and a peasant!
KOSTYA: Here—In the Embassy?
THOMAS: Catch me a peasant!
(KOSTYA *exits.* THOMAS *begins working on story, typing.* PRINCE *enters)*
Hello, Prince. What're you doing here?
PRINCE: This was the home of Snegurutchka—my father's favorite mistress.
THOMAS: The last of the Romanoffs.
PRINCE: I'm not a Romanoff. My family was more cultured. More historical—Can you change a hundred rouble note? *(Gives it to him)*
THOMAS: Why certainly, Prince. *(Looks at the note)* Your hundred franc note was a better job.
PRINCE: *(Takes note back)* You're perfectly right. *(Bows and exits)*
(COLETTE *enters with* SECRETARY*)*
SECRETARY: Do you mind waiting here, Miss. The Ambassador will be here soon.
(Exits)

THOMAS: Colette!

COLETTE: Hello, Buck.

THOMAS: Am I glad to see you! Where have you been keeping yourself?

COLETTE: I came up to interview the Ambassador.

THOMAS: Which one? There will be a new one next week.

COLETTE: I see you have taken over the Embassy. Up to your old tricks?

THOMAS: I was invited for tea, and I moved in. I like it here.

COLETTE: You haven't changed a bit!

THOMAS: That's where you're wrong. I'm not the man you knew: Devious, tricky, superficial, in short . . . a heel.

COLETTE: How well you put it.

THOMAS: Colette, no one has ever taken your place. . . . not really.

COLETTE: Only six or seven. I don't know what you want, Buck, but whatever it is, forget it. When I left you in Paris, I closed a chapter. Let's keep it closed. *(Smiles)* Shall we?

THOMAS: You don't mean that! I brought you a little gift.

COLETTE: You brought me a gift?

THOMAS: Oh, it's nothing.

COLETTE: Sure it wasn't meant for someone else?

THOMAS: It was meant for you, dear. *(Gives her JERRY'S gift)*

COLETTE: From Jerry?

THOMAS: Did he enclose a card?

COLETTE: Thank you. I've been expecting it.

THOMAS: Swell fellow, Grainger. Why don't you come back to Paris with me?

COLETTE: Wouldn't Miss Winslow object?

THOMAS: Where did you hear about Dolly?

COLETTE: All over town.

THOMAS: Oh, that's just an episode. Ours is different. *(Tries to embrace her)*

COLETTE: No, Buck. I'll see you. I'll work with you. But no nonsense.

THOMAS: No?

COLETTE: I think I'll see the Ambassador later. *(She exits)*

(KOSTYA *enters with a heavy set tall* PEASANT. *He is dressed in long coat, Russian blouse and boots, and* SOZANOFF, *the worker, dressed in leather coat and Russian blouse)*

KOSTYA: Mr. Thomas, I have brought a worker and a peasant.

THOMAS: Good. (KOSTYA *brings peasant right center.* THOMAS *goes to worker)* So this is a peasant!

KOSTYA: No, sir. *This* is a peasant. *(Indicates peasant)*

THOMAS: He's a real peasant?

KOSTYA: Yes, sir.

THOMAS: Not just a commuter? . . . Ask him what he raises.

PEASANT: *(In Russian)* I raise corn.

(KOSTYA *interprets)*

KOSTYA: He raises corn.

THOMAS: Good! That will save me a trip to the Ukraine. Ask him, does he like the government of the USSR.

PEASANT: *(Cautiously looks about, shakes his head)* No.

THOMAS: Why?

PEASANT: Government wants taxes.
(KOSTYA *interprets*)
THOMAS: Ask him if he likes the Czar's government better?
PEASANT: *(Vehemently)* No . . . No . . .
THOMAS: Then what kind of a government does he like?
(KOSTYA *asks* PEASANT)
KOSTYA: A better one.
THOMAS: Oh, a subversive. Ask him if he's happy.
(KOSTYA *does*)
PEASANT: Who is?
KOSTYA: He says: Who is?
THOMAS: Who is? . . . There's the soul of the Russian Peasant . . . Profound!
(KOSTYA *takes* PEASANT *off right*)
SOZANOFF: You are a Journalist?
THOMAS: You speak English?
SOZANOFF: I speak also French, German and Sanskrit.
THOMAS: Remarkable! . . . A common ordinary worker—And a linguist!
SOZANOFF: I am not a common ordinary worker . . . I have great news for you
  of vital importance . . .
(*Enter* KOSTYA)
SOZANOFF: Who is this man?
THOMAS: My interpreter.
SOZANOFF: Is he to be depended on? Is he reliable? You trust him?
THOMAS: Implicitly.
SOZANOFF: I don't trust him. Dismiss him!
THOMAS: Run along, Kostya.
(KOSTYA *exits*)
SOZANOFF: Take pencil—take paper—
THOMAS: Right here—
SOZANOFF: Are you ready?
THOMAS: Ready—
SOZANOFF: I wish to state to the entire world—
THOMAS: Yes?
SOZANOFF: To all thinking persons—
THOMAS: Yes?
SOZANOFF: To the comrades abroad—
THOMAS: Yes—
SOZANOFF: That Leninism is not Stalinism. Stalinism is not Marxism. Trotsky-
  ism is not Marxism. Bolshevism is not Communism. And Communism is not
  Socialism!
THOMAS: Oh, hell . . . I thought you had news.
SOZANOFF: You look upon the leader of the next Russian Revolution.
THOMAS: Revolution? When?
SOZANOFF: Tomorrow.
THOMAS: What?
SOZANOFF: The day after—next week—next year—fifty. A hundred years. What
  does time matter?
THOMAS: *(To SOZANOFF)* My boy—if you want your name in the paper study
  the front page of the *World-Tribune*. *(Gives it to him)* Look here . . . war . . .

murder . . . kidnapping . . . corruption . . . Everybody on that front page has *done* something. What have you done? You haven't even got an attempted assassination to your credit . . . How many in your party?

SOZANOFF: *(Studying the paper)* Six. *(Crossing right)* You shall hear from me!

THOMAS: Good. *(SOZANOFF exits)* Nuts make news!

(GOODHUE enters with medal on lapel of coat)

GOODHUE: Hello, Buck.

THOMAS: Well, did they throw you out on your ear?

GOODHUE: I made that speech. They gave me a medal.

THOMAS: What?

GOODHUE: *(Looking at medal)* I wonder what it is, I am?

THOMAS: They made you an Artist of the People.

GOODHUE: Do I have to draw pictures? Anyway, I got that recipe for Mrs. Goodhue, for blintzes.

(GRAINGER enters)

GRAINGER: Your Excellency, the British Ambassador, the French Ambassador, the Japanese Ambassador, Latvian Minister and the German Ambassador would like to pay their respects.

GOODHUE: Respects? Not the debts?

THOMAS: You don't want to see 'em!

GOODHUE: I don't want to see them.

GRAINGER: Wait a minute, Buck—

THOMAS: His Excellency is not in the mood.

GRAINGER: But, dammit, it's customary—It's a formality . . . The expected thing to do.

GOODHUE: Have they got any horseshoes?

THOMAS: Only in their gloves. *(To GRAINGER)* Tell them America has a new foreign policy—isolation! . . . Strict neutrality . . . We don't like any of 'em.

GRAINGER: Your Excellency—

GOODHUE: *(Sternly)* You heard the boss. *(Indicates THOMAS)*

GRAINGER: *(Turns to THOMAS)* I don't know what your game is, Buck . . . Your Excellency, it's my duty to warn you. I don't want to be impertinent . . . But I swear to you these tactics may lead to your recall.

GOODHUE: Now you're talking!

(GRAINGER exits)

THOMAS: Stinky, we've got to do something drastic, something spectacular. I'll have you thrown out of here or I'll know the reason why.

GOODHUE: Well, don't be impatient, Buck. Rome wasn't built in a day.

(GRAINGER re-enters)

GRAINGER: Your Excellency—The German Ambassador insists on seeing you. He says if you don't receive him, he'll march in. *(Starts to exit)*

THOMAS: *(To GRAINGER)* Wait a minute! I've got it! . . . Send him in!

GRAINGER: I wish I knew what you were up to.

THOMAS: You'll find out.

(Drumbeat is heard, and marching footsteps. Finally an imposing snarling figure enters, dressed in Nazi uniform. He extends hand in Nazi salute)

GERMAN AMBASSADOR: *(Snarling and spitting)* Your Excellency, I wish to establish cordial relations with you. We wish to be frrrriends. We luf you! We want your helium . . . We want your money . . . we want your trade in South

America . . . We want your army, navy and aeroplanes . . . and in return we gif you culture, you barbarian, you!

GOODHUE: *(To GRAINGER)* What am I supposed to say?

GRAINGER: Say you are pleased to accept the good wishes of His Excellency's government, and hope the present correct and cordial relations will be maintained and extended.

GOODHUE: *(To THOMAS)* Is that all right?

THOMAS: No! *(He whispers in GOODHUE'S ear)* Kick him in the belly.

GOODHUE: Shall I?

GERMAN AMBASSADOR: I am waiting!

GOODHUE: Well, here goes. *(Hops, skips and starts to kick)*

Blackout

SCENE 5

GOODHUE'S *bedroom in the Embassy.*

This bedroom is very attractive. There is a canopied bed right of center. Left of door there is a blackboard with a code book attached. Also, a small stepladder two steps high used to stand on for writing on the blackboard. At stage center there is an upholstered arm cushion chair. To the right of the chair, a small round table with lamps. Left of the chair is Goodhue's trapshooting outfit. A small candid camera is on the table.

Stage left and stage right are used for entrances.

At Rise: GOODHUE *is discovered in bed in a robe lined with red and white stripes. His foot is bandaged.*

MRS. GOODHUE: *(Enters)* How are you feeling, A.P.? How's your poor foot? The idea of that German wearing a corset!

(FRENCH AMBASSADOR and LATVIAN MINISTER enter. They are in full dress)

GOODHUE: *(Groaning—sees figures)* Who's that?

MRS. GOODHUE: It's the French Ambassador, and the Latvian minister. They insisted on coming up when I told them you were in no condition for the reception.

FRENCH AMBASSADOR: *(Leans over, confidentially)* France is proud of you. *(He kisses his cheek, then exits)*

(LATVIAN MINISTER comes over)

LATVIAN MINISTER: Latvia is proud of you. *(He kisses him, then exits)*

MRS. GOODHUE: And here's the British Ambassador.

(BRITISH AMBASSADOR enters in full dress)

BRITISH AMBASSADOR: *(Clearing his throat)* On behalf of England and the Empire—

GOODHUE: Aren't you going to kiss me?

BRITISH AMBASSADOR: Certainly not.

GOODHUE: Then I can open my eyes.

BRITISH AMBASSADOR: Britain views your deed with pride and alarm, congratulates and condemns you, and will now perform its breathtaking triple loop, suspended by a single wire, sitting in a tub of water.

GOODHUE: Did you say something?

BRITISH AMBASSADOR: We'll issue a statement in the morning, depending on which way the wind blows. *(He exits)*

GOODHUE: A lot they know! I'll bet Mr. Hull is good and mad. Buck Thomas says I'll be recalled for conduct unbecoming an Ambassador and a gentleman.

MRS. GOODHUE: I wouldn't be surprised if we got London—now.

GOODHUE: London?

MRS. GOODHUE: Why, yes—We should have had it in the first place if you were half a man. Answer me: Why haven't I got nine children like the Kennedys? *(Exits)*

GOODHUE: I'm tired.

(After MRS. GOODHUE *has left,* GOODHUE *rises in bed, begins peeling off the bandage.* GRAINGER *comes in with cable)*

GRAINGER: Should you be getting up, Mr. Goodhue?

GOODHUE: There's nothing wrong with my foot. I just don't want to go to the party. *(Gets out of bed and pulls robe around him showing the red and white stripes)*

GRAINGER: Oh! . . .

GOODHUE: They all want information on our Foreign Policy. I don't know what our Foreign Policy is. I do know what *my* policy is. Live and let live . . . only they won't let me!

GRAINGER: Your Excellency, we've got a wire.

GOODHUE: No official business. *(Goes to table and picks up candid camera)* Did you ever see this candid camera? One of the boys at the plant invented it. It's the last word in simplicity. It only takes one picture. *(He snaps* GRAINGER*)* You take out the film, and throw away the camera. *(He does)* As soon as I save up enough money out of my allowance, we're going into mass production. *(Goes over to trapshooting outfit)* This is my favorite hobby. I'm going to lobby for my hobby. *(Shoots at ducks at left)* I never miss. You see, practice makes perfect and I've got plenty of time to practice. Mrs. Goodhue runs everything. *(Puts gun down)*

GRAINGER: Your Excellency, we've got a wire from Mr. Hull.

GOODHUE: You have? Why didn't you tell me? Am I fired?

GRAINGER: We haven't decoded it yet.

GOODHUE: I'll decode it. It's the only fun I get around here. Gee, I hope he says I'm fired . . . *(He moves ladder up to blackboard, takes chalk and climbs up)*

GRAINGER: Eenie, meenie, minie, mo.

GOODHUE: *(Sings out)* Eenie, meenie, minie, mo. The twenty-third letter of the alphabet, divided by two—SO— *(Prints SO)*

GRAINGER: Beautiful Katie . . .

GOODHUE: Beautiful Katie—Beautiful Katie. Sock . . . *(He writes)* You're sure that's sock? Not sacked?

GRAINGER: No . . . Sock . . . The Glory Road.

GOODHUE: The Glory Road—The Glory Road. Second Letter H . . . skip one, purl two . . . I . . . add eight . . . HIM . . . HIM . . .

GRAINGER: Goodbye summer . . .

GOODHUE: Goodbye summer . . . AGAIN . . . Good gracious . . . SOCK HIM AGAIN!

GRAINGER: Signed . . . 3–8–7.

GOODHUE: 3–8–7. You know who. That's Mr. Hull. *(Gets down from stepladder.* THOMAS *enters. Pointing gloomily)* Look, from Mr. Hull—

THOMAS: *(Taking out wire)* From J. H . . . Amazed at your apathy . . . Do you want contract renewed?

GRAINGER: Well, I'll leave this air of gloom. Buck, I just wanted to tell you—I've dated Colette for every dance tonight. No cutting in!

THOMAS: Don't worry. I'm not in a dancing mood.

GRAINGER: Fine! *(He exits)*

THOMAS: How was I to know the whole world was waiting for someone to kick a Nazi in the belly? Stinky, I'm going to blow you out of Moscow by tomorrow. We've got to do something.

GOODHUE: I've been thinking . . . Maybe I can take some pictures of Stalin out of focus . . . I'll bet he won't like that.

THOMAS: Picayune.

GOODHUE: Picayune? I'm getting kind of discouraged. Other Ambassadors are getting recalled and I have to stay here. I feel like those fellows in Devil's Island . . .

THOMAS: This isn't definite . . . I'm just thinking aloud . . . Suppose you stole Lenin's corpse out of the mausoleum.

GOODHUE: What would I do with it?

THOMAS: *(Shakes his head, dismissing the idea)* There must be *something* you can do . . . After all, an Ambassador enjoys diplomatic immunity. He can't be arrested on foreign soil, for any crime.

GOODHUE: Is that a fact?

THOMAS: International law.

GOODHUE: I didn't know there was any . . .

THOMAS: Why, they can't even arrest you for murder . . . *(Stops)* Murder! . . . Why haven't I thought of that before?

GOODHUE: Well, that's not a nice thing to think about.

THOMAS: You're a crack shot . . . It all fits in . . . They can't possibly keep a diplomat who goes around ventilating people.

GOODHUE: But I don't want to murder anybody.

THOMAS: Who's asking you to? Scratch him . . . wing him . . . For our purposes, an attempted assassination is just as good as the real thing—Better! . . . Just as big a story and no messy consequences . . . We need somebody to shoot!

GOODHUE: *(Pensively)* Who have you got in mind?

(PRINCE ALEXANDER enters)

PRINCE: *(Bows)* Good evening, Your Excellency . . . How do you do, Mr. Thomas.

(THOMAS and GOODHUE look at each other, and then at the PRINCE. They nod their heads to each other designating that this is their man)

THOMAS: *(Awed)* The last of the Romanoffs!

PRINCE: I am not a Romanoff. *(To GOODHUE)* Your Excellency, I come to thank you personally for a magnificent dinner . . . Invite me again—and again—

GOODHUE: Mrs. Goodhue runs a pretty nice table.

THOMAS: *(Briskly)* Prince, what's your full name?

PRINCE: Alexander Ivanovitch Tomofsky . . . Why?

THOMAS: *(Taking notes)* I'm going to be writing about you.

PRINCE: Yes?

THOMAS: How old are you?

PRINCE: Guess.

THOMAS: We'll play games later.

PRINCE: Forty-four . . .

THOMAS: No living relatives?

PRINCE: No.

THOMAS: The last of the Romanoffs! What are you doing for dinner tomorrow?

PRINCE: Dinner? *(Turns to* GOODHUE*)* Am I invited here tomorrow?

GOODHUE: I wouldn't know. I only live here.

THOMAS: Come to my apartment . . . Say at six-thirty!

PRINCE: That would be nice . . . I shall come.

THOMAS: Without fail.

PRINCE: Without fail . . . *(Turns)* You know, Mr. Thomas, I came back to Moscow to die—

THOMAS: *(Guiltily)* Don't say that—

PRINCE: But I shall see you tomorrow at six-thirty. *(Exits)*

THOMAS: That's our man! Tomorrow night at six-thirty you'll be out on my balcony . . . Wing him . . . and run . . . and leave the rest to me.

GOODHUE: But wait a minute, Buck—

THOMAS: From the balcony of my room a hand comes through the curtain, and bang—bang—the last of the Romanoffs slumps to the floor.

GOODHUE: Gee, that's good . . . I'm getting goose pimples.

THOMAS: The hue and cry . . . the next day: "U. S. Ambassador Suspected . . . U. S. Ambassador Grilled . . . U. S. Ambassador Admits Shooting . . . *U. S. Ambassador Recalled . . . !*"

GOODHUE: It's just like a dream.

THOMAS: Your name will be mud around the world. What do you say, Stinky?

GOODHUE: I like it. I've got two wonderful guns. They're called the G-man's guardian and the policeman's pal. I'll go in the next room and get them. *(Exits)*

(DOLLY enters)

DOLLY: Hello, Buckie.

THOMAS: Hello, Dolly.

DOLLY: I don't often come into a gentleman's room without knocking, but I wanted to say goodbye to the Ambassador before I leave.

THOMAS: You're leaving?

DOLLY: Well, I have to go back to J. H. eventually. Now don't act silly about it. You remember that Belgian Count? He made an awful fuss. He even sent his father up. And what a time I had with the father!!

THOMAS: You innocent adorable child!

(DOLLY and THOMAS come downstage and curtain closes on bedroom. They sing: "When All's Said and Done")

(Verse)

THOMAS:

This affair has been so swell,
But we must face the fact,
That once it used to ring the bell,
But now it's out of the act.

DOLLY:

Dear Buckie, you'll go far!
What a great philosopher you are.

(Refrain)
THOMAS:

> *When all's said and done,*
> *Though I hate to see you go,*
> *When all's said and done,*
> *I must say it's best.*

DOLLY:

> *When all's said and done*
> *We've had plenty heidy-ho,*
> *It's all been sublime*
> *But I guess it's time*
> *We gave it a rest.*

THOMAS:

> *We've had so much pleasure, playing,*
> *But there's an old saying,*
> *Oh, so profound,*
> *"You can't have peaches all the year 'round."*

DOLLY:

> *So long and goodbye,*
> *It's been proven in the past*
> *The real good things never last,*
> *And we've had our fun, Baby,*

BOTH:

> *When all's said and done.*

(1st Patter)
DOLLY:

> *We've wandered 'neath the stars together,*
> *And in the rain.*

THOMAS:

> *We've opened so many bars together*
> *And so much champagne.*

DOLLY:

> *How often we did the town together*

THOMAS:

> *And ended by falling down together.*

DOLLY:

> *But now, honey, it's*
> *The end of it all, let's call it quits.*

THOMAS:

> *So long and goodbye*
> *Without even feeling sad,*
> *Because, heaven knows, we've had*
> *A whole lotta fun, Baby,*

BOTH:
When all's said and done.

    Blackout

SCENE 6

Another part of the park in Moscow.
There is a platform about two feet high with steps right of center leading up to
platform. There is an arch over steps. Painted on arch is "Park of Culture and Rest".
Over this sign is the same written in Russian.
DAUGHTERS *and* SECRETARIES *are discovered on stage and execute dance to*
"When All's Said and Done". At the conclusion of the dance, they exit. The
SHOWGIRLS *and* SINGING BOYS *enter and complete number with* DOLLY *and*
THOMAS.

OCTETTE and LES GIRLS:
When all's said and done
Though I hate to see you go,
When all's said and done, I must say it's best
When all's said and done
We've had plenty heidy-ho,
It's all been sublime
But I guess it's time
We gave it a rest.
We've had so much pleasure playing
But there's an old saying,
Oh, so profound,
So very true
The birds fly south when summer is thru
So long and goodbye,
You go your way, I'll go mine
And someday drop me a line
We've had so much fun, Baby,
When all's said and done.

(DOLLY *and* THOMAS *re-enter)*
(*2nd Patter)*
DOLLY:
Each evening, we'd set sail together,
And never stop.

THOMAS:
We nearly once went to jail together,
But you vamped the cop.

DOLLY:
How often we meant to sup together,

THOMAS:
And ended by waking up together,

DOLLY:
And now duty calls
Me back to my Dad's marble halls.

THOMAS:
So long and good-bye,

DOLLY:
You go your way, I'll go mine,

THOMAS:
And some day drop me a line

BOTH:
We've had so much fun, Baby
When all's said and done.

Blackout

SCENE 7

THOMAS' *Hotel Suite in Moscow.*
There is a double door upstage center. At stage left are French doors, opening offstage. These doors are richly draped, and are one step high which gives the effect of the balcony offstage. At stage right there are two doors, one step high. The lower door leads to bathroom, the upper door to THOMAS' *bedroom. A modernistic fireplace divides these two rooms. On mantel is a specially built clock. In front of fireplace, a desk and chair. On desk, typewriter, telephone and desk equipment. At stage left there is a single chair placed directly center of French doors. Left of center door upstage is an armchair. The entire room is furnished in excellent taste.*
At Rise: Clock on mantel chimes once. THOMAS *is typing.* GOODHUE *is standing with revolver.*

THOMAS: Six-thirty! *(Indicates batch of manuscript)* Story is written—now you know what you've got to do.

GOODHUE: I go out on the balcony . . . you put the Prince in this chair . . . I wait for the clock to strike . . . on the seventh chime, I shoot. But not in a vulnerable spot. I ping him . . . I sting him . . . I wing him . . .

THOMAS: Perfect! . . . Any questions?

GOODHUE: Should I take his picture before I shoot him or after?

THOMAS: No pictures!

GOODHUE: I thought the kids might like it.

THOMAS: Don't waste time! Get out on that balcony, and make sure you can see this chair . . .

GOODHUE: All right . . . You sit in it. *(*THOMAS *does.* GOODHUE *goes to the balcony)* When I see Mr. Hull, I'm going to tell him what I had to go through to get out of my job. *(He steps behind the curtains)*

THOMAS: Hurry up! . . . Can you see me?

GOODHUE: Just a moment. *(He steps back and adjusts* THOMAS' *head as if he were posing a subject)* The chin up, please . . . Look over there . . . That's it . . . Perfect! *(He goes back to the balcony)*

THOMAS: How is it?

GOODHUE: The pose is very good, but— *(He fires the gun, and only a click is heard)* but there's something wrong with the G-man's guardian. I wish I had the policeman's pal. *(He opens the gun)*

*(*PRINCE *enters center)*

PRINCE: Pardon me, am I late?

GOODHUE: We're not quite ready for you. Have you got a screwdriver?

PRINCE: I have a knife . . . *(Gives it to him)*

GOODHUE: That'll do . . . thanks.

PRINCE: Not at all . . . But where is the dinner?

THOMAS: There's been a slight delay. How would you like to take a bath?

PRINCE: A bath?

THOMAS: *(Crosses toward bathroom door with* PRINCE*)* Then you'll have some vodka . . . some caviar . . . some truffles . . . your favorite goose, etc., etc . . . You'll be sitting right in that chair *(He indicates)* lapping it up just as soon as you've had your bath.

PRINCE: Very well. I shall bathe. I enjoy to bathe. There is a Russian saying, "When the bird puts water on his tail, he also washes his face." *(He exits into bathroom)*

THOMAS: How's that gun?

GOODHUE: There's a screw loose—I mean in the gun. *(Gun snaps)* Now I can load it up.

(Bathroom door opens and PRINCE *emerges)*

THOMAS: *(Tensely)* What's wrong?

PRINCE: The water—it is very hot. I shall luxuriate.

THOMAS: Fine! . . .

PRINCE: I was thinking in there. What is life? A bath—dinner—a charming woman—such simple things and now so difficult to obtain. Interesting, n'est-ce pas? *(He exits)*

GOODHUE: You better lock him in.

THOMAS: Get going! Remember—the seventh chime! *(*GOODHUE *exits through balcony.* THOMAS *goes to bathroom)* How are you doing, Prince? *(*PRINCE *carols.* THOMAS *nods, satisfied. He goes to balcony. To* GOODHUE*)* Are you all right? *(*PRINCE *stops carols)*

GOODHUE: *(Sticking his head through curtain)* Just perfect! I'm raring to go. *(He sticks his head in. Door center opens and a strange apparition appears in a bathrobe. This is* MACKENZIE, *King's Messenger, crosses to bathroom)*

THOMAS: *(Stops him)* What do you want? Who are you?

MACKENZIE: I'm Mackenzie, King's Messenger . . . I believe you're Mr. Thomas . . . I've the room down the corridor and I have no bath . . . I've always used yours . . . I'm simply filthy! May I?

THOMAS: *(Leading him to door center)* Not now . . . Come back tomorrow . . . Bath's engaged.

MACKENZIE: Oh, dear . . .

THOMAS: Why don't you take an all-over sponge? *(He pushes him out and locks the door. He goes to bathroom)* You'd better hurry, Prince. Dinner is coming up any moment. *(*PRINCE *carols. Knock at the door . . . another knock . . .* THOMAS, *disgusted, goes to door, doesn't open it)* Who's there?

VOICE (COLETTE): Open the door . . . It's me, Colette . . . *(*THOMAS *opens the door. She enters.* PRINCE *carols)* Buck, I wanted to tell you—Who's that?

*(*PRINCE *stops carols)*

THOMAS: Never mind him.

COLETTE: You have guests?

(GOODHUE sticks his head out)

GOODHUE: Raring to go! *(He disappears)*

COLETTE: What's the Ambassador doing out there? What are you up to, Buck? This room smells of your intrigue.

THOMAS: Darling—

COLETTE: Why can't you leave a country in the same condition you find it?

THOMAS: Look—I'm only trying to discredit the Ambassador.

COLETTE: Some more of J. H.'s dirty work?

THOMAS: But the Ambassador wants to be discredited. He wants to go home.

COLETTE: I don't believe you, Buck.

(Knock at door)

KOSTYA: Mr. Thomas. Mr. Thomas.

THOMAS: Damn it—what does that interpreter of mine want now? *(He moves toward door.* COLETTE *follows him)*

KOSTYA: Mr. Thomas. Mr. Thomas.

THOMAS: *(At door)* Kostya—no interpreting today . . . I don't want to be disturbed.

KOSTYA: Open the door, Mr. Thomas . . . It is important! *(COLETTE unlocks door.* KOSTYA *slips in breathlessly)* Oh, Mr. Thomas, Mr. Thomas, the Foreign Minister wants to see you.

COLETTE: *(Seeing* BUCK'S *agonized reaction)* Good luck, Buck. I have a feeling you'll need it. *(She exits)*

THOMAS: Look Kostya, tell the Foreign Minister I'll see him tomorrow.

KOSTYA: But that is impossible. He is coming now.

THOMAS: Now? *Here—?*

(TWO MEN enter center, dressed in uniform)

KOSTYA: This is the secret service who go with the Foreign Minister . . . Comrade Graustein . . . and Comrade Golkin . . . *(They bow)*

THOMAS: Secret service?

(Another MAN enters. Dressed in business suit)

KOSTYA: And this is the secretary to Foreign Minister.

(FOREIGN MINISTER enters, dressed in cutaway and derby)

And this is the Foreign Minister.

FOREIGN MINISTER: How do you do, Mr. Thomas.

THOMAS: I'm—I'm delighted to meet you, Mr. Commissar . . . This is an unexpected pleasure . . . I uh . . .

FOREIGN MINISTER: *(Making his way to appointed chair)* I took the liberty of calling on you quite unofficially, knowing you are very close to the American Ambassador. May I? *(Looks at chair. He seats himself)* I ask you: Why doesn't he receive me? Why does he refuse to talk to me? Have we offended him?

THOMAS: No . . . Is that all you wanted to know? The answer is no.

FOREIGN MINISTER: No?

THOMAS: No. Well, goodbye, Mr. Commissar— *(Extends hand)*

FOREIGN MINISTER: *(He rises)* I am relieved. It has occurred to me that I have denied you an interview. Perhaps we can kill two birds with one stone. *(Sits again)*

THOMAS: You want me to interview you?

FOREIGN MINISTER: Yes. Interview me.

THOMAS: Very well . . . Is Socialism a success?

FOREIGN MINISTER: Yes.

THOMAS: *(Quickly)* Thank you very much. That's all I wanted to know.

FOREIGN MINISTER: But when I say it has been a success I do not wish to imply we've accomplished everything we've hoped for. *(Clock starts chiming)* The difficulties of foreign relations—the necessity for armaments— *(After seventh chime)*

THOMAS: DON'T SHOOT—that's the policy of our paper . . . DON'T SHOOT the Russian experiment—DON'T SHOOT the powers of progress. DON'T SHOOT anything—anybody . . . Let us have peace!

    Blackout

(In darkness, THOMAS continues)

THOMAS: DON'T SHOOT . . . innocent men, women and children . . . DON'T SHOOT a hair of yon grey head.

    (The lights come up on the balcony of THOMAS' suite. It is a continuation of the previous scene. GOODHUE is examining his gun when SOZANOFF suddenly appears right)

GOODHUE: Pardon me . . . Have you a screwdriver?

SOZANOFF: No.

GOODHUE: Have you a knife?

SOZANOFF: No. *(He seizes the gun, looks at it)* And you call yourself a revolutionist! *(Gives gun back)* Are you in my party?

GOODHUE: Are you a democrat?

SOZANOFF: I am syndicalist.

GOODHUE: How did you boys make out in the primaries?

THOMAS' VOICE: Don't shoot!

SOZANOFF: Do you hear them? Don't shoot . . . They know I'm here. They know I followed them from the Foreign Office . . . Tomorrow my picture will be on every wall . . . My statue in every park!

GOODHUE: That so? Maybe the hotel clerk has a screwdriver. Will you pardon me? I'll look for your statue in the park.

    (He exits, left. SOZANOFF waits, takes out gun. As he moves forward to French doors:)

    Blackout

(The lights come up immediately on the hotel room)

THOMAS: *(Panting)* Don't shoot the birds in the trees . . . That, in a nutshell, is the philosophy *(He pants)* of the New Deal . . . And I guess everything is all right . . . Everything is all right. *(SOZANOFF emerges with gun through French doors)* What the—!!

SOZANOFF: Up with your hands! . . . *All of you! (They lift their hands. He moves further in to chair)* I have come, Mr. Thomas, to make news. I shall do something. Just as you said. I am going to liquidate the Commissar of Foreign Affairs—

THOMAS: You're crazy!

SOZANOFF: That's what the doctors said. *(To FOREIGN MINISTER)* Do you remember me? Sozanoff wasn't good enough to be even a clerk in your office. Sozanoff couldn't spell. *(He seats himself in chair)*

THOMAS: Now look here, my man— *(THOMAS drops clock. It begins to chime)*

SOZANOFF: Silence! This is a moment in history. *(Clock chimes)*

(GOODHUE sticks his face through curtain, gets nod from THOMAS. He counts the chimes on fingers)

SOZANOFF: I am taking the power. *(Clock chimes)* And now you shiver when your clerk talks . . . you are pale . . . *(Clock chimes)* *You shall die . . . you shall all die . . .* *(Clock chimes)* *Tomorrow I shall sit in the Kremlin!* (Clock chimes)

(GOODHUE fires on seventh chime and comes in. SECRET SERVICE MEN leap on SOZANOFF and carry him off thru center door)

COMMISSAR: Your Excellency! You have saved my life. *(Kisses GOODHUE)*

(PRINCE emerges from bathroom)

PRINCE: Dinner is not yet ready?

THOMAS: *(Taking it all out on the PRINCE)* You get the hell out of here!

    Fast Curtain

(COLETTE enters in front of curtain followed by entire ENSEMBLE dressed in peasant and Russian character costumes. They sing: "Comrade Alonzo". At finish of the 1st Refrain, the curtain opens on Scene 8)

ENSEMBLE:

> *Comrade Alonzo, we love you, Russia will never forget.*
> *By the deed you have done*
> *You have proved to be one*
> *Of the biggest Bolsheviks yet.*
> *Bill Bullitt, at heart was a bourgeois and Davies played ball with the upper set,*
> *So we thank Topeka, Kan.*
> *For you, little man,*
> *The Saviour of the Soviet,*
> *No Russia will never forget.*

(ALL)

> *'Tis the final conflict, let each stand in his place,*
> *The International Soviet shall lead the human race,*
> *'Tis the final conflict, let each stand in his place,*
> *The International Soviet shall lead the human race.*

STALIN

> *Nyet, nyet, nyet, nyet,*

DOUBLE QUARTETTE

> *The greatest Ambassador yet,*

THOMAS

> *Nyet, nyet, nyet, nyet,*

DOUBLE QUARTETTE

> *Alonzo P. Goodhue, our pet.*

GOODHUE

> *Nyet, nyet, nyet, nyet,*

(ALL)

> *The Saviour of the Soviet.*

SCENE 8

Red Square.

This scene is rich in color. Direct center is a platform about four feet high—and ten feet long with four steps on each side leading up to it. This gives the impression of a grandstand.

Discovered on platform are GOODHUE, *dressed in high top silk hat, and in silk knickerbockers.* THOMAS, COLETTE, MRS. GOODHUE, STALIN *(Dressed in an exact replica of Stalin himself),* FOREIGN MINISTER *in high top hat and* GRAUSTEIN. *They have been watching parade.* ENSEMBLE *finishes number on stage.*

GOODHUE: Look, Mr. Stalin, I've been on my feet seven hours. You're used to it, but I got awful tender feet.

(STALIN leans forward and kisses him. CROWD *cheers)*

MRS. GOODHUE: I bet the Kennedys are boiling!

GOODHUE: I don't want to be kissed. I don't want to be an Ambassador. I want to go home!

THOMAS: Keep your chin up. I'll get you out of here if I have to smuggle you out of the country in the Russian Ballet. Why didn't I think of that before!

(ENSEMBLE picks up number "Comrade Alonzo" and continues until:)

Curtain

ACT TWO

SCENE 1

Red Square.

At Rise: The same people, with the exception of the FOREIGN MINISTER, *are discovered on platform as in Act One, Scene 8.* GOODHUE *is in a Cossack uniform.*

The ENSEMBLE *does one chorus of dance and sing another refrain of "Comrade Alonzo" and all exit stage left, giving the impression that the parade is continuing down the street.*

GOODHUE, MRS. GOODHUE, COLETTE *and* THOMAS *emerge from the grandstand.*

GOODHUE: *(Very tired)* Well, I guess that's over—It's been going on for two weeks. Buck, I don't want to be an Ambassador. I won't have any feet left.

MRS. GOODHUE: A.P.

COLETTE: Don't you want to leave your name in history?

MRS. GOODHUE: You owe it to me, A.P.

GOODHUE: You're all against me.

MRS. GOODHUE: I won't take London, now. I'll have you made Ambassador-at-Large!

GOODHUE: That's just how I feel. *(He exits.* MRS. GOODHUE *follows)*

COLETTE: Nice work, Buck. If you keep on discrediting the Ambassador, he will end up with the Nobel prize.

THOMAS: *(To* COLETTE*)* I failed him again. What's the matter with me?

COLETTE: You're practically perfect.

THOMAS: I used to be able to go into a country, arrange duels, assassinations, have people thrown into jail, out of jail. Took it all in my stride . . . What are you doing to me?

COLETTE: What am *I* doing?

THOMAS: Ever since I saw you in the Embassy my hand has lost its cunning. I'm thinking pure thoughts. I feel like Walter Lippman.

COLETTE: Impossible.

THOMAS: You've changed me. Don't deny it—you have. And I'm worried, Colette, I'm worried. Let's drive somewhere and think this out.

(They come downstage, looking for a Droshky as the curtain closes)

COLETTE: Droshky! Droshky! Droshky!

THOMAS: Taxi!

COLETTE: Droshky!

SCENE 2

Droshky.

Direct center on platform six inches high covered with velvet is a Russian Droshky seat.

GRAUSTEIN *enters immediately stage left.*

GRAUSTEIN: Pardon me, Mr. Thomas, I have a telegram for you. *(Gives it to him)*
(COLETTE gets into Droshky)

THOMAS: Oh, thanks. *(Reaches in pocket for tip)*

GRAUSTEIN: No tipping. In Soviet Russia, messenger tips you.

THOMAS: Propaganda.

GRAUSTEIN: Correct. *(THOMAS opens wire)* The telegram is signed Dolly . . . The message: "I took the wrong train. I am stranded in Siberia. It's snowing. Send one thousand dollars or I'll tell J.H. and I know plenty."

THOMAS: Do you make a practice of reading telegrams you deliver?

GRAUSTEIN: Of course. *(Exits)*

COLETTE: Your past catching up with you?

THOMAS: What do you think? The poor kid landed in Siberia. She wants one thousand dollars. How much money have I in the bank?

COLETTE: Twenty-three dollars overdrawn.

THOMAS: All right, I'll send her that. *(THOMAS gets into Droshky)* Tell him to —just drive . . .

COLETTE: *(In Russian)* Just drive . . . *(She moves close to him)*

(They sing: "From Now On." The Droshky moves down front, and goes down on each patter and back up on end of each)
  (1st Verse)
THOMAS:
  A fool there was
  And he made his pray'r
  To lights that glitter,
  Bugs that jitter
  And girls too bitter to care.
  But this fool that was
  Has suddenly found life solved
  Since you appeared,
  So, Baby, be it resolved

(1st Refrain)
From now on, no more philand'ring,
No more hot-spots, no scatter-brain.
From now on, my fun will be meand'ring
With my darling down lover's lane.
The old gang will never know me
When they find
I've become the kind
People call "homey",
No more yearn for something new, dear,
My address is you, dear,
From now on.

(2nd Verse)
COLETTE:
I'd like to b'lieve, cheri,
The words that you say to me,
For if I had your love
Could I ask for anything more?
But, frankly, dites-moi
Exactly, combien de fois,
When the moon shone above
Have you said before?

(2nd Refrain)
"From now on, no more philand'ring,
No more hot-spots, no scatter-brain,
From now on, my fun will be meand'rin'
With my darling, down lover's lane."
I can't b'lieve a word you say, boy,
For you see
You were born to be
Merely a play-boy.
So, put love back on the shelf, dear,
Be your charming self
From now on.

THOMAS: Happy?
COLETTE: I've never been so happy.
   (GOODHUE *enters with hitchhiking gesture. Still in Cossack uniform*)
GOODHUE: Going my way?
COLETTE: *(In Russian, to driver)* Stop!
THOMAS: Hop in, Stinky.
GOODHUE: *(Gets in)* Thanks. Mrs. Goodhue picked up some of the Les Girls and
   there wasn't room for me in the Ambassador's car.
THOMAS: Relax!
GOODHUE: I can't. I'm raging inside.
THOMAS: What's the matter?
GOODHUE: You promised to get me recalled, and instead you make me a hero!
THOMAS: Now wait a minute, Stinky. Maybe we've got the wrong slant on this

whole thing. Maybe we shouldn't try to tear you down. Maybe we should build you up!

GOODHUE: Build me up? For what?

THOMAS: I'm thinking of 1940.

COLETTE: *(To driver)* Stop! *(To* THOMAS*)* I'm home.

*(*THOMAS *and* COLETTE *get out of Droshky)*

THOMAS: Stinky, trot along to the Embassy. Don't worry, I won't let you down. Good night. *(*THOMAS *exits with* COLETTE*)*

GOODHUE: Good night. Driver, I want to go to the Americansky Embassky. *(*PEOPLE *start entering from stage right and left. He speaks to some of them)* Can you tell the driver the way to the American Embassy? *(They don't understand. Pass by. He asks another group, and they pass by. And finally he gives up and sits back in Droshky)* I want to go home!

GOODHUE: *(Sings "I Want to Go Home")*
(Verse)
When the sun goes down on the big Red Square,
I dream of Kansas a way out there
And I get so homesick I swear
I just go silly.
How I long, at the drugstore, again to sit
And order a double banana split,
And then wash it down with some rare old sars'parilly.
The trouble is with this job
You can't get corn-on-the-cob.

(1st Refrain)
I want to go home to old Topeka
And cry "Eureka,
I'm here to stay!"
I want to go home to middle-west land
'Cause that is the best land
In the world today.
When those Cossacks start to sing,
That's when I retire,
Why they couldn't show a thing
To our Baptist choir.
Topeka to some may seem a hick town,
To me it's a slick town,
And I want to go home!

(2nd Refrain)
I want to go home to old Topeka
And cry "Eureka,
I'm here to stay!"
I want to go home to middle-west land
'Cause that is the best land
In the world today.
How I long once more to go
With the folks that we know

To a double-feature show
For a game of "Beano".
Some visitors say Topeka's dirty,
To me it's so purty
And I want to go home.

(3rd Refrain)
I want to go home to old Topeka
And cry "Eureka,
I'm here to stay!"
I want to go home to middle-west land
'Cause that is the best land
In the world today.
Often, ev'nings, just for fun,
When I've ceased my labors,
I take pop-shots with my gun
Just to scare the neighbors.
Topeka to you might seem too quiet,
To me it's a riot,
And I want to go home.

(4th Refrain)
And besides her city-hall
And her other glories,
There's a pool-room where they all
Tell the darnedest stories!
Topeka to you may be the last town,
To me it's a fast town
And I want to go home.

(Dream Sequence. Alternately flashes are seen on each side of the stage)
GOOD HUMOR VENDOR: *(Dressed in white coat and hat with Good Humor box around shoulders)* Good Humor, Mister. Good Humor?
GAS STATION ATTENDANT: *(Dressed in overalls and dirty rag in hand)* Check your oil, Mister? Check your oil?
A PEANUT VENDOR: *(Dressed in white coat and cap with tray around shoulders)* Get your scorecard! Popcorn, peanuts, hot dogs!
A HORSESHOE PLAYER: *(Coatless. He throws a horseshoe)*
GOODHUE: A ringer!
MRS. GOODHUE: *(She appears with bonnet and gingham dress, sitting on gate)*
GOODHUE: Leora!
(A BARBERSHOP QUARTET enters. They are dressed in white coats and each carries a barber's tool. They join GOODHUE in a reprise of the 4th Refrain of "I Want to Go Home")

Curtain

SCENE 3

GOODHUE's *Bedroom in the Embassy.*
At Rise: GOODHUE *enters carrying boots, throws them down. Scene opens in dim light, then flash up with* GRAINGER'S *entrance.*

GRAINGER: *(Offstage)* Mr. Ambassador! Mr. Ambassador! *(He enters left and goes to bed)* Pardon me, Mr. Ambassador. Are you asleep?

GOODHUE: Only my feet.

GRAINGER: Well, Buck Thomas is downstairs kicking up a row because I don't think you should see him. It will give me a great deal of pleasure to tell him he's barred from the Embassy forever.

GOODHUE: Oh, boy. I wish *I* was!

GRAINGER: Shall I make it clear to him that his presence is not desired?
(THOMAS enters with package)

THOMAS: Stinky, I've got it!

GRAINGER: Wait a minute, Buck—

THOMAS: I've finally got it. I'll underwrite it. I'll guarantee it. We can't fail!

GRAINGER: Mr. Ambassador, I warn you. Mr. Thomas is not a good influence!

GOODHUE: He was too good for me.

THOMAS: Stinky, I'll stake everything on this—Everything!

GOODHUE: You really got something this time?

THOMAS: I've got it!

GOODHUE: All right, Grainger, I will receive him.
(GRAINGER shrugs and exits)

THOMAS: I sat down with pencil and paper. I analyzed what was wrong with everything we've done. And finally I got it. We've been barking up the wrong tree.

GOODHUE: Huh?

THOMAS: And it's all my fault. I was old-fashioned. I didn't realize the world had changed. I had you kick people in the belly, shoot somebody. Wrong, Stinky, wrong.

GOODHUE: Wrong?

THOMAS: Let me make this clear to you. In real life what happens to the innocent bystander who tries to stop a fight?

GOODHUE: Nothing.

THOMAS: He's taken to the hospital with a fractured skull. What happens to the kindly old gentleman who stops his car to let the baby carriage pass? He's given a ticket for stalling traffic.

GOODHUE: Not in Topeka!

THOMAS: Everywhere! Don't you realize it's the idealist who gets kicked in the fanny?

GOODHUE: I'm a Rotarian.

THOMAS: Get this and get this straight: There's only one way for you to get out of this job . . .

GOODHUE: How?

THOMAS: Do a good deed.

GOODHUE: Yes?

THOMAS: Take this job seriously and I'll have you out of here so fast you won't know what hit you!

GOODHUE: *(Rises)* Well, I've always thought I could do something good here— Like: Why should the Germans hate the Russians?

THOMAS: That's it! That's it!

GOODHUE: We don't understand New Yorkers in Topeka. But we don't want to kill 'em.

THOMAS: That's it! That's it!

GOODHUE: Folks can get along together.

THOMAS: *(Extending his hand)* You're practically on your way out—

GOODHUE: But I mean it!

THOMAS: I want you to mean it. I want you to be completely sincere. I want you to be a wide-eyed idealist—and *here's* a present for you. Get used to wearing it. *(Gives him package)*

GOODHUE: What is it?

THOMAS: A bulletproof vest!

    Blackout

SCENE 4

A Steppe, somewhere in Siberia.

When curtain opens it is snowing. Direct center is DOLLY'S *baggage trunk. Right of center is a Russian sign post made like a cross. On sign is painted, in Russian: "NPKYTCK".*

At Rise: DOLLY *is standing at sign post. On music cue, six* BOYS, *dressed in furs for the Siberian winter, enter and group around her as she sings "My Heart Belongs to Daddy". As the number progresses,* DOLLY *does an enticing mock strip-tease.*

DOLLY: *(Sings "My Heart Belongs to Daddy")*
(Verse)
I used to fall
In love with all
Those boys who maul
Refined ladies.
But now I tell
Each young gazelle
To go to hell—
I mean, Hades,
For since I've come to care
For such a sweet millionaire

(Refrain)
While tearing off
A game of golf
I may make a play for the caddy
But when I do
I don't follow through
'Cause my heart belongs to Daddy.
If I invite
A boy, some night
To dine on my fine finnan haddie,
I just adore
His asking for more,
But my heart belongs to Daddy
Yes, my heart belongs to Daddy.
So I simply couldn't be bad.

Yes, my heart belongs to Daddy,
Da-da, da-da-da, da-da-da, Dad!
So I want to warn you, laddie,
Tho' I know you're perfectly swell,
That my heart belongs to Daddy
'Cause my Daddy, he treats me so well.
He treats it and treats it,
And then he repeats it,
Yes, Daddy, he treats it so well.

(2nd Refrain)
Saint Patrick's day,
Although I may
Be seen wearing green
With a paddy,
I'm always sharp
When playing a harp
'Cause my heart belongs to Daddy.
Though other dames
At football games
May long for a strong undergraddy,
I never dream
Of making the team
'Cause my heart belongs to Daddy.
Yes, my heart belongs to Daddy
So I simply couldn't be bad,
Yes, my heart belongs to Daddy,
Da-da, da-da-da-da-da-da-, Dad!
So I want to warn you, laddie,
Tho' I simply hate to be frank,
That I can't be mean to Daddy
'Cause my Da-da-da-daddy might spank.
In matters artistic
He's not modernistic
So Da-da-da-daddy might spank.

Blackout

SCENE 5

Anteroom in the American Embassy, Moscow.
At center stage there is a small round gilded table with chair. Stage left: two Louis XIV armless chairs. At stage right, the same.
At Rise: FIVE DAUGHTERS *and some of the* AMBASSADORS *and* SHOWGIRLS *are discovered on in groups.* AMBASSADORS *are in uniforms and* SHOWGIRLS *in evening gowns.*
Enter some more AMBASSADORS *and* SHOWGIRLS.
BRITISH AMBASSADOR: How do you do, Your Excellency. Are you still bombing our damned ships?
ITALIAN AMBASSADOR: Italy wants England's friendship.
FRENCH AMBASSADOR: Is my country at war with your country?

YOGI AMBASSADOR: Peace. Father, it's wonderful.

(GUESTS *start filing out right.* MRS. GOODHUE *enters with* FOREIGN MINISTER. *He leaves her and exits with other guests)*

MRS. GOODHUE: *(Looking after them)* Roughriders of Europe!

*(*DAUGHTERS *come up to her)*

DAUGHTERS: Mother, what are we waiting for?

MRS. GOODHUE: Your father, as usual. He's going to read the Goodhue Plan for us before he goes into conference with the other Ambassadors.

*(*THOMAS *in full dress enters . . . holding* GOODHUE *by the hand. He is dressed in a specially designed suit with silk knickerbockers. American eagles and colors are designed on suit in conspicuous places. He wears a plumed hat like that of an Admiral. He shows suit off to* DAUGHTERS *and* MRS. GOODHUE*)*

GOODHUE: Buck, I don't feel right in this suit.

THOMAS: We must have dignity.

GOODHUE: I like the hat.

*(*THOMAS *turns to* MRS. GOODHUE*)*

THOMAS: Mrs. Goodhue—have the Ambassadors arrived?

MRS. GOODHUE: Yes, they are all here except the Japanese Ambassador. He's late.

THOMAS: I guess he mislaid his camera. Now, your Excellency, when we go into the conference room, this is what I'm going to say: "Gentlemen, His Excellency, the United States Ambassador to Moscow, and my silent partner in the Goodhue Plan and incidentally a very great man and like another great American—first in the hearts of his countrymen, will now present the Goodhue Plan." *(*THOMAS *hands* GOODHUE *speech)*

GOODHUE: Is this it?

THOMAS: That's it.

GOODHUE: Shall I read it?

THOMAS: With feeling.

GOODHUE: *(Reading)* "Applause." Now I've lost my place. *(To* THOMAS*)* Where was I?

THOMAS: *(Finding the place)* Page Two.

GOODHUE: "Page Two . . . Plank."

THOMAS: Plank Number One.

GOODHUE: "Plank number one of the Goodhue Plan is as follows: The people of each nation will admit they are no better and no worse than the people of any other nation!

"Plank Two. . . . Since for centuries the nations of Europe have fought for the possession of colonies, the Goodhue Plan abolishes colonies. *(Continues reading)* In the United States, we civilize an immigrant in one generation . . . If you can't civilize a colony in ten generations, there's something wrong . . . Maybe you don't want to civilize them." *(To* THOMAS*)* There's something in that.

THOMAS: Go ahead.

GOODHUE: "Plank Three . . . Now I come to the most important phase of the Goodhue Plan . . . I propose to keep all the benefits of war, and none of the drawbacks." *(To* THOMAS*)* That'll be quite a trick. *(Continues reading)* "We will take the case of France and Germany . . . We will say that Germany is bored. It has no more good books to burn. So they whoop up the idea of war with

France. Under the Goodhue Plan, the German Army will march into France."
(Marches goose-step, then continues reading) "But the French Army will not
stop them. Oh, no. The French Army will march into Germany." *(Marches)*
"Both Armies will be quartered in each other's countries. And not a shot fired!
Not a shot." *(To* THOMAS*)* That makes sense. *(Continues reading)* "That brings
me to the most important plank: Plank Four—Sex!" *(Looks quizzically at*
THOMAS *and* MRS. GOODHUE*)*

THOMAS: Sex!

GOODHUE: *(Continues reading)* "The French soldiers will live in German houses.
The German soldiers will live in French houses. And what are the results?"
(Takes glasses off and smiles) Fun for everybody. *(Continues reading)* "At the end
of one year, the soldiers will be home sick."

THOMAS: *(Correcting him)* Homesick.

GOODHUE: Homesick. *(Continues reading)* "The Armies march back. *(Business of
marching)* The result of a year's occupation will bring about a whole generation, not of Germans, not of Frenchmen, but Franco-Germans . . . Now . . .
Twenty years pass . . . The Franco-German Army marches into Russia . . . We
have a generation of Franco-German-Russians . . . Gentlemen, 'ere long, there
will be no nations. We will have the United States of Europe."
(SECRETARY enters)

SECRETARY: The Ambassadors are ready, Your Excellency.

THOMAS: *(To* SECRETARY*)* Thumbtacks on every chair?

SECRETARY: Yes, sir.

THOMAS: Are the cigars all loaded for the Ambassadors?

SECRETARY: Yes, sir. *(He exits)*

GOODHUE: Buck, this won't get me recalled. This is a good plan.

THOMAS: I know it is. *(Hisses are heard offstage)*

GOODHUE: What's that?

THOMAS: Just the Japanese Ambassador being polite. Come on. *(Takes* GOOD-
HUE'S *hand and leads him off)*

MRS. GOODHUE: Children, some day your father will be a bust in the Hall
of Fame.
(A group of LADIES *enter)*

A LADY: Mrs. Goodhue, could you tell us what your husband's plan is? Is it
a secret?

MRS. GOODHUE: I can't tell you, exactly . . . But roughly . . . very
roughly . . . *(Lyrically she explains. Curtain closes on anteroom and* MRS. GOOD-
HUE, SHOWGIRLS *and* SINGING BOYS *come downstage)*

MRS. GOODHUE: *(Sings "TOMORROW")*
(Verse)
Ladies and gentlemen, when my heart is sick
I've got a remedy that does the trick,
So, ladies and gentlemen, whenever you're blue
I advise you to try
My
Remedy too,
Just say

(1st Refrain)
Tomorrow, your troubles'll be done,
Tomorrow, your vict'ry'll be won,
Tomorrow, we're all gonna have fun,
'Cause there ain't gonna be no sorrow, Tomorrow.
Tomorrow, when the dawn appears, we all will be so good,
And so intent on doing just exactly as we should,
That there'll be no double-crossing, even out in Hollywood,
'Cause there ain't gonna be no sorrow, Tomorrow.
Tomorrow, you poor Jerseyites, who got such awful jars
When Orson Welles went on the air and made you all see stars,
I know you'll be relieved to hear we're giving him back to Mars,
'Cause there ain't gonna be no sorrow, Tomorrow.
Tomorrow, plumpish ladies, who are heavier than whales,
Will wake to find that suddenly they're all as thin as rails,
So little Elsa Maxwell will no longer break the scales,
'Cause there ain't gonna be no sorrow, Tomorrow.
We'll have so much spare time that each of Maurice Evans' plays
Instead of lasting seven hours will last for days and days,
And to make all Federal projects even bigger, we propose
To throw out Harry Hopkins and instead hire Billy Rose.
Tomorrow, this dear world will be so beautiful a place,
And such a happy hunting ground for all the human race,
That you'll even see John L. Lewis with a smile upon his face,
'Cause there ain't gonna be no sorrow, Tomorrow.

SCENE 6

Embassy Reception Room. It is very elaborate, beautifully decorated and furnished. At Rise: DANCING GIRLS *are discovered on.* MRS. GOODHUE *and* ENSEMBLE *finish "Tomorrow" number in the Reception Room. Then curtain is drawn on which from projection booth is flashed:* "Goodhue recalled. War averted."

(2nd Refrain)
*(*ENSEMBLE *and* MRS. GOODHUE*)*
Tomorrow, your troubles'll be done,
Tomorrow, your vict'ry'll be won,
Tomorrow, we're all gonna have fun
'Cause there ain't gonna be no sorrow, Tomorrow,
Yes, Yes, Tomorrow, it's all gonna be grand,
Tomorrow, you'll start leadin' the band,
Tomorrow, we'll live in a new land
'Cause there ain't gonna be no sorrow, Tomorrow.
There ain't gonna be
No tears in your eyes,
You ain't gonna see
No clouds in the skies,
You ain't gonna have
No worries at all,

So why do you fret and get yourself iller?
You'll feel like a killer-diller
Tomorrow, you'll wake up and feel swell,
Tomorrow, you'll start ringin' the bell,
Tomorrow, we're all gonna raise hell
'Cause there ain't gonna be no sorrow, Tomorrow.
And so why borrow
Even a small cup of sorrow?
Instead, get in your head, mio caro,
There ain't gonna be no sorrow, Tomorrow.
No, no there ain't gonna be
No sorrow for you and me
Tomorrow

Curtain

SCENE 7

Moscow Park. This time bench is direct center.
At Rise: COLETTE *in evening gown and* THOMAS *in top hat enter gaily, reading telegrams.*
THOMAS: *(Reading telegram)* "Congratulations on the Goodhue Plan. Father Divine."
COLETTE: Here's one from King Zog of Albania. *(Gives it to him)*
THOMAS: *(Reading)* "Collect!" *(Throws telegram away and reads another)* "Goodhue's recall is a disgrace to our so-called civilization." Signed "Some of The Boys and Warden Lawes."
COLETTE: The Goodhue Plan certainly worked.
THOMAS: Well, the old Buck Thomas went out in a blaze of glory. From now on, Baby, I'm going to tell J.H.: "No more of your dirty work. I'm going to be a serious journalist." I'll make John Gunther come to *me* for lessons.
COLETTE: Now you're going to write a book. *(Sits)*
THOMAS: That's right! I should write a book . . . everybody else has.
(GOODHUE enters in silk knickerbockers and high hat, humming, carrying suitcase)
GOODHUE: Hello, folks.
THOMAS: Hello, Stinky.
GOODHUE: Buck, you're a genius! I was saying to Leora: "There's a man who keeps his word. He promised to get me recalled and by God he did!"
THOMAS: Glad to do it.
GOODHUE: I've been locked out of the Embassy.
COLETTE: Who locked you out?
GOODHUE: Mrs. Goodhue. She's pretty mad. *(Goes over to* THOMAS *and whispers)* I have to go somewhere to change my pants. I don't want to be arrested for impersonating an Ambassador.
THOMAS: Why don't you change in my place?
GOODHUE: Thanks, Buck. I'll never forget what you did for me. I hope some day to do the same for you. *(Exits)*
THOMAS: Well, I'm going to get started again. I'm going to Spain. I'm going to China!

COLETTE: What about me?
THOMAS: With wife and drum!

(They sing "Far Away". On music cue DAUGHTERS and SECRETARIES in evening wraps and full dress and top hats enter and do dance. THOMAS and COLETTE re-enter and finish number on bench)
(Verse)

COLETTE:

Now that there is no question
Of my not becoming your wife,
I've a certain suggestion
As to our married life.
If you only accept it
I shall prove my gratitude,

THOMAS:

Go on, spring it,
If possible, sing it
For I'm in a lyrical mood.

(1st Refrain)

COLETTE:

I'm not suggesting to you
A drafty cottage for two
By the side of a wide waterfall,
But you must grant me, sweetheart,
That it would be rather smart
To get away, far away from it all.

THOMAS:

I'll make a row if you lease
A tumbling temple in Greece,
Or a hole in the ole China wall,
But when it's all said and done
I'll admit it would be fun
To get away, far away from it all.

COLETTE:

What a joy not to fear,
As we wander 'neath the moon,
That some radio near
Will repeat that Berlin tune.

THOMAS:

And to be certain, my dear,
That the readers of Heywood Broun
Are far away

COLETTE:

Far, Far away,

BOTH:

But me from you
Never too.

(2nd Refrain)

COLETTE:

I'm not proposing we get
A tent atop of Tibet,
Or that we cross the sea in a yawl,
But, dear, with me as your mate
You'll agree it would be great
To get away, far away, from it all.

THOMAS:

Please don't suggest that we test
The open spaces, out West,
In a shack with no back to the hall,
But if we took some nice nook
I could watch you while you cook
And get away, far away from it all.

COLETTE:

With the blue skies above,
And a peaceful habitat,
There'll be no danger of
Hearing Franklin give a chat.

THOMAS:

And we'll know also, my love,
Grover Whelan and his hat
Are far away,

COLETTE:

Far, far away,

BOTH:

But me from you
Never too
Far away.

(GOODHUE enters changed into long pants, and still wearing high hat, carrying his knickerbockers across his arms)

GOODHUE: My first long pants in Moscow! Buck, do you know who's looking for you? J. H. Brody!

THOMAS: Brody?

COLETTE: He's here? I thought he was in Paris. He must have flown in.

THOMAS: I'm going to stick him for a raise. After all he'll owe his appointment to me!

GOODHUE: I wonder what he wants to be an Ambassador for. You have to go to dinners with people you don't like, and you get indigestion. And besides, there is no future in it! *(BRODY and DOLLY enter. COLETTE moves slightly away)* We were just talking about you.

THOMAS: Chief, this is a surprise! Welcome to Moscow.

BRODY: Farley told me to wait in Moscow.

COLETTE: How do you do, Miss Winslow? Lovely evening, isn't it?

DOLLY: Is it?

BRODY: I was on my way to your hotel. Here's your new contract, Buckley. *(Hands him an envelope)*

THOMAS: Thanks, chief. It was nice of you to come to Moscow to congratulate me in person. Goodhue's recall is the greatest triumph of my career!

GOODHUE: It certainly is!

THOMAS: *(After opening envelope)* The pink slip... Fired? Why, Chief, what have I done?

BRODY: You've brought Miss Winslow to Moscow. You deceived me!

THOMAS: Our relationship was purely platonic. Dolly will bear me out.

DOLLY: I told Daddy I came to Moscow to study music, but he put two and two together.

BRODY: Buckley, I assume I'll take charge of the Embassy tomorrow. I'll be out of contact with newspapers generally. *But* I'm going to wire every newspaper publisher in America just what you've done to me. I'll have you blacklisted as no man has been blacklisted before. I'm going to cover the advertising agencies —the radio stations—motion pictures . . .

THOMAS: You can't do that to me!

GOODHUE: What about television? . . . There's the coming thing!

BRODY: As for you, Stinky, I expect you out of the Embassy tomorrow.

GOODHUE: I'm out now . . . I've been paroled.

BRODY: Come along, Dolly. Let this be a lesson to you.

DOLLY: Oh, it is . . . it is . . . I'm through with sex. *(They exit)*

COLETTE: Blacklist!

GOODHUE: Yeh, that's a funny thing to do to a man.

THOMAS: Funny! You know what it means? The relief rolls . . . WPA writing projects . . . for *me!* How the mighty have fallen . . . *(Points to bench)* . . . My future home!

GOODHUE: I've got an idea!

THOMAS: What?

GOODHUE: Maybe I can sell Brody these pants.

Blackout

SCENE 8

Railroad Station, Moscow.

It is rich in color and should look very elaborate. There are three arches in the background. Platforms, three steps high, leading up to them. Entrances upstage left and upstage right through arches, and entrances downstage left and right. On stage are two large ottomans built in circumference for eight girls to sit on. One is placed right of center, the other at left of center.

At Rise: GRAUSTEIN *is seated on ottoman right. Some of the* SINGING BOYS *and some of the* DANCING GIRLS *are also discovered on.* BRODY *and* DOLLY *enter.*

GRAUSTEIN: Cablegram for you, Mr. Brody.

BRODY: Thank you . . . What's this? . . . This is a mistake.

GRAUSTEIN: No mistake . . . The signature is Farley . . . Correct?

BRODY: Correct . . .

GRAUSTEIN: The message: "Congratulations your appointment Minister to Liberia."

BRODY: Minister to Liberia?

DOLLY: You can't be a minister. You'll have to turn your collar around.

BRODY: I'll turn Farley around! *(Exits with DOLLY)*
(PORTERS enter, followed by GOODHUE)

GOODHUE: *(Gaily)* Going home, boys. *(MRS. GOODHUE enters, followed by the DAUGHTERS)* Going home, Leora . . . Going home, children.

MRS. GOODHUE: Proud of yourself, aren't you? Couldn't let well enough alone, could you? The Goodhue Plan . . . If you ask me, it was the not so Goodhue Plan! *(LES GIRLS dance in right)*

GOODHUE: Going home, girls?

MRS. GOODHUE: Home! . . . Why, I had London right there . . . *(Indicates her palm)*

GOODHUE: *(Looking down at palm)* Where's Westminster Abbey? *(PORTER enters with trunk)*

MRS. GOODHUE: See that trunk? My presentation dress! My crown! *(PORTER exits)*

GOODHUE: *(Rapturously)* Going home!

MRS. GOODHUE: I can smell the dust bowl!

GOODHUE: Yes, sir. God's country.

MRS. GOODHUE: He's been neglecting it lately.

GOODHUE: *(Indignantly)* I won't have that. You can lock me out . . . You can order me around . . . You can insult me in front of my children . . . But you can't say a word against—*(Takes his hat off)* God's country. Topeka, Kansas! *(THOMAS enters gloomily)*

MRS. GOODHUE: The dreamer!

GOODHUE: What's the matter, Buck. You feeling bad?

THOMAS: Another man left Moscow this way. *(Puts his hand in coat)*

GOODHUE: Oh, I know. But it's no use feeling sorry for him now. He's dead. *(Hesitates)* Isn't he?

THOMAS: If I had the courage, I'd join him in Valhalla. *(He exits into telegraph office upstage right)*

GOODHUE: Valhalla—I was there once. That's in Westchester . . . Gee, that seems far away, doesn't it, Leora?

MRS. GOODHUE: Not far enough. Whenever I think of it, Her Excellency gets pooped!

GOODHUE: Ah, come on Leora.

MR. and MRS. GOODHUE and DAUGHTERS: *(Sing "From the U.S.A. to the U.S.S.R.")*

From the U.S.A. to the U.S.S.R.
Good God, it's far!
From a five-year plan, to a five-cent cigar.
Jeepers creepers, it's far!
Think of any nation so backward,
Any country so dog-gone slow
That, instead of Charlie MacCarthy,
Who's the funniest guy I know,
They still vote a fellow called Stalin
Number One on the radio!

Good God, it's far away
From the little ole U.S.A.

(PORTERS and COLETTE enter, looking for THOMAS. THOMAS comes from telegraph office)

COLETTE: Hello, Buck—

THOMAS: Coming to see me off? I've just been in to see if there were any telegrams for me. I wired every important paper in the country I was free. Not a word. It's nice of you to come down to say goodbye.

COLETTE: I didn't come down to say goodbye. I'm going with you.

THOMAS: With me?

COLETTE: Yes—

THOMAS: I haven't got a job . . . I'm unreliable . . . I'm . . . You're crazy!

COLETTE: Yes—

THOMAS: I won't let you throw your life away. *(GOODHUE enters)* I won't let you!

GOODHUE: *(Approaching him with copy of paper)* I bought a paper. *(Shows it)* See?

THOMAS: Anything in it about me?

GOODHUE: *(THOMAS turns away)* I just ran into Brody . . . Well, we had a chat . . . and he said to me: "How much do you spend a week on newspapers?" And I said: "Oh, about fifty cents." And he said: "Why not buy your own paper and save money?" That kind of got me.

THOMAS: You bought the *World-Tribune?*

GOODHUE: How would you like to work for me and cover some big fires in Chicago?

THOMAS: Fires?

GOODHUE: You got me out of Moscow. One good turn deserves another.

THOMAS: As new Executive Editor of the Chicago *World-Tribune*, Colette, take a wire . . .

(Finale: Reprise "Tomorrow" and "From Now On" with entire company)

Curtain

L/ADY IN THE D/ARK

Book by Moss Hart
Lyrics by Ira Gershwin
Music by Kurt Weill

Editor's Notes

A landmark musical of the American theatre (and one of the first of its genre to utilize psychiatry as thematic material), *Lady in the Dark* swept onto Broadway with all the impact of a cyclone. With the mercurial and virtuosic Gertrude Lawrence as the troubled heroine, Liza Elliott, and a supporting company that would have out-dazzled a lesser star, the show not only was a consistent sellout during its lengthy engagement, but, reportedly, was the first in theatre history to play to standees at every performance.

In his coverage of the premiere, Brooks Atkinson wrote in *The New York Times:* "All things considered, the American stage may as well take a bow this morning. For Moss Hart's musical play, *Lady in the Dark*, which was put on at the Alvin Theatre last evening, uses the resources of the theatre magnificently and tells a compassionate story triumphantly. Note the distinction between 'musical play' and 'musical comedy.' What that means to Mr. Hart's mind is a drama in which the music and the splendors of the production rise spontaneously out of the heart of the drama, evoking rather than embellishing the main theme.

"Eschewing for the moment his blistering style of comedy, Mr. Hart has written a dramatic story about the anguish of a human being. Kurt Weill has matched it with the finest score written for the theatre in years. Ira Gershwin's lyrics are brilliant. As for Gertrude Lawrence, she is a goddess: that's all . . . *Lady in the Dark* is a feast of plenty. Since it also has a theme to explore and express, let's call it a work of theatre art."

The critic for *Variety* summed it up as "one of the most stupendous evenings the theatre will afford in this or any other season." Other members of the press concurred: "*Lady in the Dark* is in many respects the most lavish and beautiful entertainment to reach Broadway in many seasons. Its theme is a serious and mature composition, written with some of Mr. Hart's choicest language. It is the case history of a tired and neurotic business woman, editor of a fashion magazine, who craves romance and has never been able to find it. She tells her life story to a psychoanalyst, and it is her review of past scenes, incidents and dreams that carry *Lady in the Dark* into a sphere of gorgeously bedizened make-believe that will create theatrical memories for every one who sees them."

According to theatrical legend, the creation of *Lady in the Dark* began with the author's own adventures into psychiatry. It was during that period that he began to explore the possibilities of a play involving the experiences of a troubled heroine who turned to analysis for guidance and help. Originally, Mr. Hart saw the play as a straight drama, and had envisioned Katharine Cornell in the principal role. But being a perceptive craftsman, it soon became apparent to Hart that in order to effectively blend realism and fantasy, the dream sequences would have to be musicalized. The result was a stunning blend of all components of the theatre.

According to published reports, the production involved a company of 58 performers, 51 stagehands and 4 revolving stages. It was mounted for the then-staggering cost of $130,000. (To interject a note on the current economics of the theatre, today it would be capitalized at approximately $750,000.)

Not only did the show brighten the Broadway horizon, it also zoomed to stardom a young comedian, Danny Kaye, who was making his debut in a musical play.

Enormously successful as a writer and director of Broadway plays and musicals, Moss Hart was born in New York City on October 24, 1904, in a railroad flat over his father's newsstand and stationery shop. His father, a cigar maker, would set up a newsstand whenever he couldn't get a job in a cigar factory. Mr. Hart had to quit school in the eighth grade to supplement the small family income. While holding down jobs as errand boy and stock clerk he read a great deal in libraries. With his Aunt Kate, who instilled in him a passion for the theatre, he saw many shows.

His first contact with the theatre came when he was 17. As an office boy for Augustus Pitou, a producer who specialized in dispatching road companies across the nation, Hart submitted a play under a pseudonym. It was bought, and he later confessed the authorship. The play was produced and failed. His next venture was not much more profitable. But it brought to the young playwright a sense of timing and an understanding of audiences. He became a social director for a while at summer resorts in the Catskill Mountains and there he continued to hone his craftsmanship.

In the late 1920's, talent and experience were merged, and he wrote the first draft of *Once in a Lifetime*, a satire on Hollywood. A producer liked the script and suggested that he take as collaborator George S. Kaufman, already established as a front-rank playwright. He was more than eager to comply. In his own words: "He was, to me, already a legendary figure. As a high school boy, I had been entranced by *Dulcy* and *To the Ladies*... By the time I had seen *Merton of the Movies* and *Beggar on Horseback*, I had developed one all-consuming ambition—to write plays in the Kaufman tradition.

"When I received word that he had read the play, and not only liked it but definitely wanted to collaborate on the revisions, I suppose my excitement was a little unearthly, so that I entered the office (of producer Sam H. Harris) for that first meeting wide-eyed with hero worship and drunk with my own perfume."

The play opened on September 24, 1930, was an immediate success, and ran for 406 performances. As the author recounted in his widely-acclaimed autobiography *Act One*, published in 1959, after the triumphant opening of *Once in a Lifetime*, he promptly went to Brooklyn where he lived with his family. Then, he called a taxi and took them to a hotel in Manhattan "taking not so much as a toothbrush from the old house."

Thereafter, the team of Kaufman and Hart was to enliven the Broadway sector with *Merrily We Roll Along* (1934), *You Can't Take It With You* (which won the Pulitzer Prize, 1936), the musical *I'd Rather Be Right* (1937), *The Fabulous Invalid* (1938), *The American Way* (1939), *The Man Who Came to Dinner* (1939), and *George Washington Slept Here* (1940).

In addition to *Lady in the Dark*, Mr. Hart also contributed the books to other illustrious musicals, including *Face the Music* (with songs by Irving Berlin, 1932), *As Thousands Cheer* (with Berlin, 1933), *The Great Waltz* (with music by Johann Strauss, Sr. and Jr., 1934), and *Jubilee* (with songs by Cole Porter, 1935).

On his own, the dramatist wrote and directed *Winged Victory* (1943), *Christopher Blake* (1946), *Light Up the Sky* (1948), and *The Climate of Eden* (1952).

His other directorial credits include the staging of *Junior Miss, Dear Ruth, The Secret Room, Miss Liberty, Anniversary Waltz, My Fair Lady*, and *Camelot*, which he also co-produced with Alan Jay Lerner and Frederick Loewe.

He also wrote many screenplays, notably, *Hans Christian Andersen, Prince of Players*, the Judy Garland version of *A Star Is Born*, and *Gentleman's Agreement* which won the Academy Award in 1947 as the best film of the year.

Moss Hart, who died in 1961, is survived by his widow, the actress-singer Kitty Carlisle, and their two children, Christopher and Cathy.

Ira Gershwin, the first lyricist ever to be awarded the Pulitzer Prize (*Of Thee I Sing, 1932*) was born in New York City on December 6, 1896. While attending the College of the City of New York, he began contributing "droll quatrains and comments" to several popular newspaper columns. Afterwards, he was to sell humorous pieces and verses to various periodicals.

Eventually, he was to turn to lyric writing, using the pseudonym of Arthur Francis so as not to capitalize on his brother George's emerging fame in the theatre. As "Arthur Francis," he contributed lyrics to several musicals, the most successful being *Two Little Girls in Blue* (with music by Vincent Youmans) presented in 1921.

With the 1924 production of *Be Yourself*, he used his own name professionally for the first time. As he explains it in his book, *Lyrics on Several Occasions:* "In 1924, I dropped Arthur Francis. He was beginning to be confused with lyricist Arthur Jackson; also I'd been made aware that there was an English lyricist named Arthur Francis. Besides, all who knew me knew me as a Gershwin anyway."

The famed Gershwin collaboration, which was to last until George's untimely death in 1937, officially began with a song written for Nora Bayes in *Ladies First*, but it wasn't really concretized until 1924 when they provided the words and music for *Lady, Be Good!* With Fred and Adele Astaire as stars, the show ran for 184 performances and was the Gershwins' first joint hit. Thereafter, George's tunes always were embellished with Ira's lyrics (culminating with their collaboration with DuBose Heyward on the memorable *Porgy and Bess*, which appears in this editor's earlier collection). He also occasionally worked with other composers in the theatre or in films: Vernon Duke, Jerome Kern, Harold Arlen, Arthur Schwartz, among them.

Disconsolate after the death of his brother, he did not write for the theatre again until he was persuaded by producer Sam H. Harris and Moss Hart to do the lyrics for the Kurt Weill score for *Lady in the Dark*, which reaffirmed his position as one of the most distinguished lyricists of his time.

Equally sought after by Hollywood, Ira Gershwin's lyrics have brightened almost a score of films, notably *Shall We Dance*, *A Damsel in Distress*, *The Goldwyn Follies*, *Cover Girl*, *The Barkleys of Broadway*, *An American in Paris*, and *A Star Is Born*.

A virtuoso composer, Kurt Weill (1900–1950) was born in Dessau, Germany. Under the influence of his father, a cantor, he began to compose while still in primary school and at the age of 18 was sent to Berlin to study with Engelbert Humperdinck, the noted composer of *Hänsel und Gretel*. After serving as a director of a provincial opera company, he returned to Berlin, this time to study with the pianist-composer Ferruccio Busoni who would teach him "form, technique, classical tradition, but not formulate or influence his style." He continued his studies until 1924, meanwhile composing symphonies, operas, and chamber music— music which, although in the classical tradition, was influenced occasionally by the American jazz idiom.

It was during this period that a Russian company visited Berlin and commissioned him to do a children's ballet and it was in the composition of this work that he adapted his style to the theatre, the medium through which he was to attain eventual fame.

His first opera (with a text by Georg Kaiser) was *The Protagonist*, produced by the Dresden State Opera in 1926. After composing two other operas, *The Royal Palace* and *The Czar Has Himself Photographed*, Weill joined forces with Bertolt Brecht and together they created *The Threepenny Opera (Die Dreigroschenoper)*. Adapted from John Gay's eighteenth century *The Beggar's Opera*, the Weill-Brecht work opened in Berlin on August 28, 1928. It was an outstanding success and before the Berlin run had ended, it had been produced in almost every major city in Germany as well as in many foreign countries. In 1933, it came to Broadway but apparently theatregoers were not quite prepared for the sardonic and trenchant musical for it lasted a mere 12 performances. However, in a new English-language adaptation by Marc Blitzstein, *The Threepenny Opera* was to be an off-Broadway sensation of the 1950's, playing at the Theatre de Lys for 2,611 performances.

Weill wrote several other theatre pieces with Brecht, including *The Rise and Fall of the City of Mahagonny*. In 1933, he collaborated again with Georg Kaiser on *The Silver Lake* and it incurred the wrath of the rising Nazi regime and prompted an official ban on all of the composer's works in Germany. Soon after, he and his wife, singer-actress Lotte Lenya, left Germany and went to Paris, then London.

In 1935, the composer was brought to the United States by Max Reinhardt to write the music for his production of Franz Werfel's Biblical spectacle, *The Eternal Road*. Due to production delays, however, his first American show was to be *Johnny Johnson*, presented by the Group Theatre in 1936.

Subsequently, he was to compose the scores for the following Broadway musicals: *Knickerbocker Holiday* (1938), *Lady in the Dark* (1941), *One Touch of Venus* (1943, published in this editor's earlier volume), *The Firebrand of Florence* (1945), *Street Scene* (1947), *Love Life* (1948), and *Lost in the Stars* (1949).

Among the distinguished authors who furnished the books and lyrics for the aforementioned productions are: Paul Green, Maxwell Anderson, Moss Hart, Ira Gershwin, Edwin Justus Mayer, Elmer Rice, Langston Hughes and Alan Jay Lerner.

Kurt Weill, who became an American citizen in 1943, also wrote music for several motion pictures and (with Arnold Sundgaard) the folk opera, *Down in the Valley*.

In 1941, the drama critic of *The New York Times* said of Weill: "He is not a song writer but a composer of organic music that can bind the separate elements of a production and turn the underlying motive into song."

A film version of *Lady in the Dark* (with Ginger Rogers, Ray Milland, Warner Baxter and Jon Hall) was released in 1943.

Production Notes

Lady in the Dark was first presented by Sam H. Harris at the Alvin Theatre, New York, on January 23, 1941. The cast was as follows:

Dr. Brooks, *Donald Randolph*
Miss Bowers, *Jeanne Shelby*
Liza Elliott, *Gertrude Lawrence*
Miss Foster, *Evelyn Wyckoff*
Miss Stevens, *Ann Lee*
Maggie Grant, *Margaret Dale*
Alison Du Bois, *Natalie Schafer*
Russell Paxton, *Danny Kaye*
Charley Johnson, *Macdonald Carey*
Randy Curtis, *Victor Mature*
Joe, *an office boy, Ward Tallmon*

Tom, *an office boy, Nelson Barclift*
Kendall Nesbitt, *Bert Lytell*
Helen, *a model, Virginia Peine*
Ruthie, *a model, Gedda Petry*
Carol, *a model, Patricia Deering*
Marcia, *a model, Margaret Westberg*
Ben Butler, *Dan Harden*
Barbara, *Eleanor Eberle*
Jack, *Davis Cunningham*

The Albertina Rasch Group Dancers, *Dorothy Byrd, Audrey Costello, Patricia Deering, June MacLaren, Beth Nichols, Wana Wenerholm, Margaret Westberg. Jerome Andrews, Nelson Barclift, George Bockman, Andre Charise, Fred Hearn, Yaroslav Kirov, Parker Wilson.*

The Singers, *Catherine Conrad, Jean Cumming, Carol Deis, Hazel Edwards, Gedda Petry, June Rutherford, Florence Wyman, Davis Cunningham, Max Edwards, Len Frank, Gordon Gifford, Manfred Hecht, William Marel, Larry Siegle, Harold Simmons.*

The Children, *Anne Bracken, Sally Ferguson, Ellie Lawes, Joan Lawes, Jacqueline Macmillan, Lois Volkman. Kenneth Casey, Warren Mills, Robert Mills, Robert Lee, George Ward, William Welch.*

Play Staged by *Moss Hart*
Production, Lighting and Musical Sequences by *Hassard Short*
Choreography by *Albertina Rasch*
Settings Designed by *Harry Horner*
Costumes Designed by *Irene Sharaff*
Gowns Designed by *Hattie Carnegie*
Musical Direction by *Maurice Abravanel*
Orchestrations and Vocal Arrangements by *Kurt Weill*

Act One

Scene 1: Dr. Brooks' Office.
Scene 2: Liza Elliott's Office.
  The same day.
Scene 3: Dr. Brooks' Office.
  The next day.
Scene 4: Liza Elliott's Office.
  Late that afternoon.

Act Two

Scene 1: Liza Elliott's Office.
  Late the following afternoon.
Scene 2: Dr. Brooks' Office.
  Later that evening.
Scene 3: Liza Elliott's Office.
  A week later.

Musical Numbers

Act One

Oh, Fabulous One In Your Ivory Tower	Liza Elliott's Serenaders
The World's Inamorata	Liza and her maid
One Life to Live	Liza and her chauffeur
Girl of the Moment	Ensemble
It Looks Like Liza	Entire Company
Mapleton High Choral	The High School Graduates
This is New	Randy Curtis and Liza
The Princess of Pure Delight	Liza and Children
This Woman at the Altar	Entire Company

Act Two

The Greatest Show On Earth	Ringmaster and Ensemble
Dance of the Tumblers	Albertina Rasch Dancers
The Best Years Of His Life	Charley Johnson and Randy Curtis
Tschaikowsky	Ringmaster and Ensemble
The Saga of Jenny	Liza, Jury and Ensemble
My Ship	Liza

ACT ONE

SCENE 1

The office of DR. ALEXANDER BROOKS.

A bright, cheerful, book-lined room. There are a desk, a couch, a few chairs, some pleasant pictures on the walls, a few plants of early spring flowers on the window sill, and an air about the place that is distinctly unmedical.

DR. BROOKS is seated at the desk, signing some letters. The sunlight, streaming in through the window, illuminates his strongly lined, good-humored face. He is a man in his middle forties, good-looking without being in any way handsome and, when he speaks, with an agreeable lack of the usual bedside manner.

He looks up momentarily to glance at his watch, presses the buzzer on his desk, then returns to sign and blot the last letter. MISS BOWERS, the DOCTOR'S secretary, comes in from the outer office, notebook and pencil in hand. MISS BOWERS is a jovial little woman, obviously wedded to her work, and clearly as efficient as the horn-rimmed spectacles she wears.

DR. BROOKS: I've penciled in the corrections myself, Miss Bowers. Just mail them. *(He hands her the letters)* Telephone Dr. Lindsay and see if he can have his patient see me tomorrow. If it's urgent, I'll make it late this afternoon. Did you talk to the hospital?

MISS BOWERS: Yes. The consultation is at six.

DR. BROOKS: I see. *(He glances at a paper on his desk)* A Miss Elliott waiting, isn't there?

MISS BOWERS: Yes.

DR. BROOKS: Ask her to come in.

MISS BOWERS: *(In the doorway)* Will you please come in, please?

(MISS ELLIOTT comes into the room as MISS BOWERS goes out, closing the door behind her)

DR. BROOKS: *(Rising)* How do you do, Miss Elliott. *(He motions her to a chair in front of the desk. For a moment she stands uncertainly, then crosses to the chair and sits. LIZA ELLIOTT is a woman in her late thirties, plain to the point of austerity. She wears a severely tailored business suit, with her hat pulled low over her eyes. No single piece of jewelry graces her person and her face is free of make-up. There is an air of the executive about her, of a woman always in complete control, yet at the moment she seems to be fighting hard for a moment of calm before she can speak. The* DOCTOR *regards her silently, waiting. Their eyes meet. With an effort, she turns away and looks around the room)*

LIZA: I had expected something quite different.

DR. BROOKS: *(Smiling)* Really? What, for instance?

LIZA: I don't know. Certainly not sunlight and flowers and a Harvard accent.

DR. BROOKS: *(Laughing)* I'm sorry about the sunlight and flowers—I can't help the accent.

LIZA: Well, well! Psychoanalysis with charm. Something new?

DR. BROOKS: Not entirely.

LIZA: All—this—throws me off. I know very little about psychoanalysis, Dr. Brooks, but I do feel there should be a beard and a Viennese accent around some place.

DR. BROOKS: *(Smiling)* I'm all out of them at the moment. *(He leans forward a little)* Suppose you tell me about yourself, Miss Elliott.
(A pause)

LIZA: May I smoke?

DR. BROOKS: Certainly. *(He holds a cigarette lighter toward her)*

LIZA: *(She pulls at the cigarette nervously for a moment)* Do you happen to know anything about me?

DR. BROOKS: A little. I would prefer to hear it from you.

LIZA: You know, I suppose, that I'm the editor of *Allure*, the fashion magazine?

DR. BROOKS: Yes, I do.

LIZA: I've been editor for the last ten years. *(She lapses into silence)*

DR. BROOKS: Yes?

LIZA: *(Angrily)* I can't tell you what's the matter with me. I don't know. If I knew I wouldn't be here. *(She gets up and paces)* I find this extremely humiliating.

DR. BROOKS: Why?

LIZA: I have nothing but contempt for women who spend their days pouring out their frustrations at so much per hour. *(She turns and faces him directly)* Let me get one thing straight, Dr. Brooks. There's nothing strange in my life. I have no queer twists. I am doing the kind of work I care most for and I am enormously successful at it. My love life is completely normal, happy and satisfactory. I wish there was some little phobia for you to gnaw at. But there isn't. *(She crushes out her cigarette and falteringly lights another)* Sorry. I'll try to talk in a moment.

DR. BROOKS: *(Quietly)* Take all the time you want, Miss Elliott.

LIZA: I want to say something else. I don't particularly believe in psychoanalysis. Does that matter?

DR. BROOKS: No.

LIZA: Dr. Carlton advised me to come here. There is nothing organically wrong with me whatever. That's—that's what's so maddening about it. I feel so ashamed to sit here whining about myself with a world at war. What difference does it make about the way *I* feel! But this isn't a question of happiness or unhappiness. I must make that clear. I'm here because everything in my life is imperiled—my work, all my relationships. I've turned to this in desperation, Dr. Brooks, because I've tried everything else. I've made every effort to pull myself out—and I can't.

DR. BROOKS: I don't think you need be ashamed, Miss Elliott. Can you tell me a little about the way you feel?

LIZA: *(Haltingly)* I seem to be—going to pieces. And yet there's no reason—no reason at all. Nothing has changed—nothing is different. *(Breathlessly)* I don't know what's happened to me.

DR. BROOKS: Just what do you mean by—going to pieces?

LIZA: *(Taking a moment to steady herself)* It's difficult to make it clear. I'm in a constant state of terror and anxiety.

DR. BROOKS: About what?

LIZA: I don't know. It's completely irrational. I have nothing to be afraid of. Yet every time the telephone rings I am filled with fear. I awake in the morning with a feeling of terror and I go through the day in a kind of panic.

DR. BROOKS: When did this start?

LIZA: About six months ago.

DR. BROOKS: Did anything happen at that time that might have caused it?

LIZA: No. Nothing that I remember. I was just—depressed at the time. Everyone goes through the same thing more or less.

DR. BROOKS: How long would these depressions last?

LIZA: Oh, they would vary. Two days—a week. They always passed. And I would feel superb again. I am usually quite a happy person. But I noticed, about six months ago, that my—vapours—as I called them, were lasting longer and longer and coming closer and closer together. There was a long unbroken stretch. I can't quite tell you when this other thing started. It seemed to be part of the depression at first.

DR. BROOKS: What about this—feeling of panic?

LIZA: It's just *that*—panic. I have moments when I realize how unreal it is—and then suddenly I am engulfed by it.

DR. BROOKS: Are you able to sleep at night?

LIZA: *(She laughs shortly)* As though I had taken ether. I've suffered for years with insomnia, but now I can sleep the days around. I suspect it's a kind of escape.

DR. BROOKS: Perhaps.

LIZA: I have to struggle constantly not to slip away into sleep. I get great waves of fatigue. I have to fight to keep awake.

DR. BROOKS: You've kept working?

LIZA: Two months ago I handed in my resignation. I felt that getting away from everyone and everything I ever knew might be the answer. And for a week I was well—though it was a kind of well-being that was actually painful. The fatigue disappeared. I would wake up in a state of intense excitement and go through the day in such high exhilaration that it was almost as hard to bear as the other thing. Then imperceptibly, the depression and the panic came back. So I've kept working. I've clung desperately to work to see me through the days —to try to steady myself. And now that's beginning to go. That's why I'm here. Something happened yesterday that—frightened me.

DR. BROOKS: What was it?

LIZA: We had our usual weekly staff meeting. It's a thoroughly routine affair. The editorial staff meets weekly to discuss layout, space, general policy. Next month's cover—the Easter issue—was up for discussion; whether it was to be the regulation Easter cover or a painting of the circus. I vetoed the circus cover. Our advertising manager kept insisting on it. Suddenly I picked up a paperweight from my desk and threw it at him. Afterward, I had a spell of weeping —I can't ever remember having cried before. I couldn't stop. This may seem trivial, Dr. Brooks, but it isn't. I have always been an enormously controlled person. That's why this—frightens me.

DR. BROOKS: How long have you been with the magazine?

LIZA: Twelve years.

DR. BROOKS: You've been editor for ten?

LIZA: Yes.

DR. BROOKS: What did you do before that?

LIZA: College. A year or two abroad. Free-lance articles. Nothing very exciting. The magazine was my idea.

DR. BROOKS: You started it?

LIZA: Kendall Nesbitt, the publisher, backed it for me. *(A slight pause)* It's ridiculous for me to be schoolgirlish about this. Mr. Nesbitt and I have been living together for a good many years. His wife refuses to divorce him.

DR. BROOKS: How do you feel about that?

LIZA: I no longer think about it. We are quite happy together. Our arrangement is a very agreeable one. *(Impatiently)* I've told you there's nothing strange in my life. It's a good deal more normal and successful than most. I've come to you because I know I am completely healthy in all other respects and this seems to be the only method of treating this—illness. Can you help me?

DR. BROOKS: I don't know.

LIZA: What does that mean?

DR. BROOKS: It's a little more complicated than my just saying "Yes." I don't know. It would be wrong for me to suggest that I know what your difficulty is, or how to help you. I can only advise that you embark upon a trial analysis —for a month, let us say. At the end of that time I should have enough data to at least make an honest diagnosis, and you, perhaps, may have a more complete picture of the essential trouble.

LIZA: I see. A month. *(She hesitates)* Very well. I can start next Tuesday.

DR. BROOKS: I think you should start immediately.

LIZA: Now?

DR. BROOKS: Yes.

LIZA: I couldn't. We go to press day after tomorrow. I couldn't possibly spare the time. I've had to steal even this time.

DR. BROOKS: Nevertheless, I think it quite important that you begin now.

LIZA: I'm sorry. I can't.

DR. BROOKS: *(Gently)* I'm afraid you'll have to find someone else, then.

LIZA: *(Staring at him for a moment. Angrily)* Why is this suddenly so urgent?

DR. BROOKS: I happen to think it is. If you do not feel you can trust me to know, then I think it wiser to go to someone else. I'm sorry, Miss Elliott.

(There is a pause)

LIZA: All right. *(She looks uncertainly about)* You want me to—start now?

DR. BROOKS: Yes. It's a simple procedure. It may even seem a little foolish to you. Just remove your hat, lie down on the couch, and speak any of the thoughts that come into your mind. Anything at all.

(A pause)

LIZA: You will get into your beard meanwhile, I trust.

DR. BROOKS: *(Smiling)* Yes. Just throw your hat on the chair. *(She hesitates, then tosses her hat onto the chair, and goes quickly to the couch and lies down. There is a long pause)* I am listening.

(Another pause. Then:)

LIZA: How curious—how very curious! Out of all the millions of little pieces of which my life is made up, one silly little thing keeps going round and round in my mind. It's the first thought I had and it keeps turning.

DR. BROOKS: What is it?

LIZA: It's a song—some little song I knew as a child.

DR. BROOKS: What are the words of the song?

LIZA: I don't even remember them. Just a word here and there.

DR. BROOKS: Have you ever thought of the song before?

LIZA: Yes.

DR. BROOKS: When was that?

LIZA: Oh, various times. It's a little childhood song.

DR. BROOKS: But when did you think of it? At what times?

LIZA: I don't know exactly. When I'm depressed, usually. Or when this feeling of panic hits me. I seem to remember it then.

DR. BROOKS: When did you think of it last?

LIZA: Last night. I knew I was coming here this morning—and it frightened me. The song kept running through my head. Over and over. Then I fell asleep— and the song was in the dream, too. Now that I think of it, the song is always there when I dream. It changes—but the music is always there.

DR. BROOKS: What was the dream?

LIZA: I've forgotten it.

DR. BROOKS: Try to remember it.

LIZA: I don't think I can. It was one of those confused, fantastic dreams. I knew the people—they were the people I see every day—and yet they were not the people I knew at all. *(Her hands go to her eyes and cover them)* I can't remember it.

DR. BROOKS: How did it begin?

LIZA: With the song.

DR. BROOKS: Hum what you remember of the song. It doesn't matter about the words. Just hum the music.

(There is a pause. Then softly, LIZA begins to hum the song. The lights dim. As the music swells, twelve men in faultless evening clothes, carrying lyres, march on. One carries a sign: "New York Chapter—LIZA ELLIOTT Admirers." It is early evening on Park Avenue)

ALL:

We come to serenade the lovely lady we adore.
She occupies the seventeenth to twenty-second floor.
Our lady so seraphic
May not be very near us,
And with the sound of traffic
She may not even hear us—
But love is wrong without a song, so, now as heretofore,
We come to serenade the lovely lady we adore.

THE LEADER:

Oh, Fabulous One in your ivory tower—
Your radiance I fain would see!

What Mélisande was to Pelléas,
Are you to me. . . .

Oh, Fabulous One in your ivory tower—
My heart and I, they both agree:
What Juliet was to Romeo
Are you to me. . . .

OTHERS:
What Beatrice was to Dante . . .
What Guinevere was to Lancelot . . .
What Brunhilde was to Siegfried . . .
What Pocahontas was to Captain Smith . . .
What Martha was to Washington . . .
What Butterfly was to Pinkerton . . .
What Calamity Jane was to Buffalo Bill . . .
What Carmen was to Don José
Are you to me. . . .

ALL:
Oh, Fabulous One in your ivory tower—
Oh, Sweet! This is no potpourri!
What Mélisande was to Pelléas
Are you to me!

(The music continues as SUTTON, *a maid, later to be identified as* MISS FOSTER, LIZA'S *secretary, appears)*

SUTTON:
I'm Miss Elliott's maid.
Gentlemen, I'm afraid
Your loyalty we must be testing.
She cannot be seen. She's resting.
But she wishes to thank you all for the serenade.

MEN:
Give the lady above
Salutations and love.
Advise her we leave in sweet sorrow
But that we return on the morrow
With our nightly serenade.

(Leaving, they wave to the apartment above)

Each night we serenade the lovely lady we adore
Who occupies the seventeenth to twenty-second floor.

(As they leave, the apartment entrance disappears and we are in LIZA'S *boudoir.* SUTTON *is getting* LIZA'S *clothes ready. The color theme is blue. Doorbell rings)*

SUTTON:
Come in.

(BOY enters, carrying package)

BOY:
A package for Miss Elliott.

SUTTON:
Put it on the table.
(She points upstage)
What is it?

BOY:
A coat of sable.
(He dances upstage and disappears. Bell rings)

SUTTON:
Come in.

(A tall, distinguished man, in top hat and beribboned stiff shirt, enters, followed by a Zouave carrying an enormous rose whose cellophaned stem is at least fifteen feet long)

MAN:
A flower for Miss Elliott—
Tribute to her splendor—
From His Royal Highness,
The French Pretender!

(They salute as SUTTON curtsies; then she points upstage in which direction they both dance off, to same step as boy, and disappear. Bell rings)

SUTTON:
Yes?

(BEEKMAN, later to be identified as RUSSELL PAXTON, the photographer of Allure, now appears as a chauffeur in a bright yellow uniform)
Good evening, Beekman.

BEEKMAN:
Good evening, Sutton.
(Looks at clothes strewn about)
Ah, I see a touch of blue.
She wears it as it's worn by few.

(They sing ecstatically:)

BOTH:
When as in silks our Liza goes
Then, then, methinks how sweetly flows
The liquefaction of her clothes—
The liquefaction of her clothes. . . .

BEEKMAN:
A delicate poem by Herrick—
But, surely, heavier than a derrick
Compared to our Miss Liza—she's so glamorous
She makes all other women appear Hammacher Schlammorous
(He looks at his wristwatch)

A thousand pardons—I must quit the scene
I must be off to perfume the gasoline.

(He dances off. The music swells again, this time in a romantic, glamorous mood, and LIZA appears. Her hair is now red)

LIZA:
Good evening, Sutton.

SUTTON:
Good evening, Miss Elliott.

LIZA:
Are there any messages?

SUTTON:
Quite a number.
(From dressing table SUTTON takes an assortment of letters, cables, telegrams, etc.)

Huxley wants to dedicate his book to you
And Stravinsky his latest sonata.
Seven thousand students say they look to you
To be at the Yale-Harvard Regatta.
Epstein says you simply have to pose for him.
Here's the key to the Island of Tobago.
Du Pont wants you wearing the new hose for him.
Can you christen a battleship in San Diego?

LIZA (Dreamily):
Huxley wants to dedicate his book to me.

(SUTTON finds another cable)

SUTTON:
Shostakovitch his latest cantata.

LIZA:
Seven thousand students say they look to me
To be at the Yale-Harvard Regatta.

SUTTON:
Oh, how lovely to be you!

LIZA:
How splendid!

SUTTON:
But it only is your due.

LIZA:
This must never be ended!
Epstein says I simply have to pose for him. . . .
No refusing these artistic ultimata!
Du Pont wants me wearing the new hose for him. . . .
Oh, how thrilling to be the world's inamorata!
Oh, how thrilling to be the world's inamorata!

SUTTON:
You never looked lovelier, Miss Elliott.

LIZA:
Thank you, Sutton. (MISS FORSYTHE, *the secretary, enters*)
And what are my engagements, Miss Forsythe?

(The "Huxley" melody now becomes a Viennese waltz)

MISS FORSYTHE *(From notebook):*
Dinner at the Seventh Heaven.

LIZA:
With the Maharajah and those two handsome men from Texas.

MISS FORSYTHE:
Toscanini broadcast.

LIZA:
I told the Maestro I'd drop in for half an hour or so.

MISS FORSYTHE:
Party at the Harrimans'.

LIZA:
Saroyan promises to write a play in front of us.

MISS FORSYTHE:
Skyscraper Room.

LIZA:
Ah, yes. Sacheveral and I are reviving the cake-walk.

MISS FORSYTHE:
That's all I have here.

LIZA:
I'll probably motor to Bear Mountain to see the sun rise.
You needn't wait up. Good night.

SUTTON and MISS FORSYTHE:
Good night, Miss Elliott.

(As lights dim down, waltz emerges fortissimo. LIZA is seen waltzing in spotlight until BEEKMAN is discovered. He is now in a blue uniform, standing at attention, beside a glittering car. The music stops)

BEEKMAN:
I learned it would be blue tonight. So I'm driving the blue
Duesenberg with the blue license plates and I've put the blue
Picasso in the car.

LIZA:
Very thoughtful, Beekman.

(Music starts as BEEKMAN opens door of car. LIZA enters)

BEEKMAN:
Where to, Miss Elliott?

LIZA:

> *That new nightclub. The Seventh Heaven!*
> (BEEKMAN *starts car. Green light. Then red light. Brakes*)
> *Where are we, Beekman?*

BEEKMAN:

> *Columbus Circle.*

LIZA:

> *Would you get me my blue soap box, please? I want to make a speech.*

(*The car is pulled to one side, red light dims.* BEEKMAN *jumps out of car, opens door for her.* LIZA *gets on soap box, and gestures to the crowd*)

> *There are many minds in circulation*
> *Believing in reincarnation.*
> *In me you see*
> *One who doesn't agree.*
> *Challenging possible affronts,*
> *I believe I'll only live once*
> *And I want to make the most of it;*
> *If there's a party I want to be the host of it;*
> *If there's a haunted house I want to be the ghost of it;*
> *If I'm in town I want to be the toast of it.*
>
> (*Refrain*)
> *I say to me ev'ry morning:*
> *You've only one life to live,*
> *So why be done in?*
> *Let's let the sun in*
> *And gloom can jump in the riv'!*
> *No use to beat on the doldrums—*
> *Let's be imaginative.*
> *Each day is numbered—*
> *No good when slumbered*
> *With only one life to live.*
>
> *Why let the goblins upset you?*
> *One smile and see how they run!*
> *And what does worrying net you?*
> *Nothing!*
> *The thing*
> *Is to have fun!*
> *All this may sound kind of hackneyed*
> *But it's the best I can give.*
> *Soon comes December*
> *So, please remember*
> *You've only one life to live—*
> *Just one life to live.*

BEEKMAN:

> *She says to her ev'ry morning*
> *She's only one life to live.*

LIZA:

So why be done in?
Let's let the sun in
And gloom can jump in the riv'!

What you collect at the grindstone
Becomes a millstone in time.
This is my thesis:
Why go to pieces?
Step out while you're in your prime.

(They dance back into car. Green traffic light. Suddenly the Seventh Heaven appears. Couples are dancing. LIZA makes an entrance, BEEKMAN in attendance carrying her coat. PIERRE, the headwaiter, later to be identified as KENDALL NESBITT, rushes to LIZA)

PIERRE:

Words fail me. My little establishment which, I flatter myself, is the world's most exclusive nightclub since Louis the Fourteenth ran Le Petit Trianon, is only in the smallest degree worthy of your presence.

LIZA:

You are sweet, Pierre.

PIERRE: *(Clapping for attention)*
Miss Liza Elliott!

(All turn to her. LIZA waves a greeting)

PIERRE:

Gentlemen—a toast! The *toast! The toast of toasts! Liza Elliott!*

THE CROWD:

Hip, hip! Hip, hip! Liza Elliott!

MEN: *("Girl of the Moment")*
Oh, girl of the moment
With the smile of the day
And the charm of the week
And the grace of the month
And the looks of the year—
Oh, girl of the moment,
You're my moment
Ev'ry moment of the time.

BEEKMAN:
Oh, girl of the moment
With the light in your eyes
And the sun in your hair
And the rose in your cheeks
And the laugh in your voice—
Oh, girl of the moment,
In a moment
You could make my life sublime.

In all my flights of fancy
Your image I drew—
I look at you and can see
That fancy come true.

ENSEMBLE:
Oh, girl of the moment
With the smile of the day
And the charm of the week
And the grace of the month
And the looks of the year—
Oh, girl of the moment,
You're my moment
Ev'ry time!

(Suddenly, a bugle call is heard. All stop dancing, listen; nothing happens—they shrug their shoulders and resume dancing. This time the call is louder. Then on march a SOLDIER, SAILOR and a MARINE. The MARINE is later to be identified as CHARLEY JOHNSON, advertising manager of Allure)

THE CROWD:
Oh, goodness, oh, gracious!
Our minds are capacious
But what in the world does this mean?
Although we are partial
To men that are martial
What reason brings you on the scene?

MARINE:
I bring a message for Miss Liza Elliott.

LIZA:
From?

MARINE:
The President of the United States.

THE CROWD:
Oh, goodness, oh, gracious!
Our minds are capacious
But what in the world does this mean?
Direct from the White House
He calls at the night house!
One cannot say this is routine!

LIZA:
And?

MARINE:
The President requests . . .

LIZA:
Yes?

MARINE:
That for the National unity . . .

LIZA:
Yes?

MARINE:
For the furtherance of good will . . .

LIZA:
Yes?

MARINE:
And for the advancement of cultural and artistic achievement . . .

(THE CROWD *can wait no longer.)*

ENSEMBLE:
Yes?

MARINE:
Your portrait be painted and your likeness used on the new two-cent stamp.

LIZA:
How really lovely!

THE CROWD:
Oh, how thrilled she ought to be!
At that, there's none so fair as she.

LIZA:
Who is to paint me—and where?

MARINE:
I am to paint you—and here.

(LIZA *acquiesces. The soldiers' guns become legs of an easel. A throne-like chair is brought on for* LIZA. MARINE *poses her. Starts to paint her. All this to the first half of "Girl of the Moment" which, from the instant* LIZA *has nodded her acceptance to pose, has become an oratorio with Bach-like harmonies. There is a second's silence at conclusion of singing)*

It's finished. The portrait is painted!

ENSEMBLE:
Of beauty untainted
The portrait is painted—
The portrait the nation awaits.
Oh, please, sir—unveil it!
And when can we mail it
To friends in the forty-eight States?

LIZA:
Is it Impressionistic?
Or is it American Primitive?
This work of art he's done,
Is it Pointillistic?
Is it Surrealistic?
Or is it a W.P.A.-ish one?

ALL:

Of beauty untainted
The portrait is painted—
The portrait the nation awaits.
Oh, please, sir, unveil it,
And when can we mail it,
And when can we mail it,
And when can we mail it,
And when can we mail it,
And when can we mail it
To friends in the forty-eight States?

PIERRE:

Ladies and gentlemen—my little establishment tonight becomes a shrine of historic importance.

BEEKMAN:

The portrait painted on these premises promises to produce a popular period of peace and prosperity which probably will be prolonged to perpetuity.

ALL:

Oh, how thrilled she ought to be!
At that, there's none so fair as she.

(The portrait is unveiled. It is not flattering. It is LIZA as she appeared in the doctor's office—austere, somewhat forbidding, entirely without glamor. She looks at it for a few tense seconds, screams, slaps the face of its creator, throws herself on the throne-like chair and hides her face. The crowd is at first perplexed, then becomes cynical.)

WOMAN:

It looks like Liza!

MAN:

But is it Liza?

ANOTHER WOMAN:

The looks of Liza—

ANOTHER MAN:

The size o' Liza—

ALL:

But if it's Liza
Why is Liza
So un-Liza-like?

MARINE:

I painted Liza!
It must be Liza!
The looks of Liza—
The size o' Liza—

ALL:

If she *is Liza*
(Pointing to portrait)

And she *is Liza*
(Pointing to Liza)
What is Liza really like?
What is Liza really like?
What is Liza really like?

(Imperceptibly this rhythm becomes that of "Girl of the Moment" which now is traced orchestrally as a wild bolero. All sing accusingly and, later, in the wild, semiballet formations encircling LIZA, *they point at her scornfully and laugh mockingly)*

ENSEMBLE:
Oh, girl of the moment
With the smile of the day
And the charm of the week
And the grace of the month
And the looks of the year—
Oh, girl of the moment,
Ev'ry moment
Was a waste of precious time!
Oh, girl of the moment
With the light in your eyes
And the sun in your hair
And the rose in your cheeks
And the laugh in your voice—
Oh, girl of the moment,
From this moment
To the heights no more you'll climb.

My dreams are torn asunder.
Your image I drew.
I see you now and wonder
What I saw in you.

Oh, girl of the moment
With the smile of the day
And the charm of the week
And the grace of the month
And the looks of the year—
Oh, girl of the moment,
Where's the girl
That was sublime?

(Now all become "frozen" as the lights start to dim down. The whirling light effect with which the dream began is again introduced and after a crescendo in the orchestra we are in the doctor's office. As the lights come up again, LIZA *is on the couch)*

DR. BROOKS: You seem to have remembered a great deal of the dream.

LIZA: Yes.

DR. BROOKS: Did anything about the dream strike you as very strange?

LIZA: Why—only that it seems incredible—when I think of it in relation to myself.

DR. BROOKS: Yes, but you dreamed it. No one else did. You did. Fantastic as it may seem, it came from you. And a dream, you know, is merely a daydream at night. Doesn't it strike you as strange, Miss Elliott, that in your fantasy you are the complete opposite of your realistic self?

LIZA: I don't know what you mean.

DR. BROOKS: Well, in reality, you are obviously a woman who cares very little for any of the feminine adornments most women use to enhance their attractiveness. In reality, you go to the opposite extreme—almost to the point of severity. Not only in dress, but in any form of rather innocent womanly guile. Yet, in your dream, the very opposite is true. In your fantasy you are the epitome of the glamorous woman—a woman using her femininity as a lure to all men—an enchantress. Doesn't it strike you as curious, too, that you, who have rejected beauty for yourself, in reality, at least, should spend all your days, in fact, dedicate your life to the task of telling *other* women how to be beautiful? That is the function of your magazine, isn't it?

LIZA: *(Slowly)* Yes—yes, that's true. What does it mean?

DR. BROOKS: I don't know. Perhaps we shall find out. *(He rises)* That will be all. Tomorrow at twelve-fifteen.

(LIZA rises from the couch and slowly takes her hat from the chair. She looks at him for a moment, starts to speak, then checks herself)

LIZA: Good day.

DR. BROOKS: Good day, Miss Elliott.

(She walks quickly to the door and goes out)

Curtain

SCENE 2

LIZA'S *office.*

A large oak-paneled room, done in the Georgian manner. It is an impressive room, as befits the editor of the most successful woman's magazine in the country. It is not, however, a feminine room. The desk is a man's desk, the chairs large and heavy, the curtains severe.

The office is empty at the moment, except for a life-size dummy which stands almost in the center of the room, magnificently clothed in full evening dress, and looking astonishingly like Greta Garbo. MISS FOSTER, LIZA'S secretary, a young girl of about twenty-five and very pretty, comes in from the outer office and places some opened letters on the desk. The telephone rings.

MISS FOSTER: Hello? No, this is Miss Foster. Put him on. Hello . . . No, Mr. Nesbitt, she hasn't come in yet. Just a moment. *(She glances down at a book on the desk)* She has several office appointments and a luncheon engagement. Yes, Mr. Nesbitt, I'll tell her. *(She hangs up and makes a notation on the desk-pad. MISS STEVENS, a tall, beautiful, willowy blonde girl, looks in through the doorway. She has a manner that stamps her immediately for what she is: the receptionist for the stream of celebrities who pass through the offices of Allure. She makes sure MISS FOSTER is alone—then rushes over to her)*

MISS STEVENS: *(Breathlessly)* Elinor—did you get a look at him?

MISS FOSTER: Randy Curtis?

MISS STEVENS: Yes.

MISS FOSTER: No, damn it. I was upstairs.

MISS STEVENS: Oh, God—that's all—oh, God!

MISS FOSTER: Something, eh?

MISS STEVENS: *(Fervently)* The most beautiful hunk of man I've ever seen!

MISS FOSTER: Russell promised me I could sneak into the studio and stand in the back while he was taking the pictures. Damn! I wish Miss Elliott would get here!

MISS STEVENS: Listen. He came to the reception desk and I was looking up a number in the telephone book, and he said, "I'm supposed to have my picture taken," and of course that voice went through me like a pound of cocaine. Then I looked up—and I was a dead pigeon. *(Reverently)* Elinor, you've never seen anything like it—take my word.

(MAGGIE GRANT *strolls in. A good-looking woman in her early forties. A little on the acidulous side so far as humor goes, but a lusty, earthy lady)*

MAGGIE: Miss Elliott not in *yet?*

MISS FOSTER: No. She's going to be awfully late for all her appointments.

MISS STEVENS: *(Still starry-eyed)* Miss Grant, did you get a look at Randy Curtis?

MAGGIE: A fleeting eyeful. Not bad.

MISS STEVENS: *(Outraged)* Not bad! Have you ever seen anything better?

MAGGIE: I'm an older woman, girls. I know what gives me indigestion now. Give up, dear. Even if you could have it, it's poison.

MISS STEVENS: It's a lovely way to die, though. Oh, well—I can always see him in the movies, anyway. *(She starts out, then stops as she passes the dummy)* We featuring this in the next issue, Miss Grant?

MAGGIE: Yes, if Miss Elliott okays it. *(She circles around the dummy)* Sometimes I think that Schiaparelli does a good deal of her designing at Wuthering Heights.

(LIZA *comes briskly in, murmurs a "Good morning," and makes straight for her desk, tossing off her hat as she goes. She glances quickly at her watch, then down at the appointment pad)*

LIZA: Just tell me who's waiting, Miss Foster. I want to speak to Miss Grant first.

MISS FOSTER: Mr. Johnson, the printers, Mr. Adams. Mr. Nesbitt has been trying to reach you. He's coming in to see you. I told him you had a luncheon engagement. He said to please wait for him.

LIZA: All right. I'll see Mr. Johnson in a few minutes—the others will have to wait. Send Mr. Nesbitt in when he comes. Close the door please. *(She ruffles through the letters on her desk for a moment as MISS STEVENS and MISS FOSTER go out. Then she looks up at MAGGIE)*

MAGGIE: *(Regarding her for a moment)* Been to see the Wizard of Oz?

LIZA: Yes.

MAGGIE: What did he say?

LIZA: He didn't know what was the matter with me.

MAGGIE: *(Plumping down into a chair)* Say, *I* could tell you that—at twenty dollars an hour!

LIZA: It's going to be a slow process, Maggie.

MAGGIE: Sure—it mustn't be too quick at twenty bucks a throw. What's it like —what does he do?

LIZA: He doesn't do anything.

MAGGIE: Oh, isn't that nice. *He* doesn't do *anything.* What do you do?

LIZA: Just lie on a couch and talk. He listens. It's quite amazing.

MAGGIE: Amazing? I've been doing that free for years. You get paid for it now, huh?

LIZA: *(Tiredly)* All right, Maggie.

MAGGIE: I'm sorry. *(She gets up and comes over to her)* I know you're having a tough time, Liza, but this seems such a strange thing for you to be doing—it's so unlike you. I know that other people do it—but I wish you weren't. Digging down into yourself and bringing up stuff that'll frighten the hell out of you. God, *I* could give him an earful.

LIZA: I've got to try it, anyway.

MAGGIE: Bad night?

LIZA: Ghastly.

MAGGIE: How do you feel now?

LIZA: A little better. I liked Dr. Brooks. Yes, I liked him—and I came away feeling a little steadier. At least I could talk to him about the unreality of this, and he understood. That was a great deal. *(She lights a cigarette and puffs thoughtfully for a moment)* He told me something at the end of the hour that staggered me.

MAGGIE: About yourself?

LIZA: Yes.

MAGGIE: Uh-huh. Well, I hope it works—God knows, I hope it works. But it would be awfully hard to make me believe that the reason I can't stand artichokes is because my mother put me on the pottie wrong when I was two years old.

(The door flies open and ALISON DU BOIS rushes in under full steam. A woman who could be any age between thirty and fifty, and positively alive with costume jewelry. She is actually as American as Appleton, Wisconsin, but there is nothing on the Rue de la Paix quite as French as MISS DU BOIS.)

ALISON: Liza, darling, forgive me—but I do want a moment. I want you to hear this, and please don't stick it in the back of the magazine with the girdle ads. It's too chic! Isn't it, Maggie? I read it to Maggie this morning. Listen to it, darling, it will only take a moment to get the idea. It's very French—very gay! It's called "Why Not." *(She reads from a typewritten page in her hand)* "Why not save your champagne corks and use them to tie back the curtains on your sun porch? They'll look lovely against the delphiniums! Why not take your old sable coat and make it into a play-rug for Junior? Babies love sable. Why not melt down your old silver service into a Kleenex receptacle for the boudoir? It will look stunning beside those new square bathtubs. Why not take your old dog leashes and turn them into a tie-rack for Dad?"

MAGGIE: Why not take your old babies and turn them into a chandelier? They'll look lovely in the new game room!

ALISON: Now, Maggie, dear, you know what fun you made of my "Have You Tried Doing," idea, and it was sensational. Liza, darling, don't you think it's a chic idea? You will use it, won't you?

LIZA: Leave it here, Alison—I'll read it over.

ALISON: *(Handing the papers to LIZA)* Were either of you at the opening last night? Such a chic play! Omar Kiam did the clothes. Lovely. The play itself was dreadful, but chic. *(As she passes the dummy on her way out)* A new Schiaparelli, isn't it? I loathe it. Hello, Russell, darling! *(This last is tossed over her shoulder to a flaxen-haired young man who is just entering as she goes out. RUSSELL PAXTON is the staff photographer—the Cecil Beaton of Allure. He is still in his early twenties, but very Old World in manner and mildly effeminate in a rather charming fashion)*

RUSSELL: *(Hysterical, as usual)* Girls, he's God-like! I've taken pictures of beautiful men, but this one is the end—the *end!* He's got a face that would melt in your mouth . . . Liza, you've got to entertain him for a few moments. He asked to see you. I want to do one picture of him in color as Captain of the Coldstream Guards, and the damn costume hasn't arrived. He's been sitting in the studio for the last half hour in a cowboy outfit. Maggie, did you see him? Is he a creature out of this world or not? Liza, be charming to him—he's waited around like a perfect angel. He's heaven. *(He rushes out)*

LIZA: *(Laconically)* What was all that?

MAGGIE: Randy Curtis.

LIZA: Oh, yes, of course.

MAGGIE: The whole office is in an uproar.

(There is a knock at the door)

LIZA: Come in.

(CHARLEY JOHNSON saunters into the room, his hat on the back of his head, a topcoat slung over his arm, trailing on the floor. He looks and is slightly hung-over. In his rather dissipated face, there are still the remains of great good looks. To people who go for him, CHARLEY is the charmer of the world)

CHARLEY: Think you'll get to me before lunch, Boss Lady?

LIZA: Would you mind waiting a minute, Johnson? I've got to meet Mr. Curtis. I won't keep you long. Stay right here.

CHARLEY: Thank you, Boss Lady. *(He strolls over to MAGGIE)* Want a wet kiss?

MAGGIE: *(Holding him off)* Get away from me, Charley—you reek of hangover.

CHARLEY: You're so right. *(He strolls over to the dummy and lifts up the skirt)* Good morning.

(The door opens and RUSSELL comes in, RANDY CURTIS in tow. MR. CURTIS is indeed God-like—even the cowboy outfit he is sheepishly wearing at the moment cannot detract from his overwhelming good looks. If anything, it adds to them. Tall, bronzed, sandy-haired, he is every woman's notion of what a good-looking man should be. There is none of the movie "pretty-boy" about him. He is rugged, powerful, and as MISS STEVENS so aptly phrased it, a "beautiful hunk of man")

RUSSELL: *(As though he were pronouncing a benediction)* Mr. Randy Curtis.

LIZA: *(Coming forward)* How do you do, Mr. Curtis? I'm Liza Elliott. This is Margaret Grant, our fashion editor. And Mr. Johnson, our advertising manager. *(The others murmur how-do-you-do's)* Thank you so much for posing for us.

RANDY: Glad to. Mr. Paxton said it was all right to come in here this way—I feel I ought to be leading a horse. *(Ruefully)* Movie actors have to do the goddamnedest things!

LIZA: *(Smiling)* We're fairly used to strange get-ups, Mr. Curtis—this is a fashion magazine. Please sit down.

RUSSELL: Good God, no! Those pants just button! They sent over the wrong size.

MAGGIE: *(Laughing)* You're having a helluva day, aren't you, Mr. Curtis?

RANDY: Oh, nothing fazes me any more—that mob nearly tore the trousers right off me in Grand Central Station when I got in last week. It was awful.

RUSSELL: They adore him! They absolutely worship him!

LIZA: How long are you to be in New York for, Mr. Curtis?

RANDY: I'm going back this afternoon. I only had a week between pictures. *(He smiles at her)* You don't remember me, do you, Miss Elliott? You know, we've met before.

LIZA: No! Really? I'm awfully sorry. When? Where was it?

RANDY: Oh, that's all right. It was just at dinner. But we had quite a talk afterwards.

LIZA: Oh, dear. Please forgive me—I've got a wretched memory. Where was it?

RANDY: At Mrs. Brackett's—about a year ago. I took you home, in fact. Don't you remember that? We sat in the car talking.

LIZA: Of course, of course! How stupid of me!

MAGGIE: Want to take *me* home some night, Mr. Curtis? *I'll* remember it!

LIZA: I do this all the time! Can we have a drink together before you leave? How awful of me not to remember!

RANDY: Say, it doesn't matter at all—I shouldn't have mentioned it. Please don't think twice about it. I'd love to have that drink with you, but I can't. The Century leaves at four and I've got to get back to the hotel and do some last-minute packing. We'll have it next time I'm in town.

LIZA: Please do. Perhaps we can make it dinner.

CHARLEY: *(Suddenly coming forward)* May I have your autograph, Mr. Curtis?

RANDY: *(Taken aback)* Why—why . . . *(He looks at CHARLEY)* Say, you're kidding, aren't you?

CHARLEY: *(Wide-eyed and innocent)* Oh, no. I collect autographs of all the movie stars. I have them all in a big book and on rainy days I look at them.

RUSSELL: *(Under his breath—furious)* Really!

CHARLEY: *(Pushing a piece of paper and pencil at him)* Please?

RANDY: *(Embarrassed. Gruffly)* Okay.

(MISS STEVENS, at her most willowy, drapes herself in the doorway)

MISS STEVENS: That costume has arrived, Mr. Paxton. *(Her eyes devour this extra glimpse of her hero)*

RUSSELL: *(Taking RANDY by the arm)* Come on, duck. Color photos take a long time. *(He grabs the paper and pencil out of RANDY'S hands and tosses them at CHARLEY)* Pay no attention to this one—he's just *too* funny for words! *Really!*

RANDY: *(Being hurried out by RUSSELL—calling over his shoulder)* Good-bye. Good-bye, Miss Elliott. *(The door closes)*

MAGGIE: Honestly, Charley, what a stinker you are! What did you do that for?

CHARLEY: I dunno, Maggie. Sometimes I think there's a devil in me.

MAGGIE: Oh, stop being a pixie, Charley—you're getting a little too old for it. You got a lunch date, Liza? Yes, you have—I know. I'll see you later. *(She motions to the dummy as she crosses to the door)* What about "Murder in the Rue Morgue"—are we going to use it?

LIZA: Yes.

MAGGIE: Okay. I'll have it sent down to Russell.

(She goes out. There is a little silence after the door closes. CHARLEY stands facing LIZA, whistling through his teeth an off-key, indiscriminate tune. Finally:)

LIZA: I know no way of phrasing an apology for the inexcusable. For me to apologize to you now would serve no purpose except to give me some personal satisfaction, and I think my behavior yesterday was such that I am not entitled to any.

(A pause)

CHARLEY: May I keep the paperweight? *(He takes a paperweight out of his pocket and tosses it up and down in the air)* Maybe I can tell the little ones some day what Grandpa was doing during the Second World War. Or do you think you'll want to throw it at somebody else?

LIZA: *(Angrily)* That will be all, Johnson. We won't discuss it any further. *(There is a knock at the door)* Come in.

(Two OFFICE BOYS enter)

FIRST OFFICE BOY: Miss Grant told us to take this model down to the studio, Miss Elliott.

LIZA: Yes. Tell Mr. Paxton it's to be a two-page spread in color. *(The OFFICE BOYS carry the dummy out. LIZA waits impatiently until they are gone)*

LIZA: Was there something you wanted to say to me, Johnson? I'm very busy— and not in an antic mood.

CHARLEY: *(He looks at her—then suddenly bursts into laughter)* You kill me, Boss Lady.

LIZA: *(Slamming the paper-cutter she has been toying with down on the desk)* Look here, Johnson. I don't like you. I never have. Your so-called charm has always eluded me, and I am repelled by what you consider amusing, such as that little episode with Mr. Curtis just now. You're here because you're excellent at your job and I have never allowed my personal dislikes to interfere with the magazine. *(The telephone rings)* Yes? Send him right in. *(She hangs up and walks over to the fireplace, her back to JOHNSON)* Suppose in the future you confine your remarks to your work. If you don't think you can do that perhaps you can make a pleasanter arrangement elsewhere.

CHARLEY: My, my! *(He whistles shortly, that irritating through-the-teeth whistle)* Well, good morning.

LIZA: Good morning.

(He starts out as the door opens and KENDALL NESBITT enters)

NESBITT: Morning, Johnson.

CHARLEY: Morning. Be careful. Teacher's mad!

(He goes out. NESBITT looks after him for a moment, then crosses to LIZA and takes her in his arms)

NESBITT: *(Kissing her fondly)* Hello, darling. Feeling any better?

LIZA: A little. Anything wrong, Kendall?

(He shakes his head. KENDALL NESBITT is a young fifty. A pleasant rich man's life has given him a polish that he wears with becoming elegance. He is gray in just the right places and beautifully turned out, but his face, while a handsome one, has a soft weak quality)

KENDALL: *(Running his hand over her hair)* Did you see Brooks this morning?

LIZA: Yes.

KENDALL: Well?

LIZA: He didn't say much. I'm going to try it for a month.

KENDALL: I don't think you'll have to, darling.

LIZA: What do you mean?

KENDALL: I think I've found the solution. *(He kisses her again)* I've been so worried about you, Liza—more than I ever let you know.

LIZA: *(Disengaging herself)* What are you trying to tell me, Kendall?

KENDALL: Listen . . . *(He takes her hand and draws her over to the sofa and down beside him)* I think the trouble is—*us!*

LIZA: *(Looking at him for a long moment)* I don't understand.

KENDALL: Yes, you do. Liza, we did the best we could under the circumstances. It seemed at the time to be a civilized, adult way of handling an impossible situation, didn't it? For both of us. But it never works out in the end, Liza. Someone always suffers in a set-up of this kind and usually it's the woman. Somehow—I don't know why—it's different for a man, but a woman can have no sense of fulfillment—no real peace and serenity as a woman, living out her life this way. I think that's what's been eating away at you. *(He draws her closer to him)* I had a long talk with Kate last night. We're much better friends now. *(He turns her toward him)* She's agreed to give me a divorce. At last, Liza!

LIZA: *(Falteringly)* Oh . . .

KENDALL: She's going to Mexico next week. We discussed the settlement in detail this morning. *(He shakes his head ruefully)* Kate drives a hard bargain. She gets everything but the kitchen stove, practically. I don't mind much. It's worth it. *(He becomes suddenly conscious that she isn't listening)* Liza—what's the matter? This is what we've always wanted, isn't it?

LIZA: Yes . . . Yes, of course, Kendall. *(Her hands go to her eyes)* What *is* the matter with me . . . ?

KENDALL: Liza, for God's sake, will you get out of this office and go home? Why do you keep driving yourself when you're not well? Maggie can get out the magazine—you know very well she can. Why do you persist in this "show-must-go-on" nonsense, when you're ill!

LIZA: It's better for me here—really it is. Kendall, come to dinner tonight. We can talk then.

KENDALL: I don't like the way you look. Let me take you home now.

LIZA: Please, Kendall! I know what's best for me. Just let me alone for a moment. *(MISS FOSTER opens the door and stands in the doorway)*

MISS FOSTER: Will you see Mr. Curtis, Miss Elliott?

LIZA: Mr. Curtis? Why—yes . . .

MISS FOSTER: Will you come in, Mr. Curtis? *(RANDY comes in. He wears a conservative dark business suit now)*

RANDY: Oh, I'm sorry. I . . .

LIZA: That's quite all right. This is Kendall Nesbitt. Randy Curtis. *(They exchange how-do-you-do's)*

RANDY: Why—er—I just had a call from the Coast. The shooting date has been postponed and I'm here for another three days. I—er—wondered if we could have dinner tonight.

LIZA: Oh, I'm sorry. I can't tonight.

RANDY: Tomorrow night?

LIZA: Tomorrow night—tomorrow night. Yes. Certainly. I'd be delighted. *(She nervously lights a cigarette)* Would you mind picking me up here, Mr. Curtis? About seven-thirty? We're going to press and I'll be working up to the last minute.

RANDY: Not at all. I'm glad you can make it. *(There is an awkward little silence)* Well—good-bye again. Glad to have met you, Mr. Nesbitt. *(He almost runs out of the room)*

KENDALL: *(Looking after him—he laughs)* That was rather like a bit from one of his pictures. Didn't I hear you say you were dining with the Newtons tomorrow night?

LIZA: Oh, God. Yes. I completely forgot. I'll phone him and break it. I said "yes" to get rid of him.

KENDALL: Is that a cue for me to go, too?

LIZA: Do you mind? I've got an office full of people waiting.

(He crosses to her and kisses her lightly on the forehead)

KENDALL: See you at dinner. But that *is* great news, isn't it, Liza? *(LIZA nods without speaking)* And please spare yourself a little. *(He smiles at her)* Kate may wind up with the magazine, anyway—so don't work too hard. Good-bye.

LIZA: Good-bye. *(He tosses her a kiss from the doorway, then goes out. She stands quite still for a few moments after he has gone—then she crushes out her cigarette and picks up the telephone)* See if Miss Grant has gone to lunch yet. If she hasn't, ask her to come in here right away. No—never mind. Don't do that. Tell those people who are waiting I can't see them today, and tell Miss Foster I don't want to be disturbed by anybody—I don't want to see anyone until I ring her. Anyone. Understand? Thank you. *(She reaches for her handkerchief and wipes her forehead—hangs up and leans heavily against the desk for a moment. She goes quickly to the door and turns the key in the lock. Then she walks slowly to the couch and flings herself down on it. Her arm goes across her face. There is a long moment of stillness. Then, involuntarily, without quite knowing she is doing it, LIZA begins to hum that little phrase of song)*

(The lights dim into darkness. Through the darkness the name, LIZA, is heard, weirdly sung. The lights come up somewhat and we discover the singing is being done by a group of BOYS and GIRLS, slowly moving forward. They are dressed as high-school graduates of a generation ago. They carry diplomas. They sing as a Choral. Mostly their lines are sung—a few are spoken)

CHORAL:
> *There's a girl—Liza Elliott.*
> *We all knew her. We went to high school together.*
> *We graduated with her.*

BOY:
> *She was cheerleader in the third year.*

CHORAL:
> *Mapleton High, Mapleton High,*
> *For you we will do and for you we will die!*
> *Rah, rah, rah!*

GIRL:
> *I remember Liza well,*
> *We read Les Miserables in her room on rainy days.*
> *And A Tale of Two Cities, too.*

GIRL:
> *I liked her a lot.*

GIRL:
> *I thought she was stuck up.*

BOY:
> *I remember the house she used to live in*
> *And the tree in the garden where she used to swing.*

BOY:

> *I might as well tell it now.*
> *On Graduation Day when Liza delivered the Valedictory*
> *I asked her if she'd wait for me.*
> *She smiled. She didn't take me seriously.*

GIRL:

> *I never quite understood her. She had a pretty voice, though.*

CHORAL:

> *We sing the praise of Mapleton High;*
> *Each heart is filled with loyalty.*
> *And for our school we'll do or we'll die*
> *And reach the goal of victory.*
> *Oh, Alma Mater, Mapleton High—*
> *Your bounty is on every hand*
> *And while we live we'll never deny*
> *No finer school is in the land.*

BOY:

> *She was a whiz at tennis. One time I had her 5–2, set point. She beat me, 9–7.*

BOY:

> *Remember that caricature she drew of M. D'Albert, the French teacher? Instead of getting*
> *sore at her he took it home to show to his wife.*

CHORAL:

> *Le, la, les!*
> *Parlez-vous français?*
> *Ouvrez la fenêtre,*
> *S'il vous plait!*
> *La la la la la la la, la la la la la,*
> *La la la lala la, la lala la la.*

> (To the tune of "Clair de Lune")

BOY:

> *Happy, happy days.*

CHORAL:

> *Oh, Alma Mater, Mapleton High—*
> *Your bounty is on every hand;*
> *And while we live we'll never deny*
> *No finer school is in the land.*

> (They split into two groups—opposite sides of the stage)

> *And now a Mapleton High girl is to be married.*
> (Bolero rhythm starts)
> *Liza Elliott is marrying Kendall Nesbitt.*

> (KENDALL is spotlighted. He looks around expectantly)

GIRL:

> *Kendall Nesbitt is forty-eight years old. He loves Liza and Liza loves him. They get along*
> *beautifully.*

CHORAL:

It's quite idyllic.

BOY:

He started the magazine for her. It's been most successful.

CHORAL:

They should be very happy.

(LIZA appears in a white gown. KENDALL goes to her)

And now they are buying the ring. But why is Liza hesitant?

(A salesman with tray of rings appears. It is CHARLEY JOHNSON)

Shall it be with emeralds or shall it be with diamonds?

(LIZA finally decides, points. JOHNSON bows and instead of giving her the ring proffers a small golden dagger. LIZA recoils as both men disappear and RANDY is spotlighted)

MEN'S VOICES:

Randy Curtis. Flame of the celluloid. A precious amalgam of Frank Merriwell, Anthony Eden and Lancelot.

WOMEN'S VOICES:

Forty million women see him every week and forty million women love him. In Kansas, in Patagonia, in Hollywood itself he is a man every woman wants.

(RANDY sees LIZA whose face is covered by her hands. He turns her to face him. Slowly her expression changes. Finally she smiles up at him)

RANDY:

With you I used to roam
Through The Pleasure Dome
Of Kubla Khan.
I held you tight, my love,
In the gardens of
Old Babylon.
I lost you through the centuries.
I find you once again
And find myself
The luckiest of men.

RANDY AND LIZA:

This is new—
I was merely existing.
This is new
And I'm living at last.
Head to toe,
You've got me so I'm spellbound.
I don't know
If I am heaven or hell-bound.
This is new—
Is it Venus insisting
That I'm through
With the shadowy past?
I am hurled

Up to another world
Where life is bliss
And this
Is new.

(The Second Refrain is sung by the CHORAL. LIZA *leaves* RANDY'S *arms, finds herself in* JOHNSON'S. *They dance. Six girls in red wigs, with dresses exactly like* LIZA'S, *come on.* JOHNSON *disappears.* RANDY *is again discovered. He sings to the six. As they dance* LIZA *merely watches. Finally* LIZA *is alone on the stage. Slowly she hums the beginning of that phrase of song)*

CHORAL:

Go on.

LIZA:

I can't remember any more.

CHORAL:

What's worrying you, Liza?

LIZA:

I don't know.

CHORAL:

What are you afraid of?
You should be happy.
Every woman wants to be married.
And this is the eve of your wedding day.
What are you thinking of?

VOICE OF DR. BROOKS:

Take all the time you want, Miss Elliott.

LIZA:

How curious! How very curious! Of all the things I could be thinking of at this moment, a
    little school play I acted in when I was a child keeps running through my mind.

CHORAL:

We are listening.

LIZA:

It was called "The Princess of Pure Delight."

(A PERSIAN PRINCE, *a little child, appears, along with other* CHILDREN. *They bow, then proceed to enact* LIZA'S *narrative)*

The Prince in Orange and the Prince in Blue
And the Prince whose raiment was of Lavender hue—
They sighed and they suffered and they tossed at night
For the neighboring Princess of Pure Delight. . . .
(Who was secretly in love with a Minstrel)

Her father, the King, didn't know which to choose;
There were two charming suitors he'd have to refuse.
So he called for the Dean of his Sorcerers and
Inquired which one was to win her hand.
(Which they always did in those days)

"My King, here's a riddle—you test them tonight:
What word of five letters is never spelled right?
What word of five letters is always spelled wrong?
The one who can answer will be wedded ere long.
That will be twenty gulden, please!"

The King called the three and he told them the test,
The while his fair daughter kept beating her breast.
He put them the riddle. They failed (as he feared).
Then all of a sudden the Minstrel appeared!
(Quite out of breath)

"I'll answer that riddle," cried the singer of song.
"What's never spelled 'right' in five letters is 'wrong'
And it's right to spell 'wrong'—w-r-o-n-g!
Your Highness, the Princess belongeth to me!
And I love her, anyway!"

"Be off with you, villain!" the King cried in rage,
"For my Princess a Prince—not a man from the stage!"
"But, Sire!" said the Minstrel, " 'tis love makes me say
No King who's a real King treats lovers this way!
It isn't sporting.

And if you're no real King, no Princess is she—
And if she's no Princess then she can wed me!"
"By gad," cried His Highness, "you handsome young knave,
I fear me you're right!" and his blessing he gave,
As a trumpeter began to trumpet.

The Princess then quickly came out of her swoon
And she looked at her swain and her world was in tune.
And the castle soon rang with cheer and with laughter
And of course they lived happily ever after.

(All bow as orchestra music grows louder and children gradually disappear. Suddenly wedding bells fill the air. LIZA looks wonderingly about and slowly walks to other side of stage where she discovers her office desk. As though under a spell she goes to the desk and presses a buzzer. MISS FOSTER appears)

LIZA:
Miss Foster, where is everybody? Where's Miss Grant, Miss Du Bois, Mr. Paxton, Mr. Johnson? (MISS FOSTER just looks at her and slowly backs away. LIZA frantically pushes all the buttons on the desk) Maggie! Alison! Russell! Johnson! Where are you? (Slowly they appear) Maggie, where are the proofs? Johnson, where's your layout? Alison, where's your column? What's the matter with you? What's the matter with everybody?

JOHNSON:
Why, don't you know what day this is, Boss Lady? This is your wedding day.

ALISON AND MAGGIE:
Your wedding day. You must hurry, Liza. This is your wedding day.

(Again the wedding bells ring out. As JOHNSON *backs away,* MAGGIE *and* ALISON *go to* LIZA *and lead her upstage.* RUSSELL PAXTON *appears in morning coat, high hat, striped trousers. In back of him are* BOYS *and* GIRLS *as bridesmaids and ushers and as they proceed to dress* LIZA *as a bride, the stage turns into a church. In the back a huge stained-glass window with a grotesque bride and groom as the motif, and for the altar a huge wedding cake. The wedding procession starts)*

CHORAL:

And now Liza Elliott is going to be married.
At last Liza Elliott is going to be married.
Let music fill the air!
We hail the happy pair!
Lift every voice in praise!
This is their day of days!

GUESTS:

What a lovely day for a lovely wedding.
What a lucky man to win himself such a bride.
To the gates of paradise both are heading
With love and loyalty acting as their guide.

*(*NESBITT *appears, goes to* LIZA, *offers his arm. The children now act as flower boys and girls.* RANDY *sings "This Is New" as though it were "Oh, Promise Me." The procession marches toward the altar. During the second half of "This Is New,"* CHARLEY, *who is now the minister, starts murmuring the marriage service. It becomes audible)*

CHARLEY:

If there be any who know why these two should not be joined in holy wedlock let him speak
    now or forever hold his peace.

A VOICE IN CHORAL:

The murmurings of conscience do increase
And conscience can no longer hold its peace.
This twain should ne'er be joined in holy wedlock
Or e'en in secular board and bed-lock.
This is no part of heaven's marriage plan.
This woman knows she does not love this man.

CHORAL:

This woman knows she does not love this man.

LIZA:

No, no! no, no! That isn't true!
I do! I do! I do! I do!

CHORAL:

This woman at the altar
Is not the true Liza Elliott.
Tell them about yourself, Liza Elliott.
Tell them the woman you really want to be—
Longing to be beautiful
And yet rejecting beauty.

Tell them the truth.
Tell them the truth.
This is no part of heaven's marriage plan.

LIZA:
No, no! It isn't true!

CHORAL:
This woman knows she does not love this man.

LIZA:
I do! I do! I do! I do!

(LIZA, *who has been backing away slowly, her hands pressing against her ears to shut out the accusing voices, soon disappears. RANDY starts intoning "This Is New" as the guests sing the counter melody "What a Lovely Day." It all becomes a bizarre combination of oratorio and mysterious and ominous movement winding up in a cacophonous musical nightmare)*

Curtain

SCENE 3

DR. BROOKS' *office.*
DR. BROOKS *is at the desk.* MAGGIE GRANT *sits in the chair facing him.*
MAGGIE: Now that I'm here, Dr. Brooks, I don't know what to say—I feel a little foolish.
DR. BROOKS: *(Laughing)* I think I understand, Miss Grant. You're not very partial to psychoanalysis. Is that it?
MAGGIE: In a word—yes.
DR. BROOKS: That's quite all right. I understand perfectly.
MAGGIE: God knows I don't know anything about it, but you do hear the damnedest things! One person discovers he was frightened by cornflakes as a child, and another one finds out the only trouble with him is he can't stand Radio City. So what does he do about that?
DR. BROOKS: *(Smiling)* It's not quite as bad as that, I hope, Miss Grant.
MAGGIE: No, of course not. I'm being funny, Dr. Brooks. People do get snarled up—no question about that. I'm in a little trouble myself. I'm too damn normal. That can't be right, can it? Oh, to hell with fencing around. Dr. Brooks, I'm worried sick about Miss Elliott. I want to be sure that she's doing the right thing in coming—here. I hope you don't mind my saying that.
DR. BROOKS: No.
MAGGIE: I don't know quite what I expected to say to you or to have you tell me, but I just *had* to have some reassurance. I'm beginning to get really frightened.
DR. BROOKS: Did Miss Elliott know you were coming to see me?
MAGGIE: No, no—I just did this on my own. You see—we're very great friends. We've grown up with the magazine together—and I know Liza so well that the change in her these last few months scares me. She's going through some kind of hell—and the terrible thing is that even *I* can't seem to reach her. She seems to be sinking into herself more and more. Yesterday afternoon I got kind of a shock. I came back to the office after lunch and her door was locked. I had to pound to get in. She'd fallen asleep on the divan. I'd never known her to do

anything like that before. She didn't make sense for a few minutes—she'd been dreaming. She hardly seemed to notice me. Then she started to cry. Couldn't stop. Then she seemed to get hold of herself and we started to work. But she couldn't work. She'd start and stop—pace the floor—light cigarettes—toss them away. Finally—she just walked out. And with the magazine going to press! You can't realize what a different Liza Elliott that is—she's been like a machine all the years I've known her. That's why I'm frightened, Dr. Brooks. Is she on the right track? Can you help her? Forgive my being skeptical—I'm very fond of her and very worried.

DR. BROOKS: I hope I can help her, Miss Grant. Analysis takes time and patience and courage—on Miss Elliott's part. I can't discuss details with you—I'm sure you realize that. But for your own reassurance—I'm inclined to be hopeful. I can't say any more than that.

MAGGIE: Thank you. That's very good news. You've been very nice, Dr. Brooks. And may I say that if ever I get neurotic, you'll be the first to know. In fact, I may try to develop something right away.

DR. BROOKS: *(Laughing)* Thank you. Will you go out this way, please? I believe Miss Elliott is outside.

MAGGIE: Oh. Good day, Dr. Brooks. *(She looks at him and smiles)* Yes, sir, there are times when I wish I weren't so goddamned normal.

(She goes out through the other door. DR. BROOKS makes a notation on his desk-pad, then presses the buzzer on his desk. MISS BOWERS comes in from the waiting room)

MISS BOWERS: Mr. Haskell telephoned to know if his hour could be changed to four o'clock today.

DR. BROOKS: Let me see. *(He consults his appointment book)* Yes, that will be all right. You'd better telephone the hospital and switch my appointment to five-thirty. Is Miss Elliott waiting? Have her come in, please.

MISS BOWERS: *(Turning)* Will you come in, Miss Elliott? *(She holds open the door as LIZA enters, then goes out)*

LIZA: Good morning.

DR. BROOKS: Good morning, Miss Elliott. *(LIZA tosses her hat on a chair—then goes to the couch and lies down. Silence)* I am listening.

LIZA: I can't seem to think. Just the same thing over and over and over. *(Another silence)*

DR. BROOKS: Suppose we go back to the end of the hour yesterday.

LIZA: All right. Anything.

DR. BROOKS: You had this feeling of panic when Mr. Nesbitt told you of the divorce. Is that right?

LIZA: Yes.

DR. BROOKS: Had you intended to go to sleep?

LIZA: No. I was suddenly so weary that I flung myself on the sofa. I remember that song going through my head—then that dream—then Maggie pounding on the door.

DR. BROOKS: Yes.

LIZA: I've told you. I tried to work. I couldn't. Then I called you and came here. *(A pause.)*

DR. BROOKS: Had you ever been aware before that you did not want Mr. Nesbitt to divorce his wife?

LIZA: No.

DR. BROOKS: I think the thing that still challenges us is to find out why you are so panic-stricken when it happens.

LIZA: I haven't any idea. I want to know what to do now.

DR. BROOKS: I don't think you ought to make a decision in the dark, do you?

LIZA: No. But I must make a decision.

DR. BROOKS: What do you want to do?

LIZA: I don't know. I can't seem to think.

DR. BROOKS: I suggest that you decide nothing until you know what you want to do.

LIZA: But I must do something. Can't you see that?

DR. BROOKS: Now, look here—suppose I said to you, "Go ahead and marry him," would you be able to accept that?

LIZA: No.

DR. BROOKS: And if I said, "No, don't marry him"—would that solve your problem?

LIZA: No, no, of course not. But I expect some kind of help from you. Why am I here?

DR. BROOKS: I can only suggest again that we try to learn more about your present emotional state before deciding anything. You noticed, I presume, that in this dream, too, you are again the glamorous woman.

LIZA: Yes, yes. What of it?

DR. BROOKS: Why do you think you continually dream this fantasy, and yet never attempt to act it out in your conscious life?

LIZA: I don't know.

DR. BROOKS: Have you any reason that you give yourself for the austere way you dress, for instance?

LIZA: Only the simple and valid one that I happen to like business suits and simple dresses.

DR. BROOKS: Do you think there is a chance that that may not be the real explanation?

LIZA: Suppose it isn't? What earthly difference does it make?

DR. BROOKS: Have you always felt that way about clothes? As a child, for instance?

LIZA: Yes, yes! As far back as I can remember.

DR. BROOKS: That's curious, isn't it? Children usually like pretty clothes.

LIZA: Well, I didn't! And I was a perfectly happy, normal child!

DR. BROOKS: I see. Now, these men in the dream. They are the men you usually see every day?

LIZA: Yes. All except Mr. Curtis.

DR. BROOKS: Oh, yes. And I think you told me you have an engagement with him for tomorrow night, didn't you?

LIZA: I intend to break it.

DR. BROOKS: Why?

LIZA: I only said "yes" to get rid of him. He came in just after Kendall told me about—Kate. I wanted to get him out.

DR. BROOKS: Why do you intend to break the engagement?

LIZA: Because I can think of nothing I'd like to do less.

DR. BROOKS: Really? Why?

LIZA: It just wouldn't interest me, that's all. Do we have to go on with this forever?

DR. BROOKS: Do you think most women would feel that way? Don't you think most women would be delighted to spend an evening with a man as attractive as Curtis? They might even feel flattered at being seen with him.

LIZA: I wouldn't. Do you mind?

DR. BROOKS: There's a strange contradiction here, isn't there? Remember in your dream Mr. Curtis made love to you—held you in his arms. Yet here you savagely reject him. That's a curious denial, isn't it?

LIZA: Yes, yes, what of it?

DR. BROOKS: Bear with me a little further, Miss Elliott—it's important. Then, in your dream, you are suddenly a bride—but it is Kendall Nesbitt you find at the altar. Not Randy Curtis. And the mocking voices of other women make the ceremony a nightmare—turn it into a horror you cannot face. Yet your job is to make other women beautiful, isn't it?

LIZA: We've been over that before, haven't we?

DR. BROOKS: I wonder if your scorn and hatred of other women is because you are afraid of them. You make them beautiful to appease them, but the more beautiful you make them the more they continue to rob you, and your hate and fear of them grows. Perhaps the reason for the way you dress is that it is a kind of protective armour—with it you are not forced to compete. You don't dare.

LIZA: That's not true. I reject that—all of it. You forget Nesbitt.

DR. BROOKS: No. You see, Miss Elliott, even the man you have belongs to another woman. In a sense he is a man already taken—a man that you share. And the thought of having him alone sends you into a panic. You don't dare compete as a woman.

(There is a moment's pause. LIZA rises from the couch and faces him. Her voice sounds strange, as though she could not quite control it)

LIZA: I've had enough. I'm not going any further. Send me a bill for whatever this is. Good day.

(DR. BROOKS rises, but makes no move to detain her)

DR. BROOKS: Good day, Miss Elliott. *(She goes quickly out)*

Curtain

SCENE 4

LIZA'S *office, late the next afternoon.*

RUSSELL *is sprawled full length on the couch, a lady's evening cape thrown across him as a coverlet, a rather outrageous lady's hat over his face.* ALISON *is slumped down in an easy chair, intent upon her fingernails.* MAGGIE *is nervously pacing and smoking a cigarette. They have apparently been there for hours. The office looks smoky and unkempt. Two of those life-sized dummies in formal evening attire stand at one side. Various hats, dresses, boudoir accessories, blow-up photos and proof copies of the next issue are everywhere about the room.*

MAGGIE *crushes out her cigarette and sits on the edge of the desk.*

MAGGIE: *(Violently)* Where the hell *is* she?

ALISON: Darling, she's just been delayed, somehow. *(She dabs some perfume behind her ears)*

MAGGIE: Oh, for God's sake, Alison, don't be such a jerk! Delayed! It's half-past six. *(She paces again)* Russell, take that silly-looking thing off your face. You're a great help.

RUSSELL: *(Removing the hat)* What do you want me to do, dear? Weep quietly? *(He sits up and sniffs)* Alison, is that you I smell?

ALISON: It's that new "Northwest Mounted," darling. Do you like it?

RUSSELL: You'll get a horse with it, dear, not a man. *(He yawns and stretches)* Maggie, how much longer are we going to just sit here?

MAGGIE: I don't know what to do, Russ. I hate to go ahead without her—but we've got to get to the printers. Damn! Why doesn't she show up? She's never done this before in her life!

(A pause. Then:)

RUSSELL: Look, dear. Why don't you break down and tell us.

MAGGIE: Tell you what?

RUSSELL: Did she go to that doctor today?

MAGGIE: *(Startled)* What doctor?

RUSSELL: Now, dear—don't trifle with J. Edgar. I have my own little Gestapo. I know she's going to a psychoanalyst.

ALISON: An analyst? Darling, why didn't she *tell* me? They're all awful! I went to one myself but he said there was nothing the matter with me that a good boot in the behind wouldn't cure. I go to an astrologer now who's simply divine! Absolutely saved my life.

RUSSELL: *(Ignoring this)* Did you speak to the doctor?

MAGGIE: She didn't show up there today, either.

ALISON: I do wish Liza would try Astrology—it's absolutely miraculous!

RUSSELL: *(After a pause)* She's cracking up, if you ask me.

MAGGIE: What the hell do you know about it, anyway?

RUSSELL: Listen, pet, behind this pretty little face there's just sheer intuition.

MAGGIE: I'm sure. And you understand women. Want to give us a brief talk? I'm just in the mood.

RUSSELL: Don't be bitter, dear, I worship women. But you're all such fools! A career or a baby isn't always the answer.

ALISON: Oh, I agree, darling!

RUSSELL: Sleeping around isn't either, dear. *(ALISON shuts up)* None of you ever seem to realize that anything is wrong until you're in the middle of a blitzkrieg!

MAGGIE: What do they call you at home, Professor—the Magic Bullet?

RUSSELL: Well, look around you, dear. You're all so messy—maybe that's why so much bitchery goes on.

(The telephone rings. MAGGIE leaps to it)

MAGGIE: Hello? Oh, hello, Kendall. No, she hasn't shown up yet. Any luck? I . . . *(She listens for a moment)* All right. Why don't you do that? We'll go ahead without her. I guess we have to. *(She hangs up)* Nesbitt's coming over. Now, shall we get to work or would you rather finish your report to the Rockefeller Foundation?

RUSSELL: Oh, lead your own dreary female lives. I don't know why I bother. Where did I put those pictures?

(The door opens and LIZA enters)

ALISON: *(Leaping up)* Darling, we've been frantic!

MAGGIE: Shut up, Alison.

LIZA: I'm sorry for this. We'll have to work late. Russell, talk to Adams, will you? He's outside. See if he can hold the men at the shop. Alison, call Bergdorf's for me and see if they'll hold over until the next issue. Promise them anything. Maggie, wait here a minute, will you?

ALISON: *(On her way out)* Darling, you look liverish—you ought to take a good physic. It's not very chic, but . . .

RUSSELL: *(Following her)* Come on, dear—move, move! We've been all through your upper colon, many times.

(The door closes behind them. LIZA *slowly removes her hat)*

MAGGIE: Everything under control?

LIZA: Like a runaway train. *(A slight pause)* Kate is giving Kendall a divorce, Maggie.

MAGGIE: Oh.

LIZA: He told me yesterday.

MAGGIE: I thought you wanted that, Liza.

LIZA: So did I. I went to pieces when he told me. Don't ask me why. God knows! Why have I been driving around Long Island since seven o'clock this morning? I can't think any more—I can't. *(She slumps into a chair)* What are people saying, Maggie? They must be talking! "Liza Elliott mooning around because she's unhappy. Well, who isn't? She's got more than most people right now." I wouldn't blame them—it's true. I couldn't offer any defense. But this is an illness, Maggie—a sickness. This has nothing to do with being happy or unhappy—I'm sick inside. *(Unsteadily, she lights a cigarette)* I've quit the analysis, Maggie. I couldn't stand it. I just couldn't.

MAGGIE: *(After a moment)* What did you tell Kendall yesterday?

LIZA: I lied. I wanted time to think—and I can't think. I can't get one single thought clear. I keep turning and turning in a squirrel-cage of myself. I can't go on this way much longer. I've got to do something. But I don't know what to do—I don't know.

MAGGIE: Maybe the doctor could have helped, if you'd given him time. You shouldn't have quit, Liza! You shouldn't!

LIZA: I couldn't stand it, I tell you!

MAGGIE: *(Helplessly)* I don't know what to say, Liza.

LIZA: I know, I know. What's happened to me, Maggie? What *is* this thing?

*(MISS FOSTER *appears in the doorway)*

MISS FOSTER: Mr. Nesbitt is here, Miss Elliott.

LIZA: *(A deep sigh)* Have him come in.

*(MISS FOSTER *goes)*

MAGGIE: Don't you want to put him off?

LIZA: No. Facing it can't be worse than this.

MAGGIE: I'll get things moving. Don't worry about the magazine—we'll get it out. Just try and decide about the Easter cover, will you?

LIZA: All right. Thank you, Maggie.

MAGGIE: *(As she opens the door)* Hello, Kendall.

KENDALL: 'Lo, Maggie. *(He closes the door behind him, then comes straight to* LIZA*)* Liza, what happened?

LIZA: I don't know, Kendall. I had an impulse to run away, that was all. Sorry I was such a fool.

(He lights a cigarette and paces for a moment or two. Then:)

KENDALL: Be completely honest with me, will you, Liza?

LIZA: Yes.

KENDALL: You weren't last night.

LIZA: I know that.

(A pause)

KENDALL: You don't want to marry me. Is that right? Don't be polite. Is that true?

LIZA: Yes.

KENDALL: Do you want to go on as we have before?

LIZA: I don't know. I haven't thought about it.

KENDALL: Have I been at fault?

LIZA: No.

KENDALL: Is there someone else?

LIZA: No, Kendall.

KENDALL: What is my position then, Liza? I have just rearranged my life to give you what you've always led me to believe you've wanted.

LIZA: I don't know why I don't want it now—I don't know why!

KENDALL: That isn't enough, Liza. You're too fair a person to think it is.

LIZA: I can't explain it. How can I make clear to you what I don't understand myself. There *is* no valid reason. I can't give you one. I've tried to think it out —you must know I have—but I can't. I'm ill, Kendall.

KENDALL: I won't let you off this easy, Liza. I know you're ill—but you'll be well again. Other people go through these things, too. Meanwhile, you haven't the right to trifle with other people's lives, even with this as an excuse. I won't let you.

LIZA: What do you want me to do?

KENDALL: I want you to go through with this. This—confusion—will pass. I know it will. You're behaving like a child. It's time you stopped.

LIZA: Don't talk to me like that! I won't take it—not from you or anybody! I'm fighting as hard as I know how.

KENDALL: Liza, listen to me. I can't stand aside while you proceed to destroy something very important to me.

LIZA: Kendall, give me time.

KENDALL: No, Liza. That's not facing it honestly. And you've got to. For both of us.

LIZA: *(Wearily)* All right . . . All right. Come back here for me. I'll get through as soon as I can. But don't push me into a corner, Kendall—it's no use.

KENDALL: I'm going to fight, Liza. I can't help that.

(RUSSELL comes in, his arms full of trailing chiffon and prop doves)

RUSSELL: Sorry to interrupt. Liza, you'll have to look at this. Bring it in, boys.

KENDALL: *(To LIZA)* Around eleven?

LIZA: Yes.

(He waves a hand in good-bye, and goes out, passing two boys carrying in a full-sized suit of armour)

RUSSELL: Put it right here. And wait. Ben, go and tell the girls to come in. Look, dear—the only way I can get those four models in the issue is to put them all together.

LIZA: We promised separate pictures.

RUSSELL: They won't kick—they're getting them in color.

LIZA: Why not do it and show me proofs?

RUSSELL: Because there isn't time, dear. I want your okay now. Come on in, girls. Stand over there and no talking.

(The girls come in, murmuring a "Good evening, MISS ELLIOTT.*" There are four of them, and they are very beautiful indeed. One is in a ski outfit, one in evening dress, one in an afternoon dress for Southern wear, and another in a negligee. They stand, beautiful but vacant)*

RUSSELL: Ben, hold these goddamn doves. I'm going to make Elmer pretty. *(He hands over the doves to the office boy, and begins, with great concentration, to drape the chiffon over the suit of armour)*

LIZA: *(On the telephone)* Tell Adams to bring in whatever he has. *(She hangs up)* Russell, where's that California stuff?

RUSSELL: Maggie put it on your desk. *(Staring at the armour)* Dear me, I wonder what they did in those days if they ever had a hurry call. It must have happened occasionally. What did they *do!* *(He stands back and surveys his handiwork)* Give me those doves now, Ben. *(He places a dove on each shoulder)*

(CHARLEY JOHNSON saunters in and strolls behind the girls. RUSSELL, *deep in his work, and* LIZA, *immersed in pictures spread out on her desk, are not immediately aware of him. One of the girls gives a little scream. He has evidently pinched her behind)*

RUSSELL: *(Looking up)* Oh, for God's sake! *(*LIZA *looks up, then goes back to the pictures)* Come on, girls. Over here, please. Helen, I want you here, Ruthie, you over here. Carol over on the left. And Marcia in the middle. Now drape yourselves, girls. Come on, Helen, suck up your gut and drape. That's better. Look, Liza—what about it? I'll process in a shot of a Gothic Castle in back.

LIZA: I don't like it, but go ahead if there isn't time. And rush the Bonwit Teller stuff up to me as fast as you can.

HELEN: You going to take this *tonight*, Mr. Paxton? In color? Oh, nuts! *(The other girls echo her annoyance)*

RUSSELL: Now, dear, *my* love life has been shot to hell, too. You'll be out by nine.

CHARLEY: I'll take you all over to the Stork. How about it?

HELEN: Oh, Mr. Johnson, you're a sweetie! *(The girls rush over to him and gurgle their delight)*

RUSSELL: All right, Ben. Take Errol Flynn down to the studio. Come on, girls —downstairs. And close your negligee, dear. You're giving us a bird's-eye view of the promised land. *(The girls start out, chattering)*

LIZA: Tell Miss Foster to grab a bite and come right back, Russell. And ask Maggie to come in as soon as she can, will you?

RUSSELL: Yes, ma'm. You know the printers are on double and overtime, dear? And what about the Easter cover?

LIZA: I'll let you know.

RUSSELL: See you later. *(He gestures toward* CHARLEY*)* Keep Tommy Manville out of the studio if you want that stuff out. *(He goes out)*

CHARLEY: Got a minute?

LIZA: Just about. Can it wait?

CHARLEY: Yes—but I'd like to settle it. Happens to be about the Easter cover— that ole davvil Easter cover. If you'd make up your mind and decide on a circus cover, Boss Lady, I can get a helluva tie-up with Ringling Brothers.

LIZA: When must you know?

CHARLEY: Soon as possible. I've got all the big stores lined up to splurge on circus ads in the issue and I'd like to get Paxton started on a circus layout for the whole magazine. Ringlings will give me access to all their old circus styles and dresses. We could make it a very interesting issue.

LIZA: I'll give you an answer as soon as I can.

(ALISON comes in)

ALISON: Bergdorf's will hold over—I charmed them into it, dear. *(To* CHARLEY*)* Darling, I saw you at Blake's last night. What was that fight about anyway?

CHARLEY: I don't remember any fight.

ALISON: Why, darling, they carried that man *out* after you hit him.

LIZA: Come on, Alison. Is there anything else?

ALISON: Darling, forgive me, but *would* you read this book on astrology? I know you've been going to an . . . *(She glances at* CHARLEY *and stops)* I mean it's absolutely saved my life—the stars can cure anything once you get under the right one.

LIZA: Alison, I'm very busy.

ALISON: Darling, let me leave it on your desk and just look at it when you have a moment. Will you? You just wouldn't believe what the stars can do! After all, it's a science as old as the world and they've just begun to discover it can heal and cure. Darling, you *must* promise me you'll look at it.

LIZA: Yes, yes, yes! Put it down. And bring in the Paris stuff as soon as it's set up, will you? I want to go over it.

ALISON: I will, dear. Liza, whatever is the matter with Kendall? He was positively rude! Really, if everyone took physics regularly I don't believe we'd ever have a war! *(She goes out)*

LIZA: Was that all you wanted, Johnson?

CHARLEY: Um. Too bad you can't decide on that cover. I wanted to cinch that and leave in a blaze of glory.

LIZA: Leave?

CHARLEY: This is what might be termed my resignation, Boss Lady. Please—no tears. Just a light kiss on the cheek, perhaps. Then a quick good-bye. Hot dog!

LIZA: *(After a pause)* Pretty thin-skinned, aren't you?

CHARLEY: Me? You mean you think I'm tossing in the towel because you spanked me yesterday? No-oo! Just got a better offer—that's all.

LIZA: Where?

CHARLEY: *Town and Country.*

LIZA: I'll meet it.

CHARLEY: 'Fraid you couldn't.

LIZA: I'll be the judge of that.

CHARLEY: Why? I annoy the pants off you, don't I?

LIZA: That has nothing to do with the way you do your job. I'll meet their figure. Does that settle it?

CHARLEY: Look—it has nothing to do with salary. I'm taking less. But I can get something there that I can never get here. *(He pauses slightly)* Your job. I'm afraid that's what I want.

LIZA: How nice of you to be so frank.

CHARLEY: Yah—I'm ambitious. Want to run the whole thing myself, some day. Never suspect it, would you? But I'm an eager lad, full of dreams. And there isn't a chance of that here. You married that desk years ago, Boss Lady, and you're never going to get a divorce. I know your kind.

LIZA: Do you, really!

CHARLEY: Yep. You have magazines instead of babies. Maybe you're right. There's a lot like you.

LIZA: *(Quietly)* Get out of here!

CHARLEY: Now, I didn't mean to be insolent. Honest.

LIZA: You're not only insolent. You're contemptible. I know your kind, too, Johnson. And I'm sick of that incredible side-show you put on under the guise of "the gay young man with a wicked tongue." It doesn't always excuse your being an ill-mannered boor, and I question whether that isn't the extent of your talent.

CHARLEY: *(Stung)* Rage is a pretty good substitute for sex, isn't it?

LIZA: *(Exploding)* Get out! *(She picks up a cigarette box from the desk and flings it at him)*

(He dodges it, then bows deeply)

CHARLEY: Don't think it hasn't all been charming. And if we ever need a good man over there, I'll make you an offer. *(He strolls out, whistling)*

(Suddenly LIZA crumples into the desk chair, her head and her arms on the desk. She begins to cry, violently, uncontrollably. The door opens and MISS STEVENS stands in the doorway. LIZA manages to rise and turn away just in time)

LIZA: What is it?

MISS STEVENS: *(All aglow)* Mr. Curtis is here, Miss Elliott.

LIZA: Mr. Curtis?

MISS STEVENS: Why, yes. You have a dinner engagement with him, haven't you? That's what he said.

LIZA: *(A gasp)* Oh, my God. Ask him to come in, Miss Stevens.

(MISS STEVENS goes. LIZA dabs furiously at her eyes—pulls herself together with enormous effort. The door opens)

MISS STEVENS: Mr. Curtis. *(RANDY comes in. He is resplendent in white tie and tails. The door closes behind him)*

RANDY: Good evening. Am I too early?

LIZA: *(Aghast at the picture he presents)* Hello, Mr. Curtis. No, you're not. I'm terribly sorry, I . . .

RANDY: *(Laughing)* Now, you didn't forget about me again, did you?

LIZA: No, of course not. I'm just—late. We've been so pressed. I haven't had time to . . .

RANDY: *(Eagerly)* Say—you know what? I wish you wouldn't go home and dress. Let's go out just as you are. I'll stop back at the hotel on the way and change —won't take me five minutes. Let's do that, huh? *(He hesitates)* I was so afraid I'd run into a glamour girl tonight instead of . . .

LIZA: Instead of what?

RANDY: You. As you are now. That's what I like so much about you, Miss Elliott. Just this. You don't know what a relief it is. I'm up to my hips in glamour most of the time.

LIZA: *(Grimly)* Thank you. But I *am* going to dress, Mr. Curtis. Won't take me five minutes. Will you wait outside for me please!

RANDY: Why, sure—if you'd rather. I'll wait. *(He smiles uncertainly at her. Then goes out)*

(She barely waits for the door to close. Then she rips off her dress and tosses it on the floor. Crossing the room she kicks off her shoes. She is crying again—wildly now. She goes straight to the dummy and takes off the dress and flings it on. From the other dummy she takes the evening cape and shoes. She runs to the mirror on the other side of the room, undoing the knot of her hair as she crosses. In front of the mirror she begins to fluff out her hair—half singing, half sobbing that phrase of song. MAGGIE comes in and for a moment does not realize it is LIZA at the mirror. Then:)

MAGGIE: Liza! What *is* this?

LIZA: Advertisement! From *Allure!* Magazine of Beauty! Like the line? The most alluring women are wearing it!

MAGGIE: *(Crossing to her and taking her by the shoulders)* Liza! Are you all right?

LIZA: I'm fine! Let me alone! *(She shakes her off and goes out of the door. MAGGIE stands staring after her)*

The curtain is down

ACT TWO

SCENE 1

LIZA*'s office. Late the following afternoon.*

LIZA *is at the desk intent on a layout spread before her. MAGGIE comes in, hat and coat on, drawing on her gloves.*

MAGGIE: Liza—you'll kill your eyes that way. *(She snaps on the lights)* It's as gloomy as a Willkie button in here. Can I buy you a cocktail on the way home?

LIZA: I'm staying down to work.

MAGGIE: Liza—don't push yourself this way. Come and have a drink.

LIZA: Let me be, Maggie. Please.

MAGGIE: All right.

(ALISON comes in, also on the way home)

ALISON: Darlings, do I look too dreadful to bounce into "21"—just the bar, I mean. I wouldn't dream of going upstairs this way.

MAGGIE: You look ducky. Come on—I'll drop you.

ALISON: Liza, dear, you were the absolute sensation of the Stork Club last night —you and Randy Curtis. I didn't see you come in, you know, and somebody said, "Guess who just walked in with Randy Curtis" and I said, "Let me guess —twenty questions" and of course I never even came close to guessing *you,* darling. You looked divine and he's such a dreamboat that I almost couldn't believe it when I turned around. Nobody talked of anything else all night.

MAGGIE: Not even Hemingway? Come on, Alison—Liza wants to work. Good night, Liza.

ALISON: Night, darling. Maggie, dear, do come into "21" with me—it's so un-chic to walk in alone.

MAGGIE: You must be brave, Alison. We're living in dangerous times.

(They are gone. For a moment LIZA stares unseeingly at the papers on the desk before her. Wearily she tosses her pencil down on the desk—then gets up and stands quite motionless. She goes to the window and stands looking out. Then drifts to her desk and idly picks up some letters without glancing at the contents—then lets them

fall again. She lights a cigarette and paces. Up and down. Up and down. She stops and tiredly passes her hand across her eyes. She glances down at a little side table on which ALISON *has left the book on Astrology. Impulsively, she picks it up and opens it. She sinks into a chair and slowly turns the pages. From out of nowhere, a* VOICE *speaks)*

THE VOICE: Turning to Astrology, now, eh?

ANOTHER VOICE: What will it be next—Numerology?

ANOTHER VOICE: Astrology! The stars! And you're clutching at it! Helplessly! You're clutching at anything!

(Violently, she tosses the book aside, gets up, and again the pacing begins. Suddenly she stops dead. She shakes her head—throws back her shoulders. It is an enormous effort at regaining some kind of self-control. Defiantly, she walks to the desk and picks up several large cellophane-covered drawings, takes them to the divan and sits down, spreading them out before her for consideration. For a long moment she is intent on the drawings. Then, a VOICE *again)*

THE VOICE: Can't make up your mind, can you?

ANOTHER VOICE: Can't even decide on a cover!

ANOTHER VOICE: You're not as efficient as you used to be.

ANOTHER VOICE: You used to make decisions immediately.

ANOTHER VOICE: You can't seem to work any more.

ANOTHER VOICE: Your mind seems to wander all the time.

ANOTHER VOICE: Decide on this cover. You've got to. You've got to.

*(*LIZA *is holding one drawing in front of her, staring at it as though hypnotized)*

KENDALL NESBITT'S VOICE: I won't stand aside while you proceed to destroy something very important to me. I'm going to fight, Liza. I can't help that.

CHARLEY JOHNSON'S VOICE: You married that desk years ago, and you're never going to get a divorce. I know your kind.

RANDY CURTIS'S VOICE: That's what I like so much about you, Miss Elliott. Just this. You don't know what a relief it is. I'm up to my hips in glamour most of the time.

(She passes her hand in front of her eyes—as though to drive the voices out of her head. Then:)

A VOICE: Decide on this cover. You've got to. You've got to.

ANOTHER VOICE: It's not so difficult. You can do it. The circus cover or the Easter cover.

ANOTHER VOICE: The circus cover or the Easter cover. Why can't you decide? Even this little decision frightens you now. It's getting worse. It's getting worse.

ANOTHER VOICE: You must decide this now or you'll go mad. You can't leave here without deciding. You won't sleep again. You've got to decide. You've got to.

ANOTHER VOICE: You can do it. Yes, you can. Decide. Decide. The Easter cover or the circus cover. The Easter cover or the circus cover.

(The lights have been dimming. Now, as the lights come up, LIZA *is standing with her back to the audience, silhouetted against a brilliant picture of circus performers in full costume. The walls of the office have disappeared and in their place is a huge circus cover for the magazine—the cover* LIZA *has been staring at)*

(While voices are saying "Easter cover or circus cover?" we faintly hear circus parade music. It quickly grows louder and paraders march on.)

PARADERS:
Ta ra ra, tszing, tszing, tszing—
Ta ra ra, tszing, tszing, tszing—
Ta ra ra, tszing, tszing, tszing—
Ta ra ra ra!
Ta ra ra, tszing, tszing, tszing—
Ta ra ra, tszing, tszing, tszing—
Ta ra ra, tszing, tszing, tszing—
Ta ra ra ra!
The Greatest Show on Earth!
It's Full of Thrills and Mirth!
You Get Your Money's Worth!
Come one, come all!

Come see the Midgets and the Bushman from Australia;
Come see the Cossacks in Their Dazz-l-ing Regalia!

The Flower of Womankind
Who Can't Make up Her Mind
Is A Feature You Will Always Recall!

You Get Your Money's Worth!
It's Full of Thrills and Mirth!
The Greatest Show on Earth!
Come one, come all!

RINGMASTER (RUSSELL PAXTON) *(Very operatic):*
Ladies and Gentlemen, I Take Pride in Introducing
The Greatest Show on Earth!
Liza Elliott's Gargantuan Three-Ring Circus
Featuring for the First Time
The Captivating and Tantalizing Liza Elliott . . .
The Woman Who Cannot Make up Her Mind!
In Addition, We Bring You an Assortment
Of Other Scintillating Stars of the Tanbark Ring
And a Galaxy of Clowns and Neuroses
In a Modern Miracle of Melodramatic Buffoonery
And Mental Tight-Rope Walking!
The Greatest Show on Earth!

ENSEMBLE:
The Flower of Womankind
Who Can't Make up Her Mind
Is a Feature You Will Always Recall!

You Get Your Money's Worth!
It's Full of Thrills and Mirth!
The Greatest Show on Earth!
Come one, come all!

RINGMASTER:
Order in the arena!

(Drum roll as PAGE *somersaults on. Presents parchment)*

PAGE:
The charges against Liza Elliott.

RINGMASTER:
Thank you, my dear.

(As photographer rushes on taking flashlight of LIZA*)*

LIZA: *(Bewildered)*
What is all this? Charges against me? What for? What is all this?

RINGMASTER: *(Reading from parchment)*
Whereas—

ENSEMBLE:
Whereas—

RINGMASTER:
Liza Elliott cannot make up her mind about the Easter cover or the circus cover—
Secundus—

ENSEMBLE:
Secundus—

RINGMASTER:
Liza Elliott cannot make up her mind whether she is marrying Kendall Nesbitt or not.
Moreover—

ENSEMBLE:
Moreover—

RINGMASTER:
Liza Elliott cannot make up her mind as to the kind of woman she wants to be—the executive or the enchantress—
And, inasmuchas—

ENSEMBLE:
Inasmuchas—

RINGMASTER:
In a world where tumult and turmoil reign, these indecisions of Liza Elliott only add to the confusions of an already, as indicated, confused world—
Therefore, be it resolved—

ENSEMBLE:
Be it resolved—

RINGMASTER:
That Liza Elliott be brought to trial and be made to make up her mind. (A cheer) Introducing That Death-Defying Trapeze Artist and Prosecuting Attorney, Charley Johnson!

(Fanfare as JOHNSON *marches on)*

CHARLEY:

I'm the attorney for prosecution—
Can't be bought or sold!
For the jam she's in there's no solution,
Once the story's told!

ENSEMBLE:

He's the attorney for prosecution—
Flying into space!
Will there be an electrocution
If he wins the case?

RINGMASTER:

Introducing That Thrilling Bareback Rider and Attorney for the Defense—Randy Curtis!

(Fanfare as RANDY *marches on)*

RANDY:

I'm the lawyer for the defendant—
Can't be sold or bought!
Miss Elliott's star is in the ascendant—
This will come to naught!

ENSEMBLE:

He's the lawyer for the defendant—
Bareback rider, too!
Miss Elliott's star is in the ascendant—
'Cording to his view!

(Fanfare as JURY *gets up)*

RINGMASTER:

Introducing Those Merry Madcaps and Prankish Pantaloonatics—the Jury!

JURY:

Our object all sublime
We shall achieve in time:
To let the melody fit the rhyme—
The melody fit the rhyme!

*(*RINGMASTER *bangs gavel)*

RINGMASTER:

This is all immaterial and irrelevant—
What do you think this is—Gilbert and Sellivant?

JURY:

Gilbert and Sellivant! Ha ha ha ha ha ha ha ha ha!
If this is just a sample
Then evidence is ample
You get your money's worth
At The Greatest Show on Earth!

CHARLEY:

Your Honor, Mr. Ringmaster! I would like to call That Peerless Witness and Lion Tamer,
   Kendall Nesbitt!

(RINGMASTER *snaps whip as* NESBITT *marches on)*

Mr. Nesbitt, you are divorcing your wife so you can be free to marry the defendant, isn't that so?

NESBITT:
Yes, sir.

CHARLEY:
You were led to believe the defendant would *marry you, when, as and if.*

NESBITT:
Yes, sir.

CHARLEY:
But now she refuses to make up her mind.

NESBITT:
Yes, sir.

CHARLEY:
You gave her the best years of your life
And yet she refuses to be your wife!

NESBITT:
Yes, sir!

RINGMASTER:
What a show! What a situation! Can you conceive it?
If you saw it on the stage you wouldn't believe it!

(Comes downstage to sum it up for the audience)

He gave her the best years of his life.
She was, shall we call it, his mistress?
'Twas only for her he's divorcing his wife
And now the man's in distress.

The mister who once was the master of two
Would make of his mistress his Mrs.
But he's missed out on Mrs. for the mistress is through—
What a mess of a mish mash this is!

ENSEMBLE:
But he's missed out on Mrs. for the mistress is through—
What a mess of a mish mash this is!

RANDY:
Your Honor, Mr. Ringmaster.

RINGMASTER:
Yes, Mr. Bareback Rider.

RANDY:
I would like to answer the charge just made by the prosecuting attorney.

RINGMASTER:
Go ahead. I can hardly wait.

RANDY:

> *Thank you.*

> *She gave him her heart, but not her word—*
> *This case, therefore, is so much deadwood.*
> *Her promise to wed he never heard*
> *For she never promised she wed would.*

> *It's just that a change of heart occurred*
> *And although it may have dismayed him—*
> *When a maid gives her heart but does not give her word,*
> *How on earth can that maid have betrayed him?*

(RANDY and ENSEMBLE repeat this softly as LIZA comes down to sing the counter-melody)

LIZA:

> *Tra la—I never gave my word;*
> *Tra la—This action is absurd.*
> *Tra la—I loved him at the start*
> *And then I had a change of heart.*
> *Tra la—The rights of womankind*
> *Tra la—permit a change of mind.*
> *When a maid gives her heart but does not give her word,*
> *How on earth can that maid have betrayed him?*

ENSEMBLE:

> *When a maid gives her heart but does not give her word,*
> *How on earth can that maid have betrayed him?*

RINGMASTER:

> *Charming, charming! Who wrote that music?*

JURY: *(As one)*

> *Tschaikowsky!*

RINGMASTER:

> *Tschaikowsky! I love Russian composers!*

> *There's Malichevsky, Rubenstein, Arensky and Tschaikowsky,*
> *Sapellnikoff, Dmitrieff, Tscherepnin, Kryjanowsky,*
> *Godowsky, Arteiboucheff, Moniuszko, Akimenko,*
> *Solovieff, Prokofieff, Tiomkin, Korestchenko;*

> *There's Glinka, Winkler, Bortniansky, Rebikoff, Ilyinsky;*
> *There's Medtner, Balakirev, Zolotareff and Kvoschinsky,*
> *And Sokoloff and Kopyloff, Dukelski and Klenowsky*
> *And Shostakovitsch, Borodin, Gliere and Nowakofski;*

> *There's Liadoff and Karganoff, Markievitch, Pantschenko*
> *And Dargomyzsky, Stcherbatcheff, Scriabine, Vassilenko,*
> *Stravinsky, Rimsky-Korsakoff, Moussorgsky and Gretchaninoff*
> *And Glazounoff and Caesar Cui, Kalinikoff, Rachmaninoff—*
> *Stravinsky and Gretchaninoff,*
> *Rumshinsky and Rachmaninoff*
> *I really have to stop, the subject has been dwelt upon enough!*

ENSEMBLE:
Stravinsky!

RINGMASTER:
Gretchaninoff!

ENSEMBLE:
Kvoschinsky!

RINGMASTER:
Rachmaninoff!

ENSEMBLE:
He'd better stop because we feel we all have undergone enough!

RINGMASTER:
Proceed with the trial.

CHARLEY:
Mr. Ringmaster, I would like to call Miss Liza Elliott.

RINGMASTER:
And about time, too. Introducing That Dazzling Defendant and Peerless Proponent of Mental Acrobatics—Miss Liza Elliott.

ENSEMBLE:
And now the star attraction—
The Greatest in the Land!
The Feature Attraction
Gives us Action
On the Witness Stand!

CHARLEY:
Miss Elliott, you've heard the charges against you. Have you made up your mind about any of these things?

LIZA:
No, I haven't.

CHARLEY:
Do you intend to?

LIZA:
I don't know.

CHARLEY:
Can you give this court any reasonable explanation as to why you cannot make up your mind?

LIZA:
Yes, I can.
There once was a girl named Jenny
Whose virtues were varied and many—
Excepting that she was inclined
Always to make up her mind—
And Jenny points a moral

With which you cannot quarrel—
As you will find.

ENSEMBLE:

Who's Jenny?
Never heard of Jenny!
Jenny is out of place!

LIZA:

But I am sure the court'll
Find Jenny is immortal
And has a bearing on this case!

JURY:

As, for instance?

LIZA:

Well, for instance—
Jenny made her mind up when she was three
She, herself, was going to trim the Christmas tree.
Christmas Eve she lit the candles—tossed the taper away.
Little Jenny was an orphan on Christmas Day.

Poor Jenny!
Bright as a penny!
Her equal would be hard to find.
She lost one dad and mother,
A sister and a brother—
But she would make up her mind.

JURY:

Little Jenny was an orphan on Christmas Day.

LIZA:

Jenny made her mind up when she was twelve
That into foreign languages she would delve;
But at seventeen to Vassar it was quite a blow
That in twenty-seven languages she couldn't say no.

JURY:

Poor Jenny!
Bright as a penny!
Her equal would be hard to find.

LIZA:

To Jenny I'm beholden.
Her heart was big and golden—
But she would make up her mind.

JURY:

In twenty-seven languages she couldn't say no.

LIZA:

Jenny made her mind up at twenty-two
To get herself a husband was the thing to do.

She got herself all dolled up in her satins and furs
And she got herself a husband—but he wasn't hers.

JURY:

Poor Jenny!
Bright as a penny!
Her equal would be hard to find.

LIZA:

Could have had a bed of roses
But history discloses
That she would make up her mind.

JURY:

She got herself a husband—but he wasn't hers.

LIZA:

Jenny made her mind up at thirty-nine
She would take a trip to the Argentine.
She was only on vacation but the Latins agree
Jenny was the one who started the Good Neighbor Policy.

JURY:

Poor Jenny!
Bright as a penny!
Her equal would be hard to find.

LIZA:

Oh, passion doesn't vanish
In Portuguese or Spanish—
But she would make up her mind.

JURY:

She instituted the Good Neighbor Policy.

LIZA:

Jenny made her mind up at fifty-one
She would write her memoirs before she was done.
So she wrote 'em and she published all her loves and her hates
And had libel suits in forty of the forty-eight States.

JURY:

Poor Jenny!
Bright as a penny!
Her equal would be hard to find.

LIZA:

She could give cards and spade-ies
To many other ladies
But she would make up her mind.

JURY:

There were libel suits in forty of the forty-eight States.

LIZA:

Jenny made her mind up at seventy-five
She would live to be the oldest woman alive.

But gin and rum and destiny play funny tricks
And poor Jenny kicked the bucket at seventy-six.

JURY:

Jenny points a moral
With which we cannot quarrel.
Makes a lot of common sense!

LIZA:

Jenny and her saga
Prove that you are gaga
If you don't keep sitting on the fence.

JURY:

Jenny and her story
Point the way to glory
To all man and womankind.

LIZA:

Anyone with vision
Comes to this decision:

ALL:

Don't make up—
You shouldn't make up—
You mustn't make up—
Oh, never make up—
Anyone with vision
Comes to this decision:
Don't make up your mind!

(During the continuing music, RANDY, the JURY, the RINGMASTER, all congratulate her. She finally goes back to her seat, picks up the drawing of the circus cover. CHARLEY goes to her)

CHARLEY:

A most excellent defense, Miss Elliott. May I ask what you have there?

LIZA:

Why, the circus cover.

CHARLEY:

May I see it?

LIZA:

Of course.

CHARLEY:

Thank you. (Looks at it. Goes to JURY*) Gentlemen, look at this.*

(They lean forward. The oboe sounds in the orchestra and they read the cover as though it were a piece of music. They sing the opening bars of that phrase of song)

LIZA:

No, no! Don't! don't! Don't sing that! (She rushes over and snatches the drawing from
his hand)

CHARLEY: *(To* JURY*)*

> *You see? (Goes to* LIZA*) You're afraid. You're hiding something. You're afraid of that music, aren't you? Just as you're afraid to compete as a woman—afraid to marry Kendall Nesbitt—afraid to be the woman you want to be—afraid—afraid—afraid!*

(Flutter in the orchestra. ENSEMBLE *turns on* LIZA *and laughs tauntingly and accusingly. Immediately the original circus music starts as all march, whispering in rhythm, "Make up your mind, make up your mind, make up your mind." As the lights come up again,* LIZA *is in the office of* DR. BROOKS. *It is later that evening)*

SCENE 2

DR. BROOKS' *office.*

DR. BROOKS *is at the desk—*LIZA *is pacing. There is a long moment of silence. Then:*

LIZA: I—I don't think I can lie down. Do you mind if I sit here and smoke?

DR. BROOKS: Whatever is most comfortable for you.

LIZA: Thank you.

> *(Silence again)*

DR. BROOKS: What is it?

LIZA: That dream. I can't seem to shake it off. I keep calling it a dream—it wasn't. It was a kind of hallucination, really.

DR. BROOKS: What occurs to you about it, Miss Elliott?

LIZA: Nothing. Except—that all through it, I had the feeling of remembered emotion—of having experienced it all before, somehow. I can't seem to shake it off. That's why I've come back. I had to.

> *(A pause)*

DR. BROOKS: Yes?

LIZA: In the dream, when they laughed at me, I had that same feeling of humiliation and hurt that I used to have.

DR. BROOKS: When?

LIZA: I used to have it constantly as a little girl.

DR. BROOKS: Why?

LIZA: I've never thought about it before until this moment. Isn't that strange? I must have forgotten through all these years—but it's the same. The "bad feeling" I used to call it.

DR. BROOKS: Can you possibly remember when you first felt it?

LIZA: Yes . . . Yes, I can remember. I must have been very little—three or four years old—but I can still remember it.

> *(The lights dim. The lights come up on a small group of people dressed in the evening clothes of the year nineteen hundred and four.* LIZA, *the* LIZA *of today, stands alone in a spotlight at one side. In the group, a woman of great beauty stands out from the others. It is* LIZA'S MOTHER. *She has red hair. Into the group comes a man, carrying a small child in his arms. It is* LIZA'S FATHER, *and he is carrying the* LIZA *that used to be)*

THE FATHER: Here she is! To say good-night and sing her little song, and off to bed with her!

A WOMAN: Liza, Liza! A beautiful name for a beautiful girl!

A MAN: She's lovely, Bob!

THE FATHER: *(Laughing)* Now, now! We're reconciled to Liza's looks. In fact, I'm rather pleased at having a plain child. *(He pats his wife's cheek tenderly)* One beauty in the family is enough, I can tell you! I couldn't stand two!

THE MOTHER: *(Playfully slapping his hand away)* Robert, really! You'd think I did nothing but stand in front of a mirror for hours, to hear him talk.

THE FATHER: But you do, my dear! Tim—never marry a legendary beauty. It's hell!

THE MOTHER: *(Laughing)* Hush, Robert! *(To the child)* I'm afraid you're never going to be able to wear blue, my darling, and we must be careful how we do your hair, but we shall make the most of your good points, Liza, won't we?

THE FATHER: She'll never be a beauty, Helen, no matter what you do, and I'm glad of it!

(They all laugh)

LIZA: *(In the spotlight)* I wanted to cry out: "It's not true! It's not true! I'm like my mother!" I wanted to shout and make them stop!

THE FATHER: Daddy's little ugly duckling, isn't she? Come, Liza! Sing us your song, and then a good-night kiss. *(The CHILD buries her head in his shoulder)* Why, Liza! Is this our smart little girl? Come now. That song we sing together. *(He sets her down)*

(The CHILD is silent for a moment, looking up into their faces. She seems to be struggling against tears. Falteringly, she begins the little song. It is the song we know. Only the first few bars emerge. Then suddenly the child breaks into sobs and runs from the room. The lights dim down on the group. LIZA remains alone in the spotlight)

LIZA: I ran to the nursery and looked in the mirror. I felt ugly and ashamed. When my mother came in I hated her because she was so beautiful!

(On the other side of the stage, the lights come up on a group of schoolchildren with their teacher)

THE TEACHER: Now, then! Once again. Just the end and then I shall choose who is to play the Prince and the Princess. Ready? *(She blows on a pitch pipe. The children begin. They sing a little musical Cinderella play. They finish and stand waiting, their faces eager for the decision)* That was fine, children. Now! For the Prince, I have chosen David Reed—and for the Princess, Liza Elliott.

(LIZA, now a girl of seven, jumps up and down with joy. The other children murmur politely. Suddenly DAVID REED, a boy about the same age as LIZA, steps forward and speaks)

DAVID: Miss Sullivan—I don't want to be the Prince.

THE TEACHER: Why, David! Why on earth not?

DAVID: Why can't we have a pretty Princess—like Barbara? A Princess ought to be beautiful, oughtn't she? Liza will spoil everything! I don't want to be the Prince if she's the Princess.

LIZA: *(In the spotlight)* I couldn't bear it. I wanted to hide. I wanted to crawl away and hide.

THE TEACHER: David, what a stupid thing to say! Step back into your place. I have chosen Liza for the Princess, and there will be no more talk about it, if you please.

LIZA: *(The child)* I don't want it now! I don't want it! *(She runs, sobbing, from the room)*

(The lights dim and fade)

LIZA: *(In the spotlight)* I wanted it more than anything else in the world!

(The lights come up on a little girl, sprawled full-length on the floor, reading a book and munching an apple. It is LIZA, now a child of ten. In a moment or two a buxom woman in a housekeeper's uniform comes slowly on. LIZA looks up from her book)

LIZA: Is Mother better, Mrs. Bennett?

(The WOMAN struggles to answer but cannot. Instead, she motions to the child to come to her, and when she does, takes her in her arms)

MRS. BENNETT: Liza, dear—your mother . . . *(She hugs the child tightly to her— then turns and goes. The child stands quite still for a long moment)*

LIZA: *(In the spotlight)* I wanted to cry. I knew. Yet, somehow, I couldn't. I loved my mother. But I could feel no grief. The tears wouldn't come.

(Suddenly the CHILD runs off into the darkness, and in a moment slowly returns. She is wearing a woman's evening cloak—her mother's—and in her hand she has a mirror. She turns and looks at herself in the mirror and half-smiles. Then softly, she begins to hum that childhood song. LIZA'S FATHER comes out of the sick room and stops dead as he sees the child)

THE FATHER: Liza! Liza, what are you doing! *(He rips the cloak from her shoulders and tears the mirror from her hand)* Go to your room at once!

(The lights fade)

LIZA: *(In the spotlight)* But that—feeling was gone. I don't know why. It was gone. Until . . .

(The lights come up on a group of seventeen-year-old boys and girls, dancing. The girls wear white, starched dresses, bow-knots in their hair—the boys, blue serge suits and stiff collars. One of the boys comes to LIZA)

THE BOY: May I have the rest of this dance, Liza?

LIZA: Why, yes, Ben. Thank you. *(The LIZA of today goes into his arms, and they dance with the rest)*

(A BOY stands up on a chair and claps his hands for attention)

THE BOY: Listen, everybody! The votes are all in and counted. Want to hear the results? *(They yell: "Yes! Yes!")* Here you are: The Graduating Class of Mapleton High School votes Homer Adams the Boy Most Likely to Succeed, *(Applause)* Henry Conrad the Most Brilliant Student, *(Applause)* Barbara Joyce the Most Beautiful Girl, *(Applause)* Ben Butler the Handsomest Boy, *(Applause)* and Liza Elliott the Most Popular Girl! *(Congratulatory groups cluster around the winners for a moment. Then the dance picks up again)*

LIZA: *(As they dance)* I didn't vote for you, Ben. I don't think you're the handsomest boy.

BEN: I didn't vote for you, Liza. I don't think you're the most popular girl! *(They laugh)* That was before this dance, though.

LIZA: Why, Ben—maybe you *are* the handsomest boy. I guess I never looked at you this close. *(They laugh again)*

BEN: Who you going in to supper with, Liza?

LIZA: No one, 'specially. I sort of half-promised Henry.

BEN: Will you have supper with me?

(She looks at him for a moment)

LIZA: What about Barbara, Ben?

BEN: Barbara won't mind. She's not speaking to me. And I'm not speaking to her.

LIZA: *(Laughing)* You will be, Ben, by the time we go in to supper.

BEN: No. You don't know me, Liza.

LIZA: Why, I've known you since I was seven years old!

BEN: Yes, but you don't really know me, Liza. Want to sit out this dance? It's hot in here.

(LIZA nods. They detach themselves from the dancers and walk to a bench on the opposite side of the stage. The lights dim and fade on the dancers as they disappear, and the lights come up on BEN *and* LIZA*)*

LIZA: Oh, it's nice here. The music sounds nicer far away. Why did you and Barbara quarrel, Ben?

BEN: Oh, I don't know. I just hate a girl who flirts all the time. Honest, do you think a girl should flirt all the time, Liza?

LIZA: It's hard for Barbara not to, I guess. She's so beautiful.

BEN: Too beautiful, if you ask me. I'm going to college next fall and I don't want a girl who—Oh, why do we keep on talking about Barbara, anyway. You're lots nicer.

LIZA: *(Smiling)* Ben! You've never even asked me to dance with you until tonight —and that's only because you've quarreled with Barbara. *(She laughs)* I'll bet you wouldn't ever notice me otherwise.

BEN: Maybe it took a girl like Barbara to make me see how nice you are, Liza. Who you going on the boat-ride with?

LIZA: Homer Adams.

BEN: Break it and come with me.

LIZA: Oh, I couldn't, Ben.

BEN: Yes, you could. Come on, Liza! Say you'll do it! Please!

LIZA: But . . .

BEN: But what?

LIZA: I don't understand it, Ben . . .

BEN: You don't understand what?

LIZA: You've—you've never noticed me before tonight, Ben.

BEN: Well, say—can't a fellow . . . Don't you like me, Liza?

LIZA: Yes—yes, I do, Ben. I always have.

BEN: Well, say, can't a fellow suddenly like a girl—suddenly?

LIZA: All right, Ben! I'll do it!

BEN: That's great! *(Impulsively he takes her in his arms and kisses her)*

LIZA: Ben!

BEN: I'm sorry.

LIZA: It's—it's all right.

(He takes her hand)

BEN: Gee, you're nice, Liza. We'll write to each other this summer, huh?

LIZA: Yes. *(Suddenly she covers her face with her hands)*

BEN: What's the matter?

LIZA: Nothing. I don't know. I feel funny. I guess I'm just—happy.

BEN: Me, too. Want to dance?

LIZA: I'd rather sit here awhile, Ben.

BEN: Sure. *(He puts his arm around her waist and places her head on his shoulder)* My, it's going to be summer any minute. We'll sure have a nice day for the boat-ride. *(They sit in silence for a moment or two. Then softly,* LIZA *begins to hum the song)* What's that song, Liza?

LIZA: Why, I—I didn't even know I was singing.

BEN: Go ahead and sing it—it's cute.

LIZA: I don't know whether I can remember it—I haven't thought of it in years. *(And then she sings. For the first time we hear the entire song. She sings it joyfully)*

My ship has sails that are made of silk—
The decks are trimmed with gold—
And of jam and spice
There's a paradise
In the hold.
My ship's aglow with a million pearls
And rubies fill each bin;
The sun sits high
In a sapphire sky
When my ship comes in.
I can wait for years
Till it appears—
One fine day one spring,
But the pearls and such
They won't mean much
If there's missing just one thing.
I do not care if that day arrives—
That dream need never be
If the ship I sing
Doesn't also bring
My own true love to me—
If the ship I sing
Doesn't also bring
My own true love to me.

BEN: Say, that was lovely. I didn't know you could sing, Liza.

LIZA: Oh, I don't sing. It's . . . It's—just a song I've always known. But I never could remember all the words before. *(A girl strolls casually toward them. A blonde, very beautiful girl. She laughs a little as she sees them. They turn)* Oh—hello, Barbara.

BARBARA: Hello. Excuse me for interrupting.

LIZA: That's all right.

BARBARA: Ben, could I talk to you for a minute?

BEN: What for?

BARBARA: Why, I just want to talk to you, silly.

BEN: I didn't know you were speaking to me.

BARBARA: I'm not, really. And if you just want to be rude, Ben, of course it doesn't matter.

(A slight pause)

BEN: Excuse me, Liza. I'll be right back.

(They go off into the darkness. LIZA sits motionless, waiting. In a few moments she turns and begins to look off into the darkness. Then motionless again, waiting. A BOY strolls on, whistling)

THE BOY: Hi, Liza! What you doing sitting out here? Everyone's gone to supper.

LIZA: Oh. Have they? I'm waiting for Ben—he's taking me.

THE BOY: Ben? Why, he's in there now, Liza—with Barbara. They're having supper together.

LIZA: Oh, are they? I—I—guess he must have got tired waiting. I—I—said to wait for me—but I've just been sitting here forgetting about the time—and I guess he got tired waiting.

THE BOY: Want me to take you in to supper, Liza?

LIZA: No—No—I'd just as soon sit here awhile. It's such a lovely night. Thank you, Charles, just the same.

THE BOY: See you on the boat-ride tomorrow, Liza. We're sure going to have a fine day for it!

(She nods her head up and down without speaking. THE BOY *waves a good-bye and goes. She sits immovable for a moment. Then her face plunges into her hands and she begins to weep uncontrollably. The lights fade out)*

(The lights come up again on the doctor's office. LIZA *is sitting in the chair facing him—her face averted, her hand over her eyes)*

DR. BROOKS: I'm afraid we have only a little time left today, so what I want to say I must say quickly. Shall I wait until tomorrow? I know this has been difficult for you.

LIZA: No. I'm all right.

DR. BROOKS: Let me try to fit the pieces together, if I can. We can see the pattern more clearly now, I think. A little girl, convinced of her own ugliness, rejects herself as not as good as other little girls, and then is rejected by the world.

LIZA: The world?

DR. BROOKS: Yes. That little episode in school was tragic. School and other children are a child's world, aren't they?

LIZA: But why did that—"bad feeling"—disappear when my mother died? I don't understand that.

DR. BROOKS: Perhaps because that constant reminder of beauty—of all that you were not and longed to be—was no longer there.

LIZA: And then?

DR. BROOKS: Then you blossomed as yourself until once again—and at a most crucial moment—a beautiful woman robs you. I think, then, that you withdrew as a woman. That you would no longer risk being hurt as a woman competing with other women. But the longing remained—and so did the rage and that deep sense of injustice. And what you are facing now is rebellion—rebellion at your unfulfillment as a woman.

LIZA: But that's not true! I did love Kendall. And I know he loves me. How can you answer that?

DR. BROOKS: I can't answer that yet, Miss Elliot. But there is an answer, I think, to that, too. *(He rises)* Tomorrow at the usual time?

LIZA: Yes. Good day. *(She goes quickly out)*

Curtain

SCENE 3

LIZA'S *office. A week later.*

MAGGIE *and* CHARLEY *are there, as are four of those beauteous models, in evening clothes and wraps this time, all of them distributed about the room in various attitudes of waiting.*

MAGGIE: What time is your next appointment, girls?

A MODEL: We're due over at *Vogue* at four o'clock for winter furs.

CHARLEY: *(Stretched out full-length on the divan)* Winter furs in April, a sun suit in December. If I were a model I'd wear nothing at all in September. *(The girls giggle)*

MAGGIE: *(Glancing at her watch)* I must have Miss Elliott see these first. I can't imagine what's delaying her. Look—why don't you go down to the drug store, and have an ice cream, girls? She ought to be here by the time you get back.

CHARLEY: *(Leaping up)* I'll buy you all a rich frappé—because you're sweet and beautiful and have got no minds.

MAGGIE: You'll stay right here, Johnson. Go ahead, girls, and don't be too long. Just lie down again, Charley—you're not going.

CHARLEY: Ah, me—I work in a world of women! *(He pinches the behind of one of the girls)* T'ain't bad, either! *(The girl slaps his hand away as the others laugh and exit)* You're a hard woman, Maggie.

MAGGIE: You said it. Now look—you're going to keep your word, Charley. You promised me.

CHARLEY: Yes.

MAGGIE: An apology. And no jokes. I'm staying right here to see that you do it.

CHARLEY: All right.

MAGGIE: What makes you such a heel, Charley? You're really a good guy.

CHARLEY: Look. I said a couple of things I shouldn't have. I should have just quit and that's all. I'm going to apologize to her. Do I have to take any more? I'm leaving anyway, so what difference does it make?

MAGGIE: Okay.

CHARLEY: How long have I been here? Six years. Six years is a long time to be irritated by a woman.

MAGGIE: You furnish your own share of irritation, my boy. And on purpose. I've watched you do it.

CHARLEY: Know why?

MAGGIE: No, I don't.

CHARLEY: Because I like her and admire her. I've always admired her—as a person. As a woman she makes me sick. Let me tell you something, Maggie. It's not what I say or the way I behave sometimes that gets under her skin. It's because I see through the pose. The big executive pose. She can't stand that. It frightens her. She needs that authority she wears like a thick enamel—she's afraid without it, God knows why! I knew that from the first day I walked into this office—but I could never resist chipping bits of it off and seeing what was underneath. Because underneath it, she's a helluva girl.

MAGGIE: *(Looking at him)* You kinda surprise me, baby.

CHARLEY: No, I don't. You've suspected it for a long time, you old blunderbuss. Anyhow, shut up. Want a wet kiss? *(He comes over and attempts to kiss her)*

MAGGIE: Stop it, Charley. Can't you be serious for more than a minute?

CHARLEY: Everybody likes me better when I'm cute. Know something else, Maggie? I'm kinda sick of being cute—even to myself. *(He laughs ruefully)* Yep. Here's a big secret—inside I'm romantic as hell. Outside, I pinch a model's behind because—hey—you stop this now, Maggie. Lay off me! *(RUSSELL storms in)*

RUSSELL: That bitch! That stinking blinking ruddy bloody bitch!

CHARLEY: I always thought you were fond of your mother, Russell.

RUSSELL: Oh, shut up. Where's Liza?

CHARLEY: Roping a cowboy.

RUSSELL: Maggie—either Alison leaves the magazine or I do. This is the end—the absolute end.

MAGGIE: Now, Russell . . .

RUSSELL: I mean it. She's just calmly loaned my color plates to a friend until Wednesday.

CHARLEY: Say, that's kinda new . . . "I'd like you to come up to the apartment and see my color plates."

RUSSELL: Oh, don't be so goddamn bright, Johnson—you sicken me. Maggie, you of all people know that I've put up with Alison in an absolutely God-like fashion. Now, either she goes or I do. And just before I leave I may tear out her entrails and photograph them in color. *(He storms out)*

CHARLEY: Famous last words.

MAGGIE: I didn't dare say so, but he's right, you know. Why the hell does Alison *do* these things!

(MISS FOSTER enters)

MISS FOSTER: Miss Grant, don't you think I'd better cancel Miss Elliott's appointment with Daché? It's almost three now and she isn't back yet.

MAGGIE: See if you can make it for four instead.

(MISS FOSTER nods and goes, as ALISON bustles in)

ALISON: 'Lo, darling. I had the most enchanting conversation with a traffic cop just now. He was divine! Really, the city is getting so chic! Trees on Sixth Avenue and traffic cops with oomph! It's that wonderful LaGuardia, you know. I worship him! Where's Liza?

MAGGIE: Alison, *why* did you loan Russell's color plates? He's furious!

ALISON: Oh, *that!* Darling, I didn't loan them. I dropped them and broke them —I haven't told him yet.

MAGGIE: Oh, God!

ALISON: Charles, dear, I've got the Saks and Bonwit Teller people in my office. Come along and help me convince them.

CHARLEY: Convince them of what, cookie?

ALISON: I've got an idea for a feature. I want a Bonwit Teller window-dummy, male, to fall in love with a Saks' dummy, female, and carry out the love affair in the two store windows. It's darling, isn't it, Maggie?

MAGGIE: Oh, it's chic, Alison.

ALISON: Come along, Charles, dear. Saks' is *so* conservative. I think they sometimes mix themselves up with St. Patrick's, they've been next to each other for so long!

CHARLEY: Alison, my dear, there's a touch of greatness about you!

ALISON: Darling!

CHARLEY: There's a touch of something about you—but we won't go into that. Come on.

MAGGIE: *(Calling after them as they go out)* You come back here, Charley, as soon as you've finished. *(She picks up the telephone)* Phone Le Coq D'Or—the restaurant—and find out what time Miss Elliott left there, will you? I'll be in my office.

(MAGGIE goes out. MISS FOSTER comes in and places a new batch of papers on LIZA's desk. As she starts out again, LIZA comes in followed by RANDY)

LIZA: Anything important, Miss Foster? I know I'm terribly late.

MISS FOSTER: There's a list of calls on your desk, Miss Elliott. I changed your appointment to four, with Daché.

LIZA: Good. Thank you. *(MISS FOSTER goes out)* Out of my life now, Mr. Curtis. This minute. Thank you for lunch, but you're too fascinating. You've made me late for every appointment this afternoon. *(RANDY looks at her and smiles)* What are you smiling at?

RANDY: You. You're about three different people, Liza. Today at lunch you were like someone I'd never met before—gay, and . . . I don't know—completely different from the other night. And the minute you walk into this office you're someone else again. If you want to talk about fascinating—*you're* the one!

LIZA: *(Laughing)* Which one do you like best, Randy?

RANDY: I like 'em all.

LIZA: Oh, come now. Take your pick. Maybe I can do a little homework.

RANDY: Nope. I like 'em all. Just as though I'd ordered it from a Sears Roebuck Catalogue.

LIZA: What a boy you are for saying just the right thing, Mr. Curtis.

RANDY: Well, you get the idea.

LIZA: I do, indeed. I guess I'm lucky you didn't say Macy's Basement.
    (They both laugh)

RANDY: Really got to work, huh?

LIZA: Honest.

RANDY: Couldn't possibly consider taking the afternoon off, huh? Walk through the park—it's a beautiful day—cocktails later—anything you want. I'll be fascinating—I haven't *begun* to turn it on, yet! *(LIZA laughs)* What's the matter?

LIZA: Nothing. You're just—very endearing sometimes, Randy.

RANDY: Endearing. I hope you realize you're talking to the number one box-office attraction in America, Miss Elliott. Only endearing, huh?

LIZA: Randy, you're wonderful and get out of here. I've *got* to get to work. *(She begins to propel him out)*

RANDY: Liza . . . *(He takes her hand)* Tell me something. It's not just the movie star you like, is it? Don't mind my asking that. It's because—sometimes I can't tell where the movie star leaves off and I begin. You see, I know people invite me around—not because they want *me*—they want a name and a face. And I find myself playing up all the time—giving 'em what they expect. Paying for my dinner. And it's not me at all. I get more and more lost in the shuffle. I didn't want it to be that way—with us.
    (A pause)

LIZA: *(Quietly)* It's not, Randy.

RANDY: *(Exuberantly)* Come on—take the afternoon off, Liza! Let's get drunk.
    (The door opens and CHARLEY JOHNSON appears)

CHARLEY: I beg your pardon.

LIZA: Come in, come in, Johnson. I want to see you.

CHARLEY: *(Uneasily)* I can come back later.

LIZA: No, no. I want to see you now. Good-bye, Randy. Call me.

RANDY: Good-bye, Liza. Hello, there, Mr. Johnson. How are the autographs coming?

CHARLEY: Fine—fine.
    (The door closes behind RANDY. LIZA and CHARLEY look at each other for a moment. Then:)

LIZA: Sit down for a minute, Johnson.

CHARLEY: I'm kinda busy. I thought Maggie was in here . . .

LIZA: Never mind. This is Boss Lady speaking. You see, it occurred to me, Johnson, that in all the years you've been here, in all those charming talks we've had together, *you've* always had all the answers. And now that you're leaving, I thought I'd like at least one little talk in which *I* had the answers.

CHARLEY: Yes.

LIZA: Is that the end of a sentence?

CHARLEY: Uh-huh.

LIZA: Oh, come on, Johnson. Put 'em up. It's the kid's last fight.

CHARLEY: Better not get me started, Boss Lady.

LIZA: *(After a moment)* Funny . . . It doesn't seem to matter very much now. It's gone.

CHARLEY: What?

LIZA: I used to be afraid of you. I don't know why. I used to be terrified every time you came into this office—but now I'm not. And suddenly it doesn't matter much who has the answers. All this surprise you, Johnson?

CHARLEY: In a quiet way. I could even make a rough guess at the reason—but I came in here to . . .

LIZA: Yes?

CHARLEY: You wouldn't come out and meet me on my own ground, would you?

LIZA: Which arena would that be?

CHARLEY: Would you come out into the open where *I'm* the boss, Miss Elliott? Just once? Dinner, cocktails—name it yourself. Any place away from that goddamned desk. I'll even make it my office and my desk. How about it?

LIZA: It's the best offer I've had today. Only I like being boss, Johnson.

CHARLEY: I know that. But so do I.

LIZA: I know that. But so do I.

CHARLEY: Well, sir—here we are.

LIZA: Yes, sir—here we are.

(MISS FOSTER appears in the doorway)

MISS FOSTER: Mr. Nesbitt, Miss Elliott.

(KENDALL appears in the doorway)

CHARLEY: Ah, me. *(To NESBITT)* Hello, Mr. Nesbitt. Teacher's fine again. In fact, she just used her ruler. *(He goes out)*

(For a moment NESBITT stands silent. Then he crosses to LIZA and takes her in his arms. He holds her in a tight embrace. Then he lets his arms fall to his sides and turns away)

LIZA: Kendall . . .

KENDALL: *(Huskily)* Don't leave me, Liza. I haven't any pride any more. Don't leave me.

LIZA: Kendall . . . *(She crosses to him and takes his hand in hers)* Kendall, dear, it isn't you—it's me. I know that now. Something mixed up inside myself—something I'm only dimly beginning to understand—but it's like a searchlight playing over my entire life. So many, many things are suddenly clear. It's not you, darling, it's me.

KENDALL: I need you terribly, Liza. I've been alone all my life except for you.

(ALISON bustles in)

ALISON: 'Lo, darling. 'Lo, Mr. Nesbitt. Do you know where Charley is, Liza? They said he was here.

LIZA: He's gone back to his own office.

ALISON: No, he hasn't, dear. And I . . .

LIZA: *(Sharply)* I'd go and look.

ALISON: Oh. I see. Well . . . Bonwit Teller's are being divine but I need Charley for Saks. They're positively *rural! (She goes out)*

LIZA: Kendall—help me. I'm trying to fight my way out of the dark. Help me to do the right thing. For both of us. I can't bear to see you like this—we're bound together by years of kindness and affection—we always will be, Kendall. Always. I want so desperately for you to understand now. I must make you understand.

KENDALL: *(Quietly)* It's over, Liza, isn't it? Nothing either one of us can do about that. It's over. I guess I've known for a long time, but I couldn't face it. I'm sorry—For just now. *(He takes her in his arms again)* Perhaps I do understand, Liza—in my own way. Perhaps the thing that brings people together—that need they have of each other—is a very strange one. Love is just a label for it —a word. It's not as simple as that. It's love and fear and hiding and longing and all the little pieces that go to make up the mystery and wonder of a human being. I know—because I've had a battle of my own. It's what brought us together, Liza—each in our own separate way—and now it's tearing us apart. It's the way things happen. *(He kisses her gently)* You'll do this, Liza. Fight your way through. Perhaps you'll be one of the lucky ones—the ones who come out of the dark into the sun. But some way—somewhere—find a place for me in your life, will you?

LIZA: Always, Kendall. Always. *(She kisses him tenderly)*

(MAGGIE comes briskly in—then stops dead in her tracks)

MAGGIE: Whoops! Sorry!

KENDALL: No, no. Stay right here, Maggie. I'm going. And stop looking as though you'd blundered into *True Story* magazine! Good-bye, my dear. *(He waves a kiss to LIZA and is gone)*

(LIZA stands motionless for a moment—then her hands cover her face)

MAGGIE: Liza . . . !

LIZA: It's all right, Maggie. It's just that—part of my life walked out of that door just now—part of me. You know, Maggie, I'm learning all about someone I don't think I ever really knew before—myself. It's frightening—and wonderful. Somehow, I'm going to find the courage to see it through.

MAGGIE: You will, Liza. I know that. Only I hope . . . No, what's the difference.

LIZA: I know what you mean. Will I give up all this—will my life change completely? I don't think so, Maggie. I think it only means I'll be free—at least as free as it's possible for a human being to be. I'll be through with hiding and running away.

MAGGIE: You've never run away from anything in your life, Liza.

LIZA: There are other ways of running away, Maggie. I think my whole relationship with Kendall was a flight from something I didn't dare face. And Kendall, too. He's like a lost child, really—this false front of strength that I have gave him the security he needed.

(MISS FOSTER appears in the doorway)

MISS FOSTER: Mr. Curtis wants to see you, Miss Elliott.

LIZA: Mr. Curtis! Why—he just left here.

MISS FOSTER: He said it was important. And can you come out to the Reception Room, Miss Grant? Miguel Santos is here to be photographed, and Mr. Paxton rushed out a few minutes ago.

MAGGIE: Damn! It's Russell and Alison again. Never mind—I'll tell you later. Keep your mind on Mr. Curtis—it's not a bad place for any woman's mind. Send Mr. Santos into my office, Miss Foster. *(She goes out)*

MISS FOSTER: *(In the doorway)* Will you come in, Mr. Curtis? *(She closes the door behind him)*

(RANDY stands for a moment, just looking at LIZA)

RANDY: Hello . . .

LIZA: Randy, what is it? Nothing wrong, I hope?

RANDY: No—nothing like that.

LIZA: You sound so strange. And just now you looked as though . . .

RANDY: Liza—will you marry me? *(Speechless, she just looks at him)* Don't say anything—just let me talk for a minute. This is all pretty strange to me, too. I've been walking up and down outside—then I just went to the telephone and plunged.

LIZA: Randy . . .

RANDY: No, don't, Liza—let me go on for a while. I don't know myself what I expect you to say—you've only known me for a week. Look—I want to tell you about myself. I don't give a hoot in hell for acting, and I wouldn't care if I never saw Hollywood again. I stumbled into it by dumb luck, and it's been pretty fine, because I guess if it weren't for that I'd probably be tending a gas station some place in Arizona, right now. What I'm trying to say is you wouldn't have to give up any of this for me, Liza. *(As she starts to speak)* No, wait a minute —let me get it *all* off my chest. I don't know quite how to say what I want to. I've been in love before or thought I was, but you see, Liza, you're the only woman I've ever known who's given me a feeling of peace—as though no matter what happened you'd always be there . . . I get a feeling of courage from you for the first time in my life.

LIZA: Courage—from me?

RANDY: I need someone like you, Liza—someone with your strength and courage —to lean on—to always be there. I guess the truth is, I'm a pretty frightened guy inside.

LIZA: Frightened? You, Randy?

RANDY: Maybe it goes back to when I was a kid. I was kicked out on my own at twelve—scared and desperate and needing someone to hang on to. And the funny thing is that still goes. I often think when I'm playing one of those big strongman scenes and telling everyone where to get off—boy, if they only knew! Gee, this is a helluva love scene I've just played. *(He mops his face)*

(There is a moment of silence)

LIZA: What do they always say in the movies, Randy—"This is so sudden"?

RANDY: You don't have to say anything now, Liza—I didn't expect you to.

LIZA: I want to think about it, Randy.

RANDY: Sure. I just had to tell you or explode. Now I want to get out of here —quick!

LIZA: *(Laughing)* All right.

RANDY: Phone you later? *(She nods)* Dinner, maybe?

LIZA: All right.

RANDY: Good-bye—and don't ever let my public know what a lousy lover I really am. *(And he goes)*

(She stands for a moment with a stunned expression on her face, then slowly crosses

to the desk and leans on it—that same stunned look on her face. The door flies open and RUSSELL *storms in)*

RUSSELL: Liza, I demand a showdown—an immediate and utter showdown!

LIZA: I can't talk to you now, Russell.

RUSSELL: Do you realize what that woman has done? She just calmly took my color plates and . . .

LIZA: *Please*, Russell. Not now.

RUSSELL: Not now—not now! What am I supposed to do to get some attention —*bleed* in front of you?

(The door opens and CHARLEY *strolls in)*

CHARLEY: Paxton, the Dog Department wants to see you.

RUSSELL: How darling of them! I may stay there the rest of my life. *(He goes to the door)* If you have any luck with Sleeping Beauty, let me know. Really, I could *spit!* (*He slams the door and leaves in a rage)*

CHARLEY: *(After a moment)* I'm supposed to apologize for what I said the other day—promised Maggie I would. But I've been thinking it over quietly and I've decided I'm not going to. I'm sorry—I can't help it. It's just that you've had to be the boss—always—and something in me deeply resents that. I can't help it. I know I've been pretty rotten to you—and I've kicked myself for it after-ward. But there's always been that secret battle between us—from the very beginning—and I've always had to win—because, well, because I'm me, I guess. Anyhow, I want you to know—now that I'm leaving—that for all your god-damn shenanigans I think you're fine. *(He turns away)* I've turned in the Hattie Carnegie layout to Paxton, so I guess that washes me up. Anything else?

(LIZA has been staring at him as though seeing him for the first time. Now she seems suddenly to come alive)

LIZA: Johnson—or Charley—if I may—give me back that paperweight and stay, will you?

CHARLEY: Huh?

LIZA: I know all your reasons for wanting to leave, but it appears that I'm slowly getting a divorce—from myself. I think you ought to stick around and see the fun. What do you say?

(CHARLEY looks at her for a long moment. Then:)

CHARLEY: Sorry. It wouldn't work.

LIZA: You mean—two bosses?

CHARLEY: Roughly.

LIZA: You're right. But suppose we ran it together—I might even step aside after a while if you didn't get too drunk with power.

CHARLEY: You—you mean that?

LIZA: Yes. Only—I'd like the paperweight now, as a token that you're going to stay. Because—I want you to stay—very much.

(A slight pause, then CHARLEY *crosses to her)*

CHARLEY: Here you are. Catch. *(He tosses the paperweight to her, she catches it, goes behind her desk)*

LIZA: Thank you.

(There is quite a pause, then suddenly he turns)

CHARLEY: Now look—I'd like to change the format right away—I've been sick of it for years. Got a layout on your desk?

LIZA: Yes. The July issue.

CHARLEY: Here's what I mean. To hell with the title being on top. Put it over here. See what I mean?

(MAGGIE *enters and stares amazed at the picture the two of them present*)

LIZA: Yes—yes!

CHARLEY: Then change the type—you suggested that yourself months ago.

LIZA: Change the size, too!

CHARLEY: Sure, sure. Look—let me show you something . . . !

LIZA: *(As she looks up and sees* MAGGIE*)* Maggie, be an angel and telephone Mr. Curtis at the Waldorf and tell him I can't see him tonight—I'll talk to him in the morning. But look, Charley, we can't do all that for the July issue, can we?

CHARLEY: Sure, we can! Listen—I've got a layout in my office—let me get it— be right back.

LIZA: Okay.

CHARLEY: *(To* MAGGIE, *as he rushes out)* Be nice to me, Wonderful. I'm your boss now.

MAGGIE: *(Acidly)* Would you mind telling me, Miss Elliott, exactly what the hell goes on here?

LIZA: Oh, Maggie, Maggie, I almost made a great mistake! I almost twisted up my life all over again. I might have married Randy! He seemed a refuge—a tower of strength! Those parts he plays—and the way he looks! And you know what, Maggie? He's another Kendall. Frightened and insecure—seeing in me what Kendall saw in me—needing what Kendall needed. A mother—not a wife! I almost did the same thing all over again. And I'll tell you something else—I've suddenly seen Charley Johnson for the first time—and I think I know the reason why for a great many things. *(Gaily)* Don't worry about me, Maggie! I'm going to be all right!

MAGGIE: Well, for God's sake!

(CHARLEY *dashes back in, arms full of papers)*

CHARLEY: *(Going right to the desk and seating himself)* Look—I made up this dummy just for fun a few weeks ago—See what it does to the whole magazine?

LIZA: Yes, yes . . . I like it.

CHARLEY: Now, look at this . . . The ads here . . . The color section here. What about that? It's dangerous—but if we can pull it off it can be great.

(LIZA *has apparently not heard. Intent on the papers in her hands, she begins to hum. It is that song)*

CHARLEY: *(Suddenly singing)* "And of jam and spice, there's a paradise in the hold."

LIZA: *(Looking at him—astonished)* Why—do you know that song?

CHARLEY: Yeah—haven't heard it since I was a kid, though. Go ahead—do you know it all?

LIZA: Yes—I know all the words—now. *(She smiles, then slowly begins to sing.* CHARLEY, *as the remembered words come back to him, softly joins in.* MAGGIE *looks curiously from one to the other—then elaborately sinks into a chair and folds her hands in her lap.* LIZA *is singing gaily—happily. Oblivious of* MAGGIE *they half-smile at each other. The curtain is slowly descending)*

Curtain

LOST IN THE STARS

Book and Lyrics by Maxwell Anderson
Music by Kurt Weill

(Based on the novel, *Cry, the Beloved Country*, by Alan Paton)

Editor's Notes

One of the more memorable theatrical events of the 1949–1950 Broadway season transpired on the evening of October 30, 1949 when *Lost in the Stars* had its premiere at the Music Box Theatre. The Maxwell Anderson-Kurt Weill work was described in the press as "a lyric adaptation of Alan Paton's eloquent novel of racial tragedy set in his native South Africa, *Cry, the Beloved Country*. It is a beautiful, enthralling and soaring show . . . the Messrs. Anderson and Weill have provided the lyric stage with one of its finest achievements in many a year, one that brings enormous distinction and rewarding substance to the current Broadway season."

Other members of the press corps concurred by hailing it as: "An altogether touching tale of native problems and racial unevenness stated in poetic Anderson wordage in conjunction with Weill's superlative music. It is in reality an extraordinarily luminous folk opera of South Africa. In short, not since the immortal Gershwin saga of Catfish Row, *Porgy and Bess*, have we encountered any stage exhibit of this very special sort to approach in appeal and pleasure the musical legend of Stephen Kumalo."

As John Chapman reported in the New York *Daily News:* "The Playwrights' Company (the original producers) has been understandably puzzled as to what to call *Lost in the Stars*, for this is a piece which does not fit into an ordinary category. In the program it is called 'a musical tragedy'. After having swallowed the lump in my throat and shaken the last tingle out of my spine, and composed myself for careful statement, I'd call *Lost in the Stars* a work of art.

"Here is a production for the musical stage in which all the complex elements have been put together in an inspiring manner. A novel has been adapted and has not lost its scope and character as a piece of fiction. Mr. Anderson's libretto and lyrics are the work of an artist. Mr. Weill's music fits the novel, libretto and lyrics like a true and splendid creation, which it is."

In his book devoted to the *American Musical Theatre*, David Ewen stated: "*Lost in the Stars* is stirring dramatic art, and like the novel from which it was derived, touching in its compassion and humanity and inspiring in its promise of a better life of tolerance and human understanding."

The musical ran for 273 performances in its original production and was designated as one of the ten best plays of the 1949–1950 season.

On February 19, 1972, *Lost in the Stars* received a major revival at the John F. Kennedy Center for the Performing Arts in Washington, D. C., where it once again made a decided impression upon audiences. The production then moved on to Boston where it was greeted by Elliot Norton of the *Boston Record American* as "A great American musical play" that is "enormously exciting, something to admire, respect and enjoy." Samuel Hirsch echoed the praise in the *Boston Herald Traveler:* "It soars with the kind of dramatic force that is seldom seen in the lyric theatre. It has power and relevance and stands head and shoulders above most of the musicals that have come along."

The revival proceeded to New York, opening at the Imperial Theatre on April 18, 1972. Richard Watts, Jr. of the *New York Post* lauded it as "One of the most striking and original American musicals" while his colleague on *The New York Times*, Clive Barnes, conveyed to his readers: "People talk about innovative musicals—this is a tragic musical that extended the range of the musical theatre. It brings dignity, passion and grand music to Broadway."

The musical play was made into a motion picture and released in 1974 by the

American Film Theatre. Brock Peters starred as Stephen Kumalo, the same role that brought him acclaim in the 1972 revival.

Lost in the Stars represented Maxwell Anderson's second musical collaboration with Kurt Weill. The first, *Knickerbocker Holiday*, opened in 1938 with Walter Huston starring as Peter Stuyvesant. His unforgettable rendition of "September Song" firmly established it as a classic.

Maxwell Anderson (1888–1959) was one of America's foremost dramatists. Never content to follow any one dramatic or artistic formula, he varied his themes and styles to conform with his aims as thinker and practical playwright intent upon providing entertainment for the public. During his long career he touched upon almost every conceivable dramatic genre, ranging from contemporary realistic comedy to historical verse tragedy. Undeniably, there were the high peaks and the low, yet, in retrospect, his important achievements far outweigh the occasional creative lapses.

Anderson was born in Atlantic, Pennsylvania, the son of a Baptist minister. After being educated at the University of North Dakota and Stanford University, he taught for a while, then drifted into journalism. From there it was a logical step to try his hand at drama, and his first play, *White Desert*, was produced in 1923. Undeterred by its failure, he embarked on a second theatrical project, this time in collaboration with Laurence Stallings. The result was *What Price Glory?* (1924), an enormous hit and the first play written by an American "to question the sacredness of our mission in the First World War."

A long stream of plays followed. To list some (in nonchronological order): *Saturday's Children, Elizabeth the Queen, Mary of Scotland, Both Your Houses* (which won the Pulitzer Prize in 1933), *Valley Forge, Winterset* (winner of the first New York Drama Critics' Circle Award, 1936), *High Tor* (recipient of the same award, 1937), *The Star Wagon, The Eve of St. Mark, Key Largo, Candle in the Wind, The Wingless Victory, The Masque of Kings, Joan of Lorraine, Night Over Taos, Anne of the Thousand Days, Barefoot in Athens,* and *Bad Seed.*

A point that seems to have been overlooked in most studies and treatises dealing with his work is the salient fact that Anderson often wrote in the grand manner, with strong stress upon star roles. While this may be denied by some, it is nonetheless verifiable if one takes a moment to scrutinize the list of stars who appeared in his plays: Alfred Lunt, Lynn Fontanne, Katharine Cornell, Helen Hayes, Walter Huston, Philip Merivale, Paul Muni, Ingrid Bergman, Ruth Gordon, Rex Harrison, Lillian Gish, Richard Bennett, Joyce Redman, Uta Hagen, José Ferrer, Burgess Meredith, Nancy Kelly, and dozens more. A star does not glisten without a strong role, and Anderson, a consummate man of the theatre, surely was aware of their contributions and significance to a property when planning a new play.

He also was an outspoken man. Although twice accoladed by the New York drama critics, he was not averse to heaping his scorn upon them when the occasion arose. Indeed, it was on just such an occasion in 1946 when one of his minor efforts, *Truckline Café*, received an unmerciful trouncing from the press, that he publicly labeled the Broadway critics "the Jukes family of journalism," a descriptive phrase that since has become part of theatrical folklore.

In 1938, Anderson openly expressed his dissatisfaction with the vagaries and tastes of the average commercial producer and joined forces with Robert E. Sherwood, Elmer Rice, Sidney Howard, S. N. Behrman, and attorney John F. Wharton to found The Playwrights' Company, an organization that mainly was to produce the plays of its noted officer-members. As Anderson stated at the time, its aims were "to make a center for ourselves within the theatre, and possibly rally the theatre as a whole to new levels by setting a high standard of writing and production."

The organization flourished for more than two decades and during its period of activity frequently fulfilled its initial objectives.

In spite of a growing concern over the complexities and problems of contemporary civilization and his lifelong preoccupation with poetic form, to the end Maxwell Anderson remained a man of the theatre, a conscientious and dedicated craftsman who knew that the theatre, basically, always has been and always will be a medium of inspiration and entertainment.

(NOTE: For comments on Kurt Weill, see *Lady in the Dark*.)

Production Notes

Lost in the Stars was first presented by The Playwrights' Company at the Music Box Theatre, New York, on October 30, 1949. The cast was as follows:

Leader, *Frank Roane*
Answerer, *Joseph James*
Nita, *Elayne Richards*
Grace Kumalo, *Gertrude Jeannette*
Stephen Kumalo, *Todd Duncan*
The Young Man, *La Verne French*
The Young Woman, *Mabel Hart*
James Jarvis, *Leslie Banks*
Edward Jarvis, *Judson Rees*
Arthur Jarvis, *John Morley*
John Kumalo, *Warren Coleman*
Paulus, *Charles McRae*
William, *Roy Allen*
Jared, *William C. Smith*
Alex, *Herbert Coleman*
Foreman, *Jerome Shaw*
Mrs. Mkize, *Georgette Harvey*

Hlabeni, *William Marshall*
Eland, *Charles Grunwell*
Linda, *Sheila Guyse*
Johannes Pafuri, *Van Prince*
Matthew Kumalo, *William Greaves*
Absalom Kumalo, *Julian Mayfield*
Rose, *Gloria Smith*
Irina, *Inez Matthews*
Policeman, *Robert Byrn*
White Woman, *Biruta Ramoska*
White Man, *Mark Kramer*
The Guard, *Jerome Shaw*
Burton, *John W. Stanley*
The Judge, *Guy Spaull*
Villager, *Robert McFerrin*

Singers, *Sibol Cain, Alma Hubbard, Elen Longone, June McMechen, Biruta Ramoska, Christine Spencer, Constance Stokes, Lucretia West, Leon Bibb, Robert Byrn, Clyde Turner, Russell George, Joseph James, Mark Kramer, Moses LaMar, Paul Mario, Robert McFerrin, William C. Smith and Joseph Theard.*

Production Directed and Supervised by *Rouben Mamoulian*
Settings by *George Jenkins*
Costumes by *Anna Hill Johnstone*
Conducted by *Maurice Levine*
Musical Arrangements and Orchestrations by *Kurt Weill*

Time: The Present.

Act One

Opening: Ndotsheni—A small village in South Africa
Scene 1: Stephen Kumalo's Home
Scene 2: The Railroad Station
Scene 3: Johannesburg, John Kumalo's Tobacco Shop
Scene 4: The Search: The Factory Office; Mrs. Mkize's House; Hlabeni's House; Parole Office
Scene 5: Stephen's Shanty Town Lodging
Scene 6: A Dive in Shanty Town
Scene 7: Irina's Hut in Shanty Town
Scene 8: Kitchen in Arthur Jarvis' Home
Scene 9: Arthur Jarvis' Library
Scene 10: Street
Scene 11: Prison
Scene 12: Stephen's Shanty Town Lodging

Act Two

Opening: Johannesburg
Scene 1: John Kumalo's Tobacco Shop; Arthur Jarvis' Doorway
Scene 2: Irina's Hut in Shanty Town
Scene 3: The Courtroom
Scene 4: The Prison Cell
Scene 5: Ndotsheni—Stephen's Chapel
Scene 6: Stephen Kumalo's Home

Musical Numbers

Act One

Opening:	
The Hills of Ixopo	Leader and Singers
Scene 1:	
Thousands of Miles	Stephen
Scene 2:	
Train to Johannesburg	Leader and Singers
Scene 4:	
The Search	Stephen, Leader and Singers
Scene 5:	
The Little Grey House	Stephen and Singers
Scene 6:	
Who'll Buy?	Linda
	Danced by La Vern French and Mabel Hart
Scene 7:	
Trouble Man	Irina
Scene 8:	
Murder in Parkwold	Singers
Scene 10:	
Fear	Singers
Scene 12:	
Lost in the Stars	Stephen and Singers

Act Two

Opening:
The Wild Justice   Leader and Singers
        Scene 1:
O Tixo, Tixo, Help Me   Stephen
        Scene 2:
Stay Well   Irina
        Scene 4:
Cry, the Beloved Country   Leader and Singers
        Scene 5:
Big Mole   Alex
A Bird of Passage   Villager and Singers
        Scene 6:
Thousands of Miles (Reprise)   Singers

ACT ONE

SCENE 1

   The curtain goes up in darkness and a picture of the Ixopo hills develops gradually in the background. From the orchestra pit a broad flight of steps leads up to the stage. A group of SINGERS sits on these steps, so placed that they are not in the way of the action but can comment on it or ascend to take part in it at any time. The first scene is the tiny and cheap but clean sitting room in the home of STEPHEN KUMALO, near St. Mark's Church near Ndotsheni, Natal, South Africa. As the curtain rises, we see SINGERS entering from the pit onto the center stairs, and also from right and left stage to positions on the side steps. The LEADER takes his place center stage and sits on a basket which he carries on stage.

LEADER: *(Sings)*
   There is a lovely road
   that runs from Ixopo into the hills.
   These hills
   are grass covered and rolling, and they are lovely
   beyond any singing of it.
   About you
   there is grass and bracken, and you may hear
   the forlorn crying of the titiboya bird.
   The grass of the veld is rich and matted.
   You cannot see the soil.
   The grass holds the rain and mist,
   and they seep into the ground, feeding
   the streams in every clove.
   The clove is cool and green and lovely beyond any singing of it.

ANSWERER: But sing now about the lower hills.

LEADER:
Where you stand the grass is rich and matted—
but the rich green hills break down.
They fall to the valley below—
and, falling, change.
For they grow red and bare;
they cannot hold the rain and mist;
the streams run dry in the clove.
Too many cattle feed on the grass;
it is not kept or guarded or cared for.
It no longer keeps men, guards men, cares for men.
The titihoya cries here no more.

ANSWERER: Yes, wherever the hills have broken down and the red clay shows through, there poor people live and dig ever more desperately into the failing earth.

LEADER: *(Sings)*
The great red hills stand desolate,
and the earth has torn away like flesh.
These are the valleys
of old men and old women,
of mothers and children.
The men are away.
The young men and the girls are away.
The soil cannot keep them any more.

(STEPHEN KUMALO enters and sits on a chair behind the table. As the last of the SINGERS go out the lights come up on the sitting room. GRACE KUMALO, Stephen's wife, enters, and a small Zulu girl, NITA, runs in with a letter and crosses to STEPHEN.)
NITA: *(Handing the letter to STEPHEN)* I bring a letter, umfundisi.
STEPHEN: Where did you get it, my child?
NITA: From the store, umfundisi. The white man asked me to bring it to you.
STEPHEN: That was good of you. Go well, small one.
(NITA starts to go, but pauses)
GRACE: Perhaps you might be hungry, Nita.
NITA: Not—not very hungry.
STEPHEN: Perhaps a little hungry?
NITA: Yes, a little hungry, umfundisi.
GRACE: There is a little bowl on the kitchen table, Nita. And a spoon beside it.
NITA: I thank you.
(NITA goes to the kitchen; STEPHEN sits fingering his letter; GRACE crosses to him and looks over his shoulder at the letter)
GRACE: From Johannesburg.
STEPHEN: Yes, August 9, 1949.
GRACE: "Reverend Stephen Kumalo, St. Mark's Church, Ndotsheni, Natal." It is not from our son.
STEPHEN: No. It's a writing I haven't seen.
GRACE: It may bring news of him.

STEPHEN: Yes. Let me think. Our son Absalom is in Johannesburg; my sister Gertrude is there—and my brother John is there. But he has never written to me. *(He picks up the knife from the table)* Perhaps the way to find out is to open it. *(He slits the flap with the knife and hands the letter to GRACE)* Read it, my helper. Your eyes are better than mine.

GRACE: It's from your brother John.

STEPHEN: Then this is truly an occasion. Read carefully, my helper.

GRACE: "Dear Stephen, you old faker in Christ. I don't know whether it was you who sent our dear sister Gertrude to Johannesburg or not, but if it was, for the love of your own Jesus send and fetch her back. She says she came looking for a husband who ran away from her. Maybe so. Anyway she's found plenty husbands, and the stories about the kind of house she keeps are not good for my business, because it's known here who she is. See to this soon, O brother in God, or I'll have the woman put away where she won't be so noticeable. Your affectionate brother, John." He's an evil man. *(She sits.)*

STEPHEN: *(Humorously)* No, he honestly thinks that I am a faker. He thinks all men are fakers, perhaps because he's one. But I am not concerned about that. I am concerned about Gertrude—if she has taken to bad ways.

GRACE: What will you do?

STEPHEN: I don't know.

GRACE: *(She has a plan)* If you were in Johannesburg you could find Gertrude.

STEPHEN: It's many hundreds of miles. Where would I find the money to go to Johannesburg?

GRACE: There is the St. Chad's money.

STEPHEN: Absalom's money—the money we save for his school? You would have me use that?

GRACE: Should you not, Stephen? Absalom will never go now to St. Chad's.

STEPHEN: How can you say that? How can you say such a thing?

GRACE: He is in Johannesburg. When people go to Johannesburg they do not come back.

STEPHEN: But Absalom will! Absalom went to Johannesburg for one purpose— to earn money for his education! When he returns he will bring twelve pounds of his own to put with the twelve we have saved, and then he will have enough for a year at St. Chad's, and he will go there and learn quickly! I know him!

GRACE: It's nearly a year since we had a letter from him, Stephen. We do not know him now. He has been in the mines. No young man could work in the mines and not change. Absalom will not go to school. Take the money— use it!

STEPHEN: Do you know what you are saying? If I take his school money and use it to bring Gertrude back, then I have given up Absalom! I have said by this action that he will not make a place for himself, that we shall not see him nor be proud of him again, that he is only a drop in the great river of blacks that pours into the earth and is seen no more! I will not say this! I will not think it!

GRACE: I love him as much as you, but why has he not written to us? If there's nothing wrong he could have written.

STEPHEN: O mother of little faith! A letter can be lost so easily! We must not cease to believe in him. We must love him, and not doubt him. There's a great gulf between people, Grace, between husband and wife, between parents and child, between neighbor and neighbor. Even when you live in the same house it's deep and wide, except for the love between us. But when there is love, then distance doesn't matter at all—distance or silence or years.

(He sings "Thousands of Miles")
How many miles
To the heart of a child?
Thousands of miles, thousands of miles.
When he lay on your breast
He looked up and smiled
Across tens of thousands,
Thousands of miles.
Each lives alone
In a world of dark,
Crossing the skies
In a lonely arc,
Save when love leaps out like a leaping spark
Over thousands, thousands of miles.

Not miles, or walls, or length of days,
Nor the cold doubt of midnight can hold us apart,
For swifter than wings of the morning
The pathways of the heart!
How many miles
To the heart of a son?
Thousands of miles, thousands of miles.
Farther off than the rails
Or the roadways run
Across tens of thousands,
Thousands of miles
The wires and the ways,
Reach far and thin
To the streets and days
That close him in,
But there, as of old, he turns 'round to grin
Over thousands—thousands of miles.

Not miles, or walls, or length of days,
Nor the cold doubt of midnight can hold us apart,
For swifter than wings of the morning
The pathways of the heart!
Over tens of thousands of miles.

(NITA *enters from upstage door)*
STEPHEN: Is the little bowl empty, Nita?
NITA: Yes, umfundisi. I thank you.
STEPHEN: Go well, my child.
NITA: Stay well, umfundisi. *(She skips out and off left)*
GRACE: Stephen, please take the St. Chad's money. Go to Johannesburg.
STEPHEN: You're not thinking of Gertrude. You're thinking of Absalom.
GRACE: Yes. We have heard nothing from our son for a year—go to Johannesburg. Find him.

STEPHEN: If you wish it so much, it may be that I should go, my helper. I shall bring you word of Absalom. It will be good news, that I know. *(He crosses left and looks at the clock)* I couldn't go today. The train goes at twelve, and it's past the hour. But I could go tomorrow.

GRACE: *(Her arms around him)* You are my Stephen.

> The lights dim.

SCENE 2

> *The station at Carrisbrooke, indicated only by a semaphore. As the lights come up a white* STATIONMASTER *announces the coming of the train and a group of* ZULUS *enters, singing a farewell to one of their number who has been called to work in the mines.*

STATIONMASTER: Attention! The train for Johannesburg will be here in five minutes! Have your baggage ready! Train for Johannesburg!

CHORUS:
Johannesburg, Johannesburg.
Johannesburg, Johannesburg.

LEADER:
Train go now to Johannesburg,
Farewell!

CHORUS:
Farewell!

LEADER:
Go well!

CHORUS:
Go well!

LEADER:
Train go now to Johannesburg,
Farewell!

CHORUS:
Farewell!

LEADER:
Go well!

CHORUS:
Go well!
This boy we love, this brother,
Go to Johannesburg!
White man go to Johannesburg—
He come back, he come back.
Black man go to Johannesburg—
Never come back, never come back!

YOUNG MAN: *(Speaking)* I come back.
WOMAN: Please!
YOUNG MAN: All this they say—I fool them. I come back.

CHORUS: *(Sings)*
> Black man go to Johannesburg—
> Go, go, never come back
> Go, go, never come back.
> Train go now to Johannesburg—
> Farewell, farewell,
> Go well, go well!
> This boy we love, this brother,
> Go to Johannesburg.
> White man go to Johannesburg,
> He come back, he come back.
> Black man go to Johannesburg,
> Go, go, never come back—
> Go, go, never come back, never come back
> Never come back!

(JAMES JARVIS, an Englishman of about fifty-five, enters, accompanied by his son, ARTHUR, and his grandson, EDWARD. They pause a minute to talk; the ZULUS diminish their singing to a pianissimo)

ARTHUR: We're in plenty of time.

JARVIS: Yes—I can see the plume of smoke just over the hill. The train will be here in three minutes.

EDWARD: I wonder who invented schools, and Latin grammar.

ARTHUR: It's not only your school, son. I have to get back to work, too.

EDWARD: Anyway, I'll always remember this is the year I learned to ride horseback.

JARVIS: And I'll see that Danny gets his daily oats and exercise till you're here again. Next vacation you can wear longer stirrups and take a few jumps with him.

EDWARD: Do you think he'll remember me?

JARVIS: I'm not sure just how much a horse remembers. But he'll be here, and we'll all be here, waiting for you. The old place gets pretty lonely with only your grandmother and me.

EDWARD: It was the best mid-term I ever had.

JARVIS: *(Smiling)* Thank you, Edward. *(STEPHEN KUMALO enters with his wife and crosses to center; he is carrying a small black bag)* It was among the best I ever had. You have a book to read on the train?

EDWARD: I have my Latin grammar—but I'm planning to look out the window a lot.

ARTHUR: There's Stephen Kumalo—and I haven't seen him for a year. Forgive me. *(He starts toward STEPHEN)*

JARVIS: Arthur!

ARTHUR: Yes?

JARVIS: I don't know what the customs are now in Johannesburg. They may have changed since I was there. But in our village one does not go out of his way to speak to a black.

ARTHUR: The customs have not changed in Johannesburg, Father. But I am not bound by these customs. I have friends among the Zulus. And my friends are my friends. *(He goes to STEPHEN and offers his hand)* Mr. Kumalo!

STEPHEN: Ah, Mr. Jarvis!

(They shake hands)

ARTHUR: You're making a journey?

STEPHEN: To Johannesburg, sir. It is my first long journey. And a happy one—I go to see my son!

ARTHUR: Ah! And Mrs. Kumalo goes with you?

GRACE: No, sir. I stay with the house.

ARTHUR: I'm leaving today, too. I wish I'd had time to see you while we were here.

STEPHEN: Sir, it is always a great pleasure to see you. Perhaps when you come again—

ARTHUR: That's right—there's always a next time. And I won't forget.

(ARTHUR and STEPHEN shake hands again)

STEPHEN: I know you won't, sir.

(ARTHUR returns to his father and son)

JARVIS: If you had struck me across the face you couldn't have hurt me more—or damaged me more, in the eyes of those who stand here. I suppose you know that?

ARTHUR: I don't believe that, Father. This is an old quarrel between us. We haven't time to settle it before the train goes. Perhaps we shall never settle it.

JARVIS: What you do in Johannesburg I can't alter! But here, where every eye is on us, where you are known as my son, you could avoid affronting me in such a fashion! Will you remember that in the future?

ARTHUR: Let's shake hands and agree to disagree, Father. The train is almost here.

JARVIS: You make no promises?

ARTHUR: I make no promises.

JARVIS: Then I'm not sure that I want you to come here again, Arthur!

ARTHUR: Father!

JARVIS: I'm sorry. Of course you'll come again.

ARTHUR: Not if it offends you, Father. But—my friends are my friends.

(ARTHUR and JARVIS face each other. The CHORUS begins to imitate the approaching train)

EDWARD: Good-by, Grandfather.

JARVIS: Good-by, Edward.

ARTHUR: Good-by, sir. *(He puts out his hand)*

JARVIS: Good-by, Arthur. *(He shakes hands with ARTHUR. ARTHUR and ED-WARD go to the left. STEPHEN has started to go toward the train offstage left, but steps back to let ARTHUR and EDWARD precede him. As STEPHEN and his wife go out the ZULUS shout to them)*

LEADER: Go well, umfundisi.

STEPHEN: Stay well, you who dwell here.

(The CHORUS and the LEADER, imitating the train, sing simultaneously)

LEADER:
White man go to Johannesburg,
He come back,
He come back.

CHORUS:
Clink, clink, clickety.

1ST VOICE: *(Imitating the whistle)*
Whoo-oo-oo-oo!

CHORUS:
Black man go to Johannesburg!
Never come back, never come back!
Clink, clink, clickety,
clink, clink, clickety . . .

The lights fade

SCENE 3

JOHN KUMALO'S *tobacco shop in Johannesburg. A counter with a small display of cigars, cigarettes, and tobacco.* JOHN *is conferring with some political lieutenants, all Zulus or Bantu.*

JOHN: Don't take it so hard, gentlemen, don't take it so hard. We won't get equal suffrage, we won't get social equality, we won't get any kind of equality—but those of us who are quick in the head will get along. That's the way it is everywhere, for whites and for Zulus. Use your head and you can live. Try to reform the world and somebody steals your mealies. Now—suppose a Zulu says to you, "I demand equality; I want to vote and I want to be represented!" What do you say to him? You, Paulus?

PAULUS: I say to him, "Man, our Political League is out for just that; it's out for equality. We won't get it this year. We won't get it next year. But we'll get it!"

JOHN: What else do you say to him? William?

WILLIAM: I say to him, "We've got a doctor in our League, brother. Somebody gets sick he goes to your house first. You run out of mealies maybe and need some to tide you over. Come and see me. We got a barrel in the back room just for that."

JOHN: That's right. Long-term notes, like equality, make 'em big—we're never going to pay. Short-term notes, like a bite to eat, keep 'em small. We pay 'em on the dot. And in ten years, gentlemen, our League will own Johannesburg. *(JARED, a Zulu, enters)* Yes, sir.

JARED: Some pipe tobacco, please.

JOHN: Native grown or imported?

JARED: Native grown. A quarter-pound. *(He gets his tobacco and goes out)*

JOHN: And now, gentlemen, you're part of the biggest thing that's happening in this town!
(STEPHEN KUMALO enters, holding a small Zulu boy, ALEX, *by the hand.* JOHN *looks at* STEPHEN *without recognizing him)*

JOHN: Yes, umfundisi?

STEPHEN: I've come to see you, John . . .

JOHN: It's Stephen. It's our old gospel bird, scratching 'round in the big city. You got my letter?

STEPHEN: Yes. This is Gertrude's son. Little Alex.

JOHN: Excuse me, gentlemen. My own brother, the son of our mother, has come. *(WILLIAM and PAULUS go out)* Well, any rain down your way this year?

STEPHEN: Less than we needed, John.

JOHN: You should pray, brother, you should pray. Now about Gertrude, she goes back with you to Ndotsheni?

STEPHEN: She allows the child to go with me. But she stays here.

JOHN: Brother, I want our sister out of this town. There's a limit to the number of bastard nephews a respectable tradesman can have.

STEPHEN: I asked her to come with me. She would not. And she said, "John won't put me away anywhere. He would have to find me first, and he won't find me."

JOHN: You have failed with her.

STEPHEN: Yes.

JOHN: Take her son, then, and go back to your hills and your sheet-iron chapel and your rusty god. I thought you might rid me of the woman. If you can't do that I have no further use for you.

STEPHEN: Honest and straightforward, aren't you, John? I'll go, but first there are two things I must ask. I have no room to stay in—

JOHN: There's no room here.

STEPHEN: Don't be afraid. I can pay for a room.

JOHN: Perhaps I can find you one, then. What else?

STEPHEN: My son Absalom. Did you see him while he was here?

JOHN: How much have you heard from Absalom?

STEPHEN: Four letters—from the mines—nearly a year ago. He was well, and working hard.

JOHN: I see. Well—your son left the mines and went about with my son Matthew for a while. They both stayed here. But your Absalom was not a good influence on Matthew.

STEPHEN: John!

JOHN: I had to tell them to get out.

STEPHEN: You sent them away?

JOHN: Yes.

STEPHEN: Do you know—where they went?

JOHN: Yes, I've written it somewhere.

STEPHEN: I hoped you would know. That makes it all easy. Now I thank my God —I thank my *Tixo*—

JOHN: You can leave your God out of it. He's not interested. 14 Krause Street, Doornfontein Textiles Company.

STEPHEN: Doornfontein Textiles Company, 14 Krause Street.

JOHN: That's it. And now you want a place to stay. *(He writes an address)* You think I am a hard man.

STEPHEN: Brother, you have helped me. We do what we can.

JOHN: Brother, you're right. We do what we can. I hope you know what you do. You're the white man's dog, trained to bark and keep us in order. You know that.

STEPHEN: No, brother, I do not know it.

JOHN: They pile up mountains of gold, and they pay our sons three shillings a day, and out of this wage take a heavy tax. Is that fair?

STEPHEN: No, brother, it is not fair.

JOHN: Then why do you wear their Anglican clothes and read their Testament?

STEPHEN: Because all men do evil, I among them—and I wish all men to do better, I among them.

JOHN: *(Giving* STEPHEN *the address)* Yes, blessed are the chicken-hearted. This will give you a place to sleep. It's expensive and it's in Shanty Town and it's not pleasant. Such are the customs of our city.

STEPHEN: I shan't mind. Good-by, John. *(He puts out his hand)*

JOHN: *(Taking it)* Good-by. You old faker in Christ.

STEPHEN: The same John! *(He starts out)* 14 Krause Street . . .

    The lights dim and go out

SCENE 4

The lights come up on the CHORUS *on the orchestra pit steps.*

CHORUS: *(Sings)*
14 Krause Street
Textiles Company
14 Krause Street
Textiles Company
14 Krause Street
Textiles Company.

STEPHEN: *(Alone on the street)*
Not miles, or walls, or length of days,
Nor the cold doubt of midnight can hold us apart,
For swifter than wings of the morning
The pathways of the heart!

CHORUS: *(Sings)*
14 Krause Street
Textiles Company
14 Krause Street
Textiles Company.

*(*STEPHEN *is now seen speaking with a factory* FOREMAN *who stands behind a cashier's cage. He is looking up a record in a large volume)*

FOREMAN: Yes, they did work here. Absalom Kumalo and Matthew Kumalo. But they left us some months ago.

STEPHEN: Sir, did they work well?

FOREMAN: Why, I think so. I rather liked Absalom. A good lad.

STEPHEN: Thank you, sir. He's my son, you know. Could you tell me where they went?

FOREMAN: They had a house address when they were here. They lived with Mrs. Mkize, 77 Twenty-third Avenue, Alexandra.

STEPHEN: Thank you, sir.

    The lights dim

CHORUS: *(Sings)*
Seventy-seven, Twenty-third Avenue—
Mrs. Mkize—Twenty-third Avenue.

*(*STEPHEN *is now seen at a doorway.* MRS. MKIZE *appears in it as the lights come up)*

STEPHEN: How long ago, Mrs. Mkize?

MRS. MKIZE: These many months.
STEPHEN: Do you know where he is now?

CHORUS: *(Sings)*
  Make no doubt
  It is fear that you see in her eyes!
  It is fear!

MRS. MKIZE: No, I do not know.
STEPHEN: Are you afraid of me?
MRS. MKIZE: No, I'm not afraid.
STEPHEN: But you tremble when I speak of him.
MRS. MKIZE: I don't know you. I don't know why you ask.
STEPHEN: I am his father. I wish him well—and you well.
MRS. MKIZE: His father? Then it would be better if you followed him no further.
STEPHEN: Why?
MRS. MKIZE: Umfundisi, they were friendly with a taxi driver named Hlabeni who lives near the stand in this same street. At number 25.
STEPHEN: Why should I look no further?
MRS. MKIZE: Lest you be hurt by it.
STEPHEN: What did he do?
MRS. MKIZE: In the middle of the night they brought things here, umfundisi. Clothes and watches and money. They left in haste. I think they were near to being discovered. Oh, follow him no further!
STEPHEN: Hlabeni, at 25 on this street?
MRS. MKIZE: Yes.

  The lights dim

CHORUS: *(Sings)*
  A taxi driver, known as Hlabeni,
  Taxi stand; in Twenty-third Avenue,
  What you must find is always a number,
  A number and a name.
  Though it sear the mind, say it over and over,
  Over and over,
  A boding song,
  Searing like flame.

LEADER: *(Sings)*
  Be there, my one son, be well there—

(STEPHEN *is now at* HLABENI'S *doorway)*
HLABENI: I can tell you this much; they were picked up for something they'd done, and one of them went to jail for a while.
STEPHEN: What—had they done?
HLABENI: Oh, some wild trick like boys do.
STEPHEN: Which one went to prison?
HLABENI: Absalom. I don't know why Matthew didn't go, but he got out of it somehow. And Absalom's out now. He's on parole. Or that's what I heard.
STEPHEN: Where would he be?
HLABENI: You could ask the parole officer at the government building. He might know.

STEPHEN: Is it near?

HLABENI: Four or five miles.

STEPHEN: Could I find it tonight?

HLABENI: I'll tell you what I'll do. I'll draw you a map. That might help.

    The lights dim

CHORUS: *(Sings)*
What you must find is always a number,
A number and a name,
In prison cells they give you a number,
Tag your clothes with it,
Print your shame!

LEADER: *(Sings)*
Be there, my one son, be well there—

VOICE: *(Speaking)* But how could he be well there? How could he be well?
(The lights come up on STEPHEN *standing before* MARK ELAND, *the parole officer, a young white man)*

ELAND: Yes, he's been paroled, umfundisi. We made an exception in his case, partly because of his good behavior, partly because of his age, but mainly because there was a girl who was pregnant by him.

STEPHEN: He is married, then?

ELAND: No, umfundisi. But the girl seemed fond of him, so with all these things in mind—and with his solemn undertaking that he would work hard to support the child and its mother—we let him go. He's living with the girl in Pimville.

STEPHEN: Is it far?

ELAND: It's some miles. It's among the shacks there, and at night the streets are —well, pretty hard to get about in. I think I'd have to take you.

STEPHEN: Could—could you go tonight, sir?

ELAND: Tonight I can't. But if you could come here early tomorrow—

STEPHEN: Yes, sir. Thank you.

    The lights dim out

SCENE 5

    The lights come up as we see STEPHEN *striking a match and lighting a candle in a tiny, squalid room.* ALEX *is with him.*

ALEX: Uncle Stephen?

STEPHEN: Yes, Alex.

ALEX: The room is very small here, and not clean.

STEPHEN: Yes, it's the best they had.

ALEX: I hope we won't live here.

STEPHEN: No, no, Alex; you'll live in Ndotsheni. In the country. In my home.

ALEX: Is it like this there?

STEPHEN: No, not at all like this. There are hills and valleys, and trees growing on the hills and streams running in the valleys.

ALEX: What will our house be like?

STEPHEN: It's a little grey house.

ALEX: Will there be grass in front of it?

STEPHEN: Yes, and flowers growing in the grass.

ALEX: Do you have a wife there?

STEPHEN: Yes.

ALEX: I don't like my mother. She hits me. And I hit her, too. Only she hits me harder!

STEPHEN: Nobody will hit you in my house.

ALEX: Tell me about the house. Why is it grey?

STEPHEN: Because it has not been painted.

ALEX: Is the water good when it comes from the tap, or do you have to boil it?

STEPHEN: There's no tap at all, boy. We get water from the spring. There's a tree that my son liked to climb. He built himself a place to sleep in it, like a nest. You will climb that tree.

ALEX: Is the nest still there?

STEPHEN: Yes, it's there.

ALEX: I see. I'm thinking about it. *(He looks out, imagining)*

CHORUS: *(Sings)*
What are you thinking,
Old man among the broken boxes
Of Shanty Town?

What do you see,
Child with the shining eyes,
Among the broken hopes
Of Shanty Town?

STEPHEN: *(Sings "The Little Grey House")*
There's a little grey house
In a one-street town,
And the door stands open,
And the steps run down;
And you prop up the window
With a stick on the sill,
And you carry spring water
From the bottom of the hill:
And the white star-of-Bethlehem
Grows in the yard,
And I can't really describe it
But I'm trying hard;
It's not much to tell about,
It's not much to picture out,
And the only thing special is
It's home.

CHORUS:
It's not much to sing about,
It's not much to picture out,
And the only thing special is
It's home.

STEPHEN:
It's a long road, God knows,
The long and turning iron road that leads to Ndotsheni.

How I came, God knows, by what ridges, streams, and valleys,
And how we shall return is in God's keeping.
Many bright days, many dark nights, we must ride on iron
Before I see that house again!

There's a lamp in the room,
And it lights the face
Of the one who waits there
In her quiet place,
With her hands always busy
Over needle and thread,
Or the fire in the kitchen
To bake tomorrow's bread.
And she always has love enough
To take you in,
And her house will rest you
Wherever you've been!

CHORUS:
It's not much to tell about,
It's not much to picture out,
And the only thing special is
It's home!

STEPHEN:
It's not much to tell about,
It's not much to picture out,
And the only thing special is
It's home!

(STEPHEN *carries* ALEX *up to the cot and covers him with a blanket. He blows out the candle. The lights dim out)*

SCENE 6

A dive in Shanty Town. Some strange harmonies have crept into the last few bars and now we discover that they were indications of another song that begins to come from another part of the stage, still in darkness. It's sung in the manner of a nightclub entertainer. The voice is a girl's. As the lights come up we see LINDA, *the singer,* MATTHEW KUMALO, JOHANNES PAFURI, *and* ROSE *and* SUTTY, *two girls who came with the young men.* ABSALOM KUMALO *sits alone and moody. Two* DANCERS, *a man and a girl, dance to* LINDA'S *singing.*

LINDA: *(Sings "Who'll Buy")*
Who'll buy
My juicy rutabagas?
Who'll buy
My yellow corn?
Who'll buy asparagus or carrots or potatoes?
Who wants my peppers and my ginger and tomatoes,
The best you bit into
Since you were born?
If you want to make a supper dish fit for a king

Look over what I offer, I offer everything!
So try my, buy my
Black-eyed peas;
The garden of Eden
Had nothing like these!
You'll feel like flying, like a bird on the wing;
You'll stay up there like a kite on a string:
They're satisfactory, and they got a sting!
So try my,
Buy my
Asparagus, yellow corn, black-eyed peas, tomatoes, potatoes, beans, and rutabagas—
Who'll buy
My oranges and melons?
Who'll buy
My prickly pears?
Who'll pay shillings for my lemons and persimmons,
Who wants apricots and nectarines and trimmin's,
The best you laid lip to
The last ten years?
I haven't got a license, so I can undersell,
I haven't got a license, so I treat you well!
So try my, buy my
Pure veld honey!
In the garden of Eden
They never use money!
You'll feel like flying, like a bat out of hell,
You'll own high heaven and a landing field as well!
The apples of Paradise, they always jell!
So try my—

MATTHEW *and* JOHANNES:
Try my—

LINDA:
Buy my—

OTHERS:
Buy my—

LINDA:
Oranges, prickly pears, apricots, nectarines, tangerines, apples, groundnuts, bananas—
Buy my—

OTHERS:
Buy my—

LINDA:
Oh my—

OTHERS:
Oh my—

LINDA:
Oh my—

OTHERS:
Oh my—

LINDA:
Buy my—oh my—oh my—

JOHANNES: I'll take 'em! I'll take 'em all! You're off the market!

LINDA: *(Falling into* JOHANNES' *arms)* Sold!

MATTHEW: Just one little technical problem here if you don't mind, lady. You said you had no license?

LINDA: That's right. No license. Just Johannes' little wild honey, that's all.

MATTHEW: Officer, arrest that woman and bring her before the court. *(JO-HANNES brings* LINDA *down front as if to face the judge)* In the first place, what is a—h'm—rutabaga?

LINDA: It's a vegetable, Your Lordship.

MATTHEW: You don't give that impression.

LINDA: What impression do I give, Your Lordship?

MATTHEW: Are you trying to corrupt this court?

LINDA: Yes, sir.

MATTHEW: Twenty years, hard!

JOHANNES: Your Lordship, your wig is dirty, your logic is full of holes, and your monocle don't fit you!

MATTHEW: I find you in contempt—hic! Damn that whisky and soda.

JOHANNES: What's the trouble, Your Monocle?

MATTHEW: Young man, did you address me as Your Monocle?

JOHANNES: Yes, Your Monocle.

MATTHEW: Forty years, hard!

JOHANNES: You got a little mixed here, Your Whisky and Soda! You're supposed to be trying this young lady!

MATTHEW: That's right. *(To* ROSE, *who is sitting on table)* Make a note the young man's right. Hic. Put in that hic. That was a British hic. Put it in.

ROSE: *(Imaginary writing of notes)* Yes, sir!

MATTHEW: Where's the persecution? Young man, will you persecute this young lady?

JOHANNES: I'd love to, Your Rutabaga. When do I begin?

MATTHEW: Woman, have you got anything to say?

LINDA: I throw myself on the mercy of the court. *(She throws herself into* JO-HANNES' *arms)*

MATTHEW: I'm the court, see! Throw yourself on me—not him!

ROSE: I throw myself on the mercy of the court! *(*ROSE *throws herself into* MAT-THEW'S *arms)*

JOHANNES: I demand justice!

MATTHEW: Remove that woman out of your pocket! And somebody scrape the court stenographer from the Judge's vest! Young man, you got justice, we all got justice! Justice is when the black man digs and the white man carries the briefcase! Justice is when the black woman cooks and the white woman has breakfast in bed! If you want anything extra—you pay for it!

JOHANNES: Your Honor, would you accept a little money?

MATTHEW: What! Me, sir? A judge, sir? Take money, sir?—Yes, sir! All right, scrape her off your vest, Johannes! And get out of here, all of you! We'll be with you in a minute! Wait for us.

LINDA: Where are we going to wait?

MATTHEW: Outside!

LINDA: Matthew!

MATTHEW: Outside, I said! *(They go, leaving* JOHANNES, ABSALOM, *and* MAT-THEW*)* Wake up, Absalom! Now to begin with—how do we get in?

JOHANNES: You don't have to break into the house, I tell you; he never locks his doors, day or night.

MATTHEW: Why not?

JOHANNES: I don't know. He's got some theory. He says, "If anybody wants what I've got he can come in and take it."

ABSALOM: Then why would we need a gun when we go there?

MATTHEW: Because nobody ever knows when he's going to need a gun! And you've got a gun—and we might as well have it along!

ABSALOM: But Johannes says there won't be anybody there! The white man went for a trip somewhere and the servant gets home late every night.

MATTHEW: That's the way we think it's going to be, but if somebody happens to come in we don't want to take chances.

LINDA: *(Offstage)* Matthew!

MATTHEW: *(Calling)* We'll be right with you, pretty! *(To* ABSALOM*)* So don't come without it. We might need it. What do you say?

ABSALOM: I think it's better without the gun.

MATTHEW: Well, I don't, see? And if you don't bring it you're not in on this at all. Look, I'm going to get to those new gold fields! And I'm going on my own. Now, if you want to help us raise the money to get there, you're in; you come along! But if you're scared to carry that cheap revolver of yours you're no use to us. So bring it or stay home.

LINDA: *(Offstage)* Matthew!

MATTHEW: *(To* JOHANNES*)* We'll get rid of the girls. Think it over, country boy. *(*JOHANNES *and* MATTHEW *go out to the right.* IRINA, *a young and pretty Zulu girl, enters from the left. She sees* ABSALOM *and crosses to him)*

IRINA: *(Timidly)* Absalom?

ABSALOM: Irina? What do you want?

IRINA: I came to tell you something.

ABSALOM: Yes?

IRINA: Something about the parole officer.

ABSALOM: What happened?

IRINA: He came to the cabin asking for you. And I lied. I had to lie. I told him you were at work and things were going well. But he'll be at the factory tomorrow—and if you're not there—

ABSALOM: I don't think I will be there.

IRINA: What will happen to you, Absalom?

ABSALOM: I won't be there. I won't be anywhere where he can find me. Ever again.

IRINA: What will happen to us? You and me?

ABSALOM: We'll live in a better place than Shanty Town.

IRINA: When?

ABSALOM: When I come back.

IRINA: Are you going away?

ABSALOM: Yes, but not from you! To get something for you and me! Look, Irina, suppose I went home with you now and went to work tomorrow. What kind of life would we have?

IRINA: Like others.

ABSALOM: Yes, like the others. Shanty Town. Crawling with boarders and bugs and children. You'd have your baby, and I'd keep on at the factory, and you'd have another baby, and we'd live in the same shack and pay our taxes and our rent and pretty soon we're sleeping four in a room. Ten in a room. Filth. Nothing. And that's our fun. That's our life forever. That's what we get. Isn't it?

IRINA: I'll keep our place clean, Absalom.

ABSALOM: Nobody can keep those places clean! And I can't stand it. I don't want it that way—I love you, Irina. I want you to have something better than that.

IRINA: What could we have?

ABSALOM: I've never been able to bring you a gift, Irina. We've always had—not quite enough to live on. Even the way we live. I want to come back with enough so we can set up a little shop, and be free of work gangs, and keep our own house—

IRINA: Where could you get money for this?

ABSALOM: In the new gold fields. There's a new rich strike, Irina. If you go there as a free man, not in a labor gang, you can sometimes get ahead and save something—

IRINA: *(Her arms about him)* I'm afraid for you. Come home with me.

ABSALOM: Wait for me, Irina. I'll come home when I have something—when I am something.

IRINA: Where will you get money to go to the mines?

ABSALOM: We'll get it.

IRINA: You won't steal again?

ABSALOM: We'll get it.

IRINA: Oh, Absalom, Absalom, if you were caught once more they could keep you from me a whole lifetime! Come home with me, Absalom, come home with me!

ABSALOM: Oh, God damn this world! *(He kisses her)* Yes, I'll come with you. *(They start out as MATTHEW, followed by JOHANNES, re-enters)*

MATTHEW: Where are you going, Absalom? *(He sees Irina)* It's his cook! It's his little cookie!

ABSALOM: I'm out of it.

MATTHEW: She gives the orders, huh? . . . You could be rich, you know—

ABSALOM: I'm on parole. You're not.

MATTHEW: One more black boy loose in a gold field, they'd never locate you.

ABSALOM: But even if we make money in the gold fields, we still have to come back here. And they'll get me.

MATTHEW: Why would they? You'll change your name, you'll be wearing new clothes, you'll have cash in your pocket, you can walk up and buy a shack of your own. There won't be any Absalom Kumalo. There'll be a new man! A man—not somebody's dumb ox!

ABSALOM: He's right, Irina—wait for me. It'll take a little time, but wait for me.

IRINA: Please—

ABSALOM: Go now, Irina. I'll be back.

IRINA: Oh, Absalom—

ABSALOM: Go, Irina!

IRINA: Yes, I'll go. *(She goes out)*

MATTHEW: That's more like it!

JOHANNES: You know what I heard? I heard there's sometimes loose gold you can pan out of a river if you get there before the land's all fenced.

MATTHEW: Some places you can take just a kitchen pan and wash the dirt around in it and there's gold at the bottom.

JOHANNES: It's that way beyond Rigval clove.

MATTHEW: And then, by God, we'll live like men! Johannes, you bring along that machinery you talked about?

JOHANNES: I've got it where I can pick it up quick.

MATTHEW: Then pick it up, and pick up your feet! This is the best time.

The lights dim as they go out

SCENE 7

IRINA'S *hut in Shanty Town. We see the interior of the hut and the city behind it.*
ELAND *enters, followed by* STEPHEN. ELAND *knocks at the door.*

ELAND: *(At the door)* Irina!

IRINA: *(Going to the door)* Come in, sir.

(ELAND and STEPHEN enter her room)

ELAND: Thank you, Irina. This is the Reverend Stephen Kumalo, Irina, Absalom's father. I have told him about you, and he wishes to see you and to see Absalom. We'll go on from here to the factory. Absalom's there, of course?

IRINA: No, sir.

ELAND: But—when I was here—two days ago—

IRINA: Yes, sir. I lied to you.

ELAND: Where is he?

IRINA: I do not know. He's gone, I don't know where.

ELAND: This is another of my failures, then. They're like water. They live together, they get a child, they engage to marry, and the next day both have forgotten.

STEPHEN: Could I be alone with her a moment?

ELAND: I'll wait. *(He goes out)*

STEPHEN: Irina?

IRINA: Yes—umfundisi.

STEPHEN: Perhaps my son never spoke of me to you. We love him very much, his mother and I—and I have come to Johannesburg thinking I might find him. Would you help me to find him?

IRINA: Yes, umfundisi.

STEPHEN: He has lived here with you for some time?

IRINA: Yes.

STEPHEN: You were not married in the church?

IRINA: No, umfundisi.

STEPHEN: And you are to have a child?

IRINA: Yes.

STEPHEN: Why has he left you?

IRINA: I—do not know.

STEPHEN: You distrust me?

IRINA: No, umfundisi.

STEPHEN: Do you have a family?

IRINA: I have no one.

STEPHEN: But you lived somewhere—before you met Absalom.

IRINA: I lived in Sophiatown.

STEPHEN: Alone?

IRINA: *(Picking nervously at the back of a chair)* Nobody lives alone in Sophiatown.

STEPHEN: You lived with your first—husband?

IRINA: Yes. With my first.

STEPHEN: How many have there been?

IRINA: Three.

STEPHEN: Three. And now you will seek a fourth.

IRINA: No. I wait for Absalom.

STEPHEN: I think you would do anything! You would go to anyone! I am an old man, Absalom's father, but you would come to me if I asked you! Anything!

IRINA: No. I would not.

STEPHEN: You think an umfundisi is not a man? What if I desired you—with my whole body? What if I desire you now?

IRINA: You?

STEPHEN: Yes. I.

IRINA: It would not be right.

STEPHEN: Was it right before? With the others?

IRINA: No. It was not right.

STEPHEN: Then why would you not be willing with me?

IRINA: I do not know.

STEPHEN: Then you would be willing? *(She is silent)* Would you be willing?

IRINA: No, I do not know. *(She twists her hands, looks away)*

STEPHEN: *(Savagely)* Speak! Tell me!

IRINA: I could be willing.

STEPHEN: Yes, you are a woman who would go to anyone.

IRINA: Why did you come here? How would I know what you think—or what you want? I don't know what power you have—or what you will do! I'm alone here. I'm to have a child, and Absalom is gone— *(She sits on the chair in a passion of crying)* and I love him! I want only Absalom. He brought me only trouble —but I love him!

STEPHEN: *(After a pause)* Yes, I was wrong. I should not have put you to such a test. Will you forgive me? We all do what we must do. Not what we wish but what we can. *(He crosses closer to her)* Do you forgive me?

IRINA: Yes, umfundisi.

STEPHEN: I will go now, Irina, but I will come again. I'm searching for my son. If I find him I will come to tell you. My address is on this paper. *(He hands her a slip of paper)* If he comes back to you, please let me know.

IRINA: Yes, umfundisi.

(He goes out)

IRINA: *(Sings "Trouble Man")*
Since you came first to me,
Dear one, glad one,
You bring all the worst to me,
Near one, sad one;

There's trouble in your coming,
Trouble in your laughter,
There's trouble in your going,
And trouble after.

Since you were near to me,
Lost one, mad one,
No other is dear to me,
Loved one, bad one;
I love your dark silence,
Love your bright laughter
I love the trouble you bring me,
The crying after!

Trouble man, trouble man,
Since you've been gone,
Somehow I manage
Living here alone;
All day long
You don't catch me weeping
But, oh, God help me
When it comes time for sleeping,
When it comes time for sleeping here alone!

Trouble man, trouble man, walking out there,
Maybe in a strange place, God knows where,
Maybe in a strange town, hurrying and walking,
Listen to my blood and my bones here talking,
Listen to the blood in my hands and feet,
Finding you out on a far, strange street;
Finding the footprints out where you ran,
Asking, "Aren't you coming home, trouble man?
Trouble man! Trouble man! Trouble man! Trouble man!"
Saying, "All day long you don't catch me weeping,
But, oh, God help me when it comes time for sleeping,
When it comes time for sleeping here alone!"
Trouble man! Trouble man!

> The lights dim

SCENE 8

Kitchen in ARTHUR JARVIS' *home. As the lights come up we see a* SERVANT *placing dishes on the pantry shelves. We then see* JOHANNES, ABSALOM, *and* MATTHEW *entering from the left, handkerchiefs tied over their faces.* JOHANNES *is carrying an iron bar,* ABSALOM *carries a revolver.*

SERVANT: *(Turning as he hears the noise of their entrance)* What do you want?
JOHANNES: We want money and clothes!
SERVANT: It's Johannes! I know you! You cannot do such a thing!
JOHANNES: Do you want to die?
SERVANT: *(Running to the door and opening it)* Master! Master!
  *(*JOHANNES *strikes the* SERVANT *over the head with the iron bar; the* SERVANT

falls. ARTHUR JARVIS *comes into the doorway,* ABSALOM *fires the revolver.* AR-
THUR JARVIS *falls to the floor)*

MATTHEW: Quick! Get out!

*(The three run to the left, stop in panic, turn and run off to the right. The lights go
out)*

CHORUS: *(Sings "Murder in Parkwold")*
Murder in Parkwold!

WOMAN: *(Speaking)* He was shot at night!

CHORUS:
Murder in Parkwold!

WOMAN: *(Speaking)* Nobody knows why or by whom!

WHITES:
Murder in Parkwold!

MAN: *(Speaking)* There was one shot only!

CHORUS:
Murder in Parkwold!

WOMAN: *(Speaking)* He went to help the servant!

CHORUS:
Murder in Parkwold!

MAN: *(Speaking)* The servant had called out!

WHITES:
Murder in Parkwold!

CHORUS:
Murder in Parkwold!

ALL:
In Parkwold, among the great houses,
Among the lighted streets and the wide gardens.

WOMAN: *(Speaking)* There are not enough police!
*(The lights dim. The CHORUS goes out. From offstage right comes a man's voice
singing)*

MAN:
Murder in Parkwold!

ANOTHER: *(Offstage left)*
Murder in Parkwold!

The lights come up immediately on the next scene

SCENE 9

ARTHUR JARVIS' *library. As the lights come up we see* JAMES JARVIS *seated in
a chair by a desk, motionless and alone.* ELAND *knocks and then enters.*

ELAND: Mr. Jarvis? Mr. Jarvis?

JARVIS: *(Looking up)* Yes, Eland.

ELAND: I could come later if I disturb you.

JARVIS: No—no. Come in.

ELAND: I have seen the police. They have arrested Pafuri, the one who used to work in your son's house—and he has been identified.

JARVIS: By whom?

ELAND: By the servant who was struck.

JARVIS: I think I remember the name. Pafuri. Johannes Pafuri. Yes, he was houseboy here. I suppose he could be guilty—not that it would help to fix the guilt. Our son is dead. Arthur is dead and punishment will not bring him back.

ELAND: The boy denies being involved, but he looks very guilty.

JARVIS: One thing I hope the police will remember; no man is to be punished unless guilty.

ELAND: They'll make very certain before they act, Mr. Jarvis. They assured me of that.

JARVIS: I differed sharply with my son concerning our policy toward the blacks, but in this I want what he would have wanted—that the guilty feel the penalty —no man else. I had quarreled with my son, I suppose you know that. I wish we'd had a chance to patch up that quarrel.

ELAND: I'm sure it wasn't serious.

JARVIS: Yes. It was serious. Over Negro equality. *(He rises)* And the irony of it, that an advocate of Negro equality should have been killed by a Negro. There's only one course with them—a strong hand and a firm policy. They understand nothing but discipline, respect nothing else.

ELAND: There are good and bad among them.

JARVIS: Are there? At this moment I wonder.

ELAND: We can know them only by their actions. There was a man who came into this house with a pistol, came with intent to steal, and ended by committing murder. Let us find this one man and see that he is punished. Let us not blame the whole race.

JARVIS: You think he will be found?

ELAND: He will be found.

JARVIS: May he suffer as we suffer. As my wife suffers now.

ELAND: There's something I wanted to ask you, Mr. Jarvis. If you'd rather not stay in this house—

JARVIS: I want to stay here. This is where he worked. He was here when he heard the cry from the kitchen and ran to help.

ELAND: He will be a great loss to us. To our country and to me personally. As a parole officer—well, many times I'd have given up in despair except for him.

JARVIS: And yet they killed him. What would he have said about a crime like this?

ELAND: He would have said, "They live in such poverty and fear. They see no way out of their poverty or their fear and they grow desperate."

JARVIS: Yes. *(He sits)* It sounds like him.

ELAND: You wish to be here alone?

JARVIS: Yes—I wish to be here alone.

(The lights dim. ELAND goes out. Offstage we hear again the cries repeated)

MAN: *(Sings, offstage right)*
Murder in Parkwold!

ANOTHER: *(Sings, offstage left)*
Murder in Parkwold!

SCENE 10

A street in Shanty Town. As the lights come up the street is empty. A MAN and a WOMAN run through, knocking at doors. The ZULUS come out of their houses and gather in groups around three newspapers, reading intently. There is a whistle from off right—the street empties, and the houses go dark. A POLICEMAN passes through, disappears. The people emerge from the houses, cluster again around the papers. A WHITE MAN and WOMAN enter from the right.

WOMAN: These streets are full of evil; I'm afraid!

MAN: It's all right, take my arm. This is a shabby neighborhood.

WOMAN: Hush! *(The POLICEMAN re-enters from left and meets the couple center stage. The WOMAN speaks with relief)* Good evening, officer.

(The POLICEMAN and the WHITE COUPLE go out left. The NEGRO CHORUS sings)

1ST MAN:
It is fear!

2ND MAN:
It is fear!

1ST WOMAN:
It is fear!

3RD MAN:
It is fear!

2ND MAN:
Who can enjoy the lovely land,
The seventy years,
The sun that pours down on the earth,
When there is fear in the heart?

(A group of WHITE SINGERS enters)

WHITE MAN:
Who can walk quietly in the dusk
When behind the dusk there are whispers
And reckless hands?

WHITE CHORUS:
Yes, we fear them.
For they are many and we are few!

NEGRO QUARTET:
Who can be content
When he dares not raise his voice?

WHITE CHORUS:
It is fear!

NEGRO QUARTET:
For fear of the whip, the guard, the loss of his house?

WHITE CHORUS:
It is fear!

NEGRO CHORUS:

For fear of the mines,
And the prison,
And the cell from which there is no return?
Yes, we fear them,
Though we are many and they are few!

WHITE:

Who can lie peacefully abed
When the dark without window is troubled
By those who hate you for what you are and what you do?

NEGRO:

You think you know what it is to fear or to hate?
What is there you have not taken from us except hate and fear?
Yes, we fear them, though we are many and they are few!

WHITE:

Men are not safe in the streets,
Not safe in their houses.

NEGRO:

It is fear!

WHITE:

There are brutal murders.

NEGRO:

It is fear!

WHITE:

Robberies!

NEGRO:

It is fear!

WHITE:

Tonight again a man lies dead!

NEGRO:

Yes, it is fear!

WHITE:

Yes, it is fear!

NEGRO:

Fear of the few for the many!

WHITE:

Fear of the many for the few!

NEGRO:

It is fear!

WHITE:

It is fear!

NEGRO:
It is fear!

WHITE:
It is fear!

ALL:
Fear of the few for the many,
Fear of the many for the few!

The lights go out

SCENE 11

The lights come up on ELAND, *who is pacing up and down.* STEPHEN *enters from the right, crosses to* ELAND.

STEPHEN: I came as soon as I could, sir. You say—my son is here? Absalom is here?

ELAND: Yes.

STEPHEN: Why is he here?

ELAND: It's not proved, of course—but the charge is that he killed Arthur Jarvis.

STEPHEN: He killed—

ELAND: It could not be worse. For me or you or him. Forgive me. What I feel is nothing—I know that. Only it's my life work to help. And this may destroy it all.

STEPHEN: Absalom is accused of killing Arthur Jarvis?

ELAND: Remember, it's not proved about Absalom, and I don't believe it! It cannot be true.

STEPHEN: Let me speak to Absalom. *(The lights come up on center stage; we see* ABSALOM *sitting on a stool in a cell, facing away from the entrance)* My child, my child!

ABSALOM: *(Turning)* My father!

STEPHEN: At last I have found you.

ABSALOM: Yes, my father.

STEPHEN: I have searched in every place for you—and I find you here. Why have they charged you with this terrible crime? *(There is no answer)* Answer me, my child.
*(*ABSALOM *is still silent)*

ELAND: You should rise when your father speaks to you, Absalom.

ABSALOM: Yes, sir. Oh, my father, my father! *(He reaches through the bars to his father)*

STEPHEN: My son, my son, if I had only come sooner! But we shall make it all well yet, Absalom; for the courts are just, and when they have found that you did not kill it will be only a light punishment. (ABSALOM *drops his father's hands)* And when it ends you will come back to Ndotsheni and be content in our quietness. For you were a boy without guile and without anger, at home where there are hills and trees, not in these streets where men must live by their wits and without scruple. The hills are as beautiful as ever, Absalom. You will be happy there again.

ABSALOM: My father—

STEPHEN: Yes? *(Silence)* Yes?

ABSALOM: I cannot say it.

STEPHEN: I know you so well, Absalom, that I know you could not be guilty of this crime, and so you need not fear what the judge will say. You will live again at Ndotsheni.

ABSALOM: I shall never come home.

STEPHEN: Why, my son?

ABSALOM: Because I am guilty.

STEPHEN: Of what, my son?

ABSALOM: *(After a pause)* I killed the white man.

STEPHEN: But—this cannot be true. He was shot—in his house.

ABSALOM: Yes.

ELAND: There are three men accused in this murder, Absalom. Do you try to shield someone?

ABSALOM: No, sir. There were three of us, Matthew Kumalo and Johannes Pafuri and I. It was Johannes who struck the servant, but it was I who carried the revolver, and—

STEPHEN: And—you killed this man?

ABSALOM: I did not mean to kill him. We thought he would not be there. Then suddenly he was there, and I was frightened—and—

(A GUARD comes into the shadow from the right)

ELAND: It is time for us to go.

STEPHEN: My son, I stand here, and see you, and a kind of dizziness has come over me, so that I am not sure what is real, or whether this is a true place or in a dream. Did you tell me, you, my son Absalom, that you had—had killed —a man?

ABSALOM: Yes, my father, it is true.

GUARD: I'm sorry, umfundisi, it's time for you to go.

STEPHEN: May I come again?

GUARD: Yes, umfundisi. At certain hours on certain days. The hours are ended for this day.

STEPHEN: Absalom—

ABSALOM: Yes, my father.

STEPHEN: Stay well, my child.

ABSALOM: Go well, my father.

(STEPHEN turns to go. The lights fade)

SCENE 12

The lights come up on STEPHEN *in his Shanty Town lodging, where he sits at a table trying to write.* ALEX, *in the cot near him, wakes and speaks.*

ALEX: Uncle Stephen?

STEPHEN: Yes, Alex.

ALEX: Is it very late?

STEPHEN: Yes, very late.

ALEX: But you are not asleep.

STEPHEN: No. I must write a letter.

ALEX: Do you know the best thing that ever happened to me?

STEPHEN: No.

ALEX: These shoes you bought me, with the brass toes and the brass heels. Would it be all right if I kept them in bed with me?

STEPHEN: If they're clean.

ALEX: I cleaned them on the quilt. I can see my face in the brass. I could walk all the way to Ndotsheni wearing these shoes!

STEPHEN: Please, Alex, lie and sleep. Or be silent. This is a hard letter.

ALEX: Who do you write to, Uncle Stephen?

STEPHEN: I write to my wife in Ndotsheni. To the mother at home. O *Tixo, Tixo!* O God of all lost people and of those who go toward death, tell me what to say to her! How can I say this to the mother, O my *Tixo?* That he has done this thing! That I cannot bring him home! That he will perhaps never, never come home!

ALEX: Uncle Stephen—who will not come home?

STEPHEN: My son Absalom.

ALEX: But Uncle Stephen, you are an umfundisi, and you can ask God to help you, and he will surely help you.

STEPHEN: I don't know, Alex.

(He sings "Lost in the Stars")
Before Lord God made the sea and the land
He held all the stars in the palm of his hand,
And they ran through his fingers like grains of sand,
And one little star fell alone.

Then the Lord God hunted through the wide night air
For the little dark star on the wind down there—
And he stated and promised he'd take special care
So it wouldn't get lost again.

Now a man don't mind if the stars grow dim
And the clouds blow over and darken him,
So long as the Lord God's watching over them,
Keeping track how it all goes on.

But I've been walking through the night and the day
Till my eyes get weary and my head turns grey,
And sometimes it seems maybe God's gone away,
Forgetting the promise that we heard him say—
And we're lost out here in the stars—
Little stars, big stars,
Blowing through the night,
And we're lost out here in the stars.

STEPHEN and CHORUS:
Little stars,
Big stars,
Blowing through the night,
And we're lost out here in the stars.

    Curtain

ACT TWO

SCENE 1

The curtain goes up on a dark and bare stage. The CHORUS *enters in the dark. The lights come up after the music has begun.*

LEADER and CHORUS: *(Singing "The Wild Justice")*
Have you fished for a fixed star
With the lines of its light?
Have you dipped the moon from the sea
With the cup of night?
Have you caught the rain's bow in a pool
And shut it in?
Go hunt the wild justice down
To walk with men.

Have you plotted the high cold course of a heron's flying,
Or the thought of an old man dying,
Or the covered labyrinth of
Why you love where you love?
Or, if one love you,
Why your love is true?
Only for a little, then,
Tease the wild justice down to dwell with men.
When the first judge sat in his place
And the murderer held his breath
With fear of death in his face,
Fear of death for death,
And all that could be said, for and against, was said,
And the books were balanced, and two, not one, were dead,
Was justice caught in this net?
Not yet, no, not quite yet, not yet.

No, tug first at the fixed star
On the lines of its light,
Sieve the moon up out of the sea
With the black seine of night,
Snare first the rain's bow in a pool
And close it in.
The wild justice is not found
In the haunts of men.
The wild justice is not found in the haunts of men!

(The lights come up on JOHN'S *tobacco shop.* JOHN *stands behind the counter,* STEPHEN *sits before him)*

JOHN: When you go before a judge you have to have a lawyer. Now a lawyer's paid to lie and make it sound like the truth. I'm getting a good lawyer. A white man's lawyer. And he'll do all he can for all three. There's no use trying to defend one alone—they all have to stick together in this. If they do that there's a good chance, because the fact is there's not much evidence against them.

STEPHEN: There's an identification, by the servant.

JOHN: Well, when our lawyer gets through with that, maybe not. You see, the only one the servant says he identified is Johannes Pafuri. He says he knew him because of his eyes. He's got a peculiar twitch over his eye, and the servant could see his eyes, even with the mask on—so he says he's sure it was Johannes. On the other hand, suppose it was somebody else with a twitch over his eye? With the rest of his face covered it would be hard to be sure it was Johannes, wouldn't it? Well, the lawyer will bring that up. And that'll shake the identification. And there's no other evidence against them, positively none.

STEPHEN: Except that—they were there. They will have to say that they were there.

JOHN: Why?

STEPHEN: Because it is the truth.

JOHN: The truth! Why would they tell the truth in a court? Do they want to get themselves hanged? No, if they all say they know nothing about it, they'll get off, as sure as God's got whiskers.

STEPHEN: But in a court there is a plea—guilty or not guilty.

JOHN: Yes. They'll plead not guilty. Everybody does.

STEPHEN: But Absalom says he will plead guilty.

JOHN: Good God! Why?

STEPHEN: Because he is guilty.

JOHN: Look, Stephen, if they don't all tell the same story, anything can happen to them. Surely you see that. Let them prove the boys guilty if they can. It's not up to the defense to hand 'em their case on a platter.

STEPHEN: I haven't told Absalom what to say. But he says he will not lie again. That he's done his last evil, and from now on he won't tell a lie or do any wrong. And so he will tell them that he was there. And that he shot Arthur Jarvis.

JOHN: Will he tell them Matthew was there—and Johannes?

STEPHEN: Yes.

JOHN: Well—that changes everything. You better fix that, brother, and fix it fast, or I give you my word we'll fix Absalom. Talk to him, brother.

STEPHEN: I have. He will plead guilty.

JOHN: A man who pleads guilty to murder receives the punishment of the first degree—and that's hanging by your neck with a sack over your head. They don't fool about that.

STEPHEN: He has already made a confession. He has admitted the whole charge.

JOHN: He can deny that. He can say he was out of his mind—anything.

STEPHEN: And Matthew and Johannes will plead not guilty?

JOHN: Of course they will. That's part of the game. This is what happens in a court, Stephen. The defendant may be guilty as hell but he goes in and pleads not guilty and his lawyer tries to make the evidence look as if he's not guilty. The prosecution may be weak as hell but it goes in and tries to make things look as if the defendant's guilty as a hyena. Each one tries to foul up the witnesses on the other side and make his own witnesses look good. If the defense piles up the most points, why fine, the old sheep-face of a judge says he's not guilty. If the prosecution piles up the most points, why old sheep-face says hang him up. It's a game. Truth has nothing to do with it. Now if Absalom pleads guilty it would make it look bad for all three—but don't let him do it, brother, because I'm going to get Matthew out of this, and anything Absalom says is going to be used against him. By me, if necessary. So talk to him, Stephen, talk to him as you never talked to anybody before. He doesn't want to die—and you don't want him to die. If you want him to live, tell him to plead not guilty.

(The lights dim. JOHN *goes out.* STEPHEN *is left musing alone)*

STEPHEN: *(Sings "The Soliloquy")*
What have I come to here,
At this crossing of paths?
Must he tell a lie and live—
Or speak truth and die?
And, if this is so,
What can I say to my son?
O Tixo, Tixo, help me!

Often when he was young
I have come to him and said,
"Speak truly, evade nothing, what you have done
Let it be on your head."

And he heeded me not at all,
Like rain he ran through my hands,
Concealing, as a boy will, taking what was not his,
Evading commands.

For he seemed to hear none of my words;
Turning, shifting, he ran
Through a tangle of nights and days,
Till he was lost to my sight, and ran far into evil—
And evil ways,
And he was stricken—
And struck back,
And he loved, and he was desperate with love and fear and anger,
And at last he came
To this—
O God of the humble and the broken—
O God of those who have nothing, nothing, nothing—
To this—
To the death of a man!
To the death of a man!

A man he had given to death.
Then my words came back to him,
And he said, "I shall do no more evil, tell no more untruth;
I shall keep my father's ways, and remember them."

And can I go to him now
And say, "My son, take care,
Tell no truth in this court, lest it go ill with you here;
Keep to the rules, beware"?

And yet if I say again,
"It shall not profit a man
If he gain the whole world and lose his own soul,"
I shall lose Absalom then.
I shall lose Absalom then.
(He speaks)
I must find some other way—
Some other hope.
My son did not mean to kill his son,
Did not mean to kill.
(He sings)
O Tixo, Tixo, *help me!*
(He speaks)
To whom can I appeal?
(He sings)
O Tixo, Tixo, *help me!*
(He speaks)
Where can I turn now?
(He sings)
O Tixo, Tixo, *help me!*

(The lights dim out, and come up on the door of a well-kept residence in Johannesburg. STEPHEN *goes to the door, knocks, gets no answer, and starts to go.* JAMES JARVIS *opens the door)*
JARVIS: Yes? Did you knock?
STEPHEN: I—I'm sorry, sir. I—expected a servant to answer—I—
JARVIS: There are no servants here today, umfundisi. Did you wish to see one of them?
STEPHEN: No, umnumzana. I wished to see you.
JARVIS: Yes?
STEPHEN: I— *(His body fails him. His cane clatters to the ground and he sits on the step.* JARVIS *comes down to him)* Forgive me, umnumzana— *(His hat lies beside him, he reaches for it, leaves it)*
JARVIS: Are you ill, umfundisi?
*(*STEPHEN *doesn't answer, he is trembling, looking at the ground; finally he looks up and speaks)*
STEPHEN: Forgive me—I—shall recover.
JARVIS: Do you wish water? Or food, perhaps? Are you hungry?
*(*STEPHEN *reaches for his cane, with another effort gets to his feet.* JARVIS *stands watching him, finally picks up his battered old hat and hands it to him)*
STEPHEN: Thank you, sir. I am sorry. I shall go now.
JARVIS: But you said you wished to see me.
STEPHEN: Yes, sir.
JARVIS: Well, then—?
STEPHEN: I have no words to say it.
JARVIS: You are in fear of me. I do not know why.
STEPHEN: I cannot tell it, umnumzana.
JARVIS: I wish to help whenever I can. Is it so heavy a thing?
STEPHEN: It is the heaviest thing of all my years.

JARVIS: You need not be afraid. I try to be just.

STEPHEN: Umnumzana—this thing that is the heaviest thing of all my years—it is also the heaviest thing of all your years.

JARVIS: You can mean only one thing. But I still do not understand.

STEPHEN: *(Slowly)* It was my son that killed your son.

(JARVIS *turns and walks away—then comes back to* STEPHEN)

JARVIS: Why did you come?

STEPHEN: There were three who went to rob the house, umnumzana. Two of them have lied and said they were not there. My son has told truth, that he was there, that he fired the revolver that killed your son. He will die for this truthtelling, the lawyer thinks.

JARVIS: Not for his truthtelling.

STEPHEN: Umnumzana, could you intercede for him?

JARVIS: One does not seek to influence a court.

STEPHEN: He did not mean to kill. And he tells truth. Is there not a core of good in him who tells truth?

JARVIS: My son left his doors always open. He trusted his fellow men. And for this your son killed him.

STEPHEN: He never meant to kill. But the revolver was in his hand and he heard someone coming and was frightened.

JARVIS: Have you thought what it is for me that my son is dead?

STEPHEN: I have tried. I have thought of—my son—

JARVIS: Have you thought what it is for his mother? His mother will die of this. It's in her face.

STEPHEN: I know. I can see the face of my son's mother. Forgive me, umnumzana —I know what this is to you. But—if he were only to live—even shut up—even far from us.

JARVIS: I try to be just. I know what it is to lose a son. But—I say again—one does not try to influence a court. And even if the judge were merciful, mercy can be pitiless. If your son went free ten thousand others might be misled into the death he escaped. Better that one be punished where punishment is deserved —and the ten thousand be warned.

STEPHEN: I think he did not mean evil, umnumzana. And to die—when he is loved—

JARVIS: I know about death.

STEPHEN: If I could take him back to his home, umnumzana! Away from Johannesburg. He grew up in Ndotsheni. Among the hills. There was no evil in him then. From our house we could see up through the clove to your great house. You were kind to the folk who worked the little farms. Be kind again. A terrible thing has befallen my people. We are lost. Not many have found their way to the Christ, and those who have not are lost. My son was lost. This would not have happened if there were not the gold mines, and the great city your people have built, and the little hope we have.

JARVIS: Umfundisi, there are two races in South Africa. One is capable of mastery and self-control—the other is not. One is born to govern, the other to be governed. One is capable of culture and the arts of civilization—the other is not. The difference between us is greater than that I live on a hill and you live in the valley. If my son had killed your son I would not have come to you for mercy. Nor to the judge. Whether it were my son or yours, I would have said, let him answer the law!

STEPHEN: You—you could save him—

JARVIS: You have neither heard nor understood me! There is only a handful of whites in South Africa to control the great tide of blacks—and the blacks have no control of their own! They have no mind to it—and no mind for it! It's their way to run and evade and lie and strike down in the dark! Those who will not keep order must be kept in order! Those who lift their hands to kill must know that the penalty for death is death!

STEPHEN: *(Humbly)* Umnumzana—I read my Testament carefully. Jesus has not said this.

JARVIS: No, he has not, but where there is government it's true. Have you more to say to me?

STEPHEN: No, umnumzana.

(JARVIS turns to go in. The lights dim)

SCENE 2

The lights come up on IRINA'S *hut. We see* IRINA *hanging some clothes on a clothesline.*

IRINA: *(Sings "Stay Well")*
If I tell truth to you,
My love, my own,
Grief is your gift to me,
Grief alone,
Wild passion at midnight,
Wild anger at dawn,
Yet when you're absent
I weep you gone.

Stay well, O keeper of my love,
Go well, throughout all your days,
Your star be my luckiest star above,
Your ways the luckiest ways.
Since unto you my one love is given,
And since with you it will remain,
Though you bring fear of hell, despair of heaven,
Stay well, come well to my door again.

*(*STEPHEN *enters from the left, knocks and then calls)*
STEPHEN: Irina?
IRINA: Yes?
STEPHEN: The trial will begin tomorrow. Do you wish to be there?
IRINA: Could I see him?
STEPHEN: Yes. All those in the court will see him.
IRINA: Then I wish to go. Umfundisi—is anything sure?
STEPHEN: Nothing is sure. He will be tried. It's not known what will come of it.
IRINA: He might go free?

STEPHEN: I wish I could say yes. He says he will plead guilty. He says he will speak the truth. If he does I think he will stay in the prison. For a long time.

IRINA: For a long time.

STEPHEN: For a very long time.

IRINA: So that I will never see him?

STEPHEN: It may be many years.

IRINA: Many years.

STEPHEN: Would you wait for him—if it were so long?

IRINA: Yes, umfundisi. I would wait.

STEPHEN: He has asked me—would you wish to marry him in the prison—so that your child will have his name?

IRINA: Yes.

STEPHEN: He wishes it.

IRINA: *(Running to him)* Umfundisi—

STEPHEN: Yes?

IRINA: Will they kill him?

STEPHEN: It's not known yet.

IRINA: I want him to live! I want him to come back to me!

STEPHEN: Even if it's many years?

IRINA: Yes.

STEPHEN: And you will wait?

IRINA: Yes.

STEPHEN: Even if he does not come back at all?

IRINA: I will still wait.

STEPHEN: And when the desire is on you?

IRINA: I desire only him.

STEPHEN: *(Stroking her hair)* I will come tomorrow for you. And I will tell him that you wish the marriage. Stay well, Irina.

IRINA: Go well, my father.

(STEPHEN *goes out.* IRINA *sings "Stay Well")*

When you have fled from me,
My love, my own,
I've waited quietly,
Here alone.
Some come back at midnight,
Or come back at dawn,
Now that you're absent
I weep you gone.

Go well, though wild the road and far
Stay well through darkening days,
Your star be still my luckiest star,
Your ways the luckiest ways,
Though into storm your lone bark be driven,
Though my eyes ache for you in vain,
Though you bring fear at dawn, despair at even,
Stay well, come well to my door again.

The lights dim

SCENE 3

A courtroom. The JUDGE'S *bench is at the left; the* JUDGE *is seated.* ABSALOM *and* MATTHEW *are in the prisoner's dock. In the courtroom are all those we have seen who are concerned with this case or related to the prisoners:* IRINA, LINDA, JOHN, STEPHEN, *the* SERVANT, *and many* ZULU SPECTATORS. JAMES JARVIS, ELAND, *and a number of* WHITES *sit on the opposite side of the courtroom. As the lights come up* JOHANNES PAFURI *is in the witness box, center, and* BURTON, *the defense lawyer, is questioning him.*

BURTON: Johannes, you have been identified as one of three masked men who entered the kitchen of Arthur Jarvis on October eighth, between eleven and twelve. Were you there at that time?

JOHANNES: No, sir.

BURTON: Where were you?

JOHANNES: At Mrs. Ndela's house, in End Street.

BURTON: How do you know you were there at eleven?

JOHANNES: Because we had been dancing at a place in High Street till nearly eleven, and at eleven we were at Mrs. Ndela's.

BURTON: Who else was there?

JOHANNES: Matthew Kumalo was there, and the girls Linda and Rose.

BURTON: The witness is excused. Will Matthew Kumalo take the stand? *(MAT-THEW KUMALO comes down into witness box)* Matthew Kumalo, you are accused of being one of three masked men who entered the kitchen of Arthur Jarvis on October eighth, between eleven and twelve. Were you there at that time?

MATTHEW: No, sir.

BURTON: Where were you?

MATTHEW: At Mrs. Ndela's, in End Street.

BURTON: You are sure of the time?

MATTHEW: Yes, sir. We had been dancing at the place in High Street, and when we came to Mrs. Ndela's she said, "You are late, but come in," and we saw that it was near eleven.

BURTON: Do you know Absalom Kumalo?

MATTHEW: Yes, sir. He is the son of my father's brother.

BURTON: Was he with you on this evening?

MATTHEW: No, sir.

BURTON: Do you know where he was?

MATTHEW: No, sir.

BURTON: The witness is excused for the moment. *(MATTHEW steps back to the bench and sits. BURTON crosses to the JUDGE)* Your Honor, I am about to call the third defendant, Absalom Kumalo. Before I do so I wish to explain that his plea of guilty is his own choice, and that I have not attempted to influence him in any way.

JUDGE: I understand, sir. You may proceed.

BURTON: Absalom Kumalo, will take the stand. *(ABSALOM does so)* Absalom Kumalo, you are accused of being one of three masked men who entered the kitchen of Arthur Jarvis on October eighth, between eleven and twelve in the evening. Were you there at that time?

ABSALOM: Yes, sir.

BURTON: Who were the two masked men with you?

ABSALOM: Matthew Kumalo and Johannes Pafuri.

BURTON: What was your purpose in going there?

ABSALOM: To steal something from the house.

BURTON: Why did you choose this day?

ABSALOM: Because Johannes said the house would be empty at that time.

BURTON: The same Johannes Pafuri here?

ABSALOM: Yes, sir.

BURTON: When did you three go to this house?

ABSALOM: It was after eleven at night.

BURTON: Did you go there disguised?

ABSALOM: We tied handkerchiefs over our mouths.

BURTON: And then?

ABSALOM: We went into the kitchen and there was a servant there.

BURTON: This man?

ABSALOM: Yes, that is the man.

BURTON: Tell the court what happened then.

ABSALOM: This man was afraid. He saw my revolver. He said, "What do you want?" Johannes said, "We want money and clothes." This man said, "You cannot do such a thing." Johannes said, "Do you want to die?" Then this man called out, "Master! Master!" and Johannes struck him over the head with the iron bar.

BURTON: Did he call again?

ABSALOM: He made no sound.

BURTON: What did you do?

ABSALOM: No, we were silent—and listened.

BURTON: Where was your revolver?

ABSALOM: In my hand.

BURTON: And then?

ABSALOM: Then a white man came into the doorway.

BURTON: And then?

ABSALOM: I was frightened. I fired the revolver.

BURTON: And then?

ABSALOM: The white man fell.

BURTON: And then?

ABSALOM: Matthew said, "We must go." So we all went quickly.

BURTON: Where did you go?

ABSALOM: I wandered about. I wanted to find a place to hide.

JUDGE: I have a question to ask, Mr. Burton.

BURTON: Yes, Your Honor.

JUDGE: Why did you carry a revolver?

ABSALOM: It was to frighten the servant of the house.

JUDGE: Where did you get this revolver?

ABSALOM: I bought it from a man.

JUDGE: Was this revolver loaded when you bought it?

ABSALOM: It had two bullets in it.

JUDGE: How many bullets were in it when you went to this house?

ABSALOM: One.

JUDGE: What happened to the other?

ABSALOM: I took the revolver out into the hills and fired it.

JUDGE: What did you fire at?

ABSALOM: I fired at a tree.

JUDGE: Did you hit this tree?

ABSALOM: Yes, I hit it.

JUDGE: Then you thought, "Now I can fire this revolver"?

ABSALOM: Yes, that is so.

JUDGE: And when Matthew Kumalo and Johannes Pafuri say they were not with you at the time of the murder they are lying?

ABSALOM: Yes, they are lying.

JUDGE: Do you know where they went after the crime?

ABSALOM: No, I do not know.

JUDGE: Where did you go?

ABSALOM: I went to a plantation and buried the revolver.

JUDGE: And what did you do next?

ABSALOM: I prayed there.

JUDGE: What did you pray there?

ABSALOM: I prayed for forgiveness.

JUDGE: How did the police find you?

ABSALOM: Johannes Pafuri brought them to where I was.

JUDGE: And what did you tell them?

ABSALOM: I told them it was not Johannes who had killed the white man, it was I myself.

JUDGE: And how was the revolver found?

ABSALOM: No, I told the police where to find it.

JUDGE: And every word you have said is true?

ABSALOM: Every word is true.

JUDGE: There is no lie in it?

ABSALOM: There is no lie in it, for I said to myself, I shall not lie any more, all the rest of my days, nor do anything more that is evil.

JUDGE: In fact, you repented.

ABSALOM: Yes, I repented.

JUDGE: Because you were in trouble?

ABSALOM: Yes, because I was in trouble.

JUDGE: Did you have any other reason for repenting?

ABSALOM: No, I had no other reason.

JUDGE: I have no further questions, Mr. Burton.

BURTON: The witness is dismissed.

(The lights dim on the courtroom, and the CHORUS *comes forward)*

CHORUS: *(Sings)*
And here again, in this place,
A man who has killed takes breath
With the fear of death in his face,
Fear of death for death,
And are the terms of justice clearly met?
Not yet, no, not quite yet.

(The courtroom lights come up again. The SPECTATORS *are standing; the* JUDGE *sits; they all sit except the three* BOYS *who are awaiting sentence)*

JUDGE: The evidence in this case is in many ways inconclusive, unsatisfactory, and fragmentary. Some of the witnesses are or could be interested parties. Some of the accused appear to have testified in collusion with each other or other witnesses. There are many points not clear, some of which, perhaps, will now never be clear. It seems quite possible that Matthew Kumalo and Johannes Pafuri are guilty with Absalom Kumalo of the murder of Arthur Jarvis. It was the identification of Pafuri by the servant who was struck that led to Pafuri's arrest. It was the arrest of Pafuri that led the police to arrest Absalom and later Matthew. The alibis offered by Matthew and Johannes are obviously doubtful. No reason has come to light why Absalom should involve in the robbery and murder two men who were not with him at the time and not guilty. And yet, after long and thoughtful consideration, my assessors and I have come to the conclusion that the guilt of Matthew and Johannes is not sufficiently established. *(MATTHEW and JOHANNES look at each other, puzzled)* There remains the case against Absalom Kumalo. Except for his plea and his confession the case against him remains substantially that against Johannes and Matthew. His guilt is not established in the testimony alone, but that testimony, taken together with his confession, leads us inescapably to the conclusion that he is guilty. No reason has been offered why he should confess to a deed he did not commit, and his own insistence that he had no intention to kill operates to validate the confession itself. Matthew Kumalo and Johannes Pafuri, you are discharged and may step down. *(They do so, move over right quietly; LINDA and ROSE rise and join them)* Absalom Kumalo, have you anything to say before I pronounce sentence?

ABSALOM: I have only this to say, that I killed this man, but I did not mean to kill him, only I was afraid.

JUDGE: Absalom Kumalo, *(The SPECTATORS lean toward the JUDGE, who puts a little black cap on his head)* I sentence you to be returned to custody, and to be hanged by the neck until you are dead. And may the Lord have mercy on your soul.

(IRINA rises, then STEPHEN. JARVIS gets up and crosses the courtroom. As he does so he is met by STEPHEN. JARVIS steps back to let STEPHEN pass. He goes to ABSALOM, who stands stunned and motionless)

SCENE 4

The prison cell. The lights come up on the CHORUS.

CHORUS: *(Sings "Cry, the Beloved Country")*
  Cry, the beloved country,
  Cry, the beloved land,
  the wasted childhood,
  the wasted youth,
  the wasted man!
  Cry, the broken tribes, and the broken hills,
  and the right and wrong forsaken,
  the greed that destroys us,
  the birds that cry no more!
  Cry, the beloved country,
  Cry, the lost tribe, the lost son.

(The CHORUS *parts, revealing the prison cell.* ABSALOM *is in the cell,* IRINA *near him.* STEPHEN *is reading the marriage service)*

STEPHEN: —to live together after God's ordinance in the holy estate of Matrimony? Wilt thou obey him, and serve him, love, honour, and keep him, and forsaking all others, keep thee only unto him, so long as ye both shall live?

IRINA: I will.

WOMAN: *(Sings)*
> *Cry, the unborn son,*
> *the inheritor of our fear,*
> *let him not laugh too gladly in the water of the clove,*
> *nor stand too silent*
> *when the setting sun makes the veld red with fire.*

STEPHEN: And now you are man and wife, my son, and my daughter. Irina will come with me to Ndotsheni, Absalom.

ABSALOM: I am glad, my father.

STEPHEN: We shall care for your child as if it were our own.

ABSALOM: I thank you, my father.

STEPHEN: Will you wish to say good-by to Irina?

ABSALOM: There is no way to say good-by. My father, I must go to—Pretoria.

STEPHEN: There will be an appeal.

ABSALOM: But it will not help. I am afraid. I am afraid of the hanging.

STEPHEN: Be of courage, my son.

ABSALOM: It's no help to be of courage! O *Tixo, Tixo,* I am afraid of the rope and the hanging!

*(*IRINA *kneels)*

GUARD: You must go now.

ABSALOM: Where I go there will be no wife or child or father or mother! There is no food taken or given! And no marriage! Where I go! O *Tixo, Tixo!*

CHORUS: *(Sings)*
> *Cry, the unborn son,*
> *fatherless,*
> *let him not be moved by the song of the bird,*
> *nor give his heart to a mountain*
> *nor to a valley!*

> *Cry, the beloved country!*
> *Cry, the lost son,*
> *the lost tribe—*
> *the lost—*
> *The great red hills stand desolate,*
> *and the earth has torn away like flesh.*
> *These are the valleys*
> *of old men and old women,*
> *of mothers and children.*

WOMAN: *(Sings)*
> *Cry, the beloved land.*

The lights dim

SCENE 5

As the lights come up we see ALEX *playing with a little Negro* BOY *and* GIRL. *There is a small handmade toy between them. We can see the interior of the chapel, center stage.*

ALEX: *(Sings "Big Mole")*
Big Mole was a digger of the fastest kind;
He'd dig in the earth like you think in your mind;
When Big Mole came to the side of a hill
Instead of going over he'd start in to drill.
He promised his mother a well in the town
And he brought boiling water from a thousand feet down!

Down, down, down, down,
Three mile, four mile, five mile down;
He can go through rock, he can go through coal;
Whenever you come to an oversize hole
Down at the bottom is Big Black Mole!
Big Black Mole, Big Black Mole!

When Mole was a younker they showed him a mine;
He said, "I like the idea fine,
Let me have that hose, let me have that drill."
If they hadn't shut it off he'd be boring still!
And down at the bottom he chunked all around
Till he chunked out a city six mile in the ground!

Down, down, down, down,
Three mile, four mile, five mile down;
You can bet your pants, you can bet your soul,
Whenever you come to a man-size hole
Down at the bottom is Big Black Mole!
Big Black Mole! Big Black Mole!

Big Mole had a girl who was small and sweet;
He promised her diamonds for her hands and feet;
He dug so deep and he dug so well,
He broke right into the ceiling of hell,
And he looked the old devil spang in the eye,
And he said, "I'm not coming back here till I die!"

(EDWARD JARVIS enters and stands listening)

ALEX: *(Sings)*
Down, down, down, down,
Three mile, four mile, five mile down;
He can go through rock, he can go through coal;
Whenever you come to a sure-enough hole,
Down at the bottom is Big Black Mole!
Big Black Mole, Big Black Mole, Big Black Mole!

EDWARD: Hi, there!
ALEX: Hi.

(The other two CHILDREN *get up and run off to the right)*

EDWARD: You know, there's one thing I have to say for your voice—it's loud. It reminds me of Jericho.

ALEX: Jericho?

EDWARD: Yes, the man that knocked the town over with music.

ALEX: It was Joshua that broke the walls of the city with music. Jericho was the name of the city he destroyed.

EDWARD: How do you know that?

ALEX: My uncle read it to me out of the Old Testament.

EDWARD: Well, don't sing as loud as you can around here, or some of these walls might go down. *(EDWARD laughs,* ALEX *joins him, they both laugh)*

ALEX: I'll be very careful, sir.

EDWARD: I'm waiting for my grandfather now. We live up there in the hills.

ALEX: I know. I've seen you riding around up there. On a bicycle.

EDWARD: Sometimes I ride a bicycle, sometimes a horse. I can fall off both just fine. *(They laugh again)* What have you got there?

ALEX: A digging machine.

EDWARD: Does it work?

ALEX: Not much. I made it myself.

EDWARD: What's your name?

ALEX: Alex.

EDWARD: Mine's Edward. I guess your uncle's the umfundisi here.

ALEX: Yes, he is.

EDWARD: I know a lot of Zulu words. My father taught them to me. *Ingeli* is English.

ALEX: That's right.

EDWARD: What's the word for water?

ALEX: *Amanzi.*

EDWARD: And how do you say to die?

ALEX: *Siyafa.*

EDWARD: The young *Ingeli siyafa* for *amanzi*—is that right?

ALEX: You mean the English boy is dying for water?

EDWARD: Uh-huh. I am, too. Only I'd rather have milk, out of the fridge.

ALEX: The fridge?

EDWARD: You know, the refrigerator.

ALEX: My uncle doesn't have one.

EDWARD: How do you keep the milk cold?

ALEX: We have no milk. Nobody has milk in Ndotsheni.

EDWARD: No milk!

ALEX: No. Can I get you some water?

EDWARD: Never mind. *(To himself)* No milk . . . You know, you've got a real idea here; if you had something heavy on that string, and it had a point on it, and it kept dropping on the ground, it would really dig.

ALEX: Like a nail?

*(*JAMES JARVIS *enters from the left)*

JARVIS: We're going now, Edward.

EDWARD: Yes, Grandfather. *(He rises.* ALEX *rises)*

JARVIS: The car's at the market.

ALEX: *(Afraid of* JARVIS*)* I have to go. *(He runs to the right)*

EDWARD: Good-by, Alex!

ALEX: *(Stopping)* Good-by—Edward! *(He runs off behind the chapel, waves to* EDWARD, *who also waves farewell)*

JARVIS: Edward, when you are a man, you will live your own life. You will live as you please to live. But while you live with me, never let me see this again.

EDWARD: You mean talking with this boy?

JARVIS: I mean that.

EDWARD: But I like him. He's bright and he's nice.

JARVIS: There are not many rules in my house. I am lax in many ways, and not easily angered. *(He sits—his head in his hands.* EDWARD *sits beside him)* I have lost so much that I don't know why I go on living, or what's worth saving. I don't know any more why any man should do his tasks or work for gain or love his child. I don't know why any child should obey—or whether good will come of it or evil. But I do know this; there are some things that I cannot bear to look on.

(We hear organ music. The lights come up in the chapel. PARISHIONERS *come in from the right and take their places in the chapel.* STEPHEN *and* GRACE *enter.* STEPHEN *stands before the pulpit.* JARVIS *still sits on the step)*

STEPHEN: *(Speaking from the pulpit)* I will say first the hardest thing I have to say. I am resigning from my pastorate at Ndotsheni. I shall be your umfundisi no more. It had been my hope to end my years here, but—I cannot now.

EDWARD: Aren't we going, Grandfather?

JARVIS: We'll wait a moment.

STEPHEN: My son Absalom will die tomorrow morning on the scaffold for a murder to which he confessed, and of which he was guilty. You all know of this. The man he killed was known to you, too. He was Arthur Jarvis. He was born in the hills above our little town. There was a brightness upon him even as a child. As a man he was a friend of our race, a friend of all men, a man all men could be proud of. And my son—killed him. And the mother of Arthur Jarvis is dead of grief for her son. My people, if I stay here now I become a hindrance to you, and not a help. I must go.

PARISHIONERS: You cannot go, umfundisi! You cannot go! No, umfundisi!

STEPHEN: This is a poor village, Ndotsheni, and it grows poorer. In the past when our little church was in desperate need we have sometimes turned to Arthur Jarvis, and he has helped us. He will not help here again. And no one will help you while I remain here, for the man who slew him was my son. I must go for still another reason, my dear people. When I began to serve my God and my church I had a sure faith that the God of our world ordered things well for men. I had a sure faith that though there was good and evil I knew which was good, and God knew it—and that men were better in their hearts for choosing good and not evil. Something has shaken this in me. I am not sure of my faith. I am lost. I am not sure now. I am not sure that we are not all lost. And a leader should not be lost. He should know the way, and so I resign my place.

MCRAE: Umfundisi, if you have lost your faith, I too have lost my faith.

PARISHIONERS: Yes.

MCRAE: Where does a man go, and what does he do when his faith is gone?

STEPHEN: I don't know.

PARISHIONERS: Oh, Stephen, you have always helped us. Please stay!

STEPHEN: If I keep my place, and this black thing has happened to my son and is said, little by little the few who still worship here will shrink away, the rusty roof will leak more, the floor will break till there is none, the windows will go —they will be thrown at and broken and will go—and the unpainted sides of this chapel I have loved will stand empty, roofless—and I shall live in despair beside it, knowing that I have done this thing to you and to my church by remaining. *(STEPHEN starts to go—they all reach out to him and he pauses)*

VILLAGER: *(Sings "A Bird of Passage")*
Lord of the heart, look down upon
Our earthly pilgrimage,
Look down upon us where we walk
From bright dawn to old age,
Give light not shed by any sun.

PARISHIONERS:
Lord of the heart!

MAN:
Not read on any page.

CHORUS:
Lord of the heart!
A bird of passage out of night
Flies in at a lighted door,
Flies through and on in its darkened flight
And then is seen no more.

(STEPHEN stands for a moment at the pulpit, then turns and goes out)

This is the life of men on earth:
Out of darkness we come at birth
Into a lamplit room, and then—

EDWARD: *(Speaking through the music)* What is it, Grandfather?

CHORUS: *(Sings)*
Go forward into dark again,
Go forward into dark again.

　　　The lights dim

SCENE 6

It is before daylight the next morning and STEPHEN *is sitting on a chair in front of the table in the room where we saw him in the first scene of the play. There is an extra chair upstage center added to this scene. Stephen sits watching the clock on the shelf. The* CHORUS *sings as the lights come up.*

CHORUS:
Four o'clock, it will soon be four.

IRINA: *(Coming in)* Umfundisi.

STEPHEN: Yes, Irina?

IRINA: She has fallen asleep. She meant to sit and watch with you at this hour, and she has been awake till only now—but now she sleeps.

STEPHEN: We won't wake her, Irina. If she sleeps and the hour goes past, then at least it will be past.

IRINA: Even in her sleep she reaches for my hand.

STEPHEN: Sit beside her, Irina, if you can.

IRINA: Yes, I can. *(She starts to go.* STEPHEN *stops her)*

STEPHEN: My daughter, I'm glad he found you and not some other.

IRINA: I'm glad he found me, my father. *(She goes back into the kitchen)*

CHORUS: *(Sings)*
> *Four o'clock, it will soon be four.*

LEADER: *(Sings)*
> *Why do they choose the morning,*
> *the morning, when men sleep sound?*

CHORUS: *(Sings)*
> *Four o'clock,*
> *it will soon be four.*

STEPHEN: *(Speaks)*
> If they would kill me instead
> Absalom would make a good man.
> But it will never be.
> He is waiting now.
> Sleep, O mother. Sleep sound.
> Soon Absalom will sleep.

(JARVIS enters from left, crosses to door, knocks. STEPHEN, almost unaware of what he is doing, answers)

STEPHEN: Yes—

JARVIS: *(In the doorway)* I hope you will forgive me for coming at this hour, umfundisi.

STEPHEN: *(Rising)* Why are you here?

JARVIS: May I come in?

STEPHEN: You—you wish to come into my house?

JARVIS: Yes.

STEPHEN: Come in, sir.

JARVIS: *(Entering)* I stood outside your church yesterday and heard what you said to your people, and what they said to you. I want you to know that I will help you with the roof and with the painting—and whatever must be done. I will do whatever my son would have done.

STEPHEN: I—thank you, sir. The church will thank you.

JARVIS: Whatever you need.

STEPHEN: Mr. Jarvis. *(He looks at the clock)* It's hard for me to think of the church or of—in a quarter of an hour my son is to die.

JARVIS: I know. I couldn't sleep—thinking of it.

STEPHEN: I think this does not touch you.

JARVIS: Yes. It does.

STEPHEN: I don't know how. I think it might be better if I sat here alone.

JARVIS: I know my presence pains you. I know I am the last man in the world you wish to see. And yet—may I stay for a moment?

STEPHEN: If you wish.

JARVIS: Stephen Kumalo, my wife is dead. My son is dead. I live in a house with a child who knows me only as an old man. I have thought many times I would be better dead. I thought myself alone in this desolation that used to be my home. But when I heard you yesterday I knew that your grief and mine were the same. I know now that of all the men who live near this great valley you are the one I would want for a friend. And—I have been walking about—and came and knocked here now—because I wanted to sit with you in this hour—

STEPHEN: You want to sit with me?

JARVIS: Yes, if I may.

STEPHEN: Mr. Jarvis, you know that you can give me only charity. If you were seen to touch my hand, this town, this whole valley, would turn against you.

JARVIS: I've finished with that. I haven't come here lightly. I shall take your hand wherever I like, before whom I like. I shall come and worship in your church if I wish to worship. May I sit here with you?

STEPHEN: Yes, umnumzana. *(JARVIS starts to sit)* This is not a good chair. *(He brings another chair and places it. JARVIS sits)* It's almost the hour. O God—O Tixo—it is almost now.

JARVIS: But there will be a tomorrow, Stephen. Edward will come tomorrow to see Alex. He wants to come and play.

STEPHEN: I shall be gone. I shall never see this place again. Nor the path where Absalom ran to meet me—nor the hills where he played and came late to supper —nor the room where he slept—never, never again.

JARVIS: You must stay in Ndotsheni.

STEPHEN: If I stayed, do you know what I would preach here? That good can come from evil, and evil from good! That no man knows surely what is evil or what is good! That if there is a God He is hidden and has not spoken to men! That we are all lost here, black and white, rich and poor, the fools and the wise! Lost and hopeless and condemned on this rock that goes 'round the sun without meaning!

JARVIS: Not hopeless, Stephen, and not without meaning. For even out of the horror of this crime some things have come that are gain and not loss. My son's words to me and my understanding of my son. And your words in the chapel, and my understanding of those words—and your son's face in the courtroom when he said he would not lie any more or do any evil. I shall never forget that.

STEPHEN: You think well of my son?

JARVIS: I tried not to. But you and I have never had to face what Absalom faced there. A man can hardly do better than he did when he stood before the judge. Stay in Ndotsheni, Stephen, stay with those who cried out to you in the chapel. You have something to give them that nobody else can give them. And you can be proud of Absalom.

STEPHEN: And he is forgiven, and I am forgiven?

JARVIS: Let us forgive each other.

STEPHEN: Umnumzana—umnumzana!

JARVIS: Let us be neighbors. Let us be friends.

STEPHEN: Umnumzana—before the clock strikes—I shall stay in Ndotsheni. You are welcome in this house. I have a friend.

JARVIS: I have a friend.

(The clock strikes four. STEPHEN sits and buries his head in his hands. JARVIS goes to him, puts an arm around him)

CHORUS: *(Sings)*
> *Each lives alone in a world of dark,*
> *Crossing the skies in a lonely arc,*
> *Save when love leaps out like a leaping spark*
> *Over thousands, thousands of miles!*

Curtain

WONDERFUL TOWN

Book by Joseph Fields and Jerome Chodorov
Lyrics by Betty Comden and Adolph Green
Music by Leonard Bernstein

(Based upon the play *My Sister Eileen* by Joseph Fields and Jerome Chodorov
and the stories by Ruth McKenney)

Editor's Notes

One of the highlights of the 1940–1941 Broadway season was the comedy, *My Sister Eileen*. Coauthored by Joseph Fields and Jerome Chodorov, it entertained audiences for 864 performances. In 1942, it was made into an equally successful film with Rosalind Russell. But the best was yet to come, and it did. When *Wonderful Town*, the musical version of the play, swept onto the stage of the Winter Garden Theatre on February 25, 1953, audiences and critics were equally aroused to fever pitch. Unanimously hailed in the press, Robert Coleman reported in the New York *Daily Mirror:* "A great musical called *Wonderful Town* roared into the Winter Garden last evening like a hurricane, and left a brilliant first night audience limp from applauding and hoarse from cheering." With Miss Russell repeating her screen role, now embellished with songs and dances, John Chapman of the New York *Daily News* exclaimed: *"Wonderful Town*—wonderful score—wonderful book—wonderful Rosalind Russell—wonderful production . . . This new musical moves into my sentimental heart as one of the gayest, smartest shows of recent times."

Wolcott Gibbs, generally a caustic critic, joined the cheering section by imparting to his readers of *The New Yorker:* "It is an extraordinarily charming work and I can recall fewer happier evenings than the one I spent at the Winter Garden . . . The book by Joseph Fields and Jerome Chodorov from a series of short stories contributed by Ruth McKenney has a genial and civilized air about it. Leonard Bernstein's tunes are gay and appropriate and the lyrics contributed by Betty Comden and Adolph Green are ingenious and also admirably suited to the mood of the play. The cast directed by George Abbott who has an unquestioned genius for musical comedy could hardly be better."

Others described it as: "A great, big, lovely musical . . . sunny, spirited and bursting with contagious good humor . . . Out of an entertaining play, Fields and Chodorov have made an entertaining libretto. The Comden-Green lyrics are not just clever, but humorous and light . . . and then there is Leonard Bernstein's remarkably bright score. It is one of those happy musicals that are thoroughly professional from first to last."

Wonderful Town ran for 559 performances and walked off with the season's major honors: the New York Critics' Circle Award for best musical and a number of Antoinette Perry (Tony) Awards, including one for best musical.

Joseph Fields (1895–1966) was born in New York City. The son of Lew Fields of the famed vaudeville team, Weber and Fields, he attended New York public schools and New York University where he earned his B.A. While serving in the U. S. Navy during World War I, he wrote and produced several sketches. After the war, he pursued writing sketches, contributing them to various revues, including the *Ziegfeld Follies*. He then spent some years in Hollywood writing for motion pictures, and it was there that he met his future collaborator, Jerome Chodorov.

Mr. Chodorov was born in New York City on August 10, 1911. Before turning to writing for films and the theatre he was a journalist on the staff of the *New York World*. Subsequently he too went to Hollywood, where he was engaged as a screenwriter. The first Fields-Chodorov work for the stage was *Schoolhouse on the Lot*, presented in 1938. Thereafter, they collaborated on *My Sister Eileen* (1940), *Junior Miss* (1941), *The French Touch* (1945), *Wonderful Town* (1953), the book for the musical *The Girl in Pink Tights* (1954), *Anniversary Waltz* (1954), and *The Ponder Heart* (1956).

On his own, Mr. Chodorov wrote the book for the 1964 musical, *I Had a Ball*, and also directed the Broadway productions of *Make a Million*, *The Gazebo*, and *Blood, Sweat, and Stanley Poole*.

Mr. Fields also wrote the popular wartime comedy, *The Doughgirls* (1942), and with Anita Loos, the book for *Gentlemen Prefer Blondes* (1949), which rocketed Carol Channing to stardom. His other works for the theatre include *The Tunnel of Love* (with Peter de Vries, 1957), which he also directed, and the book for the musical *Flower Drum Song* (1958), in collaboration with Oscar Hammerstein II.

Described by *Time* magazine as a "Renaissance Man (who) in an age of specialization refuses to stay put in any cultural pigeonhole," Leonard Bernstein is one of the world's most eminent conductors, a front-rank composer of serious music, pianist, author, lecturer, teacher, television personality, and the creator of the scores for four Broadway musicals: *On the Town* (1944), *Wonderful Town* (1953), *West Side Story (1957)*, and *Candide* (1956, 1973).

Leonard Bernstein was born in Lawrence, Massachusetts, on August 25, 1918. From the Boston Latin School, he went on to Harvard, where he majored in music. At the suggestion of Dimitri Mitropoulos, he turned to the study of conducting, first with Fritz Reiner at the Curtis Institute of Music in Philadelphia, then with Serge Koussevitzky at the Berkshire Music Center, Tanglewood, Massachusetts.

In 1943, he soared to fame, when as an assistant conductor of the New York Philharmonic, he was called in at short notice to take over for the ailing conductor Bruno Walter. His performance electrified the audience and the next day's press coverage exceeded that bestowed on most musical events.

His growing renown as guest conductor of some of the nation's finest orchestras brought him offers from abroad and in 1946, he began the first of a series of many international tours. In 1958, he was appointed Music Director of the New York Philharmonic, serving in this post until 1969 when he was given the lifetime title of Laureate Conductor.

In 1953, he made his operatic debut as the first American-born conductor to conduct at La Scala in Milan, Italy. Since then, he has frequently appeared at other leading opera houses of the world, including the Metropolitan in New York.

As a composer, Bernstein has been successful in ballet, symphonic composition (*Jeremiah*, *The Age of Anxiety*, and the *Kaddish Symphony*), songs, choral and chamber works, and, of course, the musical theatre.

In addition to the aforementioned Broadway musicals, he also composed the incidental music for *Peter Pan* (1950), *The Lark* (1955), and Katharine Cornell's 1958 production of *The First-born*. For films, he did the score for the Academy Award-winning *On the Waterfront*.

Mass, one of the composer's most recent major works, was specially commissioned for the opening of the John F. Kennedy Center for the Performing Arts, Washington, D. C. (September, 1971).

Charismatic as well as supremely talented, Leonard Bernstein has made more than one hundred recordings of classical music, has won countless awards, and has been decorated by at least a half-dozen foreign countries.

(NOTE: For comments on Betty Comden and Adolph Green, see *Applause*.)

Production Notes

Wonderful Town was first presented by Robert Fryer at the Winter Garden Theatre, New York, on February 25, 1953. The cast was as follows:

Guide, *Warren Galjour*
Appopolous, *Henry Lascoe*
Lonigan, *Walter Kelvin*
Helen, *Michele Burke*
Wreck, *Jordan Bentley*
Violet, *Dody Goodman*
Valenti, *Ted Beniades*
Eileen, *Edith Adams*
Ruth, *Rosalind Russell*
A Strange Man, *Nathaniel Frey*
Drunks, *Lee Papell, Delbert Anderson*
Robert Baker, *George Gaynes*

Associate Editors, *Warren Galjour, Albert Linville*
Mrs. Wade, *Isabella Hoopes*
Frank Lippencott, *Chris Alexander*
Chef, *Nathaniel Frey*
Waiter, *Delbert Anderson*
Delivery Boy, *Alvin Beam*
Chick Clark, *Dort Clark*
Shore Patrolman, *Lee Papell*
First Cadet, *David Lober*
Second Cadet, *Ray Dorian*

Policemen, *Lee Papell, Albert Linville, Delbert Anderson, Chris Robinson, Nathaniel Frey, Warren Galjour, Robert Kole*
Ruth's Escort, *Chris Robinson*
Greenwich Villagers, *Jean Eliot, Carol Cole, Marta Becket, Maxine Berke, Helena Seroy, Geraldine Delaney, Margaret Cuddy, Dody Goodman, Ed Balin, Alvin Beam, Ray Dorian, Edward Heim, Joe Layton, David Lober, Victor Moreno, William Weslow, Pat Johnson, Evelyn Page, Libi Staiger, Patty Wilkes, Helen Rice, Delbert Anderson, Warren Galjour, Robert Kole, Ray Kirchner, Lee Papell, Chris Robinson*

Production Directed by *George Abbott*
Dances and Musical Numbers Staged by *Donald Saddler*
Sets and Costumes by *Raoul Pene du Bois*
Musical Direction and Vocal Arrangements by *Lehman Engel*
Miss Russell's Clothes by *Mainbocher*
Lighting by *Peggy Clark*
Orchestrations by *Don Walker*

Scene: The play takes place in Greenwich Village in the '30s.

Musical Numbers

ACT ONE

Christopher Street	Sung by Guide and The Villagers
Ohio	Ruth, Eileen
Conquering New York	Ruth, Eileen, and the Ensemble
One Hundred Easy Ways	Ruth
What a Waste	Baker and Editors
Story Vignettes by Miss Comden and Mr. Green	
	Rexford, Mr. Mallory, Danny, Trent, and Ruth
A Little Bit in Love	Eileen

Pass the Football	Wreck and The Villagers
Conversation Piece by Miss Comden and Mr. Green	
	Ruth, Eileen, Frank, Baker, Chick
A Quiet Girl	Baker
Conga!	Ruth
	Danced by The Cadets

ACT TWO

My Darlin' Eileen	Eileen and Policemen
Swing!	Ruth and The Villagers
Reprise: Ohio	Ruth, Eileen
It's Love	Baker and The Villagers
Wrong Note Rag	Ruth, Eileen and The Villagers

ACT ONE

SCENE 1

In front of the curtain, which is a semi-abstract impression of Greenwich Village, a GUIDE *and a group of gaping* TOURISTS *enter to a musical vamp in a style highly characteristic of the 1930s.*

GUIDE: Come along!

(Singing in the brisk offhand manner of a barker and indicating points of interest in a lilting song.)

On your left,
Washington Square,
Right in the heart of Greenwich Village.

TOURISTS: *(Looking around ecstatically)*
My, what trees—
Smell that air—
Painters and pigeons in Washington Square.

GUIDE:
On your right,
Waverly Place—
Bit of Paree in Greenwich Village.

TOURISTS:
My, what charm—
My, what grace!
Poets and peasants on Waverly Place—

GUIDE: *(Reeling off his customary spiel)* Ever since eighteen-seventy Greenwich Village has been the Bohemian cradle of painters, writers, actors, etc., who've gone on to fame and fortune. Today in nineteen thirty-five, who knows what future greats live in these twisting alleys? Come along!

(As the GUIDE *and group cross to the side, the curtain opens, revealing Christopher Street. The scene looks like a cheery postcard of Greenwich Village, with Village characters exhibiting their paintings, grouped in a tableau under a banner which reads "Greenwich Village Art Contest, 1935")*

GUIDE:
> *Here you see*
> *Christopher Street,*
> *Typical spot in Greenwich Village.*

TOURISTS:
> *Ain't it quaint,*
> *Ain't it sweet,*
> *Pleasant and peaceful on Christopher Street?*

(Suddenly the tableau comes to life and all hell breaks loose. An angry artist smashes his painting over the head of an art-contest judge who retires in confusion)
VILLAGER: Here comes another judge.

(A second judge enters, examines the paintings and awards First Prize to a bewildered janitor, whose well-filled ash can the judge mistakes for an ingenious mobile sculpture. The angry artists smash another painting over the second judge's head and all freeze into another tableau)

GUIDE:
> *Here is home,*
> *Christopher Street—*
> *Right in the heart of Greenwich Village.*

VILLAGERS:
> *Life is calm,*
> *Life is sweet,*
> *Pleasant and peaceful on Christopher Street.*

(They freeze into another tableau as a cop comes in, a friend of the street, named LONIGAN. *He goes up to one of the artists, a dynamic, explosive character named* APPOPOLOUS*)*

GUIDE:
> *Here's a famous Village type,*
> *Mr. Appopolous—modern painter,*
> *Better known on this beat*
> *As the lovable landlord of Christopher Street.*

(Music is interrupted)

APPOPOLOUS: *(Breaking out of tableau. To* LONIGAN—*violently)* Throw that Violet woman out of my building!
LONIGAN: What's the beef now, Appopolous?
APPOPOLOUS: I'm very broad-minded, but when a woman gives rumba lessons all night, she's gotta have at least a phonograph!

(Music resumes. LONIGAN *enters building.* WRECK *exits from building, carrying bird cage with canary. He meets a cute young girl named* HELEN *on the street. As they kiss the stage "freezes" again)*

GUIDE:

Here's a guy known as The Wreck,
Football professional out of season,
Unemployed throughout the heat,
Living on nothing on Christopher Street.

(Music is interrupted. Freeze breaks. WRECK kisses HELEN.)

HELEN: Hi! Where you goin' with Dicky Bird?

WRECK: Takin' him down to Benny's to see what I can get for him.

HELEN: Oh, no, Wreck! You can't hock Dicky!

WRECK: Take your choice—we either hock him or have him on toast.

(Music resumes. He goes off. VIOLET comes out of building, followed by LONI-GAN)

VIOLET: Let go of me, ya big phony!

(Freeze. VIOLET drops valise on sidewalk, leans down, pointing angry finger at LONIGAN. She carries large pink doll)

GUIDE:

Here is yet another type.
Everyone knows the famous Violet,
Nicest gal you'd ever meet
Steadily working on Christopher Street.

(Music is cut off)

VIOLET: *(To LONIGAN)* Don't shove me, ya big phony!

LONIGAN: On your way, Violet.

(VIOLET is pushed off by LONIGAN)

VIOLET: *(As she goes)* You're a public servant—I pay your salary! So just you show a little respect!

(Music resumes)

ALL:

Life is gay,
Life is sweet,
Interesting people on Christopher Street.
(Everyone dances)
Such interesting people live on Christopher Street!

A PHILOSOPHER: *(Enters, carrying a sign "MEETING ON UNION SQUARE")* Down with Wall Street! Down with Wall Street!

(He freezes with the others, fist in air)

GUIDE:

Such interesting people live on Christopher Street!

YOGI: *(Enters with sign "PEACE")* Love thy neighbor! Love thy neighbor!

(Another freeze)

TOURISTS:

Such interesting people live on Christopher Street!

(Two MODERN DANCERS enter)

MODERN DANCERS: *(Working hard)*
And one—and two—and three—and four—
And one—and two—and three—and four

TOURISTS:
Such interesting people live on Christopher Street.

ALL:
Look! Look!
Poets! Actors! Dancers! Writers!

Here we live,
Here we love.
This is the place for self-expression.
Life is mad,
Life is sweet,
Interesting people living on Christopher Street!

*(*THE VILLAGERS *perform a mad dance of self-expression, which involves every-thing from a wild can-can to imitations of a symphony orchestra. It works its way up to a furious climax which ends with a last tableau like the opening one, the final punctuation being the smashing of yet another painting over the first judge's head)*

GUIDE: *(Leading* TOURISTS *off, as music fades)*
Come along,
Follow me.
Now we will see MacDougal Alley,
Patchen Place,
Minetta Lane,
Bank Street and
Church Street and
John Street
And Jane.

VALENTI: *(A strange zoot-suited character struts in)* Skeet—skat—skattle-ee-o-do—
APPOPOLOUS: Hey, Mister Valenti, my most desirable studio is about to become available, and I'm going to give you first chance at it.
VALENTI: Down there? *(Pointing to bars of a basement room below street level)* When I go back to living in caves—I'll see ya, Cornball.
(There is a scream offstage and a kid rushes in, carrying a typewriter. APPOPO-LOUS *twists him very expertly. The kid runs off, dropping the typewriter)*
EILEEN: *(Runs on)* Stop him, somebody! He grabbed it right out of my hand! Ruth!
*(*RUTH *enters with two valises)*
RUTH: *(To* APPOPOLOUS*)* Oh, you've got it! Thank goodness! Thank you, sir. Thank you very much.
APPOPOLOUS: *(Pulls typewriter back)* You're welcome, young lady.
RUTH: *(Holding out for case)* Well?
APPOPOLOUS: Only how do I know this property belongs to you? Can you identify yourself?
RUTH: Identify myself?
APPOPOLOUS: Yes, have you got a driver's license?
RUTH: To operate a typewriter?
EILEEN: Now you give that to my sister!
APPOPOLOUS: How do I know it's hers?
RUTH: The letter "W" is missing.

APPOPOLOUS: Now we're getting somewhere. *(Opens case)*

RUTH: It fell off after I wrote my thesis on Walt Whitman.

APPOPOLOUS: *(Closes case)* She's right. Here's your property. The incident is closed. Case dismissed.

RUTH: Who are you, Felix Frankfurter?

APPOPOLOUS: *(Laughs)* You can tell they're out-of-towners. They don't know me!

EILEEN: We don't know anybody. We just got in from Columbus today.

RUTH: Please, Eileen, they're not interested.

HELEN: Columbus? That's the worst town I ever played in.

EILEEN: Are you an actress? *(HELEN nods)* That's what I came to New York for —to break into the theatre—

WRECK: Well, you certainly got the face and build for it—

APPOPOLOUS: *(Steps in to RUTH)* And you, young lady, are you artistic like your sister?

RUTH: No. I haven't the face and build for it.

EILEEN: Don't listen to her. She's a very good writer—and very original.

RUTH: Yes. I'm the only author who never uses a "W." *(She picks up case and valise)* Come on, Eileen. It's getting late, and we've got to find a place.

APPOPOLOUS: *(Laughing)* Remarkable! You're looking for a place, and I got just the place! Step in—I'll show it to you personally!

RUTH: What floor is it on?

APPOPOLOUS: What floor? Let me show you the place before you start raising a lot of objections!

EILEEN: Let's look at it anyway, Ruth. What can we lose?

APPOPOLOUS: Of course! What can you lose?

RUTH: I don't know, Eileen—

APPOPOLOUS: What do you gotta know? *(He opens door)* Step in. *(EILEEN steps through. RUTH follows)* A Chinese opium den it isn't, and a white slaver I ain't! *(APPOPOLOUS steps in, closes door behind him)*

VILLAGERS:
There they go
Down the stairs.
Now they will live
In Greenwich Village.

Life is mad,
Life is sweet.
Interesting people living on
Christopher Street.

(They all dance off)

SCENE 2

The Studio: A basement horror with two daybeds, an imitation fireplace and one barred window that looks out on the street above. It's a cross between a cell in solitary confinement and an iron lung.

APPOPOLOUS: Isn't it just what you've been dreaming about?

RUTH: It's very nice, only—

APPOPOLOUS: Note the imitation fireplace— *(Steps to bed, patting it)* the big comfortable daybeds— (RUTH *goes to bed, starts to pat it;* APPOPOLOUS *takes her hand away and points to window)* Look! Life passes up and down in front of you like a regular parade! *(Some people pass by—only their legs are visible)*

RUTH: Well, really—

APPOPOLOUS: Let me point a few salient features. In here you have a model kitchenette—complete in every detail. (RUTH *goes to door—*APPOPOLOUS *closes it quickly. He goes to bathroom door. She follows)* And over here is a luxurious bathroom— (RUTH *starts to look.* APPOPOLOUS *closes door quickly)*

RUTH: They're awfully small.

APPOPOLOUS: In those two rooms you won't entertain. *(He indicates a hideous painting on the wall)* You see that landscape? That's from my blue-green period.

RUTH: You mean *you* painted that?

APPOPOLOUS: Yes, of course. This studio is merely a hobby—a sanctuary for struggling young artists—and since you are both in the arts, I'm gonna let you have this studio for the giveaway price of sixty-five dollars a month.

RUTH: Sixty-five dollars for *this?*

EILEEN: *(Weakly)* Couldn't we stay here tonight, and then if we like it—
*(*RUTH *shakes head "no")*

APPOPOLOUS: I'll do better than that. You can have the place for a month—on trial—at absolutely no cost to you!

RUTH: Oh, we couldn't let you do that—could we, Eileen?

APPOPOLOUS: And then, if you're not one hundred percent satisfied, I'll give you back your first month's rent!

EILEEN: *(Pathetically)* Please, Ruth—I've got to get to bed.
*(*RUTH *gives her a look, sighs and starts to count out some bills)*

RUTH: Twenty, forty, sixty-one, sixty-two . . .
(There is a tremendous boom from below. The girls freeze in terror as APPOPO-
LOUS *quickly grabs the money from* RUTH*)*

APPOPOLOUS: That's enough.

EILEEN: My God!

RUTH: What—what was that?

APPOPOLOUS: *(Innocently)* What was *what?*

RUTH: That noise—the whole room shook!

APPOPOLOUS: *(Chuckles)* That just goes to show how you'll get used to it. I didn't even notice it.

EILEEN: Get used to it?

APPOPOLOUS: You won't even be conscious of it. A little blasting—the new subway— *(He points to the floor)*

RUTH: You mean they're blasting right underneath us?

APPOPOLOUS: What are you worrying about? Those engineers know how much dynamite to use.

EILEEN: You mean it goes on all the time?

APPOPOLOUS: No—no—they knock off at midnight and they don't start again until six o'clock in the morning! *(Goes to door and turns)* Good night—Sleep tight! *(He goes out)*

RUTH: Yes, Eileen—sleep tight, my darling—and you were in such a hell of a hurry to get to bed!

EILEEN: Ruth, what are we going to do?

RUTH: We're gonna do thirty days. *(EILEEN exits to bathroom with suitcase. RUTH follows, looks in, and steps back in horror)* Thank God, we took a bath before we left Columbus! *(She opens her suitcase and starts to take out her things. Woman with dog passes at window, dog stops and looks through bars)* Oh! You get away from there! *(The woman and her dog go off)*

EILEEN: *(Comes out of bathroom, combing her hair. She is in her pajamas)* I wonder what Billy Honnecker thinks now?

RUTH: He's probably at the country club this minute with Annie Wilkinson, drinking himself to death.

EILEEN: He can have her.

RUTH: Don't you suppose he knows that?

EILEEN: And she can have him too—with my compliments.

RUTH: That's the advantage of not leaving any men behind—you don't have to worry what becomes of them.

EILEEN: Oh, it's different with you. Boys never meant anything in your life.

RUTH: *(Going to bathroom with pajamas)* Not after they got a load of *you* they didn't.

(She goes into bathroom. EILEEN sits on her bed and a moment later a man comes in the front door and calmly crosses to a chair and sprawls out on it)

FLETCHER: Hello. Hot, isn't it? *(He offers EILEEN a cigarette)*

EILEEN: *(Rising fearfully)* I think you're making a mistake. What apartment do you want?

FLETCHER: Is Violet home?

EILEEN: No. No Violet lives here.

FLETCHER: It's all right. Marty sent me.

EILEEN: I don't know any Marty. You'll have to get out of here!

FLETCHER: Aw, don't be like that. I'm a good fella.

EILEEN: I don't care *what* you are! Will you please go!

FLETCHER: Are you sure Violet Shelton doesn't live here?

EILEEN: If you don't get out of here, I'm going to call the police! *(He laughs)* All right—you asked for it—now you're going to get it! *(She goes to front door)*

FLETCHER: Ha! They won't arrest me—I'm a fireman!

EILEEN: *(In the hall)* Help—somebody—help!

(RUTH comes out of the bathroom, stops in surprise as she sees FLETCHER and backs away)

RUTH: Oh, how do you do?

FLETCHER: Hello.

EILEEN: *(Comes in)* Don't "how do you do" him, Ruth! He's nobody! *(She runs behind RUTH)* He just walked in and he won't go away. Make him go 'way, Ruth!

RUTH: *(Diffidently)* Now you go 'way. And stop bothering my sister.

FLETCHER: No.

(WRECK dashes in, still in his shorts)

WRECK: What's the trouble, girls?

EILEEN: This man walked in and he won't go 'way!

WRECK: *(To FLETCHER—who rises)* What's the idea of crashing in on these girls?

FLETCHER: Now don't get yourself excited. It was just a mistake.

WRECK: You bet it was a mistake! Now get movin'!

FLETCHER: *(Goes calmly to door)* Okay *(To girls)* Good evening— *(To WRECK)*

You're the hairiest Madam I ever saw! *(He runs out as* WRECK *starts after him angrily)*

EILEEN: *(Hastily)* Oh, thank you—Mr.—

WRECK: *(Turns)* Loomis—but call me The Wreck.

RUTH: The Wreck?

WRECK: That's what they called me at Trenton Tech. I would have made all-American, only I turned professional. Well, girls, if anyone busts in on you again, just holler. "I'm a ramblin' Wreck from Trenton Tech—and a helluva engineer—" *(He goes off singing)*

EILEEN: Ruth, I'm scared!

RUTH: It's all right, darling, go to bed— *(She leads* EILEEN *to a daybed, then goes to fireplace and bumps her hips)* Aw, the hell with it! Let it spread! *(RUTH switches off light. There's no perceptible difference)* Didn't I just put out the light? *(She pushes button again. Then, she pushes the button a third time)*

EILEEN: There's a lamp post right in front of the window. Pull down the shade.

RUTH: There *isn't* any shade.

EILEEN: No shade? We're practically sleeping on the street!

RUTH: Just wait till I get that Appopolous! *(Sits on bed and winces)* Boy! What Bernarr MacFadden would give for this bed!

EILEEN: Let's go to sleep.

RUTH: Maybe we can forget.

EILEEN: Good night—

RUTH: Good night—

(A kid runs by window, scraping a stick against the iron bars. It sounds like a volley of machine-gun fire. The girls sit up, terrified)

EILEEN: What was that?

RUTH: It sounded like a machine gun!

KID: *(Runs by again, shouts)* Hey, Walyo—wait for me!

EILEEN: *(Wails)* Gee, Ruth—what I got us into.

RUTH: Oh, go to sleep!

(Girls settle back wearily. Drunks are heard singing "Come to Me My Melancholy Baby." They come up to window, their legs visible)

EILEEN: *(Covering herself—shouts to window)* You go 'way from there, you drunken bums!

(Drunks stoop down, leering in)

FIRST DRUNK: Ah! A dame!

RUTH: You go 'way from there or we'll call the police!

FIRST DRUNK: Another dame! Look, Pete! There's two broads—one for you too!

(Wiggling his fingers happily at RUTH*)*

EILEEN: Ruth! Close the window!

RUTH: *Me* close the window!

FIRST DRUNK: No—the hell with her— *(To* EILEEN*)* You close it!

EILEEN: Ruth, please!

SECOND DRUNK: Don't you do it, Ruth!

FIRST DRUNK: Leave me in! I'll close it!

(The cop's legs appear, nightstick swinging)

LONIGAN: What's goin' on here? Come on! Break it up! *(The drunks hurry away.* LONIGAN *stoops, looks in window)* Oh, I get it!

RUTH: I'm awfully glad you came, Officer.

LONIGAN: *(Heavily)* Yeah, I'll bet you are.

RUTH: We just moved in today.

LONIGAN: *(Grimly)* Well, if you're smart, you'll move out tomorrow. I don't go for this stuff on my beat. I'm warning you.

(He goes off. The girls stare at each other in dismay)

EILEEN: Oh, *Ruth!*

RUTH: *(Goes to her dismally)* Now, Eileen, everything's going to be all right.

EILEEN: It's awful!

RUTH: Never mind, Eileen—try and sleep.

EILEEN: I *can't* sleep.

RUTH: Try, darling—make your mind a blank.

EILEEN: I did, but I keep thinking of Ohio. *(RUTH puts arm around EILEEN)*

RUTH: Oh, Eileen—Me too.

(They sing, plaintively)

BOTH:
Why, oh why, oh why, oh—
Why did I ever leave Ohio?
Why did I wander to find what lies yonder
When life was so cozy at home?
Wond'ring while I wander,
Why did I fly,
Why did I roam,
Oh, why oh, why oh
Did I leave Ohio?
Maybe I'd better go home.
Maybe I'd better go home.

(Music continues)

RUTH: *(Rises, defiantly)*
Now listen, Eileen,
Ohio was stifling.
We just couldn't wait to get out of the place,
With Mom saying—"Ruth, what no date for this evening?"

EILEEN:
And Pop with, "Eileen, do be home, dear, by ten—"

BOTH:
Ugh!

RUTH:
The gossipy neighbors
And everyone yapping who's going with who—

EILEEN:
And dating those drips that I've known since I'm four.

RUTH:
The Kiwanis Club Dance.

EILEEN:
On the basketball floor.

RUTH:
Cousin Maude with her lectures on sin—

BOTH:
What a bore!

EILEEN:
Jerry Black!

RUTH:
Cousin Min!

EILEEN:
Ezra Nye!

RUTH:
Hannah Finn!

EILEEN:
Hopeless!

RUTH:
Babbity!

EILEEN:
Stuffy!

RUTH:
Provincial!

BOTH:
Thank heavens we're free!

(By this time each is in her own bed, reveling in newfound freedom. There is a terrific blast from the subway below and they dash terrified into each other's arms and sing hysterically)

BOTH:
Why, oh why, oh why, oh—
Why did we ever leave Ohio?

(They cut off as music continues and go over to RUTH'S *bed, huddling together under the covers)*

BOTH: *(Quietly and sadly)*
Wond'ring while we wander,
Why did we fly,
Why did we roam,
Oh why, oh, why oh—
Did we leave Ohio?
Maybe we'd better go home, (RUTH: *O-H-I-O)*
Maybe we'd better go home.

(They sink back exhausted as the lights dim. There is a fanfare of a bugle reminiscent of "Reveille," followed by the sound of an alarm clock as the lights come up sharply. It is early morning.
RUTH *springs up as if shot from a cannon, turns off the alarm and shakes* EILEEN.
RUTH *is full of determination)*

RUTH: Come on, Eileen. Up and at 'em! Let's get an early start. We're going to take this town. Get up, Eileen!

(She starts briskly toward the bathroom, suddenly winces and clutches her aching back, but limps bravely on. The lights black out)

(There is a dance pantomime depicting the girls' struggle to get ahead in the "Big City" beginning with determined optimism and ending in utter defeat. Everywhere RUTH *goes with her manuscripts, publishers are either out to lunch, in conference, or just not interested. Everywhere* EILEEN *goes, looking for theatre work, she receives many propositions, but they are never for jobs. As the number comes to a finish the two sisters join each other sadly, collapsing glumly on each other's shoulders as the hostile city crowds sing to them "Maybe you'd better go home!" There is a blackout)*

SCENE 3

The Street, same as Scene 1.

ESKIMO PIE MAN: Eskimo Pies—Eskimo Pies—Eskimo Pies—

(RUTH enters from house with milk bottles in a sack)

RUTH: Hey, Eskimo Pies! Will you take five milk bottles? You can cash them in on the corner!

ESKIMO PIE MAN: I got no time for milk bottles! *(He goes. RUTH puts bottles down)*

EILEEN: *(Enters with a large paper bag)* Be careful, Ruth—they're valuable!

RUTH: *(Wearily)* Oh, hello, Eileen. What have you got in the bag?

EILEEN: Food.

RUTH: *(Eagerly)* Food? Let's see! Where'd you get it? *(They sit on the stoop)*

EILEEN: At the food show. I saw people coming out with big bags of samples. So I went in, and I met the nicest boy. He was the floor manager—

RUTH: *(Nods sagely)* Oh, the floor manager—

EILEEN: He loaded me up! We've got enough junk here for a week.

RUTH: *(Taking out small boxes of cereal)* "Pep-O," "Rough-O," "Vita-Bran," "Nature's Broom." We're going to have breakfast all day long.

EILEEN: It's good for you—it's roughage.

RUTH: I'd like to vary it with a little smoothage—like a steak!

(Puts stuff back in bag. VALENTI enters and crosses, snapping his fingers in rhythm)

VALENTI: Skeet—skat—skattle-o-do—

EILEEN: Oh, hello, Mr. Valenti!

VALENTI: Hi yah, gate! I got my eye on you! *Solid.* Skeet—skat—skattle-e-o-do—

RUTH: Who was *that?*

EILEEN: That's Speedy Valenti! He runs that advanced nightclub—the Village Vortex. He's a very interesting boy. He had a cow and he studied dairy farming at Rutgers and then got into the nightclub business.

RUTH: Naturally.

EILEEN: I auditioned for him this morning.

RUTH: You did? How'd he like it?

EILEEN: He said I should get myself a reputation and he'd give me a trial.

(HELEN and WRECK enter)

HELEN: Oh, girls! Can we see you a minute?

RUTH: Sure, Mrs. Loomis—what is it?

HELEN: Well, this is awfully embarrassing—I don't know how to tell you—

WRECK: It's like this. Helen got a wire that her old lady is coming on, which kind of straight-arms me into the alley.

RUTH: Haven't you room?

WRECK: You see, Helen's mother doesn't know about me.

EILEEN: You mean she doesn't know that you're married?

WRECK: Well, you might go a little deeper than that. She doesn't even know we're engaged.

(RUTH *looks at* EILEEN)

HELEN: So, while Mother's in town we thought you wouldn't mind putting The Wreck up in your kitchen?

EILEEN: What?

RUTH: You mean *sleep* in our kitchen?

HELEN: You'd feel a lot safer with The Wreck around. And he's awful handy. He can clean up and he irons swell.

WRECK: But no washing—that's woman's work.

EILEEN: Well, maybe we could do it for one night, but—

RUTH: Wait a minute—

HELEN: Oh, thank you, girls. You don't know how much you're helping us out! *(She goes)*

RUTH: But, look—we haven't—

WRECK: *(Quickly)* Gee, that's swell! *(Follows her)* I'll get my stuff together right away!

RUTH: *(Grimly)* Something tells me you weren't quite ready to leave Columbus.

EILEEN: *(Smiles guiltily and goes to door)* Coming in?

RUTH: No. I'm taking these stories down to the *Manhatter (Holding up envelope with manuscript)* and I'm going to camp beside the water cooler till that editor talks to me.
     See you later—

EILEEN: I won't be here later. I've got a date.

RUTH: With whom?

EILEEN: Frank Lippencott.

RUTH: *Who's* Frank Lippencott?

EILEEN: Didn't I tell you about the boy who manages the Walgreen drugstore on 44th Street?

RUTH: No.

EILEEN: He hasn't let me pay a single lunch check since I've been going there. Today I had a pimento sandwich, a tomato surprise, and a giant double malt —with marble cake.

RUTH: That's right, dear—keep your strength up. You're eating for two now.

EILEEN: I want you to meet him, so when *you're* in the neighborhood, you can have your lunches there too.

RUTH: Gee, since I've been in New York, I only met one man, and he said, "Why the hell don't you look where you're going?" *(Shrugs)* Maybe it's just as well. Every time I meet one I gum it up. I'm the world's leading expert on discouraging men. I ought to write a book about it. "Girls, are you constantly bothered by the cloying attentions of the male sex? Well, here's the solution for you. Get Ruth Sherwood's new best-seller—'One Hundred Easy Ways to Lose a Man.' "

(EILEEN *laughs and goes into house as* RUTH *sings in a spirit of rueful self-mockery)*

Chapter one—
Now the first way to lose a man—
(Sings with exaggerated romanticism)
You've met a charming fellow and you're out for a spin.
The motor fails and he just wears a helpless grin—
Don't bat your eyes and say, "What a romantic spot we're in."

(Spoken flatly)
Just get out, crawl under the car, tell him it's the gasket and fix it in two seconds
  flat with a bobby pin.
That's a good way to lose a man—

(Sung)
He takes you to the baseball game.
You sit knee to knee—
He says, "The next man up at bat will bunt, you'll see."
Don't say, "Oooh, what's a bunt? This game's too hard for little me."

(Spoken)
Just say, "Bunt? Are you nuts?!! With one out and two men on base, and a
left-handed batter coming up, you'll walk right into a triple play just like it
happened in the fifth game of the World Series in 1923."

(Sung)
That's a sure way to lose a man.

A sure sure sure sure way to lose a man,
A splendid way to lose a man—
Just throw your knowledge in his face
He'll never try for second base.
Ninety-eight ways to go.

The third way to lose a man—
The lifeguard at the beach that all the girlies adore
Swims bravely out to save you through the ocean's roar.
Don't say, "Oh, thanks, I would have drowned in just one second more"—

(Spoken)
Just push his head under water and yell, "Last one in is a rotten egg" and race
him back to shore!

(Sung)
That's a swell way to lose a man.

You've found your perfect mate and it's been love from the start.
He whispers, "You're the one to who I give my heart."
Don't say, "I love you too, my dear, let's never never part"—

(Spoken)
Just say, "I'm afraid you've made a grammatical error—it's not 'To who I give
my heart,' it's 'To *whom* I give my heart'—You see, with the use of the preposi-
tion 'to,' 'who' becomes the indirect object, making the use of 'whom' imperative which I can easily show you by drawing a simple chart"—
(Waving good-bye toward an imaginary retreating figure)

That's a fine way to lose a man.

A fine fine fine fine way to lose a man,
A dandy way to lose a man—
Just be more well-informed than he,
You'll never hear "O Promise Me"—

Just show him where his grammar errs
Then mark your towels "hers" and "hers"—
Yes, girls, you too can lose your man
If you will use Ruth Sherwood's plan—
One hundred easy ways to lose a man!

(She goes off as the lights dim)

SCENE 4

BAKER'S Office at the Manhatter.
At Rise: BAKER is seated behind desk. RUTH is seated in a chair opposite, talking fast.
RUTH: —So you see, Mr. Baker, I worked on the Columbus *Globe* a couple of years —society page, sports, everything—and did a lot of writing on the side—but I'm afraid my stuff was a little too sophisticated for Columbus—so I took the big plunge and came to New York—
BAKER: *(Breaks in)* Yes, I know—I did it myself but this is a mighty tough town —Maybe you should have come here gradually—by way of Cleveland first—
RUTH: Yes. They're awfully short of writers in Cleveland—
BAKER: Well, at least a few people in Ohio know you—
RUTH: That's why I left—
BAKER: *(Laughs)* Look, Miss Sherwood, I'd like to help you, but I'm so swamped now—If you just leave your stories here, somebody will read them.
RUTH: *(Puts envelope down)* Are you sure? I get them back so fast that unless I take the subway, they beat me home!
BAKER: We read them, all right— *(He takes eyeglasses from breast pocket)* I had 20–20 vision when I left Duluth.
RUTH: Duluth? Maybe *you* should've come here gradually—and stopped at St. Paul—
BAKER: *(Grimly)* Huh?
RUTH: —95 ways to go—
BAKER: What?
RUTH: Oh, dear—Mr. Baker, please—would you mind if I went out that door and came back in and started all over again?
BAKER: Forget it!
RUTH: And I was so anxious to make a good impression!
BAKER: Well, you made a strong one.
(ASSOCIATE EDITORS enter with pile of manuscripts. They put them on BAKER'S desk)
FIRST EDITOR: Light summer reading, Bob!
BAKER: Oh, no, not any more! *(To RUTH)* See what I mean? Every one of those authors is convinced he's an undiscovered genius!
RUTH: *(Looks at pile of manuscripts, then up to BOB)* Well, what do you advise me to do?

BAKER: *(From desk)*
> *Go home!*
> *Go west!*
> *Go back where you came from!*
> *Oh, why did you ever leave Ohio?*

RUTH: *(Rises)* Because I think I have talent!

BAKER:
> *A million kids just like you*
> *Come to town every day*
> *With stars in their eyes;*
> *They're going to conquer the city,*
> *They're going to grab off the Pulitzer Prize,*
> *But it's a terrible pity*
> *Because they're in for a bitter surprise.*
> *And their stories all follow one line*
> *(Pointing with his arm to* FIRST EDITOR*)*
> *Like his,*
> *(Pointing to* SECOND EDITOR*)*
> *Like his,*
> *(To himself with both hands)*
> *Like mine.*
> *(To* RUTH*)*
> *Born in Duluth,*
> *Natural writer,*
> *Published at seven—genius type—*
> *Wrote the school play,*
> *Wrote the school paper—*
> *Summa cum laude—all of that tripe—*
> *Came to New York,*
> *Got on the staff here—*
> *This was my chance to be heard.*
> *Well, since then I haven't written a word.*

BAKER AND EDITORS: *(Strumming guitars—imaginary)*
> *What a waste,*
> *What a waste,*
> *What a waste of money and time!*

*(*RUTH *turns and goes angrily as* BAKER *looks after her sympathetically)*

FIRST EDITOR:
> *Man from Detroit—*
> *Wonderful Artist—*
> *Went to Picasso—Pablo said "Wow!"*
> *Settled in France,*
> *Bought him a beret,*
> *Lived in Montmartre,*
> *Really learned how,*
> *Came to New York—had an exhibit,*

> *Art critics made a big fuss,*
> *Now he paints those toothpaste ads on the bus!*

EDITORS AND BAKER:
> *What a waste,*
> *What a waste,*
> *What a waste of money and time!*

SECOND EDITOR:
> *Girl from Mobile,*
> *Versatile actress—*
> *Tragic or comic—*
> *Any old play.*
> *Suffered and starved,*
> *Met Stanislavsky.*
> *He said the world would*
> *Cheer her some day.*
> *Came to New York,*
> *Repertoire ready,*
> *Chekhov's and Shakespeare's and Wilde's—*
> *Now they watch her flipping flapjacks at Childs'.*

EDITORS AND BAKER:
> *What a waste,*
> *What a waste,*
> *What a waste of money and time!*

BAKER:
> *Kid from Cape Cod,*
> *Fisherman's family,*
> *Marvelous singer—big baritone—*
> *Rented his boat,*
> *Paid for his lessons*
> *Starved for his studies*
> *Down to the bone—*
> *Came to New York,*
> *Aimed at the opera—*
> *Sing "Rigoletto" his wish—*
> *At the Fulton Market now he yells "Fish!"*

EDITORS:
> *What a waste,*
> *What a waste,*
> *What a waste of money and time!*

BAKER: *(Looking off after* RUTH*)*
> *Go home! Go west!*
> *Go back where you came from!*
> *(*EDITORS *go.)*
> *Go home!*

(BAKER *goes to his desk, his mind still on* RUTH, *and picks up the envelope containing her manuscripts. He takes them out and starts to read one)*

BAKER: *(Reading)* "For Whom the Lion Roars"—by Ruth Sherwood.
"It was a fine day for a lion hunt. Yes, it was a good clean day for an African lion hunt—a good clean day for a fine clean kill."
(The lights go up on stage left as BAKER continues reading. In the ensuing STORY VIGNETTES, played stage left and musically underscored, RUTH portrays all the heroines. These are RUTH'S ideas of sophisticated writing, and are acted in exaggerated satiric style)
BAKER: *(Reading)* "Sandra Mallory stalked into the clearing with the elephant gun."
(SANDRA MALLORY [RUTH] enters dazzlingly attired in a glamorous version of an African hunting outfit, a huge gun tucked casually under her arm)
BAKER: *(Reading)* "Just behind Sandra was Harry Mallory, her husband, and Randolph Rexford, the guide."
(They enter. REXFORD is an open-shirted, tight-lipped Gary Cooper type and HARRY is a small, ineffectual-looking man in an obvious state of terror, his gun shaking in his hands)
BAKER: *(Reading)* "Nearby they could hear the fine clean roar of the lion."
(There is a loud ominous lion roar)

REXFORD: *(Pointing out front)*
There he is, right in front of you, Mr. Mallory! *(MALLORY points his gun toward the oncoming roars, which become louder and louder as REXFORD continues)* No, not yet—wait until you see his eyes. That will be the fine, clean way to bag the Simba. No—not yet—Not yet, Mr. Mallory—
(MALLORY dashes off, screaming)

SANDRA: *(Flatly)*
My cigarette has gone out. *(She holds her cigarette up to her mouth. Contemptuously)* He ran—Harry, the brave hunter! *(Her hand is trembling exaggeratedly)*

REXFORD: *(Tensely)*
Your hand is trembling, Mrs. Mallory— *(He grabs her hand, helping her light the cigarette)*

SANDRA: *(Conscious of his grasp)*
It is nothing.

BAKER: *(Reading)* "He gripped her hard. It was a clean fine grip. She remembered Harry's grip. Like clean, fine oatmeal. Suddenly Sandra Mallory felt the beat, beat, beat of Africa—"
(Drums heard nearby)

SANDRA: *(Sexily to REXFORD as she undulates to the rhythm)*
Rexford—why do you hate me?

REXFORD: *(Tight-lipped)*
I have my job—Mrs. Mallory—and Mr. Mallory is your husband.

(There is a roar and terrified scream from offstage)

SANDRA: *(Calmly)*
He *was* my husband. *(She drops her gun and walks toward him passionately)*
Rexford—

REXFORD: *(Moving toward her with equal passion)*
  Mrs. Mallory—

SANDRA: *(Stepping nearer)*
  Rexford—

REXFORD: *(Nearer—and now seething)*
  Sandra—

SANDRA: *(Throwing her arms around him)*
  Randolph! *(He bends her backwards in a movie kiss)*

BAKER: *(Incredulous)* No!
  (There is a blackout on the African scene, as BAKER *picks up the next manuscript a little more cautiously)*

BAKER: *(Reading)* "Twentieth-Century Blues." "It was squalid in that one room flat in Williamsburg without the windows, with the gray peeling plaster and the sound of rats scurrying inside the walls and the scratching phonograph across the hall screaming gee I'd like to see you lookin' swell baby diamond—" *(BAKER finally has to take a deep breath and plunge on)* "—bracelets Woolworth doesn't sell baby and Danny coming in gray and drawn like the gray plaster coming in clutching his guts with the gray rats inside his walls too yeah the gray rat pains of hunger yeah the twentieth-century hunger yeah—"
  (DANNY enters, a ragged proletarian figure in his undershirt, in the depths of despair and hunger. He is followed by ESSIE [RUTH], *ludicrously ragged and obviously somewhat with child. They speak in the singsong Brooklynese used in the social-problem dramas of the '30's)*

ESSIE: *(Dully)*
  Danny—when we gonna get married?

DANNY:
  When—when—when—always naggin'—

ESSIE:
  They're talkin'—the neighbors are talkin'. Mamma looks at me funny like.

DANNY:
  It takes money, dream boat, to get married. The green stuff with the pictures of Lincoln—

ESSIE:
  Lincoln should see me now. Remember how swell life was gonna be— We was gonna have everything—a four-star trip to the moon—diamonds —yachts—shoes!

DANNY:
  Baby—

ESSIE:
  What's left, Danny—what's left?
  (They approach each other lumberingly with the same growing passion as in the first vignette)

DANNY:
(Stepping closer, arms open)
Baby—

ESSIE:

Danny—

DANNY:

Baby—

ESSIE: *(Clutching him in an embrace)*
Danny!

BAKER: No!
(There is a blackout on the vignette as he hurls the script down and very warily picks up the third.)
"Exit Laughing"—"Everyone agreed that Tracy Farraday was marvelous. Everyone agreed that this was her greatest acting triumph. Everyone agreed that her breath-taking performance in 'Kiss Me, Herman' was the climax of a great career."
(The lights go up on elegantly dressed party. Guests are discovered in a tableau)
"Everyone agreed that the plush opening night party at the Astor Hotel was a memorable occasion."
(Everyone is indulging in upper-class merriment, with laughter and hysterical chitchat. TRENT FARRADAY, a stuffy society type, is kissing a girl as he holds her in a deep embrace)

WOMAN GUEST: *(Looking off)*
Here comes Tracy now!

ALL GUESTS:
Tracy!
(TRACY enters in superb evening clothes—the perfect picture of the glamorous actress. She takes a glamorous pose)

BAKER: *(Reading)* "Everyone agreed that perhaps Tracy drank a bit too much."
(TRACY suddenly staggers in cross-eyed, exaggerated drunkenness)

TRACY: *(Tallulah-ish)*
Has anyone seen that silly old husband of mine?
(TRACY staggers to TRENT—taps him on shoulder. He is still deep in the embrace)
O, Trent—*(TRENT looks up from kiss)* Have you got a match?

TRENT:

Tracy—I'm leaving—I have found someone who needs me—appreciates me—

TRACY:

You cahn't!

TRENT: *(Exiting with girl)*
You are not a woman, Tracy. You are a billboard.

TRACY: *(After him)*
No, no, Trent—I'll be different—I will—Don't go!

BAKER: *(Reading)* "Everyone agreed that Tracy was a hypochondriac. Otherwise, why did she always carry a bottle of iodine?"
(TRACY, throughout speech, is rummaging through her purse, pulls out red bottle of iodine and downs the contents)

TRACY: *(With bitter abandon, giving her greatest performance)*
   Everybody! On with the party!
    (She executes a wild fandango—then suddenly clutching her midriff in a paroxysm of agony, she crashes to the floor)

MALE GUEST:
   Tracy!

WOMAN GUEST:
   Ah—she's just passing out!

TRACY: *(Pulling herself up on one elbow with difficulty—gallant to the end)*
   Yes! Everyone agrees—I'm just passing out—exit laughing! Ha—Ha—Ha—Ha!
   (She laughs wildly and falls back dead, after a last convulsive twitch)

GUESTS: *(Raising glasses in a toast to a noble lady, singing in solemn chorale fashion)*
What a waste,
What a waste,
What a waste of money and time!

(BAKER joins in the chorus—hurling his script down on the desk)

  Blackout

SCENE 5

The Street. At Rise: MRS. WADE *and* HELEN *come on.*
MRS. WADE: Whatever possessed you to move into a dreadful neighborhood like this, Helen? How do you ever expect to meet a nice young man down here?
HELEN: Oh, Mother, please! Let me live my own life!
MRS. WADE: *(Climbing steps—turning from top before going into house)* Life! You're just a child! You don't know what life is!
*(Exits into house—*HELEN *following.* VALENTI *enters, followed by two* BOP GIRLS. FRANK LIPPENCOTT *enters. He carries a box of candy)*
VALENTI: Skeet—skat—skattle-e-o-do— *(To girls)* Don't bother me, kids! Wait until you grow up!
(He's off, followed by kids. EILEEN *comes on and sees* FRANK *peering in their window)*
EILEEN: Oh, hello, Frank!
FRANK: Hello, Eileen! I just came down during my lunch hour. I've been thinking about you all morning.
EILEEN: You have?
FRANK: I brought you some chocolate-covered cherries we're running. We're featuring them all this week during our annual one-cent sale.
EILEEN: *(Taking candy from him)* You're sweet.
FRANK: Well, I've got to get back to the drugstore. It's pandemonium down there.
EILEEN: Don't forget—we expect you for dinner tonight. I want you to meet my sister—she's in your neighborhood a lot.

FRANK: Oh—I'll be here all right.

EILEEN: Thanks for the chocolate-covered cherries.

FRANK: 'Bye, Eileen—

EILEEN: 'Bye, Frank!

(She watches him go off and, starry-eyed, starts to sing)
Mm—Mmm—
I'm a little bit in love.
Never felt this way before—
Mm—Mmm—
Just a little bit in love
Or perhaps a little bit more.

When he
Looks at me
Everything's hazy and all out of focus.
When he
Touches me
I'm in the spell of a strange hocus-pocus.
It's so
I don't know
I'm so
I don't know
I don't know—but I know
If it's love
Then it's lovely!

Mm—Mmm—
It's so nice to be alive
When you meet someone who bewitches you.
Will he be my all
Or did I just fall
A little bit
A little bit in love?

(BOB BAKER enters, goes to grill window and looks in. EILEEN *pulls ribbon off candy box, goes to steps. She sees* BAKER *and stares coldly)*

EILEEN: *Well?*

BAKER: *(Looking up from window)* I was just looking for the young lady who lives in there—my name's Baker—Robert Baker—

EILEEN: Did *Marty* send you?

BAKER: I beg your pardon.

EILEEN: I hate to ruin your afternoon, Mr. Baker, but Violet doesn't live here any more.

BAKER: Violet?

EILEEN: You might tell Marty and all the boys. It'll save them a trip.

BAKER: I'm afraid you've got me confused with somebody else.

EILEEN: I have?

BAKER: Yes. I'm looking for Ruth Sherwood. She lives here, doesn't she?

EILEEN: Who—are you, Mr. Baker?

BAKER: I'm an associate editor of the *Manhatter*.

EILEEN: Oh, oh, I'm terribly sorry! Ruth'll be furious—I'm her sister, Eileen.

BAKER: How do you do, Miss Sherwood?

EILEEN: Ruth isn't in right now, but I'm sure she'll be right back. Won't you come in and wait?

BAKER: No, thanks. I'll drop by later.

EILEEN: You're sure, now?

BAKER: Oh, yes—

EILEEN: Because I know Ruth must be terribly anxious to see you—

BAKER: Well?

EILEEN: How about a nice, cool drink?

BAKER: Not now—thanks, Miss Sherwood—

EILEEN: Oh—*Eileen!*

BAKER: Eileen—

EILEEN: Mr. Baker—I mean, Robert—I have a wonderful idea! Why don't you come back and take pot luck with us?

BAKER: Well, I don't know—

EILEEN: Oh, please! I'm making a special dish tonight!

BAKER: Okay—what time?

EILEEN: Any time after seven!

BAKER: Swell, Eileen—see you later.

EILEEN: 'Bye, Bob!

(*She watches him go—and, with the same starry-eyed look as before, she sings*)

Mm—Mmm—
I'm a little bit in love
Never felt this way before
Mm—Mm—
(*Music continues*)

(LONIGAN *enters slowly*)
O hello, Officer!

LONIGAN: (*Suspiciously*) Yeah.

(THE WRECK *enters and goes to house. He is carrying a rolled-up Army mattress*)

WRECK: I borrowed a mattress, Eileen. That floor in your place is awful hard!

(WRECK *disappears into house.* LONIGAN *looks warily to* EILEEN, *who turns, startled, and puts a hand to her mouth*)

Blackout

SCENE 6

The Back Yard. This is the "garden" that APPOPOLOUS boasts about. It's a dismal place, sunk deep among the tenements that surround it. There are a moldy tree, a couple of chairs and a bench. Across from the girls' kitchen we see the back entrance of NINO'S, an Italian restaurant.

At Rise: WRECK is at an ironing board, pressing some of the girls' things.

WRECK: "I'm a rambling Wreck—From Trenton Tech—And a helluva engineer—"

(WAITER *comes out of* NINO'S *and is joined by Italian* CHEF)

CHEF: E arrivato la padrone— E meglio cominciare a lavorare.

WAITER: Peccato. Si sta cosi bene qui fuore.

CHEF: Be. Cosi e la vita.

(RUTH *comes in from kitchen)*

RUTH: Any mail?

WRECK: Yeah, one of your stories came back.

RUTH: From the *Manhatter?*

WRECK: No, *Collier's.* (RUTH *picks up manuscript in envelope at windowsill, changing address with a pencil)* Hot, ain't it?

RUTH: Yah. I feel as if I'm living in my own little world, mailing these to myself.

WRECK: Hey, which way do you want these pleats turned?

RUTH: *(Glances at him wearily)* Toward Mecca.

(The phone rings. WRECK *goes to windowsill and answers it)*

WRECK: The Sherwood residence—who do you want?—Eleanor? You mean Eileen—She's not in. *(Annoyed)* This is the butler—Who the hell are *you?*

RUTH: *(Grabbing phone)* Wreck! Hello? . . . Who is this, please? . . . Chick Clark? Oh, yes, Mr. Clark. This is her sister—Ruth . . . No, she's not in right now . . . any minute . . . I'll tell her . . . 'Bye. *(Hangs up. Makes note on pad at windowsill)*

WRECK: That Eileen does all right for herself. And the funny part of it is, she's a good girl.

RUTH: *(Eyeing him)* When did you find *that* out?

WRECK: No, you sense those things. I never made a pass at you, but I could swear *you're* all right.

RUTH: That's the story of my life.

(She goes off with manuscript as HELEN *enters)*

WRECK: Hy'ah, Sugar Foot!

HELEN: Hi.

WRECK: Do you miss me, honey?

HELEN: Of course I miss you. Now *I* have to do all the housework. *(Looking at laundry)* Huh! You never ironed that good for me!

WRECK: Now look, honey—!

*(MRS. WADE *appears in street above them.* HELEN *ducks behind ironing board, her rear facing the audience)*

MRS. WADE: *(Staring at* WRECK*)* Well, I never!

WRECK: What are *you* lookin' at, you old bat?

MRS. WADE: How dare you! *(She goes off indignantly)*

WRECK: *(Shouts after her)* Didn't you ever see a man in shorts before?

HELEN: *(Wails)* Wreck! That was Mom!

WRECK: You mean that old wagon was your mother?

HELEN: You've got to get out of here!

WRECK: Where am I gonna sleep?

HELEN: If we could scrape up a few dollars you could stay at the "Y" till Mother leaves.

WRECK: We're tryin' to dig up a coupla bucks and your mother's got a mattressful!

HELEN: If only we had somethin' left to hock.

WRECK: Hey—wait a minute! *(Goes to kitchen)* If anyone comes, whistle "Dixie."

(There is a blast from the subway. HELEN *jumps as* WRECK *reappears with APPOPOLOUS' "blue-green" canvas)*

HELEN: That's one of Appopolous'. They won't lend you a dime on it!

WRECK: This fancy frame might be good for a coupla bucks. Take it over to Benny's and see what you can get on it!

(HELEN exits with picture. DELIVERY KID enters from street with basket of vegetables)

KID: *(Adoringly)* Hey, Wreck—getting ready for the football season?

WRECK: Oh, I keep in shape!

KID: *(Centering the "ball"—a head of cabbage)* Hey—signals?

WRECK: 45—26—7—hip! *(WRECK catches ball)*

CHEF: *(Enters in front of NINO'S—to KID)* E tu che diavalo fai con quel cavalo?

KID: *(To WRECK)* Pass.

(WRECK passes to KID—who passes to WAITER, who catches cabbage in his stomach)

CHEF: Che pazzerela! *(Waving an angry hand at KID, who passes him basket with vegetables. CHEF exits)*

KID: Well, you certainly look in good shape for the football season.

WRECK: Yeah—for all the good it does me! *(Goes wearily back to ironing and sings)*

Look at me now
Four years of college
Famous professors
Tutoring me
Scholarship kid
Everything paid for
Food and vacations
All of it free
Day that I left
Everyone gathered
Their cheering still rings in my ears—

(Carried away by memories, he executes some of the old cheers with great vigor)

Ray Wreck rah
Rah Wreck ray
Rah Wreck
Wreck rah
Rah Wreck Wreck
W-e-c, R-e-k, R-e-q
Wreck, we love you!
(Singing bravura)
'Cause I could pass a football
Like nothin' you have ever seen!

(A crowd has gathered on the street, watching him. They cheer)

Couldn't spell a lick
Couldn't do arithmetic
One and one made three
Thought that dog was c-a-t
But I could pass a football
Like nothing you have ever seen

Couldn't write my name
Couldn't translate "je vous aime"

Never learned to read
Mother Goose or André Gide
But I could pass a football
Like nothing you have ever seen

Couldn't figure riddles
Puzzles made me pout
Where the hell was Moses when the lights went out?
I couldn't even tell red from green
Get those verbs through my bean
But I was buddies with the Dean
Like nothing you have ever seen

Passed without a fuss
English Lit and Calculus
Never had to cram
Even passed the bar exam
Because I passed that football
Like nothing you have ever seen

Then there was the week
Albert Einstein came to speak
Relativity
Guess who introduced him? Me!
'Cause I could pass a football
Like nothing you have ever seen

Had no table manners
Used ta dunk my roll
Always drunk the water from the fingerbowl
Though I would not get up for any she
The Prexy's mom—age ninety-three
Got up and gave her seat to me
Like nothing you did ever see

In our Hall of Fame
There's a statue with my name
There we stand, by heck
Lincoln, Washington and Wreck
'Cause I could pass that football
Like nothing you have ever seen!

(WRECK and CROWD of assorted VILLAGERS do a "football" dance, with WRECK ending up with a pile of players, hopelessly outclassed. He sticks his head out from under, weakly)

'Cause I could pass that football!
Like nothing you have ever—ever seen!

(CROWD pulls away. WRECK staggers and collapses in their arms. At the end of number, the CROWD goes off. HELEN enters with pawn ticket)
HELEN: Two bucks—here's the ticket.
EILEEN: *(Enters from studio)* Gee, Wreck—the laundry looks swell.
HELEN: *(Coldly)* Too bad he's leaving, isn't it?
EILEEN: Oh, is he?

HELEN: Yes, and it's about time, too.

(RUTH *enters from alley)*

WRECK: Stop racin' your motor! I told her there was nothing to it!

RUTH: Nothing to *what?*

EILEEN: Ruth, do you know what she had the nerve to insinuate?

RUTH: Was it something with sex in it?

WRECK: Why, if I thought about Eileen in that way—May God strike me dead on this spot! *(He raises his hand solemnly and there's a tremendous Boom! from below. He shrinks guiltily)*

RUTH: *(Looking up)* He's everywhere all right.

HELEN: Come on, Wreck!

(They go off. VIOLET enters from house)

VIOLET: *(Cheerfully)* Hello, girls.

RUTH: *(Stares)* Hello.

VIOLET: I'm Violet. I used to live in this fleabag before you girls got it.

EILEEN: Oh, so *you're* Violet.

VIOLET: Say, have I had any callers the last coupla weeks—since you kids moved in?

RUTH: *(Grimly)* One or two.

VIOLET: I thought so. A lot of my friends don't know I moved yet. In case they come around—would you mind giving out my new cards? *(She takes thick pack of calling cards from purse and hands them to* EILEEN*)* Thanks loads. So long. *(She goes)*

RUTH: The spiritual type.

(EILEEN carries cards to windowsill)

EILEEN: *(Looking at note pad)* Oh, did Chick Clark call?

RUTH: Yes. Who's he?

EILEEN: He's a newspaperman. I met him in an elevator. We got to talking and I told him about you. He seemed very interested in you.

RUTH: So interested in me, I'll bet he can't wait to get you alone.

EILEEN: What've we got for dinner, Ruth?

RUTH: What do you think? Spaghetti and meat balls.

EILEEN: Haven't we polished that off yet? We've had it all week!

RUTH: *(Flatly)* It closes tonight.

EILEEN: Well, we simply can't give that to Bob.

RUTH: Bob? I can't keep up with you. Who's *Bob?*

EILEEN: You know, Bob Baker, from the *Manhatter.* Don't play dumb!

RUTH: Mr. Baker! No! *(Turns* EILEEN *around)* Where did you meet him?

EILEEN: He dropped by to see you, and naturally I asked him to dinner.

RUTH: Naturally! *(Grabs* EILEEN, *kisses her)* Oh, darling! You are terrific! I'd never have the nerve!

EILEEN: Well, for goodness sake, why not? He's just a *boy*—

RUTH: *(Looks around helplessly)* How can we fix this dump up a little? *(Closing kitchen door)* Eileen, promise me you won't take him in there!

EILEEN: Of course not. We'll eat in the garden—al fresco.

RUTH: Ah—

EILEEN: Oh, dear—I just remembered. I asked Frank over tonight.

RUTH: Who?

EILEEN: You know—Walgreen's—

RUTH: Oh, no! How can you mix a soda jerk with an editor?

EILEEN: He's *not* a jerk! He's the manager!

RUTH: Okay—okay—Gee, if a man like Mr. Baker comes to see me personally, he must really be interested!

EILEEN: Of course he's interested.

RUTH: And we can't even offer him a cocktail.

EILEEN: We could tell him it's too hot to drink.

RUTH: *(Nods)* But cold enough for spaghetti.

EILEEN: Hmmm—smell that chicken cacciatore at Nino's. Maybe I ought to have a little talk with Mr. Nino.

RUTH: Do you know him, too?

EILEEN: No, but I will—he's our neighbor, isn't he?
(She goes into NINO'S. CHICK CLARK enters from street above)

CHICK: Hello. *(Coming down stairs, consulting matchbook)* I'm lookin' for a party named Sherwood—Eleanor Sherwood.

RUTH: You mean Eileen. You must be Mr. Clark?

CHICK: Yeah. Who are you?

RUTH: I'm her sister.

CHICK: *(Doubtfully)* Her sister? She's a blonde, *good-looking* kid, ain't she?

RUTH: *(Grimly)* Yes, she's a blonde, good-looking kid.

CHICK: *(Loosening his collar)* Wow, it's absolute murder down here, ain't it? *(Staring overhead)* What is this—an abandoned mine shaft?

RUTH: Are you planning to be with us long, Mr. Clark?

CHICK: Eileen asked me to take pot luck with her.

FRANK: *(Offstage)* Hello? Anyone home? *(FRANK appears at window in studio)* Oh, hello, the front door was open. Is Eileen home?

RUTH: You're Mr. Lippencott, aren't you? Come in.
(She motions to steps. Door opens. LIPPENCOTT appears, carrying bottle of red wine. Trips down stairs. Recovers himself. Pulls out comb and combs hair)

FRANK: Gee, I'm sorry. I didn't know there was any—*(Shakes hands with RUTH)*

RUTH: Oh, that's all right. Everybody does that.

FRANK: I guess you're Eileen's sister. I can see a family resemblance, all right.

RUTH: Why, I'm very flattered.

FRANK: Of course, you're a different type.

RUTH: Yes, I see what you mean. Eileen'll be back in a minute—*(Glancing to café)* She's just fixing dinner. *(Looking at CHICK)* Oh, I want you to meet Mr. Clark—
(FRANK goes to CHICK, to shake hands. CHICK ignores his hand)

CHICK: There ain't too much oxygen down here as it is.

RUTH: Mr. Lippencott is with Walgreen's.

CHICK: Yeah? I buy all my clothes there.

FRANK: No, it's a drugstore.

CHICK: *(Groans and looks at bottle with interest)* What's in the bottle?

FRANK: *(To CHICK coldly)* A very fine California Burgundy-type wine. *(To RUTH)* I thought it would go good with the spaghetti. *(Hands her wine)* It's a special we're running this week.

RUTH: *(Looking at bottle sadly)* So's our spaghetti.

FRANK: Huh?

RUTH: Has this heat affected your business?

FRANK: Why, we pray for heat waves.

CHICK: Oh, you *do*, eh?

FRANK: Our fountain turnover is double. I'm lucky to get away at all.

RUTH: Oh, *we're* the lucky ones.

EILEEN: *(Entering, to FRANK)* Oh, Frank, I'm terribly sorry I wasn't here to greet you! *(To RUTH)* Ruth, what do you think?

RUTH: What?

EILEEN: Mr. Nino's in Italy. He won't be back till Labor Day. *(To CHICK, in dismay)* Oh, hello, Mr. Clark!

CHICK: Hy'ah, gorgeous!

EILEEN: Oh, Ruth, this is that newspaper gentleman I was telling you about who was so interested in you.

CHICK: That's right. I gave the city editor a big pitch already—*(Lasciviously)* You won't believe this, baby, but I've been turnin' you over in my mind all afternoon.

(EILEEN laughs uneasily as RUTH nods)

FRANK: Gee, this is great. I always wanted to live in the Village in a place like this.

RUTH: What stopped you?

FRANK: Well, in my position in the drugstore you've got to keep up appearances.

RUTH: I see. Where the Liggetts speak only to the Walgreens and the Walgreens speak only to God.

(CHICK grabs EILEEN'S hand. She pulls away)

EILEEN: I'd better set the table. *(Goes to kitchen)* Where shall we dine—inside or outside?

CHICK: Which is *this?*

(BOB BAKER appears from street, waving envelope with manuscript)

BAKER: Hello!

EILEEN: Oh, hello, Bob!

RUTH: Hello, Mr. Baker! Sorry I wasn't in when you called.

BAKER: That's all right—

RUTH: I'd like you to meet Mr. Clark—Mr. Lippencott—This is Mr. Baker—

FRANK: Pleased to meet you. *(Holds out his hand, which BAKER shakes)*

CHICK: What the hell is this, a block party?

RUTH: You're quite a card, aren't you, Mr. Clark? *(Puts wine on windowsill)* Mr. Lippencott brought you some wine, dear.

EILEEN: Oh, how sweet! Shall we sit down? *(She motions the others to join her and there is a general embarrassed shuffling about for chairs. She pulls BOB down beside her on her chair. CHICK brings a chair forward and RUTH, assuming it is for her, goes toward it, but CHICK sits on it himself. She gets her own and the five wind up in a tight uncomfortable group facing one another with nothing to say. EILEEN, after a pause)* Well—here we are—all together—

(There is a dry discordant vamp in the orchestra expressing the atmosphere of embarrassed silence, which is repeated during every pause in the following song and conversation. It seems to grow more mocking and desperate at each repetition. After another pause they all start speaking at once very animatedly and then dwindle off. Pause again. EILEEN giggles nervously. Pause)

FRANK: *(Starting bravely)* At the bottom of the vanilla— *(He has a terrific coughing fit.* BAKER *slaps his back, and he sits down—and combs his hair)* It's nothing. *(Vamp)*

EILEEN: *(Singing, over-brightly, after a pause)*
Mmmm—mmmm—it's so nice to sit around—
And chat—
Nice people, nice talk,
A balmy summer night,
A bottle of wine—
Nice talk—nice people,
Nice feeling—nice talk—
The combination's right
And everything's fine—

Nice talk—nice people
It's friendly—it's gay
To sit around this way.
What more do you need?
Just talk—and people.
For that can suffice
When both the talk and people are so nice—

(She finishes lamely as the vamp is played again. Pause)

FRANK: *(Settling back in chair with a hollow, unconvincing laugh)* Ha ha—Funny thing happened at the counter today—Man comes in—Sort of tall-like—Nice-looking refined-type—Red bow tie—and all. Well, sir, he orders a banana split —That's our jumbo special—twenty-eight cents—Three scoops—chocolate, strawberry, vanilla—choice of cherry or caramel sauce—chopped nuts— whipped cream—Well, sir, he eats the whole thing—I look at his plate and I'll be hornswoggled if he doesn't leave the whole banana—doesn't touch it—not a bite—Don't you see?—If he doesn't like bananas, what does he order a banana split for?—He coulda had a sundae—nineteen cents—Three scoops—Chocolate —Strawberry—Vanilla— *(He dwindles off as vamp is played again)*

RUTH: *(Making a noble attempt to save the day)* I was re-reading *Moby Dick* the other day and—Oh, I haven't read it since—I'm sure none of us has—It's worth picking up again—It's about this whale— *(Her futile attempt hangs heavy on the air. Vamp again)*

CHICK: *(Even he is driven by desperation to attempt sociability)* Boy, it's hot! Reminds me of that time in Panama—I was down there on a story—I was in this, well, dive—And there was this broad there—What was her name?—Marquita? —Maroota? *(Warming to his subject)* Ahh, what's the difference what her name was—That dame was built like a brick—

(A sharp drum crash cuts him off and the vamp is played with hysterical speed and violence. The four others spring to their feet horrified and, as CHICK stands by puzzled, they cover up with a sudden outburst of animated talk and laughter expressed by a rapid rendition of "Nice People, Nice Talk" with EILEEN singing an insane coloratura obbligato as the music builds to a thunderous close)

ALL:
Nice people, nice talk,
A balmy summer night,

A bottle of wine—
Nice talk, nice people,
Nice feeling—nice talk.
The combination's right
And everything's fine.

Nice talk, nice people—
It's friendly, it's gay
To sit around this way.
What more do you need?
Just talk and people.
For that can suffice
When both the talk and people are so nice
It's nice!

(A closing orchestra chord)

RUTH: *(Gets bottle)* Let's have a drink, shall we?

EILEEN: *(To* FRANK*)* Do we need ice?

FRANK: No, this wine should be served at the temperature of the room.

CHICK: Then you'd better cook it a coupla hours.

APPOPOLOUS: *(Entering from stairs)* Congratulate me, young ladies! Today is the big day! I'm entering my painting in the WPA Art Contest! *(He goes into studio)*

BAKER: Ruth, who's that?

RUTH: Our landlord—Rasputin.

APPOPOLOUS: *(Comes back, heavily)* What kind of a funny game is going on here? Where is it? Who took it?

RUTH: What?

APPOPOLOUS: You know everybody who goes into your apartment.

RUTH: We don't know *half* of them.

APPOPOLOUS: Please, I know you girls are hard up. Tell me what you did with it and there'll be no questions asked.

EILEEN: You don't think we stole it?

APPOPOLOUS: If you didn't—who did?

RUTH: Maybe it was the same gang that swiped the Mona Lisa.

APPOPOLOUS: *(Goes angrily)* You won't be so humorous when I come back with a cop!

RUTH: *(To* BAKER, *anxiously)* I hope you don't take any of that seriously, Mr. Baker.

BAKER: Of course not.

FRANK: *(Scared)* Do you think he's really going to call the police?

EILEEN: The police won't pay any attention to him—he's always calling them!

CHICK: Well, let's crack that bottle before the wagon gets here!

EILEEN: I'll open it and get some glasses. Do you want to help me, Frank?

CHICK: *(Stepping in)* I'll help ya, Eleanor—*(Turning to* FRANK*)* You stay out here and hand them a few laughs.

(EILEEN starts in to house. CHICK follows)

FRANK: Oh, is that so? *(Trips up steps into house)*

RUTH: *(To* BAKER, *sadly)* If you'd like to make your getaway now, Mr. Baker, I'll understand.

BAKER: No, I'm enjoying it.

RUTH: Did you get a chance to read those stories?

BAKER: I certainly did!

(WRECK *and* HELEN *appear in street*)

RUTH: Well, what did you think?

WRECK: *(Coming down stairs)* Oh, I'm sorry, Ruth—didn't know you had company.

HELEN: *(With him)* Can we come in?

RUTH: *(Groans)* Yes, please do. *(To kitchen)* Two more glasses, Eileen!

WRECK: I talked it over with Helen, and she wants to apologize.

RUTH: *(Quickly)* That's not necessary—Mr. Baker—This is Mr. Loomis—and his intended. *(They shake hands.* BAKER *eyes his shorts anxiously)* Mr. Loomis is in training.

BAKER: Oh.

(FRANK *enters from studio with tray and glasses of wine.*)

FRANK: *(From top of steps)* This wine was—*(Stepping carefully down)* made by a Frenchman in California.

(EILEEN *comes through studio door, carrying two more glasses*)

EILEEN: Oh, hello there—*(She hands glass to* RUTH. CHICK *follows through studio door, carrying his own glass.* FRANK *passes tray to* WRECK *and* HELEN *and moves upstage with tray)* What a magnificent bouquet!

RUTH: Drink up, everyone—it's later than you think! Here's to us and Burgundy, California!

(They all have raised glasses in toast. There's a "boom" from below. FRANK jumps and spills his wine all over his new white suit.)

FRANK: Gee, what was that?

EILEEN: *(Stares at the wine stain miserably)* Oh, Frank, I'm terribly sorry!

FRANK: *(Looking down at his suit pathetically)* What—what happened?

RUTH: The new subway—*(Wipes off wine)*

FRANK: *(Wails)* Does red wine stain?

EILEEN: Not if you rub salt on it. *(Wipes off wine)*

CHICK: You better get a bagful!

FRANK: I just got this suit. It's brand new!

CHICK: Ah, you can't even notice it!

(He starts to laugh. They all join in, hysterically. FRANK stands in the center, stricken. HELEN sinks to the floor in her laughter)

FRANK: *(Backing to stairs, he starts up them)* Well, if you think it's so funny, I'll go!

EILEEN: *(Starts to follow)* Frank—don't go! Wait! *(Turning to the others)* Oh, dear —he's really angry.

MRS. WADE: *(Offstage)* Helen, are you in there?

HELEN: Yes, Mother.

RUTH: Won't you come in, Mrs. Wade?

MRS. WADE: *(Entering)* Most certainly not. Helen, I want you to come out of there immediately!

HELEN: But, Mother.

MRS. WADE: I will not have you associating with those depraved women and their consort!

RUTH and EILEEN: *What?*

WRECK: *Who's* a consort?

HELEN: Please, Mother—

MRS. WADE: Not another word. You come right along with me. Don't you dare talk to my Helen again. You're not fit to associate with decent people! *(She pushes* HELEN *out)*

WRECK: I'm gonna wait till Mother's Day—*(Making fist)* and sock her! *(He goes)*

EILEEN: Bob, I don't know what you must think of us, but really, it isn't so.

BAKER: *(Grins)* I'm sure it isn't.

RUTH: Well, you must admit—for a place with a bad location and no neon sign, we're doing a hell of a business.

EILEEN: *(Brightly)* Dinner, anyone?

BAKER: Fine!

EILEEN: *(Going to kitchen)* I'd better heat the entrée.

CHICK: *(Following close behind)* We'll warm it up together, Eleanor! *(They go off)*

RUTH: Funny, I'm not a bit hungry.

BAKER: I'm starving. And I smell something delicious!

RUTH: *(Looks at* NINO'S*)* Trade Winds.

EILEEN'S VOICE: Mr. Clark, please! Not while I'm trying to cook!

BAKER: While we have a minute, before anything else happens, I'd like to talk to you about your stories—

RUTH: Oh, do, please! You mean you actually read them yourself?

BAKER: I certainly did—You have a lot of talent, Miss Sherwood—

RUTH: Do you really think so?

BAKER: Yes, I do—*(*RUTH *turns away, tearfully)* What's the matter?

RUTH: Nothing—

BAKER: You're crying—

RUTH: *(Turning back to him)* It's just an allergy I have to good news—

BAKER: You really should have more faith in yourself—

RUTH: Thanks, I'm beginning to—

BAKER: And once you get on the right track, you're going to do some good work.

RUTH: Right track?

BAKER: Look Ruth. Have you ever gone on a safari in the African veldt?

RUTH: No.

BAKER: And have you ever lived in a cold-water tenement?

RUTH: No.

BAKER: Then why do you write that stuff? Write about something you know— something you've actually experienced.

RUTH: I write the things I feel! I put myself in every one of those characters!

BAKER: Then you must be hopelessly repressed.

RUTH: That's a terrible thing to say! I'm the most normal person you'll ever meet!

BAKER: That's a sure sign. All inhibited people think they're normal.

RUTH: Oh! So now I'm inhibited!

BAKER: *(Turns to her)* I'm afraid so—if you claim you're really those frustrated heroines.

RUTH: Repressed! Inhibited! Frustrated! What *else* am I?

BAKER: Don't take it personally—

RUTH: How else can I take it?

BAKER: I'm just trying to help you—

RUTH: What are you, an editor or a psychoanalyst?

BAKER: I should've known better—You can't take it—You'll never get anywhere till you learn humility—

RUTH: When did you learn yours? *(Runs into studio quickly.* BAKER *watches her)*

BAKER: *(With weary anger)*
All right! Good-bye!
You've taught me my lesson!
Get mixed up with a genius from Ohio!
It happens over and over—
I pick the sharp intellectual kind.
Why couldn't this time be different,
Why couldn't she—only be
Another kind—A different kind of girl

(As the lights dim, he pictures the kind of relationship he would like to have, but has never known)

I love a quiet girl,
I love a gentle girl
Warm as sunlight,
Soft, soft as snow.

Her smile, a tender smile,
Her voice, a velvet voice,
Sweet as music,
Soft, soft as snow.

When she is near me
The world's in repose.
We need no words
She sees—She knows.

But where is my quiet girl,
Where is my gentle girl,
Where is the special girl,
Who is soft, soft as snow?

Somewhere—
Somewhere—
My quiet girl.

(As he walks slowly off, RUTH *enters from the kitchen and watches him go, with the hopeless feeling of having lost him)*

RUTH: *(Sings)*
I know a quiet girl,
Hoping—waiting—
But he'll never know.

(The music continues. There is a crash of dishes from the kitchen. RUTH *turns suddenly—looks toward kitchen—her reverie broken)*

EILEEN: *(Offstage)* Now look what you made me do! *(Entering from studio,* CHICK *follows)* The spaghetti—it's all over the kitchen floor! Really, Mr. Clark!

CHICK: You're so darn jumpy—! *(Goes to stairs)* Okay, I'll run down to the corner and get some sandwiches and beer! Be right back! *(He's off)*

EILEEN: Where's Bob?

RUTH: Gone.

EILEEN: Isn't he coming back?

RUTH: If he does, he's crazy after the way I treated him.

EILEEN: Gee, Ruth, what happened?

RUTH: I'd rather not discuss it—I'm too frustrated. *(There's a "boom" from below. She looks down wearily)* Go on! Blow us up and get it over with!

EILEEN: Gee, Ruth, if you start to feel that way, who's going to hold me up?

RUTH: Oh, I'm not worried about you—not while there's a man alive.

EILEEN: After all, men are only an escape.

(The phone rings. EILEEN hurries to it)

RUTH: Comes another escape—

EILEEN: *(On phone)* Sherwood residence—Miss *Ruth* Sherwood?

RUTH: For *me?*

EILEEN: Who's calling please?—What? Wait a minute—Just a second! *(To RUTH)* Ruth, it's Chick Clark's paper. Mr. Bains of the city room wants to talk to you—

(EILEEN hands phone to RUTH)

RUTH: Hello?—Yes—yes, Mr. Bains. This is she—*her*—she. Thank you, Mr. Bains. That's wonderful! Yes, yes, of course. *(To EILEEN)* Paper and pencil quick. Take this down!

(EILEEN reaches over for pad and pencil from window)

EILEEN: What is it? What happened?

RUTH: Yes, Mr. Bains—I'm ready! Sands—Street—Brooklyn—I understand— Yes, right away, Mr. Bains! Thank you—thank you very much. *(She hangs up, looks up excitedly)* I can't believe it!

EILEEN: What did he say? What did he want?

RUTH: He's giving me a chance to show what I can do—an assignment over in Brooklyn!

EILEEN: Brooklyn? What happened there?

RUTH: A Brazilian training ship just came in—like Annapolis—only these fellows are all young coffee millionaires. I'm going aboard to get a human-interest story.

EILEEN: Coffee millionaires! Well, you're not going over there with a run in your stocking! Take it off! *(They sit on bench. Both remove stockings, exchange them. Conversation continues throughout)*

RUTH: What a break! Isn't it wonderful! I'll show him!

EILEEN: Who?

RUTH: Never mind! Inhibited, huh?

EILEEN: What?

RUTH: I'll get a job on my own! Who does he think he is? *(Finished with stocking, she jumps up)* Have you got any money?

EILEEN: Who—*me?*

RUTH: How am I going to get over there?

EILEEN: The milk bottles!

(RUTH picks up bottles near door, grabs her hat and rushes to stairs)

RUTH: *(Climbing stairs)* Wish me luck!

(EILEEN follows)

EILEEN: Good luck!

(RUTH exits noisily, milk bottles clanging. EILEEN turns back, picks up tray with wine glasses, exits into studio. WAITER enters with gallon glass jug of cheap wine. CHEF enters with two Chianti bottles in straw and funnel.)

CHEF: Il vino?

WAITER: Porta qui le bottiglie. Eco! *(Pulls two straw bottles from behind back. WAITER pours from cheap bottle into straw one. When first bottle is full, CHEF takes funnel and puts it into second bottle)*

CHICK: *(Entering from street carrying package from grocery store. EILEEN comes out of studio)* Dinner for two—comin' right up!

EILEEN: *(Takes sandwiches)* Oh, how nice!

CHICK: Let's go in the kitchen. It's stiflin' out here!

(CHEF and WAITER go off with bottles)

EILEEN: *(Going to bench)* Oh, this is much pleasanter! *(CHICK sits next to her and makes a pass at her shoulder which she shrugs off. She puts bag with food between them)* It was awfully sweet of you to get Ruth a chance. *(Opening wrapper, pulling out sandwich)*

CHICK: A pleasure! *(He pats her hand and puts arm around her. She hands him sandwich in hand which has been groping around her back. He puts sandwich on bench, his arms around her again)*—And the next thing, we're gonna get your career straightened out.

EILEEN: *(Struggling, rises)* Please! You'll have to excuse me, Mr. Clark!

CHICK: Excuse ya! After all the trouble I went to get rid of that eagle-eyed sister of yours.

EILEEN: *(Staring)* What? That call Ruth got was from the editor, wasn't it?

CHICK: What are you worryin' about? I'm handling it—

EILEEN: It was *you!* You sent Ruth on a wild goose chase!

CHICK: *(Shrugs)* I'll give her a coupla bucks for her trouble.

EILEEN: She was so excited. How am I ever going to tell her? You get out of here!

CHICK: Now that's a lousy attitude to take! *(Phone rings)* Let it ring!

EILEEN: Hello? Oh, Mr. Baker—hello, Bob!

CHICK: *(Into phone)* Call back later!

EILEEN: *(To CHICK)* How dare you! *(Into phone)* Oh, just somebody who's leaving —*(To CHICK)* Now stop this nonsense! *(EILEEN, into phone)*—Ruth? No, she's gone to Brooklyn—*(To CHICK—hand over phone)* Skunk! *(Into phone, elegantly)* Oh, you don't have to apologize—we never got to dinner anyway. Me? I guess I'll wait for Ruth—I always feel silly eating alone—

CHICK: Alone! How about me and them baloney sandwiches!

EILEEN: *(Into phone)* Why, Bob, how nice! I'd love to have dinner with you— *(Glaring at CHICK)* Yes, I'll be waiting—*(Hangs up. Picks sandwich from windowsill)*

CHICK: That's the worst double-cross I ever got! A fine little sneak you turned out to be! *(EILEEN starts to eat sandwich. CHICK grabs it from her hand, as she is taking a bite. CHICK goes to bench, picks up empty bag, stuffs EILEEN'S sandwich into it)* I ain't fattenin' you up for someone else!

Blackout

SCENE 7

The Navy Yard. At Rise: SHORE PATROLMAN *doing sentry duty.* RUTH *enters, passing* SHORE PATROLMAN.

SHORE PATROLMAN: Just a minute, Miss! Where's your pass?

RUTH: Oh, it's all right—Press—I'm a reporter—

SHORE PATROLMAN: You gotta have a pass.

RUTH: I just want to interview those Brazilian cadets.

SHORE PATROLMAN: Look—I'm tryin' to tell you—a pass—

RUTH: Well, where can I get one?

SHORE PATROLMAN: You can't—Commandant's office is closed. Tomorrow.

RUTH: Oh, please—my job depends on it!

SHORE PATROLMAN: So does mine.

(BRAZILIAN CADET enters)

FIRST CADET: *(Eyeing* RUTH *with some interest. After all, she's a woman)* Hello.

RUTH: *(To* SHORE PATROLMAN*)* Is that one of them? *(*SHORE PATROLMAN *nods. She steps to* CADET*)* Excuse me, Admiral. I'm from the press, and I'd like to ask you a few questions—

*(*CADET *shrugs his shoulders, blankly)*

SHORE PATROLMAN: That means he don't understand.

RUTH: Thanks. I know that much Portuguese myself. *(Seven more* CADETS *enter, enveloping* RUTH *in their midst, and talking loudly)* Ah! Any of you Admirals speak English?

SECOND CADET: Si! English!

RUTH: What do you think of America?

SECOND CADET: American dance—Conga!

RUTH: No, no! Conga's a Brazilian dance!

FIRST CADET: No—Cubano!

SECOND CADET: Conga *American* dance! You show Conga!

RUTH: Then will you tell me?

ALL: Si! Si!

RUTH: It's like this. One, two, three, kick. One, two, three, kick. *(She shuffles from side to side in Conga step. They follow clumsily. She ad-libs: That's fine! You've got it! That's right! But they don't quite stop. Music:)*

What do you think of the USA—NRA—TVA,
What do you think of our Mother's Day,
What do you think of the—

ADMIRALS:
Conga!

(They dance. She attempts to get her interview, but each time the ADMIRALS *cut in with shrieks of "Conga!" As the number becomes more violent and* RUTH *is hurled about from one* CADET *to the other, she remains grimly resolved to disregard them and get her story)*

RUTH:
What do you think of our native squaws,
Charles G. Dawes,
Warden Lawes—

What's your opinion of Santa Claus,
What do you think of the—

ADMIRALS:

Conga!
(They dance)

RUTH:

Good neighbors—Good neighbors,
Remember our policy—
Good neighbors—I'll help you
If you'll just help me—

ADMIRALS:

Conga!

(They dance. RUTH gets more and more involved)

RUTH:

What's your opinion of Harold Teen,
Mitzi Green,
Dizzy Dean.
Who do you love on the silver screen—
What do you think of the—

ADMIRALS:

Conga!

(More dancing, with RUTH struggling to get out of it)

RUTH:

What do you think of our rhythm bands,
Monkey glands,
Hot-dog stands.
What do you think of Stokowski's hands—
What do you think of the—

ADMIRALS:

Conga!
(Dance)

RUTH:

Good neighbors—Good neighbors,
Remember our policy—
Good neighbors—I'll help you
If you'll just help me—

ADMIRALS:

Conga!
(By now the dancing is abandoned and wild)

RUTH:

What's your opinion of women's clothes,
Major Bowes,
Steinbeck's prose.

How do you feel about Broadway Rose—
What do you think of the—

ADMIRALS:
Conga!

RUTH:
What do you think of our rocks and rills,
Mother Sills sea-sick pills.
How do you feel about Helen Wills—
What do you think of the—

ADMIRALS:
Conga!

RUTH:
Good neighbors—Good neighbors,
Remember our policy—
Good neighbors—I'll help you
If you'll just help me!!

(ADMIRALS sing serenade, strumming on imaginary guitars while RUTH *stands totally exhausted. They yell "Conga!" again, and lift her on their backs. Careening about,* RUTH *still tries to get her interview)*

Stop!
What do you think of our double malts,
Family vaults,
Epsom Salts,
Wouldn't you guys like to learn to waltz?
I know—You just want to—Conga!

(She is whirled about piggy-back in Conga rhythm, her hat over her eyes—and finally lifted aloft and carried offstage—as the music builds to a frenetic finish.)

SCENE 8

The Back Yard. RUTH *enters, immediately after rise, on street, followed by* ADMIRALS.
RUTH: Good night! Au revoir! Auf wiedersehn! Good-bye! *(To* EILEEN, *who enters from studio)* Eileen. Eileen!
EILEEN: What's going on?
RUTH: The Fleet's in!
EILEEN: *(To* ADMIRALS*)* How do you do?
RUTH: Listen, Emily Post—How do you say, "Get the hell out of here" in Portuguese?
EILEEN: Why? What's the matter?
RUTH: Suppose *you* take 'em outside and walk 'em around! I'm sick of having kids whistle at me.
EILEEN: You mean they don't understand any English at all?
RUTH: Yes—three words—American dance—conga!
A CADET: Conga! Da-da-da-da-da-da! *(He starts to dance. The others restrain him hastily)*
RUTH: Listen boys—Go! Leave! Good-bye! *(She waves.* ADMIRALS *return wave,*

mutter happily "Goo-bye." RUTH *turns back to* EILEEN, *shrugs and steps back to her)*

EILEEN: What did you bring them here for?

RUTH: Bring them! They've been on my tail ever since I left the Brooklyn Navy Yard.

EILEEN: What do they want anyway?

RUTH: What do you *think* they want?

EILEEN: Oh, my God! We've got to get them out of here! Make them go, Ruth!

RUTH: Suppose you take a crack at it.

EILEEN *(Sweetly)* Look, boys. Go back to your boat. Boat!

(She salutes. ADMIRALS *snap to attention, salute in return)*

RUTH: Admiral Sherwood, I presume.

(They drop salute)

EILEEN: Boys—go way—please!

(Supplicating—her arms extended—they take it wrongly—howl and step forward after her. EILEEN *shrieks, runs back to* RUTH*)*

RUTH: That's fine.

EILEEN: Gee, they can't be *that* dumb.

RUTH: They're *not* that dumb.

EILEEN: What are we going to do?

RUTH: I've tried everything. I guess, Eileen, we'll just have to stand here grinning at each other.

(She turns to ADMIRALS *and grins broadly.* ADMIRALS *all grin back. She motions helplessly, steps back in to* EILEEN*)*

EILEEN: Look—boys—sick! Very sick! *(Sits on bench—leans all the way back—on "bed")* Bed! Bed!

(The ADMIRALS *rush in at her.* EILEEN *jumps up, shrieks, makes a dash for* RUTH, *swings behind her for protection)*

RUTH: For God's sake, don't let 'em get any wrong ideas!

EILEEN: You brought them here! The least you can do is help me get rid of them!

(The ADMIRALS *start to toss coins)* What are they tossing for?

RUTH: I don't know, but I've got a hunch it's not me!

(An ADMIRAL *goes to them gravely)*

FIRST ADMIRAL: *(Bowing)* Senorita, eu tive e grande prazer de a ganhar esta noite.

RUTH: Isn't it a romantic language?

EILEEN: No understando—no spikee Portuguese—

FIRST CADET: American dance—Conga!

(He turns EILEEN, *takes her by the wrist and other* ADMIRALS *join in.* RUTH *dances backwards, in front of* EILEEN*)*

RUTH: Eileen, we've got to get them out of here.

(There is a blast from below. The ADMIRALS *stop and cross themselves in fear)*

EILEEN: Run—Earthquake!

*(*EILEEN *runs to doorway, hides against it, to see if* ADMIRALS *disperse.* ADMIRALS *make for the stairway.* WAITERS *and* CHEF *enter from* NINO'S. *Passers-by stop on the street to stare down. The* ADMIRALS *stop on steps, look at one another and laugh)*

RUTH: What a performance! Helen Hayes couldn't have done better. Listen, I've got an idea. Lead 'em out through the alley and lose them on the street!

EILEEN: Okay, but tell Bob I'll be right back.

RUTH: Bob?

EILEEN: Yes, I'm having dinner with him. *(To* ADMIRALS*)* Come on, boys—Conga!

(Boys make line. EILEEN *exits into alley,* ADMIRALS *Congaing after her.* RUTH *stares off unhappily. The* WAITERS *from* NINO'S *start to Conga gaily.* BAKER *enters from street and looks strangely at* CHEF *and two* WAITERS *in Conga line. He goes to* RUTH*)*

BAKER: Ruth, what's going on?

RUTH: *(Looks at him and starts to Conga by herself)* Oh, a few friends dropped in. We're losing our inhibitions!

(She grabs piece of celery from WAITER, *puts it between her teeth, starts to Conga wildly. She starts her own line, with* CHEF, *and* WAITERS *following. As they go off they are met by* EILEEN *coming back, still followed by the* ADMIRALS *and a huge snake line of mixed* VILLAGERS. RUTH *backs away, in dismay)*

EILEEN: I couldn't lose them!

*(*MRS. WADE *comes on with* LONIGAN *and another cop. Whistles are blown by* LONIGAN. *Meanwhile* RUTH *has been hoisted up in the air by* ADMIRALS. COP *makes a grab for* EILEEN, *picks her up. She turns in the air, kicks* LONIGAN *in the stomach. He drags her off.* MRS. WADE *has made for the stairs and stands on the first landing, motioning wildly.* RUTH *gets down from her perch and desperately starts to run across after* EILEEN. *She is grabbed by one of the* ADMIRALS, *carried, slid back and overhead by the* ADMIRALS. BAKER *runs after* EILEEN *as* RUTH *is congaed aloft amidst a swirl of village figures, all caught up in the frenzy of the Conga rhythm)*

Curtain

ACT TWO

SCENE 1

The Christopher Street Station House. A couple of COPS *are talking as* WRECK *and* HELEN *enter.* WRECK *is carrying a dress of* EILEEN'S.

COP: Hey, what are you doing in here?

HELEN: Good morning.

WRECK: Can we see Miss Sherwood, please?

COP: What do you think this is, the Barbizon Plaza? Miss Who?

HELEN: Eileen Sherwood.

COP: Eileen? Why didn't you say so? *(Calls offstage)* Oh, Eileen!

EILEEN: *(Offstage)* Yes? What is it, Dennis? *(Enters. Sees* WRECK *and* HELEN. *She is carrying a malted milk)* Oh, hello, Wreck—Helen—

WRECK: Hi, Eileen!

HELEN: The Wreck ironed this dress especially. He thought you'd want to look fresh in court.

EILEEN: *(Taking dress)* Oh, thanks, Wreck. That's awfully sweet of you. *(To* COP*)* Dennis—

COP: Yeah, Eileen.

EILEEN: *(Hands dress to him)* Dennis, would you mind hanging this up in my cell?

COP: Sure, Eileen.

(He goes off, holding dress carefully over arm. SECOND COP *enters)*

SECOND COP: Oh, Eileen.

EILEEN: Yes, Dan—

SECOND COP: There's a man on the phone—wants to talk to you—says it's important.

EILEEN: Who is it, Dan?

SECOND COP: Chick Clark. Says he knows you.

EILEEN: *(Angrily)* You tell Mr. Clark I'm not in to him and hang up on him if he ever calls again!

SECOND COP: Leave it to me, Eileen. *(He pats her shoulder and goes)*

HELEN: *(To WRECK)* And we were worried about her!

EILEEN: Oh, I'm fine. How are you two getting along?

WRECK: Pretty good. If everything works out all right we'll be leavin' on our honeymoon next week.

EILEEN: Congratulations! Are you getting married?

HELEN: We decided not to wait for the football season.

WRECK: Yeah. Ya see, Helen went to the doctor—

HELEN: *(Turns to him)* Wreck!

WRECK: Anyway, the decision was taken out of our hands.

HELEN: Yes, we've got a plan and Appopolous is puttin' up all the dough.

EILEEN: Appopolous!

HELEN: Yes, as soon as I collect my dowry, he'll get his back rent.

EILEEN: Good luck. I hope you'll be very happy.

WRECK: Well, we've been happy so far—I don't see why marriage should change it. *(They go off)*

EILEEN: *(To COP)* And to think I was always afraid of being arrested!

THIRD COP: Ah, that Lonigan's a bum sport—Just because you kicked him!

FOURTH COP: *(Enters)* Eileen, there's a girl outside—claims she's your sister—

EILEEN: Ruth? Send her in please!

(COP waves RUTH on)

RUTH: *(Embracing EILEEN tearfully)* Eileen! Oh, you poor kid!

EILEEN: *(Startled)* What happened?

RUTH: What do you mean, what happened? This!

EILEEN: Oh—Oh, yes—this!

RUTH: I've been all over New York, trying to raise your bail—Maybe I'd better send a wire to Dad.

EILEEN: Gee, don't do that! He'll ask a lot of foolish questions—

RUTH: Well, we've got to do something.

EILEEN: I'm all right! Everybody's very sweet to me here!

FIRST COP: *(Enters)* Phone, Eileen.

EILEEN: Who is it, Dennis?

FIRST COP: A Mr. Lippencott. He'd like to know when he can call on you.

EILEEN: *(Thoughtfully)* Tell him—anytime before five.

RUTH: *(Stares)* Tell me, Eileen, how many do you keep in help here?

EILEEN: Huh?

RUTH: I just love the way you've done this place. Well, I've got to get to work!

EILEEN: Where?

RUTH: The Village Vortex. Your old pal Speedy Valenti gave me a job.

EILEEN: Doing what?

RUTH: *(Hesitates)* Well, it pays—

FOURTH COP: *(Enters)* Eileen, there's a gentleman to see you. *(Hands* EILEEN *a business card)*

EILEEN: *(Reading)* Robert Baker! Why, it's *Bob!* Send him in, please.

RUTH: *(Turning unhappily)* I'd better go.

BAKER: *(Enters)* How are you, Eileen? *(Turns to* RUTH*)* Oh, hello, Ruth—

RUTH: *(Flatly)* Hello.

BAKER: What happened to you, Ruth? I looked for you after the patrol wagon left.

RUTH: I went for a walk—had a lot of things to think over—

BAKER: You do look a little tired.

RUTH: I am. I didn't sleep all night—*(To* EILEEN*)*—worrying about *you*—So I sat at that typewriter and wrote the story about the Brazilian Admirals. It's a darn good story—I know it is! I took your advice—a slice of my own life—and I sent it to Chick's city editor—Mr. Bains. *(Sadly)* But they didn't print it, so I guess it wasn't so good after all—

BAKER: Want *me* to read it?

RUTH: If you feel up to it—*(To* EILEEN*)* Sorry to eat and run, darling—but I've got to get to work! *(Kisses her)*

BAKER: *(To* RUTH*)* Did you get a job? What are you doing?

RUTH: Oh, it's in the advertising game. *(Looks at wristwatch)* Cocktail time, already? Well, I've got to fly! 'Bye, dear—lovely party—such fun! *Do* ask me again! *(She hurries off)*

EILEEN: Poor Ruth! I didn't have the heart to tell her. There isn't any Mr. Bains.

BAKER: What?

EILEEN: It was all a big lie! That Chick Clark's an utter snake! Oh, if I could only get out of here, I'd—

BAKER: Look, I'm working on this. I'm going to get you out. I just tried to pay your fine, but they haven't set it yet.

EILEEN: Why not?

BAKER: I don't know. Washington wants them to hold you here.

EILEEN: *(Gasps)* Washington—D.C.?

BAKER: Something about Pan-American relations.

EILEEN: Oh, my God!

BAKER: But don't worry—I'm working on this.

FOURTH COP: *(Entering, making a butler's announcement)* Frank Lippencott.

EILEEN: Send him in, Pat.

BAKER: I'm going over to see the Brazilian Consul right now.
   (He starts out. FRANK *enters. They collide.* FRANK *carries small box)*

FRANK: Oops! Sorry—*(*BAKER *exits irritatedly.* FRANK *combs his hair quickly)* Gee, this is the first time I was ever in a police station.

EILEEN: It's *my* first time, too.

LIPPENCOTT: I brought you an electric fan we're running. I thought it would cool off your cell. *(Holds box out to her)*

EILEEN: Isn't that thoughtful!

LIPPENCOTT: It's given away free with every purchase over five dollars.

EILEEN: Thanks.

FRANK: *(Opening box)* Somebody forgot it.

EILEEN: You're sweet.

FRANK: *(Removing small rubber fan from box)* You'd be surprised at the breeze that little thing gives off—*(He spins blade, holds it up to* EILEEN'S *face)* Everybody in the store's got a cold. *(He hands her fan.* FOURTH COP *enters)*

EILEEN: *(To* COP*)* Pat, would you mind putting these things in my cell? *(She gets suitcase, hands it to him)*

FOURTH COP: Yes, sure.

EILEEN: Thank you.

(FOURTH COP exits)

FRANK: Eileen, I want to ask you something—it's the most important decision I ever made in my life—

EILEEN: Frank, you're a very sweet boy, and I'm fond of you, but I'm really not thinking of getting married.

FRANK: No, neither am I.

EILEEN: You're not?

FRANK: No.

EILEEN: Then what are you thinking of?

FRANK: Listen, Eileen—I suddenly realize I've been wasting my life—

EILEEN: What are you talking about?

FRANK: You know—*Life*—the way you girls live it—free to follow your natural bent whatever it is—

EILEEN: What's all that got to do with me?

FRANK: Don't you see? We'd have our freedom and we'd have each other. I thought we could have a sort of ideal relationship, like Helen and The Wreck.

EILEEN: *(Aghast)* Timothy!

FRANK: Gee, Eileen, it was only an idea!

EILEEN: Show this gentleman out—and don't ever let him in here again!

(He goes quickly. As he passes COP, COP *stamps his foot menacingly.* FRANK *quickens speed, exits)*

FIFTH COP: *(Enters excitedly)* Eileen! Did you see the paper?

EILEEN: No.

FIFTH COP: Look! You're in it!

FIRST COP: *(Enters)* Eileen's in the papers.

FIFTH COP: A big story! Your picture and everything!

EILEEN: Oh, for goodness sakes!

FOURTH COP: *(Comes in with others)* Hey! That's me! Not bad, huh?

FIRST COP: That jerk Lonigan has his back to the camera! He'll fry!

SECOND COP: Look, Lonigan!

(LONIGAN enters)

FOURTH COP: You're famous, Eileen!

EILEEN: Do you think so? I wonder if Mr. Valenti saw it? *(To* LONIGAN*)* Oh, John, it's on your beat. Would you do me a great favor? Would you take this over to the Village Vortex and show it to Speedy Valenti personally?

THIRD COP: He'd better!

LONIGAN: Sure, Eileen. I'll serve it on him!

THIRD COP: Atta boy, John! *(To* EILEEN *as music begins)* Oh, Eileen, you brought a breath of the old country into the station house.

FOURTH COP: *(In greatly exaggerated Irish brogue)* Sure and I been feelin' twice as Irish since you came into our lives.

(Singing à la John McCormack)
Take it from me,
In Dublin's fair city
There's none half so pretty
As pretty Eileen.

Take it from me,
The Mayor of Shannon
Would shoot off a cannon
And crown ye the queen.

ALL:
Darlin' Eileen,
Darlin' Eileen,
Fairest colleen that iver I've seen.
And it's oh I wish I were back in the land of the green
With my darlin' Eileen.

FIRST COP:
I've seen them all—
There's Bridget and Sheila

SECOND COP:
There's Kate and Deli—lah
And Moll and Maureen.

THIRD COP:
I've seen them all—
Not one can compete with—

FIRST COP:
Or share the same street with
My darlin' Eileen.

ALL:
Darlin' Eileen—Darlin' Eileen,
Fairest colleen
That iver I've seen—
And it's oh I wish I were back
In the land of the green
With my darlin' Eileen.

(They dance a lusty jig of the Old Country, lumbering but full of life, all vying for her attention)

EILEEN: *(Somewhat apprehensive, cutting them off)*
Listen, my lads,
I've something to tell you
I hope won't impel you to cry and to keen.
Mother's a Swede and Father's a Scot—
And so Irish I'm not—And I never have been—

ALL: *(They will not hear of this)*
  Hush you, Eileen! Hush you, Eileen!
  Fairest colleen that iver I've seen.
  Don't you hand us none of that blarney—
  You come from Killarney,
  You're Irish, Eileen!

(The dance resumes and ends in a "hats-off" salute to the girl of their dreams,
EILEEN*)*

  Blackout

SCENE 2

The Street. At Rise: MRS. WADE *sitting on a camp stool, posing;* APPOPOLOUS
painting her picture.
MRS. WADE: May I look?
APPOPOLOUS: No, it's still an embryo. Let it kick and breathe first. As a model
  you will be immortalized like Van Gogh's herring!
  (The WRECK *and* HELEN *enter.* HELEN *pushes him in. He wears navy-blue suit,
  carries hat. She motions to his head. He puts hat on, starts to step in.* HELEN *grabs
  him, motions to glasses. He puts bone glasses on.* HELEN *goes off as* WRECK *crosses
  to* APPOPOLOUS *and looks over his shoulder at canvas)*
WRECK: Bravo! Magnificent! You've captured the inner soul of this lovely lady!
APPOPOLOUS: Thank you, Mr. Loomis. *(MRS. WADE looks at WRECK)* That's
  indeed a compliment coming from a great collector like you!
WRECK: Not at all!
APPOPOLOUS: May I present you? Mr. Loomis—Mrs. Wade—
MRS. WADE: Pleased to meet you.
WRECK: *(Removing his hat)* I'm delighted. Maestro, I'd like to add this to my
  collection. Is it for sale?
APPOPOLOUS: Sorry! I'm presenting this to Mrs. Wade!
  (HELEN enters)
HELEN: Hello, Mother.
MRS. WADE: Oh, Helen. Come here a moment! I want you to meet someone! This
  is my daughter, Helen—Mr. Loomis.
WRECK: Daughter? You're spoofing! You look more like sisters!
HELEN: I'm very pleased to meet you, Mr. Loomis.
WRECK: Likewise, I'm sure! Well, this is delightful! May I invite you all to tea
  at the Purple Cow?
MRS. WADE: Oh.
APPOPOLOUS: Fine! You young people go along, and we'll join you in a minute.
  (WRECK smiles, offers his arm to HELEN. She takes it)
HELEN: Do you get down to the Village very often, Mr. Loomis? *(They go off)*
MRS. WADE: Who *is* he?
APPOPOLOUS: He comes from a very aristocratic family from Trenton Tech.
  *(APPOPOLOUS and MRS. WADE go off. RUTH enters with MAN with sign.
  As passers-by come on, they turn on electric signs reading "VORTEX" across
  their chests)*
RUTH: *(To MAN)* I feel like a damn fool!
MAN: *(Shrugs)* It's a living.

(Another couple passes by. RUTH *and* MAN *turn on signs)*

VILLAGER: You ever been there?

SECOND VILLAGER: Yeah, last night. *(They go off)*

RUTH: I'm really a writer, you know.

MAN: I'm really an architect, but they haven't built anything since the Empire State Building.

RUTH: *(Spotting someone offstage)* Oh, this is awful!

MAN: What's the matter?

RUTH: Here comes someone I know! Please, don't light up!

MAN: Sure! Don't worry about it.

(RUTH turns, faces MAN, simulates fixing his tie. BAKER enters. After he has passed RUTH, she and MAN turn and stroll off. BAKER recognizes RUTH, turns)

BAKER: *Ruth!*

RUTH: *(Turns, brightly)* Oh, hello there! *(Hastily she folds her arms across the electric sign)*

BAKER: Well, this is a surprise! Going out?

RUTH: Yes, we are—to the opera. Mr. Stevens, I'd like you to meet Mr. Baker. Mr. Stevens is in Washington with the Reconstruction Finance Corporation. *(They shake)*

BAKER: *(To* RUTH*)* I read your piece about the Brazilian Navy. Now that's the idea! It's fine!

RUTH: Really? No repressions? No inhibitions?

BAKER: No, just good clean fun. I gave it to the boss to read. I'm sure he'll go for it.

RUTH: Oh, thank you, Bob. That's wonderful of you!

(VALENTI enters)

MAN: *(To* RUTH*)* Hey, Ruth, we're going to be late for the opera!

RUTH: Just a minute, please. This is important!

MAN: So is this! More important! *(Points to* VALENTI*)*

VALENTI: What's going on here? Get on the ball! *(MAN snaps light on,* BAKER *stares in wonder.* RUTH *looks at him unhappily)* Well? What's with you, sister —run out of juice?

RUTH: *(Lights up and smiles feebly at* BAKER*)* Well, it's a healthy job. Keeps me out in the air!

BAKER: *(Pats her arm reassuringly)* Good girl. *(He smiles at her and goes off)*

VALENTI: No socializing on my time. *(Goes to* MAN*)* Here's a pitch. You take Sheridan Square. *(Hands flyer to* MAN *who exits and then hands her flyer)* Here's your spiel—come on, get a mob around you. Make with the pitch. Get hep. *(He exits)*

RUTH: *(Tentatively)* Yes, sir—hep. *(Reading from flyer—very tentatively to passers-by)* Step up—step up—*(Embarrassed)* Get hep—get hep—*(Suddenly, loudly)* Step up!

(Rhythm starts in orchestra. RUTH *still reading from flyer, giving a very "square" rendition)*

Step up! Step up!

Get hep! Get hep!

(While she reads a crowd of '30's hepcats, VILLAGERS, *gathers around her)*

Come on down to the Village Vortex

Home of the new jazz rage—Swing!

Rock and roll to the beat beat beat
Of Speedy Valenti and his krazy kats!

(Sings falteringly)
Swing! Dig the rhythm!
Swing! Dig the message!
The jive is jumpin' and the music goes around and around—
Whoa-ho—!
Goes around and around—
Cat, make it solid!
Cat, make it groovy!
You gotta get your seafood, Mama, your favorite dish is fish,
It's your favorite dish.
Don't be square,
Rock right out of that rockin' chair;
Truck on down and let down your hair;
Breathe that barrel-house air!
The Village Vortex!
Swing! Dig the rhythm!
Swing! Dig the message!
The jive is jumpin' and the music goes around and around—
Get full of foory-a-ka-sa-ke,
Get full of the sound of swing,
The solid, jivy, groovy sound of swing!

VILLAGERS: *(Singing and showing* RUTH *how to get hep)*
Swing! Dig the rhythm!
Swing! Dig the message!
The jive is jumpin' and the music goes around and around—
Whoa-ho—!

RUTH: *(Getting the idea)*
Oh!

VILLAGERS:
Cat, make it solid!
Cat, make it groovy!
You gotta get your seafood, Mama;
Your favorite dish is fish—

RUTH: *(Catching on still more and beginning to enjoy it)*
Oh!

VILLAGERS:
Don't be square,
Rock right out of that rockin' chair;
Truck on down and let down your hair;
Breathe that barrel-house air—
You gotta get with the whoa-ho-de-ho!

RUTH: *(Answering in Cab Calloway fashion)*
Whoa-ho-de-ho.

VILLAGERS:
The gut-gut-bucket.

RUTH:
The gut-gut-bucket.

VILLAGERS:
Skid-dle-ee-oh-day!

RUTH:
Skid-dle-ee-oh-day!

VILLAGERS:
Heedle heedle heedle.

RUTH:
Heedle heedle heedle.

VILLAGERS:
Well, all right then, cats!

RUTH:
Well, all right then, cats!

VILLAGERS:
Yes, yes, baby I know!

RUTH: *(By this time RUTH is in a glaze-eyed hypnotic trance, having got the message and as the hepcats gather around her she delivers patter in a husky dreamlike monotone)*

Well, yes yes, baby, I know!
That old man Mose
Kicked the bucket,
The old oaken bucket that hung in the well—
Well, well, well, baby, I know—
No no; was it red?
No no no! Was it green green—
Green is the color of my true love's hair—
Hair-breadth Harry with the floy floy doy
Floy doy, floy doy, floy doy, boy!
Hoy dre(h)eamt boy dwe(h)elt in ma(h)arble halls—
Well that ends well, well, well—
Baby I know—No, no,
Was it green?
No no no
Was it red sails in the sunset callin' me me me
You good for nothin'
Mi-mi mi-mi
Me Tarzan, you Jane,
Swingin' in the trees,
Swingin' in the trees,
Swingin' in the trees—

(This develops into an abandoned dance in which RUTH not only joins but finally leads the hepcats to a "sent" finish)

VILLAGERS:
> *Swing—swing—swing—swing—swing—swing*
> *Swing—Chu-chu-chu-chu-chu-chu-chu-chu-chu-chu*
> *Swing—Chu-chu-chu-chu-chu-chu-chu-chu-chu-chu*
> *Swing—Chu-chu-chu-chu-chu-chu-chu-chu-chu-chu*

RUTH:
> *Floy-doy floy-doy floy-doy boy!*

VILLAGERS:
> *Sh-sh-sh.*

RUTH:
> *Gesundheit.*

VILLAGERS:
> *Thanks.*

RUTH:
> *You're welcome.*

VILLAGERS:
> *Whoa!*
> (Motioning to RUTH*)*
> *Come on, Jackson, you're getting hep.*
> *Come on, Jackson, you're getting hep.*
> *Come on, Jackson, you're getting hep.*

RUTH:
> *I want my favorite dish.*

VILLAGERS:
> *Fish.*

RUTH:
> *Gesundheit.*

VILLAGERS:
> *Thanks.*

RUTH:
> *It's nothing!*

VILLAGERS:
> *Solid, groovy, jivy sound of swing—*

FIRST MAN:
> *Ah—do it.*

SECOND MAN:
> *Solid, Jackson.*

FIRST GIRL:
> *Seafood, Mama.*

SECOND GIRL:
> (A long banshee wail)

VILLAGERS:
> *Go go go—yah—*
> *Swing—oh swing it,*
> *Swing—oh swing it.*

(The dance continues, as the VILLAGERS *back out, followed by* RUTH *in a trance)*

RUTH: *(In a hoarse, hypnotic whisper)*
> *Swing—Swing*
> *Green, no—red, no*
> *Me Tarzan—No, no, no*
> *That old man Mose*
> *He kicked that bucket*
> *Down in the well—well, well, well*
> *My favorite dish*
> *Ahhh—fish!*

VILLAGERS:
> *Gesundheit.*

RUTH:
> *Thank you.*

VILLAGERS:
> *You're welcome.*

RUTH: *(Her hands before her, mesmerized. Walks off in a trance)*
> *Swing—swing—swing—swing—swing—*

(She disappears)

> Blackout

SCENE 3

The Studio. At Rise: Stage empty. Through window, VIOLET'S *legs pass by, then man's legs.* VIOLET *stops, half-turns. Man comes back and joins her. They stand, then go off together.*

During this scene, APPOPOLOUS *enters carrying blue-green painting. He steps on bed, looks about for something to stand on, picks up manuscripts off typewriter next to bed, and slips one under each foot. He hangs painting, jumps down, takes valise from under* RUTH'S *bed, puts it on top of bed, takes typewriter from chair next to bed, puts it on bed, gets books and candlesticks off and puts them on bed.* RUTH *enters from bathroom in her slip. She screams.*

RUTH: Ah! What are you doing with my things? *(She takes robe from bathroom and slips it on)*

APPOPOLOUS: You're being dispossessed! I only hope your sister has sense enough to give the wrong address!

RUTH: Yes, imagine what bad publicity could do to this dump!

APPOPOLOUS: *(Pointing to painting)* I found my masterpiece in Benny's. For the frame, two dollars—for my painting, nothing! At six o'clock your current occupancy terminates! *(Knock on door)* Remember! If you're not out by the stroke of six, you'll find your belongings in the street! *(He goes out through kitchen. There is another knock on the door)*

RUTH: Come in. *(BAKER enters)* Oh, Bob—

BAKER: *(Sadly)* Oh, hello, Ruth.

RUTH: What's the matter?

BAKER: *(Angrily)* All I can say is, he wouldn't know a good story if he read one!

RUTH: Who?

BAKER: His Highness—king of the editors—pompous ass. (APPOPOLOUS *sticks head in from kitchen door)*

APPOPOLOUS: Fifteen minutes! *(Disappears again)*

BAKER: What was *that?*

RUTH: Bulova Watch Time.

BAKER: I'm sorry, Ruth. He just didn't like it.

RUTH: *(Shrugs)* Well, maybe it wasn't any good.

BAKER: It's just one man's opinion.

RUTH: That's enough.

BAKER: I still think it's a hell of a good story and I'm going to tell him so!

RUTH: Please, Bob, don't get into any trouble on my account.

BAKER: This has nothing to do with you. It's a matter of principle. Either I know my business or I don't!

RUTH: *(Nods slowly)* I see.

(EILEEN *enters from street with* LONIGAN, *who is carrying her suitcase)*

EILEEN: Ruth!

RUTH: *(Embracing her)* Eileen! Darling, you're out! How did it happen?

EILEEN: Bob fixed everything. Thanks, Bob.

(CHICK CLARK *appears at window)*

CHICK: Hello, kids.

EILEEN: Chick Clark! You get away from there, you big snake!

CHICK: Now wait a minute, Eileen! Gimme a chance.

EILEEN: You had enough chances!

RUTH: What are you talking about?

EILEEN: Ruth, when I tell you what he did—

CHICK: Wait! The city editor's read your Brazilian story and he thinks it's the absolute nuts!

RUTH: *(Going to window. Hopefully)* He does?

EILEEN: Don't believe him, Ruth! He's the biggest liar!

CHICK: Go ahead—call him up! Mr. Wilson! You know the number!

RUTH: Wilson? I thought his name was Bains?

EILEEN: You see, Ruth, he's lying again! *(To* LONIGAN*)* John, will you do me a great favor and chase him away from there?

LONIGAN: Glad to! *(He runs out)*

CHICK: Now wait a minute, Eileen. You're gonna louse it up! Tell her to call Mr. Wilson—the city editor—I keep tellin' her all the time! (CHICK *runs off as* LONIGAN *stops at window)*

LONIGAN: *(Kneels down, offering her whistle)* Oh, Eileen, if anything else happens, here's a police whistle.

EILEEN: *(Taking whistle)* Thanks, John.

(LONIGAN *goes)*

RUTH: Next week you'll have your own hook and ladder.

APPOPOLOUS: *(Sticking head through kitchen)* Five minutes!

EILEEN: What's that about?

RUTH: We're being dispossessed.

BAKER: Where are you going?

RUTH: *(Hands EILEEN suitcase)* I don't know—home, I guess.

EILEEN: We can't. What would people say?

RUTH: "Did you hear the dirt about those Sherwood girls? On account of them, we almost lost the Naval Base in Brazil."

BAKER: It's ridiculous. You can't go home now.

RUTH: But, Bob—

BAKER: I haven't time to argue about it. *(Looks at his watch)* I've got to get up to the office before His Highness leaves. He wants to see me—and I want to see him a damn sight more! *(Goes to door)* Now I want you to promise me you'll wait right here till I get back.

RUTH: You'd better hurry, or you may find us out in the street.

BAKER: Half an hour. Top. *(He's off)*

EILEEN: Isn't he nice?

RUTH: *(Sits on bed wearily)* Um—You like him a lot, don't you, Eileen?

EILEEN: You know, Ruth, he's the first boy I've ever met who really seemed to care what happened to me—how I got along and everything.

RUTH: Yes, I know. *(Shrugs)* I guess it doesn't make any difference now anyway.

EILEEN: What?

RUTH: *(Close to tears)* I said we're going home—so it doesn't matter about Bob.

EILEEN: *(Goes slowly to RUTH, putting an arm around her)* Gee, Ruth, I never dreamed. You mean you like him, too?

RUTH: Strange as it may seem—

EILEEN: Well, why didn't you say anything?

RUTH: What was there to say?

EILEEN: After all—you're my sister.

RUTH: *(Smiles at her through her tears)* That's the side of you that makes everything else seem worthwhile.

EILEEN: Gee, Ruth—I'm sorry we ever came here.
(Puts her head on RUTH'S shoulder)

BOTH:
> *Why, oh why, oh why—oh*
> *Why did we ever leave Ohio?*
> *Why did we wander to find what lies yonder*
> *When life was so cozy at home?*
>
> *Wond'ring while we wander,*
> *Why did we fly,*
> *Why did we roam—*
> *Oh, why oh why oh*
> *Did we leave Ohio?*
> *Maybe we'd better go home.*

(APPOPOLOUS enters:)

APPOPOLOUS: Time's up! Your occupancy is officially terminated.

RUTH: We're not ready yet.
(VALENTI enters)

VALENTI: Skeet—skat—skattle-ee-o-do! *(He carries newspaper)* Where is she? I knew it! I said it! I meant it! You hit me in my weak spot—*(Slaps newspaper)* Right on the front page!

EILEEN: Oh, Mr. Valenti! How did you like it?

RUTH: *(Takes newspaper, reading headline)* Like what? "Beautiful Blonde Bombshell Sinks Brazilian Navy." Oh, my—now we *can't* go home!

VALENTI: *(To EILEEN)* You're in the groove, babe! I'm gonna put you in my saloon for an audition tonight. If you make good, I'll sign you!

EILEEN: Oh, Mr. Valenti! Speedy! That's wonderful! *(To RUTH)* Ruth, it's a job! My first break in the theatre. *(They embrace)*

APPOPOLOUS: Girls, I'm gonna extend your time until six o'clock tomorrow morning. Make good and you can be with me for life! *(He goes)*

VALENTI: *(To EILEEN)* Get over there right away!

EILEEN: Yes, yes. *(To RUTH)* Only what about Bob?

RUTH: We'll leave a note on the door.

EILEEN: What'll I wear, Mr. Valenti?

VALENTI: I'll lend you a dress. I'll lend your sister one, too—*(RUTH looks up)*— and without the lights. Now get over there. *(Goes to door)* What are you gonna sing, Babe?

EILEEN: Ruth, remember the song we always used to do at the Kiwanis Club? The "Wrong Note Rag"?

RUTH: Oh, yes—do that one.

VALENTI: It's an oldie, but you'll never know it when I back you up with the licorice stick.

RUTH: The what?

VALENTI: My clarinet. Then for an encore—Tell me, kid—did you ever take 'em off?

EILEEN: What?

VALENTI: You know, *strip?*

RUTH: My sister doesn't strip.

VALENTI: Too bad. We're always looking for new faces!

Blackout

SCENE 4

The Street in front of the Vortex. At Rise: HELEN *and* WRECK *enter, followed by* MRS. WADE *and* APPOPOLOUS.

HELEN: That was a lovely dinner, Mr. Loomis!

APPOPOLOUS: *(Grimly)* Yes, he's certainly a fine host—everything out of season!

WRECK: Why not? You only live once!

APPOPOLOUS: Only the champagne I didn't expect!

MRS. WADE: It's good, though! Hit the spot!

WRECK: There! You see, Maestro?

HELEN: Come on! Let's get a good table!

WRECK: Yeah.

(They go off. APPOPOLOUS takes MRS. WADE'S arm)

APPOPOLOUS: One moment, Ella. They make a lovely couple, don't they?

MRS. WADE: Yes! Do you think his intentions are serious?

APPOPOLOUS: I'll vouch for it.

MRS. WADE: Did you notice he was holding Helen's hand under the table? My, I'd love to see my Helen settled down!

APPOPOLOUS: *(Offers his arm)* Don't worry, Ella, she'll be settled down and you'll be a grandmother before you expect it!

(They go off. RUTH and EILEEN hurry on)

EILEEN: Oh, dear, I'm so frightened!

RUTH: Now look, Eileen, you're not afraid of anything. I know you better than that!

EILEEN: You do?

(CHICK CLARK runs on)

CHICK: Hey, kids! I gotta talk to you!

EILEEN: Chick Clark, for the last time, stop annoying us!

CHICK: I tell ya! I got it all fixed!

EILEEN: All right! You asked for it—now you're going to get it! *(She puts whistle, attached to her wrist, to her lips and blows several times)*

CHICK: What are you doin'? Ya crazy!

(LONIGAN dashes on, CHICK runs off. EILEEN points in CHICK'S direction. LONIGAN follows him off)

RUTH: Eileen, are you sure you're doing the right thing?

EILEEN: Some day I'll tell you the truth about Mr. Chick Clark! *(Clutches her stomach)* Oh, gee—I'm all upset again! I feel nauseous!

RUTH: You do? Well, look—walk up and down in the air—and breathe deeply— That's right. I'll take your case and get you some black coffee. *(She goes off)*

EILEEN: Oh, thanks, Ruth.

(BAKER enters with piece of paper)

BAKER: Eileen—I found your note—this is wonderful news! *(Takes her hands)*

EILEEN: Thanks, Bob.

BAKER: Now, no more of that nonsense about going home.

EILEEN: Oh, no. No.

BAKER: And I'll get something for Ruth—just as soon as I land a job myself.

EILEEN: Job! What happened?

BAKER: Well, I left the *Manhatter*—uh—a difference of opinion—

EILEEN: Oh, Bob—I'm awfully sorry—But I think it's wonderful that you feel that way about Ruth!

BAKER: Well, I'm very fond of her—

EILEEN: Fond? It must be more than that if you got fired on her account.

BAKER: I left on a matter of principle!

EILEEN: Principle! Don't play dumb!

BAKER: Dumb?

EILEEN: Well, you must be if you don't know what's going on in your own mind!

BAKER: Will you please tell me what's going on in my mind?

EILEEN: I suppose you don't know why you fought with your editor about Ruth's story—or why you're picking a fight with me right now! Poor Bob—you're in love with Ruth and you don't even know it!

(Sings)
It's love! It's love!

BAKER: *(Sings)*
Come on now—Let's drop it.

EILEEN:
> *It's love! It's love!*
> *And nothing can stop it.*

BAKER:
> *You're a silly girl—It's a sign of youth.*

EILEEN: *(Shakes head)*
> *You're a silly boy—You're in love with Ruth.*
> *It's love! It's love!*
> *Come on now—Just try it.*

BAKER: *(Tentatively)*
> *It's love! It's love!*

EILEEN:
> *Don't try to deny it,*
> *I know the signs,*
> *I know it when I see it—*
> *So just face it,*
> *Just say it.*

BAKER:
> *It's love,*
> *It's love,*
> (BAKER *sings*—Big)
> *It's love!!*
> (EILEEN *watches him a moment—then exits*)
> *Maybe—It's love! It's love!*
> *(As the realization grows)*
> *Well, who would have thought it*
> *If this is love,*
> *Then why have I fought it?*
> *What a way to feel—*
> *I could touch the sky.*
> *What a way to feel—*
> *I'm a different guy!*
>
> *It's love, at last,*
> *I've someone to cheer for—*
> *It's love, at last,*
> *I've learned what we're here for—*
> *I've heard it said,*
> *"You'll know it when you see it."*
> *Well, I see it—I know it—*
> *It's Love!*

> *(Exits happily)*

SCENE 5

The Village Vortex, a surrealistic nightclub, hung with paintings from every artist who couldn't pay his tab, and dominated by a huge revolving mobile, hung from the ceiling. VALENTI *leads the band with his clarinet as the crowd dances a slow, writhing jitterbug, packed tightly together like anchovies.*

VALENTI: *(As dance ends and a bedlam of sound from the crowd bubbles up)* Settle down! Settle down!

(WRECK has opened bottle of champagne. Rises with bottle and glass)

WRECK: Folks, here's a toast to my future mother-in-law. Long may she wave!

PATRON: *(From balcony)* Sit down, you bum!

(WRECK starts to remove his coat and glasses, shakes an angry fist at patron)

HELEN: *(To WRECK)* Please, Mr. Loomis—

(WRECK subsides)

VALENTI: Cat and Gates! You've read about her, you've talked about her! Now here she is in person, fresh from a cellar in Christopher Street—Miss Eileen Sherwood!

(RUTH and EILEEN enter. RUTH is pushing EILEEN, fixing her hair at the last minute)

Give the little girl a great big hand!

(He leads applause. EILEEN climbs steps—RUTH sits on bottom step)

CHICK: *(Enters)* Hey, Ruth, I gotta square myself with you.

RUTH: Go away—my sister's going to sing!

EILEEN: You get out of here, Chick Clark!

FRANK: *(Stepping in)* Is he annoying you, Miss Sherwood?

CHICK: *(Pushing FRANK)* Go on back to your drugstore! No! Look, Ruth! I got your press card, signed by the city editor! You start Monday!

RUTH: Is it true?

CHICK: It's official—I tell ya!

LONIGAN: *(To CHICK)* All right you—come on! *(Takes CHICK'S arm)*

CHICK: Ruth, tell this clown I'm okay!

RUTH: No, no, Officer—he's all right!

EILEEN: Yes, John—you can let him go now.

LONIGAN: *(Disgustedly)* Ah!

RUTH: Oh, thanks, Chick! Eileen, I can't believe it! Look, it's a press card! I've got a job—I can go to work! *(They embrace)*

EILEEN: Ruth, that's wonderful!

VALENTI: What is this—a nightclub or an employment agency?

VOICES: Come on! Sing it! Let's hear her sing!

VALENTI: Come on, what are you cryin' for?

EILEEN: I'm happy!

RUTH: We're both happy!

VALENTI: Well, I ain't! And the customers ain't! Sing or blow!

RUTH: She'll sing! Go on Eileen—

EILEEN: I can't—I can't just stop crying and start singing!

RUTH: Of course, you can!

EILEEN: Do it with me, Ruth, please!

RUTH: In front of all those people!

VALENTI: Come on! Come on!

EILEEN: Ruth!

RUTH: Should I, Mr. Valenti?

VALENTI: Sure! Do something—do anything!

RUTH: All right! Play the band—the "Wrong Note Rag"!

(RUTH and EILEEN stand up. RUTH explains the routine. RUTH and EILEEN hurriedly whisper directions to each other during the announcement)

VALENTI: Folks, something new has been added. Another glorious voice joins us. The "Wrong Note Rag"—Hit it, boys!

(There is an old-fashioned blaring introduction and RUTH *and* EILEEN *march forward and perform the number they have known since their early childhood. They work in a dead-pan sister-act, style circa 1913)*

RUTH AND EILEEN:

Oh there's a new sensation that is goin' aroun'—
Goin' around—Goin' around—Goin' around—
A simple little ditty that is sweepin' the town,
Sweepin' the town—Swee—eepin' the town—
Doo—Doo—Doo
Doo—Doo—Doo—Doo—Doo—Doo
They call it the Wrong Note Rag!

It's got a little twist that really drives ya insane,
Drives ya insane, drives ya insane, drives ya insane,
Because you'll find you never get it out of your brain,
Out of your brain—Ou-Out of your brain!
Doo—Doo—Doo—
They call it the Wrong Note Rag!

(The music and the girls' spirit and energy become infectious and the crowd joins in)

ALL:

Bunny Hug!
Turkey Trot!
Gimme the Wrong Note Rag!

GIRLS:

Please play that lovely wrong note
Because that wrong note
Just makes me
Doo—Doo Da—Doo, Doo—Doo—Da—Doo, Doodoo!

That note is such a strong note
It makes me

EILEEN:

Rick-ricky-tick rick-ricky-tick tacky.

RUTH:

Wick-wicky-wick wick-wick-wick wacky.

GIRLS:

Don't play that right polite note
Because that right note
Just makes me
Blah-blah-bla-blah, blah-blah-bla-blah blah blah!

Give me that new and blue note
And sister
Watch my dust,
Watch my smoke
Doin' the Wrong Note Rag!

(They break out into a corny ragtime dance, and the couples at the Vortex, loving it, pick up the steps and join them, building the number to a high-spirited finish. There is wild enthusiasm from the Vortex patrons as RUTH *and* EILEEN *hug each other happily)*

VALENTI: Well, that's what drove 'em out of Ohio. What are you gonna do for an encore?

EILEEN: Encore? Did I get one?

RUTH: Of course you did! You were terrific! Go on!

VALENTI: What's it gonna be? *(*EILEEN *whispers,* "It's Love"! *She goes upstage and all face her.* RUTH *sits on a step downstage)* For an encore our little premier donna is gonna get nice and mellow—Keep it low, folks.

(The music to "It's Love" starts and EILEEN *sings—all eyes on her. She is in a spotlight—and so is* RUTH, *watching her)*

EILEEN: *(As she sings)*
It's love! It's love!
Well, who would have thought it.

*(*BAKER *enters, looks about, sees* RUTH, *he goes to her and touches her shoulder. She turns, shushes him and turns back to watch* EILEEN*)*

If this is love
Then why have I fought it?

*(*RUTH *does a take as she realizes it is* BAKER, *but she shushes him again. This time he takes her in his arms and kisses her. Still dazed, she pushes him away, saying, "Ssh!" Then suddenly realizing what is happening, she turns back to him and rushes into his arms)*

What a way to feel—
I could touch the sky.
What a way to feel—
I have found my guy.

BAKER: *(Holding* RUTH, *as all turn to watch them,* EILEEN *beaming happily at them across the club)*
It's love at last,
I've someone to cheer for.

RUTH:
It's love at last—
I've learned what we're here for.

ALL: *(Singing)*
I've heard it said,
"You'll know it when you see it."

*(*RUTH *and* BAKER, *holding hands, oblivious to everything but each other)*

Well, I see it—I know it—
It's love!

    The Curtain Falls

FIORELLO!

Book by Jerome Weidman and George Abbott
Lyrics by Sheldon Harnick
Music by Jerry Bock

Editor's Notes

Winner of Broadway's triple crown, the Pulitzer Prize, the New York Drama Critics' Circle Award and the Antoinette Perry (Tony) Award, *Fiorello!* opened on November 23, 1959, to rave reviews and sellout houses. A musical celebration of the life and times of one of New York's most beloved mayors, Fiorello H. La Guardia, it ran for 795 performances, a record that he, too, would have approved. Indeed, Brooks Atkinson noted in *The New York Times* that: "*Fiorello!* is not the least of the Little Flower's gifts to the city he loved . . . Jerome Weidman and George Abbott, old pros in excellent standing, have written the legend of La Guardia's preliminary years in poster style—admiring and enjoying their hero as they go along . . . Everything falls into place with the most cheerful precision."

Other first-night judges lauded it with such phrases as: "*Fiorello!* scored a smashing victory at the polls with humor, heart and zest . . . A warm, humorous and melodic panorama of the New York scene during (and before) the Tempestuous Twenties . . . It tells a heartening story well, and the music is in complete sympathy . . . It is a hard-boiled tale, raucous, honest and blisteringly funny . . . The audience began cheering long before the final curtain."

Walter Kerr, then writing for the *New York Herald Tribune*, summed up the event with: "When Mr. Abbott makes a musical, it's a beaut!"

A leading American author, Jerome Weidman (coauthor with George Abbott of the book for *Fiorello!*) was born in New York City on April 4, 1913. He was educated at the College of the City of New York and the New York University Law School. His initial prominence came with the best-selling novel about Manhattan's garment industry, *I Can Get It for You Wholesale*, published in 1937. Many other novels were to follow. To name some: *What's in It for Me?*, *I'll Never Go There Any More*, *The Price Is Right*, *The Hand of the Hunter*, *Give Me Your Love*, *Before You Go*, *The Sound of Bow Bells*, *They Told Me You Were Dead*, and *The Enemy Camp*.

A prolific writer, he also has published a number of collections of short stories, among them: *The Horse That Could Whistle "Dixie"*, *The Captain's Tiger*, *My Father Sits in the Dark*, *The Nine Stories*, and a travel book, *Letter of Credit*.

As a playwright, Mr. Weidman made his Broadway debut with *Fiorello!* This was followed by collaborating once again with Mr. Abbott on the book for *Tenderloin* (with lyrics by Sheldon Harnick, music by Jerry Bock, 1960); and the musical version of his popular novel, *I Can Get It for You Wholesale* (with lyrics and music by Harold Rome, and which introduced a newcomer to the Broadway stage, Barbra Streisand, 1962).

In addition to his many books and works for the theatre, Jerome Weidman has written extensively for television and motion pictures; in the latter mediums are his screenplays for *The Damned Don't Cry*, *House of Strangers*, and *I Can Get it for You Wholesale*.

The grand doyen of the American theatre, George Abbott was born in Forestville, New York, on June 25, 1887. He first became interested in the theatre while attending the University of Rochester, from which he graduated with a B.A. He then went to Harvard University to study playwriting with George Pierce Baker, who was one of the most vital influences in the formation of modern dramatic literature and theatre.

Mr. Abbott first came to the New York theatre as an actor in the 1913 production, *The Misleading Lady*. His acting career continued well into the twenties, after which (with only occasional forays into performing again) he devoted all his energies to writing, directing and producing, and became one of the outstanding men on Broadway. His first major success as a dramatist occurred in 1925 when he collaborated with James Gleason on the comedy, *The Fall Guy.*

To list all of the productions that he was associated with thereafter, either as author, director or producer (or a combination of all three) would require at least a half-dozen pages. Thus, in the interest of conciseness, the editor has chosen merely to list his most successful and better-known achievements.

The plays, in nonchronological order, include: *Broadway, Chicago, Gentlemen of the Press, Jarnegan, Louder Please, Twentieth Century, Four Walls, Coquette, Page Miss Glory, Three Men on a Horse, Boy Meets Girl, Small Miracle, Brother Rat, Room Service, The Primrose Path, What a Life, Jason, Kiss and Tell,* and *Take Her, She's Mine.*

Then there are the musicals, once again in nonchronological order: *Jumbo, On Your Toes, The Boys from Syracuse, Best Foot Forward, Too Many Girls, Beat the Band, Pal Joey, Look, Ma, I'm Dancin'!, Once Upon a Mattress, High Button Shoes, Where's Charley?, Barefoot Boy with Cheek, On the Town, Billion Dollar Baby, New Girl in Town, Me and Juliet, Call Me Madam, The Pajama Game, Damn Yankees, A Tree Grows in Brooklyn, Wonderful Town,* and *A Funny Thing Happened on the Way to the Forum.*

Once described as "a modern Molière," the hallmarks of an Abbott show were pace, humor and a steady level of efficient action.

In addition to his endless contributions to the American stage (and to the entertainment of millions of theatregoers), he also has written and directed many films, and in 1963, to celebrate his fiftieth year in the theatre, he published his autobiography, *Mr. Abbott.*

Jerry Bock (music) and Sheldon Harnick (lyrics) first came into joint view with the 1958 production of *The Body Beautiful.* Although that musical could hardly be classified as a success, it was an important (and catalytical) event for the songwriting duo, for their work so impressed producer Harold Prince, his late partner, Robert Griffith, and George Abbott that they commissioned the collaborators to take on the assignment of creating the songs and musical numbers for *Fiorello!* The success of the production propelled the team of Bock and Harnick to the forefront of the American musical theatre. It also was the harbinger of their record-breaking work, *Fiddler on the Roof* (with book by Joseph Stein, it ran for 3,225 performances) and the start of their long and successful association with Harold Prince under whose managerial banner they also collaborated on *Tenderloin* (1960) and *She Loves Me* (1963).

With their 1966 Broadway musical, *The Apple Tree* (based on stories by Mark Twain, Frank R. Stockton and Jules Feiffer), Bock and Harnick entered a new phase of collaboration: in addition to creating the words and music, they also functioned as coauthors of the book.

Jerry Bock was born in New Haven, Connecticut, in 1928, raised in Flushing, New York, and attended Flushing High School (where he began his composing career) and the University of Wisconsin. He received his baptism as a "professional" composer at Camp Tamiment in the Poconos, and later wrote much of the music for television's "Your Show of Shows." He also contributed songs (with Larry Holofcener as lyricist) to the revue *Catch a Star* and an edition of the *Ziegfeld Follies.* His first full Broadway score was written for the Sammy Davis, Jr. vehicle *Mr. Wonderful* (1956).

Born in Chicago in 1924, Sheldon Harnick was inspired by his mother's passion for commemorating all occasions in verse and while still at grammar school picked up the thread and commenced to write poems himself, "mostly doggerel and mostly nonsense." In 1943, he entered the army and it was while in service that he first started seriously to write songs which he performed at various USO shows, sandwiching them in between his violin solos.

In 1946, he returned to Chicago and enrolled at Northwestern University where he contributed songs to the annual student musicals and doubled as a fiddle player with the show's orchestra. After graduation from Northwestern, he worked for a while as a violinist with Xavier Cugat's orchestra, then after being fired for "swaying to the left instead of the right," he headed for New York and a career as a songwriter.

Prior to teaming up with Jerry Bock, Mr. Harnick contributed his talents to *New Faces of 1952* (notably, with the number "Boston Beguine"). During this period (the 1950's), some other revues that included his work were *Two's Company, The Littlest Revue, Take Five, Kaleidoscope,* and *John Murray Anderson's Almanac.*

In 1970, Bock and Harnick had another Broadway success with *The Rothschilds* (based on Frederic Morton's book and with a libretto by Sherman Yellen); it ran for 507 performances.

At the moment, the team is working separately. Jerry Bock is contemplating a new project while Sheldon Harnick has completed the lyrics for the musical *Rex* (with book by Sherman Yellen and music by Richard Rodgers) which is scheduled to open on Broadway in 1976.

Production Notes

Fiorello! was first presented by Robert E. Griffith and Harold S. Prince at the Broadhurst Theatre, New York, on November 23, 1959. The cast was as follows:

Announcer, *Del Horstmann*	Sophie, *Lynn Ross*
Fiorello, *Tom Bosley*	First Heckler, *Bob Bernard*
Neil, *Bob Holiday*	Second Heckler, *Michael Scrittorale*
Morris, *Nathaniel Frey*	Third Heckler, *Jim Maher*
Mrs. Pomerantz, *Helen Verbit*	Fourth Heckler, *Joseph Toner*
Mr. Lopez, *H. F. Green*	Thea, *Ellen Hanley*
Mr. Zappatella, *David Collyer*	Senator, *Frederic Downs*
Dora, *Pat Stanley*	Judge Carter, *Joseph Toner*
Marie, *Patricia Wilson*	Commissioner, *Michael Quinn*
Ben, *Howard Da Silva*	Politician, *H. F. Green*
First Hack, *Stanley Simmonds*	Mitzi, *Eileen Rodgers*
Second Hack, *Del Horstmann*	Frankie Scarpini, *Michael Scrittorale*
Third Hack, *Michael Quinn*	Florence, *Deedy Irwin*
Fourth Hack, *Ron Husmann*	Reporter, *Julian Patrick*
Fifth Hack, *David London*	First Man, *Scott Hunter*
Sixth Hack, *Julian Patrick*	Second Man, *Michael Scrittorale*
Seedy Man, *Joseph Toner*	Tough Man, *David London*
Nina, *Pat Turner*	Derby, *Bob Bernard*
Floyd, *Mark Dawson*	Frantic, *Stanley Simmonds*

Singers, *David Collyer, Barbara Gilbert, Del Horstmann, Deedy Irwin, Mara Landi, David London, Julian Patrick, Ginny Perlowin, Patsy Peterson, Silver Saundors, Ron Husmann.*

Dancers, *Charlene Carter, Bob Bernard, Elaine Cancilla, Ellen Harris, Patricia Harty, Scott Hunter, Bob La Crosse, Lynda Lynch, James Maher, Gregg Owen, Lowell Purvis, Dellas Rennie, Lynn Ross, Dan Siretta, Michael Scrittorale, Pat Turner.*

Production Directed by *George Abbott*
Choreography by *Peter Gennaro*
Scenery, Costumes and Lighting by *William* and *Jean Eckart*
Musical Direction: *Hal Hastings*
Orchestrations by *Irwin Kostal*
Dance Music Arranged by *Jack Elliott*

> *Act One:* New York City, shortly before World War I.
> *Act Two:* Ten years later.

Musical Numbers

Act One

On the Side of the Angels	Bob Holiday, Nathaniel Frey, Patricia Wilson
Politics and Poker	Howard Da Silva and Politicians
Unfair	Tom Bosley, Pat Stanley and Girls
Marie's Law	Patricia Wilson and Nathaniel Frey
The Name's LaGuardia	Tom Bosley and Company
The Bum Won	Howard Da Silva and Politicians
I Love a Cop	Pat Stanley
I Love a Cop (Reprise)	Pat Stanley and Mark Dawson
Till Tomorrow	Ellen Hanley and Company
Home Again	Company

Act Two

When Did I Fall in Love	Ellen Hanley
Gentleman Jimmy	Eileen Rodgers and Dancing Girls
Gentleman Jimmy (Reprise)	Company
Little Tin Box	Howard Da Silva and Politicians
The Very Next Man	Patricia Wilson
The Very Next Man (Reprise)	Patricia Wilson
Finale	

PROLOGUE

After the "Overture" the orchestra plays a few bars of the "Marine Hymn."
ANNOUNCER: Ladies and gentlemen, His Honor Fiorello H. La Guardia, Mayor of New York.
FIORELLO: *(Voice)* Well, children, I guess you've been wondering what's happened to little Shirley Shorthand. Patience and fortitude!
(The lights come up gradually. FIORELLO *is sitting in a radio station, holding up a*

comic paper. Above his head an electric sign reads "ON THE AIR." He is talking into a microphone marked "WNYC")

FIORELLO: In this first box we see Shirley leaving for the office. Her mother stands in the door. Mrs. Shorthand says: "Goodbye, Shirley dear, be a good girl." Now in this next box what do we see? Oh, ho! A fierce-looking fellow —Shirley's boss—Alderman P. T. Pickel, a very, very corrupt man. And I can remember when we had a lot of corrupt men running our dear city—way back before the First World War, when I had my law office in Greenwich Village . . .

(The lights begin to fade. The stage is in total darkness as we hear NEIL'S voice)

ACT ONE

SCENE 1

Time: Shortly before the First World War.

Place: Law offices of FIORELLO H. LAGUARDIA in Greenwich Village. Two simple rooms: a private office at left; a combination reception room and outer office at right.

At Rise: It is late afternoon. NEIL, the bright young law clerk, is at the switchboard. MORRIS, the doleful, resigned, pessimistic office manager, is standing near the filing cabinets, talking on the phone. MRS. POMERANTZ, a plump, squat matron in her fifties, is seated on the client's bench.

NEIL: *(Into switchboard phone)* Yes, I'll give him the message. *(Switchboard buzzes)* Office of Fiorello H. LaGuardia, good afternoon. *(He listens, then turns)* Morris, on Saperstein versus Kriewald, General Sessions, Tuesday—will Mr. La Guardia be there?

MORRIS: I don't think so.

NEIL: You're kidding.

MORRIS: Mr. LaGuardia never has time for people who pay their bills. He'll be taking care of some charity case.

NEIL: Aw—come on.

MORRIS: Sure, he'll be there.

(MR. LOPEZ, a shabbily dressed man, enters and looks around)

MR. LOPEZ: Excuse—?

MRS. POMERANTZ: I'm waiting first!

NEIL: *(Into phone)* Yes, sir. Yes, he'll be there. *(He hangs up and makes a note on his pad)*

MR. LOPEZ: My papers. I got trouble.

(Buzzer sounds. MR. ZAPPATELLA, an elderly Italian, enters)

NEIL: *(To LOPEZ)* One second, please. *(Into phone)* Office of Fiorello H. La-Guardia.

MRS. POMERANTZ: *(To ZAPPATELLA)* I'm waiting first.

NEIL: *(To ZAPPATELLA)* Just have a seat, please. *(To MORRIS)* Morris, it's your wife.

ZAPPATELLA: Excuse—

MORRIS: *(Picking up phone)* Yes, Shirley?

ZAPPATELLA: *(To NEIL)* Mr. LaGuardia he help me?

NEIL: He'll be here directly.

LOPEZ: *(Reassuringly, to* ZAPPATELLA*)* Mr. LaGuardia he help anybody.
MRS. POMERANTZ: I'm waiting first.
ZAPPATELLA: *(To* NEIL*)* He help me—you sure?
NEIL: Yes, I'm sure he'll help you—don't worry. *(Goes into private office and places a slip of paper on* FIORELLO'S *desk)* Mr. LaGuardia will help you. *(He sings "On the Side of the Angels")*

What a man!
What a job!
All these people
Who look to us for justice—
Trust us!

What a boss to work for
What a fine upstanding man he is
I'll follow in his footsteps
And do my level best
To earn a reputation like his.

I promise I'll proudly endure
The hardships I'll share
Working with this man
On the side of the angels.

My life will be selfless and pure
Like Upton Sinclair
Working with this man
On the side of the angels.

We're marching forward
Incorruptible, he and I
Battling with evil
Fighting till we drop
What a way to die!

So give me your tired, your poor,
And scoundrels, beware!
Here we stand in chorus
He and I and Morris
Standing firm, side by side,
On the side of the angels!

(He goes back to the switchboard)
MORRIS: *(At phone)* Shirley, how can I tell you when to put the roast in? No, Shirley, only God and Mr. LaGuardia know when I'll be there, and neither one tells me till the last minute. I would ask him, but he hasn't come in yet. What a man is right. *(He sings "On the Side of the Angels")*

What a job!
What a man!
What an office!
That line of poor and friendless—
Endless!

Call the fire department
There's another kitten up a tree
Up goes Fiorello
And everybody cheers
And what does he use for a ladder?
Me?

Your life is an island of grief
Surrounded by woe
When you choose to work
On the side of the angels.

My hours of leisure are brief
My wages are low
Working with this man
On the side of the angels.

That bench stays crowded
It's a regular wailing wall
Penniless and helpless
Ignorant and scared
He collects 'em all!

There's never a moment's relief
But this much I know
Each poor soul I see there
Could be me there
So I stay with this man
On the side of the angels!

NEIL: *(At phone, covering mouthpiece)* Morris, will Mr. LaGuardia be willing to play cornet at the Saturday night dance for the First Hibernian Sick and Benevolent Association?

MORRIS: If they promise not to pay him. I think it will be okay. Check with Miss Fischer.

DORA: *(Enters)* Pardon me—

NEIL: *(Into phone)* His secretary isn't here just now, but—

DORA: Miss Fischer, please.

MRS. POMERANTZ: I'm waiting first.

NEIL: *(To DORA)* One second—*(He turns back to the phone)*

DORA: It's terribly important. Somebody's in jail.

   (MARIE enters from the outside, carrying a cornet. She is an attractive, wholesome, efficient girl)

DORA: *(Turning from NEIL and hurrying toward MARIE)* Marie! Thank Heaven!

MARIE: Dora! What's the matter?

DORA: Marie, please, you've got to get Mr. LaGuardia to help us. They've arrested Thea.

MARIE: Come in here.

MRS. POMERANTZ: President Wilson's daughter!

MARIE: *(She takes DORA into the inner office)* Now for goodness' sake, calm down. What happened?

DORA: Thea's our leader. She's the one got us to go out on strike in the first place. She's the only one dares talk back to them. And now they arrested her.

MARIE: For picketing? They can't do that.

DORA: Marie, not for picketing—for soliciting.

MARIE: For what?

DORA: Yes, soliciting. That crooked cop, he claims she was trying to pick up somebody.

MARIE: And she wasn't?

DORA: No, she was just carrying a banner.

MARIE: She wasn't—oh—flirting with anybody? Or wiggling or anything? *(She twitches her hips just a trifle to illustrate)*

DORA: No, no, she wasn't. She's not that kind at all. Somebody's just got to help us. You've got to help us—

MARIE: Now, now—

DORA: She's in jail, Marie, she's in jail.

MARIE: Now please, Dora, don't get so excited. Cut it out. Gee whiz, Mr. La-Guardia will do something. I know he will. Now come on! You sit out here and just wait.

(MARIE takes DORA into the outer office. In the other room, the conversation now resumes)

MR. ZAPPATELLA: Look, I no want to go to jail.

MRS. POMERANTZ: Who wants to go to jail?

MR. ZAPPATELLA: My daughter she come home it's after eleven o'clock. She's out with a bad boy. I say: Don't go again or I hit. She go again. I hit. She call a policeman. He give me this summons.

(The room freezes into silence as FIORELLO strides in through the outer door, wearing his famous sombrero, and, with scarcely a look at the people in the outer office, goes through to the inner office. He hangs up his hat and sits at the desk as though in the throes of great excitement. Meanwhile, after he has shut the door, the people in the outer office begin to murmur again. We don't notice them, however. We watch FIORELLO. Suddenly he gives the desk a slap with the flat of his hand and jumps to his feet)

FIORELLO: *(With exalted decision)* Yes! *(He hurries back into the outer office. As he enters, all talking ceases abruptly. He looks around, spots MARIE, points a finger at her, and returns to his own office. MARIE jumps up, follows him in, and shuts the door)* Sit!

MARIE: Mr. LaGuardia, something terrible has just happened.

FIORELLO: *(An impatient wave of the hand)* Later.

MARIE: My friend Dora, she's here about a girl they arrested for soliciting.

FIORELLO: *(Preoccupied)* Marie, look. Ben Marino. The Republican leader of the Fourteenth District—you told me you knew him. What I'd like, Marie, I want you—*(Pause, then sharp)* Soliciting? A friend of yours?

MARIE: Yes. But it's just a frame-up. They just do it to break the strike.

FIORELLO: The strike?

MARIE: The shirtwaist strike.

FIORELLO: Marie, I'll take care of your friend's friend in just a moment. But first, I want you to arrange to introduce me to Ben Marino.

MARIE: But—

FIORELLO: I just heard he's having trouble finding a candidate for Congress, and I want the nomination.

MARIE: *(Incredulous)* In the Fourteenth? Mr. LaGuardia, Tammany has that district sewed up. No Republican has ever gone to Congress from the Fourteenth. I can't believe you're serious.

FIORELLO: Try. Because I'm counting on you to introduce me to Ben. Why do you suppose I've spent all that time down at Silky Hetzel's Club in the Twelfth?

MARIE: I thought it was business.

FIORELLO: I was waiting for an opening. And now that I've found it, let's not waste any time. Bring your friend in. *(Sees cornet)* Oh, it's fixed. Good.

(MARIE goes to the outer office. FIORELLO blows a note on the cornet)

MARIE: Dora—

MRS. POMERANTZ: *(Rising)* I'm waiting first.

(DORA follows MARIE into the inner office)

DORA: Mr. LaGuardia, I can't tell you how—

FIORELLO: I've heard about that shirtwaist strike. First time women have been on the picket line.

DORA: They've arrested our leader. We've been out for six weeks and our money's about gone, and they arrested her, and the most awful part is it's for soliciting!

FIORELLO: And she wasn't?

DORA: No, sir. Just picketing. And Mr. Schirmer, the owner, he promised us if we'd work through the busy season we'd get a living wage, and then he broke his word. Honest, Mr. LaGuardia, they treated us just terrible.

FIORELLO: My dear girl, I understand Mr. Schirmer and people like him. They'll stop at nothing. They murdered my father. *(He turns to MARIE)* Marie! Telephone Ben Marino and tell him we're on the way over. *(He turns back to DORA as MARIE starts out of the room)*

DORA: They murdered your father?

FIORELLO: They did. *(Turns to MARIE)* Marie! Never mind. It's better just to walk in and surprise him. *(To DORA, as MARIE stops and turns back)* They poisoned him.

DORA: *(Aghast)* The Nifty Shirtwaist Corporation?

FIORELLO: *(Impatient)* No, the exploiters. That's the trouble with this younger generation. You don't grasp issues. You see the little things, and miss the big ones. They sold rotten food to the Army in the Spanish-American War—and my father died. *(To MARIE)* Send Morris in here. *(To DORA, as MARIE goes out to fetch MORRIS)* These same crooks will wear out your young lives working you twelve hours a day, then try to intimidate you by framing an innocent young girl and ruining her life—while they drive around in their great big shiny cars earned by the exploitation of children. *(MORRIS enters)* Morris, I want you to go right over to Ike Feeney's and arrange for a bail bond for a friend of this girl's.

MORRIS: Yes, sir.

FIORELLO: *(To* DORA*)* Meantime, you go on back to strike headquarters and I'll meet you there.

DORA: Thank you, Mr. LaGuardia.

MORRIS: This way, miss.

FIORELLO: *(To* DORA, *as he moves into outer office)* And don't be afraid of Morris. Under that melon he calls a face, he's got a kind heart. *(*FIORELLO *goes to the waiting group on the client's bench)* All right, my friends. Who's first?

*(*MARIE *remains in* FIORELLO'S *office. Music starts for "On the Side of the Angels")*

MR. ZAPPATELLA: *(Singing)*
I no want to go to jail

MR. LOPEZ: *(Singing)*
Tell me what I gotta do

MRS. POMERANTZ: *(Singing)*
I got such a lot of trouble and grief

ALL THREE:
I need relief
That's why I come to you.

(The following is sung in counterpoint)

MR. ZAPPATELLA:
I no want to go to jail

MARIE:
As long as he wants me, I know

MR. LOPEZ:
Tell me what I gotta do

I'll always be here

MRS. POMERANTZ:
I got such a lot of trouble and grief

Working with this man

ALL THREE:
I need relief
That's why I come to you.

On the side of the angels.

MR. ZAPPATELLA:
I'm in trouble with the law

NEIL:
Wherever he sends me, I'll go

MRS. POMERANTZ:
Don't know what it's all about

My duty is clear

LOPEZ:
I no got a lot of money to pay

Working with this man

ALL THREE:
People they say you help me out.

On the side of the angels.

MORRIS: *(Solo, pointing to* DORA*)*
Here's one more client
Who's another financial gem
I've yet to see the meek
Inheriting the earth
But we inherit them!

(In counterpoint)

ALL THREE:

   I was worried where to go
   So I talk to all my friends
   Everybody say when you want the best
   You go to Fiorello
   Sure, they say you very smart
   But more than that
   They say you got a heart
   Just like the angels.

MARIE, MORRIS, NEIL:

   I know that he needs me, and so
   I'll make my career
   Working by his side
   And proud to be allowed to
   Side by side with this man
   On the side of the angels.

   Blackout

SCENE 2

Place: The main room of the Ben Marino Association on West Third Street. Over a large round poker table covered with green baize, hangs a single electric bulb shielded by one of those porcelain shades that look like inverted ice-cream cones— white on the inside, green on the outside. In the background, through a haze of cigar smoke, we can see all the other recognizable symbols of a battered, musty political meeting house.

At Rise: BEN'S POLITICAL HACKS are seated around the table. They are playing five-card stud. BEN MARINO is not in the game. He paces back and forth.

FIRST HACK: What do you say, Ben? You gonna take a hand?

BEN: Not now. Too much on my mind to play poker. Gotta settle on that damn candidate. *(SEEDY MAN enters)* Well, look who's here, my old friend Eddie Brown. How are you, Eddie?

SEEDY MAN: *(Correcting him)* No, Harry.

BEN: Sure, Harry, isn't that what I said? Here—*(Takes a dollar from the pot)*—vote Republican—carfare.

SEEDY MAN: You bet, Mr. Marino. You can count on me. *(He exits)*

BEN: I doubt it.

THIRD HACK: That's your man, Ben. Run him.

BEN: May come to that yet. How about you? All you have to do—

THIRD HACK: I know, I know—

FIFTH HACK: He's done it twice.

THIRD HACK: Nothing doing. This time get yourself a brand-new sucker.

FIRST HACK: *(To BEN)* Sure you don't want to be dealt in?

BEN: No, go ahead.

   (They sing)

FIRST HACK:

   King bets.

SECOND HACK:

   Cost you five.
   Tony, up to you.

THIRD HACK:

   I'm in.

FOURTH HACK:
So am I.

FIFTH HACK:
Likewise.

FIRST HACK:
Me, too.

BEN: *(While the cards are being dealt)*
Gentlemen, here we are, and one thing is clear:
We gotta pick a candidate for Congress this year.

FIRST HACK:
Big ace.

SECOND HACK:
Ace bets.

THIRD HACK:
You'll pay—through the nose.

FOURTH HACK:
I'm in.

FIFTH HACK:
So am I.

FIRST HACK:
Likewise.

SECOND HACK:
Here goes.

FIRST HACK: *(Examining the hands)*
Possible straight,
Possible flush,
Nothing.

BEN:
Gentlemen, how about some names we can use?
Some qualified Republican who's willing to lose?

SECOND HACK:
How's about we should make Jack Riley the guy?

THIRD HACK:
Which Riley are you thinking of? Jack B. or Jack Y.?

BEN:
I say neither one,
I never even met 'em.

FOURTH HACK:
I say:
When you got a pair of jacks,
Bet 'em!

ALL:
Politics and poker
Politics and poker

Shuffle up the cards
And find the joker.
Neither game's for children,
Either game is rough.
Decisions, decisions, like:
Who to pick,
How to play,
What to bet,
When to call a bluff.

BEN: *(Speaking)* All right, now, fellas, politics or poker? Which is more important?

FIRST HACK: *(Singing)*
Pair of treys.

SECOND HACK:
Bet 'em.

THIRD HACK:
Little treys,
Good as gold.

FOURTH HACK:
I'll stay.

FIFTH HACK:
Raise you five.

FIRST HACK:
I'll call.

SECOND HACK:
I'll fold.

THIRD HACK:
Raise you back.

FOURTH HACK:
I think you're bluffin'.

THIRD HACK:
Put your money where your mouth is.

BEN:
Gentlemen, knock it off, and let's get this done.

FIFTH HACK:
Try Michael Paniaschenkowitz, I'm certain he'd run.

BEN:
Mike is out. I'm afraid he just wouldn't sell
Nobody likes a candidate whose name they can't spell.

FIRST HACK:
How about Dave Zimmerman?

BEN:
Davy's too bright.

SECOND HACK:
What about Walt Gustafson?

BEN:
Walt died last night.

THIRD HACK:
How about Frank Monahan?

FOURTH HACK:
What about George Gale?

BEN:
*Frank ain't a citizen, and
George is in jail.*

FIFTH HACK:
We could run Al Wallenstein.

BEN:
He's only twenty-three.

FIRST HACK:
What about Ed Peterson?

SECOND HACK:
You idiot! That's me!

ALL:
*Politics and poker
Politics and poker
Playing for a pot
That's mediocre.
Politics and poker,
Running neck and neck.
If politics seems more
Predictable that's because usually you can stack the deck!*

(Enter MARIE)
MARIE: Mr. Marino.
BEN: Well, if it isn't my old friend Miss Fischer. How are you, Miss Fischer?
MARIE: I came over because I want you to make the acquaintance of my boss, Mr. LaGuardia.
THIRD HACK: Huh!
BEN: Who?
THIRD HACK: That little wop with the big hat. *(Contemptuous)* Fiorello. You know him. He hangs around Silky Hetzel's in the Twelfth.
*(*FIORELLO *enters)*
FIORELLO: There are no little wops. Just big ones. As I'm ready and willing to demonstrate.
THIRD HACK: A modest guy, huh?
FIORELLO: No, just a guy who happens to believe the way to beat Tammany is not—*(Reaches over, takes the* THIRD HACK'S *cards, and tosses them to center of table)*—by throwing in your cards. I came over to get this nomination.
FIRST HACK: Is he kiddin'?
FIORELLO: I never kid about serious issues, and I'm sitting on one right now that's

big enough and hot enough to elect a Congressman from this district.

MARIE: Ben, what have you got to lose?

BEN: *(Dry)* Just another election, that's all.

FIORELLO: You've been doing that long enough. Here's your chance to win for a change.

BEN: With what?

FIORELLO: The people of your own district. You think the men and women of the Fourteenth like the tenth-rate tinhorns they've had representing them in Congress for years?

BEN: And you think—?

FIORELLO: You give me the nomination, and I'll give you a Congressman.

BEN: And if you don't?

FIORELLO: *(Holds up his large sombrero)* See this hat?

BEN: You might get indigestion.

FIORELLO: I'll take my chances on that. Do I get the nomination?

BEN: *(Shrugging)* Why not?

MARIE: Congratulations, Mr. Marino, you've just got yourself a wonderful candidate.

FIORELLO: Call me tomorrow and I'll show you how to lay out the campaign. Right now, I've got to go take care of the hot issue that's going to help elect me. Come on, Marie.

(FIORELLO and MARIE exit)

BEN: *(Dry)* Well, we got that settled.

(The music starts. The players sing)

THIRD HACK:
Gimme three.

FOURTH HACK:
Likewise.

FIFTH HACK:
None for me. Standing pat.

FIRST HACK:
Up to you.

SECOND HACK:
I'm in.

THIRD HACK:
I'm out.

FOURTH HACK:
I'm flat.

FIFTH HACK: *(Staring in direction taken by FIORELLO)*
Wonder why any guy would lead with his chin
Don't Fiorello realize he ain't gonna win?

SECOND HACK:
Ain't it obvious the
Odds are too great?

BEN:
Some guys
Always gotta try to fill an inside straight.

(He speaks)

If they didn't, where the hell would the fun be in the game? *(He joins the game)*

ALL:

Politics and poker
Politics and poker
Makes the av'rage guy
A heavy smoker.
Bless the nominee,
And give him our regards,
And watch while he learns
That in poker and politics,
Brother, you gotta have
That slippery haphazardous commodity
You gotta have the cards!

Blackout

SCENE 3

Place: The street outside strike headquarters, which is in a store next to the Nifty Shirtwaist Factory.

At Rise: DORA, NINA, BELLA, LENA, SOPHIE and others are moving in a picket circle, holding their signs overhead. They have very little spirit. They are singing "Unfair."

GIRLS:

Management's unfair
Management's unfair
Management is terribly unfair!

(They are being taunted and jeered at by male HECKLERS. A policeman, FLOYD, is standing by, watching)

FIRST HECKLER: Go get pants!

THIRD HECKLER: Go home, why don't you!

GIRLS: *(Singing)*
We've worked for a living all our lives
We're dreadfully underpaid
If you want to help your sisters and wives
Your mothers and daughters
Aid the lady strikers.

FIRST HECKLER: *(Speaking)* Says you! You want the vote? Go on home!

THIRD HECKLER: *(Speaking)* Woman's place is in the kitchen!

SECOND HECKLER: *(Speaking)* You wanna strike like men, you gotta dress like men!

NINA: Oh, shut up!

FIRST HECKLER: Go get pants!

NINA: We know why you're here—

DORA: Yes!

NINA: —insulting helpless women—'cause the company pays you to do it, that's why.

FIRST HECKLER: Woman's place is in the kitchen.

SOPHIE: *(Tearful)* How'd you like it if your sister had to work twelve hours a day, six days a week, for four dollars?

FIRST HECKLER: Go get pants!

SECOND HECKLER: Make a deal with you, girls! We'll teach you how to picket, if you teach us how to cook!

(*All* HECKLERS *laugh*)

NINA: *(At breaking point)* Somebody ought to teach you common decency! *(She stumbles. She pauses to adjust the cardboard in the torn sole of her shoe)*

FLOYD: *(Poking* NINA *with his nightstick)* Keep moving. No loitering allowed.

NINA: I'm not loitering. I've got a hole in my shoe. *(She hops along on one foot)*

FLOYD: Keep moving, I tell you. *(He pushes her)*

DORA: Hey, you stop that! What are you doing to that girl?

FLOYD: Another county heard from.

FIRST HECKLER: Wear pants!

FLOYD: And how does your big-mouthed girl friend like things over at the jail?

DORA: You can ask her—'cause she'll be back here in a couple of minutes. We got a lawyer now—and he got her out.

FLOYD: Stop all that lying and keep movin'. *(He pushes* DORA*)*

DORA: You get your hands off me, you cossack! *(*HECKLERS *yell tauntingly)* We got rights. Mr. LaGuardia says so.

FLOYD: And who, may I ask, is Mr. LaGuardia?

DORA: He's our lawyer.

NINA: Yeah—so there!

DORA: And we got a right to march—and you should be keeping those goons from bothering us, instead of joining in with them.

*(*HECKLERS *yell derisively)*

FIRST HECKLER: Wear pants!

FLOYD: Now look. *(Walks along with* DORA*)* I got me duty to do.

DORA: *(Hands him sign)* Hold this, will you, please? *(She hops along, fixing the cardboard in her shoe)*

FLOYD: What is this? Has everybody got holes in their shoes?

SOPHIE: Sure we have.

NINA: Where we going to get new shoes on our pay?

FLOYD: Then why don't you be sensible and go back to work?

SECOND HECKLER: Look!

THIRD HECKLER: He's joined them!

FLOYD: *(Becomes aware that he is carrying sign)* Here. What do you think you're doing to me? *(He thrusts the sign back into* DORA'S *hands)*

SOPHIE: We know why you want us to go back to work.

NINA: 'Cause you're just a Tammany grafter like all the rest of them.

FLOYD: I don't want that kind of language.

NINA: Then you leave us alone.

FIRST HECKLER: Pull 'em in!

SECOND HECKLER: Lock 'em up!

FIRST HECKLER: Do your duty, Officer.

DORA: He doesn't dast to touch her.

FLOYD: Oh, I don't, eh?

NINA: No, you don't!

FLOYD: Well, you close that big mouth or I'll take you over to the station right now.

NINA: On what charge?

FLOYD: Solicitin'. I saw you wigglin'. I saw you trying to get those men over there. They'll testify.

DORA: All right, then, arrest me. Look, I'm wigglin'. *(She wiggles vigorously. The HECKLERS cheer)* Go ahead! Why don't you? And I'll get over there and we'll have a doctor's examination, and I guess that'll prove who's a liar. That'll prove whether I'm one of those women or not.

FLOYD: Oh, you're a pure thing, eh?

DORA: You're God damn right I am! *(FIORELLO and MARIE enter)* Oh, Mr. LaGuardia. This copper—this policeman—

FIORELLO: All right, all right. I'll take charge. I'd like a word with you, Officer.

FLOYD: And who are you?

FIORELLO: You'll learn in the course of the next few weeks. *(To DORA)* You girls got a headquarters?

DORA: In the store.

FIORELLO: All go in there.

DORA: And stop picketing?

FIORELLO: For the moment. We'll have a little meeting.

NINA: Stop picketing?

DORA: Do what he says. He's a lawyer. He knows what he's talking about.
(The girls go out as FIORELLO continues the scene with FLOYD)

FIORELLO: The name is Fiorello H. LaGuardia, and you better get it firmly in your mind because you're going to hear a good deal about me in the next few months.

FLOYD: I am, eh?

FIORELLO: If there is any further interference with these girls in the exercise of their constitutional rights, I'll slap a writ of interdictum on each and every perpetrator of such interference—beginning with you.

FLOYD: *(Suddenly uneasy)* I'm just doing my duty, Counselor.

FIORELLO: I suggest you do it the way you promised under oath when you joined the force. I know what goes on behind the scenes, my friend. I know that this sweatshop and others like it have bought protection, and I intend to fight every one of them. I wouldn't like to see a nice intelligent fellow like you get caught in the middle.

FIRST HECKLER: Listen to him!

THIRD HECKLER: You gonna stand for that?

FLOYD: *(Blustering at them to save face)* Keep moving! Don't loiter! None of your lip! *(Crosses and waves the HECKLERS off the stage. Returns to FIORELLO)* I'll go back to the station house and report what you—what you just said about—about—you know.

FIORELLO: And if the Lieutenant has any difficulty understanding, I'll be glad to explain it to him, too. *(Hands FLOYD a card)* That's my office number. I answer calls from anybody.
(FLOYD goes)

MARIE: I do admire you so.

FIORELLO: Well, I tell you, Marie. There's nothing like being right.

MARIE: I'll go back to the office and check on a few more bail bondsmen.

FIORELLO: Good.

MARIE: Good night. *(She starts out)*

FIORELLO: Marie. *(She turns)* Would you care to have dinner with me tonight?

MARIE: What?

FIORELLO: That is, if you're not busy?

MARIE: Oh no, I'm not.

FIORELLO: Well?

MARIE: Of course. Yes. Yes, I would.

FIORELLO: I was going into an explanation—you know, the employer and his relations with people in the office—

MARIE: Oh, Mr. LaGuardia, I understand.

FIORELLO: But I have always wanted to know you better, Marie.

MARIE: I accept your invitation.

FIORELLO: Good. I'll pick you up at the office in about an hour.

    (MARIE exits. Cheers are heard. DORA comes running in) What's the matter?

DORA: She's here! She's back!

FIORELLO: Well, that's fine.

    (SOPHIE runs in without shoes)

SOPHIE: She wants to see Mr.—She's back—Oh, excuse me. Thea—*(SOPHIE exits)*

FIORELLO: *(Surprised as he stares offstage)* That girl? That's the girl they arrested?

DORA: She's a model. She works in the front. But she's joined us.

FIORELLO: That girl?

DORA: She's our leader.

    (Several girls enter)

NINA: She's out!

SOPHIE: That'll show 'em!

DORA: Put one over on the cossacks that time!

NINA: Now we'll win!

GIRLS: We'll win! *(MORRIS pushes through with THEA)*

FIORELLO: You did well, Morris.

MORRIS: She's out on Ike Feeney's five hundred dollars and her own recognizance. But I promised the judge that you'd be personally responsible. I'd have had her here sooner, but she insisted on washing her face.

FIORELLO: I can see that.

THEA: Thank you.

FIORELLO: Morris, you'd better line up a few more bondsmen. Then you can call Shirley and tell her to put the roast in the oven.

MORRIS: *(Morose)* Sure. Good night. *(He exits)*

FIORELLO: Girls!

DORA: Yes, sir?

FIORELLO: You got any running water in there? *(He points offstage)*

DORA: Yes, sir.

FIORELLO: Soap, too?

DORA: Uh-huh.

FIORELLO: All right. I don't want to see only one clean face. I want a lot of clean faces. In short, when you come back, I want you to look like girls again.

DORA: *(Rubbing her dirty face)* Yes, sir.

FIORELLO: And meantime I'll go over a few plans with this young lady.

DORA: *(Introduces THEA to him as the girls exit)* Miss Almerigatti.

FIORELLO: That's a good name. If you want to, you can call her Joan of Arc.

DORA: You bet. *(She exits)*

FIORELLO: *(Indicating a battered soapbox)* Won't you sit down, my dear young

lady? I know what you've been through—even though we don't let them know.
(THEA sits. He walks up and down)
THEA: Can we win?
FIORELLO: We can.
THEA: Somehow I believe you. But then I know, of course, that's not realistic.
   Lots of times I believe things can win and they don't come out that way.
FIORELLO: You've got a just cause.
THEA: Oh, I know that, but—
FIORELLO: And you've got me. Believe in your cause and believe in me. This is
   my issue. As of today, I make it mine. For two reasons. Because I believe in
   your cause, and to be perfectly frank with you, because it will help me. A little
   thing like this is just what I need. Maybe it's the issue that will send me to the
   Congress of the United States of America. You think I'm talking a lot of
   nonsense, don't you? I'm the candidate from the Fourteenth District.
THEA: Well, if we can help, I'm sure that—
FIORELLO: You can—you can. Maybe you can help in more ways than one. You're
   an Italian girl—you're beautiful—you're smart. You can help me. One of the
   things I'm going to do is organize the Italian-Americans into political clubs.
THEA: I should think it's about time that—
FIORELLO: When people think of Italians, I want them to think of Michelangelo,
   Caruso, Garibaldi; not of Ponzi and the Mafia. Where you from?
THEA: *(Rises proudly)* Trieste, an Italian city now being ground under the heel
   of the imperialistic Austrian invader.
FIORELLO: Well! *Dunque siete veramente una Triestina?*
THEA: *(Smiles with pleasure) Lo potete capire dal mio accento.*
FIORELLO: When I was a kid, before I studied law, I was U. S. Consul in Fiume.
THEA: Fiume? Why, that's just across from—!
FIORELLO: Of course. I've been in Trieste many times.
THEA: Well, then, you know that isn't justice, is it? That's what I mean when you
   say we'll win. Trieste didn't win.
FIORELLO: You must be patient and believe in me.
THEA: I do, don't misunderstand me. *(Laughter offstage)* Listen! Look what you've
   done for us already, Mr. LaGuardia. That's the first laughter in days.
FIORELLO: And what you did, facing arrest—I don't forget that—that took cour-
   age. I admire it.
THEA: Do you really think we could win?
FIORELLO: I told you we could win this strike.
THEA: But do you know all about this situation?
FIORELLO: I don't know anything about it, but you're going to tell me.
THEA: There are so many problems. Are you going to have some time?
FIORELLO: Of course.
THEA: Right now, I mean?
FIORELLO: Certainly.
THEA: Could you perhaps take me to dinner?
FIORELLO: *(Hesitates, then, slowly)* Yes. Of course I could. That would be fine—
   just fine.
THEA: I'll wait for you, then.
FIORELLO: Good.
   (The girls enter singing)

GIRLS:

> *Management's unfair, management's unfair,*
> *Management is terribly unfair.*

FIORELLO: Girls, girls—that's not the way to win.

> *(Sings)*
> *You'd think that a human heart would break*
> *At such a display as this*
> *But warm-hearted men with money at stake*
> *Can turn into heartless*
> *Misbegotten misers*
> *Now a strike isn't played like tic-tac-toe*
> *And soft-spoken tactics just don't go*
> *Ladies you've got no choice*
> *You've got to holler and howl*
> *In your most unladylike voice*
> *Unfair!*

GIRLS: *(Timidly)*

> *Unfair . . .*

FIORELLO:

> *Louder—unfair!*

GIRLS:

> *Unfair!*

FIORELLO:

> *Again—unfair!*

GIRLS:

> *Unfair!*

FIORELLO:

> *Good!*
> *Let's put a stop*
> *To the sweatshop*
> *That's the disease we want to cure*
>
> *Proudly we picket*
> *The men who pick the pockets*
> *Of the poor hard-working poor*
>
> *While we stitch, stitch, stitch*
> *Someone's getting rich*
> *By the sweat of his sister's brow*

GIRLS:

> *Right!*

FIORELLO:

> *Let's fix the wagon*
> *Of this gold-hungry dragon*
> *Let's trim the fat*
> *From this sacred cow!*
> *You've got to howl at the top of your voice*

GIRLS:
Unfair!

FIORELLO:
Holler and howl at the top of your voice

GIRLS:
Unfair!

FIORELLO:
Keep yelling foul at the top of your voice

GIRLS:
Unfair!

Let's put a stop
To the sweatshop
Let's end the evil of the age

Fight to the finish
To win the war we're waging
For a decent living wage

Must we sew, and sew
Solely to survive
So some low so-and-so
Can thrive?
No!
He'll fry in Hades
If it's up to the ladies
Waistmaker's union
Local twenty-five!
(Shouting)
Unfair! Unfair! Unfair! Unfair!

(All exit left)

Blackout

SCENE 4

FIORELLO'S *office immediately following the preceding scene.* MORRIS *is on the phone in the outer office;* MARIE *is on the phone in the inner office.*

MARIE: *(Into phone)* It's only just in case, Mr. Lamberti.

MORRIS: *(Into phone)* Ike Feeney went to five hundred for one of them, but she was the leader. For the others, in case they're arrested, it won't be more than two fifty—three hundred top. They're very small girls. *(Pause)* Thanks, George. *(He hangs up and makes a note on his pad)*

MARIE: *(Into phone)* That's very nice of you, Mr. Lamberti. Mr. LaGuardia will appreciate it. *(She hangs up and makes a note on her pad)*

MORRIS: *(Calls to her)* How do we stand?

MARIE: *(Examining her list)* It's all right.

MORRIS: Then we're okay as long as they don't get arrested for anything worse than soliciting. *(The phone rings.* MORRIS *speaks into phone)* Hello? Yes, she is. Just a moment, Mr. LaGuardia. *(To* MARIE*)* It's for you.

(MARIE *comes to him*)

MARIE: *(Eager, into phone)* Hello? *(Pause)* Yes, Mr. LaGuardia? *(Pause)* Mr. La-
Guardia, is something wrong? *(Pause)* Yes. *(Pause)* No, no, that's all right. I
understand. *(Pause. Then, with forced brightness)* No, I don't mind. *(Pause)* Of
course. Good night, Mr. LaGuardia. *(She hangs up slowly)*

MORRIS: *(Quiet)* Anything wrong?

MARIE: *(Quick)* No, my list is complete.

MORRIS: You know what I mean. What's the matter?

MARIE: Nothing. *(Suddenly angry)* I'm just a damn fool, that's all.

MORRIS: There's no law against that.

MARIE: Well, there ought to be.

MORRIS: Now . . . now.

MARIE: I'd like to make the laws.

MORRIS: I bet they'd be good.

MARIE: Oh, would they! Would they! You bet they would. Here—take a law—
write this down.

(She sings "Marie's Law")
My law shall state
To whom it may concern

MORRIS: *(Singing)*
Your law shall state
To whom it may concern

MARIE:
When a lady loves a gentleman
He must love her in return

MORRIS:
Loves a gentleman he must love her in re . . .

MARIE:
In re, my law
Ad hoc, to wit, to woo

MORRIS:
In re, your law
Ad hoc, to wit, to woo

MARIE:
When a lady feels affectionate
Then the man must follow through

MORRIS:
Feels affectionate then the man must follow . . .

MARIE:
Here's another law we women'll
Do our best to legislate
It shall be completely criminal
For a man to break a date
Each offender shall be rapidly
Thrown in jail where he belongs
Thus we'll right our bill of wrongs

My law is what
The world is waiting for

MORRIS:
Your law is what
The world is waiting for

MARIE:
Every unrequited lover will be grateful when it
Meets the full approval of the House and Senate
Such enthusiasm as you never saw
Will greet my lovely law.

In re, my law
It should be understood

MORRIS:
In re, your law
It should be understood

MARIE:
With the help of women everywhere
We shall outlaw bach'lorhood

MORRIS:
Women everywhere you shall outlaw bach'lorhood . . .

MARIE:
What's more . . . in lieu

MORRIS:
Marie, before you're through
I've got some things
I'd like to say. If you
Have got to outlaw anything
You should outlaw in-laws, too.

MARIE:
I'm concerned with what the man must do

Every girl shall have a boneymoon
Which shall last at least a year
During which aforesaid boneymoon
Every care shall disappear
Ipso facto, let the government
Get the bride and groom alone
After that they're on their own.

Whereas

MORRIS:
Whereat

MARIE:
Hereby

MORRIS:
Hereof

MARIE:
Therein

MORRIS:
They're out and furthermore

MARIE:
My law

MORRIS:
Your law

MARIE:
Is what

MORRIS:
Is what

MARIE:
The world

MORRIS:
The world is waiting for

MARIE:
We are going to rid the country
Of contempt of courtship

MORRIS:
Legally replacing it
With davenportship

BOTH:
Such enthusiasm as you never saw
Will greet (my/your) lovely law.

    Blackout

SCENE 5

   Place: A street corner.
   At Rise: Enter NEIL, BEN MARINO *and* MIKE, *carrying a stepladder platform.*

BEN: *(To* NEIL, *as they move across the stage)* Well, this is a good time to break the ice, kid. Maybe you'll become a great orator. You'll have a crowd around you in no time. All right, this way to the LaGuardia rally.

NEIL: *(Mounting stepladder)* And I'm going to ask you to vote for Fiorello H. LaGuardia. *(*NEIL *stands on the stepladder, stage left, addressing a small crowd. A couple of the Republican politicians are standing near the ladder.* DORA *and some of the girl strikers are in the crowd.* FLOYD *is off at one side, watching. Later he works his way across to talk to* DORA*)* I want to ask you to consider not only the issues but the man. I know this man and he is just great—that's what I'm telling you—he's just great. If you knew him as I do, you'd realize what a great thing it would be to have such a great man represent you in Congress. Now he'll be here a little later to talk to you himself, but in the meantime, here's another speaker who wants to address you.

   (The politicians lead a little applause. NEIL *gets down to make way for* THEA, *who is helped up the ladder. While this is going on,* FLOYD *addresses* DORA*)*

FLOYD: Now, miss, you mustn't hold that against me. Anyhow, I hear you won the strike.

DORA: Yes—we did.

FLOYD: *(Shakes hands)* Congratulations. I'm glad.

THEA: *(On platform)* I'm a working girl. I model for the Nifty Shirtwaist Company. And I see that some of you are working people, too. *(Laughter and applause)* The girls in that factory were working twelve hours a day for four dollars a week. They were promised a living wage; they didn't get it; they struck. Who would help us? Nobody. Until one man, one man who hates injustice and tyranny of any type, took up our cause, and got us our rights, and that's why I'm for him. And here he is to talk to you himself—Fiorello H. LaGuardia.

(They help her down. FIORELLO comes in followed by MARIE. He mounts the ladder)

FIORELLO: Friends, I want each and every one of you to take a long deep breath! Like this! *(He illustrates)* You know what that smell is? Tammany! They've been stinking up this district long enough. It's time to get the garbage off the doorsteps, and I've got the shovel to do it with. Your vote! Put that pencil cross next to the name of Fiorello H. LaGuardia! L-A-G-U-A-R-D-I-A!

(He sings)
Now here's another name
T-A-M-M-A-N-Y, what's that?

VOICE: *(Speaking)* Tammany?

FIORELLO: *(Speaking)* Wrong!

(Singing)
The answer's tyranny
Tammany spells tyranny
Like r-a-t spells rat!

Now there's a double "M" in Tammany
And a double "L" in gall
Just like the double-dealing
Double-crossing
Double-talking
Double-dyed duplicity
Of Tammany Hall!

But you can change it all
Go use the ballot box
And cast your spell come next election day
The name's LaGuardia
L-A-G-U-A-R-D-I-A!

CROWD:
L-A-G-U-A-R-D-I-A!

(The lights go down quickly and come up at stage right, where an Italian audience is being addressed by THEA)

THEA: . . . and who is against tyranny of every type, and who believes that Trieste should go back to the Italian people—*(Cheers)* And here he is, Fiorello La-Guardia!

(Cheers. She gets down and FIORELLO *mounts the ladder.* DORA *comes in accompanied by* FLOYD*)*
FIORELLO: *(In Italian) Amici!*
A MAN: *Amici!*
FIORELLO: *Trieste deve esser libera e noi dobbiamo esser liberi.*
   (The crowd cheers)
FIORELLO: *Attenti!*
ANOTHER MAN: *Attenti!*
FIORELLO: *(He sings the song in Italian. The lyrics spelled phonetically)*

   Kees-tuh vay vaw-lyoh dee
   Ah-tee-tee-eh-en-tee-ee, ah tahm-mah-nee

   Kay fays see vay vaw fah
   Vay-nee-tay toot-tee kwahn-tee toot-tee
   Kwahn-tee ahk-kah, noon fah-tay-vay'ngahn-nah!

CHORUS: *(Singing)*
   Ah tahm-mah-nee
   Bravo, LaGuardia, bravo!

(The lights go down and come up again at stage left, where another part of the city is indicated. MORRIS *is on a platform addressing a crowd, many of whom are Jewish)*
MORRIS: . . . and a fearless man and an honest man—a man who will look after your interests.
HECKLER: Look after the Italian interest, you mean!
MORRIS: I mean all interests without fear or favor. And my name is not King Victor Emmanuel—it's Morris Cohen!
WOMAN: Moisha Cohen!
   (Laughter and applause)
MORRIS: And here he comes now—he'll tell you himself.
   (DORA and FLOYD appear at the edge of the crowd)
DORA: *(Smiling at FLOYD)* It's very nice of you to walk me over.
   (FIORELLO is on the ladder. Applause)
FIORELLO: Friends—I've just come from Mulberry Street.
HECKLER: Little Italy, huh? You're always talking about your Italian background. I hear you're half Jewish. How come you never brag about your Jewish background?
FIORELLO: I figure if a man is only half Jewish it isn't enough to brag about.

(FIORELLO sings a Yiddish version of the song. The lyrics are spelled phonetically)
   Ich bin LaGvardia

MRS. POMERANTZ: *(Speaking)* Mr. LaGuardia!

FIORELLO:
   Doss is La-med A-leph Gim-mel A-leph Raysh
   Doll-ed yood eyen dee far-guess doss nischt
   Ich zug tsu eye-ich, Tammany is nisht kosher

Habb doss in zinnen
Und beatzich foon zay!

CHORUS:
La-med A-leph Gim-mel A-leph Raysh Doll-ed
Yood eyen meer veln doss nisht far-guessen
La-med A-leph Gim-mel A-leph Raysh Doll-ed
Yood eyen meer veln doss nisht far-guessen.

(The crowd erupts in a wildly enthusiastic street dance into which are drawn
FIORELLO, THEA, *and* MORRIS*)*

CHORUS: *(Singing. Exultant)*
The name's LaGuardia
L-A-G-U-A-R-D-I-A!

Blackout

SCENE 6

BEN MARINO *and his political hacks come straggling out on stage. They carry newspapers. They look dazed. They sing "The Bum Won."*

BEN: *(Singing)*
Even without our help
Look at the way he won
Everyone sold him short!

FIRST HACK: *(Speaking)* You think they'll ask for a recount?

BEN: *(Singing)*
We got a winner
But what good is that to us?
Not if he doesn't feel
Grateful for our support

FIRST HACK: *(Speaking)* You mean no patronage, huh, Ben?

BEN:
I gotta talk to him.

SECOND HACK: *(Singing)*
Someone pinch me
Maybe this is just a beautiful dream
I'm in a bad state of shock

SECOND and THIRD HACK: *(Singing)*
I'd like to know just how the hell it happened
What we did right
Fellas, the whole thing is cockeyed.

FIRST, FOURTH and FIFTH HACK:
We got a winner at last
We got a star which is in the ascendant

BEN:
If he feels that we sloughed him off
He could become, God forbid, independent.

SIXTH HACK:
> *Who'd ever guess that the people would go*
> *To the polls and elect a fanatic?*
> *People can do what they want to*
> *But I got a feeling it ain't democratic*

BEN:
> *This is a guy that is gonna go further*
> *Than anyone ever suspected*

SIXTH HACK:
> *Yesterday morning I wrote him a note*
> *That I'm sorry he wasn't elected!*

(In counterpoint)

BEN:
> *Even without our help*
> *Look at the way he won*
> *Everyone sold him short*
> *We got a winner*
> *But what good is that to us*
> *Not if he doesn't feel*
> *Grateful for our support*

SECOND and THIRD HACKS:
> *Someone pinch me*
> *Maybe this is just a beautiful dream*
> *I'm in a bad state of shock*
> *I'd like to know just how the hell it happened*
> *What we did right*
> *Fellas, the whole thing is*
> *cockeyed*

FIRST, FOURTH and FIFTH HACKS:
> *We got a winner at last*
> *We got a star which is in the ascendant*
>
> *If he feels that we sloughed him off*
> *He could become, God forbid, independent.*

SIXTH HACK:
> *Who'd ever guess that the people would go*
> *To the polls and elect a fanatic?*
> *People can do what they want to*
> *But I got a feeling it ain't democratic*
> *This is a guy that is gonna go further*
> *Than anyone ever suspected.*
> *Yesterday morning I wrote him a note . . .*

BEN:
> *I had to go take an amateur from the ranks*
> *Make him the nominee*
> *What does he do? He wins!*

FIRST HACK: *(Speaking)* Kind of makes you believe in miracles, huh, Ben?

SIXTH and FOURTH HACKS:
> *The bum won*

SECOND and THIRD HACKS:
> *The bum won*

BEN: *(Mournful)*
> *God forbid, independent!*

FIRST and FIFTH HACKS:
> *We gotta talk to him.*

(They begin to straggle off listlessly, repeating lines from "The Bum Won" until they are offstage)

> Blackout

SCENE 7

Place: A dreary Greenwich Village tenement roof with one cheerful spot—a table with a bright cloth and tea things. Two hatboxes are at one side.

At Rise: DORA, *in a neat dress, sits at the table. She is pouring tea—a second cup.* FLOYD, *his back to us, is looking over the parapet toward the street.*

FLOYD: *(Calls down)* You ain't in no rush. Sure it's important. Ten minutes. *(Turns and comes to her. His coat is unbuttoned)* Riley's a good egg—he's in no hurry. *(He tries to kiss her)*

DORA: Oh, Floyd—not in the middle of the day.

FLOYD: My feelings don't watch the clock. I get thinking of that kiss you gave me last night and then I can't think of nothing else.

DORA: Floyd, think of duty. You got to go to work. Besides, Marie is coming over.

FLOYD: Which Marie—the dopey one?

DORA: Floyd, you're going to make me very angry.

FLOYD: I love you when you're angry. *(He chases her)*

DORA: Floyd—not now, you brute! *(Pounds his chest with her fists)* You cossack!

FLOYD: *(Releases her)* Okay. That's one you owe me. What's that Marie want of you anyway?

DORA: She wants to borrow a hat. She's going to Washington.

FLOYD: Down to see the little wop, huh? Boy, is that big mouth getting himself in trouble down there.

DORA: He is, Floyd?

FLOYD: Is he? He's trying to get us into war. Didn't you read the papers?

DORA: Not lately.

FLOYD: Me neither. But I listen. I hear things. Oh, they hate him—his own district—they hate him. He couldn't get elected again. Not to nothing.

DORA: Mr. LaGuardia won our strike, that's all I know.

FLOYD: Huh!

DORA: And he got to Congress, didn't he?

FLOYD: That's another thing. They was talkin' about it over to the Wigwam. How come they let that little squirt walk off with the Fourteenth District right from under their noses? And I give my opinion: overconfidence, I says. And one of the very important guys there, he says to me: Floyd McDuff, you're only walking a beat now, but mark my words, he says, one of these days I expect you to be a sergeant, he says. And maybe even higher, he says.

DORA: I bet you will, too. I believe in you, Floyd.

FLOYD: And you know what he says? He says—with a kind of a wink, you know —he says: You may not be the smartest guy on the force, but you're loyal.

DORA: And what did you say to him?

FLOYD: I says, Judge, thank you.

DORA: That was real smart.

(A knock. MARIE *pokes her head out through stair door)*

MARIE: Dora, can I come out?

DORA: Marie! I'm so glad to see you. *(Runs to embrace her)*

FLOYD: Ah, hello there, Marie. How are you?

MARIE: Fine.

DORA: Come on out.

FLOYD: Well, my sidekick is waiting for me down there. Goodbye, Marie.

MARIE: Good-bye.

FLOYD: See you tonight, Dora. Thanks for the tea—*(He gives her a meaningful bump with his hip)* and the sugar.*(He laughs and hurries out, buttoning his tunic)*

MARIE: Your new admirer seems in high spirits.

DORA: Sure. He's very good-natured. Want some tea?

MARIE: No, thanks. I just stopped down at the corner and had a Moxie.

DORA: Marie, you shouldn't drink Moxie.

MARIE: No? Why not?

DORA: Didn't you know that Moxie is bad for the teeth?

MARIE: Moxie?

DORA: Floyd says if you put an ordinary molar in a glass of Moxie, and you keep it there overnight, in the morning you'll find the tooth is completely disappeared.

MARIE: Floyd told you that?

DORA: Yes.

MARIE: Well, as long as you're happy, that's the main thing.

DORA: Oh, I am, I'm happy. But, Marie—I'm miserable, too!

MARIE: You don't act it.

DORA: Life is so complicated.

(She sings "I Love a Cop")
I love a cop
I love a cop
What a situation; ain't it awful?
Life is really grim . . .
I can only say that it's unlawful
How I feel towards him . . .

I love a cop
I love a cop
If I introduce him as my steady
Down at where I work,
I can hear the rumor spread already
Dora's gone beserk!

Then there's Thea . . . Oh, how gruesome!
Can you see me introduce 'em?
"You remember her—
She detested you."
"You remember him,
He arrested you!"

I'm so confused
I'm so confused
If I loved a dentist or a doctor
I'd be up on top
But I . . . love . . . a cop!

I love a cop
I love a cop
Though it wasn't easy to accept him

Now I think he's sweet
You should hear him tell the way I swept him
Off his big flat feet.

I love a cop
I love a cop
I can see his drawbacks clear as crystal
Still I testify
Once you take away his club and pistol
Floyd won't hurt a fly.

Floyd's ambitious and he's forceful
Energetic and resourceful
I can see how far
This will carry him
If he'd get an honest job
I would marry him.

That's how it is
He's mine . . . I'm his
Little did I know when Floyd first kissed me
And I whispered, "Stop!"
You can't . . . stop . . . a cop!

(Speaking) Ah, Marie, it's so wonderful for two people to be in love.

MARIE: Yes, even for one people.

DORA: What?

MARIE: Nothing.

DORA: Is that why you're going to Washington? Did Mr. LaGuardia invite you?

MARIE: No, Ben Marino.

DORA: Is he your latest?

MARIE: It's business, Dora, just business.

DORA: *(Grinning)* Monkey business.

MARIE: Oh, Dora, don't be so romantic.

DORA: *(Runs to the hatboxes)* Well, I brought my two best hats up. See—put this on—it'll knock him dead.

MARIE: *(Puts on hat)* How do I look?

DORA: I don't know. Take a look.

MARIE: *(Examines herself in a mirror)* I'll tell you the truth, Dora, I'm going because Mr. Marino thinks I have influence. He thinks I can tell Mr. LaGuardia what to say in Congress—which is utterly ridiculous. But oh, well, at least I'll get a chance to see Washington.

DORA: You better take a good look, Marie, because Floyd says if Mr. LaGuardia doesn't stop trying to send American boys over there to fight for those foreigners—Floyd says he'll never get elected again.

MARIE: Well, at least that would keep him in New York.

DORA: *(Grinning)* I knew it! I can see right through you. I knew it!

MARIE: Thank you for the hat. Thanks loads. Good-bye.

(She exits. DORA dances a wistful, impish, wordless refrain to "I Love a Cop")

Blackout

SCENE 8

Place: LaGuardia's office in the House Office Building in Washington.

At Rise: FIORELLO *sits at his desk, working. He is writing a speech. He puts his glasses on, writes a few words, stops, takes the glasses off, gestures with them, puts them back on, mutters a few phrases inaudibly. He even rises at one point to practice a high spot in his oration.*

The buzzer sounds. FIORELLO *lifts receiver of desk box and listens.*

FIORELLO: *(Into box)* Send the senator in, and let me know the minute the Ben Marino party gets here. *(He hangs up, pushes the glasses up on his forehead, and sits waiting. A* SENATOR *is ushered in. He is the old-school conservative type—ponderous and benign.* FIORELLO *rises and shakes his hand)* Senator.

SENATOR: Congressman. Thank you for letting me intrude upon you at this time. I understand you're busy.

FIORELLO: Trying to earn my money.

SENATOR: Congressman, I've often wanted to have a chance to exchange ideas with you. And I do hope such an opportunity develops before long.

FIORELLO: Thank you, Senator.

SENATOR: Right now I come in here upon a matter which concerns you and me both, because it concerns our party. I've been told that you're planning to make a speech.

FIORELLO: That is correct.

SENATOR: You've been very active in things in Washington, Congressman La-Guardia, and that's as it should be. But as you undoubtedly know, there's an unwritten law, a piece of cherished etiquette, I might say, that a freshman member does not speak on the floor of the House during his first term.

FIORELLO: Yes, I've heard about that. It seems ridiculous, doesn't it?

SENATOR: You don't believe that tradition has its value, Congressman?

FIORELLO: Not very much, I guess.

SENATOR: But you could be wrong, of course.

FIORELLO: *(Casual)* That's possible.

SENATOR: And you could be wrong in this rash support you are proposing to give to the Draft Act.

FIORELLO: *(Firm)* Only I'm not. When the Congressman from Milwaukee takes the floor again, I shall take the floor. The pacifists are poisoning the thought of the country. They have to be answered. Breaking a rule of etiquette is a small, small price for the House to pay.

SENATOR: Only the House won't pay, my dear LaGuardia—you will pay.

FIORELLO: That's all right with me. I can't remain quiet any longer. Did you read his speech yesterday? When you boil away all the phony blubber, you find what this genius has been telling us is that we can win this war without men. Let the Allies do the fighting, he says. All we have to do is write a few checks. And look at our allies. France? Senator, you know what a shirt looks like when it's made one trip to the laundry too many? *(He snatches up a shirt from the desk, and pulls it on over his head. The material is so threadbare, it tears)* That's France. Completely worn out. Who else? England? Ever have a tooth yanked, Senator? The dentist fills the hole with a fake. You have enough of them yanked, you get enough fakes as replacements, and pretty soon you've got a complete set of china choppers. *(Pulls a pair of false teeth from his coat pocket)* They look all

right, but there's damned little bite in them. And after four years of replacements, that's what the British Army is like today—damned little bite in it.
Italy? One pork chop, Senator. *(Snatches up a raw pork chop and brandishes it
under the* SENATOR'S *nose)* That's the daily food ration of the average Italian
soldier.

SENATOR: All that may be very true, sir, but the fact remains—

FIORELLO: When you're in a war, Senator, there are no buts. You have only two
choices. You can win, or you can lose. If we depend on France—*(Tugs at the
torn shirt he is wearing)*—on England—*(Snatches up the false teeth and drops them
on the desk)*—on Italy—*(Snatches the pork chop and slaps it down on the desk)*
—we sure as hell won't win this one!

SENATOR: Now, wait one minute, sir!

FIORELLO: We can't spare that minute, Senator. We can't wait. Because we're in
terrible danger. We've got to prepare before it's too late. We've got to get the
men—American men—to save our American lives!

SENATOR: Please, sir—

FIORELLO: And there's only one fair and honest and democratic way to get those
men—a Draft Act! *(The intercom buzzes. He snatches up receiver and speaks into
the box)* Yes? Good. *(Hangs up, then speaks to the* SENATOR*)* Excuse me. *(Hurries
out, leaving the door open. Offstage voices are heard.* FIORELLO *says, "Welcome,
welcome," to which* BEN MARINO *replies, "Good to see you, Congressman." The*
SENATOR *fumes, then starts out as* FIORELLO *re-enters)* Senator—I'm
sorry.

SENATOR: *(Pompous)* I don't believe there is anything else we can discuss at this
moment. Thank you very much. *(He exits)*

FIORELLO: Thank you. *(Turning toward the open door)* Come in—come in. *(*MARIE
and BEN *enter)* Well, I told you I'd be here and here I am. How do you
like it?

*(*BEN *and* MARIE *stare at him)*

MARIE: Lovely. *(She giggles)*

FIORELLO: What's the matter?

MARIE: Is that what the well-dressed Congressman wears?

FIORELLO: *(Looks down at himself)* Oh! Oh, this. It's to illustrate a point. I'm using
it in my speech tomorrow. *(He takes off the shirt)*

BEN: *(Incredulous)* You're going to wear that thing down on the floor of the
House?

FIORELLO: Why not?

BEN: *(Dry, to* MARIE*)* Maybe we got here just in time.

FIORELLO: In time for what, Ben?

BEN: Marie—talk to him.

FIORELLO: Talk to me about what?

MARIE: We all want you to be successful.

FIORELLO: Never mind about that. Talk to me about what?

MARIE: The Draft Act.

FIORELLO: I see.

MARIE: Up in the Fourteenth the people are—they're terribly upset by the—by
the way you—they're angry, Mr. LaGuardia, because you're backing the Draft
Act.

FIORELLO: I'm sorry about that. I must have fallen down on the job of keeping them informed. I thought I'd explained the issue clearly. I thought they understood what's at stake.

MARIE: Oh, they do, Mr. LaGuardia. They understand the issue.

FIORELLO: Then how can they be angry?

MARIE: They—you see, they don't care about the issue. They just want to keep their boys at home.

FIORELLO: So do I.

BEN: *(An angry outburst)* If you're telling the truth, if you really want to keep the boys at home, why do you want to go yelling your head off down there on the floor of the House? Why all this let's pass this Draft Act right away in a hurry this minute fast or we're all dead ducks?

FIORELLO: *(Very quiet)* Because when the people of the Fourteenth voted for me, and sent me down here, they changed me a little. They may not have known they were doing it—they may not even be aware they've done it—but they made me a little different from themselves. I can no longer think the way they think, as a single individual, a father or a mother thinking about a son. I have to think about the whole country, all the people in it, what's best for all of them. I'm not a guy hanging around a political club any more, Ben. I'm a Congressman now.

BEN: *(Sore)* I wonder how your thinking would go if this Draft Act applied not only to people but also to Congressmen?

FIORELLO: *(Quiet)* You can stop wondering about that. I enlisted this morning.

Blackout

SCENE 9

Place: A street.

At Rise: Several soldiers walk across the stage. They meet NEIL *as he enters.*

FIRST SOLDIER: It's at the Ben Marino club. They got the yard all fixed up.

SECOND SOLDIER: Hi, Neil. Comin' to the party?

NEIL: Sure. First I gotta pick up my girl. *(A drunk enters carrying a sign: "Good-bye, FIORELLO."* NEIL *laughs)* There's somebody who's going, all right.

(The drunk staggers off. DORA *and* FLOYD *enter.* FLOYD *is in civilian clothes)*

NEIL: Hello, Dora. How are you, Mr. McDuff?

(The soldiers and NEIL *exit.* DORA *and* FLOYD *start across the stage. Then* FLOYD *stops suddenly)*

FLOYD: *(Sullen)* Listen, Dora, I'm not going.

DORA: Now, Floyd, have we got to go all through that again?

FLOYD: When I see those guys in uniform . . .

DORA: Well, it's not your fault. You tried. You can't help it if you've got flat feet.

FLOYD: I know what they say about me. I can see them looking at me.

DORA: Floyd, I've got to go to Mr. LaGuardia's farewell party, and I couldn't have any fun without you. I'd just be miserable. Now please come with me. I'm so proud of you. You're so handsome, and you're going up in the world.

FLOYD: Well, maybe I am.

DORA: Oh, I know you are.

FLOYD: I'm started, ain't I?

DORA: That's what I say. And now you got this job in the sewer department, who

knows where it will all end? Floyd, if you just go to the party and be nice—
then afterward—tonight—*(She kisses him)*
FLOYD: *(Hoarse, as he comes up out of the kiss)* What?

DORA: *(Reprises "I Love a Cop")*
> *I love a cop*
> *I love a cop*
> *I will not allow my friends to taunt you*
> *Honest, Floyd, that's true*
> *Even if your Uncle Sam don't want you*
> *Mister, I sure do!*
>
> *I know why they won't enlist you*
> *It's because they never kissed you*
> *Even though your feet are a wee bit flat*
> *Maybe I can help you forget all that.*
>
> *Now, Floyd Mc "D",*
> *You come with me*
> *Little did I know when I first met you*
> *One day I'd be yours*
> *And you'd . . . be . . . in sewers!*

(Enter SOLDIERS and GIRLS. DORA pantomimes a request for their help in per-suading FLOYD)

DORA, SOLDIERS, GIRLS: *(Singing)*
> *We love a cop*
> *We love a cop*

(The soldiers seize FLOYD and start dragging him to the party)

FLOYD: *(Singing)*
> *I don't wanna argue with you doughboys*
> *Let's get one thing clear*
> *Either you decide to let me go, boys,*
> *Or we'll have a private war right here.*

(He shakes himself free but is promptly seized by the girls)

GIRLS:
> *We know you're a patriot, Floyd*
> *In a uniform or not, Floyd*
> *No one thinks of you as an also-ran*
> *We prefer to think you're a plain-clothes man*

ALL:
> *We love a cop*
> *We love a cop*
> *Come along and join our friendly send-off*
> *You have stalled enough*
> *So lead . . . on . . . McDuff!*

(They exit with FLOYD)

Blackout

SCENE 10

Place: The main room of the Ben Marino Association on West Third Street.

At Rise: Music and cheers are heard from the yard, which is shut off, so that only the small set in the center of the stage is exposed. MARIE *is sitting at card table. She is affected by the sadness of* FIORELLO'S *departure.*

MORRIS *stands at the door, looking out at crowd dancing in the yard. The dancing stops; the crowd applauds.*

MORRIS: They sure are giving him a great send-off.

MARIE: Yes. *(She lowers her face to cover her quivering lip)*

MORRIS: *(Turns)* What's the matter, Marie?

MARIE: *(Very small voice)* What if I never see him again?

MORRIS: *(Touches her shoulder reassuringly)* You will.

MARIE: I'm sorry, Morris.

MORRIS: They can't kill him.

MARIE: Bullets can kill anybody.

MORRIS: No, not him.

FIORELLO: *(His voice is heard out in the yard)* Let's get out of it for a couple of seconds. *(FIORELLO and THEA come in. FIORELLO wears a flier's uniform; THEA, a party dress)* Hello, you two.

MORRIS: Great turnout, Mr. LaGuardia.

THEA: Isn't it wonderful? Everybody, just everybody! Aren't you proud, Marie?

MARIE: *(Managing to control her voice)* Oh, yes. *(She goes out)*

FIORELLO: Where is she going?

MORRIS: Those papers, you know, before you go. I'll check on it. *(He goes out after her)*

THEA: Dear Marie, she's so upset about your going away.

FIORELLO: I don't want her to be. I told her I was going to come back.

THEA: I know you will.

FIORELLO: Thea—this is our last chance to talk.

THEA: No, it isn't. We'll talk when you come back.

FIORELLO: You know what's going to happen when I come back, don't you?

THEA: You're going to run for President.

FIORELLO: Better yet—I'm going to marry you.

THEA: Do we have to discuss marriage?

FIORELLO: Thea—you're in my thoughts constantly. Now, I'm not an idiot. And I know you have other men who are in love with you—as I am. So I want to have you tell me now—before I go away—what's the score? That's what I want to know—what's the score?

THEA: I do admire you so much—you know that—and I respect you. But is that enough for marriage?

FIORELLO: I thought we were very close, Thea.

THEA: Oh, yes. We have been—and when you helped us win our strike, and when I helped you win your seat in Congress—those were wonderful days.

FIORELLO: We'll have more of them.

THEA: I'm so confused. I've been asking a little advice.

FIORELLO: If you want advice, you come to me.

THEA: I asked a friend of mine, Father O'Rourke. I asked him did he think it a good idea for an Italian Catholic girl to marry an Italian Jewish Episcopalian.

FIORELLO: *(Dry)* You chose the right person to ask all right.

THEA: You know what he said?

FIORELLO: Of course, I know. What could he say? But I notice something else.

THEA: What?

FIORELLO: I notice you're thinking about marrying me or you wouldn't have asked him.

THEA: Oh—you noticed that.

FIORELLO: Yes, and I notice something else.

THEA: What else?

FIORELLO: I know you're not going out steady with any of these lounge lizards who are hanging around you.

THEA: Oh!

FIORELLO: So quit arguing. After I get Trieste for you—when I come back—

THEA: *(Impulsive)* Not for me—for justice! That's why we should get Trieste!

FIORELLO: I'm going to capture it for you, personally.

THEA: Oh, Fiorello, if you do—*(She kisses him on the cheek)*

FIORELLO: If I do, you're going to have to kiss me better than that. *(Starts to embrace her, but there is a knock at the door)* Who is it?

(MORRIS sticks his head in)

MORRIS: I think we'd better get this done before they close in on you, Mr. LaGuardia.

FIORELLO: Oh, yes, of course, come in, Morris. *(MORRIS and MARIE enter)* Marie, give me those papers. I'll sign them. Let's get it over with. *(He sits at the table and signs papers as MARIE places them in front of him one at a time)*

THEA: Morris, you think your wife will let you dance with me?

MORRIS: *(Giving her his arm)* She better, after all the money I spent at Roseland! *(They go out into the yard)*

FIORELLO: There—and those—I hope you checked them.

MARIE: Yes, I did.

FIORELLO: *(Touches her hand as she gathers the papers)* Thank you, Marie, for many things. *(He looks out the window)* Now, look at that—isn't that pretty? I like dancing.

MARIE: I do, too.

FIORELLO: You do? That's a surprise to me. All right, come on now, let's see if we can keep in step.

(They dance awkwardly in the room, while the set revolves and opens up, revealing the yard. Everyone is dancing. Many men are in uniform. All the girls wear party frocks. BEN mounts a platform. The crowd grows quiet and waits)

BEN: And now, friends, it's time to say good-bye. My boy *(Puts a hand on FIOREL-LO'S shoulder)*—in addition to all the other great things he's done down there in Washington—he's now going over there to clean up the map of Europe for good old Uncle Sam. *(Applause)* Ladies and gentlemen, with all our thanks and all our best wishes, and a prayer from right here in our hearts—we say good-bye and good luck and God bless you and give the Kaiser a good swift kick you-know-where from all of us. *(Crowd laughs)* Captain LaGuardia has asked for no speechmaking. Instead he thinks we'd all like music. *(He motions to* THEA *to lead singing)*

THEA: *(Sings "Till Tomorrow")*
Twilight descends
Everything ends
Till tomorrow, tomorrow

Since we must part
Here is my heart
Till tomorrow, tomorrow

Clouds drifting by
Echo a sigh
Parting is such sweet sorrow

I'm drifting, too,
Dreaming of you
Till tomorrow comes.

COMPANY: *(Final chorus)*
Twilight descends
Everything ends
Till tomorrow, tomorrow

Since we must part
Here is my heart
Till tomorrow, tomorrow

Clouds drifting by
Echo a sigh
Parting is such sweet sorrow

I'm drifting, too,
Dreaming of you
Till tomorrow comes.

Blackout

SCENE 11

A movie screen is lowered.

Picture: The Pathé News rooster crowing.

Caption: Camp Dix, New Jersey, First Draftees Report for Training
Picture: American draftees in camp having their teeth examined.

Caption: Washington, D.C., Flying Congressman, F. H. LaGuardia, Clears Desk on Which He Helped Shape the Draft Act.
Picture: Fiorello in civilian clothes at his desk, busily signing papers.

Caption: Somewhere in France, LaGuardia Squadron Prepares for Action
Picture: Fiorello and his men gathered around a biplane.

Caption: ACTION!
Picture: Aerial dogfight.

Caption: The Major's First Scalp!
Picture: Fiorello in close-up at controls of plane. German plane is hit, plummets to earth.

Caption: Trieste, King Victor Emmanuel Reclaims Trieste for Italy
Picture: Victor Emmanuel amid cheering throng.

Caption: Trieste's Favorite Son
Picture: Fiorello in flier's uniform.

Caption: "Aw, shucks, it was nothing."
Picture: Fiorello rocking back and forth and smiling shyly at camera.

Caption: Armistice
Picture: Exultant throngs, Times Square, newspapers proclaiming Armistice, flags waving, etc.

Caption: New York Harbor: HOME AGAIN! *(The orchestra underscores "Home Again")*
Picture: Troop ship entering New York Harbor, passing the Statue of Liberty, pulling into a dock, soldiers waving and coming down gangplank.

(The picture dissolves into a real gangplank. The stage is full of returning soldiers. FIORELLO *walks to the gangplank. The crowd cheers)*
FIORELLO: My friends—it's good to be back in this wonderful country—this wonderful city. It's good to be home.

COMPANY: *(Singing softly, "Home Again")*
Home again
Home again
What a day

Home again
Home again
Home again to stay.

*(*FIORELLO *walks down the gangplank, passes the eagerly waiting* MARIE, *hurries to* THEA*)*
FIORELLO: Thea, I brought you a present—a key to the city—Trieste.
THEA: Oh, Fiorello!
FIORELLO: Now what's the score?
THEA: Yes!
(They embrace. The crowd sings "Home Again" while confetti falls)

COMPANY:
Home again
Home again
Home to stay

Home again
Home again
In the U.S.A.

Curtain

ACT TWO

SCENE 1

Place: The LAGUARDIA *home.*

At Rise: THEA, *wearing a kimono and mules, is setting out breakfast. From the bedroom, offstage,* FIORELLO'S *voice is heard raised cheerily in a snatch of opera. The phone rings.* THEA *hurries to answer it.*

THEA: *(Into phone)*Hello? Yes, this is Mrs. LaGuardia. Put him on. Oh, hello, Ben.

(FIORELLO stops singing)

FIORELLO: *(Enters from the bedroom. He wears a shirt, tie, underdrawers. No pants)* Hey, honeybunch! I can't find my pants.

THEA: Ben wants to talk to you.

FIORELLO: Where's my black suit? *(Sits down beside her and takes the phone)* Yes, Ben? I said what? My war record? What's the matter with it? I don't care if it was ten years ago—facts are facts. I'm busy, Ben. Good-bye. *(To THEA)* Thinks I talked too much about my war record in that interview. These nickel-and-dime ward heelers! Where's my black suit?

THEA: In the kitchen. I'm sending it out to be pressed.

FIORELLO: *(Crosses toward the kitchen door)* How do you expect me to beat Jimmy Walker if I wear pressed pants? *(The phone rings. He exits into the kitchen)*

THEA: *(Into phone)* Hello. Oh, Ben—I'm sorry. You know how he is on the first day of the campaign. *(She stops as* FIORELLO *re-enters. He is carrying a crumpled black suit all balled up in a wad under his arm)* Oh, darling, no, you're not going to wear that!

FIORELLO: *(Surprised, as he shakes out the crumpled suit)* Why not?

THEA: You're an important man. You're running for Mayor. You can't go around looking like a—

FIORELLO: I've got a big speech at a Hundred Twenty-fifth Street tonight. I want to look like the people I'll be talking to. Not like that tinhorn tailor's dummy they've got down in City Hall. *(He exits into the bedroom)*

THEA: *(Into phone)* Ben, he's busy just now. Can I take a message. All right, I understand. *(The door buzzer sounds)* Good-bye. *(She hangs up and hurries to answer the door)*

FIORELLO'S VOICE: *(Shouts)* Hey, honeybunch! Those notes I was making last night on my speech?

DORA: *(Offstage)* Hello!

THEA: Hello!

(DORA enters wearing street clothes)

DORA: I hope you don't mind my dropping in on you like this, Thea.

THEA: Of course not, Dora.

DORA: Floyd's got another job.

THEA: Another one?

DORA: Every year another promotion. I'm so excited.

FIORELLO: *(Enters, wearing pants and fastening his belt)* Hi, Dora.

DORA: Good morning, Mr. LaGuardia.

THEA: They're right here, darling!

FIORELLO: *(Taking the papers from THEA)* How's the sewer business?

DORA: That's what I came over to tell Thea about. I'm so excited. Floyd's just given up sewers.

FIORELLO: Too bad. I thought it suited him. *(He disappears into the bedroom with the papers)*

THEA: You mustn't mind Fiorello's jokes about Floyd. *(They go to the table, where* THEA *pours coffee)*

DORA: Oh, I don't mind. You ought to hear what Floyd says about him. Politics! Ish-ke-bibble—we just have to go along with our men—that's all. Guess what happened? Floyd's going into garbage!

THEA: Is that better than sewers?

DORA: He has the city's disposal contract for lower Manhattan.

(FIORELLO comes in. He is buttoning his vest with one hand)

FIORELLO: There was a yellow sheet, with some figures, the amount of city funds Walker spent to put a private steam room into his City Hall office.

THEA: Right here, darling.

FIORELLO: Oh—thanks. *(He exits)*

THEA: Well, I'm very happy for you and Floyd.

DORA: Thea, it's just wonderful. The people we meet and the social events. The other night at Luchow's Jimmy Hines stopped and said, "How do you do," and Al Smith was practically next to me—except on the other side of the restaurant. Honestly! I'm so excited!

(The phone rings)

THEA: *(Into phone)* Hello? Oh, hello, Ben. No, I haven't had a chance yet. He's —*(FIORELLO appears at the bedroom door, studying notes)* Wait a minute, Ben. *(To* FIORELLO, *as she puts down the phone)* He's calling back about your speech tonight. *(FIORELLO is crossing toward the phone)* Ben thinks you should let somebody else represent you uptown, while you go out to Staten Island tonight and—

FIORELLO: *(Stops moving toward the phone and, annoyed, turns)* Tell him to stick to poker and I'll stick to running my own campaign! *(He exits into the bedroom)*

DORA: Well, I've got to run. I'm meeting Floyd at our new penthouse. That's what he got me to celebrate the promotion.

THEA: *(Walking DORA to the door, she picks up the phone)* He's sweet as well as loyal. Give him my best.

DORA: I will, darling. *(She exits)*

THEA: Good-bye, Dora. *(Into phone)* I'm sorry, Ben. I can't get him now. But I'll give him your message.

DORA: *(Re-enters)* Oh, gosh, isn't this awful?

THEA: Yes, Ben. Good-bye. *(She hangs up)*

DORA: I'm so excited about Floyd, I forgot all about you! Thea, what did the doctor say?

THEA: *(Glancing nervously toward the bedroom door)* It's nothing, nothing at all.

DORA: You sure?

THEA: Forget it, please. Forget I ever said a word. I'm all right. I'm a little tired, the doctor says, and maybe a little run-down, and all I need is rest.

DORA: Well, now, you see that you get it. You hear?

THEA: Of course I will.

DORA: Because health, boy, I'm telling you, Thea, without your health you can have swell clothes, and be going out in society and everything wonderful, and you have one little pain in your stomach and the whole thing gives you a pain in the stomach. You know what I mean? Take care of yourself.

(She exits. FIORELLO *enters, now completely dressed, and goes toward the breakfast table)*

FIORELLO: Well, I'm on my way. *(Suddenly stops and looks through his pockets)* Wait a minute—I had some figures on Alderman Marconi's bank deposits. *(Finds the papers)* Oh, here they are. *(He sits down and sips coffee hastily as he fusses with the papers)*

THEA: Joe Marconi?

FIORELLO: *(Grimly)* The same.

THEA: Is he in trouble?

FIORELLO: Now, honeybunch, I know he heads the charity for Trieste and all the Italians are soft on him, but a crook is a crook. If Morris or Marie call, tell them I'm on my way.

THEA: I haven't seen Marie in weeks. Why don't you ask her to dinner some night?

FIORELLO: All right, honeybunch, when you're feeling a little stronger.

THEA: Is she going steady with anyone now?

FIORELLO: How do I know? You women!

THEA: Well, she should get married.

FIORELLO: Then what'll I do?

THEA: Darling! *(She gives him a reproving glance)*

FIORELLO: No, I didn't mean it. If she finds the right man, I'll scream to high heaven, but I'll be happy for her. *(He rises, kisses her, and goes to door as he talks. She follows)* Now don't send any more suits out to be pressed until this campaign is over. I don't know when I'll be home. This rally starts at eleven. But if you're still awake, and you keep your window open, around about midnight you should hear a long loud scream. *(He gives* THEA *another quick kiss and snatches up his ten-gallon hat)* That will be Jimmy Walker yelling Uncle!

(He slaps the hat on his head and exits. THEA *stares after him for a moment. Standing alone, she sings the ballad: "When Did I Fall in Love?")*

THEA: *(Singing)*
> *There he goes, my Congressman,*
> *Starting his day hurrying right to a fight*
> *There he goes, Sir Galahad,*
> *Galloping off, riding his white Willy's-Knight.*
>
> *Out of the house ten seconds and I miss him*
> *I miss him more with each good-bye*
> *Out of the house ten seconds and I miss him*
> *And no one's more astonished than I.*
> *I never once pretended that I loved him*
> *When did it start*
> *This change of heart?*
>
> *When did I fall in love*
> *What night*
> *Which day*
> *When did I first begin to feel this way*

How could the moment pass
Unfelt
Ignored
Where was the blinding flash
Where was the crashing chord

When did I fall in love
I can't recall
Not that it matters at all
It doesn't matter when, or why, or how
As long as I love him now.
When did respect first become affection
When did affection suddenly soar
What a strange and beautiful touch
That I love him so much
When I didn't before.

When did I fall in love
What night
Which day
When did I first begin to feel this way
How could the moment pass
Unfelt
Ignored
Where was the blinding flash
Where was the crashing chord

When did I fall in love
I can't recall
Not that it matters at all
I'm where I want to be
His love, his wife
Until the end of my life.

Blackout

SCENE 2

Place: The terrace of FLOYD *and* DORA MCDUFF'S *penthouse home.*
At Rise: The butler is putting a punch bowl down on the table. DORA *enters.*
DORA: Chadwick!
BUTLER: Yes, madame?
DORA: Did you fix a place for the actresses to change?
BUTLER: Yes, madame, in the blue room.
DORA: Oh, good.
*(*FLOYD *enters)*
FLOYD: Say, Chadwick, the bootlegger's late, so we better get out some of that gin I made last week.
BUTLER: Very good, sir. *(He goes out)*
FLOYD: *(Disappointed)* Jimmy Hines ain't coming. He just phoned, but a lot of other big Tammany politicians will be here so I want everything to go off swell.

DORA: I don't see how it can be so swell when they aren't even bringing their wives.

FLOYD: It's a business meeting.

DORA: With a lot of chorus girls?

FLOYD: With a celebrated music comedy star—Mitzi Travers.

DORA: Oh sure, and those others down there—you ought to hear them. "It's cute! —You're cute!—I'm cute!"

FLOYD: Listen, stupid—Jimmy Hines is givin' me the honor of running this rally. You ought to be proud I asked those big shots here.

DORA: Big shots! And a gangster like Frankie Scarpini—what's he doing here?

FLOYD: The Commissioner wants to see him. Now mind your own business or I'll give you a clout. *(He raises his hand to strike her. She faces up to him, nose to nose)*

DORA: *(Chin out)* Just you try it! Just you try it! Just once!

(FLOYD falters, drops his hand, crosses, and sits)

FLOYD: *(Defeated, pleading)* Listen, Dora. I asked him here because I wanted to show off the penthouse, and the oil paintings and everything. Dora, please, I don't care about those girls. I ain't never looked at no other dame but you since we first met up.

DORA: *(Contrite)* I'm sorry. *(She sits in his lap)* I'll be good.

(Voices are heard offstage. DORA gets off FLOYD'S lap. The JUDGE enters)

JUDGE: Evening, Floyd.

FLOYD: Oh, Judge, come on in. Sweetheart, you know Judge Carter.

DORA: How do you do, Judge? *(She goes out)*

JUDGE: Nice place you got here, Floyd.

FLOYD: It's comfortable. It's home. By the way, Judge, the Chief wanted me to thank you for your help in killing that indictment. Nice to know we can count on you.

JUDGE: Thank you.

(Several men enter)

COMMISSIONER: Well, I'm telling you—

POLITICIAN: Nobody pays any attention to what LaGuardia says.

COMMISSIONER: I'm getting damn sick and tired of being insulted by that man. And so is Hines and Marconi and a lot of others.

POLITICIAN: But if the public thinks we get a hoodlum like Frank Scarpini to—

COMMISSIONER: The public won't think—'cause they won't know.

FLOYD: Commissioner—everybody knows that LaGuardia is just a loudmouth.

COMMISSIONER: Suppose he was saying these things about you?

POLITICIAN: Maybe we could shut Fiorello up if we could get something on him.

FLOYD: What?

A MAN: How about women?

FLOYD: Women, hell—he won't even listen to a dirty story. Not a chance.

JUDGE: Floyd, how about letting him get hit by a truck?

FLOYD: I don't know if it's practical. He's awful fast on his feet.

(Enter several chorus girls)

CUTIE: All right for we girls to come out here?

FLOYD: Come right along, certainly.

CUTIE: Oh, this is cute. Oh, what a gorgeous view. You can see the roof of our theatre.

(DORA *enters, followed by* MITZI)

DORA: Floyd, here's Miss Travers.

MITZI: How nice!

FLOYD: Gentlemen—the star of the evening. Miss Mitzi Travers.

FIRST MAN: Miss Travers.

FOURTH MAN: Nice to have you on our side, Miss Travers.

MITZI: I don't know much about politics, although I certainly hope I'm not stupid.

FLOYD: All right, folks, now let's pay attention. Maybe we'll put this song just in front of Jimmy Walker's big speech. Introducing that wonderful little actress, the golden-voiced star of *Yoo-Hoo Yah-Hoo*, Miss Mitzi Travers! *(He applauds)*

MITZI: *(Sings "Gentleman Jimmy")*
Live and let live
Love and let love
There are no finer sentiments than those

Live and let live
Love and let love
That's what Jimmy tells the world
Where e'er he goes

In London, in Paris
Bermuda and Rome
They love him
Just like we do at home

Who's that genial gentleman in the
Silk hat
Gray spats
Striped pants
Why that's
Gotta be him
Gentleman Jimmy

Who's that swell celebrity with the
Glad hand
Quick wit
New York's
Fav'rite
That'll be him
Gentleman Jimmy
Say, Jim, we promise on voting day
We will love you in November as we do in May
Hey!

Who's that dapper happy-go-lucky
Son of Broadway
We love James J. Walker.

Why, he's as graceful as Fred Astaire
He's the man who kept the subway to a five-cent fare
So there!

Who's that dapper, happy-go-lucky
Son of Broadway
We love James J.
'Cause under him Manhattan is just a
Syn . . . o . . . nym for
Generous . . . Gentleman . . .
James J. Walker!

(The girls all talk at the end of the song)
FIRST CUTIE: You were wonderful!
SECOND CUTIE: That'll be the biggest hit!
THIRD CUTIE: It's cute! It's so cute!
FOURTH CUTIE: And so meaning! The words and everything!
FLOYD: Well, we all agree that goes in.
ANOTHER MAN: That'll be the hit of the rally, Miss Travers. *(Enter FRANK SCARPINI with BODYGUARDS)* Hi, Frankie!
FIRST MAN: Oh—here's Frankie.
FRANKIE: *(To BODYGUARDS)* Okay, boys.
   (BODYGUARDS exit)
COMMISSIONER: Come on in. We've been waiting for you.
FLOYD: All right, girls. Now let's see what you're going to do.
CUTIE: Where's our shoes? I gave that man our shoes. *(Enter BUTLER)* Oh—here they are.
DORA: This way, girls. *(She leads the girls out to the blue room)*
COMMISSIONER: *(To SCARPINI)* We've been talking over that little problem.
MITZI: *(To FLOYD)* I could introduce my number by saying that I'm a personal friend of Jimmy's.
FLOYD: I tell you, Mitzi, Mr. Hines says let's keep personal things out of it—on account of possible trouble with—you know.
FRANKIE: *(To COMMISSIONER)* When he makes this speech at a Hundred Sixth Street—
COMMISSIONER: That's next week!
FRANKIE: Yah—*(DORA enters and crosses to FLOYD. FRANKIE leans close to the COMMISSIONER)* Well, here's the idea.
DORA: *(To FLOYD as she eyes SCARPINI)* I think he's a terrible-looking man.
FLOYD: *(Nervous)* Easy, kid, he'll hear you. He ain't so bad when you get to know him.
DORA: Is there one good thing about him?
FLOYD: Yes. He's loyal.
DORA: He's very mean-looking.
FLOYD: For God's sake, keep quiet. You want to get me bumped off?
COMMISSIONER: There's a roof right over the platform where he's going to speak.
FRANKIE: The Commish—he's not so dumb.
COMMISSIONER: And you'll have somebody up there ready to drop it on him, is that it?
FRANKIE: We'll brain him—don't worry.
POLITICIAN: But what's this about the fire alarm?
   (CUTIE enters)

CUTIE: You ready for we girls?

FLOYD: All ready, gentlemen?

COMMISSIONER: Maybe Frankie and I should go downstairs and—?

FRANKIE: *(Ogling the* CUTIES*)* No, wait. I want to see the tomatoes.

FLOYD: Okay, kids.

CUTIE: Line up, everybody.

FLOYD: If we like this, we can tack it right on to Mitzi's song.

CUTIE: Oh, Mr. McDuff, you'll like it. It's very original.

(The girls come out, tap dancing to the "Gentleman Jimmy" music)

GIRLS' FEET:

Clomp, Clomp, Clomp
Clippety Cloppety . . .

CUTIE:

Hey-hey!

GIRLS' FEET:

Tap tap tap . . .

Blackout

SCENE 3

Place: FIORELLO'S *law office.*

At Rise: In the private office, FIORELLO *is seated behind his desk. A* REPORTER *is in the chair beside the desk.* BEN MARINO *is standing at one side. In the outer office,* MARIE *is at the filing cabinet.* NEIL, *now more mature-looking than when we last saw him, is working at a desk.* MORRIS, *who also looks older, is talking on the phone. A new girl,* FLORENCE, *is at the switchboard.*

MORRIS: *(Patient, dead-pan, into phone)* Shirley, I just don't know. Listen, dear —election will be over in another week. Then I'll get some friends to introduce us. And I'll come to dinner nearly every night.

(Enter MR. ZAPPATELLA*)*

MR. ZAPPATELLA: *(To* FLORENCE*)* I come see Mr. LaGuardia, please?

NEIL: *(Calls)* Oh, hello, Mr. Zappatella.

MR. ZAPPATELLA: *(Turning from* FLORENCE *to* NEIL*)* Counselor, do I got the house?

NEIL: You certainly have. Here, sit down, please. *(He motions to the chair beside his desk.* MR. ZAPPATELLA *takes it)* Mr. LaGuardia couldn't attend the closing himself, so I appeared as the attorney of record. If you'll just sign here, please.

(He places some papers in front of MR. ZAPPATELLA *and hands him a pen.* MR. ZAPPATELLA *begins very laboriously to sign his name)*

MORRIS: *(Into phone)* Shirley, you and the twins go ahead and eat. Me, I'll just—

NEIL: *(Indicating another place on the documents)* And here, please.

*(MR. ZAPPATELLA *begins again the laborious business of signing his name)*

MORRIS: *(Irritable, into phone)* I can't help it if they're forgetting what their daddy looks like. Sometimes I can't remember myself. *(He hangs up and addresses* MARIE*)* Be happy you're not married.

MARIE: Oh yeah?

MORRIS: *(Contrite)* Marie!

MARIE: *(Pinches his cheek forgivingly)* You're cute.

(The voices die down in the outer office and come up in the inner office)

REPORTER: *(Wad of folded copy paper and pencil in hand)* Would you mind repeating that, Mr. LaGuardia?

FIORELLO: I said, when the ballot boxes are opened you will find that I have beaten Mayor Walker by at least three hundred and fifty thousand votes.

REPORTER: *(Scribbling)* Three hundred and fifty thousand.

FIORELLO: If the weather is good, you can raise that figure to half a million. The voters know me, they know my war record.

(BEN MARINO rolls his eyes to heaven in disgust)

REPORTER: Then you expect to keep the Italian vote?

FIORELLO: *(Rising)* Now, look here, young man—what do you mean by that?

BEN: *(Warningly)* Major!

FIORELLO: Why shouldn't I keep the Italian vote?

REPORTER: I thought maybe—

FIORELLO: You thought what? Come on, don't waste my time with a lot of mumbling. What did you think maybe?

REPORTER: You called Alderman Marconi a crook.

FIORELLO: Well, isn't he?

REPORTER: He's very popular with the Italian people.

FIORELLO: I didn't call him a crook. I called him a thief. A chiseling tinhorn pickpocket who has robbed the city for years.

REPORTER: May I print that?

FIORELLO: In capital letters.

REPORTER: Thank you, Mr. LaGuardia. *(He goes)*

FIORELLO: I guess that will hold him.

BEN: *(Slowly)* I guess so. *(He starts for the door)*

FIORELLO: Where you going?

BEN: For some fresh air. *(Pauses, looks at FIORELLO, then starts out again)* See you tonight.

FIORELLO: Ben! *(BEN stops)* What's the matter with you?

BEN: I've got a delicate stomach. Some kinds of things upset me.

FIORELLO: Like what?

BEN: Like the way you been running this campaign, Major.

FIORELLO: You think you can do better?

BEN: I could make a few suggestions.

FIORELLO: Like the way you did in that lousy district of yours before I took it over?

BEN: I thought you'd bring that up.

FIORELLO: Just to remind you that I've been right, and you've been wrong. That's all.

BEN: Yes, Major, you've been right, and you've done a hell of a lot of things that nobody thought you could, but once in a while you used to listen to some of us dumb bastards make a suggestion. You're going to lose, Major. Why? Because you can't play ball—not for one minute. We all know about your war record. We all know how incorruptible you are. You don't have to prove it so many times a day. You had to throw the Italian vote out the window to prove you're a fearless leader. You're not trying to win an election. You're just hoping that someday they'll put your statue up in Central Park.

FIORELLO: That's quite a speech, Ben.

BEN: That's the short version.

FIORELLO: Well, take it home and work on it—and don't come back.

BEN: I'll come back.

FIORELLO: *(Furious)* I don't need you. I don't want you. Get out of here. *(The phone rings)* Good-bye.

BEN: Good-bye, Major. *(BEN goes to outer office and, as he exits, he addresses FIORELLO'S staff)* So long, chumps.

(The phone rings. FIORELLO grabs it)

FIORELLO: *(Angry, into phone)* I told you I don't want to be bothered!

FLORENCE: Mr. LaGuardia, it's Doctor Marsini. He says—

FIORELLO: Oh. Oh, well—yes—I'll talk to him.

(DORA enters the outer office from the street)

DORA: Marie!

MARIE: Dora, come on in.

FLORENCE: *(Into phone)* All right, Dr. Marsini, here's Mr. LaGuardia.

FIORELLO: *(Into his phone)* That's all right. Of course, of course.

DORA: I gotta talk to you, Marie. Very private.

MARIE: My gosh. Something wrong? Sure, dear, right over here. *(She leads DORA to a deserted corner of the outer office)*

NEIL: *(Jogging the documents into a neat pile)* That does it, Mr. Zappatella, the house is yours.

(FIORELLO has finished talking on the phone. He hangs up and comes into the outer office)

FIORELLO: Florence, get my wife, please.

MR. ZAPPATELLA: Thank you, Mr. LaGuardia. I now can tell my Rosa it's true. We got our own house. *(He exits)*

FLORENCE: I have Mrs. LaGuardia.

(FIORELLO hurries back into his private office and picks up the phone)

DORA: *(To MARIE)* Now remember, you promised. And you've got to make him promise.

MARIE: Oh, he will, Dora. You don't have to worry about that. I know Mr. LaGuardia will feel the way I do, that you've been a real friend.

DORA: Gee whiz, Marie, a person gets so mixed up. I want to be loyal to Floyd. He's really a good, decent person, really he is. But I also can't forget what Mr. LaGuardia once did for all of us. Gee, I want to do the right thing.

MARIE: You did. You don't have to worry about it, Dora. Nobody will ever know. I promised. I double promised.

(DORA nods her head, believing MARIE, and goes out. MARIE sees her as far as the door)

FIORELLO: *(On the phone in the inner office)* Now, honeybunch, what's the use of paying the doctor good money if you don't do what he tells you to do? You've heard me make speeches before, and you'll hear me make plenty more. So you can forget about this one tonight and take care of yourself. I want you to go to bed and stay there. The doctor says you need rest. *(MARIE knocks on his office door. FIORELLO turns toward the door)* Well—? *(MARIE sticks her head in. FIORELLO speaks into phone)* I've got to hang up now, Thea. *(To MARIE)* Come in, Marie. *(MARIE enters. He continues into phone)* Something important has come up. Now I want you to listen, honeybunch. You go to bed. And when I come home, I'll do the whole damn speech over for you. Is that clear? You bet. You bet your life. Now, you do that. Good-bye. *(Hangs up. To* MARIE*)* What's wrong?

MARIE: First, Mr. LaGuardia, you must understand—what I'm going to tell you is an absolute secret.

FIORELLO: I understand.

MARIE: Absolute!

FIORELLO: Marie, I said I understand.

MARIE: Because Dora could get in terrible trouble.

FIORELLO: Nobody's getting into trouble. Now spill it.

MARIE: Dora heard some men talking to her husband. They're going to start some trouble at your speech tonight.

FIORELLO: Oh, they are?

MARIE: First they're going to turn in a fire alarm at Madison and a Hundred and Fifth. Then some other thugs are going to be up on a roof and they're going to have a baby carriage full of paving blocks. And then in all the excitement they're going to push it off the roof on top of your head!

FIORELLO: Now, isn't that typical? Good! It shows they're frightened.

MARIE: But it's murder! They're going to try to kill you!

FIORELLO: *(Striding to the outer office)* The whole damn German air force tried that once, and look what happened to them! *(At the door)* Neil!

NEIL: Yes, Major?

FIORELLO: Morris!

MORRIS: *(Who has been talking on the phone)* Never mind, Shirley, give the twins my share.

(He hangs up and, with NEIL, *hurries after* FIORELLO *into the private office)*

FIORELLO: *(After they have shut the door)* Neil.

NEIL: Yes, Major?

FIORELLO: There's a fire-alarm box at Madison and a Hundred and Fifth. During my speech tonight, someone may try to send in an alarm. Don't let him. Got it?

NEIL: Yes, sir. *(Pause)* Suppose there's a fire?

FIORELLO: Not tonight! Your job is to see that nobody pulls that lever. Morris, get hold of someone at headquarters and have some guards put on the roof over the platform where I'm speaking. If they see any baby carriages, throw them down the stairs.

MORRIS: *(Stunned)* Major! Baby carriages?

FIORELLO: They'll be full of paving blocks. Well, Neil, what about it? Get moving.

NEIL: I was just thinking, Major, suppose it's a policeman?

FIORELLO: Tell him if the law won't protect us, we'll have to protect ourselves. Get tough with him. And if you have to—hit him. Don't hesitate.

NEIL: *(Incredulous)* Sock a cop?

FIORELLO: Yes. Punch him in the eye. Come on, get moving.

(He leads the way out, followed by MORRIS *and* NEIL*)*

MORRIS: *(To* FLORENCE*)* Call Shirley and tell her I'm in jail.

Blackout

SCENE 4

Place: Madison Avenue and One Hundred and Fifth Street. There is a fire-alarm box downstage left.

At Rise: We can hear sounds of a political rally: FIORELLO'S *voice rising and falling, occasional cheers, etc.* NEIL *walks up and down, looking around, on guard. Three young men walk through from left to right.*

FIRST MAN: It's a rally. You know, speeches, vote for me, I'm a great guy.

SECOND MAN: Jimmy Walker?

FIRST MAN: No, no, it's that nut LaGuardia. What a kill-joy that guy is. He wants to reform everything. Geez, I think Jimmy Walker's got the right idea.

(They go out. NEIL *has strolled over right. A* TOUGH MAN *comes in furtively and goes over to the alarm box. He unhooks the little hammer to break the glass.* NEIL *hurries up to him)*

NEIL: Hey! What are you doing?

TOUGH MAN: Just reading this here sign. Got any objections?

NEIL: Got no objection to your reading.

TOUGH MAN: All right, mister, then how's about minding your own business?

NEIL: Just don't pull the handle.

TOUGH MAN: Why not shouldn't I pull the handle?

NEIL: 'Cause the fire department is tired.

TOUGH MAN: And what's that to you?

NEIL: *(Sore)* I'm on duty here. I got orders not to bother the fire department tonight, see?

TOUGH MAN: *(Giving* NEIL *a wide berth)* Good for you. *(Turns and retreats)* I got a couple of friends I'll tell about that.

(He goes off. Cheers are heard offstage. Two men and a woman walk through from left to right)

DERBY: What do you mean vote Republican? They're against the people, ain't they?

FEDORA: Vote Independent, I say.

DERBY: That's a lot of malarkey. What does that get you?

(As they go out, a FRANTIC MAN *runs in left and seizes the little metal hammer of the fire-alarm box)*

FRANTIC: Fire! Fire!

NEIL: *(Grabs him and shoves him away)* Just a second, buddy. Keep your hands off that!

FRANTIC: There's a fire!

NEIL: Keep your hands off that!

FRANTIC: My room is on fire! *(NEIL pushes him back again)* The building is burning up!

NEIL: Let it burn.

FRANTIC: Get out of my way, I tell you! *(NEIL pushes him back violently and he falls)* God damn you, you'll pay for this. Are you crazy? What's the matter with you? *(He gets up)*

NEIL: I don't think there is any fire.

FRANTIC: My house is on fire, I tell you!

NEIL: Where do you live?

FRANTIC: Huh?

NEIL: I thought so. Well, you can just wait until after the speech is over to have your house burn down.

FRANTIC: Wise guy, huh?

(A couple of other tough-looking characters enter to back up FRANTIC. MORRIS enters)

MORRIS: Neil.

NEIL: Just in time, Morris. I may want you to identify this guy in court.

FRANTIC: I'll show you some identifying, you fresh mug. Me and one or two others.

(He joins his gang, and they go out to reconnoiter. Cheers are heard offstage)

NEIL: *(To MORRIS)* This is a busy little assignment the Major gave me. How long do you suppose before he's finished with that speech?

MORRIS: Neil—I got a message.

NEIL: Message?

MORRIS: Neil—she died—Mrs. LaGuardia. They called up—I didn't know what to do.

NEIL: But it can't be!

MORRIS: About an hour ago.

NEIL: God damn!

MORRIS: Come on, Neil, I got a car out there.

NEIL: Sure, sure.

(They hurry out. Cheers offstage. FRANTIC, backed up by several others, comes in. He looks around, sees there is no guard, and rushes to the alarm box. He breaks the glass and pulls the lever and they quickly disappear in all directions. The speech is heard offstage for a second; there are cheers. Then the sounds of the fire-alarm sirens become audible and gradually grow until they fill the theatre)

Blackout

SCENE 5

Place: FIORELLO'S *office.*

At Rise: MARIE *is alone. She wears a hat. She stands at the switchboard, talking into phone.*

MARIE: *(Distressed)* And then the problem of his speeches. He has about twenty speeches scheduled between now and election. No, Doctor. We haven't been able to reach him yet. He's still on the speaker's platform. But Morris and Neil are there. As soon as he finishes speaking, they'll— *(Enter MORRIS and NEIL)* Here they are now. Good-bye, Doctor. *(She hangs up)* Did you tell him?

MORRIS: No.

MARIE: No?

MORRIS: We couldn't get to him.

NEIL: That baby carriage full of paving blocks. They dropped it—

MORRIS: I could kill myself.

NEIL: And in all the excitement—

MARIE: Is he hurt?

(Enter FIORELLO, his face smudged, his clothes dirty, his manner sardonic)

FIORELLO: How the hell would they know?

MARIE: *(Frightened by his appearance)* Mr. LaGuardia, you're hurt!

FIORELLO: *(Impatient)* No, no. All I need is a whisk broom and some soap and water. I can't go home looking like this. Get Thea on the phone. She'd have a relapse if she saw me like this. Thanks to them. *(Jerks his head sarcastically toward* MORRIS *and* NEIL *as he slaps dust from his jacket)* What a team! You got any bridges that have to be held? Send for these two! They'll foul things up but good. Any of your dikes spring a leak lately? Send for Neil and Morris, and watch your whole damn country get flooded away before the night's over! *(To* NEIL*)* Where were you when that alarm was pulled? *(To* MORRIS*)* Did you have anybody on that roof? Or were you just too damn busy on the phone telling Shirley when to put the roast in?

MORRIS: *(Halting)* Something happened—

FIORELLO: You bet it did. Or almost, anyway. Next time I want protection, I know two guys I'll send in the opposite direction.

MORRIS: Major, Dr. Marsini called.

FIORELLO: The doctor?

MARIE: Yes.

FIORELLO: Dr. Marsini?

MORRIS: I pulled Neil away from the fire-alarm box because—

FIORELLO: *(Sharp)* Is Thea worse?

MARIE: It was my fault.

(They stare helplessly at him)

FIORELLO: Well, come on, what is it? *(To* MARIE*)* What are you doing here at night?

MARIE: Morris called me.

MORRIS: It happened very suddenly. Dr. Marsini tried to—he—Major, it happened—that's why—it happened—the worst—she died.

*(*FIORELLO *reacts, then turns quickly and goes out)*

NEIL: Should we go with him?

MORRIS: No, no, leave him alone.

NEIL: Sure. *(He bolts out door)*

MORRIS: Marie, will you close the office?

MARIE: I will. Yes.

*(*MORRIS *goes. She turns out lights in inner office, then stands motionless and looks straight forward)*

Blackout

SCENE 6

Out of the darkness comes the voice of a radio ANNOUNCER.

ANNOUNCER'S VOICE: . . . several more hours, of course, before the final tabulations are complete. But it is perfectly clear now that James J. Walker has been returned to office by one of the most overwhelming landslides ever rolled up by a candidate in this city. Out of a total of just slightly less than one million, two hundred thousand votes cast, Fiorello LaGuardia has gone down to defeat by well over half a million ballots.

(During the radio speech the sound of crowds cheering becomes louder and louder, and when the lights come on, the stage is filled with jubilant celebrants who sing and dance their victory song, "Gentleman Jimmy")

COMPANY:
We kept our promise on voting day
That we'd love you in November
As we did in May
Hey!

Who's that dapper happy-go-lucky
Son of Broadway
We love James J.
'Cause under him Manhattan is just a
Synonym for generous Gentleman James
That's him
That's Jimmy . . . Jimmy . . . Jimmy
Jimmy . . . Jimmy . . . Jimmy . . . Jimmy

(Dancers and singers exit. FIORELLO, MARIE, MORRIS, NEIL *come in. They move slowly, a defeated group)*

NEIL: *(A sudden eruption)* Major, it's just rotten luck.

FIORELLO: *(Stops and turns)* Luck! Luck has nothing to do with it. Don't you know the people always vote for the better man?

MARIE: *(Angry)* You know that isn't so. He's not fit to shine your shoes. You know that.

FIORELLO: Damn right I do! *(Pause)* I beg your pardon, Marie.

MARIE: Oh, I've heard the word before. I've said it quite a few times tonight, too.

FIORELLO: Look here now. Why do you keep following me around? You think I need somebody to hold my hand?

MORRIS: It's a black night for all of us, Major.

(FIORELLO, embarrassed and touched, walks away, then comes back and speaks quietly)

FIORELLO: You go home now. It's good to have friends. I appreciate it. But I want to be alone now. *(They start out, each saying "Good night." Suddenly his manner changes. He becomes dynamic)* We'll work.

MORRIS: *(Turns)* What is it, Major?

FIORELLO: There's work to do. Everyone gets hit in the head with a baseball bat once in a while. Sometimes twice in succession. I don't want to feel sorry for myself and I don't want you to feel sorry for me. *(Points)* They're out there and we'll fight them. If we can't fight them in City Hall, we'll fight them in the courts. I'll see you in the office tomorrow morning at nine o'clock.

MORRIS: Yes, Major. Good night.

(They exit. FIORELLO *is alone on the stage)*

FIORELLO: *(Sings "The Name's LaGuardia")*
The name's LaGuardia
L-A-G-U-A-R-D-I-A!

(He strides off)

Blackout

SCENE 7

Place: The main room of the Ben Marino Association on West Third Street. Over the same large round poker table, covered with green baize, still hangs the same single

*electric bulb shielded by one of those porcelain shades that look like ice-cream cones;
white on the inside, green on the outside. In the background, through a haze of cigar
smoke, we can still see all the other recognizable symbols of a battered, musty political
meeting house.*

At Rise: BEN'S POLITICAL HACKS *are still seated around the table. They are still
playing five-card stud.*

FIRST HACK: These poor Tammany crooks must have bad dreams about Judge
Seabury every night.

(Laughter. BEN *deals)*

SECOND HACK: *(Reading from a newspaper)* Listen. Then after he gets this joker
on the stand and he's sworn in, Judge Seabury says, "From 1929 when Mayor
Walker appointed you till today in 1933 your official salary totaled forty thousand dollars."

BEN: "Will you please tell the investigating committee how you were able to
maintain a Wall Street brokerage account?"

THIRD HACK: No, that was the Commissioner of Hospitals yesterday.

SECOND HACK: With this boy it's a seventy-five-thousand-dollar mansion in
Teaneck, New Jersey.

THIRD HACK: And you know where he got it?

BEN: *(Grinning)* Out of a little tin box his wife keeps on the kitchen shelf. *(He gets
up and takes the newspaper)*

SECOND HACK: That's right.

BEN: *(Slapping newspaper)* Give 'em hell, Judge. Give 'em hell.

SECOND HACK: Your witness!

(They sing "Little Tin Box")

FOURTH HACK:

Mr. "X," may we ask you a question?
It's amazing is it not?
That the city pays you slightly less
Than fifty bucks a week
Yet you've purchased a private yacht!

BEN:

I am positive Your Honor must be joking
Any working man can do what I have done
For a month or two I simply gave up smoking
And I put my extra pennies one by one

Into a little tin box
A little tin box
That a little tin key unlocks
There is nothing unorthodox
About a little tin box

MEN:

About a little tin box
About a little tin box
In a little tin box
A little tin box
That a little tin key unlocks

BEN:

There is honor and purity

ALL:

Lots of security
In a little tin box

FIFTH HACK: *(Speaking)* Next witness.

FIRST HACK:

Mr. "Y," we've been told you don't feel well
And we know you've lost your voice
But we wonder how you managed on the salary you make
To acquire a new Rolls Royce

BEN:

You're implying I'm a crook and I say no sir!
There is nothing in my past I care to hide
I've been taking empty bottles to the grocer
And each nickel that I got was put aside

MEN:

That he got was put aside

BEN:

Into a little tin box
A little tin box
That a little tin key unlocks
There is nothing unorthodox
About a little tin box

MEN:

About a little tin box
About a little tin box
In a little tin box
A little tin box
There's a cushion for life's rude shocks

BEN:

There is faith, hope and charity

ALL:

Hard-won prosperity
In a little tin box.

FIFTH HACK: *(Speaking)* Next witness! Take the stand!

SIXTH HACK:

Mr. "Z," you're a junior official
And your income's rather low
Yet you've kept a dozen women
In the very best hotels
Would you kindly explain, how so?

BEN:

I can see Your Honor doesn't pull his punches
And it looks a trifle fishy, I'll admit

But for one whole week I went without my lunches
And it mounted up, Your Honor, bit by bit

MEN:
Up Your Honor, bit by bit.
It's just a little tin box
A little tin box
That a little tin key unlocks
There is nothing unorthodox
About a little tin box
About a little tin box
About a little tin box
In a little tin box
A little tin box
All a-glitter with blue chip stocks

BEN:
There is something delectable

ALL:
Almost respectable
In a little tin box
In a little tin box!

BEN: *(Speaking)* Tammany won't roll over and play dead.
THIRD HACK: But if we get the right man—
FIRST HACK: Who is it, Ben? Who we gonna run?
BEN: We're gonna run just exactly whoever Judge Seabury picks to run.
SECOND HACK: LaGuardia?
BEN: I hope not. Maybe Frank Streeter.
FOURTH HACK: He's a Democrat.
BEN: It's a Fusion ticket.
SECOND HACK: What'll we get out of it?
BEN: That's what I'm gonna be told this afternoon.
   (MARIE enters)
MARIE: Hello.
BEN: Well, Miss Fischer.
MARIE: Hello, Ben. Boys.
SECOND HACK: *(Shaking hands)* Long time no see.
MARIE: Ed.
BEN: Social or business?
MARIE: What?
BEN: Come over here with a message of any kind?
MARIE: Oh, my, no. I came over to see you personally.
BEN: Have a seat.
FIRST HACK: See you later, eh, Ben?
   (The men start to straggle out)
BEN: I'll be here.
SEVENTH HACK: Good to see you, Marie.
   (The men go. BEN pulls up a chair near MARIE and sits)
BEN: So?
MARIE: Ben, Mr. LaGuardia needs you.

BEN: His bootblack quit?

MARIE: I think he might be running for office again. He needs your advice. He needs your criticism.

BEN: My criticism? Oh, sure. He thrives on that!

MARIE: He does thrive on it. You know he has a deep affection for you.

BEN: Has he mentioned my name once in three years? *(No answer)* I thought so.

MARIE: We all know what he is.

BEN: A megalomaniac, that's what he is—and I've had it.

MARIE: Oh, Ben, you're too big for that—honestly—don't you want to beat Tammany?

BEN: I do—with a candidate who appreciates me. Good God, Marie. I should think you'd have had it, too. You going to wait around for him all your life?

MARIE: No, I'm not. *(MORRIS enters)* After this campaign, I'm quitting, but that doesn't mean I won't always be loyal to him.

MORRIS: Hello.

BEN: What is this? A class reunion? Hi, Morris.

(They shake hands. SEVENTH HACK pokes his head in the door)

SEVENTH HACK: Ben, Frank Streeter—on the phone. *(He pulls his head out)*

BEN: Make yourselves at home. *(He hurries out)*

MARIE: Did you find out?

MORRIS: I did.

MARIE: Well?

MORRIS: The answer is yes.

MARIE: Oh, Morris, isn't that exciting. Now we've got to do something. We've got to.

MORRIS: What did you mean telling him you're quitting?

MARIE: Morris, I talk too much. Now when Ben gets back—

MORRIS: You're quitting what? Quitting the office?

MARIE: This isn't the place to talk about my private troubles.

MORRIS: We've got to wait for Ben, so we've got to talk about something. Sit down. Have a cigar. Quitting what?

MARIE: Nothing, nothing, Morris, please!

MORRIS: You're among friends.

MARIE: Oh, I know that. You heard the Major yelling at me this morning, I suppose—

MORRIS: Sure.

MARIE: I'd made a date the night before.

MORRIS: Date?

MARIE: He didn't like it! I had my hat and coat on, ready to leave the office, and he wanted me to stay while he redictated a brief. *(Music plays softly)* Remember the last time we were here? Morris, I want to get married.

MORRIS: Sure.

MARIE: I've been taking a long hard look at life.

MORRIS: You're really serious?

MARIE: Yes, pal, I'm out to catch a husband—and I think making dates is the way to do it.

MORRIS: That's how Shirley caught me.

MARIE: So far, they've all bored me to tears—but I'll keep trying.

Dolly Winslow (Mary Martin) proclaims in
song that "My Heart Belongs to Daddy." One
of her avid listeners, at her right, is Gene
Kelly. *Courtesy of The Spewack Collection.*

Leave It to Me

(Above) The newly appointed American Ambassador to the Soviet Union, Alonzo P. Goodhue (Victor Moore), his wife (Sophie Tucker), and their five daughters in a Paris railway station en route to Moscow. (Below) The reviewing stand in Moscow. From left to right: Tamara, William Gaxton, Victor Moore, "Stalin," and Sophie Tucker. Both courtesy of The Spewack Collection.

Lady in the Dark

(Right) Liza Elliott (Gertrude Lawrence) swings out "The Saga of Jenny." (Below) Liza Elliott in the office of her psychoanalyst, Dr. Brooks (Donald Randolph). *Both from the Theatre Collection, New York Public Library.*

Liza's circus dream sequence. At left: Liza, Randy Curtis (Victor Mature). At far right: Kendall Nesbitt (Bert Lytell) and Russell Paxton (Danny Kaye). *Theatre Collection, New York Public Library.*

(Opposite, top) Reverend Stephen Kumalo (Todd Duncan) bids his wife
Grace (Gertrude Jeannette) farewell before leaving his home in
Ndotsheni, South Africa, for Johannesburg. *(Opposite, bottom)*
Stephen Kumalo consoles Irina (Inez Matthews), the mother of his son
Absalom's unborn child. *(Below)* Stephen Kumalo visits his son Absalom
(Julian Mayfield) in his jail cell where he awaits execution for murder.
All courtesy of Pix, Inc.

Wonderful Town

(*Above, left*) Ruth (Rosalind Russell) and her sister Eileen (Edith Adams) ponder in song why they ever left "Ohio." (*Above, right*) Ruth and the Brazilian Cadets in an extremely lively "Conga." (*Below*) Ruth and Eileen, center, leading The Village Vortex patrons in the "Wrong Note Rag." *All from the Theatre Collection, New York Public Library.*

Fiorello!

(Right) Fiorello LaGuardia (Tom Bosley)
meets Thea (Ellen Hanley) outside the strike
headquarters of the Nifty Shirtwaist Factory.
(Below) Ben (Howard Da Silva), fourth from
the left, and his Political Hacks sing about
"Politics and Poker." *Both courtesy of
Joseph Abeles Studio.*

Camelot

(*Opposite*) King Arthur (Richard Burton) peers through the branches of a tree on a hilltop near the castle at Camelot as he awaits the arrival of Guenevere. *(Inset, opposite bottom)* Guenevere (Julie Andrews) and Lancelot (Robert Goulet) share a romantic moment in the Queen's bedchamber. *Both courtesy of Joseph Abeles Studio.*

(*Above*) Don Quixote (Richard Kiley) and the Innkeeper (Ray Middleton) in the court-yard of the inn. *(Left)* "The Abduction": Aldonza and the Muleteers. *Both courtesy of Joseph Abeles Studio.*

Man of La Mancha

(Above) Sally Bowles (Jill Haworth), center, performing the song that typifies her philosophy, "Cabaret." Clifford Bradshaw (Bert Convy) applauds at table number three. (Left) Master of Ceremonies (Joel Grey) and one of the Kit Kat Klub girls in "The Money Song." (Opposite) Fraulein Schneider (Lotte Lenya) and Herr Schultz (Jack Gilford) sing "It Couldn't Please Me More" as he presents her with a pineapple. *All courtesy of Joseph Abeles Studio.*

Cabaret

Applause

(*Opposite*) Margo Channing (Lauren Bacall) singing "But Alive" in a Greenwich Village bar after her triumphant opening night. *(Below)* A party at Margo Channing's, with the star leading two of the guests in "Fasten Your Seat Belts" as the other guests look on. *Both courtesy of Joseph Abeles Studio.*

A Little Night Music

(Right) The dinner sequence, presided over by Madame Armfeldt. Desirée (Glynis Johns) stands center, below table. (Below) Desirée sings of "The Glamorous Life" she busily leads as a celebrated stage actress. She is flanked on her left by her daughter Fredrika (Judy Kahan) and on her right by her mother, Madame Armfeldt (Hermione Gingold).
Both courtesy of Joseph Abeles Studio.

MORRIS: You'll never be able to quit.

MARIE: Won't I?

MORRIS: No.

(MARIE *sings "The Very Next Man"*)

MARIE:

I shall marry the very next man who asks me,
You'll see.
Next time I feel
That a man's about to kneel
He won't have to plead or implore
I'll say "yes" before his knee hits the floor.

No more waiting around
No more browsing through True Romance
I've seen the light so while there's a chance
I'm gonna marry the very next man
Who asks me.

Start rehearsing the choir
Tie some shoes on my Chevrolet
Pelt me with rice and catch my bouquet
I'm gonna marry the very next man

If he adores me
What does it matter if he bores me?
If I allow the man to carry me off
No more will people try to marry me off

No more living alone
No more cheating at solitaire
Holding my breath for one special man
Why I could smother for all he'd care
I'm through being wary
I'll marry the very next man

No more daydreams for me
Find the finest of bridal suites
Chill the champagne and warm up the sheets
I'm gonna marry the very next man

And if he likes me
Who cares how frequently he strikes me
I'll fetch his slippers with my arm in a sling
Just for the privilege of wearing his ring

New York papers, take note!
Here's a statement that you can quote:
Waiting for ships that never come in
A girl is likely to miss the boat
I'm through being wary
I'll marry the very next man.

(BEN MARINO enters)

BEN: Well, boys and girls, I just had a very cooperative talk with a certain candidate for Mayor. Honest but grateful.

MARIE: Ben, I've got to tell you something. If Mr. LaGuardia will take it, he's to get the nomination—that's definite.

BEN: How would you know?

(MARIE nods toward MORRIS)

MORRIS: I got a cousin who works in the stenographic pool at Seabury's office. I just came from there. Seabury's going to proposition the Major tomorrow morning.

BEN: You don't say.

MORRIS: Of course, I'm not sure he'll accept.

BEN: He always accepts.

MARIE: He's in a very strange mood, Ben. But if you came to him, if you were in his office tomorrow at ten, I think he would.

BEN: Tell him to call me. Tell him to get in touch.

MARIE: Ben, he can't. You know him as well as we do. He can't. Now don't be such a stubborn fool.

BEN: Good God, you sound like Fiorello. It's catching.

MARIE: Wouldn't it be fun to start another campaign? All together? I'm going to call some of the leaders from the other districts. I know they'll come. It's too good to miss. You've got to be there.

(The poker players straggle in)

FOURTH HACK: We too early?

BEN: Not at all. Shuffle the cards. I'll be right with you.

THIRD HACK: Who's dealing?

FOURTH HACK: Ben is.

MARIE: We'll see you, eh, Ben?

BEN: Now wait a minute, I didn't say so.

MARIE: Good-bye.

MORRIS: Good-bye, Ben.

BEN: Good-bye.

(MARIE and MORRIS go)

SECOND HACK: *(With newspaper)* Guess who Seabury has got on the rack now?

BEN: I'll tell you who. Me.

(They sing "Politics and Poker")

ALL:
Politics and poker
Politics and poker
Everyone is broke
And getting broker
Everybody knows
The trouble that we're in
So here we sit playing at poker and politics
Waiting to nominate a candidate
Who's good enough and smart enough
And strong enough to win.

Blackout

SCENE 8

Place: FIORELLO'S *office.*

At Rise: When the lights come on, we are interested in the outer office, where NEIL *is sitting at his desk, talking on the phone. In the inner office, dimly seen, are* FIORELLO, *at his desk, and* MRS. POMERANTZ, *sitting in front of it.*

NEIL: *(Into phone)* Me on a committee? I don't understand. No, Mr. LaGuardia hasn't said anything to me about it. Well, yes, sure, I can be reached at this number, but— Sure. Yes. Okay. *(He hangs up and turns to* MORRIS*)* Morris, is the Major going back into politics?

MORRIS: Why do you ask?

NEIL: Some guy from Judge Seabury's office just called me about being on a fund-raising committee for this Fusion ticket I been reading about.

FLORENCE: *(Looking up from the switchboard)* Neil, excuse me, but I got somebody asking for a Mr. Ben Marino?

NEIL: Ben Marino hasn't been in this office for three years.

(The lights come up in the inner office and our attention is directed to FIORELLO *and* MRS. POMERANTZ*)*

FIORELLO: Mrs. Pomerantz, if I succeed in getting Noonan into court, you'll get your money. I guarantee that. The question is purely one of time.

MRS. POMERANTZ: By me also. Forty years I'm saving my Lennie should be a doctor.

FIORELLO: I'll do my best, Mrs. Pomerantz. But the law doesn't always move as fast as we'd like.

MRS. POMERANTZ: The best, naturally, this I know you'll do, like always. But the law for once you'll have to give it a little bit a shake.

(The phone rings. FIORELLO *picks it up)*

FIORELLO: Yes?

NEIL: *(On the phone in the outer office)* Major—the Noonan case has been taken off the docket.

FIORELLO: *(Into phone)* I'll talk to you in one minute. *(He hangs up)* All right, Mrs. Pomerantz, just try to be patient. *(He rises)*

MRS. POMERANTZ: *(Rising)* Me, I'm patient—but the clock—?

FIORELLO: I'll call you. *(He shows her to the outer office)*

MRS. POMERANTZ: *(To* FIORELLO, *as* NEIL *comes in)* So please, do me a favor, don't get sick till Lennie graduates. From then on, the rest of your life, you should live to be a hundred and twenty, a doctor's bill you'll never have to pay.

(She exits. The moment MRS. POMERANTZ *disappears,* FIORELLO'S *manner changes. He turns angrily)*

FIORELLO: *(Pointing at* NEIL*)* Now say that again! I don't think I heard you right. The Noonan case has been taken off the docket?

NEIL: *(Nervous)* Yes, sir.

FIORELLO: *(Thunders)* Why?

NEIL: The clerk of the court—said he didn't know why—except that it was done by order of Judge Carter.

FIORELLO: *(Sharp)* Which Judge Carter?

NEIL: Joseph F., sir.

FIORELLO: *(Incredulous)* General Sessions?

NEIL: Yes, sir.

FIORELLO: *(Roars)* What the hell is a General Sessions judge doing with the New York Supreme Court docket?

MORRIS: *(Enters with an armful of folders, speaks quietly)* Why don't you ask Jimmy Hines?

FIORELLO: *(Angry)* He's not on my staff! You two are!

MORRIS: *(Laying down the folders one by one on* FIORELLO'S *desk)* The same thing that happened on Bienstock versus Cowan. Delfino versus Eberhardt. Fisher versus Geoghan. And the four billion others we've worked on these last three years. It's hopeless.

FIORELLO: Nothing is hopeless. Haven't you worked here long enough to learn that?

MORRIS: I've worked here long enough to learn the difference between law and politics.

FIORELLO: *(Scornfully sarcastic)* A Solomon—a Solomon come to judgment!

MORRIS: You don't think I'm right?

FIORELLO: Of course you're right!

(MARIE enters the outer office)

MARIE: Florence, were there any men asking for me?

FLORENCE: No, but there were some messages. *(She hands message slips to* MARIE*)*

FIORELLO: If any crook has a friend at the Wigwam he doesn't have to go to court. Don't you think I see the termites eating up my city? Don't you think I know something should be done? God damn it, you were there. You've been with us. Didn't I try? *(MARIE is attracted to his door by his loud voice. She knocks)* Well! *(MARIE enters)* All right, get out, you two—I'll talk to you later. *(MORRIS and* NEIL *exit. To* MARIE*)* I'm sorry. I don't know what's come over me these days.

MARIE: *(Quiet)* I do. *(He turns to look at her)* If a person loves something—or somebody—as much as you love this city, Mr. LaGuardia, it's not easy to stand by and watch, without saying a word, or lifting a finger—

FIORELLO: *(Shakes his head wearily)* I can't, Marie. I can't. They turned their backs on me. They didn't want me.

MARIE: That's not true, Mr. LaGuardia. They didn't turn their backs on you. They just weren't looking. They didn't have to look. They were making too much money. They were having too much fun. But things are different now. The fun is over. People are starving. They'll listen now, Mr. LaGuardia.

FIORELLO: I'm awfully tired, Marie.

MARIE: *(Taking her courage in her hands)* No, you're not. You're scared. *(His head comes up sharply)* You're afraid they'll turn their backs on you again. That's what's wrong. You're scared you'll lose a second time.

(He glares at her. She is frightened but she stands her ground and stares back at him. The lights come up in the outer office)

FIRST HACK: *(Enters and addresses* FLORENCE*)* Is Mr. Ben Marino here?

FLORENCE: No, sir, he hasn't been here in three years.

FIRST HACK: I know that. What about Miss Fischer?

FLORENCE: What's the name please?

FIRST HACK: I have an appointment with Mr. Ben Marino. *(MARIE enters)* Oh— here she is.

MARIE: *(Shaking hands with* FIRST HACK*)* Hello, Ed. The others will be here shortly.

*(*BEN *enters behind them)*

BEN: Well, the old place hasn't changed such a hell of a lot.

MARIE: Thank you for coming.

BEN: I'll probably get thrown out, but I always enjoy short visits.

(Two other men enter behind them)

FIRST MAN: Oh, here he is.

BEN: Hello, Ed. Hello, Louis.

SECOND MAN: Hi ya, Ben. We got a quorum?

NEIL: Ben—Ben Marino! Well!

BEN: Morris! Neil!

MORRIS: How are you, Ben?

*(*FIORELLO *appears in the doorway of his private office)*

FIORELLO: Who? *(Stops in astonishment)* Well, this is a great honor. What the hell are you doing in this office?

BEN: I came to help, Fiorello.

FIORELLO: Help? Has somebody around here been asking for help? Help what?

BEN: Help you in your next campaign.

FIORELLO: I have no campaign.

BEN: Hasn't Judge Seabury talked to you?

FIORELLO: I give him a little advice once in a while. Of course, he's talked to me.

BEN: About running for Mayor?

FIORELLO: No, not exactly.

BEN: On a Fusion ticket. You know what I'm talking about.

MORRIS: *(Close behind* FIORELLO*)* Judge Carter, Special Sessions.

FIORELLO: *(Wheels on him)* What did you say?

MORRIS: I think you said it, Major. Nothing is hopeless.

(Politicians enter from outside)

POLITICIAN: Well, here we are.

FIORELLO: More politicians, huh?

FLORENCE: Excuse me, Mr. LaGuardia. Judge Seabury is on the phone.

(The room is very quiet. FIORELLO *hesitates, then turns toward the door of his inner office. He stops and comes back)*

FIORELLO: And if I should decide to run again, I want all you politicians to know that my chief qualification for Mayor of this great city is my monumental ingratitude. *(He goes into the office and picks up the phone and is seen in conversation during the following)*

BEN: The old fire-eater hasn't changed such a hell of a lot.

MARIE: Do you want him to?

BEN: What good'll it do me?

MORRIS: Hooray! *(He throws the files on the floor)*

BEN: What's the matter with you?

MORRIS: I'm happy! We're going to run again!

(He begins an impromptu dance. FIORELLO *hangs up the phone, comes into the outer office.* MORRIS *stops dancing. All stare at* FIORELLO. *He points at* MARIE. *She follows him into his inner office)*

BEN: *(Laughing)* That guy kills me. He just plain kills me. *(More politicians appear from outside)* Come in, boys.

(Lights come up in the inner office, where MARIE *stands penitently waiting to hear what* FIORELLO *has to say)*

FIORELLO: Did you ask Ben Marino to come here?

MARIE: Yes, I thought—

FIORELLO: Thought what? That I couldn't do my own thinking?

MARIE: Thought if you were going to run for Mayor, you'd need friends. True friends, like Ben.

FIORELLO: It's nice to know you're taking over running my life. You're getting very independent lately.

MARIE: I'm sorry.

(There is a pause. She starts back for the outer office. He calls her)

FIORELLO: Wait a minute—come here. You're fired!

MARIE: Fired?

FIORELLO: As of now.

MARIE: Just because I—?

FIORELLO: No. The reason is different. I can't court a girl who's working for me.

MARIE: Mr. LaGuardia!

FIORELLO: Will you marry me? *(She moves away from him and sits down. Music starts softly)* I know it's kind of sudden.

MARIE: Sudden! Yes, it is.

FIORELLO: But, honestly, Marie, I think you can learn to love me.

MARIE: Yes, I think I can. I've been practicing for fifteen years.

FIORELLO: *(Speaking)*	MARIE: *(Singing)*
Good. It's a deal. I've got plans, Marie. I'm not very good at expressing my feelings, but I'm good at making plans. We have so many things to share, so much in common. It's going to be all right, Marie—dear Marie.	*Start rehearsing the choir* *Tie some shoes on my Chevrolet* *Pelt me with rice and catch my bouquet,* *for I start changing my name today* *I'm through being wary* *I'll marry the very next man.*

(Politicians sing in the outer office)

MEN: *(Soft)*
  We want LaGuardia
  L-A-G-U-A-R-D-I-A
  (Loud)
  We want LaGuardia
  L-A-G-U-A-R-D-I-A!

(MARIE takes FIORELLO'S hand and leads him into the outer office. He faces the politicians and raises his arms to indicate that he will accept the nomination to run again for Mayor of New York. MARIE beams. The politicians sing lustily)

  Let every racketeer and reprobate
  Start to say a silent prayer
  We've got the man who's going to turn the town
  Both inside out and upside down

LaGuardia! His Honor the Mayor!
Yes, you can change it all
The people want you to
So cast your spell come next Election Day
The name's LaGuardia
L-A-G-U-A-R-D-I-A!

Curtain

CAMELOT

Book and Lyrics by Alan Jay Lerner
Music by Frederick Loewe

(Based on *The Once and Future King* by T. H. White)

Editor's Notes

The fanfare and publicity generated by the press prior to the New York premiere of *Camelot* on December 3, 1960, could almost be equated to the anticipation of a Second Coming. Most had envisaged a sequel to the creators' *My Fair Lady*. But while the former was steeped in the Shavian reality of Bernard Shaw, *Camelot* was embedded in fantasy and legend.

The production made news from the initial pronouncement that Alan Jay Lerner, Frederick Loewe and Moss Hart were engaged in a musical project derived from the novel by T. H. White. As Mr. Lerner, in his preface to the original publication of *Camelot*, wrote: "It was the show that was to follow the highly successful *My Fair Lady*, written and directed by the same three, and the hot spotlight of newspaper interest shone on it continuously."

After many vicissitudes (duly and daily reported in the press) during its tryout tour, it finally reached Broadway and settled down to a run of 873 performances.

John Chapman of the New York *Daily News* summarized the occasion when he reported: "*Camelot* is magnificent. Its songs are lovely and unfailingly right. Its cast is superb. The sets and costumes of its twenty scenes have far more than splendor; together they make a single, thrilling work of art. Good taste—the instinctive knowledge of what is right and proper—is paramount.

"Since *Camelot* was written by Alan Jay Lerner and Frederick Loewe and directed by Moss Hart, the gentlemen who blessed us all with *My Fair Lady*, many will ask if the new musical is as good as the older one, and the only answer to this query is to quote (Shakespeare's) Constable Dogberry and reply 'comparisons are odious.' The only real point of similarity between the two is the aforementioned good taste."

Other professional first-nighters described it as "a very handsome musical play with many lovely and imaginative things in it . . . it has gaiety and grandeur and its beauty is almost unbelievable . . . It ranks with the very best musicals hatched in this heartland of musicals" for "the inspired creators of *My Fair Lady* appear to have passed another miracle."

Camelot (with Laurence Harvey and Elizabeth Larner) also achieved success in London where it ran at the Drury Lane Theatre for 518 performances; and in 1967, a film version of the musical was released with Richard Harris and Vanessa Redgrave as stars.

Alan Jay Lerner, author of the book and lyrics, was born in New York City on August 31, 1918. He was educated in England and at Choate and Harvard University. While at Harvard, he contributed material to two Hasty Pudding Shows and after graduation wrote for radio.

Frederick Loewe studied piano in his native Vienna. At thirteen, he appeared as soloist with the Berlin Symphony Orchestra and later he was awarded the Hollander Medal, then the prize most sought by young European musicians. Coming to America in 1924, he had established himself as a concert pianist of note before meeting with Mr. Lerner. Their meeting proved to be a providential occasion for they were destined to become one of the most renowned teams in the history of the American musical theatre.

Their first joint effort was *The Life of the Party*, presented in Detroit in 1942. In the following year, they made their Broadway debut as a team with the musical *What's Up?* Although its engagement was comparatively brief, it clearly indicated promise for Lerner and Loewe and they came to near-fulfillment with the charming but surprisingly underrated *The Day Before Spring* (1945).

True and unqualified success was to come in 1947 with the memorable production of *Brigadoon* (published in this editor's earlier collection.) This was followed by *Paint Your Wagon* (1951), the record-breaking *My Fair Lady* (1956), and *Camelot* (1960).

In 1958, the magic of Lerner and Loewe was transferred to the screen with one of the most honored films of all time, *Gigi*. Named the best picture of the year, it received a total of nine Academy Awards, including one for Mr. Lerner's screenplay and for the team's title song.

In addition to his work with Frederick Loewe, Alan Jay Lerner wrote the book and lyrics for Kurt Weill's *Love Life* (1948), *On a Clear Day You Can See Forever* (with music by Burton Lane, 1965), and *Coco* (with music by André Previn). With the incantatory Katharine Hepburn making her musical stage debut as the legendary French *couturière*, Gabrielle Chanel, *Coco* was an outstanding success of the 1969–1970 Broadway season.

Mr. Lerner also wrote the story and screenplay for *An American in Paris* which brought him his first Hollywood Academy Award in 1951.

The team of Lerner and Loewe were reunited when the composer came out of retirement to provide the score for Lerner's lyrics and screenplay for the musical film based on Antoine de Saint-Exupéry's *The Little Prince* and the stage adaptation of their award-winning screen musical, *Gigi*, which opened in New York in 1973.

Production Notes

Camelot was first presented by the Messrs. Lerner, Loewe and Hart at the Majestic Theatre, New York, on December 3, 1960. The cast was as follows:

Sir Dinadan, *John Cullum*
Sir Lionel, *Bruce Yarnell*
Merlyn, *David Hurst*
Arthur, *Richard Burton*
Guenevere, *Julie Andrews*
Nimue, *Marjorie Smith*
Lancelot, *Robert Goulet*
Mordred, *Roddy McDowall*
A Page, *Leland Mayforth*
Squire Dap, *Michael Clarke-Laurence*

Pellinore, *Robert Coote*
Sir Sagramore, *James Gannon*
Clarius, *Richard Kuch*
Lady Anne, *Christina Gillespie*
Lady Sybil, *Leesa Troy*
A Knight, *Michael Kermoyan*
A Knight, *Jack Dabdoub*
Morgan Le Fey, *M'el Dowd*
Tom, *Robin Stewart*

Knights and Ladies, *Joan August, Mary Sue Berry, Marnell Bruce, Judy Hastings, Benita James, Marjorie Smith, Shelia Swenson, Leesa Troy, Dorothy White, Frank Bouley, Jack Dabdoub, James Gannon, Murray Goldkind, Warren Hays, Paul Huddleston, Michael Kermoyan, Donald Maloof, Larry Mitchell, Paul Richards, John Taliaferro, Virginia Allen, Judi Allinson, Laurie Archer, Carlene Carroll, Joan Coddington, Katia Geleznova, Adriana Keathley, Dawn Mitchell, Claudia Schroeder, Beti Seay, Jerry Bowers, Peter Deign, Randy Doney, Richard Englund, Richard Gain, Gene GeBauer, James Kirby, Richard Kuch, Joe Nelson, John Starkweather, Jimmy Tarbutton*

Production Staged by *Moss Hart*
Choreography and Musical Numbers by *Hanya Holm*

Scenic Production by *Oliver Smith*
Costumes Designed by *Adrian* and *Tony Duquette*
Lighting by *Feder*
Musical Director: *Franz Allers*
Orchestrations by *Robert Russell Bennett* and *Philip J. Lang*
Dance and Choral Arrangements by *Trude Rittman*
Hair Styles by *Ernest Adler*

Act One

Scene 1: A Hilltop near Camelot. A long time ago.
Scene 2: Near Camelot. Immediately following.
Scene 3: Arthur's Study. Five Years later.
Scene 4: A Countryside near Camelot. A few months later.
Scene 5: A Garden near the Castle. Immediately following.
Scene 6: A Terrace of the Castle. Two weeks later.
Scene 7: The Tents outside the Jousting Field. The following day.
Scene 8: The Jousting Field.
Scene 9: The Terrace. Early evening of the same day.
Scene 10: A Corridor in the Castle. Immediately following.
Scene 11: The Grand Hall. Immediately following.

Act Two

Scene 1: The Main Terrace of the Castle. A few years later.
Scene 2: The Terrace of the Castle. A month later.
Scene 3: A Forest near Camelot. The following day.
Scene 4: The Forest of Morgan Le Fey. Immediately following.
Scene 5: A Corridor to the Queen's Bedchamber. Later that night.
Scene 6: The Queen's Bedchamber. Immediately following.
Scene 7: Camelot.
Scene 8: A Battlefield outside Joyous Gard. A week later.

Musical Numbers

Act One

Scene 1:

I Wonder What the King Is Doing Tonight?	Arthur
The Simple Joys of Maidenhood	Guenevere
Scene 2:	
Follow Me	Nimue
Scene 4:	
C'est Moi	Lancelot
Scene 5:	
The Lusty Month of May	Guenevere and Ensemble
Scene 6:	
How to Handle a Woman	Arthur
Scene 8:	
The Jousts	Arthur, Guenevere and Ensemble

Scene 9:
Before I Gaze at You Again   Guenevere

Act Two
Scene 1:
If Ever I Would Leave You   Lancelot
The Seven Deadly Virtues   Mordred
Scene 2:
What Do Simple Folk Do?   Guenevere and Arthur
Scene 4:
The Persuasion   Mordred and Morgan Le Fey
Scene 6:
I Loved You Once in Silence   Guenevere
Scene 7:
Guenevere   Ensemble
Scene 8:
Camelot (Reprise)   Arthur

ACT ONE

SCENE I

Scene: A Hilltop near the Castle at Camelot. There is a large tree with great branches reaching high and out of sight, and a small hillock beyond the tree. A light snow is falling.

Time: Afternoon.

At Rise: The Overture has ended. A spotlight discovers SIR DINADAN *standing on the hillock, peering through a crude telescope into the distance. Around him can be seen Ladies and Gentlemen of the Court, arranged decoratively.*

DINADAN: *(A pompous young lord, easily astonished, suddenly quite astonished)* My Sainted Mother! The carriage has stopped! Someone is getting out. A lady.

LIONEL: Are you sure it's her carriage?

(MERLYN enters. He is a rococo figure of a man, with a huge pointed hat; flowing, heavily embroidered robes; and the legendary apparel of wisdom—a long white beard)

DINADAN: It's pure white. The horses are pure white. It's plainly and obviously a bridal carriage. *(He rushes to* MERLYN*)* Merlyn, here's a calamity. Guenevere's carriage has halted below the hill.

MERLYN: I know. I remembered she would.

DINADAN: But it was officially arranged for her to stop here at the top of the hill. Royal brides are always greeted atop the hill. What should we do?

MERLYN: Dunce! Sound the trumpet, assemble the Court and march to the bottom.

DINADAN: *(Stunned)* It's wildly untraditional.

MERLYN: I hereby proclaim from this time henceforth that all new queens shall be met at the foot of the hill. There! A brand-new tradition! Does that solve it?

DINADAN: *(Placated)* Sound the trumpet! We shall greet Lady Guenevere at the foot of the hill in traditional fashion.

(The Ladies and Gentlemen assemble formally and, with banners flying, parade across the stage and off. MERLYN pauses before the tree and, without looking at it, speaks)

MERLYN: Arthur, come down out of the tree. *(There is no response)* Your Majesty, I know you're up there. Come down at once. *(There is no response)* Wart, come down at once! You're perfectly safe. There's no one here.

(KING ARTHUR peers through the branches)

ARTHUR: Why so angry, Merlyn? I know you are because you called me Wart.

MERLYN: Yes, Wart. Your schoolboy's nickname. That's what your behavior warrants. Perched in a tree trying to steal a look at your bride. Will you never learn patience?

(ARTHUR jumps down. He is a boyish young man in his mid-twenties)

ARTHUR: *(Imperiously)* I'm the King. Others must learn patience. *(Then, with sudden nervous enthusiasm)* How is she, Merlyn? Is she beautiful?

MERLYN: I don't recall.

ARTHUR: *(Irritably)* Rubbish. Are you pretending you don't see into the future?

MERLYN: When you live backwards in time as I do, and have the future to remember as well as the past, occasionally you do forget a face.

ARTHUR: *(Dictatorially)* Merlyn, as your King, I command you to tell me if she is . . .

MERLYN: *(Giving up)* She's beautiful.

ARTHUR: *(Suddenly almost frightened)* Quite, or very?

MERLYN: Very.

ARTHUR: *(Frustrated by his own discomfort)* Merlyn, why have you never taught me love and marriage?

MERLYN: Don't scramble them together that way. They are two different things. Besides, I did give you a lesson once, but your mind was, as usual, elsewhere. You had better heed me well from now on. I shan't be here long.

ARTHUR: Why not?

MERLYN: I've told you, I'm due to be bewitched by a nymph named Nimue, who will steal my magic powers and lock me in a cave for several centuries.

ARTHUR: Nimue! Fiddlesticks! Whenever you're displeased with me, you threaten with this creature Nimue.

MERLYN: It's not a threat; it will happen.

ARTHUR: When you know she is near, change yourself into a bat. *(At his most youthful and charming)* Merlyn, do you remember when I was a boy and you changed me into a hawk? What a feeling, sailing through the air! For old times' sake, do it again. Right this minute. One last soar through the sky.

MERLYN: So you can soar through the sky to her carriage and see her through the window? No.

ARTHUR: *(Furious)* Merlyn, there are times when I insist that you remember who I am. Make me a hawk, or I'll have your head cut off.

MERLYN: It's you who keep forgetting who you are. Think of the joy you've brought to Camelot. A radiant young princess, never before out of her castle, come by treaty to bring peace between peoples. A royal marriage. A new Queen. And where is the King? Swinging in the trees. Thank heaven History never knew. Thank heaven Mallory and Tennyson never found out. Thank heaven your people are not aware of your behavior. Now go back to the castle, my boy. At once. *(He exits)*

ARTHUR: *(Rebelliously)* My people indeed! As if they give a thought to what I'm doing tonight. *(Shouting his defiance)* Oh, good and loyal subjects of the Crown, are you really peering up at the castle with a question mark in each eye, churning to know how stands the King on his bridal eve, throbbing with curiosity about the King's humor on his prenuptial night? *(Defeatedly)* Yes, you are. That's precisely what you're doing. Every last, blessed one of you. *(He sings)*

I know what my people are thinking tonight,
As home through the shadows they wander.
Ev'ryone smiling in secret delight,
They stare at the castle and ponder.
Whenever the wind blows this way,
You can almost hear ev'ryone say:

I wonder what the King is doing tonight.
What merriment is the King pursuing tonight?
The candles at the Court, they never burn'd as bright.
I wonder what the King is up to tonight.
How goes the final hour
As he sees the bridal bower
Being legally and regally prepared?
(Angrily)
Well, I'll tell you what the King is doing tonight:
He's scared! He's scared!
(He paces up and down, debating the subject with himself)

You mean that a king who fought a dragon,
Whack'd him in two and fix'd his wagon,
Goes to be wed in terror and distress?
(Admits angrily)

                   Yes!

A warrior who's so calm in battle
Even his armor doesn't rattle,
Faces a woman petrified with fright?
(Fairly shouting his rage)

                   Right!

You mean that appalling clamoring
That sounds like a blacksmith hammering
Is merely the banging of his royal knees?
(Painfully)

                  Please!

You wonder what the King is wishing tonight . . .
He's wishing he were in Scotland fishing tonight.

What occupies his time while waiting for the bride?
He's searching high and low for some place to hide.

And oh, the expectation,
The sublime anticipation
He must feel about the wedding night to come!
Well, I'll tell you what the King is feeling tonight:
He's numb!
        He shakes!
He quails! He quakes!
Oh, that's what the King is doing tonight.

(Something, or someone, offstage catches his eye, and he scrambles back into his place of hiding in the tree. Suddenly GUENEVERE, *in a flaming red cloak, flies fearfully across the stage. She stops. She looks behind to see if she has been followed. She satisfies herself that she is momentarily safe, and seats herself at the foot of the tree. She is very, very young and very, very lovely. She clasps her hands and looks heavenward)*

GUENEVERE: *(Sings)*
St. Genevieve! St. Genevieve!
It's Guenevere. Remember me?
St. Genevieve! St. Genevieve!
I'm over here beneath this tree.
You know how faithful and devout I am.
You must admit I've always been a lamb.
But, Genevieve, St. Genevieve,
(With vehement rebellion)
I won't obey you any more!
You've gone a bit too far.
I won't be bid and bargain'd for
Like beads at a bazaar.

St. Genevieve, I've run away,
Eluded them and fled;
And from now on I intend to pray
To someone else instead.
(Suddenly lost, she becomes suddenly plaintive again)
Oh, Genevieve, St. Genevieve,
Where were you when my youth was sold?
Dear Genevieve, sweet Genevieve,
Shan't I be young before I'm old?

(She speaks)
Shan't I, St. Genevieve? Why must I suffer this squalid destiny? Just when I reach the golden age of eligibility and wooability. Is my fate determined by love and courtship? Oh, no. *(Bitterly)* Clause one: fix the border; Clause two: establish trade; Clause three: deliver me; Clause four: stop the war; five, six: pick up sticks. How cruel! How unjust! Am I never to know the joys of maidenhood? The conventional, ordinary, garden variety joys of maidenhood?

(She sings)
Where are the simple joys of maidenhood?
Where are all those adoring, daring boys?
Where's the knight pining so for me
He leaps to death in woe for me?
Oh, where are a maiden's simple joys?

Shan't I have the normal life a maiden should?
Shall I never be rescued in the wood?
Shall two knights never tilt for me
And let their blood be spilt for me?
Oh, where are the simple joys of maidenhood?

Shall I not be on a pedestal,
Worshipped and competed for?
Not be carried off, or betterst'll,
Cause a little war?

Where are the simple joys of maidenhood?
Are those sweet, gentle pleasures gone for good?
Shall a feud not begin for me?
Shall kith not kill their kin for me?
Oh, where are the trivial joys . . . ?
Harmless, convivial joys . . . ?
Where are the simple joys of maidenhood?

(She turns dejectedly towards the foot of the tree. A branch cracks, and ARTHUR *drops to the floor.* GUENEVERE, *startled out of her wits, runs)*

ARTHUR: A thousand pardons, Milady. Wait! Don't run. *(She stops in the corner of the stage and looks at him coweringly)* Please! I won't harm you.

GUENEVERE: You lie! You'll leap at me and throw me to the ground.

ARTHUR: *(Amazed, protesting)* I won't do any such thing. *(He takes a step toward her. She takes a step backwards. He stops)*

GUENEVERE: Then you'll twist my arm and tie me to a tree.

ARTHUR: But I won't.

GUENEVERE: Then you'll sling me over your shoulder and carry me off.

ARTHUR: No, no, no! I swear it! By the Sword Excalibur! I swear I won't touch you.

GUENEVERE: *(Hurt)* Why not? *(Sudden rage)* How dare you insult me in this fashion. Do my looks repel you?

ARTHUR: No. You're beautiful.

GUENEVERE: Well, then? We're alone. I'm completely defenseless. What kind of a cad are you? Apologize at once.

ARTHUR: *(At once)* I apologize. I'm not certain what I've done, but from the depths of my heart, I apologize.

GUENEVERE: *(With sudden wisdom)* Ah! I think I know. You heard me praying.

ARTHUR: I couldn't help it, Milady. You prayed rather loudly.

GUENEVERE: And you know who I am.

ARTHUR: You're Guenevere.

GUENEVERE: Yes, of course. You're afraid because I may be your Queen. That accounts for your respectful, polite, despicable behavior.

ARTHUR: Milady, I would never harm you for any reason. And as for what to do with you, I'm at a loss. I know you are to be Queen and I should escort you back to your carriage. At the same time, you're a maiden in genuine distress. It's chivalry versus country. I can't quite determine which call to obey.

GUENEVERE: *(Looking off toward the foot of the hill)* You'd better decide quickly. They'll soon reach the carriage and discover I'm gone. Then all of Camelot will be searching for me. At least *that* will be exciting. Unless of course everyone in Camelot is like you and they all go home to deliberate.

ARTHUR: *(Thrown off balance, enamored, captivated, and overcome by a great sense of inadequacy)* Oh, why isn't Merlyn here! He usually senses when I need him and appears. Why does he fail me now?

GUENEVERE: Who?

ARTHUR: Merlyn. My teacher. He would know immediately what to do. I'm not accomplished at thinking, so I have Merlyn do it for me. He's the wisest man alive. He lives backwards.

GUENEVERE: I beg your pardon?

ARTHUR: He lives backwards. He doesn't age. He youthens. He can remember the future so he can tell you what you'll be doing in it. Do you understand? *(She comes toward him. He never takes his eyes off her, as the wonder of her comes nearer)*

GUENEVERE: *(Now at ease)* Of course I don't understand. But if you mean he's some sort of fortune-teller, I'd give a year in Paradise to know mine. I can never return to my own castle, and I absolutely refuse to go on to that one.

ARTHUR: *(Sadly)* You refuse to go on—ever?

GUENEVERE: Ever. My only choice is . . . Don't stare. It's rude. Who are you?

ARTHUR: *(After a thought)* Actually, they call me Wart.

GUENEVERE: Wart? What a ridiculous name. Are you sure you heard them properly?

ARTHUR: It's a nickname. It was given to me when I was a boy.

GUENEVERE: You're rather sweet, in spite of your name. And I didn't think I'd like anyone in Camelot. Imagine riding seven hours in a carriage on the verge of hysteria, then seeing that horrible castle rising in the distance, and running away; then having a man plop from a tree like an overripe apple . . . You must admit for my first day away from home it's quite a plateful. If only I were not alone. Wart, why don't you . . . Is it really Wart?

ARTHUR: Yes.

GUENEVERE: Wart, why don't you run away with me? *(She is enchanted by the notion)*

ARTHUR: I? Run away with you?

GUENEVERE: Of course. As my protector. Naturally, I would be brutalized by strangers. I expect that. But it would be dreadful if there were no one to rescue me. Think of it! We can travel the world. France, Scotland, Spain . . .

ARTHUR: What a dream you spin, and how easily I could be caught up in it. But I can't, Milady. To serve as your protector would satisfy the prayers of the most fanatic cavalier alive. But I must decline.

GUENEVERE: *(Angrily)* You force me to stay?

ARTHUR: Not at all.

GUENEVERE: But you know you're the only one I know in Camelot. Whom else can I turn to?

ARTHUR: Milady, if you persist in escaping, I'll find someone trustworthy and brave to accompany you.

GUENEVERE: Then do so immediately. There's not much time.

ARTHUR: Oh, do look around you, Milady. Reconsider. Camelot is unique. We have an enchanted forest where the Fairy Queen, Morgan Le Fey, lives in an invisible castle. Most unusual. We have a talking owl named Archimedes. Highly original. We have unicorns with silver feet. The rarest kind. And we have far and away the most equitable climate in all the world. Ordained by decree! Extremely uncommon.

GUENEVERE: Oh, come now.

ARTHUR: *(Sings)*
> *It's true! It's true! The crown has made it clear:*
> *The climate must be perfect all the year.*
>
> *A law was made a distant moon ago here,*
> *July and August cannot be too hot;*
> *And there's a legal limit to the snow here*
> *In Camelot.*
>
> *The winter is forbidden till December,*
> *And exits March the second on the dot.*
> *By order summer lingers through September*
> *In Camelot.*
>
> *Camelot! Camelot!*
> *I know it sounds a bit bizarre;*
> *But in Camelot, Camelot*
> *That's how conditions are.*
>
> *The rain may never fall till after sundown.*
> *By eight the morning fog must disappear.*
> *In short, there's simply not*
> *A more congenial spot*
> *For happ'ly-ever-aftering than here*
> *In Camelot.*

GUENEVERE: *(Sarcastically)* And I suppose the autumn leaves fall in neat little piles.

ARTHUR: Oh, no, Milady. They blow away completely. At night, of course.

GUENEVERE: Of course.
(She moves away from him, as if to leave. He leaps after her and blocks her way)

ARTHUR:
> *Camelot! Camelot!*
> *I know it gives a person pause*
> *But in Camelot, Camelot*
> *Those are the legal laws.*
>
> *The snow may never slush upon the hillside.*
> *By nine p.m. the moonlight must appear.*
> *In short, there's simply not*

A more congenial spot
For happ'ly-ever-aftering than here
In Camelot.

(DINADAN enters suddenly, accompanied by one or two Ladies and Gentlemen of the Court)

DINADAN: *(To the others)* There she is!

GUENEVERE: *(Running to ARTHUR for protection)* Wart, please . . .

DINADAN: *(To ARTHUR)* Your Majesty, forgive me. I did not see you for a moment.

(He bows. GUENEVERE looks at ARTHUR in amazement. ARTHUR avoids her gaze and steps aside, as the Court parades on in stately fashion. The men bow first to the King, and then to the Queen. The Ladies give flowers to GUENEVERE. The formality over, the Court departs. GUENEVERE stares at the King, at a loss for words)

ARTHUR: *(Turning away)* When I was a lad of eighteen, our King died in London and left no one to succeed him; only a sword stuck through an anvil which stood on a stone. Written on it in letters of gold it said: "Whoso pulleth out this sword of this stone and anvil is rightwise King born of all England." Many chaps tried to dislodge it, and none could. Finally a great tournament was proclaimed for New Year's Day, so that all the mightiest knights in England would be assembled at one time to have a go at the sword.

I went to London as squire to my cousin, Sir Kay. The morning of the tournament, Kay discovered he'd left his sword at home and gave me a shilling to ride back to fetch it. On my way through London, I passed a square and saw there a sword rising from a stone. Not thinking very quickly, I thought it was a war memorial. The square was deserted, so I decided to save myself a journey and borrow it. I tried to pull it out. I failed. I tried again. I failed again. Then I closed my eyes and with all my force tried one last time. Lo, it moved in my hand. Then slowly it slid out of the stone. I heard a great roar. When I opened my eyes, the square was filled with people shouting: "Long live the King! Long live the King!" Then I looked at the sword and saw the blade gleaming with letters of gold.

That's how I became King. I never knew I would be. I never wanted to be. And since I am, I have been ill at ease in my crown. Until I dropped from the tree and my eye beheld you. Then suddenly, for the first time, I felt I was King. I was glad to be King. And most astonishing of all, I wanted to be the wisest, most heroic, most splendid King who ever sat on any throne. *(There is a moment of silence)* If you will come with me, Milady, I will arrange for the carriage to return you to your father. *(He moves across the stage. She doesn't follow. He stops)* This way.

GUENEVERE: *(Slowly and tenderly)*
I hear it never rains till after sundown.
By eight the morning fog must disappear.
In short, there's simply not
A more congenial spot
For happ'ly-ever-aftering than here
In Camelot.

(The music continues. It takes ARTHUR *a moment to realize his stroke of fortune. Then he goes to her and kisses her hand)*

GUENEVERE: I'm afraid, Your Majesty.

ARTHUR: Afraid?

GUENEVERE: Marriage is rather frightening, isn't it?

ARTHUR: *(Placing her hand on his offered arm)* I must confess, Your Ladyship, it did occur to me. But now not marrying seems infinitely more terrifying.

(They take a step or two, then stop)

GUENEVERE: What would have happened if we hadn't? To the treaty?

ARTHUR: It would have been broken. War would have been declared.

GUENEVERE: War? Over me? How simply marvelous!

(He laughs. Then she begins to laugh. She takes his arm and they exit, still laughing. The lights dim, and before the stage is dark, a light shines on the tree, and MERLYN *appears from behind it)*

MERLYN: At last! At last! He's ambitious at last! How foolish of me not to have realized sooner. He didn't need a lecture. He needed a queen.

(As he walks downstage, the drop falls discreetly behind him)

SCENE 2

Scene: Near Camelot.

Time: Immediately following.

At Rise: SIR DINADAN *and a Lady enter.* MERLYN, *in front of the drop, continues.*

MERLYN: *(To* DINADAN*)* All his life I've tried to teach him to think.

DINADAN: Who are you talking about, Merlyn?

MERLYN: Arthur. All in vain, of course. Then over the hill comes his fated maiden, and for her he wants to be Caesar and Solomon. I tell you, Dinadan, I have waited years for this moment. And now it begins. What a joy it will be to watch! *(A Knight and two other Ladies enter and listen)* To see him putting together the pieces of his destiny. It won't go quickly. One year . . . two years . . . what does it matter? I can see a night five years from now . . .

(Suddenly a distant voice is heard. It is a high feminine voice. MERLYN *stops. Suspended)*

VOICE: *(Singing)*
Far from day, far from night . . .
Out of time, out of sight . . .

DINADAN: Go on. What about five years from now?

MERLYN: Yes! After the Battle of Bedegraine. That's the night it will happen!

(The voice is heard again. Again MERLYN *is caught by it)*

VOICE:
Follow me . . .
Dry the rain, warm the snow . . .
Where the winds never go . . .

DINADAN: Go on. That's the night *what* will happen?

MERLYN: *(His face clouded)* I can't remember. That voice. Don't you hear it?

DINADAN: What voice?

MERLYN: *(In hushed fear)* Nimue, is that you? Oh, please . . . not yet. I must find out what will happen to him.

VOICE:

In a cave by a sapphire shore
We shall walk through an em'rald door.
And for thousands of evermores
to come, my life you shall be.

*(*MERLYN'S *behavior is much too eccentric for* DINADAN. *He exits, followed by the others)*

MERLYN: Oh, Nimue! So it's you! Must you steal my magic now? Couldn't you have waited a bit longer? *(The music swells.* MERLYN *walks forlornly toward the voice. Then he stops)* Wait! Have I told him everything he should know? Did I tell him of Lancelot? *(A vision of* LANCELOT *is revealed behind him)* I did. *(Fearfully)* But Lancelot and Guenevere! Did I warn him of Lancelot and Guenevere? And Mordred? *(A vision of* MORDRED *also appears)* Mordred! I didn't warn him of Mordred, and I must! *(The visions begin to fade)* I remember nothing of Lancelot and Guenevere. And Mordred! *(With hopeless resignation)* It's all gone. My magic is gone.

(The music swells, and the voice sings clear, and MERLYN *walks slowly toward it)*

VOICE:

Only you, only I,
World farewell, world goodbye,
To our home 'neath the sea,
We shall fly,
Follow me . . .

(Just before he exits, he looks back at Camelot for the last time)

MERLYN: Goodbye, Arthur. My memory of the future is gone. I know no more the sorrows and joys before you. I can only wish for you in ignorance, like everyone else. Reign long and reign happily. Oh, and, Wart! Remember to think!

(The music swells, and the lights dim slowly, as MERLYN *follows the voice to his cavernous destiny)*

SCENE 3

Scene: ARTHUR'S *Study.*
Time: Early evening. Five years later.
At Rise: GUENEVERE *is at a tapestry easel working with needle and thread.* ARTHUR *is standing next to her.*

ARTHUR: *(Heatedly)* You cannot deny the facts! Did I or did I not pledge to you five years ago that I would be the most splendid king who ever sat on any throne?

GUENEVERE: You did.

ARTHUR: And in five years, have I become the most splendid king who ever sat on any throne?

GUENEVERE: You have.

ARTHUR: Rubbish! I have not, and you know it well. I'm nothing of what I pledged to you I would be. I'm a failure, and that's that.

GUENEVERE: Arthur, it's not true. You're the greatest warrior in England.

ARTHUR: But for what purpose? Might isn't always right, Jenny.

GUENEVERE: Nonsense, dear, of course it is. To be right and lose couldn't possibly be right.

ARTHUR: *(Thinking)* Yes. Might and right, battle and plunder. That's what keeps plaguing me. Merlyn used to frown on battles, yet he always helped me win them. I'm sure it's a clue. If only I could follow it. I'm always walking down a winding dimly lit road, and in the distance I see the outline of a thought. Like the shadow of a hill. I fumble and stumble, and at last I get there; but when I do, the hill is gone. Not there at all. And I hear a small voice saying: "Go back, Arthur, it's too dark for you to be out thinking."

GUENEVERE: My poor love. Let me see you do it. Walk out loud.

ARTHUR: All right. *(He crosses to the end of the stage)* Proposition: It's far better to be alive than dead.

GUENEVERE: Far better.

ARTHUR: *(Taking a step forward)* If that is so, then why do we have battles, where people can get killed?

GUENEVERE: *(Chews on it a moment)* I don't know. Do you?

ARTHUR: Yes. Because somebody attacks.

GUENEVERE: *(Sincerely)* Of course. That's very clever of you, Arthur. Why do they attack?

(ARTHUR leaves "the road" and comes to her)

ARTHUR: Jenny, I must confess something I've never told you before for fear you would not believe me.

GUENEVERE: How silly, Arthur, I would never not believe you.

ARTHUR: You know Merlyn brought me up, taught me everything I know. But do you know how?

GUENEVERE: How?

ARTHUR: By changing me into animals.

GUENEVERE: I don't believe it.

ARTHUR: There, you see? But it's true. I was a fish, a bobolink, a beaver and even an ant. From each animal he wanted me to learn something. Before he made me a hawk, for instance, he told me that while I would be flying through the sky, if I would look down at the earth, I would discover something.

GUENEVERE: What did you discover?

ARTHUR: Nothing. Merlyn was livid. Yet tonight, on my way home, while I was thinking, I suddenly realized that when you're in the sky looking down at the earth, there are no boundaries. No borders. Yet that's what somebody always attacks about. And you win by pushing them back across something that doesn't exist.

GUENEVERE: It *is* odd, isn't it?

ARTHUR: Proposition: We have battles for no reason at all. Then why? Why?

GUENEVERE: Because knights love them. They adore charging in and whacking away. It's splendid fun. You've said so yourself often.

ARTHUR: It *is* splendid fun. *(Steps forward)* But that doesn't seem reason enough. *(He steps back)* I think it is. And from a woman's point of view, it's wonderfully exciting to see your knight in armor riding bravely off to battle. Especially when you know he'll be home safe in one piece for dinner.

GUENEVERE: I think it is. And from a woman's point of view, it's wonderfully exciting to see your knight in armor riding bravely off to battle. Especially when you know he'll be home safe in one piece for dinner.

ARTHUR: That's it! It's the armor! I missed that before. Of course! Only knights are rich enough to bedeck themselves in armor. They can declare war when it suits them, go clodhopping about the country slicing up peasants and foot soldiers, because peasants and foot soldiers are not equipped with armor. All that can happen to a knight is an occasional dent. *(He takes a long run to the fireplace)* Proposition: Wrong or right, they have the might, so wrong or right, they're always right—and that's wrong. Right?

GUENEVERE: Absolutely.

ARTHUR: *(Excitedly)* Is that the reason Merlyn helped me to win? To take all this might that's knocking about the world and do something with it. But what?

GUENEVERE: Yes, what?

(ARTHUR sighs with resignation)

ARTHUR: It's gone. I've thought as hard as I can, and I can walk no further. *(He walks around and sits on the chaise longue)* You see, Jenny? I'm still not a king. I win every battle and accomplish nothing. When the Greeks won, they made a civilization. I'm not creating any civilization. I'm not even sure I'm civilized.. . .

GUENEVERE: *(Tenderly)* Dear Arthur. You mustn't belabor yourself like this. Let us have a quiet dinner, and after, if you like, you can stroll again.

ARTHUR: Bless you. *(He takes her hand, kisses her, rises and moves to exit. Then he stops and turns)* Jenny, suppose we create a *new* order of chivalry?

GUENEVERE: Pardon?

ARTHUR: A new order, a new order, where might is only used for right, to improve instead of destroy. And we invite all knights, good or bad, to lay down their arms and come and join. Yes! *(Growing more and more excited)* We'll take one of the large rooms in the castle and put a table in it, and all the knights will gather at the table.

GUENEVERE: And do what?

ARTHUR: Talk! Discuss! Make laws! Plan improvements!

GUENEVERE: Really, Arthur, do you think knights would ever want to do such a peaceful thing?

ARTHUR: We'll make it a great honor, very fashionable, so that everyone will want to be in. And the knights of my order will ride all over the world, still dressed in armor and whacking away. That will give them an outlet for wanting to whack. But they'll whack only for good. Defend virgins, restore what's been done wrong in the past, help the oppressed. Might for right. That's it, Jenny! Not might is right. Might *for* right!

GUENEVERE: It sounds superb.

ARTHUR: Yes. And civilized. *(Calls)* Page! *(To GUENEVERE)* We'll build a whole new generation of chivalry. Young men, not old, burning with zeal and ideals. *(The PAGE enters)* Tell the heralds to mount the towers. And to have their trumpets. And assemble the Court in the yard. Send word there is to be a proclamation.

PAGE: Yes, Your Majesty! *(He exits)*

GUENEVERE: Arthur, it will have to be an awfully large table! And won't there be jealousy? All your knights will be claiming superiority and wanting to sit at the head.

ARTHUR: Then we shall make it a round table so there is no head.

GUENEVERE: *(Totally won)* My father has one that would be perfect. It seats a hundred and fifty. It was given to him once for a present, and he never uses it.

ARTHUR: *(Suddenly doubting)* Jenny, have I had a thought? Am I at the hill? Or is it only a mirage?

(The PAGE *enters)*

PAGE: The heralds await, Your Majesty. Shall I give the signal, Your Majesty?

ARTHUR: No, wait. I may be wrong. The whole idea may be absurd. If only Merlyn were here! He would have known for certain. *(Disparagingly)* Knights at a table . . .

GUENEVERE: *(Correcting him)* A round table.

ARTHUR: *(Corrected)* Round table. Might for right, a new order of chivalry, shining knights gallivanting around the countryside like angels in armor, sword-swinging apostles battling to snuff out evil! Why, it's naïve . . . it's adolescent . . . it's juvenile . . . it's infantile . . . it's folly . . . it's . . . it's . . .

GUENEVERE: It's marvelous.

ARTHUR: Yes, it is. It's marvelous. Absolutely marvelous. *(To the* PAGE*)* Page, give the signal.

PAGE: Yes, Your Majesty. *(He exits)*

ARTHUR: *(Sings)*
We'll send the heralds riding through the country;
Tell ev'ry living person far and near . . .

GUENEVERE: *(Interrupting him)*
That there is simply not
In all the world a spot
Where rules a more resplendent king than here
In Camelot.

(The heralds appear in the towers and sound their horns. ARTHUR *embraces* GUENEVERE *and goes to the window to make his proclamation)*

Dim Out

SCENE 4

Scene: A Countryside near Camelot.
Time: The First of May. A few months later.
At Rise: LANCELOT DU LAC *enters and looks fervently at Camelot in the distance. He is a striking figure of a young man, with a stern jaw and burning eyes. His face is unlined for he has never smiled.*

LANCELOT: *(Sings)*
Camelot! Camelot!
In far off France I heard your call.
Camelot! Camelot!
And here am I to give my all.
I know in my soul what you expect of me;
And all that and more I shall be!

A knight of the table round should be invincible;
Succeed where a less fantastic man would fail;
Climb a wall no one else can climb;
Cleave a dragon in record time;

Swim a moat in a coat of heavy iron mail.
No matter the pain he ought to be unwinceable,
Impossible deeds should be his daily fare.
But where in the world
Is there in the world
A man so extraordinaire?

C'est moi! C'est moi,
I'm forced to admit!
'Tis I, I humbly reply.
That mortal who
These marvels can do,
C'est moi, c'est moi, 'tis I.
I've never lost
In battle or game.
I'm simply the best by far.
When swords are cross'd
'Tis always the same:
One blow and au revoir!
C'est moi! C'est moi,
So admir'bly fit;
A French Prometheus unbound.
And here I stand with valor untold,
Exception'lly brave, amazingly bold,
To serve at the Table Round!

The soul of a knight should be a thing remarkable:
His heart and his mind as pure as morning dew.
With a will and a self-restraint
That's the envy of ev'ry saint,
He could easily work a miracle or two!
To love and desire he ought to be unsparkable.
The ways of the flesh should offer no allure.
But where in the world
Is there in the world
A man so untouch'd and pure?

(Speaking modestly)
C'est moi

C'est moi! C'est moi,
I blush to disclose,
I'm far too noble to lie.
That man in whom
These qualities bloom,
C'est moi, c'est moi, 'tis I!

I've never stray'd
From all I believe.
I'm bless'd with an iron will.
Had I been made

The partner of Eve,
We'd be in Eden still.
C'est moi! C'est moi,
The angels have chose
To fight their battles below.
And here I stand as pure as a pray'r,
Incredibly clean, with virtue to spare,
The godliest man I know . . . !
C'est moi!

(DAP, his squire, enters, dragging a fallen Knight)

DAP: I cannot bring him to, Lancelot. You gave him a shattering blow. The echo broke several branches in the trees.

(He lowers the Knight to the ground)

LANCELOT: There's water in the flask. Toss it in his face. And hurry. *(DAP throws water in the Knight's face. LANCELOT looks up at CAMELOT)* Oh, King Arthur, what caliber of man you must be. To have conceived of the Table! To have created a new order of life. I worship you before knowing you. No harm must befall you. Beware, enemies of Arthur! Do you hear me? Beware! From this moment on, you answer to me.

(The fallen Knight lifts his head, removing his vizor. It is KING ARTHUR)

ARTHUR: What a blow! What a blow! Magnificent. Simply magnificent.

LANCELOT: Now that you have recovered, Sir, I bid you good day. And the next time you raise a spear at me, remember you challenge the right arm of King Arthur. *(He starts to leave)*

ARTHUR: *(Rising)* Wait! I am King Arthur.

(DAP falls to his knees)

LANCELOT: *(Stunned)* The King?

ARTHUR: Almost the late King.

LANCELOT: *(Grief-stricken)* I . . . struck *you?* Oh, my God! *(He crashes to his knees before ARTHUR)* Your Majesty, I am Lancelot du Lac. I heard of your new Order in France and came to join. Oh, I beg Your Majesty to forgive me. Not because I deserve it, but because by forgiving me, I'll suffer more.

ARTHUR: Really, dear chap, I don't want you to suffer at all. I want to congratulate you. Please rise. And you, too, Squire.

(DAP rises. LANCELOT doesn't)

LANCELOT: I can't, Your Majesty. I am too ashamed to lift my head.

ARTHUR: Then I command you. *(LANCELOT rises, his head still down)* I tell you, I've never felt a bash in the chest like it. It was spectacular. Where did you learn to do it?

LANCELOT: My skill comes from training, Your Majesty. My strength from purity.

ARTHUR: Oh. A unique recipe, I must say.

DAP: He's a unique man, Your Majesty. At the age of fourteen he could defeat any jouster in France. His father, King Ban, made me his squire when he was only . . .

ARTHUR: King Ban? Of Benwick? What did you say your name was?

LANCELOT: *(Still pronouncing it in French)* Lancelot du Lac, Your Majesty.

ARTHUR: *(In French)* Lancelot? *(In English)* Lancelot! My word, you're Lancelot. Of course! I was told you were coming.

LANCELOT: You were told, Your Majesty?

ARTHUR: By Merlyn, our court magician. He said to me one day: "Arthur, keep your eye out for Lancelot du Lac from the castle of Joyous Gard. He will come to the Court of Camelot, and he will be . . ." What was it . . . ?

LANCELOT: Your ally, if you'll take me? Your friend, who asks not friendship? Your defender, when you need one? Whose heart is already filled with you? Whose body is your sword to brandish? Did he prophesy that, Your Majesty? For all that, I am.

ARTHUR: *(Flattered and almost embarrassed by the effusion)* Really, my dear fellow, it's almost more than one could hope for, more than one should ask.

LANCELOT: Then you'll accept me?

ARTHUR: Oh, yes. Without hesitation. *(LANCELOT kneels)* We must arrange for your knighthood immediately.

LANCELOT: *(Rising)* No, Your Majesty. Not immediately. Not till I have proven myself. All you know of me now is words. Invest me because of deeds, Sire. Give me an order.

ARTHUR: Now?

LANCELOT: Yes, now! This moment! Send me on a mission. Let me perform for you. Is there some wrong I can right? Some enemy I can battle? Some peril I can undertake?

ARTHUR: Well, actually, there's not much going on today. This is the First of May, and the Queen and some of the Court have gone a-Maying. I was on my way to surprise her when you surprised me.

LANCELOT: Gone a-Maying, Your Majesty?

ARTHUR: *(A little embarrassed and covering it with excessive joviality)* Why, yes. It's a sort of picnic. You eat grapes and chase girls around trees . . . and . . .

LANCELOT: A picnic, Your Majesty?

ARTHUR: Yes. It's a custom we have here. England, you know. It's the time for flower gathering.

LANCELOT: *(Stunned)* Knights gathering flowers, Your Majesty?

ARTHUR: Someone has to do it.

LANCELOT: But with so much to be done?

ARTHUR: Precisely because there is so much to be done.

LANCELOT: Of course, Sire.

ARTHUR: Besides, it's civilized. Civilization should have a few gentle hobbies. And I want you to meet the Queen.

LANCELOT: I should be honored. *(To DAP)* Dap, take the horses to the castle, feed them and dress them for battle.

ARTHUR: *(Mildly)* For battle? But there's no one to fight today.

LANCELOT: One never knows, Your Majesty. Enemies seldom take holidays.

ARTHUR: I suppose not. You know, Merlyn . . . *(He stops himself, for a moment lost in thought)*

LANCELOT: What is it, Sire? Have I offended you? Did I say something that displeased you?

ARTHUR: No, no, Lancelot. I suddenly remembered what Merlyn said of you. How strange. How wondrous. He said you would be the greatest knight ever to sit at my table. But that was long before I had thought of a table. So, he knew it would exist! I thought he meant a dining table. But he meant this: the Round Table. And I have stumbled on my future. I have done the right thing.

LANCELOT: Did you ever doubt it, Your Majesty?

ARTHUR: Of course. Only fools never doubt. *(He holds out his hand)* Welcome, Lancelot. Bless you for coming, and welcome to the Table!
(They clasp arms)

    Dim Out

SCENE 5

Scene: A garden near the Castle. It is lush with the green of spring, and fountains are playing among the trees.

At Rise: The music is heard, and GUENEVERE and her Knights and Ladies, all in various shades of green, white and gold, are indulging choreographically in spring games.

At the height of the gaiety, the music stops abruptly, and all eyes turn to the Queen.

GUENEVERE: *(Sings)*
Tra la! It's May!
The lusty month of May!
That lovely month when ev'ryone goes
Blissfully astray.

Tra la! It's here!
That shocking time of year!
When tons of wicked little thoughts
Merrily appear.

It's May! It's May!
That gorgeous holiday;
When ev'ry maiden prays that her lad
Will be a cad!

It's mad! It's Gay!
A libelous display.
Those dreary vows that ev'ryone takes,
Ev'ryone breaks.
Ev'ryone makes divine mistakes
The lusty month of May!

Whence this fragrance wafting through the air?
What sweet feelings does its scent transmute?
Whence this perfume floating ev'rywhere?
Don't you know it's that dear forbidden fruit!
Tra la tra la. That dear forbidden fruit!
Tra la la la la.

KNIGHTS *and* LADIES:
Tra la la la la!

GUENEVERE:
Tra la la la la!

KNIGHTS *and* LADIES:
Tra la la la la!

GUENEVERE:
Tra la!

KNIGHTS *and* LADIES:
Tra la!

GUENEVERE:
Tra la!

KNIGHTS *and* LADIES:
Tra la!

GUENEVERE:
Tra la la la la la la la la la la la
La la! It's May!
The lusty month of May!
That darling month when ev'ryone throws
Self-control away.

It's time to do
A wretched thing or two.
And try to make each precious day
One you'll always rue.

It's May! It's May!
The month of "yes, you may,"
The time for ev'ry frivolous whim,
Proper or "im."

It's wild! It's gay!
A blot in ev'ry way.
The birds and bees with all of their vast
Amorous past
Gaze at the human race aghast
The lusty month of May!

GUENEVERE, KNIGHTS *and* LADIES:
Tra la! It's May!
The lusty month of May!
That lovely month when ev'ryone goes
Blissfully astray.

Tra la! It's here!
That shocking time of year!
When tons of wicked little thoughts
Merrily appear.

It's May! It's May!
The month of great dismay;
When all the world is brimming with fun,
Wholesome or "un."

It's mad! It's gay!
A libelous display.
These dreary vows that ev'ryone takes,
Ev'ryone breaks.
Ev'ryone makes divine mistakes
The lusty month of May!

(A man in clanking, rusty armor enters. In one hand he carries a lance. In one eye he wears a monocle. Trailing beside him is a rather seedy mongrel, named HORRID. *The Knight's name, as we will discover, is* KING PELLINORE*)*

PELLINORE: Forgive the interruption. Anyone here seen a beast with the head of a serpent, the body of a boar and the tail of a lion, baying like forty hounds?

DINADAN: *(Coming forward)* On your knees, Knight. *(Indicating* GUENEVERE*)* You are in the presence of Her Majesty Guenevere, Queen of England.

PELLINORE: *(To* GUENEVERE*)* Oh, really? Howdyado, Your Majesty. Will have to forego the bending. Beastly hinges need oiling. Been sleeping out for eighteen years. Do forgive, what? Know it isn't proper, but there you are. Stiff as a door, what? *(Removes helmet)* Oh, it stopped raining.

GUENEVERE: *(Amused)* Who are you, Milord?

PELLINORE: Name of King Pellinore. May have heard of me, what? What? What? *(He looks around for recognition, which he does not receive)* No matter. *(To* GUENEVERE*)* You say you haven't seen a beast with the head of a serpent, the body of a boar . . .

GUENEVERE: Please, I beg you, don't describe it again. It sounds much too revolting. We have not seen it.

PELLINORE: Called the Questing Beast, what? The Curse of the Pellinores. Only a Pellinore can catch her; that is, or his next of kin. Family tradition. Train all the Pellinores with that idea in mind. Limited education, what?

GUENEVERE: What?

PELLINORE: What? By the way, where am I now?

GUENEVERE: Don't you know?

PELLINORE: Haven't the foggiest. *(A few members of the Court laugh.* PELLINORE *is now a little angry)* Oh, very easy to laugh, what? But nothing jocular about it to Yours Truly . . . always mollocking about after that beastly Beast. Nowhere to sleep, never know where you are. Rheumatism in the winter, sunstroke in the summer. All this horrid armor that takes hours to put on. Then sitting up all night polishing the beastly stuff . . . But I'm a Pellinore, amn't I? It's my fate. Oh, but sometimes I do wish I had a nice house of my own to live in, with beds in it, and real pillows and sheets. Oh, dear, what? Where did you say I was?

GUENEVERE: I didn't, but I will.

PELLINORE: Please do.

GUENEVERE: You're in Camelot.

PELLINORE: Thank you. Camelot? *(Looks at the dog)* Horrid, we've been through here, haven't we? *(The dog, who is lying down, looks up at him)* Oh, you wouldn't know. All you can see is hair. But I remember. Spent a lovely day here years ago with a nice young chap named Wart. *(To* GUENEVERE*)* Ever meet him, Milady?

GUENEVERE: Constantly. He's my husband, King Arthur of England.

PELLINORE: By Jove! Is he? Is he, is he? Good for him. Well done! Yours Fondly thought he was grand. Simply grand. Do say hello to him for me. Won't take any more of your time, M'am. Have to mollock on, what? *(To* HORRID*)* Come along, Horrid. *(The dog rises)* The King of England. By jove. Isn't that well done, Horrid?

GUENEVERE: Milord, I am sure the King would love to see you again. Wouldn't you care to spend the night?

PELLINORE: *(Thunderstruck)* Spend the night?

GUENEVERE: Yes.

PELLINORE: In a house?

GUENEVERE: In a bed.

PELLINORE: A bed?

GUENEVERE: A feather bed.

PELLINORE: Would it have pillows?

GUENEVERE: Down pillows.

PELLINORE: Oh, I'd love that. By George, I would. That's wonderly kind of you, M'am. Wonderly. *(Points to the dog)* But could he sleep somewhere else?

GUENEVERE: Of course. Where would you like him to sleep?

PELLINORE: Oh, anywhere around the castle will do. The moat. I don't really like him very much, you know. No earthly use to me. Oh, he's a bit of company. But he's . . . a dog. Easily do without him.

GUENEVERE: He shall sleep in the stable. Clarius, would you escort our guest to the castle?

CLARIUS: *(Coming forward)* With pleasure, Milady.

PELLINORE: This is too nice for words, M'am. Most grateful. Come along, Horrid. *(*HORRID *rises.* PELLINORE *starts to go)* What a glorious day! There's even a hint of summer in the air. *(Looks at the dog)* Or is that you? *(They exit. Everyone starts to laugh uproariously)*

GUENEVERE: *(Imitating* PELLINORE*)* By jove, what a curse, what? Mollocking about after that beastly Beast, what? What? What?

(There is much laughter. And it is at this frivolous, unknightly moment that LANCE- LOT *and* KING ARTHUR *enter. The Knights and Ladies, still laughing, immediately bow and curtsey)*

ARTHUR: What, what, what, what?

GUENEVERE: *(Laughing)* What a delightful surprise, Arthur.

ARTHUR: *(Reacting to the laughter)* What's happened here? Jenny, I want you to meet the son of . . .

GUENEVERE: Forgive us, Arthur. We have just encountered an absolute cartoon of a man, called King Pellinore.

ARTHUR: Pellinore? Why, I remember him from my boyhood. A delicious fellow. Jenny, this is Lancelot du Lac.

GUENEVERE: Milord.

LANCELOT: *(Bowing)* Your Majesty.

ARTHUR: This is the Lancelot Merlyn spoke of. He's come all the way from France to become a Knight of the Round Table.

GUENEVERE: Welcome, Milord. I hope your journey was pleasant.

LANCELOT: *(To* GUENEVERE*)* I am honored to be among you, Your Majesty. And allow me to pledge to Her Majesty my eternal dedication to this inspired cause.

GUENEVERE: *(Slightly startled)* Thank you, Milord. *(To* ARTHUR*)* How charming of you to join us, Arthur. This afternoon . . .

LANCELOT: This splendid dream *must* be made a universal reality!

GUENEVERE: Oh, absolutely. It really must. Can you stay for lunch, Arthur? We're planning . . .

LANCELOT: I have assured His Majesty that he may call upon me at any time to perform any deed, no matter the risk.

GUENEVERE: Thank you, Milord. That's most comforting. Arthur, we have . . .

LANCELOT: I am always on duty.

GUENEVERE: Yes, I can see that. Can you stay, Arthur?

ARTHUR: With pleasure, my love. *(He seats himself)* I want you to hear the new plan we've been discussing. Explain it, Lancelot.

LANCELOT: To Her Majesty, Sire? Would Her Majesty not find the complicated affairs of chivalry rather tedious?

GUENEVERE: *(Frosting a bit)* Not at all, Milord. I have never found chivalry tedious . . . so far. May I remind you, Milord, that the Round Table happens to be my husband's idea.

LANCELOT: Any idea, however exalted, could be improved.

GUENEVERE: *(Miffed)* Really!

LANCELOT: Yes. I have suggested to His Majesty that we create a training program for knights.

GUENEVERE: *(Looking at* ARTHUR*)* !!

ARTHUR: Marvelous idea, isn't it?

GUENEVERE: A training program!?

ARTHUR: Yes. It's a program for training.

LANCELOT: *(To* ARTHUR*)* Yes, Your Majesty. There must be a standard established, an unattainable goal that, with work, becomes attainable; not only in arms, but in thought. An indoctrination of noble Christian principle.

GUENEVERE: Whose abilities would serve as the standard, Milord?

LANCELOT: Certainly not mine, Your Majesty. It would not be fair.

GUENEVERE: Not fair in what way?

LANCELOT: I would never ask anyone to live by my standards, Your Majesty. *(Overcome by his lot in life)* To dedicate your life to the tortured quest for perfection in body and spirit. Oh, no, I would not ask that of anyone.

GUENEVERE: Nor would I. Have you achieved perfection, Milord?

LANCELOT: Physically, yes, Your Majesty. But the refining of the soul is an endless struggle.

GUENEVERE: I daresay. I do daresay. Do you mean you've never been defeated in battle or in tournament?

LANCELOT: Never, Your Majesty.

GUENEVERE: I see. And I gather you consider it highly unlikely ever to happen in the future?

LANCELOT: Highly, Your Majesty.

ARTHUR: *(Into the breach)* How was the Channel? Did you have a rough crossing?

GUENEVERE: Now tell me a little of your struggle for the perfection of the spirit.

ARTHUR: *(Rising and coming between them)* But I want you to hear about the training program, Jenny.

GUENEVERE: I'm much more interested in his spirit and his noble Christian principles. Tell me, Milord, have you come to grips with humility lately?

LANCELOT: *(Not understanding)* Humility, Your Majesty?

ARTHUR: *(Quickly)* I think we had better discuss the training program elsewhere. Not here and not now. *(To GUENEVERE)* You look far too beautiful, my dearest, to have anything on your mind but frolic and flowers. *(He kisses her hand)* Have a lovely day. *(To the others)* And all of you. Come, Lance. Quickly!

(ARTHUR exits)

LANCELOT: Good day, Your Majesty.

GUENEVERE: Good day to you, Milord.

(LANCELOT exits)

DINADAN: *(To LIONEL)* By George, that Frenchman is an unpleasant fellow.

LIONEL: He seems to have the King wrapped around his finger.

LADY SYBIL: *(To DINADAN)* He's so poisonously good.

DINADAN: He probably *walked* across the Channel.

GUENEVERE: *(After a moment)* Sir Dinadan . . .

DINADAN: *(Coming forward)* Your Majesty.

GUENEVERE: When is the next tournament?

DINADAN: A week from Saturday, Your Majesty.

GUENEVERE: And who are our three best jousters?

DINADAN: Sir Lionel, Sir Sagramore and, with all "humility," I, Your Majesty.

LIONEL: *(Coming forward* He shall have my challenge in the morning.

GUENEVERE: *(Pleased)* Thank you, Sir Lionel.

SAGRAMORE: *(Coming forward)* And mine.

GUENEVERE: *(Delighted)* Thank you, Sir Sagramore.

DINADAN: And mine.

GUENEVERE: *(Ecstatic)*
  Tra la! It's May!
  The lusty month of May!
  That darling month when ev'ryone throws
  Self-control away.

GUENEVERE, KNIGHTS *and* LADIES:
  It's mad! It's gay!
  A libelous display.
  Those dreary vows that ev'ryone takes,
  Ev'ryone breaks.
  Ev'ryone makes divine mistakes
  The lusty month of May!

(They dance gaily)

  Dim Out

SCENE 6

Scene: A Terrace of the Castle. There is an entrance to a castle room. On a table are a decanter of port and three glasses.

Time: Sundown. Two weeks later.

At Rise: PELLINORE and ARTHUR are playing backgammon. They are both standing eying the board like two field commanders.

Behind the table stands LANCELOT, reading from a scroll, paying no attention to the game.

A PAGE *stands at attention off to one side.*

ARTHUR: I'm afraid I've got you, Pelly.

PELLINORE: Not yet. Yours Hopefully hasn't given up. *(He throws the dice)* Oh, fishcakes!

ARTHUR: If you lose, you'll owe me Italy, Spain and Egypt.

PELLINORE: When did I lose Spain?

ARTHUR: Last night.

PELLINORE: So I did. Oh bosh, who wants it anyway? Filthy place, Spain. All that heel-clicking nonsense. *(He flamencoes for a moment)* Stepping on bugs, that's what they're doing, what?

ARTHUR: Come along, Pelly. Don't try to rattle me with amusement. It's your move. Get on with it.

(PELLINORE steps back to survey the board. The right move comes to him and he moves forward to make it, when—)

LANCELOT: *(Exuberantly)* Bravo, Arthur! *(The brilliant move is startled out of PEL-LINORE'S mind and lost forever)* I agree completely. Let armor fight armor! Let knights fight fairly! It is not chivalry when only peasants get killed. Bravo!

ARTHUR: It's certainly more civilized. Well, Pelly. I'm waiting.

(PELLINORE steps back to survey, finds the move again and steps forward to make it)

LANCELOT: *(Explosively)* C'est magnifique, Arthur! *(PELLINORE is staggered. The move is lost)* When our knights go abroad through the land, our enemies will know what they will have to face. No more immunity. Death or reformation. C'est merveilleux!

ARTHUR: But read on! *(To PELLINORE)* Come on, Pelly. Either play or give up.

(PELLINORE watches LANCELOT and moves quickly before he is thrown off again)

PELLINORE: There!

(ARTHUR quickly throws the dice and removes two markers from the board)

ARTHUR: Egypt's mine.

PELLINORE: Oh, bulrushes! How can a chap make the right move with the town crier blasting away in his ear? *(To LANCELOT)* I know this is admirable work you're doing, but couldn't you do it in your own room? What? Your own chambre de coucher?

LANCELOT: I'm terribly sorry, Pellinore. I didn't mean to throw you off your game.

PELLINORE: Really, my dear chap! Don't you ever do anything but run around the Round Table? Have you no hobbies? Don't you ever go fishing? Collect things? Catch butterflies? Aren't you interested in astronomy, or making models of things?

LANCELOT: *(Simply)* No, Pellinore, I'm not.

PELLINORE: Well, Arthur, if this is the sort of knight you intend to breed, you'll bore History to death. And furthermore, that idea of knights fighting knights is perfectly frightful. God's feet! What's the sense of being a knight if you can get killed like everyone else? I guarantee you, Arthur, the chaps downstairs won't cotton to this at all.

ARTHUR: All new ideas are resisted, Pelly. But they'll get used to it in time.

PELLINORE: *(Referring to LANCELOT)* But he never gets off it! Why can't he come home in the evening, hang up his spear and shield and frolic about a bit the way other chaps do?

ARTHUR: Be patient, Pelly. He will.

LANCELOT: *(Gently)* No, Arthur. I won't. Pellinore is quite right. I am irritating. I always will be. *(To* PELLINORE*)* All fanatics are bores, Pellinore, and I'm a fanatic. Even when I was a child I irritated the other children. I wanted to play their games, but I knew I could not. Even then I was filled with a sense of divine purpose. I'm not saying I enjoy it. All my life I've locked the world out. And, you know, when you lock the world out, you're locked in.

PELLINORE: I don't know what you're talking about.

ARTHUR: Never mind, Pelly. I do. *(*ARTHUR *motions to the* PAGE *to remove the backgammon table, which he does. To* LANCELOT*)* Are you truly satisfied with the proclamation, Lance? Is there anything you would like to add?

LANCELOT: Not at all, Arthur. It's perfect. Of course, there are one or two changes I'd like you to consider.

PELLINORE: Naturally.

(The PAGE *enters with a rose on a salver)*

ARTHUR: *(Taking the rose. There is a note pinned to it. He calls out)* Jenny, it's for you! *(Indicating the scroll)* Where, Lance?

LANCELOT: *(Rolling up the scroll quickly)* It's not pressing, Arthur. We can do it tomorrow.

ARTHUR: No. I want to hear it now!

LANCELOT: I'd rather not, Arthur. *(Moving to go)* If you'll excuse me . . . *(He starts to leave and meets* GUENEVERE *entering)*

GUENEVERE: *(Haughtily)* Good evening, Milord.

LANCELOT: *(Uncomfortably but politely)* Good evening, Your Majesty.

GUENEVERE: While I was napping, did I miss any improvements in chivalry?

LANCELOT: No, Your Majesty. If you will excuse me . . . *(He starts to go)*

GUENEVERE: Milord! *(*LANCELOT *stops)* When you're arranging things with God tonight, do be sure and give us nice weather tomorrow.

LANCELOT: No one could refuse your wish, Milady. Good night, Sire. Good night, Milord. *(He exits)*

PELLINORE: Terrible chap. Doesn't take after his father, I'll tell you that. I knew the old King. Good man. Had a bad attack of liver last time I saw him. Yellow as a buttercup. Horrible!

ARTHUR: Jenny, why do you persist in baiting the boy?

GUENEVERE: Baiting? Not at all. Haven't you heard his latest claim? He says he can perform miracles!

PELLINORE: Miracles, what!

ARTHUR: Oh, come now. Both of you. It's quite obvious it was merely a figure of speech.

GUENEVERE: Nonsense. He announced to the Knights as clear as a bell that his purity gives him miraculous powers.

PELLINORE: Purity, what?

ARTHUR: And I tell you clear as a bell he was referring to his physical prowess, which is vast indeed.

PELLINORE: Well, we shall see about his physical prowess in the tournament tomorrow. Sagramore, Lionel and Dinadan have all challenged him to a joust. Three damn strong men.

*(*ARTHUR *gives* GUENEVERE *the rose. She reads the note)*

ARTHUR: He's accepted to fight all three on one and the same day?

PELLINORE: Quite. I tell you, Arthur, in all my travels I've never met anyone like him. Doesn't drink. Has no lady. Talks to no one but you and God. Crammed full of religion. An all around unpleasant fellow.

GUENEVERE: Pelly, please tell the Chamberlain the order of jousts tomorrow will be Dinadan, Sagramore and Lionel.

PELLINORE: The big chap last, what? Splendid arrangement. By jove, what a day. Yours Merrily can hardly wait. Good night, Arthur. Good night, M'am. The big one last, eh? Oh, ho, ho, ho. *(He exits)*

GUENEVERE: A note of thanks from Sir Lionel. I'm allowing him to carry my kerchief tomorrow.

ARTHUR: Jenny, I would be grateful if you'd withdraw your permission from Sir Lionel.

GUENEVERE: At this late date, Arthur? It would be rather awkward.

ARTHUR: Then let Lancelot carry your kerchief against Sagramore.

GUENEVERE: I promised it to Sagramore.

ARTHUR: Then against Dinadan.

GUENEVERE: He asked so prettily, I couldn't refuse.

ARTHUR: *(Angrily)* What? This is appalling! Jenny there are issues involved here which obviously you've overlooked. It will seem to the Court as if you're rooting for his downfall, championing his defeat.

GUENEVERE: We don't know he'll be defeated. Besides, he knocked you unconscious and you woke up his bosom friend. Perhaps he'll knock them out, too, and they'll all take a house by the sea together.

ARTHUR: *(Exasperated)* Jenny, at the risk of disappointing the other knights, I ask you to withdraw your permission from all.

GUENEVERE: Arthur, I believe you're jealous of the Knights and their attentions to me. Are you, my love?

ARTHUR: *(Fuming)* Jealous?! Jealous?! What absolute rubbish! You know perfectly well I'm delighted the Court adores you. I'd be astonished if they didn't. And I trust you as I do God above. They've carried your kerchief in tournament a hundred times, and . . . and . . . and . . . Jenny, you've dragged me off the subject and I want to get back on it. Will you withdraw your permission?

GUENEVERE: *(Quietly and firmly)* Only if you command me—as King.

ARTHUR: *(Gently)* And if I do, will you forgive me?

GUENEVERE: Never.

ARTHUR: If I ask as your husband, will you, as a favor?

GUENEVERE: No. The Knights are against him, and I quite agree with them. I find him just as overbearing and pretentious as they do.

ARTHUR: *(At the peak of exasperation)* That is not the issue. The issue is your kerchief. Can we not stay on the subject?

GUENEVERE: *(Calmly)* There is nothing more to be said. If the King wishes me to withdraw permission, let him command me! And Yours Humbly will graciously obey. What? What? *(She turns and exits)*

ARTHUR: What!! *(Raging)* Blast! *(He paces up and down)* Blast you, Merlyn! This is all your fault! *(He sings)*

You swore that you had taught me ev'rything from A to Zed,
With nary an omission in between.
Well, I shall tell you what

You obviously forgot:
That's how a ruler rules a Queen!

(He continues pacing)

And what of teaching me by turning me to animal and bird,
From beaver to the smallest bobolink!
I should have had a whirl
At changing to a girl,
To learn the way the creatures think!

(He paces again. Then a thought occurs to him)

But wasn't there a night, on a summer long gone by,
We pass'd a couple wrangling away;
And did I not say, Merlyn: What if that chap were I?
And did he not give counsel and say . . .

(He tries to remember)

What was it now? . . . My mind's a wall.
Oh, yes! . . . By jove, now I recall.

How to handle a woman?
There's a way, said the wise old man;
A way known by ev'ry woman
Since the whole rigmarole began.

Do I flatter her? I begged him answer . . .
Do I threaten or cajole or plead?
Do I brood or play the gay romancer?
Said he, smiling: No indeed.

How to handle a woman?
Mark me well, I will tell you, Sir:
The way to handle a woman
Is to love her . . . simply love her . . .
Merely love her . . . love her . . . love her.

(The music continues. ARTHUR *doesn't move from his position. He ponders a moment, then turns his head and looks in the direction of* GUENEVERE*)*
What's wrong, Jenny? *(He walks a few steps, then stops and looks off again)* Where are you these days? What are you thinking? *(He walks again and stops again)* I don't understand you. *(After a moment)* But no matter. Merlyn told me once: Never be too disturbed if you don't understand what a woman is thinking. They don't do it often. *(He walks again)* But what do you do while they're doing it? *(He smiles as he remembers)*

How to handle a woman?
Mark me well, I will tell you, Sir:
The way to handle a woman . . .
Is to love her . . . simply love her . . .
Merely love her . . . love her . . . love her.

(He stands quietly, as:)

The Lights Dim Out

SCENE 7

Scene: The Tents outside the Jousting Field.
Time: The following day.
At Rise: The tents are occupied by the following: SIR LIONEL, SIR DINADAN, SIR
SAGRAMORE *and* LANCELOT.
*A Knight enters and goes to each of the three challengers, clasping arms with each
in a gesture of good luck. He passes* LANCELOT *by.*
A trumpet sounds. The joust is about to begin.
LANCELOT: *(Sincerely)* I wish you success, Milords.
LIONEL: *(With a smile)* Thank you, Milord. Are you being chivalrous or ironic?
LANCELOT: Neither. I mean it truly.
LIONEL: Then save your wishes for your continuing good health.
DINADAN: Have you prayed, Milord?
LANCELOT: I have, Sir Dinadan. I have prayed for us all.
DINADAN: How benevolent. How benevolent. Do you know what I shall be
    thinking, Lancelot, when I see you on your horse? There he is, the Sermon on
    the Mount.
    (He marches off. They all follow)

SCENE 8

Scene: The Jousting Field. There is a grandstand in the rear.
Time: Immediately following.
At Rise: The stage is filled. ARTHUR *and* GUENEVERE *are standing in the royal box
of the grandstand. Two heralds flank them.*
*The music is playing gaily, as several of the Court Jesters perform a mock joust. They
exit.*

FIRST KNIGHT: *(Sings)*
Sir Dinadan's in form and feeling in his prime.

ALL:
Yah! Yah! Yah! Oh, we'll all have a glorious time!

SECOND KNIGHT:
Sir Sagramore is fit, and Sir Li'nel feels sublime.

ALL:
Yah! Yah! Yah! Oh, we'll all have a glorious time!
(Suddenly pointing to the field)
Now look you there! Sir Dinadan's astride.
It's obvious he will be the first to ride.
(Calling)
Good fortune, Dinadan! We hail you, Dinadan!
Yah! Yah! Yah! Yah! Yah! Yah! . . .

(The joust begins, and the crowd gathers together and watches excitedly)

Sir Dinadan! Sir Dinadan!
Oh, there he goes with all his might and main.
He's got a steady grip upon the rein.
Sir Dinadan! Sir Dinadan!
Oh, try to gallop by him on the right,

For that's the arm where you have all the might.
By jove, they're coming near!
Sir Dinadan is raising up his spear!
Oh, charge him, Dinadan!
You have him now, so charge him, Dinadan!
Here comes the blow! Here comes the blow!
(Catastrophe!)
Oh, no!

(They shuffle about in disgust)

FIRST KNIGHT:
'Twas luck, that's all it was; pure luck and nothing more.

A LADY:
Sagramore will even up the score.

SECOND KNIGHT:
The Frenchman struck him first, but the blow was not that great.

SECOND LADY:
Sagramore will open up his pate.

(They suddenly see SAGRAMORE *on the field)*

A GROUP:
Sir Sagramore! He's riding on the field!

SECOND KNIGHT:
Oh, there's the black and crimson of his shield.

(The joust begins)

ALL:
There he goes! There he goes!
He's bending low and spurring on his steed.
He's charging him at record breaking speed.
Sagramore! Oh, make his armor crack and split in two . . .
A mighty whack as only you can do.
Now, look you through the dust!
Sir Sagramore is ready for the thrust!
And now they're circling 'round!
Sir Sagramore will drive him to the ground!
Here comes . . . the blow! Here comes . . . the blow!
(Disaster)
Oh, no!

(Gloom descends)

ARTHUR: *(Pointedly)*
He did that rather well, don't you think, dear?

GUENEVERE: *(Tightly)*
That horse of Sagramore's is too old.

ARTHUR:
But felling Dinadan with one blow, dear . . .

GUENEVERE:

Sir Dinadan, I am told, has a nasty cold.

(The third joust begins, and the crowd becomes electric. And desperate)

ALL:

Sir Lionel! Sir Lionel!
Oh, charge at him and throw him off his horse!
Oh, show him what we mean by English force!
Sir Lionel! Sir Lionel!
I've never seen him ever ride as fast!
That Frenchman will be hopelessly outclass'd!
His spear is in the air!
I tell you Lancelot hasn't got a pray'r!
His shield is much too low!
A good hard thrust and downward he will go!
And here's the blow! Here comes . . . the blow!
(Horror)
Oh, no! Oh, no!
(They are aghast)
Sir Lionel is down!
Dear God, it isn't true!
Sir Lionel is dead!
The spear has run him through!

(Two Knights run from the scene. A moment later they return, carrying the fallen body of SIR LIONEL on a litter. ARTHUR descends from the grandstand and comes to LIONEL. He kneels down beside him and pulls the blanket over his face. The crowd is in shocked silence. GUENEVERE, who has descended from the stand, stands to one side, grief-stricken.

LANCELOT enters. The crowd falls back to let him pass, eying him with disapproval. Seemingly oblivious to them all, he walks to LIONEL and kneels beside him. He takes his limp hand in his and bows his head in prayer, pressing LIONEL'S hand against him, as if trying to force his own life into the lifeless man before him.

Suddenly a finger twitches. LIONEL'S hand moves! Then his arm! Then an eyelid flickers! And SIR LIONEL slowly, painfully, dazedly, lifts himself to one elbow. The crowd gasps.

LANCELOT rises. It seems as if he has poured so much of his own life into LIONEL that for a moment he is drained. Without a word, he slowly crosses the stage. As he passes each Knight and Lady, each bows and curtsies low and humble before him.

The last person he passes is GUENEVERE. He stops before her and bows. He rises, and their eyes look deep into each other's. She curtsies before him, with her hand to her heart. They stand transfixed by each other's eyes. ARTHUR watches with fearful sadness.

The music swells as:)

The Lights Fade

SCENE 9

Scene: The Terrace.
Time: Early evening of the same day.

At Rise: ARTHUR *is seated on a bench in troubled thought.* PELLINORE *is standing near him.*

PELLINORE: A miracle, Arthur! A miracle! By jove! Absolutely miraculous, what? Imagine restoring that chap to life. And that's a big chap, Arthur. An enormous, big chap. I mean, however the boy did it, it took an awful lot of whatever it is he uses, what? *(An idea)* I say! Do you think he could help my rheumatism? Or does he only go in for bigger things? I mean, from sleeping out all those years, I have a pain that starts about here . . . *(He reaches around to his back)*

ARTHUR: *(Impatiently)* I don't know, Pellinore. I don't know. The boy is in the hall. Go down and ask him. The walk will do you good, and the quiet will do me good.

PELLINORE: I say! That's a bit snappy, Arthur. Very well, I shall. *(He starts to exit)*

ARTHUR: Wait, Pelly. It was a bit "snappy." I apologize.

PELLINORE: Of course. Unimportant. *(He goes to the decanter)* Have a spot, what?

ARTHUR: No, thank you. You've never been in love, have you, Pelly?

PELLINORE: No time, old man. Been too busy chasing the Beast. Now I'm not young enough. Or old enough.

ARTHUR: *(Almost to himself)* And I'm too young and too old. Too old not to be uncertain of fears that may be phantom, and too young not to be tormented by them.

PELLINORE: How's that, Arthur? *(*GUENEVERE *enters.* ARTHUR *stares at her. She avoids his glance and finds a chair)* Well, M'am, it was quite a day, what?

GUENEVERE: Yes, it was, Pelly.

PELLINORE: I must say, you were very generous with the boy, M'am. When he stood there looking at you and you stood there looking at him, it was very touching. Didn't you think so, Arthur?

ARTHUR: *(Subdued)* Pelly, summon the Chamberlain. Alert the Court there are to be festivities this evening.

PELLINORE: *(Starting to go)* Right.

ARTHUR: Have him come to my study. And bring the names of those awaiting knighthood.

PELLINORE: Right. *(Stops)* Festivities, eh? By jove, I'd better skip over to the blacksmith's and pick up my formal togs. *(He exits)*

ARTHUR: *(After watching* GUENEVERE *for a moment)* You seem tired, Jenny.

GUENEVERE: I am, rather.

ARTHUR: I'm sorry to have to put you through a formal affair tonight, but I thought Lance should be invested immediately.

GUENEVERE: Oh, I agree. I shall be all right.

*(*ARTHUR *goes to her)*

ARTHUR: Jenny, tomorrow why don't you take Lady Anne and go to the lodge for a few days? She always amuses you with her gossip of the Court. I'll join you for the weekend. It might do you good to get away from Round Tables and chivalry for a little while. Don't you think? *(*GUENEVERE *doesn't answer)* Don't you think? *(She still doesn't answer. He turns and exits. The music begins.* GUENEVERE *covers her face with her hands)*

GUENEVERE: *(Desperately)* Oh, Lance, go away. Go away and don't come back. *(She sings)*

Before I gaze at you again
I'll need a time for tears.

Before I gaze at you again
Let hours turn to years.
I have so much
Forgetting to do
Before I try to gaze again at you.

Stay away until you cross my mind
Barely once a day.
Till the moment I awake and find
I can smile and say

That I can gaze at you again
Without a blush or qualm,
My eyes a-shine like new again,
My manner poised and calm.

Stay far away!
My love, far away!
Till I forget I gazed at you today . . . today.

(LANCELOT *enters.* GUENEVERE *doesn't see him at first)*
LANCELOT: Forgive me, Milady. I didn't mean to disturb you, but I was told that Arthur wanted to see me.
GUENEVERE: *(As casually as possible)* I believe he does. And you're not disturbing me at all. You are to be knighted.
LANCELOT: *(Troubled)* When, Milady?
GUENEVERE: This evening.
LANCELOT: I wish he would not.
GUENEVERE: Why?
LANCELOT: I'm not worthy of it, Milady. I don't deserve it.
GUENEVERE: Not deserve it, Lancelot! What greater wonder could you ever perform? Oh, no, I'm sure Arthur will insist. Now, if you'll excuse me, I must change for dinner. *(She starts to leave)* Do wait here. Arthur will be . . .
LANCELOT: *(Quietly)* Jenny, don't go. *(She pauses, hearing him say her name for the first time, almost knowing what he is about to say)* Jenny, I love you. God forgive me, but I do.
GUENEVERE: God forgive us both, Lance.
LANCELOT: I have known it since the first afternoon. Not when we met; but when I walked away. When . . .
(GUENEVERE *turns to him.* ARTHUR *enters. She turns away)*
ARTHUR: Lance! What a stunning achievement, my boy! And the Court! You could almost hear everyone's heart break open to you. *(Good-humoredly)* Surely I may arrange for your knighthood now. Unfortunately, sainthood is not in my power.
LANCELOT: I shall be honored, Arthur.
ARTHUR: You both must hurry and dress. But before you do, I think we three should have a quiet drink together. If you'll make an exception, Lance. *(He turns to the decanter and starts to pour the first glass)* Do you have any idea the impact the miracle will have on the country? *(LANCELOT and GUENEVERE turn slowly toward each other as he pours, until their eyes meet. They take an involuntary step toward each other. ARTHUR turns back with one glass filled, and sees their look. He continues talking, looking from one to the other, feverishly—painfully)*

When this is known, they'll be flocking to the Round Table from one end of England to the other . . . from Scotland . . . Wales . . . and all those quests we've been planning for the Knights may not even be necessary . . . I mean, when people hear . . . what has happened at Camelot . . . they may lay down their arms and come of their own free will . . . it's quite possible no one will bear arms at all any more . . . and that there will really be peace . . . all borders will disappear . . . and all the things I dreamed . . . I dreamed . . . I dreamed . . .

(His voice trails off in utter defeat, and he stands motionless in an abject trance. The sound of the March to the Grand Hall is heard in the orchestra, as:)

The Lights Dim Out Slowly

SCENE 10

Scene: A Corridor in the Castle.
Time: Immediately following.
The Knights of the Court parade to the Grand Hall with banners aflying in ceremonial drill.

SCENE II

Scene: The Grand Hall. Two thrones dominate the scene. Looking down on the hall and surrounding it, is a balcony.
Time: Immediately following.
At Rise: Ladies and Gentlemen of the Court are filing in to appropriate music in choreographed pattern.
ARTHUR *and* GUENEVERE *enter in full regal splendor, and take their places before the thrones.*
PELLINORE *stands next to* ARTHUR, *holding Excalibur.* LANCELOT *stands off to the side of* PELLINORE. DINADAN *stands next to* GUENEVERE, *holding a scroll. The music continues under.*
ARTHUR: Excalibur! *(He takes the sword from* PELLINORE*)*
DINADAN: To be invested Knights of the Round Table of England: of Brackley, Colgrevance. *(*COLGREVANCE *comes forward, kneels before the King and is touched on each shoulder with the Sword Excalibur. As he does, his banner swoops down from the balcony and hangs over the hall. He rises, bows again before* GUENEVERE, *and returns to his place)* Of Winchester, Bliant. *(The same)* Of Wales, Guilliam. *(The same)* Of Cornwall, Castor. *(The same)* Of Joyous Gard, Lancelot du Lac.
*(*LANCELOT *comes forward and bows.* ARTHUR *pauses, then very slowly, knights him.* LANCELOT *rises and returns to his place. The music swells. The Court files out.*
GUENEVERE *descends from the throne and exits.* DINADAN *and* PELLINORE *await the King.* ARTHUR *descends from the throne slowly, then stops and stands lost in his own thoughts,* PELLINORE *senses the King wishes to be alone and makes a brief sign to* DINADAN. *They exit.* ARTHUR *slowly looks up)*
ARTHUR: Proposition: If I could choose, from every woman who breathes on this earth, the face I would most love, the smile, the touch, the voice, the heart, the laugh, the soul itself, every detail and feature to the smallest strand of hair— they would all be Jenny's.
Proposition: If I could choose from every man who breathes on this earth a

man for my brother and a man for my son, a man for my friend, they would all be Lance.

(His bitterness mounts)

Yes, I love them. I love them, and they answer me with pain and torment. Be it sin or not sin, they betray me in their hearts, and that's far sin enough. I see it in their eyes and feel it when they speak, and they must pay for it and be punished. I shan't be wounded and not return it in kind. I'm done with feeble hoping. I demand a man's vengeance!

(He moves violently, then tries to control himself)

Proposition: I'm a king, not a man. And a civilized king. Could it possibly be civilized to destroy what I love? Could it possibly be civilized to love myself above all? What of their pain and their torment? Did they ask for this calamity? Can passion be selected?

(His voice rising)

Is there any doubt of their devotion . . . to me, or to our Table?

(He raises high the sword in his hand)

By God, Excalibur, I shall be a King! This is the time of King Arthur, and we reach for the stars! This is the time of King Arthur, and violence is not strength and compassion is not weakness. We are civilized! Resolved: We shall live through this together, Excalibur: They, you and I! And God have mercy on us all.

(The decision made, he becomes almost relaxed, almost at peace)

They're waiting for us at the table. *(He starts to walk off)* Let's not delay the celebration.

(The music swells, as:)

The Curtain Falls

ACT TWO

SCENE I

Scene: The Main Terrace of the Castle. Beyond the flower-covered walls at the rear can be seen the green rolling hills of the English countryside. Far in the distance is the tree in which ARTHUR first hid so many years ago.

Time: Afternoon. Several years later.

At Rise: GUENEVERE is seated at a table, LANCELOT at a small bench a distance away. He has a scroll, which he now unrolls to read. The music is playing. Just as he is about to read, a few couples move by across the rear of the stage. He looks over his shoulder and waits for them to pass. When they do, he reads and sings.

LANCELOT:
Toujours j'ai fait le même voeux,
Sur terre une déesse, au ciel un Dieu.

Un homme désire pour etre heureux
Sur terre une déesse, au ciel un Dieu.

Years may come; years may go;
This, I know, will e'er be so:

The reason to live is only to love
A goddess on earth and a God above.

(The music continues)

GUENEVERE: Did you write that, Lance?

LANCELOT: Yes.

GUENEVERE: Why do you always write about you? Why don't you ever write about me?

LANCELOT: I can't write about you. I love you too much. *(Desperately)* Jenny, I should leave you and never come back. I've said it to myself day after day, year after year. But how can I? Look at you. *When* would I? *(He sings)*

If ever I would leave you
It wouldn't be in summer;
Seeing you in summer, I never would go.
Your hair streaked with sunlight . . .
Your lips red as flame . . .
Your face with a luster
That puts gold to shame.

But if I'd ever leave you,
It couldn't be in autumn.
How I'd leave in autumn, I never would know.
I've seen how you sparkle
When fall nips the air.
I know you in autumn
And I must be there.

And could I leave you running merrily through the snow?
Or on a wintry evening when you catch the fire's glow?

If ever I would leave you,
How could it be in springtime,
Knowing how in spring I'm bewitch'd by you so?
Oh, no, not in springtime!
Summer, winter or fall!
No, never could I leave you at all.

(He walks to her. She raises her hand to stop him and, with a look, reminds him that he must not draw too near. He walks away, but turns to her again)

If ever I would leave you,
How could it be in springtime,
Knowing how in spring I'm bewitch'd by you so?
Oh, no, not in springtime!
Summer, winter or fall!
No, never could I leave you at all.

(She gazes at him tenderly)

LANCELOT: Jenny, do you think Arthur knows?

GUENEVERE: Don't speak of it, Lance. Of course he doesn't. If he ever did, I wouldn't want to live. And neither would you.

LANCELOT: No, he couldn't know. As much as he loves us, not even Arthur could . . .

(A few Ladies, led by LADY ANNE, *enter.* GUENEVERE *rises immediately, interrupting* LANCELOT*)*

GUENEVERE: *(Lightly)* It is time to go, Lady Anne?

LADY ANNE: *(Approaching)* Yes, Milady.

(The Ladies come to GUENEVERE *and put her cloak around her)*

GUENEVERE: *(To* LANCELOT, *easily)* I have a thrilling engagement this afternoon, Lancelot. I'm giving the prizes at the cattle show. *(To* LADY ANNE*)* I can't wait to see who wins.

LADY ANNE: I have the list of winners for you, Milady. *(She hands her a card)*

GUENEVERE: *(Taking it)* Oh, lovely! The Aberdeen Angus for a change. *(To* LANCELOT*)* I'm so pleased for him. He's been trying so hard, and he's been losing to the Short Horns for years. Thank you for waiting with me, Lancelot.

LANCELOT: Thank you for allowing me, Milady.

*(*GUENEVERE *exits with the Ladies.* LANCELOT *looks after her and exits. A young man enters from behind a column. His attire is foppish, his eyes mischievous, his smile wicked. His name is* MORDRED. *He casts a glance in the direction of* GUENEVERE, *and one in the direction of* LANCELOT*)*

MORDRED: Ah, Camelot. Where the King gives freedom and the Queen takes liberties. You poor things. Perhaps we can arrange a little rendezvous for you.

*(*ARTHUR'S *voice is heard.* MORDRED *drops back and out of sight as* ARTHUR *enters)*

ARTHUR: *(Entering)* Lance! I have it solved . . .*(*PELLINORE *follows him.* ARTHUR *turns to him. He does not see* MORDRED*)* Oh, I thought Lance was here, Pelly.

MORDRED: *(Coming forward, innocently)* He just left, Your Majesty. He was here with the Queen.

PELLINORE: *(Outraged)* You're not a member of this Court. How dare you enter these grounds unannounced!

MORDRED: *(Genially)* But I was announced, Milord. Did the Chamberlain not say that there was a young man from Scotland who came with royal greetings?

PELLINORE: And were you not informed all visitors were to return tomorrow afternoon?

MORDRED: I shall be busy tomorrow afternoon.

PELLINORE: By Jove, what impertinence! He shall be taught a lesson. *(He reaches for his sword and takes a step in* MORDRED'S *direction)*

MORDRED: *(Shrinking away in fear)* Keep away! Don't touch me! I'm unarmed!

ARTHUR: Call the guard, Pelly, and have this young ass thrown out.

MORDRED: *(Regaining his composure)* That's not a very kind way to treat the son of Queen Morgause.

*(*ARTHUR *is stunned to the roots. He slowly turns and, almost fearfully, looks at* MORDRED*)*

MORDRED: *(Delighted at the reaction)* Yes, Your Majesty. I am Mordred.

ARTHUR: *(Shaken)* Wait, Pelly. Mordred?

MORDRED: *(Bowing low)* Your Majesty.

ARTHUR: Leave us, Pellinore.

PELLINORE: I shall be waiting nearby, if you need me, Arthur. *(He exits)*

MORDRED: *(Cheerfully)* I bring you greetings, Your Majesty, from Queen Morgause and King Lot.

ARTHUR: I trust your mother is well, Mordred.

MORDRED: The Queen is splendid, thank you. As witchy as ever. Still beautiful, which of course she would be, with all her magic and sorcery. I've been wandering about the castle. I hope you don't mind. It's quite grand, really. I love the way you've mixed English with French. Very tasteful.

ARTHUR: And King Lot?

MORDRED: The King? Never happier. He was so delighted I left. He's always hated me, you know. Do you know what he did to me once? Mother had a youth potion that took off ten years. When I was nine, he gave it to me to make me minus one. I kept asking Mother why he disliked me so, and . . .

ARTHUR: *(Acidly)* What brings you to Camelot, Mordred?

MORDRED: A desire of blood, Your Majesty. I have quite a family here, you know. My dear aunt, Morgan Le Fey, whom I've never seen.

ARTHUR: *(Pressing him)* Nor has anyone else. The castle where she and her court live is quite invisible. It hardly seems reason for making this long journey.

MORDRED: *(Looking him square in the eye)* And there's you, Your Majesty. As I was saying, I kept asking Mother why King Lot despised me so, and one day not long ago, she told me the marvelous news: he's not my father. How once, when she was visiting England, she met an attractive lad named Arthur, invited him to her room, and bewitched him for the night. Is that the way the story goes, Your Majesty?

ARTHUR: Yes. That's the way the story goes, Mordred.

MORDRED: You can imagine her surprise when later he became the King of all England.

ARTHUR: *(Sternly)* Very well, Mordred. Now you are here. What are your plans?

MORDRED: That's for you to decide, Your Majesty.

ARTHUR: Very well. Then I shall tell you what I suggest, what I offer, what I wish. That you stay here and become a Knight of the Round Table. You have youth, brains and a proper heritage. Much could be done, if you apply yourself.

MORDRED: How generous of you, Your Majesty! I can think of nothing that would please me more than to win your confidence.

ARTHUR: I'm certain of that. And I shall be watching carefully, very carefully, to see if you deserve it. *(In full command)* Tonight you will have dinner with the Queen and me, and we will try to get to know each other better. Tomorrow your training will begin. But I must warn you, Mordred, no favoritism will be shown. You must earn the right to knighthood by virtue and proper deeds.

MORDRED: I shall try, Your Majesty.

ARTHUR: The adage, "Blood is thicker than water," was invented by undeserving relatives.

(ARTHUR exits. MORDRED looks after him and sticks out his tongue.)

MORDRED: *(Sings)*
Virtue and proper deeds, Your Majesty?
Like what?
Courage, Milord?
Purity and Humility, my liege?
Diligence? Charity? Honesty? Fidelity?
The seven deadly virtues?
No, thank you, Your Majesty.

The seven deadly virtues,
Those ghastly little traps,
Oh, no, Milord, they weren't meant for me.

Those seven deadly virtues,
They're made for other chaps,
Who love a life of failure and ennui.

Take Courage! Now there's a sport—
An invitation to the state of rigor mort!

And Purity! A noble yen!
And very restful ev'ry now and then.

I find Humility means to be hurt;
It's not the earth the meek inherit, it's the dirt.

Honesty is fatal and should be taboo.
Diligence? A fate I would hate.
If Charity means giving, I give it to you,
And Fidelity is only for your mate.

You'll never find a virtue
Unstatusing my quo,
Or making my Be-elzebubble burst.
Let others take the high road,
I will take the low;
I cannot wait to rush in
Where angels fear to go.
With all those seven deadly virtues,
Free and happy little me has not been cursed.

(He folds his arms and chuckles to himself)

    Dim Out

SCENE 2

Scene: The Terrace of the Castle.
Time: Late afternoon, a month later.
   At Rise: ARTHUR is standing in thought. GUENEVERE is seated, doing her embroidery, which she holds on her lap.
ARTHUR: *(Suddenly)* Jenny, I feel old.
GUENEVERE: Nonsense, dear.
ARTHUR: It's true. I was thinking of it this morning. I walked briskly as ever to my study and arrived much later than I expected to. The days seem longer; the nights seem shorter; and my horse seems higher.
GUENEVERE: You don't get enough fresh air, Arthur. You spend far too much time in your precious civil court.
ARTHUR: I can't help it. I only mean to stay for a moment, but I become absolutely transfixed. Not because I'm proud of it, which I am. But it's so exciting. Before, when disputes were settled by physical combat, I always knew the outcome, because I could tell at a glance which was the better swordsman. But now, with a jury and a judge, you never know till you hear the verdict. It's positively riveting.
GUENEVERE: I know it is. But I do worry about the jury, Arthur. They don't know the parties involved. They don't really care who wins. Are you sure it's wise to trust decisions to people so impartial?

ARTHUR: But that's the point . . .

(PELLINORE *enters in high dudgeon*)

PELLINORE: Arthur . . . ! *(To* GUENEVERE*)* Good evening, M'am.

GUENEVERE: Good evening, Pelly.

PELLINORE: Damn it, Arthur. *(To* GUENEVERE*)* Forgive me, damn it . . . *(To* ARTHUR*)* But, damn it! I've just left the chaps downstairs, and I can't stand it any longer. Yours Miserably has got to speak up.

ARTHUR: About what, Pelly?

PELLINORE: About what? Not about "what." About who, what? Mordred. That's what.

GUENEVERE: Oh, please, Pelly. Let's not talk about Mordred. This is the first night in a month he's not coming for dinner, and I feel as if I were going to a party.

PELLINORE: I'm sorry, M'am, but I must. Arthur, you have to face it: you have sired a snake! And to top it all, you've set him loose to poison your own Court. Do you have any idea what foul things he's saying and doing?

ARTHUR: *(Troubled, but calm)* Yes, I do.

PELLINORE: *(With indignant sarcasm)* Oh, you do, do you? Are you aware of the snaky way he's stirring up the Knights?

ARTHUR: Yes. He's preying on their provincialism and trying to make them yearn for their own lands.

PELLINORE: *(Surprised)* Oh, you know that. *(Ominously)* But, when he disappears every afternoon, do you have any idea what he's up to?

ARTHUR: He's searching the forest for his aunt, Morgan Le Fey.

PELLINORE: *(Taken aback)* Oh, you know that too? But I'll wager you don't know what he's saying about chivalry?

ARTHUR: Yes. He's mocking it with vulgar limericks.

PELLINORE: He's mocking it with vulgar . . . You know all that?!

ARTHUR: Yes. And I know why. To destroy me and those I love—and make his inheritance come faster.

PELLINORE: Then why, in the holy name of heaven, don't you stop him, Arthur? Arthur, you've simply got to stop thinking thoughts and think of something.

GUENEVERE: *(Gravely)* Is this true, Arthur?

ARTHUR: Yes, it is. *(Firmly)* But we practice civil law now, and we cannot take the law back into our own hands. Talking is not a crime, nor is walking in the woods. When he violates the law, the law shall deal with him.

PELLINORE: Do you mean to say, Arthur, a chap has to wait till he's killed before he can attack?

ARTHUR: *(After a moment)* Pelly, I'm afraid I have no answer to that.

PELLINORE: Well, I never thought I'd hear myself say it, but, Arthur, what you need is a new idea.

GUENEVERE: *(Actually reassuring Arthur)* And one will be found, Pelly. You shall see.

PELLINORE: I hope so, M'am. I hope so. I'm very worried. You know, M'am, in many ways chasing the Beast is much easier than living with people. It's true, when you're questing, the winter chills you and the summer scorches; the wind slaps you about a bit and the rain drenches you. But it's orderly. You can count on it. And they never all get together and do it to you at the same time. But people . . . ? *(Shudders)* I'm not referring to you, M'am. Or to you, Arthur. You're . . . special people. That's why I stay on, I suppose.

ARTHUR: I'll tell you, Pelly, I could do with some fresh air. Let's get away from people tomorrow and go partridge shooting.

PELLINORE: I'd love that, Arthur. *(To* GUENEVERE*)* Well, goodnight, M'am. Goodnight, Arthur. *(He exits happily)*

GUENEVERE: Arthur, I hope you suffer no guilt about Mordred. I feel nothing about him, and neither should you. *(Lightly, to ease him)* God knows you're not the first king to have one of those things running around.

ARTHUR: No. I do feel nothing for him. And there's no escaping the fact he's an appalling specimen.

GUENEVERE: Amen. The one thing I can say for him is that he's bound to marry well. Everybody is above him.

ARTHUR: Yet, there he is, Jenny. And even if he were banished, he would remain a constant menace to the throne. And to us. Jenny, don't you wish you'd never been born a queen?

GUENEVERE: Oh, occasionally. It's never being alone that bothers me most. Do you know, I have never been without someone around me in my entire life? Neither at Camilliard, or Camelot. I mean, completely, totally, solitarily alone? Sometimes I wish the castle were empty, everyone gone, no one here but me. Do you know what I would do? I would bolt every door, lock every window, take off all my clothes and run stark naked from room to room. I would go to the kitchen, naked; prepare my own meals, naked; do some embroidery, naked; and put on my crown, naked. And when I passed a mirror, I would stop and say: *(With a broad cockney accent)* " 'Ello, Jenny old thing! Nice to see you!" *(*ARTHUR *laughs)* But I must say, on the whole, being a queen can be . . . *(She pauses)*

ARTHUR: Can be what?

GUENEVERE: *(With sudden dejection)* A weary load. That dreadful boy. One more added burden we could quite well do without.

ARTHUR: Yes, but a burden we can't escape.

GUENEVERE: Royalty never can. Why is that, Arthur? Other people do. They seem to have ways and means of finding respite. What do they do? Farmers, cooks, blacksmiths . . .

(She sings)
What do the simple folk do
To help them escape when they're blue?
The shepherd who is ailing,
The milkmaid who is glum,
The cobbler who is wailing
From nailing
> *His thumb?*

When they're beset and besieged,
The folk not noblessely obliged . . .
However do they manage
To shed their weary lot?
Oh, what do simple folk do
We do not?

ARTHUR: *(Seriously)*
> *I have been informed*
> *By those who know them well,*
> *They find relief in quite a clever way.*
> *When they're sorely pressed,*
> *They whistle for a spell;*
> *And whistling seems to brighten up their day.*
> *And that's what simple folk do;*
> *So they say.*

GUENEVERE: They whistle?

ARTHUR:
> *So they say.*

(GUENEVERE hopefully begins to whistle. ARTHUR, at first surprised, joins in. They whistle away for a moment. Finding small comfort, he stops and looks at her hopelessly. She, too, stops and sighs)

GUENEVERE:
> *What else do the simple folk do*
> *To perk up the heart and get through?*
> *The wee folk and the grown folk*
> *Who wander to and fro*
> *Have ways known to their own folk*
> *We throne folk*
> > *Don't know.*

> *When all the doldrums begin,*
> *What keeps each of them in his skin?*
> *What ancient native custom*
> *Provides the needed glow?*
> *Oh, what do simple folk do?*
> *Do you know?*

ARTHUR:
> *Once along the road*
> *I came upon a lad*
> *Singing in a voice three times his size.*
> *When I asked him why,*
> *He told me he was sad,*
> *And singing always made his spirits rise.*
> *So that's what simple folk do,*
> *I surmise.*

GUENEVERE: They sing?

ARTHUR:
> *I surmise.*

(They throw themselves into happy song)

GUENEVERE *and* ARTHUR:
> *Arise, my love! Arise, my love!*
> *Apollo's lighting the skies, my love.*

The meadows shine
With columbine
And daffodils blossom away.

Hear Venus call
To one and all:
Come taste delight while you may.
The world is bright,
And all is right,
And life is merry and gay . . . !

(GUENEVERE *stops short and turns to him with frustrated disgust*)

GUENEVERE:
What else do the simple folk do?
They must have a system or two.
They obviously outshine us
At turning tears to mirth;
Have tricks a royal highness
Is minus
   From birth.

What then I wonder do they
To chase all the goblins away?
They have some tribal sorc'ry
You haven't mentioned yet;
Oh, what do simple folk do
To forget?

ARTHUR:
Often I am told
They dance a fiery dance,
And whirl til they're completely uncontrolled
Soon the mind is blank,
And all are in a trance,
A vi'lent trance astounding to behold.
And that's what simple folk do,
So I'm told.

(They burst into a surprisingly wild hornpipe together. It proves hardly a cure)

GUENEVERE:
What else do the simple folk do
To help them escape when they're blue?

ARTHUR:
They sit around and wonder
What royal folk would do.
And that's what simple folk do.

GUENEVERE: *(Sadly)* Really?!
ARTHUR: I have it on the best authority.

GUENEVERE *and* ARTHUR:
Yes, that's what simple folk do.

(They look at each other forlornly)

Dim Out

SCENE 3

Scene: A Forest near Camelot. At this moment, it is shrouded and obscure, and the scene is played before a transparent curtain.
Time: Late afternoon the following day.
At Rise: MORDRED is discovered with two large baskets of candy. As he calls into the forest, he darts from side to side, listening for an answer.
MORDRED: Morgan Le Fey? . . . Morgan Le Fey? . . . Sister of my mother, it's I, Mordred, who comes to visit you . . . Can you hear me, dear Aunt? . . . Am I near your invisible castle? . . . Am I, dear Morgan? . . . dear sweet Aunt Morgan? . . . dear sweet Queen Aunt Morgan? Can you not hear me?
MORGAN LE FEY: *(Her drawling, cooing voice is heard in the distance)* Go away, Mordred. Go away! You were a nasty little boy, and I'm told you've become a nastier little man.
MORDRED: I beseech you, Your Majesty. Give me a moment of your time.
MORGAN LE FEY: *(Lazily irritated)* Not now, Mordred. I am eating my dinner and shan't be finished till tomorrow.
MORDRED: What a pity! I have chocolates.
MORGAN LE FEY: *(A touch of excitement in her voice)* Chocolates? You say you have chocolates?
MORDRED: Hard candies and caramels! Cherry creams—with soft centers?
MORGAN LF FEY: *(Feverishly)* Cherry creams with soft centers? Don't move, my darling nephew! Your darling aunt is on her way. Court!
(The music swells and a forest begins to rise before his eyes. He disappears with the candy to hide it, as the lights come up behind him)

SCENE 4

Scene: The Forest of MORGAN LE FEY. It is a labyrinth of tanglewood.
Time: Immediately following.
At Rise: MORDRED appears. Before his eyes, weird and startling figures, half human, half animal, all members of MORGAN LE FEY'S Court, appear in choreographic pantomime. Finally the way is paved for the entrance of MORGAN LE FEY herself.
She seems in her late twenties, quite wild and quite beautiful, her hair flowing, her gown flimsy. MORDRED kneels at her feet.
MORDRED: Your Majesty.
MORGAN LE FEY: *(Waving the Courtiers off with her hand)* Arise, Mordred. And give me the candy.
MORDRED: *(Rising)* I have your candy, dear Aunt. Baskets and baskets, in sugary profusion. But first let us discuss what you shall do for me.
MORGAN LE FEY: I shall do nothing for you, nothing at all. Why should I do anything for anyone? I have all I want of life: passionate afternoons, gluttonous nights, and slovenly mornings.
MORDRED: Very well, then.
MORGAN LE FEY: Give me my candy, or I shall go home and continue eating my dining room.

MORDRED: Eating your dining room?

MORGAN LE FEY: And why not? My chairs are made of vegetables; my table's made of cheese, and my doors are gingerbread.

MORDRED: And the floor?

MORGAN LE FEY: Roast beef, wall to wall. But, candy I never get, so I desire it most of all.

MORDRED: Then why should you be denied it, when all I ask is to play a prank on King Arthur?

MORGAN LE FEY: King Arthur? Oh, Wart! I used to watch him from my invisible window out walking with Merlyn. He was a dear little boy. No. I don't wish to harm him.

MORDRED: No harm.

MORGAN LE FEY: You're the son of a wicked mother, Mordred, and I know you're up to mischief.

MORDRED: No mischief at all. Just a delicious little game that will amuse you. Arthur is out hunting. Lure him to your forest, and detain him for the night.

MORGAN LE FEY: Detain him for the night? No. Such games are for the afternoon. At night, I eat. And I'm more ravenous every minute.

MORDRED: Please, dear Aunt? Make him drowsy and build a wall around him? The invisible kind you do so well.

MORGAN LE FEY: How do you know I build invisible walls?

MORDRED: Mummy told me. Please, dear Aunt?

MORGAN LE FEY: No! I will not harm little Wart. *(She calls)* Court! *(The music begins)* Farewell, nasty Mordred!

(The Court reappears, as MORGAN prepares to depart)

MORDRED: *(Sings)*
Enough candy I'll bring
To furnish a new wing.

(MORGAN LE FEY hesitates, tempted. Then, with courageous resolve, she continues her departure)

Masses and masses
Of gummy molasses.

(The thought of it bewitches her. She finds it difficult to leave)

Fudge by the van!

(She's sorely tempted)

Fresh marzipan!

(Her defenses crumble, and she reaches for his outstretched hand)

All yours it will be
If you'll build me a wee
Little wall.

(They begin to dance together)

MORGAN LE FEY:
Do you promise, you devil,
It's all on the level?

MORDRED:

I solemnly swear
It's a harmless affair.

MORGAN LE FEY:

On your honor, dear lad?

MORDRED:

Honor? You're mad!

MORGAN LE FEY:

Ye gods, but you're low!
My answer is "No,"
And that's all!

(She turns away from him)

MORDRED:

A basket or two
Of marshmallow goo . . . !

(She stops)

A licorice stick
That takes two years to lick . . . !

MORGAN LE FEY: *(She can stand it no longer)*
Where's the King?

Bring the King!

I shall build him a wall
Three and seven feet tall!
I'll hurry and mix
Some invisible bricks.

MORDRED:

Oh, Queen! You're a joy!

MORGAN LE FEY:

Be gone, nasty boy!

(MORDRED exits gleefully. A strange, birdlike creature is summoned by MORGAN LE FEY. *The creature leaps onto the stage. An arrow flies towards him. He catches it and disappears.* MORGAN LE FEY *darts behind the tree, as* ARTHUR *and* PELLINORE *enter)*

PELLINORE: Where's the bird, Arthur? Where's the bird? You hit it. I saw it. Where did it go?

ARTHUR: *(Looking around, puzzled)* Strange, Pelly. I've never seen this forest before. I used to play in this valley when I was a boy. But it was like a meadow. There were no trees.

PELLINORE: Nature, old boy. Things pop up, you know. Where's the bird?

ARTHUR: Sh-h-h. It's awfully quiet around here, isn't it? *(MORGAN LE FEY appears from behind the tree and listens)* Not a leaf rustling, not a whisper in the woods. It makes one rather drowsy. Would you care to rest a bit?

PELLINORE: No thank you, old man. I want to find that bird, what? I mean, if you hit a bird with an arrow, it ought to fall down like a gentleman.

(He exits. ARTHUR *sighs drowsily and seats himself before a tree stump)*

ARTHUR: *(Sleepily)* Merlyn, do you remember how often we walked this valley when I was a boy? *(He yawns)* Do you know what I miss of those days? Not my youth. My innocence. My innocence . . .

(He closes his eyes and sleeps. MORGAN LE FEY *and her Court appear from the woods, carrying imaginary bricks. In balletic pantomime, flying back and forth across the stage with more and more bricks, they construct a high invisible wall around the sleeping King. When it is complete,* MORGAN LE FEY *"pats it" all around, to make certain it is perfect. Finding it to her pleasure, she disappears, followed by her Court.* PELLINORE *enters)*

PELLINORE: Arthur? *(*ARTHUR *awakens)* The bird's hopeless, Arthur. Let's push on.

ARTHUR: Where am I? What's happened? How long have I been asleep? Pelly, we must get back to the castle. I have strange feelings.

PELLINORE: Righto. If you want.

(He starts to walk away. ARTHUR *tries to follow and collides with the invisible wall)*

ARTHUR: Good God! *(He feels his way around the wall)*

PELLINORE: Well, old man, are you coming or aren't you?

ARTHUR: I'm trapped!

PELLINORE: *(Coming to him)* I say, Arthur. Who are you waving at? What's wrong with you? *(He runs into the wall)* I say! What is this? It feels like a wall! But I don't see it.

ARTHUR: *(With tragic awareness)* It is a wall.

PELLINORE: Where did it come from? How did it get here?

ARTHUR: Morgan Le Fey! Morgan Le Fey! Is this your sorcery? *(To* PELLINORE, *desperately)* Pelly, get back to the castle. Find Lance. Find Jenny. Warn them to be careful.

PELLINORE: *(Stunned)* You know, Arthur?

ARTHUR: Do as I say, Pelly! *(*PELLINORE *exits)* Morgan Le Fey! Morgan Le Fey! Morgan Le Fey!

Dim Out

SCENE 5

Scene: The Corridor to the Queen's Bedchamber.
Time: Later that night.
At Rise: LADY ANNE *and* LADY SYBIL *bow onto the stage, addressing the Queen, who is offstage.*

LADY ANNE: Good night, Milady.

LADY SYBIL: Good night, Your Majesty.

LADY ANNE: Sleep well, Your Majesty.

(They cross the stage to exit. LANCELOT *walks quietly on behind them. He watches until they are out of sight. He takes one quick look around and exits in the direction of the Queen's chamber.* MORDRED *appears at the other end of the corridor. He moves furtively across the stage and looks off after* LANCELOT. *He snaps his fingers. Five Knights enter, their swords strapped tight. He goes to them. Before he can speak,* PELLINORE *enters behind him)*

PELLINORE: You, there!

MORDRED: The name is Mordred. And if I were you, I'd remember it.

PELLINORE: Well, I'm not you, and I intend to forget it. Where's Lancelot?

MORDRED: *(Insinuatingly)* Lancelot? Now, where would you expect to find Lancelot at this hour?

PELLINORE: I looked in the chapel. He's not there. Has the Queen retired for the night?

MORDRED: That, Milord, is an iffy question.

PELLINORE: Look here, whatever-your-name-is. I don't know what slushes through that swampy little mind of yours, but while the King is away, I am in charge of this palace. And I'm not a believer in all this civil law nonsense. You make one false move, and you'll face the jury in two sections, what? Carry the head in myself. Gladly. *(He starts to exit)* Oh, wouldn't I love that! *(He exits)*

MORDRED: Pellinore, in a little while, I shall be in charge of this castle. And shortly after that, gentlemen, the kingdom. *(He draws a sword from one of the men and beckons them to follow)*

Dim Out

SCENE 6

Scene: The Queen's Bedchamber. It is a large, beautiful room. The moonlight streams in through the window.

Time: Immediately following.

At Rise: GUENEVERE, in a white loosely flowing gown, is seated at her dressing table, slowly brushing her long hair. The music of "If Ever I Would Leave You" is playing softly.

LANCELOT enters quietly. He wears no armor and has only a dagger in his belt. He looks around the bedroom as he enters, as if seeing it for the first time, which in truth he is. He pauses a few feet from GUENEVERE.

LANCELOT: *(Hushed; tremulously, fearfully)* Jenny . . . ? *(GUENEVERE rises quickly and looks at him in astonishment. He goes to her)* Jenny, I was in the yard . . . I couldn't sleep . . . I saw the light in your window . . . I knew you were alone . . . I tried to stay away . . . I tried, but I . . . Jenny, I . . . *(He takes her in his arms and they embrace passionately. Suddenly she withdraws in fear)*

GUENEVERE: Did anyone see you?

LANCELOT: No one. The castle is dark. I was careful. Jenny, don't be afraid.

GUENEVERE: But I am afraid.

LANCELOT: I swear we're alone. No one saw me enter. Jenny, there's nothing to fear. Arthur won't be back until . . . *(He stops himself, ashamed)* Forgive me, Jenny.

GUENEVERE: *(Sadly)* We're not alone, are we, Lance? *(He takes her in his arms tenderly)*

LANCELOT: *(Fervently)* We are, we are.

GUENEVERE: We're not. Here you are, with your arms around me, and the first thing we think of is him. *(She leaves him)*

LANCELOT: *(Pleadingly)* But you love me, Jenny.

GUENEVERE: Of course, I do. And I always shall. Night after night I've thought of you here and wished for it with all my being. And suddenly, we're less alone than ever.

LANCELOT: But why?

GUENEVERE: Now that the people are gone, can't you see the shadow between us? It's wider than the sea. It fills the room. Perhaps it would have been better if we had never said a word to each other at all.

(She sings)
I loved you once in silence,
And mis'ry was all I knew.
Trying so to keep my love from showing,
All the while not knowing
You loved me too.

Yes, loved me in lonesome silence;
Your heart filled with dark despair . . .
Thinking love would flame in you forever,
And I'd never, never
Know the flame was there.

Then one day we cast away our secret longing;
The raging tide we held inside would hold no more.
The silence at last was broken!
We flung wide our prison door.
Ev'ry joyous word of love was spoken . . . !

And now there's twice as much grief,
Twice the strain for us;
Twice the despair,
Twice the pain for us
As we had known before.

LANCELOT: *(Desperately)* Jenny, it's because we're here, here in Camelot that everything is so wretched.
GUENEVERE: No, Lance.
LANCELOT: Jenny, come away with me. To Joyous Gard. Let us have it open and above board at last.
GUENEVERE: Lance, I've told you a thousand times I shall never leave Arthur. Ever. Now, let us say no more about it.
LANCELOT: *(Raging)* But this agonizing torment! Day after day, year after year. Would God I had your talent for acceptance, your invincible English calm!
GUENEVERE: *(Turning on him)* Oh, the insensitivity of sensitive men! Always suffering so much they can suffer nothing for others. You think you're the only one in torment. I'm just as tortured, just as anguished as you. But what would you have us do to this man we both love? Run away! Leave him! Make him publicly miserable! Force him to declare war on you, where either one of you, if not both, would be killed, as well as hundreds of others. What sort of heart-breaking solution is that?
(For a moment they are silent)
LANCELOT: *(With quiet resignation)* Forgive me, Jenny. I shall never mention it again. I swear. Nor shall I come to you again. I swear that, too. *(He moves to leave)*
GUENEVERE: Lance? *(He stops)* Have we no more tender words to say to each other?

(She sings)
The silence at last was broken!
We flung wide our prison door.
Ev'ry joyous word of love was spoken . . .
And after all had been said,
Here we are, my love,
Silent once more
And not far, my love . . .
From where we were be . . .

(He puts his arms around her tenderly. Five Knights and MORDRED tiptoe silently into the room)

MORDRED: *(Quietly)* Lancelot . . . Don't touch your dagger. *(LANCELOT whirls around. GUENEVERE turns, horror-stricken)* I accuse you of treason, and order you both to stand trial for your crime. Surrender in the name of the King.

(LANCELOT walks toward MORDRED to surrender. Then suddenly he leaps forward and snatches the sword from MORDRED'S hand. For a second the Knights are too startled to move. MORDRED shrinks away in terror. LANCELOT backs up, his sword held high menacingly, and with his free hand, reaches for the outstretched hand of the Queen. The Knights spread out slowly to surround him, waiting for him to make the first move)

LANCELOT: *(To GUENEVERE, without taking his eyes off the Knights)* If I escape, I shall come and rescue you. If I am killed, send word to Joyous Gard. Someone will come.

(Then he jumps at the Knights. They all freeze into a tableau as:)

The Lights Dim Out Slowly

SCENE 7

Scene: Camelot. Two towers rise into the air. The rest is an endless blue.
At Rise: A hooded figure appears. He sings. As he does, the stage fills with similarly garbed figures, who slowly move into one group beside the singer.

THE SINGER:
Out of the room, down the hall,
Through the yard, to the wall;
Slashing fiercely, left and right,
Lance escaped them and took flight.

On a day, dark and drear,
Came to trial Guenevere.
Ruled the jury for her shame
She be sentenced to the flame.

As the dawn filled the sky,
On the day she would die,
There was wonder far and near:
Would the King burn Guenevere?

(ARTHUR enters forlornly and stands alone)

THE CHORUS:
Would the King let her die?
Would the King let her die?
There was wonder far and near:
Would the King burn Guenevere?

(MORDRED enters)

MORDRED: *(With wicked joy)* Arthur! What a magnificent dilemma! Let her die, your life is over; let her live, your life's a fraud. Which will it be, Arthur? Do you kill the Queen or kill the law?
ARTHUR: *(Defiantly, resolutely, tragically)* Treason has been committed! The jury has ruled! Let justice be done.
(MORDRED disappears)

THE CHORUS:
She must burn. She must burn.
Spoke the King: She must burn.
And the moment now was here
For the end of Guenevere.

(GUENEVERE enters. She is accompanied by a priest, carrying a cross, and two soldiers to guard her. She approaches ARTHUR. She pauses and looks up at him. He slowly turns and looks at her. Their eyes hold a moment. She continues. She exits. But ARTHUR has crumbled inside)

THE CHORUS:
Slow her walk, bowed her head,
To the stake she was led . . .

(A herald mounts the tower)

THE HERALD: The Queen is at the stake, Your Majesty. Shall I signal the torch?
(ARTHUR cannot answer. The herald calls frantically) Your Majesty . . . ! Your Majesty . . . ! *(But the King has no answer)*

THE CHORUS:
In his grief, so alone
From the King came a moan . . .

(MORDRED appears)

ARTHUR: I can't! I can't! I can't let her die!
MORDRED: Well, you're human after all, aren't you, Arthur? Human and helpless.

A SINGER:
Then suddenly earth and sky were dazed by a pounding roar.
And suddenly through the dawn an army began to pour.
And lo! Ahead the army, holding aloft his spear,
Came Lancelot to save his dear
Guenevere!

ARTHUR: *(Crying out)* Lance! Lance! Come save her.
HERALD: *(Desperately)* Shall I signal the torch, Your Majesty?

DINADAN: *(Rushing in)* Arthur, an army from Joyous Gard is storming the gate. Shall I double the guard? *(ARTHUR shakes his head dazedly)* Arthur, you're inviting a massacre! *(DINADAN rushes off)*

ARTHUR: Save her, Lance! Save her!

THE CHORUS:
> *By the score fell the dead,*
> *As the yard turned to red.*
> *Countless numbers felt his spear*
> *As he rescued Guenevere.*

MORDRED: Sweet heaven, what a sight! Can you see it from there, Arthur? Can you see your goodly Lancelot murdering your goodly Knights? Your table is cracking, Arthur. Can you hear the timbers split?

ARTHUR: *(In anguish)* Merlyn! Merlyn, make me a hawk. Let me fly away from here!

MORDRED: *(With mad glee)* What a failure you are, Arthur! How did you think you could survive without being as ruthless as I?

ARTHUR: Merlyn! . . . Merlyn! . . .

THE CHORUS:
> *In that dawn, in that gloom,*
> *More than love met its doom.*
> *In the dying candles' gleam*
> *Came the sundown of a dream.*

DINADAN: *(Entering)* Most of the guard is killed, Arthur, and over eighty Knights. They're heading for the Channel. I'll make ready the army to follow. Arthur, we want revenge! *(DINADAN turns to leave. His face runs with blood)*

ARTHUR: *(Broken)* Oh, God, is it all to start again? Is my almighty fling at peace to be over so soon? Am I back where I began? Am I? Am I? *(MORDRED screams with laughter and exits. Five soldiers enter with the King's armor and sword. He stands like a prisoner being shackled while they fasten his armor to him)*

THE CHORUS:
> *Guenevere, Guenevere!*
> *In that dim, mournful year,*
> *Saw the men she held most dear*
> *Go to war for Guenevere.*
>
> *Guenevere! Guenevere!*
> *Guenevere! Guenevere!*
> *Saw the men she held most dear*
> *Go to war for Guenevere!*
> *Guenevere! Guenevere! Guenevere!*

(The sky turns red. More soldiers enter)

The Lights Dim

SCENE 8

Scene: A Battlefield outside Joyous Gard. Tents can be seen in the distance, and there is one large tent downstage.

Time: Early dawn. A week later.

At rise: ARTHUR *stands alone on the battlefield.* LANCELOT *appears in the shadows.*

LANCELOT: Jenny. He's here!

(GUENEVERE *enters. She goes to* ARTHUR. *He turns to her)*

ARTHUR: Was either of you injured in the escape?

LANCELOT: Untouched, Arthur.

GUENEVERE: Arthur, we want to return with you to England. No matter the cost, we must try to put things right.

LANCELOT: This war will do horrible harm to the Table, Arthur. We must stop it before it grows.

GUENEVERE: Let us pay for what we have done.

ARTHUR: At the stake? No! I won't take you back. I shan't let you return. For what end! Justice? They've forgotten justice. They want revenge! Revenge! That most worthless of causes. It's too late, Lance. The Table is dead. It exists no more.

GUENEVERE: What?

ARTHUR: Over half the Knights were killed in the yard. Mordred has fled to Orkney, taking some with him. I suppose to organize an army against me. The rest are waiting in their tents, itching for dawn, cheerful to be at war. It's the old uncivilized days come back again. Those dreadful days we all tried to put to sleep forever.

LANCELOT: *(Unbelievingly)* It's your wish, Arthur, that this dread battle go on?

ARTHUR: No, it's not my wish, Lance. But I can think no longer what to do but ride the tide of events. Oh, what a blight thinking is. How I wish I'd never tried to think at all. All we've been through, for nothing but an idea! Something you cannot taste or touch, smell or feel; without substance, life, reality or memory. *(Trumpets sound in the distance)* The charade begins soon. You must go back to Joyous Gard.

LANCELOT: Jenny is not at Joyous Gard, Arthur. She stays with the holy sisters. Is there nothing to be done?

ARTHUR: Nothing, but play out the game and leave the decisions to God. Now go. *(*LANCELOT *goes to* ARTHUR. *They quietly and solemnly clasp arms.* LANCELOT *pauses for a moment, and looks at* GUENEVERE. *Then, without a word, exits quickly)* You must go, too, Jenny.

GUENEVERE: I know. So often in the past, Arthur, I would look up in your eyes, and there I would find forgiveness. Perhaps one day in the future it shall be there again. But I won't be with you. I won't know it. *(He holds out his arms. She goes into them. As she withdraws, she looks up into his face)* Oh, Arthur, Arthur, I see what I wanted to see.

ARTHUR: Goodbye, my love . . . *(*GUENEVERE *exits, taking a different path from* LANCELOT*)* . . . My dearest love. *(He stands for a moment in silence. A rustling is heard behind the tent)* Who's there? Who's there? Come out, I say!

(A young lad, about fourteen, appears from behind the tent. His name is TOM*)*

TOM: *(Frightened)* Forgive me, Your Majesty. I was searching for the Sergeant of Arms and got lost. I didn't wish to disturb you.

ARTHUR: Who are you, boy? Where did you come from? You ought to be in bed. Are you a page?

TOM: I stowed away on one of the boats, Your Majesty. I came to fight for the Round Table. I'm very good with the bow.

ARTHUR: And do you think you will kill people with this bow of yours?

TOM: Oh yes, Milord. A great many, I hope.

ARTHUR: Suppose they kill you?

TOM: Then I shall be dead, Milord. But I don't intend to be dead. I intend to be a Knight.

ARTHUR: A Knight . . . ?

TOM: Yes, Milord. Of the Round Table.

ARTHUR: When did you decide upon this nonexistent career? Was your village protected by Knights when you were a small boy? Was your mother saved by a Knight? Did your father serve a Knight?

TOM: Oh, no, Milord. I had never seen a Knight until I stowed away. I only know *of* them. The stories people tell.

ARTHUR: From the stories people tell you wish to be a Knight? *(A strange light comes into his eyes)* What do you think you know of the Knights and the Round Table?

TOM: I know everything, Milord. Might for right! Right for right! Justice for all! A Round Table where all Knights would sit. Everything!

*(*ARTHUR *walks away. Then suddenly he turns to the boy with a trembling inner excitement)*

ARTHUR: Come here, my boy. Tell me your name.

TOM: It is Tom, Milord.

ARTHUR: Where is your home?

TOM: In Warwick, Milord.

ARTHUR: Then listen to me, Tom of Warwick. You will not fight in the battle, do you hear?

TOM: *(Disappointed)* Yes, Milord.

ARTHUR: You will run behind the lines and hide in a tent till it is over. Then you will return to your home in England. Alive. To grow up and grow old. Do you understand?

TOM: Yes, Milord.

ARTHUR: And for as long as you live you will remember what I, the King, tell you; and you will do as I command.

TOM: *(No longer disappointed)* Yes, Milord.

ARTHUR: *(Sings)*

> *Each evening from December to December*
> *Before you drift to sleep upon your cot,*
> *Think back on all the tales that you remember*
> *Of Camelot.*

> *Ask ev'ry person if he's heard the story;*
> *And tell it strong and clear if he has not:*

That once there was a fleeting wisp of glory
Called Camelot.

Camelot! Camelot!
Now say it out with love and joy!

TOM: *(Bursting with it)*
Camelot! Camelot!

ARTHUR: *(His arm around the boy's shoulder)*
Yes, Camelot, my boy . . .

Where once it never rained till after sundown;
By eight a.m. the morning fog had flown . . .
Don't let it be forgot
That once there was a spot
For one brief shining moment that was known
As Camelot . . .

(PELLINORE enters carrying the Sword Excalibur)

PELLINORE: Arthur . . . ?

ARTHUR: *(Feverishly)* Give me the sword.

PELLINORE: *(Handing it to him)* Here.

ARTHUR: Kneel, Tom. Kneel. *(The boy does)* With this sword, Excalibur, I knight you Sir Tom of Warwick. *(He touches the boy on each shoulder)* And I command you to return home and carry out my orders.

TOM: *(Rising)* Yes, Milord.

PELLINORE: What are you doing, Arthur? You have a battle to fight.

ARTHUR: Battle? I've won my battle, Pelly. Here's my victory! *(The music swells behind him)* What we did will be remembered. You'll see, Pelly. Now, run, Sir Tom! Behind the lines!

TOM: *(Radiantly)* Yes, Milord. *(He runs off)*

ARTHUR: *(His eyes following the boy)* Run, Sir Tom! Run boy! Through the lines!

PELLINORE: Who is that, Arthur?

ARTHUR: One of what we all are, Pelly. Less than a drop in the great blue motion of the sunlit sea. *(He smiles. There is jubilance in his voice)* But it seems some of the drops sparkle, Pelly. Some of them do sparkle! Run, boy!
(The music swells. He takes a firm grip on his sword and moves to exit, as:)

The Curtain Falls

MAN OF
LA MANCHA

Written by Dale Wasserman
Lyrics by Joe Darion
Music by Mitch Leigh

Editor's Notes

A triumph in every respect, *Man of La Mancha* is one of the most honored musicals of the American theatre. Winner of the New York Drama Critics' Circle Award as best musical of the 1965–1966 season, it also received five Antoinette Perry (Tony) Awards, including one for best musical play, the Outer Circle Award, and three citations in *Variety*'s Poll of New York Drama Critics. Opening on November 22, 1965, it ran for 2,328 performances in its original engagement. Such was the power and appeal of the musical, that it was revived (with the same principal performers) at the Vivian Beaumont Theatre, Lincoln Center, in 1972 for 140 capacity performances. It also has had almost 30 major productions in cities around the world; and was made into a motion picture (released in 1972) with Peter O'Toole and Sophia Loren.

The drama critics were just as ecstatic as the audiences who nightly gave it a standing ovation. Richard Watts, Jr. of the *New York Post* imparted to his readers: "*Man of La Mancha*, the new musical adapation of *Don Quixote*, is a triumph of creative imagination and stagecraft . . . It is a thoroughly triumphant enterprise, faithful to the spirit of the Spanish classic." John Chapman of the New York *Daily News* called it "an enthralling, exquisite musical play" while others found it "a dream of a musical" that has "charm, gallantry and delicacy of spirit . . . *Man of La Mancha* is grand and glorious . . . musical theatre at its finest . . . eloquent, bold and original . . . This is a lusty, rowdy, thrilling show."

Author Dale Wasserman was born in Rhinelander, Wisconsin, on November 2, 1917. He entered show business at the age of 19 and racked up several successful careers (as director, lighting designer, and for more than seven years, manager of Katherine Dunham's dance troupe) before turning to writing in 1954.

His initial plays were written for television and in 1954 his *Elisha and the Long Knives* was voted the Top Television Play of the Year. This was the first of almost 50 Wasserman scripts, all of which, without exception, have been produced or are in production for stage, screen and television.

Among his other award-winning television plays are *The Power and the Glory* (which starred Laurence Olivier), *The Fog*, *The Eichmann Story*, *The Stranger and I*, *The Lincoln Murder Case*, and *I, Don Quixote*, which later was to become *Man of La Mancha*.

For films, he wrote *The Vikings*, *Mister Buddwing*, *Quick Before It Melts*, and the first of the many scripts for the Elizabeth Taylor-Richard Burton *Cleopatra*.

In 1957, Mr. Wasserman made his New York stage debut with the book (written in collaboration with Bruce Geller) for the musical *Livin' the Life*. Produced at the Phoenix Theatre, it was based on Mark Twain's Mississippi stories.

He next was represented on Broadway in 1963 with *One Flew Over the Cuckoo's Nest*, based on the novel by Ken Kesey. It starred Kirk Douglas and ran for 82 performances. But that was not quite the end of the property. It was re-staged off Broadway in 1971 and ran for 1,025 performances, making it the eighth longest-running presentation in off-Broadway history. It now is being made into a film.

The versatility of Dale Wasserman seems endless for in addition to his work in all branches of the entertainment industry, he also has contributed short stories and articles to numerous magazines including *Redbook*, *True*, *Cavalier* and *Argosy*.

At present, Mr. Wasserman has his own film company in Hollywood in partnership with director Delbert Mann and Douglas Laurence.

Joe Darion (lyrics) is a native New Yorker. He was educated in New York schools and at City College. During World War II, he served in the U. S. Navy.

His popular songs, which have sold more than ten million records, include "Changing Partners" and "Midnight Train."

His previous Broadway musical, *Shinbone Alley*, was presented in 1957. Based on the *archy and mehitabel* stories by Don Marquis, he wrote the lyrics and collaborated on the book with Mel Brooks. The production co-starred Eddie Bracken and Eartha Kitt as the legendary Marquis characters.

Among his other major works is the oratorio *Galileo* (in collaboration with Ezra Laderman) which was written for and produced on network television.

Mitch Leigh (music) was born in New York City on January 31, 1928. He attended New York schools, then studied with Paul Hindemith at the Yale School of Music. After returning to New York, he organized and founded Music Makers, Inc., an enormously successful company that has won most major awards for radio and television commercial music. Mr. Leigh composes in a wide range— from jazz to opera. He also has contributed incidental music for several Broadway plays, including *Too True to Be Good* (1963) and *Never Live Over a Pretzel Factory* (1964). *Man of La Mancha* represents his first score for a Broadway musical.

A Note on Miguel de Cervantes

Like his contemporary, William Shakespeare, Miguel de Cervantes y Saavedra lived a life only sparsely documented, many years of which are veiled in shadow. These things are known: he was born in 1547 to a proud but impoverished hidalgo family; he was a soldier, suffered serious wounds at the battle of Lepanto, was taken captive and spent five years as a slave in Africa. Above all he loved the theatre; in twenty years he wrote some forty plays, none of which were successful. In 1597 he was excommunicated for "offenses against His Majesty's Most Catholic Church," narrowly escaping more drastic punishment. He served at least three, and possibly five terms in prison on various charges. Aging, infirm, an utter failure, he undertook the writing of *Don Quixote* to make money. Volume I, published in 1605 when Cervantes was 58, brought him fame but little profit. Volume II, appearing ten years later, insured his immortality as author of the world's greatest novel, but he was already broken in body if not in spirit. He died in 1616, within ten days of the death of Shakespeare. His burial place is unknown.

Author's Preface

Man of La Mancha was born fortuitously and underwent several metamorphoses before it was exposed to a New York audience. It had its inception in Madrid in 1959 when I read in a newspaper that my purpose in Spain was research for a dramatization of *Don Quixote*. The item was laughing-matter, for like the great majority of people who know *Don Quixote*, I had never read it. Madrid seemed a place appropriate to repair of that omission, however, so I waded in, emerging from Volume Two with the conviction that this monument to human wit and folly could not, and should not, be dramatized.

What *had* snared my interest was not the book but its author. For one learns that the life of Miguel de Cervantes was a catalogue of catastrophe. What sort of man was this—soldier, playwright, actor, tax-collector and frequently jailbird—who could suffer unceasing failure and yet in his declining years produce the staggering testament which is *Don Quixote?* To catch him at the nadir of his career, to persuade him toward self-revelation which might imply something of significance concerning the human spirit—*there*, perhaps, was a play worth writing.

I wrote it first for television in a ninety-minute version. It was produced with considerable éclat and garnered a number of awards but left me profoundly dissatisfied, for the strictures of television and its assertive naturalism had defeated both my design and intentions. I thereupon rewrote it for the Broadway stage and it was promptly optioned. But I felt a sense of relief when the option period ran out without production, for I knew that while it might conceivably have been successful I still should have deemed it a failure. The play had not yet achieved the form which the material demanded: a form disciplined yet free, simple-seeming yet intricate, and above all bold enough to accomplish that ephemeral objective which is called "total theater." My brooding on the matter had brought me to the edge of an inescapable conclusion when Albert Marre (whom I had never met) telephoned to say, "Your play is superb, but it *must* become some sort of a musical."

Precisely.

The adventure began. I use the word advisedly, for the writing of *Man of La Mancha* was an adventure, in form, technique, and in philosophy. My collaborators, Joe Darion, Mitch Leigh, and Albert Marre made enormous contributions as we groped our way toward a kind of theater that was, at least within the boundaries of our experience, without precedent.

It would be heartening to say that the finished play immediately ensnared the interest of producers and backers. It didn't. They regarded it as too radical, too "special" and, most crushing of all, too intellectual. *Man of La Mancha* floundered rather than marched toward production, sustained only by the tenacity of those among us who shared the Quixotic dream.

But there came a night when lights glowed on Howard Bay's island-stage, and the audience responded to the performance with fervor that stunned even the most sanguine of us. It was a phenomenon we were to grow familiar with at each performance: a sort of electricity crackling randomly among the audience for a time, then polarizing toward a massive discharge of emotion. Or as Mr. Marre succinctly put it, "They're not just watching a play, they're having a religious experience."

To me the most interesting aspect of the success of *Man of La Mancha* is the fact that it plows squarely upstream against the prevailing current of philosophy in the theater. That current is best identified by its catch-labels—Theater of the Absurd, Black Comedy, the Theater of Cruelty—which is to say the theater of alienation, of moral anarchy and despair. To the practitioners of those philosophies *Man of La Mancha* must seem hopelessly naïve in its espousal of illusion as man's strongest spiritual need, the most meaningful function of his imagination. But I've no unhappiness about that. "Facts are the enemy of truth," says Cervantes-Don Quixote. And that is precisely what I felt and meant.

If there was a guiding precept for the whole endeavor it lay in a quotation I found long ago in Unamuno: "Only he who attempts the absurd is capable of achieving the impossible." But on the simplest level, and philosophies aside, the play is my way of paying tribute to the tough and tender spirit of Miguel de Cervantes.

Dale Wasserman

Production Notes

Man of La Mancha was first presented by Albert W. Selden and Hal James at the ANTA Washington Square Theatre, New York, on November 22, 1965. The cast was as follows:

Don Quixote (Cervantes), *Richard Kiley*
Sancho (The Manservant), *Irving Jacobson*
Captain of the Inquisition, *Renato Cibelli*
Aldonza, *Joan Diener*
The Innkeeper (The Governor), *Ray Middleton*
Dr. Carrasco (The Duke), *Jon Cypher*
The Padre, *Robert Rounseville*
Antonia, *Mimi Turque*
The Housekeeper, *Eleanore Knapp*
The Barber, *Gino Conforti*

Pedro, Head Muleteer, *Shev Rodgers*
Anselmo, A Muleteer, *Harry Theyard*
Jose, A Muleteer, *Eddie Roll*
Juan, A Muleteer, *John Aristedes*
Paco, A Muleteer, *Antony de Vecchi*
Tenorio, A Muleteer, *Fernando Grahal*
Maria, The Innkeeper's Wife, *Marceline Decker*
Fermina, A Servant Girl, *Gerrianne Raphael*
The Guitarist, *David Serva*
The Horses, *Eddie Rolland, Fernando Grahal*

Guards and Men of the Inquisition, *Ray Dash, Phill Lipman, Dwight Frye, John Rossi* and *Roger Morden*

Book and Musical Staging by *Albert Marre*
Choreography by *Jack Cole*
Settings and Lighting by *Howard Bay*
Costumes by *Howard Bay* and *Patton Campbell*
Musical Direction and Dance Arrangements by *Neil Warner*
Musical Arrangements by *Music Makers, Inc.*

Musical Numbers

Man of La Mancha (I, Don Quixote)	Don Quixote, Sancho and Horses
It's All the Same	Aldonza and Muleteers
Dulcinea	Don Quixote
I'm Only Thinking of Him	Padre, Antonia, Housekeeper, and Dr. Carrasco
I Really Like Him	Sancho
Little Bird, Little Bird	Anselmo and Muleteers
Barber's Song	The Barber
Golden Helmet of Mambrino	Don Quixote, Sancho, Barber and Muleteers
To Each His Dulcinea	The Padre
The Quest (The Impossible Dream)	Don Quixote
The Combat	Don Quixote, Aldonza, Sancho and Muleteers
The Dubbing	Innkeeper, Aldonza, Sancho
The Abduction	Aldonza and Muleteers
Moorish Dance	Ensemble
Aldonza	Aldonza
The Knight of the Mirrors	Ensemble
A Little Gossip	Sancho

Dulcinea (Reprise)	Aldonza
The Quest (Reprise)	Aldonza and Don Quixote
Man of La Mancha (Reprise)	Don Quixote, Aldonza and Sancho
The Psalm	The Padre
The Quest (Reprise)	Company

LOCALE: *Spain at the end of the sixteenth century. A prison in the city of Seville and various places in the imagination of* MIGUEL DE CERVANTES.

SETTING: *The common room of a stone prison vault whose furthest reaches are lost in shadow. It has niches and crannies where the prisoners make their nests. It is below ground, reached by a stairway which may be raised and lowered, drawbridge-style, and is lighted by scant cold rays sifting through a grille overhead. A trap in the floor may be raised to permit access to a level still lower. Stage right there is a fire covered by a grille, and stage left an open well. Other scenic elements are placed and removed by the prisoners as indicated.*

The prison vault is actually a single basic setting within whose architecture the DON QUIXOTE *scenes devised by* CERVANTES *play. In nature it is an abstract platform whose elements are fluid and adaptable. The primary effect is that of improvisation; it must seem as though all scenic, prop and costume items are adapted from materials already on stage, augmented by effects from* CERVANTES' *theatrical trunk.*

Only in the inner play—as devised by CERVANTES—*is there musical style and form. The prison scenes framing the inner play are not "musicalized" in the sense that there is no singing or dancing in these except as may be motivated realistically. The play is performed without intermission.*

There is an overture, then the orchestra is lost to sight as lights fade in on the common room of a prison vault. Some of the PRISONERS *lie huddled in the shadows. One strums a guitar; another dances a jaded, sensual* seguiria gitana *to its rhythm.*

Sound and motion cease as the door at the head of the stairway opens and light streams down into the vault. The stairs are lowered and a little procession descends: first a uniformed CAPTAIN OF THE INQUISITION; *then a* SOLDIER *or two assisting a chubby* MANSERVANT *with a sizable but shabby straw trunk; then* CERVANTES *himself.*

MIGUEL DE CERVANTES *is tall and thin, a man of gentle courtliness leavened by humor. He is in his late forties but his dominant qualities are childlike—ingenuousness, a grave and endless curiosity about human behavior, candor which is very nearly self-destructive. He has, too, the child's delight in play-acting, but since he is in actuality a trained actor, when called upon to perform he translates this delight into stylish verve and gusto. On his entrance he is carrying a wrapped oblong package under one arm. It is heavy.*

CERVANTES' MANSERVANT *is as old or older than his master, short, rotund, suspicious and pragmatic. The relationship between the two is obviously of long standing; indeed, they are rather like husband and wife who bicker yet are deeply devoted.*

Now the SOLDIERS *go back up the stairs.* CERVANTES *peers about, uncertainly.*

CAPTAIN: *(Watching* CERVANTES; *sardonically)* Anything wrong? The accommodations?

CERVANTES: No, no, they appear quite . . . interesting.

CAPTAIN: The cells are below. This is the common room, for those who wait.

CERVANTES: How long do they wait?

CAPTAIN: Some an hour . . . some a lifetime . . .

CERVANTES: Do they all await the Inquisition?

CAPTAIN: Ah, no, these are merely thieves and murderers. *(Starting to leave)* If you need anything, just shout. *(An afterthought)* If you're able.

(He goes and the stairway is withdrawn)

MANSERVANT: *(Apprehensively)* What did he mean by that?

CERVANTES: Calm yourself. There is a remedy for everything but death.

MANSERVANT: That could be the very one we need!

(The PRISONERS *are moving, circling, approaching like animals who scent prey)*

CERVANTES: *(With great courtliness)* Good morning, gentlemen . . . ladies. I regret being thrust upon you in this manner, and hope you will not find my company objectionable. In any case I shall not be among you very long. The Inquisition—

(With a yell, the PRISONERS *attack.* CERVANTES *and the* MANSERVANT *are seized, tripped up, pinned to the floor. The* PRISONERS *are busily rifling their pockets as* THE GOVERNOR, *a big man of obvious authority, awakens from sleep)*

THE GOVERNOR: *(In a roar)* Enough! Noise, trouble, fights . . . kill each other if you must but for God's sake, do it quietly! *(To* CERVANTES*)* Who are you? Eh? Speak up!

CERVANTES: *(Gasping as his throat is freed)* Cervantes. Don Miguel de Cervantes.

THE GOVERNOR: *(With mock respect)* A gentleman!

CERVANTES: *(Painfully getting to his feet)* It has never saved me from going to bed hungry.

THE GOVERNOR: *(Indicating the* MANSERVANT*)* And that?

CERVANTES: My servant. May I have the honor—?

THE GOVERNOR: They call me The Governor. What's your game?

CERVANTES: My game . . . ?

THE GOVERNOR: *(Impatiently)* Your specialty, man. Cut-purse? Highwayman?

CERVANTES: Oh, nothing so interesting! I am a poet.

THE DUKE: *(A prisoner of draggle-tail elegance)* They're putting men in prison for that?

CERVANTES: No, no, not for that.

THE DUKE: *(Sardonically)* Too bad!

THE GOVERNOR: *(Clapping his hands)* Well, let's get on with the trial!

CERVANTES: *(As he is seized by two of the more villainous-looking* PRISONERS*)* Excuse me, sir. What trial?

THE GOVERNOR: Yours, of course.

CERVANTES: But what have I done?

THE GOVERNOR: We'll find something.

CERVANTES: You don't seem to understand. I'll only be here a few—

THE GOVERNOR: *(Patient but firm)* My dear sir, no one enters or leaves this prison without being tried by his fellow prisoners.

CERVANTES: And if I'm found guilty?

THE GOVERNOR: Oh, you will be.

CERVANTES: What sort of a sentence . . . ?

THE GOVERNOR: We generally fine a prisoner all his possessions.

CERVANTES: *(Hard-hit) All* of them . . .

THE GOVERNOR: Well, it's not practical to take more.

CERVANTES: One moment! These things are my livelihood.

THE GOVERNOR: *(Puzzled)* I thought you said you were a poet.

CERVANTES: Of the theater!

THE GOVERNOR: *(Crossing to the trunk, digs out a sword and pulls it from its scabbard)* False!

CERVANTES: Costumes and properties. You see, actually I am a playwright and an actor. So of course these poor things could not possibly be of any use to . . . to . . .

(He comes to a halt, reading the inimical faces. He makes a sudden grab for the sword, but THE GOVERNOR tosses it over his head to another PRISONER. A cruel game ensues, the PRISONERS plundering the contents of the trunk, tossing them about as CERVANTES and the MANSERVANT stumble about, trying vainly to retrieve them)

CERVANTES: *(Panting, realizing the futility)* Very well—take them.

MANSERVANT: Oh, no, Master!

CERVANTES: Take them, take them I say. Only leave me—*(Clutching the package to him)*—this.

(THE DUKE adroitly snatches the package from him, tosses it to THE GOVERNOR, who catches it and weighs it in his hands)

THE GOVERNOR: Heavy! *(Shrewdly)* Valuable?

CERVANTES: To me!

THE GOVERNOR: We might let you ransom it.

CERVANTES: I have no money.

THE GOVERNOR: How unfortunate. *(Tears it open; angrily)* Paper!

CERVANTES: Manuscript!

THE GOVERNOR: Still worthless. *(He strides toward the fire with the intention of throwing the package in)*

CERVANTES: *(Desperately)* Wait! You spoke of a trial. By your own word, I must be given a trial!

THE GOVERNOR: *(Hesitating; then peevishly)* Oh, very well. I hereby declare this court in session! *(CERVANTES and the MANSERVANT are shoved into an improvised dock, and the "court" arranges itself)* Now, then. What are you here for?

CERVANTES: I am to appear before the Inquisition.

(There is a stir among the PRISONERS, one or two of whom cross themselves)

THE GOVERNOR: Heresy?

CERVANTES: Not exactly. You see, I had been employed by the government as a tax-collector . . .

THE GOVERNOR: Poet, actor, *tax-collector?*

CERVANTES: A temporary thing to keep us from starvation.

THE GOVERNOR: How does a tax-collector get in trouble with the Inquisition?

CERVANTES: I made an assessment against the monastery of La Merced. When they wouldn't pay, I issued a lien on the property.

THE GOVERNOR: You did *what?*

MANSERVANT: He foreclosed on a church.

THE GOVERNOR: But why are *you* here?

MANSERVANT: *(Dolefully)* Someone had to serve the papers. *(With his thumb he indicates himself)*

THE GOVERNOR: These two have empty rooms in their heads!

CERVANTES: The law says treat everyone equally. We only obeyed the law!

THE DUKE: Governor, if you don't mind, *I* should like to prosecute this case.

THE GOVERNOR: Why?

THE DUKE: Let us say I dislike stupidity. Especially when it masquerades as virtue. Miguel de Cervantes! I charge you with being an idealist, a bad poet, and an honest man. How plead you?

CERVANTES: *(Considering a moment)* Guilty.

THE GOVERNOR: Bravo! *(He rises, crossing toward the fire once more)*

CERVANTES: Your Excellency! What about my defense?

THE GOVERNOR: *(Pausing; puzzled)* But you just pleaded guilty.

CERVANTES: *(With charm)* Had I said "innocent" you surely would have found me guilty. Since I have admitted guilt, the court is required to hear me out.

THE GOVERNOR: For what purpose?

CERVANTES: The jury may choose to be lenient.

THE GOVERNOR: *(Thinks, then chuckles appreciatively)* Clever!

THE DUKE: He is trying to gain time!

CERVANTES: Do you have a scarcity of *that?*

THE GOVERNOR: *(To the* PRISONERS *)* Any urgent appointments?

(A groan for answer. He waves CERVANTES *to continue)*

CERVANTES: It is true I am guilty of these charges. An idealist? Well, I have never had the courage to believe in nothing. A bad poet? This comes more painfully . . . still . . . *(He makes a wry gesture of acquiescence)*

THE GOVERNOR: *(Skeptically)* Have you finished your defense?

CERVANTES: Ah, no, scarce begun! If you've no objection I should like to continue in the manner I know best . . . in the form of a charade—

THE DUKE: Charade?

CERVANTES: An entertainment, if you will—

THE GOVERNOR: *(Intrigued)* Entertainment!

CERVANTES: At worst it may beguile your time. And since my cast of characters is large, I call upon all here to enter in, to play whatever roles—

THE DUKE: *(Hotly)* Governor! I should like to protest!

THE GOVERNOR: No, no, let's hear him out!

CERVANTES: Then . . . with your kind permission . . . may I set the stage? *(THE GOVERNOR waves assent. The PRISONERS shift position to become audience as CERVANTES gestures to his MANSERVANT, who scurries, like a well-trained stage-manager, to assist. Music begins, softly, as CERVANTES, seated center, begins a makeup transformation as he speaks)* I shall impersonate a man . . . enter into my imagination and see him! His name is Alonso Quijana . . . a country squire, no longer young. Bony and hollow-faced . . . eyes that burn with the fire of inner vision. Being retired, he has much time for books. He studies them from morn to night, and often through the night as well. And all he reads oppresses him . . . fills him with indignation at man's murderous ways toward man. He broods . . . and broods . . . and broods—and finally from so much brooding his brains dry up! He lays down the melancholy burden of sanity and conceives the strangest project ever imagined . . . to become a knight-errant and sally forth into the world to right all wrongs. No longer shall he be plain Alonso

Quijana . . . but a dauntless knight known as—Don Quixote de La Mancha!!!
(The PRISONERS *giggle appreciatively as the transformation of* CERVANTES *into* DON QUIXOTE *takes place before their eyes. The* MANSERVANT, *who will become* SANCHO PANZA, *assists with costume elements, props, and so forth)*

DON QUIXOTE: *(Singing, a little tongue-in-cheek; an actor aware that he's performing)*

> *Hear me now, oh thou bleak and unbearable world!*
> *Thou art base and debauched as can be;*
> *And a knight with his banners all bravely unfurled*
> *Now hurls down his gauntlet to thee!*

> *I am I, Don Quixote,*
> *The Lord of La Mancha,*
> *My destiny calls and I go;*
> *And the wild winds of fortune will carry me onward,*
> *Oh whithersoever they blow.*

> *Whithersoever they blow,*
> *Onward to glory I go!*

SANCHO:

> *I'm Sancho! Yes, I'm Sancho!*
> *I'll follow my master till the end.*
> *I'll tell all the world proudly*
> *I'm his squire! I'm his friend!*

DON QUIXOTE:

> *Hear me, heathens and wizards and serpents of sin!*
> *All your dastardly doings are past;*
> *For a holy endeavor is now to begin,*
> *And virtue shall triumph at last!*

(They mount the "horses"—two dancers with wooden frames attached—and ride away. As they ride, the horses dance a spirited flamenco and DON QUIXOTE *points out to* SANCHO *the sights along the way. They sing together)*

DON QUIXOTE:	SANCHO:
I am I, Don Quixote,	*I'm Sancho! Yes, I'm Sancho!*
The Lord of La Mancha,	*I'll follow my master till the end.*
My destiny calls and I go;	*I'll tell all the world proudly*
And the wild winds of fortune will carry	*I'm his squire!*
me onward,	*I'm his friend!*
Oh whithersoever they blow!	

DON QUIXOTE and SANCHO:

> *Whithersoever they blow,*
> *Onward to glory we go!*

(At the conclusion of the song, they dismount and SANCHO *leads the "horses" to the well to drink)*

DON QUIXOTE: Well, Sancho—how dost thou like adventuring?
SANCHO: Oh, marvelous, Your Grace. But it's peculiar—to me this great high-

way to glory looks exactly like the road to El Toboso where you can buy chickens cheap.

DON QUIXOTE: Like beauty, my friend, 'tis all in the eyes of the beholder. Only wait and thou shalt see amazing sights.

SANCHO: What kind?

DON QUIXOTE: There will be knights and nations, warlocks, wizards . . . a cavalcade of vast, unending armies!

SANCHO: They sound dangerous!

DON QUIXOTE: They *are* dangerous. But one there'll be who leads them . . . and he will be most dangerous of all!

SANCHO: Well, who is he? Who?

DON QUIXOTE: The Great Enchanter. Beware him, Sancho . . . for his thoughts are cold and his spirit shriveled. He has eyes like little machines, and where he walks the earth is blighted. But one day I shall meet him face to face . . . and on that day—! *(He shakes his lance ferociously)*

SANCHO: *(Sensibly)* Well, I wouldn't get upset, Your Grace. As I always say, have patience and shuffle the cards.

DON QUIXOTE: Do you never run out of proverbs?

SANCHO: No, Your Grace. I was born with a bellyful of them. I always say—

DON QUIXOTE: *(Looking off as the projected shadows of a great windmill's sails cross the stage)* Aah-hah!

SANCHO: What is it?

DON QUIXOTE: How long since we sallied forth?

SANCHO: About two minutes?

DON QUIXOTE: So soon shall I engage in brave, unequal combat!

SANCHO: Combat? Where?

DON QUIXOTE: Can'st not see? *(Pointing)* A monstrous giant of infamous repute!

SANCHO: *(Looking vainly; the "horses" are interested, too) What* giant?

DON QUIXOTE:
It is that dark and dreaded ogre
By the name of Matagoger!
You can tell him by the four great arms awhirling on his back!

SANCHO: It's a windmill.

DON QUIXOTE: *(Shouting)*
Ho! Feckless giant standing there!
Avast! Avaunt! On guard! Beware!
(He charges off)

SANCHO: No, no, Your Grace, I swear by my wife's little black mustache, that's not a giant, it's only a—*(Offstage a crash; the horses run for cover. To musical accompaniment the combat continues as SANCHO dances about, dodging first QUIXOTE's helmet which comes flying back onstage, then the butt of his lance, splayed and splintered. The final crash; and QUIXOTE crawls back into view, his sword a corkscrew. A doleful picture, he comes rolling downstage as SANCHO hurries to plump himself down and stop him)* Didn't I tell you? Didn't I say, "Your Grace, that's a windmill"?

DON QUIXOTE: *(Hollowly)* The work of my enemy.

SANCHO: The Enchanter?

DON QUIXOTE: He changed that giant into a windmill at the last moment. He will take any advantage in order to— *(A pause; an illumination)* Sancho, it comes to me!

SANCHO: What, Your Grace?

DON QUIXOTE: How he was able to upset me. It is because I have never properly been dubbed a knight.

SANCHO: That's no problem. Just tell me how it's done and I'll be glad to take care of this drubbing.

DON QUIXOTE: Dubbing. Thank you, my friend, but it may only be done by another knight.

SANCHO: *(Dismayed)* That's a problem. I've never *seen* another knight.

DON QUIXOTE: The lord of some castle would do. Or a king or a duke.

SANCHO: *(Helping QUIXOTE to his feet)* Very well. I'll keep an eye out for any kings or dukes as we go.

DON QUIXOTE: *(Looking off)* Ahaaa!

SANCHO: *(Apprehensively)* Now what?

DON QUIXOTE: The very place!

SANCHO: Where?

DON QUIXOTE: There!

SANCHO: If Your Grace would just give me a hint . . . ?

DON QUIXOTE: There in the distance. A castle!

SANCHO: *(Peering vainly)* Castle.

DON QUIXOTE: Rockbound amidst the crags!

SANCHO: Crags.

DON QUIXOTE: And the banners—ah, the brave banners flaunting in the wind!

SANCHO: Anything on 'em?

DON QUIXOTE: *(Shielding his eyes)* I see a cat crouching on a field tawny . . . and beneath it the inscription "Miau"!

SANCHO: Oh, that's fine, Your Grace. Maybe this is where you can get yourself drubbed.

DON QUIXOTE: Dubbed. *(Excitedly)* Blow thy bugle that a dwarf may mount the battlements and announce our coming!

SANCHO: *(Under the spell, lifts his bugle then hesitates)* But I don't *see* a castle. I do see something . . . maybe it's an inn.

DON QUIXOTE: *(Sadly)* An inn.

SANCHO: We'd better pass it by, Your Grace. Those roadside places are full of rough men and women.

DON QUIXOTE: Come. We shall ride straight to the drawbridge of yon castle, and there thy vision may improve!

(The lights fade to transition lighting as QUIXOTE *and* SANCHO *drop out of character.*

CERVANTES *beckons to the* PRISONERS *who will become* MULETEERS *in the next scene; they and the* SERVANT *proceed to set up the Great Room of an inn as he speaks)*

CERVANTES: Here is an example of how to the untrained eye one thing may seem to be another. To Sancho, an inn. To Quixote, a castle. To someone else, whatever his mind may make of it. But for the sake of argument, let us grant Sancho *his* vision. An inn . . . *(He gestures to* THE GOVERNOR—*then to a lady prisoner)* A kindly innkeeper . . . his less kindly wife . . . *(He picks out some of the other* PRISONERS*)* Rough men—muleteers—fifteen miles on the road today. Rough women—in most particular a woman called—Aldonza!

MULETEERS: *(Making a chant of her name, banging their tin dishes on the table)* Aldonza, Aldonza, Aldonza!

(A pan comes sailing in; the men dodge it to prevent being hit. ALDONZA enters; a savage, dark alley-cat, survivor if not always victor of many back-fence tussles)

ALDONZA: *(With a pot of stew in her hands; roughly)* You want it on the table or over your lousy heads?

(The MULETEERS laugh. She sets down the tureen with a crash, and spits into it)

ALDONZA: There, swine. Feed!

(She starts to distribute goatskins of wine. The MULETEERS, of whom there are seven, are variously called JOSE, TENORIO, PACO, JUAN, ANSELMO and PEDRO. The seventh, nameless, is the prisoner with the guitar. JOSE is the runt of the gang; PEDRO, the biggest, is its leader)

JOSE: *(Amorously)* I brought you something.

ALDONZA: Keep it till it grows up. *(PACO whispers in her ear)* Little dogs have big ideas!

JUAN: Tonight?

ALDONZA: Payment in advance?

(He gets on his knees wanting her to pour the wine into his mouth; she pours it onto his head)

PEDRO: *(Laughing)* Aldonza! Sweetheart. Come here.

ALDONZA: Talk with your mouth, not your hands!

PEDRO: *(Pulling her close; confidentially)* I've got a nice thick bed of hay in the stable.

ALDONZA: *(As confidentially)* Good. Eat it.

PEDRO: You would refuse Pedro?

ALDONZA: Try me. *(She walks away from him)*

PEDRO: My *mules* are not as stubborn! *(He snaps his whip at her)*

ALDONZA: Fine! Make love to your mules! *(The MULETEERS laugh, then sing)*

MULETEERS:
> *I come for love,*
> *I come for love,*
> *I come to Aldonza for love!*

ALDONZA: *(Contemptuously)* Love! *(She sings)*
> *One pair of arms is like another,*
> *I don't know why or who's to blame,*
> *I'll go with you or with your brother,*
> *It's all the same, it's all the same!*
>
> *This I have learned: that when the light's out,*
> *No man will burn with special flame,*
> *You'll prove to me, before the night's out,*
> *You're all the same, you're all the same!*
>
> *So do not talk to me of love,*
> *I'm not a fool with starry eyes,*
> *Just put your money in my hand,*
> *And you will get what money buys!*

One pair of arms is like another,
I don't know why or who's to blame,
I'll go with you or with your brother,
It's all the same, it's all the same!

(The MULETEERS *reach for her, roughly; she pushes them off)*

Oh, I have seen too many beds,
But I have known too little rest,
And I have loved too many men
With hatred burning in my breast.

I do not like you or your brother,
I do not like the life I live,
But I am me, I am Aldonza,
And what I give I choose to give!

*(*PEDRO *offers money to* ALDONZA, *throws it on the floor. She spits on it and backs away, luring him. He follows and presses the money into her hand)*

One pair of arms . . . is like another
It's all the same, it's all the same!

(She exits)

ANSELMO: *(Laughing)* Payment before delivery!

PACO: She won't deliver.

PEDRO: She'll deliver!

(The INNKEEPER *enters with his wife,* MARIA, *and another serving-girl,* FERMINA*)*

INNKEEPER: Well gentlemen, everything in order?

(He surveys the interior of his inn which is somewhat the worse for wear after the violence of the preceding number. MARIA *and* FERMINA *begin to clean up)*

ANSELMO: Did you feed the mules?

INNKEEPER: They're eating as well as you.

PEDRO: God forbid!

INNKEEPER: He jokes! It's well known that I set the finest table between Madrid
    and Malaga. My patrons have always—
    (From offstage there comes the blast of a bugle horribly blown)

PEDRO: What in the name of—?
    (The bugle sounds again)

INNKEEPER: *(His face lighting up)* The pig-butcher! I didn't expect him till tomor-
    row. *(Hurrying to the door)* Coming, Señor Butcher, coming!
    (He stops short as DON QUIXOTE *and* SANCHO *enter.* QUIXOTE *has replaced his lance with the limb of a tree)*

DON QUIXOTE: *(Haughtily)* Is the lord of the castle at hand? *(No reply from the flabbergasted* INNKEEPER*)* I say, is the Castellano here?

INNKEEPER: *(With an effort)* I am in charge of this place.

DON QUIXOTE: *(Coldly)* We waited, sire, for a dwarf to mount the battlements
    and announce us, but none appeared.

INNKEEPER: The . . . the dwarfs are all busy.
    *(*QUIXOTE *makes a haughty signal to* SANCHO, *who delivers himself of a re-hearsed speech)*

SANCHO: Noble lords and ladies. My master, Don Quixote, knight-errant and defender of the right and pursuer of lofty undertakings, implores the boon of hospitality!

(The INNKEEPER *looks open-mouthed at the* MULETEERS, *who look back in kind)*

DON QUIXOTE: Well, sir? Is it granted?

INNKEEPER: *(Pulling himself together)* Absolutely! This inn—I mean, this castle—is open to everybody.

MARIA: *(To the* INNKEEPER, frightened*)* A madman!

INNKEEPER: *(Aside, to* MARIA*)* Madmen are the children of God. *(To* QUIXOTE*)* Sir knight, you must be hungry.

DON QUIXOTE: Aye, that I am.

INNKEEPER: There's food aplenty, and for your squire, too. I'll just help him stable your animals.

(He motions to SANCHO *to follow, and they exit)*

DON QUIXOTE: *(Approaching the others)* Gentle knights! Fair chatelaine! If there be any among you that require assistance, you have but to speak and my good right arm is at your service. Whether it be a princess held for ransom, an army besieged and awaiting rescue, or merely ... *(*ALDONZA *has emerged laden with things for the table. She stops, puzzled at the silence.* DON QUIXOTE *is gazing at her, stricken)* Dear God . . . it is she! *(*ALDONZA *stares. He averts his eyes worshipfully)* Sweet lady . . . fair virgin . . . I dare not gaze full upon thy countenance lest I be blinded by beauty. But I implore thee—speak once thy name.

ALDONZA: *(A growl)* Aldonza.

DON QUIXOTE: My lady jests.

ALDONZA: Aldonza!

DON QUIXOTE: *(Approaching her)* The name of a kitchenscullion ... or mayhap my lady's serving-maid?

ALDONZA: I told you my name! Now get out of the way, or I'll—

DON QUIXOTE: *(Smiling)* Did my lady think to put me to a test? Ah, sweet sovereign of my captive heart, I shall not fail thee, for I *know*. *(Singing)*

I have dreamed thee too long,
Never seen thee or touched thee, but known thee with all of my heart,
Half a prayer, half a song,
Thou hast always been with me, though we have been always apart.

Dulcinea . . . Dulcinea . . .
I see heaven when I see thee, Dulcinea,
And thy name is like a prayer an angel whispers . . .
Dulcinea . . . Dulcinea!

If I reach out to thee,
Do not tremble and shrink from the touch of my hand on they hair.
Let my fingers but see
Thou art warm and alive, and no phantom to fade in the air.

Dulcinea . . . Dulcinea . . .
I have sought thee, sung thee, dreamed thee, Dulcinea!
Now I've found thee, and the world shall know thy glory.
Dulcinea . . . Dulcinea!

INNKEEPER: *(Entering; to* QUIXOTE*)* Come along, Señor Knight! I'll show you to your quarters.
(He maneuvers QUIXOTE *offstage)*
MARIA: *(Mocking, to* ALDONZA*)* Ay, Dulcinea!
(The MULETEERS *launch into an elaborate parody of the song)*

MULETEERS: *(Singing)*
Dulcinea . . . Dulcinea . . .
I see heaven when I see thee, Dulcinea.

ANSELMO:
And thy name is like a prayer an angel whispers . . .
Dulcinea . . . Dulcinea . . .

MULETEERS:
Dulcinea . . . Dulcinea . . .
I have sought thee, sung thee, dreamed thee, Dulcinea!
Now I've found thee, and the world shall know thy glory,
Dulcinea . . . Dulcinea!

(By the end ALDONZA *has driven them about the stage, belaboring them in fury —as the lighting changes back to the prison.* THE DUKE *is in the center of the arena, shouting the others down)*
THE DUKE: Governor! Governor! If you don't mind—this man proposed to offer a defense!
CERVANTES: This *is* my defense.
TI IE DUKE: The most curious I've ever heard!
CERVANTES: But if it entertains . . . ?
THE DUKE: *(Waspishly)* The word is "diverts." I think *your* purpose is to divert us from *ours.*
CERVANTES: *(Cheerfully)* Precisely! And now if I may get on with it . . . ?
THE GOVERNOR: Continue your defense!
(CERVANTES, again the scene-master, selects people and arranges the next sequence as he speaks)
CERVANTES: Imagine now the family our brave knight left behind! Not the lords and ladies and retainers of Don Quixote de La Mancha, but the simple womenfolk of a country squire known as Alonso Quijana. *(A musical underscore begins as he beckons to three of the* PRISONERS, *handing them costumes)* Imagine their shock as news of the master's madness reaches them! To his niece, Antonia— who is worried about its effect on her forthcoming marriage. To his housekeeper of many years—who is worried about even darker matters. To the local Padre who has known Alonso all of his life. *(To* THE DUKE*)* And shortly there will enter a character whose philosophy may appeal—enormously—to you! *(He slings a costume to* THE DUKE*)* Alonso's niece and his housekeeper hurry to the neighborhood church. *(To his* MANSERVANT*)* May we have a church, please? Anguished by this terrible situation—and not unaware of what the neighbors may think—they seek help and advice from the Padre. *(The* PRISONER *selected for the* PADRE, *now costumed, giggles with delight in his role.* CERVANTES *wipes the smile from his face, adjusts his posture)* The Padre. *(The* PRISONER *composes himself instantly, walks into the scene. Setting and lighting have changed; we are now in a simple country church. There are confes-*

sional screens left and right. The PADRE *is between, listening alternately to the plaints of the two women beyond their respective screens where* CERVANTES *has positioned them, puppet-like)* But in spite of the trouble which the Squire's madness may bring down upon *their* heads, you may be sure they are only thinking of him!

(He snaps his fingers, and the people come to life, singing)

ANTONIA:
I'm only thinking of him,
I'm only thinking of him,
Whatever I may do or say,
I'm only thinking of him!
In my body, it's well known,
There is not one selfish bone—
I'm only thinking and worrying about him!

I've been told he's chasing dragons and I fear it may be true.
If my groom should hear about it, heaven knows what he will do!
Oh, I dearly love my uncle but for what he's done to me
I would like to take and lock him up and throw away the key!
But if I do . . .
But if I do . . .
There is one thing that I swear will still be true . . .

ANTONIA and HOUSEKEEPER:	PADRE:
I'm only thinking of him;	*I know, I know, my dear,*
I'm only thinking of him;	*Of course you are, my dear;*
I'm only thinking and worrying about him.	*I understand.*

HOUSEKEEPER:
Oh, I think he's been too lonely, living years without a spouse,
So when he returns I fear I may have trouble in the house;
For they say he seeks a lady, who his own true love shall be;
God forbid that in his madness he should ever think it's me!

(The PADRE *steals a look around the screen at her, incredulously)*

If he should try
I'll surely die,
And I will grimly guard my honor as I cry—

HOUSEKEEPER:	PADRE:	ANTONIA: *(Her wail continues throughout)*
I'm only thinking of him,	*I know, I know, my dear;*	*Woe, woe, woe . . .*
I'm only thinking of him,	*Of course you are, my dear;*	
I'm only thinking and worrying about him.	*I understand.*	

HOUSEKEEPER:
Woe!

(Her wail makes the PADRE *wince and recoil toward* ANTONIA*)*

ANTONIA:
Woe!

(The PADRE *winces and recoils in the other direction)*

PADRE: *(Slipping to his knees; addressing God)*	HOUSEKEEPER:	ANTONIA:
They're only thinking of him,	*Woe, woe . . .*	*Woe, woe . . .*
They're only thinking of him,		
How saintly is their plaintive plea—		
They're only thinking of him!		
What a comfort, to be sure		
That their motives are so pure—		
As they go thinking and worrying about him!		

(CERVANTES appears in the lights, ushering forward THE DUKE, *now dressed in academic cap and gown)*

CERVANTES: And now there appears on the scene a man of breeding . . . intelligence . . . logic. He is Antonia's fiancé, Doctor Sansón Carrasco—Bachelor of Science—graduate of the University of Salamanca! *(Drily)* A man who carries his own self-importance as though afraid of breaking it. *(Places* CARRASCO *in one corner of the stage. The quartet immediately starts arguing.* CERVANTES *claps his hands for silence)* I had forgotten that family quarrels have a way of getting out of hand. With so much at stake in the game, let us rearrange the pieces! *(Moving* ANTONIA *to a second corner)* The queen—cunning! *(Moving the* HOUSEKEEPER *to a third corner)* The castle—formidable! *(Moving the* PADRE *to the fourth corner)* The bishop—charmingly diagonal! *(Sitting center)* And now —the problem of the knight!

ANTONIA: Sansón!

PADRE: Have you heard?

DR. CARRASCO: On my way here I was informed by at least ten people. *(To* ANTONIA*)* My dear, your uncle is the laughingstock of the entire neighborhood. Padre? What do you know of this?

PADRE: Only that the good Señor Quijana has been carried away by his imagination.

DR. CARRASCO: Señor Quijana has lost his mind and is suffering from delusions.

PADRE: Is there a difference?

DR. CARRASCO: Exactitude of meaning. I beg to remind you, Padre, that I am a doctor.

ANTONIA: Please don't argue, we must *do* something about him!

DR. CARRASCO: I'm a little more concerned about *us*.

ANTONIA: What do you mean, us?

DR. CARRASCO: Our marriage, my dear. There is a certain embarrassment at having a madman in the family. In the eyes of others—

PADRE: *(Alarmed at this drift)* Oh, come, come, Doctor.

DR. CARRASCO: I do not relish claiming a lunatic as uncle!

HOUSEKEEPER: *(Nodding, a sibyl)* The innocent must pay for the sins of the guilty.

PADRE: Guilty of what? A gentle delusion!

DR. CARRASCO: How do you know it is gentle? By this time who knows what violence he has committed! He was armed?

HOUSEKEEPER: With sword and lance.

(CARRASCO throws up his hands)

ANTONIA: *(Voice forlorn, wistful)* Sansón. I had hoped for so much for us. For *you*, really. Everything was to be for you. My uncle's house . . . his lands . . .

PADRE: *(The devil's advocate)* True, Doctor. In time they would all be yours. After all, if one is to serve science, one must have the means.

DR. CARRASCO: *(Outraged)* Are you priest or pawnbroker?

PADRE: *(Swiftly revising his approach)* What I meant was—consider the challenge.

DR. CARRASCO: Challenge?

PADRE: Think what cleverness it would take to wean this man from madness. To turn him from his course and persuade him to return home.

(CERVANTES rises: clever approach)

DR. CARRASCO: *(Pondering)* Hmmm . . . that *is* a challenge.

PADRE: Impossible.

DR. CARRASCO: He can't have gotten far?

PADRE: No more than a day's journey!

DR. CARRASCO: Get ready, Padre. We shall go after him. *(As they prepare to leave, the DOCTOR sings)*

> But as we go . . .
> But as we go . . .
> There is one thing that I want the world to know!

PADRE: *(Singing, aside)*
> I feel, with pain,
> That once again,
> We now will bear a very often heard refrain.
> *(They sing in chorus)*

DR. CARRASCO:
> I'm only thinking of him—

PADRE:
> He's only thinking of him,

ANTONIA and HOUSEKEEPER:
> You're only thinking of him—

> He's only thinking of him, just him.

ANTONIA, HOUSEKEEPER and DR. CARRASCO:
> Whatever we may do or say,
> We're only thinking of him.

> In our bodies it's well known
> There is not one selfish bone . . .

ANTONIA, HOUSEKEEPER and DR. CARRASCO:
We're only thinking and worrying about him!

PADRE:
They're only thinking and worrying about him!

(Lights dim out on them as CERVANTES, isolated in his own light, steps forward)

CERVANTES: Let us return now to the inn. To the *kitchen* of the inn. A kitchen, ladies, if you please? Thank you. *(Taking the pots, sniffing as he places them)* Ah yes, tomorrow's onion stew. Chicken tripes, with . . . pepper. Now then! As everyone knows, it is imperative that each knight shall have a lady—for a knight without a lady is like a body without a soul. To whom would he dedicate his conquests? What vision sustain him when he sallies forth to do battle with ogres and with giants? *(He points to the stage area where lights come up on ALDONZA, seated in what is now the kitchen, gobbling her supper. SANCHO is seen approaching. CERVANTES hands him a sheet of paper)* Don Quixote, having discovered his lady, sends his faithful squire to her with a missive.

(The transition is complete; CERVANTES exits)

ALDONZA: *(To SANCHO, suspiciously)* Missive? What's a missive?

SANCHO: A sort of a letter. He warned me to give it only into your hand.

ALDONZA: *(Darkly)* Let's see it. *(She takes the rolled sheet from SANCHO, inspects both sides. Sullenly)* I can't read.

SANCHO: Neither can I. But my master, foreseeing such a possibility, recited it to me so I could commit it to heart.

ALDONZA: *(Angrily)* What made him think I couldn't read?

SANCHO: Well, as he explained it, noblewomen are so busy with their needle-work—

ALDONZA: *Needlework?*

SANCHO: Embroidering banners for their knights. He said they had no time for study.

ALDONZA: *(Contemptuously)* What's it say?

(SANCHO takes the letter from her, holds it before him, and closes his eyes. Music: the quotations from the letter are sung. All other lines are spoken)

SANCHO:
"Most lovely sovereign and highborn lady—"

ALDONZA: *(Continuing to gobble her supper)* Ho.

SANCHO:
"The heart of this, thy vassal knight, faints for thy favor."

ALDONZA: Ha.

SANCHO:
"Oh, fairest of the fair, purest of the pure; Incomparable Dulcinea—"

ALDONZA: *That* again. My name is Aldonza!

SANCHO: *(Patiently)* My master calls you Dulcinea.

ALDONZA: *(Glowering)* Why?

SANCHO: I don't know, but I can tell you from experience that knights have their own language for everything, and it's better not to ask questions because it only gets you into trouble. *(ALDONZA makes a contemptuous gesture for him to continue)*

"I beg thee grant that I may kiss the nethermost hem of thy garment—"

ALDONZA: Kiss my *which?*

SANCHO: If you keep interrupting, the whole thing will be gone out of my head!

ALDONZA: Well, what's he *want?*

SANCHO: I'm getting to it!

"*—And send to me a token of thy fair esteem that I may carry as my standard into battle.*"

ALDONZA: What kind of a token?

SANCHO: He says generally it's a silken scarf.

ALDONZA: Your master's a crackbrain!

SANCHO: Oh, no!

ALDONZA: *(Mimicking)* Oh, yes!

SANCHO: Well, they say one madman makes a hundred and love makes a thousand.

ALDONZA: What's that mean?

SANCHO: I'm not sure.

ALDONZA: You're crazy, too! *(A pause)* Well, what are you waiting for?

SANCHO: *(Patiently)* The token.

ALDONZA: I'll give him a token. Here! *(She flings him the filthy, tattered dishcloth she has been using)*

SANCHO: *(Examining it in dismay)* But my lady—

ALDONZA: Don't you "my lady" me too or I'll crack you like an egg! *(SANCHO retreats)* Wait a minute. Come here. Sit. *Sit! (She pats the stool and* SANCHO *sits, she beside him on the floor)* Tell me—why do you follow him?

SANCHO: Well, that's easy to explain, I . . . I . . . *(The reason seems to elude him)*

ALDONZA: Why?

SANCHO: I'm *telling* you. It's because . . . because . . .

ALDONZA: *Why?*

SANCHO: *(Giving up; simply, he sings)*
I like him.
I really like him.
Tear out my fingernails one by one, I like him!

I don't have
A very good reason.
Since I've been with him cuckoonuts have been in season—

But there's nothing I can do,
Chop me up for onion stew,
Still I'll yell to the sky,
Though I can't tell you why,
That I like him!

ALDONZA: It doesn't make any sense!

SANCHO: That's because you're not a squire.

ALDONZA: All right, you're a squire. How does a squire squire?

SANCHO: Well, I ride behind him . . . and he fights. Then I pick him up off the ground . . .

ALDONZA: But what do *you* get out of it?

SANCHO: What do *I* get? Plenty! Why, already I've gotten . . .

ALDONZA: You've gotten nothing! So why do you *do* it?

SANCHO: *(Sings)*
> *I like him.*
> *I really like him.*
> *Pluck me naked as a scalded chicken, I like him!*

> *Don't ask me*
> *For why or wherefore,*
> *'Cause I don't have a single good "Because" or "Therefore."*

> *You can barbecue my nose,*
> *Make a giblet of my toes,*
> *Make me freeze, make me fry,*
> *Make me sigh, make me cry,*
> *Still I'll yell to the sky*
> *Though I can't tell you why,*
> *That I . . . like . . . him!*

(He exits, in his own kind of dignity, leaving ALDONZA puzzled and less sure.
A cross-dim in the lighting, out on the kitchen; up the well stage left where CER-VANTES is entering with the MULETEERS, prompting them in the next song they are to sing. Night lighting; the mood lyric, sentimental. Satisfied that they are singing it properly, CERVANTES exits, and the MULETEERS, lounging about the coping of the well, swell into full harmony to the guitarist's accompaniment)

MULETEERS: *(During this, ALDONZA picks up a bucket and crosses the courtyard to the well. Lights will fade out in the kitchen. As ALDONZA approaches, the lines sung by the MULETEERS have focused upon her with mocking, though light-hearted double-entendre. She pushes one or two of them out of the way in order to get to the well. They sing the last lines of the song to her legs)*

> *Little bird, little bird,*
> *In the cinnamon tree,*
> *Little bird, little bird,*
> *Do you sing for me?*

> *Do you bring me word*
> *Of one I know?*
> *Little bird, little bird, I love her so,*
> *Little bird, little bird, I have to know,*
> *Little bird, little bird.*

> *Beneath this tree, this cinnamon tree,*
> *We learned to love, we learned to cry;*
> *For here we met and here we kissed,*
> *And here one cold and moonless night we said goodbye.*

> *Little bird, little bird,*
> *Oh have pity on me,*
> *Bring her back to me now*
> *'Neath the cinnamon tree.*

> *I have waited too long*
> *Without a song . . .*
> *Little bird, little bird, please fly, please go,*

Little bird, little bird, and tell her so,
Little bird, little bird!

ALDONZA: *(Dispassionately)* I spit in the milk of your "little bird."
(She bends over to fill the bucket from the well. PEDRO *spies the letter)*
PEDRO: Here, what's this? *(He snatches it)*
ALDONZA: Give it back!
PEDRO: *(Fending her off)* It's a letter.
ALDONZA: That shows how stupid you are; it's a missive!
PEDRO: *Missive? (Holding it up)* Who reads?
*(*ANSELMO *holds up a hand.* PEDRO *tosses him the letter.* ALDONZA *would try to retrieve it but is held by* PEDRO *and another of the* MULETEERS)*
PEDRO: *(Reprovingly, closing her mouth with a hand)* Sh-h-h!
ALDONZA: Sons of whores! *(She bites him)*
ANSELMO: *(Haltingly, mispronouncing words)* "Most lovely sovereign and high-born lady—!" It's from her knight. A love letter!
ALDONZA: A stupid joke!
TENORIO: Then why so hot about it?
PEDRO: Has he touched your heart?
ALDONZA: Nobody touches *my* heart.
ANSELMO: All these fine words . . . !
ALDONZA: *(Snatching back the letter)* Fine words. He's a man, isn't he? All right, he wants what every other man wants.
(She picks up her bucket of water and starts off. PEDRO *stops her)*
PEDRO: Hey, Aldonza . . . now?
ALDONZA: *(Sullenly)* Later . . . when I'm through in the kitchen.
(She exits. The MULETEERS *continue singing softly as the* PADRE *and* DR. CAR-RASCO *enter.* FERMINA *enters and crosses to them. They indicate in pantomime that she bring* DON QUIXOTE *to them. She exits)*
PADRE: I confess I shall not know what to say to him.
DR. CARRASCO: In that case, leave it to me.
PADRE: He may not even know us!
DR. CARRASCO: I am prepared for that contingency. Should he fail to recognize us . . . *(He is interrupted)*
DON QUIXOTE: *(From offstage; he enters during the course of his speech)* Who is it crieth help of Don Quixote de La Mancha? Is there a castle beleaguered by giants? A king who lies under enchantment? An army besieged and awaiting rescue? *(Surprised, he advances toward them)* Why, what is this? *(With cordial welcome)* My friends!
DR. CARRASCO: *(Taken aback)* You know us?
DON QUIXOTE: *(Equally puzzled)* Should a man not know his friends, Dr. Carrasco? *(With great warmth, taking his hand)*—Padre Perez!
PADRE: *(In deep relief)* Ah, Señor Quijana—
DON QUIXOTE: *(In cool reproof)* I should prefer that you address me properly. I am Don Quixote, knight-errant of La Mancha.
(The PADRE *quails and sinks to a seat)*
DR. CARRASCO: Señor Quijana—
DON QUIXOTE: Don Quixote.
DR. CARRASCO: There are no giants. No kings under enchantment. No

chivalry. No knights. There have been no knights for three hundred years.

DON QUIXOTE: *(To the* PADRE, *pityingly)* So learned, yet so misinformed.

DR. CARRASCO: These are *facts*.

DON QUIXOTE: Facts are the enemy of truth.

SANCHO: *(Entering)* Your Grace—

DON QUIXOTE: *(Eagerly)* Well? Did she receive thee? *(SANCHO nods)* Ah, most fortunate of squires! The token. What of the token? *(SANCHO proffers the ragged dishcloth.* QUIXOTE *takes it with reverence)* Sheer gossamer. *(Turning away)* Forgive me. I am overcome.

SANCHO: *(To the* PADRE *and* CARRASCO, *confidentially)* It's from his lady.

DR. CARRASCO: *(Pouncing)* So there's a woman!

DON QUIXOTE: A *lady!* *(Softening)* The lady Dulcinea. Her beauty is more than human. Her quality? Perfection. She is the very meaning of woman . . . and all meaning woman has to man.

PADRE: *(With a sad smile)* To each his Dulcinea.

(A happy caroling is heard from someone approaching the inn)

DON QUIXOTE: *(Hearing and turning)* Someone approaches . . . !

SANCHO: It's just an ordinary traveler.

DON QUIXOTE: But see what he wears upon his head! Get thee to a place of hiding, Sancho.

SANCHO: *(Apprehensively)* Oh, dear!

(He hides as QUIXOTE *too conceals himself to one side)*

BARBER: *(Singing offstage)*
Oh, I am a little barber
And I go my merry way,
With my razor and my leeches
I can always earn my pay.

Though your chin be smooth as satin,
You will need me soon I know,
For the Lord protects His barbers,
And He makes the stubble grow.

BARBER: *(Enters. He carries a bundle of equipment, and on his head is wearing a brass shaving basin. He sings to the* MULETEERS)

If I slip when I am shaving you
And cut you to the quick,
You can use me as a doctor,
'Cause I also heal the sick.

(QUIXOTE comes up behind him and prods him with his sword. The BARBER turns, unbelieving)

By the beard of St. Anthony—I could swear I see before me a knight in full armor! *(He chuckles)* Ridiculous. There aren't any knights. *(QUIXOTE roars, raising his sword. The BARBER falls to his knees)* I was wrong! Forgive me, Your Highness, I thought I'd been touched by the sun!

DON QUIXOTE: Thou wilt be touched by worse if thou dost not speedily hand over that Golden Helmet!

BARBER: Golden helmet? What? Where? *(Takes the basin off, examines it)* Why, this is nothing but a shaving basin!

DON QUIXOTE: *(With fine contempt)* Shaving basin.

SANCHO: *(Examining it)* I must say, Your Grace, it *does* look like a shaving basin.

BARBER: *(Eagerly)* Of course! You see, I am a barber. A barber? I ply my trade from village to village, and I was wearing this on my head to ward off the rays of the sun, so that's how Your Highship made the mistake of—

DON QUIXOTE: *Silence!* *(The* BARBER *flinches and is silent. Impressively, to* CARRASCO *and the* PADRE*)* Know thou what that really is? The Golden Helmet of Mambrino! When worn by one of noble heart it renders him invulnerable to all wounds! *(To the* BARBER*)* Misbegotten knave—where didst thou steal it?

BARBER: I didn't steal it!

DON QUIXOTE: Hand it over.

BARBER: But it cost me half a crown!

DON QUIXOTE: Hand it over or I shall—!

(He takes a mighty swipe with his sword. The BARBER *yelps and tumbles out of the way, abandoning the basin which* SANCHO *catches)*

SANCHO: *(With satisfaction)* It *is* worth half a crown.

DON QUIXOTE: Fool! *(His face lights up; he tosses away his old casque, handling the basin with reverence and pleasure. He sings)*

Thou Golden Helmet of Mambrino,
With so illustrious a past,
Too long hast thou been lost to glory,
Th'art rediscovered now at last!

Golden Helmet of Mambrino,
There can be no
Hat like thee!

Thee and I, now,
'Ere I die, now,
Will make golden
History!

BARBER:
I can hear the cuckoo singing in the cuckooberry tree . . .

SANCHO:
If he says that that's a helmet, I suggest that you agree . . .

BARBER:
But he'll find it is not gold and will not make him bold and brave . . .

SANCHO:
Well, at least he'll find it useful if he ever needs a shave!

*(*SANCHO *and the* BARBER *move toward* QUIXOTE *who has indicated that the* PADRE *should "crown" him with the golden helmet as he kneels. Just as* QUIXOTE *is about to be crowned, he remembers the token, takes it from inside his tunic and hands it to* SANCHO *indicating that it be attached to the helmet before the crowning is completed.* SANCHO *does so, handing the helmet back to*

the PADRE *who completes the coronation. All this has happened to the amaze-*
ment of the MULETEERS, *the utter disbelief of the* BARBER, *and the worshipful*
attendance of SANCHO)

DON QUIXOTE:
Thou Golden Helmet of Mambrino,
Thy deeds the world will not forget;
Now Don Quixote de La Mancha
Will bring thee greater glory yet!

Golden—

DON QUIXOTE:	THE OTHERS:
—Helmet of Mambrino	*—Helmet of Mambrino,*
There can be no	*There can be no*
Hat like thee!	*Hat like thee!*
Thee and I, now,	*Thee and he now,*
'Ere I die now	*We can see, now*
Will make golden	*Will make golden*
History!	*History!*

(SANCHO *slowly drags the astounded* BARBER *off and away from* QUIXOTE,
as the MULETEERS, *one of them sobbing uncontrollably at the amazing sight, drift*
off. The PADRE *and* DR. CARRASCO, *apparently giving up their mission, also*
leave. Lights dim down and the INNKEEPER *enters)*

INNKEEPER: *(Surprised to find* QUIXOTE *alone)* Your friends have departed?

DON QUIXOTE: *(Turning on his knees)* Sir Castellano—I would make a confession.

INNKEEPER: To me?

DON QUIXOTE: I would confess that I have never actually been dubbed a knight.

INNKEEPER: Oh. That's bad!

DON QUIXOTE: And yet I am well qualified, my lord. I am brave, courteous, bold,
   generous, affable and patient.

INNKEEPER: *(Judiciously)* Yes . . . that's the list.

DON QUIXOTE: Therefore I would beg a boon of thee.

INNKEEPER: Anything! Within reason.

DON QUIXOTE: Tonight I would hold vigil in the chapel of thy castle, and at
   dawn receive from thy hand the ennobling stroke of knighthood.

INNKEEPER: Hmm. There's one small difficulty. No chapel.

DON QUIXOTE: What?

INNKEEPER: *(Hastily)* That is—it's being repaired. But if you wouldn't mind
   holding your vigil someplace else . . . ?

DON QUIXOTE: *(A happy thought)* Here in the courtyard. Under the stars . . . !

INNKEEPER: Fine! At sunrise you'll be dubbed a knight.

DON QUIXOTE: I thank thee.

INNKEEPER: *Now* will you have some supper?

DON QUIXOTE: Supper? Before a vigil? Nay, my lord, on this night I must fast
   and compose my spirit.

   (He and the INNKEEPER *exit separately as the lights pick up the* PADRE *and*
CARRASCO)

PADRE: There is either the wisest madman or the maddest wise man in the world.

DR. CARRASCO: He is mad.

PADRE: Well . . . in any case we have failed.

DR. CARRASCO: *(Tightly)* Not necessarily. We know the sickness. Now to find the cure. *(He exits)*

PADRE: *(Reflecting for a moment)* The cure. May it be not worse than the disease. *(Music: as he sings we will see* QUIXOTE *in half-light reverentially affixing the token to his helmet; and in half-light also,* ALDONZA *in the kitchen studying with mixed emotions the missive which she cannot read)*

To each his Dulcinea,
That he alone can name . . .
To each a secret hiding place
Where he can find the haunting face
To light his secret flame.

For with his Dulcinea
Beside him so to stand,
A man can do quite anything,
Outfly the bird upon the wing,
Hold moonlight in his hand.

Yet if you build your life on dreams
It's prudent to recall,
A man with moonlight in his hand
Has nothing there at all.

There is no Dulcinea,
She's made of flame and air,
And yet how lovely life would seem
If every man could weave a dream
To keep him from despair.

To each his Dulcinea
Though she's naught but flame and air!

(The lights on the PADRE *dim out, and he exits. Music resumes in another motif as the lighting in the courtyard—moonlight—comes to full.*

QUIXOTE *is now pacing back and forth, lance in hand, holding vigil over his armor)*

DON QUIXOTE: *(Pausing)* Now must I consider how sages of the future will describe this historic night. *(He strikes a pose)* "Long after the sun had retired to his couch, darkening the gates and balconies of La Mancha, Don Quixote with measured tread and lofty expression held vigil in the courtyard of a mighty castle!" *(He hears the pompous echo of his voice, bows his head, ashamed)* Oh, maker of empty boasts. On this, of all nights, to give way to vanity. Nay, Don Quixote—take a deep breath of life and consider how it should be lived. *(He kneels)*

Call nothing thy own except thy soul.
Love not what thou art, but only what thou may become.
Do not pursue pleasure, for thou may have the misfortune to overtake it.
Look always forward; in last year's nest there are no birds this year.

*(*ALDONZA *has entered the courtyard en route to her rendezvous with* PEDRO. *She stops, watching* DON QUIXOTE *and listening)*

Be just to all men. Be courteous to all women.
Live in the vision of that one for whom great deeds are done . . . she that is
called Dulcinea.

ALDONZA: Why do you call me that?
DON QUIXOTE: *(He opens his eyes)* My lady!
ALDONZA: Oh, get up from there. Get up! *(DON QUIXOTE rises worshipfully)*
Why do you call me by that name?
DON QUIXOTE: Because it is thine.
ALDONZA: My name is Aldonza!
DON QUIXOTE: *(Shakes his head respectfully)* I know thee, lady.
ALDONZA: My name is Aldonza and I think you know me *not*.
DON QUIXOTE: All my years I have known thee. Thy virtue. Thy nobility of
spirit.
ALDONZA: *(Laughs scornfully, whips the rebozo from her head)* Take another look!
DON QUIXOTE: *(Gently)* I have already seen thee in my heart.
ALDONZA: Your heart doesn't know much about women!
DON QUIXOTE: It knows all, my lady. They are the soul of man . . . the radiance
that lights his way. A woman is . . . glory!
ALDONZA: *(Anger masking uncertainty)* What do you want of me?
DON QUIXOTE: Nothing.
ALDONZA: Liar!
DON QUIXOTE: *(Bows his head)* I deserved the rebuke. I ask of my lady—
ALDONZA: *Now* we get to it.
DON QUIXOTE: . . . that I may be allowed to serve her. That I may hold her in
my heart. That I may dedicate each victory and call upon her in defeat. And
if at last I give my life I give it in the sacred name of Dulcinea.
ALDONZA: *(Draws her rebozo about her shoulders and backs away, shaken)* I must
go . . . Pedro is waiting . . . *(She pauses. Vehemently)* Why do you do these
things?
DON QUIXOTE: What things, my lady?
ALDONZA: These ridiculous . . . the things you do!
DON QUIXOTE: I hope to add some measure of grace to the world.
ALDONZA: The world's a dungheap and we are maggots that crawl on it!
DON QUIXOTE: My lady knows better in her heart.
ALDONZA: What's in *my* heart will get me halfway to hell. And you, Señor Don
Quixote—you're going to take such a beating!
DON QUIXOTE: Whether I win or lose does not matter.
ALDONZA: What does?
DON QUIXOTE: Only that I follow the quest.
ALDONZA: *(Spits in vulgar contempt)* That for your quest. *(She turns, marches
away, then stops. Music: very softly, as she comes back)* What does it mean—
quest?
DON QUIXOTE: The mission of each true knight . . . his duty—nay, his privilege!
(He sings)

To dream the impossible dream,
To fight the unbeatable foe,
To bear with unbearable sorrow,
To run where the brave dare not go.

To right the unrightable wrong,
To love, pure and chaste, from afar,
To try, when your arms are too weary,
To reach the unreachable star!

This is my Quest, to follow that star,
No matter how hopeless, no matter how far,
To fight for the right without question or pause,
To be willing to march into hell for a heavenly cause!

And I know, if I'll only be true to this glorious quest,
That my heart will lie peaceful and calm when I'm laid to my rest.

And the world will be better for this,
That one man, scorned and covered with scars,
Still strove, with his last ounce of courage,
To reach the unreachable stars!

ALDONZA: *(Is quite still after the song. Then pleading suddenly)* Once—just once
—would you look at me as I really am?

DON QUIXOTE: *(Lowering his eyes to gaze into hers)* I see beauty. Purity. I see the
woman each man holds secret within him. Dulcinea.

*(ALDONZA moans in inexpressible despair. She backs away from the steady eyes,
shaking her head. She turns to run—and gasps as she collides with* PEDRO, *who has
approached unseen. He grips her in fury)*

PEDRO: Keep me waiting, will you?

ALDONZA: I wasn't—I didn't—

PEDRO: *(Mocking ferociously)* My lady. My princess! *(And he slaps her so that she
goes spinning to the ground)*

DON QUIXOTE: *(A roar of outrage)* Monster!

PEDRO: Stay clear!

DON QUIXOTE: *(Advancing)* Thou wouldst strike a woman?!

PEDRO: Stand back or I'll break your empty head!

DON QUIXOTE: Oh, thou heart of flint and bowels of cork! Now shall I chastise
thee!

PEDRO: I warn you—ai-e-ee! *(DON QUIXOTE, clubbing his lance, catches* PEDRO
alongside the head, sending him sprawling. Music begins under. PEDRO *groans)*
Oh-h-h, I am killed. *(In a yell, staying on the ground)* Jose! Tenorio! Muleteers!

(The MULETEERS *approach on the run.* ALDONZA *is back on her feet, and has
sheltered herself behind the watering-trough.* SANCHO *comes running from the inn)*

DON QUIXOTE: *(Facing the reinforcements)* Come one, come all! Don Quixote will
vanquish armies!

PEDRO: Beware the lance!

ALDONZA: *(Stepping out)* Let him be!

PEDRO: Back, whore!

ALDONZA: I said let him be! He's worth a thousand of you!

PEDRO: *(Diverted from* DON QUIXOTE*)* You want the same, eh?

(He lurches toward her. ALDONZA *snatches* DON QUIXOTE*'s sword from the
watering-trough, swings it in a mighty arc, and the flat of the blade sends* PEDRO
bowling butt over elbow.

Music comes up full, as QUIXOTE *charges back into the fray. A comic-choreo-*

graphic treatment of the conflict. QUIXOTE *wields the lance.* ALDONZA *swings hugely with the flat of the sword, and* SANCHO *makes himself useful to both. The battle rages, and finally the* MULETEERS, *with cries, groans, and howls of pain, fall hors de combat. The music fades out)*

DON QUIXOTE: *(Gasping but joyful)* Victory!

SANCHO: Victory!

ALDONZA: *(Brandishing the sword) Victory!*

(The INNKEEPER *roused from sleep, comes rushing on, wearing nightgown and bedcap)*

INNKEEPER: What is this? All the noise—! *(He sees the* MULETEERS *where they lie groaning in an untidy heap and is aghast)* Oh! Oh! What dreadful thing . . . ?

ALDONZA: What *glorious* thing!

DON QUIXOTE: *(Gasping)* Sir Castellano—I would inform you—that the right has triumphed. *(He sags to the ground)*

SANCHO: *(Hurrying to him)* Your Grace! Are you hurt?

DON QUIXOTE: Nay . . . a little weakness . . .

ALDONZA: Oh, he *is* hurt!

(She drops the sword and hurries to help. MARIA, *frightened and in nightclothes, comes running out)*

MARIA: What is it? *(Sees* QUIXOTE*)* The madman! I knew it!

INNKEEPER: Fetch bandages! Hurry!

ALDONZA: *(Tearing bandages from her petticoat)* Poor warrior . . .

MARIA: *(Bitterly)* Poor lunatic!

INNKEEPER: Go back to bed, Maria.

MARIA: I warned you what would happen!

INNKEEPER: *Go to bed.*

(MARIA exits haughtily, as the INNKEEPER *hauls one of the* MULETEERS *out of the well.* DON QUIXOTE *stirs and moans)*

SANCHO: He's coming around!

DON QUIXOTE: *(Opens his eyes and is looking at* ALDONZA, *weakly but with pleasure)* Ah . . . might I always wake to such a vision!

ALDONZA: Don't move.

SANCHO: I must say, Your Grace, we certainly did a job out here.

DON QUIXOTE: We routed them, did we?

ALDONZA: Ha! *That* bunch'll be walking bowlegged for a week!

DON QUIXOTE: *(Distressed)* My lady! It is not seemly to gloat over the fallen.

ALDONZA: Let 'em rot in hell!

(By now the last of the MULETEERS *have been helped from the courtyard)*

INNKEEPER: *(Agitated, to* DON QUIXOTE*)* Sir, I am a tame and peaceful man. Please, Sir Knight—I don't like to be inhospitable—but I must ask you to leave as soon as you are able.

DON QUIXOTE: *(With dignity)* I am sorry to have offended the dignity of thy castle and I shall depart with daylight. But first, my lord, I must remind thee of thy promise.

INNKEEPER: Promise?

DON QUIXOTE: True, it is not yet dawn, but I have kept vigil and proven myself in combat. Therefore I beg thou dub me knight.

INNKEEPER: *(Remembering)* Oh-h. Certainly. Let's get it over with.

DON QUIXOTE: *(To* SANCHO*)* Wilt be good enough to fetch my sword? *(Warmly,* *as* ALDONZA *assists)* Lady, I cannot tell thee how joyful I am that this ceremony should take place in thy presence.

ALDONZA: *(As he sways)* Be careful, now!

DON QUIXOTE: It is a solemn moment which seals my vocation . . .

(SANCHO hands QUIXOTE*'s sword to the* INNKEEPER*)*

INNKEEPER: *(Handling the sword gingerly)* Are you ready?

DON QUIXOTE: I am.

INNKEEPER: Very well, then. Kneel! *(Music begins as* DON QUIXOTE, *with* AL-DONZA *and* SANCHO *assisting on either side, gets down to his knees. He intones)* Don Quixote de La Mancha!

I hereby dub thee knight.

(He touches him with the sword on each shoulder, then hands the sword back to SANCHO *and starts to exit)*

DON QUIXOTE: *(As music continues)* Your Lordship.

INNKEEPER: Didn't I do it right?

DON QUIXOTE: *(Humbly)* If Your Lordship would make some mention of the deeds I performed to earn this honor . . . ?

INNKEEPER: Oh . . . of course. *(He gets the sword back from* SANCHO. *He intones)* Don Quixote de La Mancha,

Having proven yourself this day

In glorious and terrible combat

And by my authority as lord of this castle—

I hereby dub thee knight!

(He gives the sword back to SANCHO, *again starts to leave)*

DON QUIXOTE: Your Lordship . . .

INNKEEPER: *(Stopping again)* Something else?

(This time SANCHO *hands the sword back to him)*

DON QUIXOTE: It is customary to grant the new knight an added name. If Your Lordship could devise such a name for me . . . ?

INNKEEPER: Hmmm. *(He reflects a moment, looking at the battered face. He gets an inspiration and sings)*

Hail, Knight of the Woeful Countenance,
Knight of the Woeful Countenance!
Wherever you go
People will know
Of the glorious deeds of the Knight of the Woe—
Ful Countenance!

Farewell and good cheer, oh my brave cavalier,
Ride onward to glorious strife.
I swear when you're gone I'll remember you well
For all of the rest of my life!

Hail, Knight of the Woeful Countenance,
Knight of the Woeful Countenance!
Wherever you go,
Face to the foe,
They will quail at the sight of the Knight of the Woe—
Ful Countenance!

Oh valorous knight, go and fight for the right,
And battle all villains that be.
But oh, when you do, what will happen to you
Thank God I won't be there to see!

INNKEEPER, ALDONZA and SANCHO:
Hail, Knight of the Woeful Countenance!
Knight of the Woeful Countenance!
Wherever you go
People will know
Of the glorious deeds of the Knight of the Woe—
Ful count—te—nance!

DON QUIXOTE: *(Ecstatically)* I thank thee.
INNKEEPER: *(Handing the sword to* QUIXOTE*)* Now, Sir Knight, I am going to bed. And I advise you to do the same! *(He exits)*
DON QUIXOTE: *(Still on his knees; raptly)* Knight of the Woeful Countenance . . .
ALDONZA: *(In tears)* It's a *beautiful* name.
SANCHO: Come, Your Grace. *(Helping him to his feet)* Let's get you to bed.
DON QUIXOTE: Not yet. I owe something to my enemies.
ALDONZA: *That* account's been paid!
DON QUIXOTE: No, my lady. I must raise them up and minister to their wounds.
ALDONZA: *(Aghast) What?*
DON QUIXOTE: Nobility demands.
ALDONZA: It does?
DON QUIXOTE: Yes, my lady. Therefore I shall take these—
ALDONZA: *(Firmly, snatching up the bandages)* No, you won't. *I'll* take them. *I'll* minister.
DON QUIXOTE: But—
ALDONZA: *(Simply)* They were my enemies, too.
DON QUIXOTE: *(With emotion)* Oh, blessed one . . . !
SANCHO: *(Helping* QUIXOTE*)* Come, Your Grace.
DON QUIXOTE: *(As they exit)* Blessed one! Ah, blessed one . . . !
   (The lighting changes as ALDONZA enters the interior of the Inn. The MULETEERS lie about the room, moaning, licking their wounds. PEDRO lifts his head as he sees her)
PEDRO: *(In a growl)* What do you think you're doing?
ALDONZA: *(Matter-of-factly)* I'm going to minister to your wounds.
PEDRO: You're . . . *what?*
ALDONZA: Nobility demands. *(Kneeling beside* JOSE*)* Turn over, you poxy goat.
   (JOSE's eyes light up with cat-and-mouse savagery as ALDONZA bends over him. With a shout he seizes her, and the other MULETEERS pounce upon her, also.
   Music: a sardonic version of "Little Bird" as with methodical, ritualistic brutality, in choreographic staging the MULETEERS bind, gag, beat and ravage ALDONZA. She fights back as best she can but the fight is hopeless and she must submit. FERMINA enters and watches, sadistically gleeful over the humiliation of ALDONZA.
   Finally PEDRO, realizing that ALDONZA is unconscious, signals the others to stop. JOSE slings the brutalized ALDONZA over his back and the MULETEERS exit, carrying

her off. As they do so, the lights pick up QUIXOTE *and* SANCHO *at another area of the stage)*

DON QUIXOTE: *(Raptly)* Ah, Sancho, how I do envy my enemies.

SANCHO: *Envy?*

DON QUIXOTE: To think they know the healing touch of my lady Dulcinea! *(An ecstatic sigh)* Let this be proof to thee, Sancho. Nobility triumphs. Virtue always prevails. *(Uplifted)* Now in the moment of victory do I confirm my knighthood and my oath. For all my life, this I do swear—*(Singing)*

To dream the impossible dream,
To fight the unbeatable foe,
To bear with unbearable sorrow,
To run where the brave dare not go!

(Off, faintly at first, then growing, is heard the "Inquisition Theme." QUIXOTE *falters and falls silent.* CERVANTES, *losing the character of* QUIXOTE, *comes forward as the volume of the theme grows and the setting alters back to the prison. The* PRISONERS *are immobile, cocking their heads to listen)*

CERVANTES: *(Uncertainly)* That sound . . . ?

THE GOVERNOR: The Men of the Inquisition.

CERVANTES: What does it mean?

PRISONER: They're coming to fetch someone.

PRISONER: They'll haul him off—put the question to him.

PRISONER: Next thing he knows—he's burning!

CERVANTES: Are they coming for me?

THE DUKE: Very possibly. What, Cervantes? Not *afraid?* (CERVANTES *shakes his head dumbly. Mockingly)* Where's your courage? Is that in your imagination, too? (CERVANTES *is retreating,* THE DUKE *following inexorably)* No escape, Cervantes. This is *happening.* Not to your brave man of La Mancha, but to *you.* Quick, Cervantes—call upon him. Let him shield you. Let him save you, if he can, from *that!*

(On the stairway the MEN OF THE INQUISITION *appear. They are robed, hooded, frightening in aspect.* CERVANTES *is paralyzed with fear, only his eyes moving, following them as they descend into the vault. As they approach* CERVANTES, *the* GUARDS *open the floor-trap and drag up a prisoner. They haul him up the stairs.* CERVANTES *sinks to a bench, faintly.*

The "Inquisition Theme" recedes, fading as the stairway is withdrawn. THE GOVERNOR *snaps his fingers at a* PRISONER, *who brings a goatskin of wine, hands it to* CERVANTES, *who takes it with trembling hands and drinks deeply)*

THE GOVERNOR: Better?

CERVANTES: *(Faintly)* Thank you . . .

THE GOVERNOR: Good, let's get on with your defense!

CERVANTES: If I might rest a moment . . .

THE DUKE: *(With tolerant contempt)* This La Mancha—what is it like?

THE GOVERNOR: An empty place. Great wide plains.

PRISONER: A desert.

THE GOVERNOR: A wasteland.

THE DUKE: Which apparently grows lunatics.

CERVANTES: I would say, rather . . . men of illusion.

THE DUKE: Much the same. Why are you poets so fascinated with madmen?

CERVANTES: I suppose . . . we have much in common.

THE DUKE: You both turn your backs on life.

CERVANTES: We both select from life what pleases us.

THE DUKE: A man must come to terms with life as it is!

CERVANTES: I have lived nearly fifty years, and I have seen life as it is. Pain, misery, hunger . . . cruelty beyond belief. I have heard the singing from taverns and the moans from bundles of filth on the streets. I have been a soldier and seen my comrades fall in battle . . . or die more slowly under the lash in Africa. I have held them in my arms at the final moment. These were men who saw life as it is, yet they died despairing. No glory, no gallant last words . . . only their eyes filled with confusion, whimpering the question: "Why?" I do not think they asked why they were dying, but why they had lived. *(He rises, and through the following speech moves into the character of* DON QUIXOTE *as a musical underscore and change of setting begin)* When life itself seems lunatic, who knows where madness lies? Perhaps to be too practical is madness. To surrender dreams—this may be madness. To seek treasure where there is only trash. Too much sanity may be madness. And maddest of all, to see life as it is and not as it should be.

(The music has stated the "I Am I, Don Quixote" theme thinly during the preceding speech, and the prison and PRISONERS *have disappeared.* CERVANTES *is isolated in limbo; the "horses" have appeared. The lights change)*

DON QUIXOTE: *(Singing)*
> *I am I, Don Quixote,*
> *The Lord of La Mancha,*
> *Destroyer of evil am I,*
> *I will march to the sound of the trumpets of glory,*
> *Forever to conquer or die!*

SANCHO: I don't understand.

DON QUIXOTE: What, my friend?

SANCHO: Why you're so cheerful. First you find your lady, then you lose her.

DON QUIXOTE: Never lost!

SANCHO: Well, she ran off with those mule drivers . . . ?

DON QUIXOTE: Ah, but undoubtedly with some high purpose.

SANCHO: High purpose with those low characters?

DON QUIXOTE: Sancho, Sancho, always thine eye sees evil in preference to good.

SANCHO: *(Stubbornly)* There's no use blaming my eye; it doesn't make the world, it only sees it. *(A band of* MOORS *appears)* Anyway, there's something my eye sees truly enough. Moors! Let's make a wide track around them, for they're a scurvy lot and Your Grace can't deny *that*.

DON QUIXOTE: There, thou fallest into the trap of thy peasant mind again.

SANCHO: They're *not* thieves and murderers?

DON QUIXOTE: Do not condemn before thou knowest! *(The* MOORISH GIRL *undulates toward them)* Sh-h-h—a young innocent approaches. *(The girl dances lasciviously as her* PIMP *encourages her, whining a nasal obligato)* Charming!

SANCHO: *(In protest)* But she's a trollop, and he—why he's nothing but a—!

DON QUIXOTE: Have done with these foul suspicions! Dost not understand what they are saying? These two are brother and sister, offspring of the noble

African lord, Sidi ben Mali. *(The girl approaches* QUIXOTE*)* Sweet maiden, what wilt thou?

SANCHO: I think *I* know what she wilt!

(The GIRL *seizes one of* QUIXOTE*'s hands and presses it to her right breast)*

DON QUIXOTE: She wishes me to feel the beating of her heart. And such is her innocence she does not even know where it is.

(The GIRL *seizes* QUIXOTE*'s other hand and presses it to her other breast)*

SANCHO: *(Cynically)* Or even how many she has!

(The MOORS *dance and wail; the* PIMP *caterwauls, beating his breast)*

DON QUIXOTE: *(Listening gravely)* Much as I surmised.

SANCHO: What's he saying?

DON QUIXOTE: A most grievous tale. The noble Sidi ben Mali hath been taken captive and even now lies deep in a dungeon not five leagues from here. While these, his faithful family and retainers, travel the countryside in hope of raising a ransom. *(The* GIRL *dances, putting a coin on her forehead)* See, Sancho, how quaint the customs of these Africans! In this charming manner they ask that I make contribution to their cause.

SANCHO: Don't do it!

DON QUIXOTE: *(Incredulously)* Thou would'st ignore a fellow knight in jeopardy? Here, sweet maiden—with all my heart. *(He gives money to the* GIRL, *and the other* MOORS *take the opportunity to lift his money pouch and other belongings. Meanwhile, to* SANCHO*)* Shame on thee for a reluctant Christian! Shame on thee for a parsimonious wretch! Shame on thee for a small-hearted peasant! Shame on thee, Sancho, multiple shame! *(*SANCHO, *overcome by the rebuke, drops a coin in* QUIXOTE*'s golden helmet which the* GIRL *is holding)* Ah, Sancho, I knew it, I knew thy heart was good! *(The* MOORS *dance wildly)* How inspiring is their gratitude. Let us celebrate in their fashion!

*(*QUIXOTE *and* SANCHO *join the dance; the* MOORS *steal everything in sight, including the "horses."* QUIXOTE *and* SANCHO *finally fall, exhausted but happy. Then, as they discover with dismay what has befallen them, the lights black out.*

The lights come up on the courtyard of the Inn. The INNKEEPER, *humming happily, is crossing the courtyard. From offstage, the discordant bleat of* SANCHO*'s bugle. He stops and turns a haunted face toward the gates.* MARIA *comes crashing from the inn)*

MARIA: *(A shriek)* Don't open the gates! Don't let him in!

INNKEEPER: *(His face clearing)* It's the pig-butcher. Don't you remember? We expected him yesterday.

MARIA: No, no! Don't open!

(The INNKEEPER *goes to the gates as* QUIXOTE *and* SANCHO *appear, supporting each other.* MARIA *screams and runs off)*

INNKEEPER: Not *again?* *(Trying to bar the way)* This place is closed. This castle has gone out of business!

DON QUIXOTE: *(Feeble but stern)* What, sir? Deny the right of sanctuary?

INNKEEPER: I hate to, but—

DON QUIXOTE: *And* to a knight dubbed by thy own hand?

INNKEEPER: *(Wavering)* It *doesn't* seem right . . .

DON QUIXOTE: Not by any rule of chivalry!

(The INNKEEPER, *yielding with a sigh, allows them to enter.* QUIXOTE *and* SAN-

CHO *totter into the courtyard—footsore and in very bad shape. The* INNKEEPER *looks them over)*

INNKEEPER: More muleteers?

SANCHO: *(Hollowly)* Moors. They stole our money.

DON QUIXOTE: Have done, Sancho.

SANCHO: They stole our animals.

DON QUIXOTE: Must thou harp on it?

SANCHO: They stole everything we *had.*

INNKEEPER: *(With pity)* Why don't you declare a truce?

DON QUIXOTE: And allow wickedness to flourish?

INNKEEPER: I'm afraid wickedness wears thick armor.

(In the background, unseen by the three, ALDONZA *enters)*

DON QUIXOTE: *(Roused)* And for that wouldst thou have me surrender? Nay, let a man be overthrown ten thousand times, still must he rise and again do battle. The Enchanter may confuse the outcome, but the effort remains sublime!

ALDONZA: *(Bitterly)* Lies. Madness and lies.

INNKEEPER: *(Horrified at her bruises, her tattered rags)* Aldonza! What happened?

ALDONZA: Ask *him.*

INNKEEPER: *(Calling as he exits)* Maria! Maria!

DON QUIXOTE: *(Rising, aghast)* I shall punish them that did this crime.

ALDONZA: Crime! You know the worst crime of all? Being born. For that you get punished your whole life!

DON QUIXOTE: Dulcinea—

ALDONZA: Enough of that! Get yourself to a madhouse. Rave about nobility where no one can hear!

DON QUIXOTE: My lady—

ALDONZA: *(Passionately)* I am not your lady! I am not any kind of a lady! *(Singing)*

I was spawned in a ditch by a mother who left me there
Naked and cold and too hungry to cry;
I never blamed her, I'm sure she left hoping
That I'd have the good sense to die!

Then, of course, there's my father—I'm told that young ladies
Can point to their fathers with maidenly pride;
Mine was some regiment here for an hour,
I can't even tell you which side!

So of course I became, as befitted my delicate birth,
The most casual bride of the murdering scum of the earth!

DON QUIXOTE: And still thou art my lady.

ALDONZA: And still he torments me! Lady! How should I be a lady? *(Singing)*

For a lady has modest and maidenly airs
And a virtue I somehow suspect that I lack;
It's hard to remember those maidenly airs
In a stable laid flat on your back.

Won't you look at me, look at me, God, won't you look at me,
Look at the kitchen slut reeking of sweat!
Born on a dungheap to die on a dungheap,
A strumpet men use and forget!

If you feel that you see me not quite at my virginal best,
Cross my palm with a coin and I'll willingly show you the rest!

DON QUIXOTE: *(Tenderly)* Never deny, thou art Dulcinea.

ALDONZA: *(Ever more frantically)* Take the clouds from your eyes and see me as I really am! *(Singing)*

You have shown me the sky, but what good is the sky
To a creature who'll never do better than crawl?
Of all the cruel bastards who've badgered and battered me,
You are the cruelest of all!

Can't you see what your gentle insanities do to me?
Rob me of anger and give me despair!
Blows and abuse I can take and give back again,
Tenderness I cannot bear!

So please torture me now with your "Sweet Dulcineas" no more!
I am no one! I'm nothing! I'm only Aldonza the whore!

DON QUIXOTE: Now and forever thou art my lady Dulcinea!

ALDONZA: *(A wail)* No-o-o!

(She collapses, despairing. DON QUIXOTE moves toward her compassionately— but suddenly, off, there is a fanfare of trumpets. Brazen, warlike, ominous in quality. SANCHO scurries to look, then backs away from what he sees)

SANCHO: *(Choking with fear)* Master . . . !

(Music continues as the gates swing open. A strange cavalcade enters; liveried attendants preceding a KNIGHT, tall and terrifying in fantastic armor. He wears a chain-mail tunic on which are mounted tiny mirrors that glitter and dazzle the eye. On his head is a masklike casque, only his eyes visible through slits. From the crest of the casque spring great plumes, accentuating what seems already incredible stature. In his hand is a naked, shining sword. The music cuts as the cavalcade comes to a halt)

KNIGHT OF THE MIRRORS: *(His voice harsh, clangorous)* Is there one here calls himself Don Quixote de La Mancha? If there is—and he be not afraid to look upon me—let him stand forth!

DON QUIXOTE: *(At length, voice shaking)* I am Don Quixote, Knight of the Woeful Countenance.

KNIGHT OF THE MIRRORS: *(Voice magnified and metallic within the casque)* Now hear me, thou charlatan! Thou art no knight, but a foolish pretender. Thy pretense is a child's mockery, and thy principles dirt beneath my feet!

DON QUIXOTE: *(Trembling with anger)* Oh, false knight! Discourteous! Before I chastise thee, tell me thy name.

KNIGHT OF THE MIRRORS: Thou shalt hear it in due course.

DON QUIXOTE: Then say why thou seekest me out!

KNIGHT OF THE MIRRORS: *(Mockingly)* Thou called upon *me*, Don Quixote. Thou reviled me and threatened.

DON QUIXOTE: The Enchanter! *(A moan from SANCHO. The music, under, is the "Enchanter's Theme."* DON QUIXOTE *tears off his left gauntlet, flinging it at the KNIGHT'S feet)* Behold at thy feet the gage of battle!

SANCHO: *(Anguished)* Master—no!

(He runs, scrambles for the gauntlet, but the KNIGHT pins it with his sword)

KNIGHT OF THE MIRRORS: *(Suddenly very cold)* On what terms do we fight?

DON QUIXOTE: Choose thine own!

KNIGHT OF THE MIRRORS: Very well. If thou art beaten thy freedom is forfeit and thou must obey my every command. *(DON QUIXOTE bows coldly)* And thy conditions?

DON QUIXOTE: If thou art still alive thou shalt kneel and beg mercy of my lady Dulcinea.

KNIGHT OF THE MIRRORS: *(Mockingly)* Where shall I find this lady?

DON QUIXOTE: There she stands.

(The KNIGHT OF THE MIRRORS *turns his eyes to* ALDONZA—*her rags, her bruises, her ruined face. He begins to laugh in cruel derision)*

KNIGHT OF THE MIRRORS: Thy lady . . . is an alley cat!

DON QUIXOTE: *(Drawing his sword in fury)* Monster! Defend thyself!

KNIGHT OF THE MIRRORS: *(Stepping back)* Hold! Thou asked my name, Don Quixote. Now I shall tell it. I am called—the Knight of the Mirrors! *(Music: the "Enchanter's Theme," as the* KNIGHT *swings forward his shield. Its surface is polished steel, a mirror which blinds and bewilders* DON QUIXOTE. *The* ATTEND-ANTS *reveal similar mirrors. In a choreographic pattern* QUIXOTE *will reel from one to the other, fetching up always against his own image)* Look, Don Quixote! Look in the mirror of reality and behold things as they truly are. Look! What seest thou, Don Quixote? A gallant knight? Naught but an aging fool! *(DON QUIXOTE recoils from his own image, only to be brought up against another)* Look! Dost thou see him? A madman dressed for a masquerade! *(Attempting escape,* QUIXOTE *finds himself facing another mirror)* Look, Don Quixote! See him as he truly is! See the clown! *(QUIXOTE reels away, only to find the mirrors converging as the* KNIGHT *and his* ATTENDANTS *close down upon him)* Drown, Don Quixote. Drown—drown in the mirror. Go deep—the masquerade is ended! *(QUIXOTE collapses to his knees)* Confess! Thy lady is a trollop, and thy dream the nightmare of a disordered mind!

DON QUIXOTE: *(In dazed desperation)* I am Don Quixote, knight-errant of La Mancha . . . and my lady is the Lady Dulcinea. I am Don Quixote, knight-errant . . . and my lady . . . my lady . . . *(Beaten, weeping, he sinks to the floor)*

KNIGHT OF THE MIRRORS: *(Removing the casque from his head)* It is done!

SANCHO: *(Thunderstruck)* Your Grace! It is Doctor Carrasco! It is only Sansón Carrasco!

DR. CARRASCO: Forgive me, Señor Quijana. It was the only way.

(Lights dim down to DON QUIXOTE, *huddled weeping on the floor.* ALDONZA *comes toward him, her face devastated by loss and pity. Music bridges as the lighting alters back to that of the prison, and the* CAPTAIN OF THE INQUISITION *is seen entering)*

CAPTAIN: *(Shouting)* Cervantes! Cervantes! Prepare to be summoned!

CERVANTES: *(Confusedly)* By whom?

CAPTAIN: The Judges of the Inquisition!

THE GOVERNOR: Captain! How soon?

CAPTAIN: Soon! *(He exits)*

THE GOVERNOR: But not yet. *(To* CERVANTES, *with satisfaction)* Good. You'll have time to finish the story.

CERVANTES: But the story is finished.

THE GOVERNOR: *What?*

CERVANTES: At least so far as I know it.

THE GOVERNOR: I don't think I like this ending. *(A growl from the* PRISONERS*)* I don't think the jury likes it, either.

THE DUKE: Well, then—he's failed!

THE GOVERNOR: Miguel de Cervantes. It is the sentence of this court—

CERVANTES: *(Panicky)* Wait!

THE GOVERNOR: For what?

CERVANTES: If I could have a little more time?

THE GOVERNOR: *(After a glance at the* PRISONERS*)* Oh, *I'll* grant it. But the Inquisition . . . ?

CERVANTES: A few moments only! Let me improvise . . .

(He snaps his fingers, pointing out the PRISONERS *who are to play in the following scene. Music underscores: a melancholy version of "I'm Only Thinking of Him" as the setting is improvised in the shape of a bedroom in* ALONSO QUIJANA's *home. Lighting alters to shafts of dying sun as the bed and its occupant—*DON QUIXOTE *—are revealed.*

QUIXOTE's *eyes are open but deep-hollowed and remote, windows on a mind that has retreated to some secret place. There is silence a while but for the music)*

ANTONIA: *(Voice low, to* CARRASCO*)* Can you do *nothing?*

PADRE: *(With soft compassion)* I'm afraid there'll be more need of my services than his. *(Waves a hand slowly across* QUIXOTE's *unseeing eyes)* Where is he, I wonder? In what dark cavern of the mind?

DR. CARRASCO: According to recent theory—

PADRE: Doctor. Please.

DR. CARRASCO: *(Resentfully)* Don't you think I did right?

PADRE: *(Sighing)* Yes. There's the contradiction . . .

(SANCHO enters timidly, hat in hand)

ANTONIA: You again?

DR. CARRASCO: Tell him to go away.

PADRE: *(Wearily)* What harm can he do?

ANTONIA: Yes—it's all been done! *(She lets him pass, grudgingly)*

SANCHO: *(Bobbing his head to the* PADRE*)* Your Reverence. *(Diffidently)* Could I talk to him?

PADRE: I'm afraid he won't hear you.

SANCHO: Well, then, I won't say much.

DR. CARRASCO: And no mention of knight-errantry!

SANCHO: Of course not. Does one speak of the rope in the house of the hanged? Oh—excuse me, Your Grace.

ANTONIA: *(Bitterly)* Your Grace.

SANCHO: *(Seating himself by the bed)* Just a few words . . . to lighten his heart. *(Music: he sings)*

A little gossip . . . a little chat . . .
A little idle talk . . . of this and that . . .

I'll tell him all the troubles I have had
And since he doesn't hear, at least he won't feel bad.
(To QUIXOTE*)*
When I first got home my wife Teresa beat me,
But the blows fell very lightly on my back.
She kept missing every other stroke and crying from the heart
That while I was gone she'd gone and lost the knack!

(Spoken)
Of course I hit her back, Your Grace, but she's a lot harder than I am, and you
know what they say—"Whether the stone hits the pitcher or the pitcher hits
the stone, it's going to be bad for the pitcher." So I've got bruises from here
to—
(An admonishing look from the PADRE. *He sings)*

A little gossip . . . a little chat . . .
A little idle talk . . . of this and that . . .
If no one listens, then it's just as well,
At least I won't get caught in any lies I tell!
(Conspiratorially to QUIXOTE*)*
Oh, I haven't fought a windmill in a fortnight,
And the humble joys get duller every day.
Why, when I'm asleep a dragon with his fiery tongue a-waggin'
Whispers, "Sancho, won't you please come out and play?"

DR. CARRASCO: *(Roused)* That's enough now.
SANCHO: Why? What did I do?
DR. CARRASCO: I warned you!
SANCHO: I didn't do anything, I was only trying to—
DON QUIXOTE: *(Barely audible)* My friend.
SANCHO: *(Politely, as all turn, startled)* Did Your Grace say something?
DON QUIXOTE: You're a fat little bag stuffed with proverbs.
SANCHO: Yes, Your Grace. Well, as I was saying—
ANTONIA: *(Running to* QUIXOTE*)* Uncle!
DON QUIXOTE: My dear . . . *(His eyes go to the others)* Good morning, Padre
    . . . or is it evening?
PADRE: Alonso . . .
DR. CARRASCO: How do you feel, sir?
DON QUIXOTE: Not well, my friends.
DR. CARRASCO: Can you speak your name?
DON QUIXOTE: *(Puzzled)* Should a man not know his own name?
DR. CARRASCO: If you would say it . . . ?
DON QUIXOTE: *(In surprise)* Alonso Quijana. *(*DR. CARRASCO *gives a triumphant
    look to the others)* Padre . . .
PADRE: Here beside you.
DON QUIXOTE: I should like to make a will.
PADRE: Of course. *(He exits to get materials)*
ANTONIA: *(Anxiously, as* DON QUIXOTE *closes his eyes and is silent)* Uncle . . . ?
DON QUIXOTE: *(Faintly)* Forgive me, my dear. When I close my eyes I see a pale
    horse . . . and he beckons me—mount.

ANTONIA: No, Uncle. You will get well!

DON QUIXOTE: *(Smiling)* Why should a man get well when he is dying? It's such a waste of good health. *(With a feeble gesture)* Come closer, my friends. *(They come to the bedside)* In my illness I dreamed so strangely . . . Oh, such dreams! It seemed I was a . . . no . . . I dare not tell you lest you think me mad.

ANTONIA: Put them from your mind!

DON QUIXOTE: *(Deeply weary)* They are gone, my dear . . . nor do I know what they meant. *(As the PADRE re-enters)* Padre . . . ?

PADRE: Speak, my friend, and I shall write.

DON QUIXOTE: I, Alonso Quijana . . . with one foot in the stirrup and the agony of death already upon me . . .

(The PADRE's pen scratches busily. From the front of the house the thudding of the doorknocker is heard)

ANTONIA: *(To the HOUSEKEEPER as she goes to see)* Don't admit *anyone*.

DON QUIXOTE: . . . do hereby make the following disposition of my estate. The bulk I bequeath to my beloved niece, Antonia Quijana . . . *(From off comes a racket of voices in vehement argument)*—with the exception of certain personal bequests which are as follows—

(The HOUSEKEEPER backs in, pushed roughly by ALDONZA. Everyone speaks at once)

HOUSEKEEPER: *(In fear and frenzy)* You cannot! I say you cannot!

ANTONIA: What is this? Sansón!

ALDONZA: Get out of my way, you hag—

DR. CARRASCO: It's that slut from the Inn.

HOUSEKEEPER: I tried to stop her! She threatened to—

ALDONZA: Tear your eyes out!

DR. CARRASCO: *(Advancing on ALDONZA grimly)* Get out of here.

ALDONZA: And if you touch me again, by God—

DR. CARRASCO: Get out of here!

ALDONZA: Not before I see him!

DR. CARRASCO: I'm warning you—go quietly or I'll—

DON QUIXOTE: *(Voice weak but commanding)* Let be.

DR. CARRASCO: Señor Quijana—

DON QUIXOTE: In my house there will be courtesy! *(DR. CARRASCO reluctantly steps aside)* Come closer, girl. *(ALDONZA approaches)* Now. What is it you wish?

ALDONZA: *(Incredulously)* Don't you know me?

DON QUIXOTE: *(Puzzled)* Should I?

ALDONZA: I am Aldonza!

(A movement forward from the others. A pause)

DON QUIXOTE: *(Blankly)* I am sorry. I do not recall anyone of that name.

ALDONZA: *(Looks about wildly. Sees SANCHO. Points to him)* He knows! *(DON QUIXOTE's eyes go to SANCHO, who steps forward as though to speak. DR. CARRASCO warns him fiercely with a gesture. SANCHO closes his mouth, shrugs feebly. Panicky, to DON QUIXOTE)* Please, my lord!

DON QUIXOTE: *(Curiously)* Why do you say "my lord"? I am not a lord.

ALDONZA: You are my lord, Don Quixote!

(The others react, then hold very still)

DON QUIXOTE: Don Quixote. *(Rubs his forehead, troubled)* You must forgive me. I have been ill . . . I am confused by shadows. It is possible I knew you once, but I do not remember.

(ALDONZA is stunned. DR. CARRASCO smoothly steps forward and takes her by the arm)

DR. CARRASCO: *(Moving her along)* This way.

(ALDONZA allows herself to be led. But she stops, pulls loose suddenly, and in a rush comes back and flings herself to her knees beside the bed)

ALDONZA: Please! Try to remember!

DON QUIXOTE: *(With helpless compassion)* Is it so important?

ALDONZA: *(Anguished)* Everything. My whole life. You spoke to me and everything was—different!

DON QUIXOTE: I . . . spoke to you?

ALDONZA: And you looked at me! And you called me by another name! *(She sings, pleadingly)*

> *Dulcinea . . . Dulcinea . . .*
> *Once you found a girl and called her Dulcinea,*
> *When you spoke the name an angel seemed to whisper—*
> *Dulcinea . . . Dulcinea . . .*

(DR. CARRASCO takes her by the arm, leads her toward the door but she resists, holding back to sing)

> *Dulcinea . . . Dulcinea . . .*
> *Won't you please bring back the dream of Dulcinea . . .*
> *Won't you bring me back the bright and shining glory*
> *Of Dulcinea . . . Dulcinea . . .*

DR. CARRASCO: I'm afraid I must insist—

DON QUIXOTE: Let be! *(Disturbed, mind stirring)* Then perhaps . . . it was not a dream . . .

ALDONZA: You spoke of a dream. And about the Quest!

DON QUIXOTE: Quest?

ALDONZA: How you must fight and it doesn't matter whether you win or lose if only you follow the Quest!

DON QUIXOTE: The words. Tell me the words!

ALDONZA: *(Speaking to music)*
> "To dream the impossible dream . . ."

But they're your own words!
> "To fight the unbeatable foe . . ."

Don't you remember?
> "To bear with unbearable sorrow . . ."

You must remember!
> "To run where the brave dare not go—"

DON QUIXOTE: *(Remembering, speaks, then sings)*
> *To right the unrightable wrong,*

ALDONZA: *(A whisper)* Yes . . .

DON QUIXOTE:
> *To love, pure and chaste, from afar,*

ALDONZA: Yes . . .

DON QUIXOTE:
> To try, when your arms are too weary,
> To reach the unreachable star!

ALDONZA: *(Seizing his hand, kisses it)* Thank you, my lord!

DON QUIXOTE: But this is not seemly, my lady. On thy knees? To me?

ALDONZA: *(In protest as he tries to rise)* My lord, you are not well!

DON QUIXOTE: *(Growing in power)* Not well? What is sickness to the body of a knight-errant? What matter wounds? For each time he falls he shall rise again —and woe to the wicked! *(A lusty bellow)* Sancho!

SANCHO: Here, Your Grace!

DON QUIXOTE: My armor! My sword!

SANCHO: *(Delightedly, clapping his hands)* More misadventures!

DON QUIXOTE: Adventures, old friend! *(Rising from the bed, and as* ALDONZA *and* SANCHO *support him on either side, he sings)*

> Oh the trumpets of glory now call me to ride,
> Yes, the trumpets are calling to me,
> And wherever I ride, ever staunch at my side,
> My squire and my lady shall be . . .
>
> I am I, Don Quixote—

DON QUIXOTE, ALDONZA and SANCHO:
> The Lord of La Mancha,
> Our destiny calls and we go!
> And the wild winds of fortune shall carry us onward
> Oh, whithersoever . . .

*(*DON QUIXOTE *falters)*

ALDONZA: *(A cry of apprehension)* My lord—!

SANCHO: Master—!

DON QUIXOTE: *(Reassuring them, sings on)*
> Whithersoever they blow,
> Onward to glory—

(A sudden cry. A whisper)
. . . I . . . go . . .
(He crumples to the floor)

ANTONIA: Uncle!

*(*DR. CARRASCO *pushes* ALDONZA *aside and kneels to* DON QUIXOTE*'s left. He bends over and places his ear to* QUIXOTE*'s heart, then rises and goes to* ANTONIA, *who is weeping softly. The* PADRE *comes to* QUIXOTE *and kneels. He crosses himself and chants in Latin)*

PADRE:
> De profundis clamo ad te
> Domine, Domine,
> *(*ALDONZA *goes slowly to* SANCHO*)*
> Audi vocem meam
> Fiant aures tuae intentae
> Ad vacem obse creationis meae

Si delictarum
Memoriam
Serva neris . . .

SANCHO: *(Stunned, pathetically)* He is dead. My master is dead.

ALDONZA: *(Quietly)* A man died. He seemed a good man, but I did not know him.

SANCHO: But—

ALDONZA: Don Quixote is not dead. Believe, Sancho. Believe.

SANCHO: *(In confused hope)* Aldonza . . . ?

ALDONZA: *(Gently)* My name is Dulcinea.

(The PADRE*'s hymn concludes as the lights dim out. In the darkness comes the snarling roll of the drums of the Inquisition; it gives way to chanting as lights fade in on the prison. The* CAPTAIN *enters at the head of the* MEN OF THE INQUISITION. *They descend to the vault.* CERVANTES, *kneeling, is removing the* DON QUIXOTE *beard and makeup)*

CAPTAIN: *(Unrolling a scroll)* Under authority of the Holy Office of the Inquisition! *(Reading)* "By reason of certain offenses committed against His Majesty's Most Catholic Church, the following is summoned to give answer and submit his person for purification if it be so ordered: Don Miguel de Cervantes."

CERVANTES: *(With wry bravado)* How popular a defendant I am. Summoned by one court before I've quite finished with another. Well? How says the Judge?

THE GOVERNOR: *(Musingly, weighing the package now held in his hands)* I think I know what this contains. The history of your mad knight? *(*CERVANTES *nods assent. Handing him the package)* Plead as well there as you did here and you may not burn.

CERVANTES: I've no intention of burning. *(To his* MANSERVANT, *buoyantly)* Well, old friend? Shall we go? *(He sees that the* SERVANT *is rigid with fear; comes to put a reassuring arm about his shoulder)* Courage!

(He leads him toward the stairs)

THE GOVERNOR: Cervantes. *(*CERVANTES *pauses)* I think Don Quixote is brother to Don Miguel.

CERVANTES: *(Smiling)* God help us—we are both men of La Mancha.

(The CAPTAIN *and the* HOODED MEN *about-face as the "Inquisition Theme" resumes. The cortège forms toward an exit, starts ascending the stairs.*

The PRISONER *playing* ALDONZA *is standing apart from the other prisoners as she always does)*

PRISONER: *(*ALDONZA*) (Singing, softly at first)*
  To dream the impossible dream,
  To fight the unbeatable foe,

(The other PRISONERS *join in one by one, their eyes following* CERVANTES*)*

  To bear with unbearable sorrow,
  To run where the brave dare not go . . .

  To run where the brave dare not go,
  Though the goal be forever too far,
  To try, though you're wayworn and weary,
  To reach the unreachable star . . .

(And now the song, swelling in full chorus, overwhelms the "Inquisition Theme")

To reach the unreachable star,
Though you know it's impossibly high,
To live with your heart striving upward
To a far, unattainable sky!

The lights fade out and the play ends

CABARET

Book by Joe Masteroff
Lyrics by Fred Ebb
Music by John Kander

(Based on the play by John van Druten and stories by Christopher Isherwood)

Editor's Notes

One of the most accoladed and successful musical plays of its decade, *Cabaret* opened on November 20, 1966, to almost unanimous critical approbation and immediate audience response. Within hours after its premiere, it became the season's "hottest" ticket.

Based on the prize play, *I Am a Camera*, which had an engagement of 214 performances in 1951, and Christopher Isherwood's stories, the saga of Sally Bowles' adventures in Berlin "when the Nazis were breaking the thin crust of a dream world," the property was converted into a masterful musical with book by Joe Masteroff and words and music by Fred Ebb and John Kander—all under the inspired direction of Harold Prince.

Walter Kerr declared in *The New York Times* that *Cabaret* was: "A stunning musical. Brilliantly conceived. It opens the door to a fresh notion of the bizarre, crackling, harsh and yet beguiling uses that can be made of song and dance." Richard Watts, Jr. of the *New York Post* wrote: "It is the glory of *Cabaret* that it can upset you while it gives theatrical satisfaction. It is disturbing, provocative, meaningful, believable and highly entertaining."

Others described it as: "A scintillating unconventional musical play" that employs "a colorful explosion of wit and intelligence. Here is a musical of unusual distinction."

Richard Gilman of *Newsweek* magazine conveyed to his readers: "*Cabaret* is serious, which is to say it accepts the premise that mature themes aren't inimical to the musical genre. It is also fun in a salty, grown-up way—sensual, elaborate, honest and yeasty, full of accurate perceptions translated into sharp and savory theatre."

The musical, which ran for 1,165 performances, won the New York Drama Critics' Circle Award for best musical of the season, eight Antoinette Perry (Tony) Awards, including one for best musical play, five citations in *Variety*'s Poll of New York Drama Critics, as well as an Outer Circle Award.

In 1972, a film version of *Cabaret* was released. Starring Liza Minnelli, Joel Grey and Michael York, it won eight Academy Awards.

Joe Masteroff was born in Philadelphia on December 11, 1919. He was educated at Temple University, graduating with a B.S. in 1940. During World War II, he served for four years in the U. S. Air Force. Deciding to pursue a career in the theatre, he studied at the American Theatre Wing from 1949 through 1951.

After it had toured nationally, he finally made his Broadway debut as a playwright when his comedy, *The Warm Peninsula*, opened on October 20, 1959 at the Helen Hayes Theatre. The cast included Julie Harris, June Havoc, Farley Granger and Larry Hagman and ran for 86 performances.

Mr. Masteroff's first musical book was *She Loves Me* which opened in New York on April 23, 1963. With music and lyrics by Jerry Bock and Sheldon Harnick, the Harold Prince production ran for 301 performances and was cited as one of the ten best plays of the season.

Fred Ebb was born in New York City on April 8, 1932, and was educated at New York University and Columbia University. Before teaming with John Kander, he wrote both the book and lyrics for *Morning Sun*, presented at the Phoenix Theatre in 1963. He also contributed the lyrics to many revues including *Put It in Writing* and *From A to Z*, and sketches for the television show, *That Was The Week That Was.*

John Kander was born in Kansas City, Missouri, on March 18, 1927. He attended Oberlin College where he received his B.A. and Columbia University where he earned his M.A.

Mr. Kander first worked in the theatre at Oberlin College when he composed *Second Square, Opus Two* and *Requiem for Georgie.* Subsequently, he was choral director and conductor for the Warwick (Rhode Island) Musical Theatre. He conducted a revival of Noël Coward's *Conversation Piece* at the Barbizon-Plaza Theatre, New York, in 1957. The next step was to Broadway to do the dance arrangements for *Gypsy* (1959) and *Irma La Douce* (1960). He collaborated on the Broadway musical *A Family Affair* in 1962 and later in the same year composed the incidental music for the comedy *Never Too Late.*

Kander and Ebb first combined talents to create the song, "My Coloring Book" which soon became number one on the record charts. They followed this with a Barbra Streisand hit, "I Don't Care Much."

Their initial Broadway venture together was the Harold Prince-George Abbott 1965 musical *Flora, the Red Menace,* for which its star Liza Minnelli won a Tony Award.

This was followed in 1966 by the fabulously successful *Cabaret,* and as of June 3, 1975, the team of Kander and Ebb are represented again on Broadway with the music and lyrics (Ebb also is coauthor of the book with Bob Fosse) for the new musical, *Chicago,* co-starring Gwen Verdon, Chita Rivera and Jerry Orbach.

Production Notes

Cabaret was first presented by Harold Prince, in association with Ruth Mitchell, at the Broadhurst Theatre, New York, on November 20, 1966. The cast was as follows:

Master of Ceremonies (Emcee), *Joel Grey*
Clifford Bradshaw, *Bert Convy*
Ernst Ludwig, *Edward Winter*
Customs Officer, *Howard Kahl*
Fraulein Schneider, *Lotte Lenya*
Fraulein Kost, *Peg Murray*
Herr Schultz, *Jack Gilford*
Girl, *Tresha Kelly*
Sally Bowles, *Jill Haworth*
Girl Orchestra, *Maryann Burns, Janice Mink, Nancy Powers, Viola Smith*
Two Ladies, *Mary Ehara, Rita O'Connor*
Maitre D', *Frank Bouley*
Max, *John Herbert*
Bartender, *Ray Baron*

German Sailors, *Bruce Becker, Steven Boockvor, Roger Briant, Edward Nolfi*
Frau Wendel, *Mara Landi*
Herr Wendel, *Eugene Morgan*
Frau Kruger, *Miriam Lehmann-Haupt*
Herr Erdmann, *Sol Frieder*
Kit Kat Girls:
   Maria, *Pat Gosling*
   Lulu, *Lynn Winn*
   Rosie, *Bonnie Walker*
   Fritzie, *Marianne Selbert*
   Texas, *Kathie Dalton*
   Frenchie, *Barbara Alston*
Bobby, *Jere Admire*
Victor, *Bert Michaels*
Greta, *Jayme Mylroie*
Felix, *Robert Sharp*

Directed by *Harold Prince*
Dances and Cabaret Numbers by *Ronald Field*
Scenery by *Boris Aronson*
Costumes by *Patricia Zipprodt*
Lighting by *Jean Rosenthal*
Musical Direction by *Harold Hastings*
Orchestrations by *Don Walker*
Dance Arrangements by *David Baker*

Scene: Berlin, Germany
Time: 1929–1930. Before the start of the Third Reich
Note: There is no curtain. As the audience enters the theatre, the stage is bare and dark. Street lamps on both sides of the stage recede dimly into the distance. A large mirror hanging center stage reflects the auditorium, thus allowing the audience to see itself. A spiral staircase is on the left side of the proscenium arch.

Musical Numbers

Act One

Willkommen	Emcee and the Company
So What?	Fraulein Schneider
Don't Tell Mama	Sally and the Girls
Telephone Song	The Company
Perfectly Marvelous	Sally and Cliff
Two Ladies	Emcee and Two Ladies
It Couldn't Please Me More	Fraulein Schneider and Herr Schultz
Tomorrow Belongs to Me	Emcee and Waiters
Why Should I Wake Up?	Cliff
The Money Song	Emcee and the Cabaret Girls
Married	Fraulein Schneider and Herr Schultz
Meeskite	Herr Schultz
Tomorrow Belongs to Me (Reprise)	Fraulein Kost, Ernst and Guests

Act Two

If You Could See Her	Emcee and the Girls
Married (Reprise)	Herr Schultz
If You Could See Her (Reprise)	Emcee and Bobby
What Would You Do?	Fraulein Schneider
Cabaret	Sally
Finale	Cliff, Sally, Fraulein Schneider, Herr Schultz, Emcee and the Company

ACT ONE

SCENE 1

In the darkness, a large sign is illuminated—letter by letter. It reads: Cabaret. *Then it disappears.*

There is a roll of the drums. Then the MASTER OF CEREMONIES *(*EMCEE*) enters in a spotlight upstage. He is a bizarre little figure—much lipstick, much rouge, patent-leather hair parted in the middle. He walks toward the footlights and greets the audience.*

EMCEE: *(Singing)*
Willkommen, bienvenue, welcome
Fremde, étranger, stranger
Glücklich zu sehen
Je suis enchanté
Happy to see you
Bleibe, reste, stay
Willkommen, bienvenue, welcome
Im Cabaret, au Cabaret, to Cabaret!

Meine Damen und Herren—Mesdames et Messieurs—Ladies and Gentlemen! Guten abend—bon soir—good evening! Wie geht's? Comment ça va? Do you feel good? Ich bin euer confrencier—je suis votre compère—I am your host! *(He sings again)*

Und sage—
Willkommen, bienvenue, welcome
Im Cabaret, au Cabaret, to Cabaret!

Leave your troubles outside! So—life is disappointing? Forget it! In here life is beautiful—the girls are beautiful—even the orchestra is beautiful! *(A GIRL OR-CHESTRA appears on stage and plays a chorus of "Willkommen")* And now—presenting the Cabaret Girls! *(The GIRLS enter. The mirror tilts upward—reflecting the stage rather than the auditorium)* Each and every one a virgin. You don't believe me? Well, don't take my word for it. Go ahead. Ask her! Outside it is winter. But here it is so hot—every night we have the battle to keep the girls from taking off all their clothing. So don't go away. Who knows? Tonight we may lose the battle!

GIRLS: *(Singing)*
Wir sagen—
Willkommen, bienvenue, welcome
Im Cabaret, au Cabaret, to Cabaret!

EMCEE: And now to serve you—
*(*WAITERS, BUSBOYS, ENTERTAINERS *appear)*

ALL: *(Singing)*
Willkommen, bienvenue, welcome
Fremde, étranger, stranger

Glücklich zu sehen
Je suis enchanté
Happy to see you
Bleibe, reste, stay
Willkommen, bienvenue, welcome
Im Cabaret, au Cabaret, to Cabaret!

Blackout

SCENE 2

A compartment of a European railway train. It appears to be in motion.
CLIFFORD BRADSHAW *is alone in the compartment—asleep. He is in his late twenties, pleasant-looking, intelligent, reserved. His suitcase and portable typewriter are on the rack above his head.*
ERNST LUDWIG *enters. He is German, about thirty, friendly and likable. He carries a suitcase, a brown leather briefcase and a magazine. He seems rather nervous.*
ERNST: Occupied? *(CLIFF opens his eyes and shakes his head)* It is permitted?
CLIFF: Please.
(ERNST places his suitcase on the rack over the seat opposite CLIFF. He puts his briefcase on the floor beside his legs as he sits down)
ERNST: English?
CLIFF: American.
ERNST: German. Berlin. Ernst Ludwig.
(They shake hands)
CLIFF: Clifford Bradshaw. Pennsylvania. Are we slowing down for the German border?
ERNST: Ja.
CLIFF: You've taken this trip before?
ERNST: Many many times. *(ERNST shows increasing signs of nervousness)* You are a tourist?
CLIFF: *No!* Not exactly. I'm a writer and I give English lessons. *(The train stops. ERNST gets up and surveys the corridor)* Would you care for a cigarette? *(There is no answer)* Herr Ludwig?
ERNST: *(Absently)* Ja?
CLIFF: A cigarette?
ERNST: No. Thank you.
(ERNST suddenly sits down and pretends to be absorbed in a magazine. Two German CUSTOMS OFFICERS enter the compartment)
OFFICER: Deutsche Grenzkontrolle. Ihre pässe, bitte.
CLIFF: I beg your pardon?
OFFICER: Your passport, if you please. *(CLIFF hands his passport to the OFFICER)* Welcome to Germany, Mr. Bradshaw. *(The OFFICER indicates CLIFF'S bags)* Yours? *(CLIFF nods. The OFFICER puts a Customs mark on his bags without even taking them off the rack. Then he turns to ERNST, who is deep in his magazine)* Ihren pass, bitte. *(ERNST hands over his passport)* Sie waren geschäftlich in Paris?
ERNST: Nein. Auf einer urlaubreise.
OFFICER: Offen sie ihre tasche. *(ERNST takes down his suitcase and opens it. The OFFICER goes through it. While the OFFICER's back is turned ERNST takes his*

briefcase off the floor and puts it on the rack over CLIFF'S *head.* CLIFF *is surprised, but says nothing. The* OFFICER *marks* ERNST'S *bag)* Haben sie nur diese eine tasche?

ERNST: Ja. Das ist alles.

OFFICER: *(To* CLIFF*)* I wish you will enjoy your stay in Germany. And a most Happy New Year. *(The* OFFICER *exits.* ERNST, *very relieved, retrieves the briefcase)*

CLIFF: What's in the bag?

ERNST: *(Too casual)* What? Baubles from Paris: perfume . . . silk stockings . . . But more than is permitted. You understand?

CLIFF: *(Nods)* I guess I've done a little smuggling myself.

ERNST: *(With new vigor)* You are most understanding. I thank you very much. And I would like to see to it that Berlin will open its arms to you! We begin tonight—New Year's Eve—the Kit Kat Klub! The hottest spot in Berlin. Telephones on every table. Girls call you. You call them. Instant connections.

CLIFF: *(Shaking his head)* Thanks—but I've still got to find a room.

ERNST: You have no room! But this is no problem! *(He takes out a card and writes on it)* I know the finest residence in all Berlin. Just tell Fraulein Schneider that Ernst Ludwig has recommended you.

CLIFF: I can't afford the finest residence in Berlin. I need something inexpensive.

ERNST: But this *is* inexpensive! Very inexpensive! She has this kind of room and that kind of room. Absolute satisfaction!

CLIFF: I don't care if it's awful—as long as it's cheap.

ERNST: But this *is* awful. You will love it!

(The train starts again. ERNST *hands* CLIFF *the card.* CLIFF *reads it)*

CLIFF: Fraulein Schneider . . .

ERNST: You see! You see! You have a new friend—Ernst Ludwig! You have a fine place to live! And you have perhaps even your first English pupil! *(He indicates himself.* CLIFF *is quite surprised)* Ja! So welcome to Berlin, my friend. Welcome to Berlin! *(They shake hands. The train moves upstage and disappears as the* EMCEE *crosses downstage)*

EMCEE: *(Singing)*
Welcome to Berlin!
Willkommen, bienvenue, welcome
Fremde, étranger, stranger
Glücklich zu sehen
Je suis enchanté
Happy to see you
Bleibe, reste, stay!

SCENE 3

A room in FRAULEIN SCHNEIDER*'s flat. The furnishings are ugly and ponderous: a bed, a table with two chairs, an armoire, and, behind a curtain, a washstand.*

As the lights come up, FRAULEIN SCHNEIDER *enters. She is about sixty: full of vitality, interested in everything, probably indestructible. She wears a flowered dressing gown and carpet slippers.*

CLIFF *follows her, carrying his bags.*

FRAULEIN SCHNEIDER: You see! All comforts! And with breakfast only one hundred marks!

CLIFF: It's very nice, Fraulein Schneider. In fact—too nice. You don't have something cheaper?

FRAULEIN SCHNEIDER: But for a friend of Herr Ludwig . . .

CLIFF: I've very little money.

FRAULEIN SCHNEIDER: But you will give English lessons. Many pupils will come. And they will pay you. And then you will pay *me*. No?

CLIFF: *(Shaking his head)* Fifty marks. That's my absolute limit. *(FRAULEIN SCHNEIDER shrugs her shoulders)* If you've anything else . . . I don't care how small, how far from the bathroom . . .

FRAULEIN SCHNEIDER: But for a *professor*—this is more suitable.

CLIFF: I am *not* a professor. Think of me as a starving author. What do you have for a starving author?

FRAULEIN SCHNEIDER: An author! A poet! You have the look!

CLIFF: A novelist.

FRAULEIN SCHNEIDER: And you will be most famous. There is no doubt. You will have *this* room. Here is for your clothing. Look—there is even a table for writing. Come . . . sitz. *(She pulls out the chair at the writing table and invites* CLIFF *to try it. He does)* Good? *(CLIFF nods)* You need a cushion . . . *(She stuffs a cushion in behind him)* Besser? *(Then she stands back and admires the scene)* A novelist! It is like—years ago—when in all my rooms—persons of real quality . . .

CLIFF: But I can still only pay fifty marks.

FRAULEIN SCHNEIDER: This room is worth one hundred. More than one hundred. *(She looks at* CLIFF *hopefully. He shakes his head)* Fifty? *(CLIFF nods.* FRAULEIN SCHNEIDER *suddenly surrenders)* Sitz! *(She sings)*

You say fifty marks,
I say one hundred marks;
A difference of fifty marks,
Why should that stand in our way?
As long as the room's to let,
The fifty that I will get
Is fifty more than I had yesterday, ja?
When you're as old as I—
Is anyone as old as I?
What difference does it make?
An offer comes, you take.

For the sun will rise and the moon will set,
And you learn how to settle for what you get.
It'll all go on if we're here or not,
So who cares? So what?
So who cares? So what?

When I was a girl my summers were spent by the sea, so what?
And I had a maid doing all of the housework, not me, so what?
Now I scrub up the floors and I wash down the walls,
And I empty the chamber pot.
If it ended that way then it ended that way, and I shrug and I say, so what?

For the sun will rise and the moon will set,
And you learn how to settle for what you get.
It'll all go on if we're here or not,
So who cares, so what?
So who cares, so what?

When I had a man, my figure was boyish and flat, so what?
Through all of our years he was so disappointed in that, so what?
Now I have what he missed and my bosom is full,
But he lies in a churchyard plot.
If it wasn't to be that he ever would see the abundance of me,
So what?

For the sun will rise and the moon will set,
And you learn how to settle for what you get.
It'll all go on if we're here or not,
So who cares, so what?
So who cares, so what?

So once I was rich, and now all my fortune is gone, so what?
And love disappeared and only the memory lives on, so what?
If I've lived through all that, and I've lived through all that,
Fifty marks doesn't mean a lot.
If I like that you're here, and I like that you're here,
Happy New Year, my dear, so what?

For the sun will rise and the moon will set,
And you learn how to settle for what you get.
It'll all go on if we're here or not,
So who cares . . . so what?
So who cares . . . so what?
It all goes on,
So who cares? Who cares? Who cares? So what?

(FRAULEIN SCHNEIDER *starts checking the room. She takes out a blanket)* An additional blanket. The telephone is in the hall. I will bring towels. *(There is a knock on the door)* Come in!

(FRAULEIN KOST *enters. She is thirtyish, a large and happy woman who works diligently at her profession)*

FRAULEIN KOST: Fraulein Schneider! There you are! There is no hot water in the bathroom! The second time this week!

FRAULEIN SCHNEIDER: *(To* CLIFF*)* If you will excuse me, Herr Bradshaw.

FRAULEIN KOST: *(She notes* CLIFF *and starts giving him the eye)* So you have finally rented this room.

FRAULEIN SCHNEIDER: Here is Herr Clifford Bradshaw—the world-famous American novelist.

(FRAULEIN KOST *starts toward* CLIFF. FRAULEIN SCHNEIDER *steps between them)*

CLIFF: How do you do?

FRAULEIN KOST: *(Flirtatiously)* I am Fraulein Kost. Across the hall . . . Please feel free at any time . . .

(A GERMAN SAILOR *runs in)*

SAILOR: Schatzi—where are you . . . ?

(FRAULEIN KOST is a little embarrassed to have CLIFF see the SAILOR)

FRAULEIN KOST: *(Making it up quickly)* My nephew! He is visiting me. From Hamburg.

FRAULEIN SCHNEIDER: *(To FRAULEIN KOST)* Come! We talk outside. We are disturbing Herr Bradshaw. And bring your nephew with you—from Hamburg! *(When they are gone, she turns back to CLIFF)* My apologies, Herr Bradshaw. I guarantee she will not bother you again.

CLIFF: Bother me?

(There is a knock at the door)

FRAULEIN SCHNEIDER: What is it now?

(HERR SCHULTZ enters. He is in his fifties, very warm and cheerful. He dresses neatly, but it would appear that he needs a woman to tell him what tie goes with what. He is carrying a bottle of schnapps)

SCHULTZ: Fraulein Schneider—

FRAULEIN SCHNEIDER: Ah, Herr Schultz! Is it eleven o'clock? I have been showing Herr Bradshaw his room. Herr Bradshaw—Herr Schultz, who also lives here.

CLIFF: Pleased to meet you.

SCHULTZ: Honored!

FRAULEIN SCHNEIDER: Herr Bradshaw is from America.

SCHULTZ: America! I have a cousin in Buffalo.

FRAULEIN SCHNEIDER: And Herr Schultz is proprietor of the finest fruit market on the Nollendorfplatz.

SCHULTZ: Seville oranges. Delicious.

FRAULEIN SCHNEIDER: I will dress now. *(To CLIFF)* Herr Schultz has been kind enough to invite me to join him in a glass of schnapps for the New Year.

SCHULTZ: And a little fruit.

FRAULEIN SCHNEIDER: And—after all—why not? Otherwise I am in bed with a hot-water bottle.

SCHULTZ: Perhaps Herr Bradshaw . . .

CLIFF: No. But thanks for asking.

SCHULTZ: Another time! *(SCHULTZ shakes hands with CLIFF)* I want to wish you *mazel* in the New Year.

CLIFF: *Mazel?*

SCHULTZ: Jewish. It means luck!

CLIFF: Thank you. The same to you.

SCHULTZ: I come to you, Fraulein—in ten minutes—with the schnapps!

FRAULEIN SCHNEIDER: And the fruit! *(HERR SCHULTZ exits. FRAULEIN SCHNEIDER turns to CLIFF)* And now—please—anything you require—knock on my door. Day, night. Also—welcome to Berlin! *(She exits)*

CLIFF: Welcome to Berlin—famous novelist. *(He puts his typewriter on the table)* Open the Remington . . .

(A beautiful GIRL appears, sitting at a café table. She is singing into a telephone. She does not look at CLIFF)

GIRL: Hello? Hello?

(CLIFF is unaware of the GIRL. He looks gloomily at the typewriter)

CLIFF: That's what you came here for.

GIRL: *(Singing)*
> *Sitting all alone like that,*
> *You happened to catch my eye.*
> *Would you like to buy a girl a drink?*

(CLIFF opens the typewriter half-heartedly)
CLIFF: Welcome to Berlin—famous novelist . . .

GIRL: *(Singing)*
> *Ja? You would? Come on over!*

(CLIFF closes the typewriter, takes his coat, and exits out the door)

SCENE 4

The GIRL is sitting in the middle of the Kit Kat Klub, an establishment in which all the tables have telephones on them so that guests can call each other. At the moment, the Klub is packed. It is New Year's Eve, 1930.

CLIFF enters the Klub and is seated at a table. The EMCEE appears; there is fanfare from the GIRL ORCHESTRA.

EMCEE: Meine Damen und Herren—Mesdames et Messieurs—Ladies and Gentlemen— And now the Kit Kat Klub is proud to present a beautiful young lady from England. She is so beautiful, so talented, so charming that I have asked her to marry me. And now there is only one thing standing in our way: my wife! *(He pantomimes cutting his throat. A few members of the audience laugh)* I give you: the toast of Mayfair—Fraulein Sally Bowles!

(SALLY BOWLES enters. She is in her early twenties, rather pretty, rather sophisticated, rather child-like, exasperating and irresistible)

SALLY: *(Singing)*
> *Mama thinks I'm living in a convent,*
> *A secluded little convent*
> *In the southern part of France.*
> *Mama doesn't even have an inkling*
> *That I'm working in a nightclub*
> *In a pair of lacy pants.*
>
> *So please, sir, if you run into my mama,*
> *Don't reveal my indiscretion—*
> *Give a working girl a chance.*
> *Hush up, don't tell Mama,*
> *Shush up, don't tell Mama,*
> *Don't tell Mama whatever you do.*
>
> *If you had a secret,*
> *You bet I could keep it.*
> *I would never tell on you.*
> *I'm breaking every promise that I gave her,*
> *So won't you kindly do a girl a great big favor?*
>
> *And please, my sweet patater,*
> *Keep this from the mater,*
> *Though my dance is not against the law.*

You can tell my papa, that's all right,
'Cause he comes in here every night,
But don't tell Mama what you saw!

(The CABARET GIRLS *appear*)

GIRLS: *(Singing)*
Mama thinks I'm on a tour of Europe
With a couple of my school-chums
And a lady chaperone.
Mama doesn't even have an inkling
That I left them all in Antwerp
And I'm touring on my own.
So please, sir, if you run into my mama,
Don't reveal my indiscretion—
Just leave well enough alone.

GIRLS:
Hush up—

SALLY:
Don't tell Mama.

GIRLS:
Shush up—

SALLY:
Don't tell Mama

SALLY and GIRLS:
Don't tell Mama whatever you do.

SALLY:
If you had a secret,
You bet I could keep it.

GIRLS:
We would never tell on you.

SALLY:
You wouldn't want to get me in a pickle,
And have her go and cut me off without a nickel,

SALLY and GIRLS:
So let's trust one another.
Keep this from my mother,
Though I'm still as pure as mountain snow.

SALLY:
You can tell my uncle, here and now,
'Cause he's my agent anyhow.

GIRLS:
But don't tell Mama what you know.

SALLY:

> You can tell my grandma, suits me fine,
> Just yesterday she joined the line.

GIRLS:

> But don't tell Mama what you know.

SALLY:

> You can tell my brother, that ain't grim,
> 'Cause if he squeals on me, I'll squeal on him.

SALLY and GIRLS:

> But don't tell Mama, bitte,
> Don't tell Mama, please, sir,
> Don't tell Mama what you know!

SALLY:

> If you see my mummy, mum's the word!

(During this number SALLY *has gradually become aware of* CLIFF. *She has sung to him, almost as if he were the only one in the audience. At the end of the number* SALLY *and the* GIRLS *dance off.* SALLY *reappears soon afterward.* CLIFF *watches her intently as she goes to a "Reserved" table for two. She sits there alone for a moment. Then she picks up the phone)*

SALLY: Table number three.

(The phone on CLIFF'S *table lights up)*

CLIFF: *(Into the phone)* Hello?

SALLY: *(Into the phone)* You're English!

CLIFF: I wish I were.

SALLY: American?

CLIFF: I'm sorry.

SALLY: But you *speak* English! You speak it beautifully! Will you just—keep talking—please? You can't imagine how starved I've been!

CLIFF: Okay. Let me think. *(He recites)*

> The sea is calm tonight.
> The tide is full, the moon lies fair
> Upon the straits: —on the French coast the light
> Gleams and is gone; the cliffs of England stand,
> Glimmering and vast, out in the tranquil bay.
> Come to the window, sweet is the night air!

SALLY: Yes—yes—don't stop—please!

CLIFF: I'm afraid that's all I know. My name is Cliff Bradshaw. I come from Harrisburg, Pennsylvania. You know where that is?

SALLY: Such a beautiful language.

CLIFF: Well, it's ninety miles west of Philadelphia. May I come to your table?

SALLY: It's like music! *(Pause)* Why did you stop?

CLIFF: I asked you a question. I'd like to join you at your table.

SALLY: Oh. I see. Well—I'm not absolutely sure that's possible—at this time. *(A man, rather middle-aged and quite Germanic-looking, walks up to* SALLY'S *table and sits down next to her. He looks rather irritated with her)* As a matter of fact, I rather doubt it.

(The man snatches the phone out of SALLY'S *hand and hangs it up. There is fanfare from the orchestra. The* EMCEE *appears, dressed as Father Time)*

EMCEE: Meine Damen und Herren, Mesdames et Messieurs, Ladies and Gentlemen. It is almost midnight! Husbands, you have only ten seconds in which to lose your wives! Five—four—three—two—Happy New Year!

(Then the stage goes black. In the darkness, there is enormous jubilation. The EMCEE *changes into Infant New Year, 1930. Then a match is lit in the darkness. It is* SALLY *lighting a cigarette in a long, long cigarette holder. She is sitting at* CLIFF'S *table)*

SALLY: Would you recite that again—about the coast of England?

CLIFF:
The sea is calm tonight,
The tide is full—

(He has a better idea. He kisses her) Happy New Year.

SALLY: I'm Sally Bowles. Are you new in Berlin?

CLIFF: Yes, I've only been here three hours.

(The man who was sitting with SALLY *has risen and is heading toward* CLIFF'S *table. As he approaches,* CLIFF *sees him and starts to get up politely.* SALLY *puts her hand on* CLIFF'S *arm, indicating that he should keep seated.* SALLY *glances briefly at the man—as if challenging him. The man hesitates for a moment. Then he goes away.* SALLY *turns back to* CLIFF *)*

SALLY: Three hours! And how long are you planning to stay?

CLIFF: *(Shrugs his shoulders)* I'm working on a novel. I'll stay till it's finished.

SALLY: *(Impressed)* You're a writer! Would I know your books?

CLIFF: It's highly unlikely. Anyway, it's *book*—singular.

SALLY: Was it a huge success?

CLIFF: They said it showed promise.

SALLY: Promise?

CLIFF: *(He puts his arm around her)* Let's talk about Sally Bowles. What part of England are you from? *(No answer)* London? *(No answer)* Stratford-on-Avon? *(No answer)* Stonehenge?

SALLY: Oh, Cliff, you mustn't ever ask me questions. If I want to tell you anything, I will. Why did you come to *Berlin* to do your novel?

CLIFF: I'd already tried London, Rome, Venice . . .

SALLY: Just looking for a place to write?

CLIFF: Something to write about.

SALLY: Where are you staying?

(CLIFF shows her the card ERNST *gave him)*

CLIFF: And you, where do *you* live? A hotel?

SALLY: No. Not really. It's more of a flat—actually.

CLIFF: You live alone? *(SALLY shakes her head)* You think your roommate would mind if I came up for just a few minutes?

SALLY: I'm afraid so. You see, Max is most terribly jealous.

CLIFF: Max? *(SALLY nods again)* Your husband?

SALLY: Oh, no! He's just the man I'm living with *(CLIFF looks a little surprised)* —this week. *(She studies his face)* I say—am I shocking you—talking like this?

CLIFF: *(Mocking)* I say, are you trying to shock me?

SALLY: Trying to . . . ? *(But she likes him for having seen through her)* You're quite right, you know. *(She kisses him; the* EMCEE *appears and signals to her. She rises)* Good luck with your writing!

(And she is gone. CLIFF'S *phone lights up)*

CLIFF: Hello?

GIRL ON PHONE: *(Singing)*
Hello.
Sitting alone like that,
You happened to catch my eye.
Would you like to buy a girl a drink?

CLIFF: Sorry.

GIRL ON PHONE:
Ach! Goodbye.

(CLIFF exits)

FIRST BOY: *(Into phone)*
Hello

FIRST GIRL: *(Into phone)*
Hello—table four is calling number nine
How are you, mister?

FIRST BOY:
Danke—fine

FIRST GIRL:
Sitting all alone like that,
You happened to catch my eye.
Would you like to give a girl a dance?

FIRST BOY:
Yah—why not?

BOTH:
Goodbye!

(They dance)

SECOND BOY: *(Into phone)*
Hello

SECOND GIRL: *(Into phone)*
Hello

THIRD BOY: *(Into phone)*
Hello

THIRD GIRL: *(Into phone)*
Hello

SECOND and THIRD GIRL:
Table seven calling number three.
How are you, handsome?

SECOND and THIRD BOY:
You mean me?

SECOND and THIRD GIRL:
We can see you—can you see us?
Would you like to have a dance
The minute that the music's hot?
Maybe we can talk it over, Ja?

THIRD BOY:
Ja!

SECOND BOY:
Of course!

SECOND and THIRD BOY:
Why not!

(Both couples dance)

FOURTH and FIFTH BOY: *(Into phone)*
Alone—alone
You shouldn't sit alone like that
Alone—alone
Not on a night like this.

ALL:
Alone—alone
You shouldn't sit alone like that
Alone—alone
Not on a night like this.

(They dance, and from different parts of the stage—right, center, left—the dancers alternately say "Hello")

ALL:
Sitting all alone like that,
You happened to catch my eye.

GIRLS:
Would you like to buy a girl a drink?

BOYS:
Would you like to buy a man a drink?

ALL:
Would you like to buy a boy a drink?

(They dance, and from different parts of the stage—right, center, left—the dancers alternately say, "You will," "Why not?" "Goodbye")

ALL: *Ja!*

Blackout

SCENE 5

CLIFF'S *room.* ERNST *is referring to a dictionary.* CLIFF *watches him.*
ERNST: You know what is the trouble with English? It is not like German. It is

not an exact language. Or one must memorize fifty thousand words or one cannot speak it correctly.

CLIFF: *Either* one must memorize—*or* one cannot speak . . .

ERNST: Aha! *Either*—or—*(ERNST happily makes a notation in his notebook, then closes it and stands up)* The time is now finished.

CLIFF: I'm in no hurry.

ERNST: But the lesson is one hour. No? Another pupil is waiting.

CLIFF: *What* other pupil?

ERNST: No other pupil? *(CLIFF shakes his head)* Then I make a suggestion! I will telephone my lady friend. She will bring a friend for you. Elsa! A genuine flapper.

CLIFF: Not tonight, Ernst.

ERNST: But you have not seen this Elsa! Hot stuff, believe me! In one minute, I guarantee, you are making a pass after her.

CLIFF: A pass *at* her.

ERNST: Aha!! A pass *at* her!

CLIFF: The trouble is, I've *got* a date tonight. *(He indicates his typewriter)*

ERNST: A typewriter? But what can one do with a typewriter?

CLIFF: Not very much—lately.

ERNST: Then come with me! We make a large whoopee!

CLIFF: *(Shakes his head)* For one thing, I've got a budget. And it only allows for a very small whoopee. Unfortunately.

ERNST: Then you are *my* guest!

CLIFF: Thanks, but . . . *(He shakes his head negatively)*

ERNST: It is difficult, you know—adjusting to the idea of a *poor* American. But I tell you a secret. There is no need for this—poverty. Ja! If you are willing, I show you a most excellent way to supplement your income.

CLIFF: Doing what?

ERNST: Oh—by taking very brief trips—to Paris! Perhaps a few days each time. Nothing more. But it will pay you well, extremely well.

(There is a knock at the door)

CLIFF: Come in.

(FRAULEIN SCHNEIDER enters. She wears her flowered dressing gown. She is quite excited)

FRAULEIN SCHNEIDER: Herr Bradshaw, there is a young lady to see you! A young lady in a fur coat!

CLIFF: A young lady?

FRAULEIN SCHNEIDER: Fraulein Bowles . . . ?

CLIFF: Bowles? *(FRAULEIN SCHNEIDER nods)* Ask her to come in.

(FRAULEIN SCHNEIDER exits)

ERNST: You are old friends—you and Fraulein Bowles? From London, perhaps . . . ?

CLIFF: From the Kit Kat Klub. Last night.

ERNST: Last night! You are some snappy operator!

(SALLY enters wearing a fur coat, smoking a cigarette in a cigarette holder. FRAU-LEIN SCHNEIDER follows her)

SALLY: Cliff!! *(She kisses CLIFF)* Ernst, darling! *(She kisses ERNST. To CLIFF)* Will you be a dear and get my bag? *(She surveys the room approvingly)* It's *lovely*, Fraulein Schneider! All these wonderful old pieces! *(CLIFF enters with her bag. To CLIFF)* Just put it anywhere. I'll unpack later.

FRAULEIN SCHNEIDER: Unpack? But Herr Bradshaw did not mention . . .

SALLY: I'll just be here temporarily.

FRAULEIN SCHNEIDER: But I am sorry. This is not possible.

SALLY: *(To* CLIFF*)* How much are you paying?

CLIFF: Fifty marks.

SALLY: *(To* FRAULEIN SCHNEIDER*)* Sixty marks?

FRAULEIN SCHNEIDER: *(Shaking her head)* It is not the money—

SALLY: Seventy?

FRAULEIN SCHNEIDER: I cannot permit—

SALLY: Eighty?

   *(*FRAULEIN SCHNEIDER *mulls this over for a moment. She is very, very tempted)*

FRAULEIN SCHNEIDER: But this room is worth one hundred marks. More than one hundred.

SALLY: Eighty.

FRAULEIN SCHNEIDER: Eighty-five! *(They shake hands)* And now—please make yourself cosy—*Frau* Bradshaw.

   *(*FRAULEIN SCHNEIDER *exits.* ERNST *looks at his watch)*

ERNST: *(To* CLIFF*)* Such a to-do! I will see you Friday for the next lesson. But I tell you something: I think I am taking from you the *wrong kind* of lessons.
   *(*ERNST *exits.* SALLY, *still in her fur coat, collapses onto the bed)*

CLIFF: Sally, now what's this all about?

SALLY: Did you guess I was terrified?

CLIFF: Were you?

SALLY: What if you'd—thrown me out? Can you imagine how *that* would feel—being thrown out twice in one day?

CLIFF: You mean—Max . . . ?

SALLY: Dear Max. And you know whose fault it was? *(She points at* CLIFF*)* If you hadn't come to the Kit Kat Klub—and been so dreadfully attractive—and recited poetry—*(She suddenly sits up)* You know what I'd love? A spot of gin.

CLIFF: Gin?

SALLY: You've *got* some? I mean—I think one *must.*

CLIFF: No, I don't have any . . .

SALLY: Oh, well, Prairie Oysters, then.

CLIFF: Prairie Oysters?

SALLY: I practically live on them. It's just a raw egg whooshed around in some Worcestershire sauce. It's heaven for a hangover.

CLIFF: I haven't got a hangover. *(*SALLY *takes eggs, salt, pepper and Worcestershire sauce out of her coat pocket.* CLIFF *watches her)* That's quite a coat.

SALLY: It should be. It cost me all I had. Little did I dream how soon I'd be unemployed.

CLIFF: What about your job at the Klub?

SALLY: Well, that's rather complicated. You see, one of the owners of the Klub . . .

CLIFF: Dear Max?

SALLY: You're divinely intuitive! I do hope I'm not going to fall madly in love with you. Are you in the theatre in any way? *(*CLIFF *shakes his head)* Then you're safe—more or less. Though I do believe a woman can't be a truly great actress till she's had several passionate affairs—and had her heart broken. *(Manufacturing the Prairie Oysters,* SALLY *breaks the eggs on this line)* I should have let Ernst pay my cab fare. He's got all that money from Paris.

CLIFF: From Paris?

SALLY: He smuggles it in for some political party.

CLIFF: Ernst is in politics?

SALLY: You didn't know? He goes to Paris about once a month and brings back pots of money.

CLIFF: He has to smuggle it in?

SALLY: It's terribly dangerous. But Ernst is so resourceful. He's discovered the Customs people almost never open the bags of non-Germans. So, just before the border, he finds some innocent-looking Englishman—or American . . . *(She completes the Prairie Oysters)*

CLIFF: It's hard to imagine an American *that* gullible.

(SALLY hands him his drink. She toasts)

SALLY: Hals and beinbruch. It means neck and leg break. It's supposed to stop it happening. Though I doubt it does.

CLIFF: *(Toasting)* Look—it's about time we—

SALLY: Drink!

(SALLY drinks her Prairie Oyster. Then CLIFF sips his)

CLIFF: It's amazing! You know what this tastes like? Peppermint!

SALLY: Oh—well, it's your toothbrush glass. I should have rinsed it. *(SALLY wanders over to the writing table. She picks up a book)* This is your novel! *(She opens it)* It's in German! *(She looks at the cover)* Mein Kampf?

CLIFF: It's not my novel. I thought I should know *something* about German politics.

SALLY: Why? You're an American! You know, I've never *known* a novelist. Will I be allowed to watch you work? I promise to be incredibly quiet . . .

CLIFF: I don't think I can write with someone else—on the premises.

SALLY: But I'm hardly noticeable—really. *(Imploring)* I'll go out when you're writing—take long invigorating walks!

CLIFF: In the middle of the night? And there's another thing: I'm not a prude. At least, I don't think I'm a prude. No—no—I've got work to do. I could never explain this arrangement. It's too peculiar.

SALLY: Peculiar? No, not in the least!

(Spoken, but the music is playing)

I think people are people. I really do, Cliff, don't you?

I don't think they should be made to apologize for anything they do.

For example, if I paint my fingernails green—

And it happens I do paint them green—

Well, if someone should ask me why,

I think it's pretty.

I think it's pretty, *that's* what I reply.

So, if anyone should ask about you and me one day,

You have two alternatives:

You can either say: "Yes, it's true we're living in delicious sin,"

Or you can simply tell them the truth, and say . . .

(SALLY sings)

I met this perfectly marvelous girl

In this perfectly wonderful place

As I lifted a glass to the start of a marvelous year.

Before you knew it she called on the phone, inviting.

Next moment I was no longer alone,
But sat reciting some perfectly beautiful verse
In my charming American style.
How I dazzled her senses was truly no less than a crime.
Now I've this perfectly marvelous girl
In my perfectly beautiful room,
And we're living together and having a marvelous time.

CLIFF: Sally, I'm afraid it wouldn't work. You're much too distracting.
SALLY: Distracting? No, inspiring! *(She sings)*

She tells me perfectly marvelous tales
Of her thrillingly scandalous life
Which I'll probably use as a chapter or two in my book.
And since my stay in Berlin was to force
Creation,
What luck to fall on a fabulous source
Of stimulation.
And perfectly marvelous too
Is her perfect agreement to be
Just as still as a mouse when I'm giving my novel a whirl.
Yes, I've a highly agreeable life
In my perfectly beautiful room,
With my nearly invisible,
Perfectly marvelous girl.

(There is a noise at the door) Oh, it's the taxi man! *(The door bursts open, and there is the taxi man with a mountain of luggage)* Hello, taxi man. Just put them any-where. I'll unpack later. (CLIFF, *a little dazed, points to all the baggage)* Things *do* accumulate. I'll throw most of it away—tomorrow! I promise! (CLIFF *helps the taxi man bring in the bags.* SALLY *starts counting the pieces)* One—two—three—four—five— *(She gives up)* There's really not much point in counting. I never remember how many there're supposed to be. *(To* CLIFF*)* Can you let me have three marks? That includes the tip. (CLIFF *hands her a bill)* Thank you. *(*SALLY *hands the bill to the taxi man, who tips his cap and exits. There is a pause)* So quite seriously, Cliff—please may I stay?
CLIFF: Sally, I can't afford—
SALLY: Only for a day or two—please?

CLIFF: *(Singing)*
I met this truly remarkable girl
In this really incredible town,
And she's skillfully managed to talk her way into my room.

SALLY: Oh, Cliff!

CLIFF:
I have a terrible feeling I've said a dumb thing;
Besides, I've only got one narrow bed.

SALLY:
We'll think of something.

CLIFF:
And now this wild, unpredictable girl

SALLY:
And this perfectly beautiful man

BOTH:
Will be living together and having a marvelous time.

(They are in each other's arms as the lights fade)

SCENE 6

The EMCEE *appears, followed by two sexy* LADIES.

EMCEE: Everybody in Berlin has a perfectly marvelous roommate. Some people have two people!

FIRST LADY: *(Singing)*
Beedle-dee-deedle-dee-dee

SECOND LADY:
Beedle-dee-deedle-dee-dee

EMCEE:
Beedle-dee-deedle-dee
Deedle-dee-deedle-dee-dee!

LADIES:
Beedle-dee-deedle-dee-dee

EMCEE:
Two ladies

LADIES:
Beedle-dee-deedle-dee-dee

EMCEE:
Two ladies

LADIES:
Beedle-dee-deedle-dee-dee

EMCEE:
And I'm the only man, Ja!

LADIES:
Beedle-dee-deedle-dee-dee

EMCEE:
I like it.

LADIES:
Beedle-dee-deedle-dee-dee

EMCEE:
They like it.

LADIES:
Beedle-dee-deedle-dee-dee

EMCEE:
> *This two for one.*
> *Beedle-dee-deedle-dee-dee*

LADIES:
> *Two ladies*

EMCEE:
> *Beedle-dee-deedle-dee-dee*

LADIES:
> *Two ladies*

EMCEE:
> *Beedle-dee-deedle-dee-dee*

LADIES:
> *And he's the only man!*

EMCEE:
> *Ja!*

ALL:
> *Beedle-dee-deedle-dee-dee*

FIRST LADY:
> *He likes it.*

EMCEE:
> *Beedle-dee-deedle-dee-dee*

SECOND LADY:
> *We like it.*

EMCEE:
> *Beedle-dee-deedle-dee-dee*

LADIES:
> *This two for one.*

FIRST LADY:
> *I do the cooking.*

SECOND LADY:
> *And I make the bed.*

EMCEE:
> *I go out daily to earn our daily bread.*
> *But we've one thing in common—*

FIRST LADY:
> *He!*

EMCEE:
> *She*

SECOND LADY:
> *And me!*

FIRST LADY:
> *The key!*

EMCEE:
Beedle-dee

SECOND LADY:
The key!

EMCEE:
Beedle-dee
The key!

LADIES:
Beedle-deedle-deedle-dee

(They dance)

EMCEE:
We switch partners daily
To play as we please.

LADIES:
Twosie beats onesie,

EMCEE:
But nothing beats threes.
I sleep in the middle.

FIRST LADY:
I'm left.

SECOND LADY:
And I'm right.

EMCEE:
But there's room on the bottom if you drop in some night.

LADIES:
Beedle-dee-deedle-dee-dee

EMCEE:
Two ladies
Beedle-dee-deedle-dee-dee

LADIES:
Two ladies
Beedle-dee-deedle-dee-dee
And he's the only man, Ja!

ALL:
Beedle-dee-deedle-dee-dee

EMCEE:
I like it.

ALL:
Beedle-dee-deedle-dee-dee

EMCEE:
We like it.

ALL:

Beedle-dee-deedle-dee-dee
This two for one
Beedle-dee-deedle-dee-deedle-dee-deedle-dee-dee

(They exit)

Blackout

SCENE 7

FRAULEIN SCHNEIDER'S *living room. It is dominated by a large sofa which nestles between two hideous end tables. An old Gramophone lurks in the background.*

Doors lead from the living room to the rooms of FRAULEIN KOST *and* HERR SCHULTZ—*also to the bedroom of* FRAULEIN SCHNEIDER. *A large double door leads outside. A hallway extends offstage, leading to still more rooms.*

As the lights come up FRAULEIN KOST *is entering through the double door with a* GERMAN SAILOR. *He pinches her. She screams. And* FRAULEIN SCHNEIDER *zooms out of her room to accost them.*

FRAULEIN SCHNEIDER: That sailor! Out of my house!

FRAULEIN KOST: That sailor— dear lady—is my brother!

FRAULEIN SCHNEIDER: Out! Out! Out!

(The GERMAN SAILOR *exits through the double door)*

FRAULEIN KOST: Wait! Wait! How dare you! You think it is easy— finding a sailor? This was only my second one since New Year's. And what is it now? April!

FRAULEIN SCHNEIDER: Your second? Your *second?* You think I do not know what goes on here? Sailors—all the time. In—out—in—out! God only knows what the neighbors must think I have here—a battleship? *(Outraged)* Fraulein Kost, I give you warning! One sailor more—I call the police!

FRAULEIN KOST: And if I cannot pay the rent?

FRAULEIN SCHNEIDER: The rent is due each Friday—as always.

FRAULEIN KOST: No sailors. No rent. I move.

FRAULEIN SCHNEIDER: Move?

FRAULEIN KOST: Move!

FRAULEIN SCHNEIDER: *(Upset)* And what am I supposed to do with your room? Out of the blue—she tells me "I move"! Is that gratitude? Only last week I gave you another new mattress!

FRAULEIN KOST: All right! I will leave the end of the week—since you insist.

FRAULEIN SCHNEIDER: *I* insist? *You* insist!

FRAULEIN KOST: And what about the sailors?

FRAULEIN SCHNEIDER: The sailors? *(She mulls it over and reaches a decision)* Fraulein Kost—if you wish to continue living here, do not let me *catch* you bringing in any more sailors? You understand?

FRAULEIN KOST: *(Haughtily)* Very well. So it is the same as always. *(She goes into her room and closes the door)*

FRAULEIN SCHNEIDER: It is *not* the same as always! *(She knocks on* FRAULEIN KOST'S *door)* Fraulein Kost! You hear me? I have put my foot down! *(She knocks again)* Fraulein Kost! Fraulein Kost!

(Meanwhile, HERR SCHULTZ *has emerged from his room, wearing his best suit and carrying a brown paper bag)*

SCHULTZ: Fraulein Schneider—Good evening!

(FRAULEIN SCHNEIDER *sees* HERR SCHULTZ. *She quickly and adroitly switches from AC to DC)*

FRAULEIN SCHNEIDER: Herr Schultz! Such a surprise!

SCHULTZ: You are occupied?

FRAULEIN SCHNEIDER: No. No. Free as a bird. Please forgive my appearance. *(She indicates her dress. If necessary, she could wear it to the opera—and she knows it)*

SCHULTZ: But it is most becoming.

FRAULEIN SCHNEIDER: Thank you.

SCHULTZ: *(Indicating the paper bag)* I have brought you a little something from the shop.

FRAULEIN SCHNEIDER: *Another* little something?

(HERR SCHULTZ hands her the bag)

SCHULTZ: With my compliments. (FRAULEIN SCHNEIDER *feels the bag)*

FRAULEIN SCHNEIDER: So heavy! But what can it be? Pears? *(She shakes her head merrily)* Last Wednesday you brought me pears. And such pears! Apples, possibly? *(She rejects the idea)* Friday was apples.

SCHULTZ: *(Nods)* Friday was apples.

FRAULEIN SCHNEIDER: So I cannot guess . . .

SCHULTZ: Then open!

(FRAULEIN SCHNEIDER peers into the bag)

FRAULEIN SCHNEIDER: Herr Schultz! Can I believe what I see? *(HERR SCHULTZ nods proudly)* But this is—too much to accept. So rare—so costly—so luxurious. *(She sings)*

If you bought me diamonds,
If you bought me pearls,
If you bought me roses like some other gents
Might bring to other girls,
It couldn't please me more
Than the gift I see—
(She takes a large pineapple out of the bag)
A pineapple for me!

SCHULTZ: *(Singing)*
If, in your emotion,
You began to sway,
Went to get some air,
Or grabbed a chair
To keep from fainting dead away,
It couldn't please me more
Than to see you cling
To the pineapple I bring.

BOTH:
Ah, ah, ah, ah, ah, ah, ah, ah

FRAULEIN SCHNEIDER:
I can hear Hawaiian breezes blow.

BOTH:
Ah, ah, ah, ah, ah, ah

SCHULTZ:
It's from California.

FRAULEIN SCHNEIDER:
Even so,
How am I to thank you?

SCHULTZ:
Kindly let it pass.

FRAULEIN SCHNEIDER:
Would you like a slice?

SCHULTZ:
That might be nice,
But frankly, it would give me gas.

FRAULEIN SCHNEIDER:
Then we shall leave it here—
Not to eat, but see.

BOTH:
A pineapple

FRAULEIN SCHNEIDER:
For me!

SCHULTZ:
From me!

BOTH:
Ah, ah, ah, ah, ah ah
Ah, ah, ah, ah, ah ah
(They dance)

FRAULEIN SCHNEIDER: But you must not bring me any more pineapples! Do you
hear? It is not proper. It is a gift a young man would present to his lady love.
It makes me blush!

SCHULTZ: But there is no one—no one in all Berlin—who is more deserving! If
I could, I would fill your entire room with pineapples!

(FRAULEIN SCHNEIDER *is quite surprised by this.* HERR SCHULTZ *is even more*
surprised. He had no idea he was going to say it)

BOTH: *(Singing)*
A pineapple . . .

SCHULTZ:
For you!

FRAULEIN SCHNEIDER:
From you!

BOTH:
Ah, ah, ah, ah, ah, ah
(The music continues)

FRAULEIN SCHNEIDER: I think I will lie down for a few minutes. My head is
spinning.

SCHULTZ: Good evening, Fraulein.

FRAULEIN SCHNEIDER: Good evening, Herr Schultz. *(They shake hands. FRAU-LEIN SCHNEIDER opens her bedroom door, then turns to HERR SCHULTZ)* I am —overwhelmed!

(She goes in and closes the door. The music ends. HERR SCHULTZ is all atingle. He makes a decision. He is about to knock on FRAULEIN SCHNEIDER'S door when suddenly he hears a sound. He jumps back from the door. He kneels down as if looking for something. FRAULEIN KOST opens her door and comes out. She wonders why HERR SCHULTZ is so far from his own door)

FRAULEIN KOST: Good evening, Herr Schultz.

SCHULTZ: Good evening, Fraulein Kost. I am looking for—I think I dropped— a small coin—a groschen. It rolled this way.

FRAULEIN KOST: You're looking for a groschen? *(Meaningfully)* I'm looking for two marks.

(FRAULEIN KOST exits. HERR SCHULTZ goes again to FRAULEIN SCHNEIDER'S door. He knocks. Immediately the door swings open. He swiftly enters. The door closes)

Blackout

SCENE 8

A group of WAITERS are seen on the spiral staircase. They are handsome, well-scrubbed, idealistic. The EMCEE is seated stage right.

WAITERS: *(Singing)*
The sun on the meadow is summery warm,
The stag in the forest runs free,
But gather together to greet the storm,
Tomorrow belongs to me.

The branch of the linden is leafy and green,
The Rhine gives its gold to the sea,
But somewhere a glory awaits unseen,
Tomorrow belongs to me.

(The EMCEE joins the WAITERS in song)

Oh, Fatherland, Fatherland, show us the sign
Your children have waited to see.
The morning will come when the world is mine,
Tomorrow belongs to me.

(The WAITERS disappear upstage, leaving a leering EMCEE alone as the lights dim)

SCENE 9

CLIFF'S *room.* SALLY'S *things are everywhere—on the floor, bulging out of the drawers, peeking out of the closets.*

CLIFF *is at the writing desk, typing.* SALLY *enters with groceries, kisses* CLIFF, *takes off her fur coat, and comes over to see what he is writing.*

CLIFF: It's not the novel. It's a letter to my mother—thanking her for the check.

SALLY: It finally arrived!

(CLIFF indicates the check from his mother)

CLIFF: Everyone at home's very thrilled the novel's going so well. Any day now they're expecting to see it in the bookstores.

SALLY: Oh, Cliff—

CLIFF: I may not be a good novelist, but I'm a very good liar. And I write a hell of a letter.

SALLY: It's my fault. If I weren't always dragging you off to party after party . . .

CLIFF: But I *like* those parties. The truth is, I like this whole city. It's so tacky and terrible—and everyone's having such a great time. If this were a movie, you know what would happen? A volcano would erupt—or there'd be a tidal wave . . .

SALLY: Maybe you should write for films! And I'll star in them! Oh, Cliff— wouldn't that be heaven!

CLIFF: Heaven! Just as soon as I finish the novel.

SALLY: There must be *something* to write about?

CLIFF: Or someone? Sally Bowles? Who would ever believe it?

SALLY: You're right—I'm much too strange and extraordinary! Much! And much too distracting . . .

CLIFF: Distracting? Nonsense! What about Venice? What about Rome? There was no Sally Bowles then—and no novel either. I was just drifting . . .

SALLY: And now you're sleepwalking. Is that better?

CLIFF: Sleepwalking? Who said that?

SALLY: *You* did. Last night.

CLIFF: I was drunk last night. Anyway—I said it was *possible* I was sleepwalking. And—if I am—who cares? What's the point in opening my eyes? *(Singing)*

> *Why should I wake up?*
> *This dream is going so well.*
> *When you're enchanted,*
> *Why break the spell?*
> *Drifting in this euphoric state,*
> *Morning can wait.*
> *Let it come late.*
> *Why should I wake up?*
> *Why waste a drop of the wine?*
> *Don't I adore you?*
> *And aren't you mine?*
> *Maybe I'll someday be lonely again.*
> *But why should I wake up till then?*

SALLY: Even so, Cliff—I've always said: When you want me to go, I'll go . . . even this very minute. I've never stayed so long with anyone.

CLIFF: Let's not talk about that! *(Singing)*

> *Drifting in this euphoric state,*
> *Morning can wait.*
> *Let it come late.*
> *Why should I wake up?*
> *Why waste a drop of the wine?*
> *Don't I adore you?*

And aren't you mine?
Maybe I'll someday be lonely again.
But why should I wake up,
Why should I wake up till then?

There's a letter for you from England.
SALLY: England? *(She is afraid to take the letter from him)*
CLIFF: It won't bite.
SALLY: Don't be too sure. *(She picks up the letter and looks at the envelope)* It's from Sybil! She's just a mad girl I used to go to school with! We were utterly wild —smoking cigarettes and not wearing bloomers! Our parents predicted we'd both come to a bad end—and the truth is—*she did.*
CLIFF: Why? What happened?
SALLY: She met this absolutely dreary boy and fell hopelessly in love with him and married him and now they have two children. *(She indicates the letter)* Probably another one on the way. *(Pause)* It looks as if *everybody's* got one on the way.
(There is a pause. CLIFF looks at SALLY)
CLIFF: What? Are you sure? *(SALLY nods)* How long have you known?
SALLY: Oh—a day or two.
CLIFF: Good God! How do you feel about it?
SALLY: I don't know, Cliff. I was going to ask how *you* feel.
CLIFF: Terrible! How else could I feel? I haven't got a dime! I haven't got— anything!
SALLY: It does seem—a bad idea. Good heavens, if you find *me* distracting—can you imagine a baby!
CLIFF: It's just not the time.
SALLY: I think you're perfectly right. So what shall we do? *(Pause)* The usual thing? *(No answer)* Cliff . . . ?
CLIFF: It's not the first time—is it?
SALLY: Oh, Cliff—remember—you mustn't ever ask me questions! The truth is, I should never have told you about the baby. But I thought if *you* didn't mind —perhaps I wouldn't mind. It might even have been rather—nice. But now we know where we stand. The subject is closed.
CLIFF: Will I ever be able to figure you out?
SALLY: After all, it's as much my fault as yours.
CLIFF: You are the world's craziest girl. It's no easy matter, you know, being in love with the world's craziest girl. *(They kiss)* Who says I'd be a terrible father?
SALLY: But is it the time?
CLIFF: Yes! It's time. Time I got a job.
SALLY: What about your novel?
CLIFF: If I'm going to be a writer, I'll be a writer—in the evening, in the morning, in the bathtub. This might be the best thing that ever happened to me.
SALLY: And I'll go back to the Kit Kat Klub!
CLIFF: Oh, no! *(There is a knock on the door)* Come in!
(The door opens and ERNST LUDWIG is there)
ERNST: Clifford—Sally— *(They shake hands)* I do not wish to intrude, but I have urgent business.
SALLY: Would you like something? A drink?

ERNST: Only if you will join me.

(CLIFF *nods.* SALLY *starts pouring three glasses of whiskey*)

CLIFF: *(To* ERNST*)* What's on your mind?

ERNST: You remember—I mentioned the possibility of an occasional business trip to Paris . . . (CLIFF *nods*) If you are interested—I think—in the next few days . . .

CLIFF: What would I have to do?

ERNST: It is so very simple. You go to an address I will give you—you pick up a small briefcase—you bring it back to Berlin. And then I pay you seventy-five marks!

SALLY: Seventy-five marks! Cliff—it's a gift from heaven!

ERNST: And I promise you are giving help to a very good cause.

CLIFF: Well, whatever it is, please don't tell me. I don't want to know.

ERNST: As you wish. But you will go?

SALLY: Of course he will!

ERNST: Clifford?

CLIFF: You see how it is? And we're not even married yet.

ERNST: Married! But such a surprise! My congratulations! Sally, congratulations. And when is the wedding to be?

(CLIFF *shrugs his shoulders*)

CLIFF: We haven't decided yet. This all just happened *today.*

ERNST: Today?

SALLY: Of course. We only *found out* today.

(ERNST *looks at* SALLY *very quizzically.* CLIFF *quickly raises his glass of whiskey*)

CLIFF: That we're going to be rich! Here—drink up! I mean, Prosit!

(SALLY *and* ERNST *raise their glasses*)

SALLY, ERNST and CLIFF: Prosit!

(*They drink as the lights fade*)

SCENE 10

At the top of the spiral staircase, the EMCEE appears. He wears expensive clothes and flashy jewelry.

EMCEE: Prosit! You see? There's more than one way to make money! (*He sings*)

My father needs money,
My uncle needs money,
My mother is thin as a reed.
But me, I'm sitting pretty—
I've got all the money I need.

My dearest friend Fritzy
Is out of his wits, he
Has four starving children to feed.
But me, I'm sitting pretty—
I've got all the money I need.

I know my little cousin Eric
Has his creditors hysterical,
And also Cousin Herman
Had to pawn his mother's ermine,

And my sister and my brother
Took to hocking one another, too.

But I've got some talents
Which build up my balance,
So even my bankers agreed
That me, I'm sitting pretty—
I've got all the money I need.

You wonder where I get my money? I have something to sell. Love! For all tastes! From all over! Meet Olga, my Russian ruble! *(A beautiful RUSSIAN GIRL enters, her bosom covered with rubles. The EMCEE helps himself to a few rubles.)* The Russian ruble will never collapse! Sushi, my Japanese yen! *(A stunning JAPANESE GIRL enters, a yen on each breast. The EMCEE takes one yen)* I have one yen. *(He takes the other)* I have two yen. *(He turns to the audience)* You have a yen? My French franc! Voilà! *(A gorgeous FRENCH GIRL enters with a French franc in her hand, which she gives the EMCEE)* And now—Ladies and Gentlemen —My American buck! *(A beautiful AMERICAN GIRL enters, an American dollar in the beak of the eagle headdress she wears. He takes the dollar and sings)*

I know my little cousin Eric
Has his creditors hysterical,
And also Cousin Herman
Had to pawn his mother's ermine,
And my sister and my brother
Took to hocking one another, too.

But, I'm not a nincompoop.
I've got an income you
Put in the bank to accrue.
Yes, me, I'm sitting pretty—
Life is pretty sitting with you!

(They dance)
And now, Brünnhilde, my German mark—you can't keep that girl down!
(She rises from behind the piano and "flies" straight up in the air. She poses for a brief moment, and as she is descending, he hits the gong that is between her legs)

ALL: *(Singing)*
Life is pretty sitting with,
Pretty sitting with,
Pretty sitting with you!

Blackout

SCENE II

FRAULEIN SCHNEIDER'S *living room is empty. Then* FRAULEIN KOST'S *door opens slowly.* FRAULEIN KOST *looks out. All seems to be clear. A* SAILOR *emerges.*
Just at this moment, FRAULEIN SCHNEIDER *opens her bedroom door. The two ladies spot each other.*
FRAULEIN KOST: All right! There is no need to say it! I know it by heart already!
(The SAILOR *exits. For some strange reason,* FRAULEIN SCHNEIDER *says nothing)*
So no lectures—please—about sailors! They are just lonesome, patriotic boys!

I have a duty! *(FRAULEIN SCHNEIDER still says nothing. She looks vaguely uncomfortable. Inexplicably, FRAULEIN SCHNEIDER goes back into her bedroom and closes the door. FRAULEIN KOST is quite surprised. She goes into her room. A moment later, FRAULEIN KOST opens her door and another SAILOR emerges. As she is about to close her door, FRAULEIN SCHNEIDER'S door opens and HERR SCHULTZ peeks out. FRAULEIN KOST sees him but he doesn't see her. Both doors close. After a while, FRAULEIN SCHNEIDER'S door opens and HERR SCHULTZ starts out, followed by FRAULEIN SCHNEIDER. At this point, FRAULEIN KOST opens her door and she comes out—very brazenly—followed by yet another SAILOR. For FRAULEIN SCHNEIDER'S benefit, FRAULEIN KOST hugs and kisses the SAILOR at great length)* Goodnight, Karl.

SAILOR: *(Correcting her)* Fritz.

FRAULEIN KOST: Fritz—you must be sure to come back again soon. At any time. *(Taking money from him)* Bring your friends. *(The SAILOR exits. FRAULEIN KOST waltzes up to FRAULEIN SCHNEIDER)* Ah—good evening, Fraulein Schneider. A busy evening, no? I see we are—after all—sisters under the skin.

SCHULTZ: Fraulein Kost!

FRAULEIN KOST: Yes?

SCHULTZ: This fine lady is *not* your sister! She has just honored me by consenting to give me her hand in marriage!

FRAULEIN KOST: *(Really amazed)* Marriage!

SCHULTZ: We marry in—three weeks.

FRAULEIN KOST: Three weeks!

SCHULTZ: So a little respect for the future Frau Schultz—if you please!

FRAULEIN KOST: Ja! Ja! Frau Schultz? *(Chastened—she exits into her room)*

FRAULEIN SCHNEIDER: Herr Schultz. You were—supreme.

SCHULTZ: But what else could I do?

FRAULEIN SCHNEIDER: Such a magnificent lie—to preserve my reputation.

SCHULTZ: But why did I say three weeks? Why not three months? Three years? This way she will find out the truth so quickly. Unless—

FRAULEIN SCHNEIDER: Unless?

SCHULTZ: Unless what?

FRAULEIN SCHNEIDER: You said "unless"!

SCHULTZ: But it is foolish! I mean—after all—who would have *me?* An elderly widower—with gray hair—and heartburn—and a little fruit . . .

FRAULEIN SCHNEIDER: Am I such a bargain then? An unbeautiful spinster with a few rooms to let—poorly furnished.

SCHULTZ: I work fourteen hours a day.

FRAULEIN SCHNEIDER: I do my own scrubbing.

SCHULTZ: My right leg bothers me.

FRAULEIN SCHNEIDER: I have such palpitations.

SCHULTZ: I'm not a well man.

FRAULEIN SCHNEIDER: Am I a well woman?

SCHULTZ: What are we talking about? We're *alive!* And what good is it—alone? So if you would even consider—marriage . . . ?
(There is a long pause)

FRAULEIN SCHNEIDER: I will consider it.

SCHULTZ: But take your time, by all means. No hurry.

FRAULEIN SCHNEIDER: Yes. I will consider it. *(They shake hands)* But this much
I can tell you. You have good reason to be very, very optimistic.
(FRAULEIN SCHNEIDER goes to her room. HERR SCHULTZ, shaken, sings)

SCHULTZ:
How the world can change,
It can change like that
Due to one little word—
Married.

See a palace rise
From a two-room flat
Due to one little word—
Married.

And the old despair
That was often there
Suddenly ceases to be.
For you wake one day,
Look around and say,
Somebody wonderful
Married me.

(The lights come up in FRAULEIN SCHNEIDER'S *bedroom. Through the wall, we
see* FRAULEIN SCHNEIDER *sitting thoughtfully on the edge of her bed)*

FRAULEIN SCHNEIDER: *(Singing)*
How the world can change,
It can change like that
Due to one little word—

SCHULTZ and FRAULEIN SCHNEIDER:
Married.

FRAULEIN SCHNEIDER:
See a palace rise
From a two-room flat
Due to one little word—

SCHULTZ and FRAULEIN SCHNEIDER:
Married.

FRAULEIN SCHNEIDER:
And the old despair
That was often there
Suddenly ceases to be.

SCHULTZ and FRAULEIN SCHNEIDER:
For you wake one day,
Look around and say,

SCHULTZ:
Somebody wonderful,

FRAULEIN SCHNEIDER:
Somebody wonderful

SCHULTZ and FRAULEIN SCHNEIDER:
Married me.

(The light goes out in FRAULEIN SCHNEIDER'S *bedroom. She comes out of her door and back to the living room)*
FRAULEIN SCHNEIDER: Herr Schultz—I have considered your proposal.
SCHULTZ: So quickly?
FRAULEIN SCHNEIDER: *(Nods)* I can think of no arguments *against* it. And so—
  if you still desire me—I am yours.
SCHULTZ: *If* I desire . . . ? *If?* I must tell someone the good news! I must tell
  everyone! Good news! Good news! *(He rushes to one of the doors and starts
  knocking on it)* Is anyone there? I have news! Exciting news!
FRAULEIN SCHNEIDER: But that is your own door!
SCHULTZ: Oh! Good news! Good news! Come and hear!
(SALLY enters through the double door)
SALLY: What's going on?
SCHULTZ: Fraulein Sally! Good news! Fraulein Schneider and I are to be
  married!
SALLY: Married! How wonderful! It's in the air! It must be!
SCHULTZ: I am so happy! *(He sits down)* I never thought—I never thought I
  would be so fortunate.
SALLY: I've got the most perfect idea! When Cliff comes back from Paris, we're
  giving you an engagement party!
FRAULEIN SCHNEIDER: Engagement party? For two old people—it is not suitable.
SCHULTZ: *What* old people? I do not see any old people! But *I* will give the party!
  I will give it at my shop! And there will be music—dancing.
FRAULEIN SCHNEIDER: And who will dance? How many people do we know?
SALLY: I'll do the inviting! I know lots of people!
FRAULEIN SCHNEIDER: I still think it is foolish—this party—a waste of money!
SCHULTZ: Have you ever had an engagement party?
FRAULEIN SCHNEIDER: Of course not.
SCHULTZ: And neither have I. So—I ask you—what are we waiting for? It's *time!*
  (The lights fade, except for a spot on FRAULEIN SCHNEIDER'S *Gramophone as*
FRAULEIN SCHNEIDER *and* HERR SCHULTZ *waltz off)*

SCENE 12

The lights come up on HERR SCHULTZ's *fruit shop—all decorated for the party,
which is in full swing. Prominent among the guests are the performers and* GIRL
ORCHESTRA *from the Kit Kat Klub.*
  CLIFF *enters—carrying his suitcase and* ERNST'S *briefcase.* SALLY *kisses him.*
SALLY: Cliff! Was Paris divine?
CLIFF: Divine.
SALLY: *(Indicating the briefcase)* Was there any trouble?
CLIFF: No. But I'll be happy to get rid of it. Is Ernst here?
SALLY: Not yet. (CLIFF *takes off his overcoat and puts the briefcase with it on a
  counter)* Come see the lovely gift we're giving Fraulein Schneider and Herr Schultz.
  (CLIFF embraces FRAULEIN SCHNEIDER)
CLIFF: Fraulein . . . *(Asking* HERR SCHULTZ'S *approval to kiss her)* May I? (HERR
  SCHULTZ *nods.* CLIFF *kisses* FRAULEIN SCHNEIDER) Congratulations.
SALLY: *(To* FRAULEIN SCHNEIDER) Now open our present. Be careful.

(FRAULEIN SCHNEIDER undoes the ribbon from a large white gift box)

FRAULEIN SCHNEIDER: Ah—Herr Schultz—look! Crystal!

SALLY: Cut crystal. It's for fruit.

FRAULEIN SCHNEIDER: Beautiful.

SCHULTZ: Thank you. And I will keep it filled. I promise—as long as we live—this bowl will not be empty.

(Everyone applauds. The door opens and FRAULEIN KOST enters)

FRAULEIN KOST: Fraulein Schneider—I am welcome?

FRAULEIN SCHNEIDER: Fraulein Kost—forgive me! I did not invite you. But only because I know you work in the evening.

FRAULEIN KOST: Tonight I am free.

FRAULEIN SCHNEIDER: *(Aside)* I should live that long.

(She indicates that FRAULEIN KOST is welcome. FRAULEIN KOST points to the door)

FRAULEIN KOST: My cousins?

FRAULEIN SCHNEIDER: From Hamburg? *(FRAULEIN KOST nods)* In!

FRAULEIN KOST: My cousins! *(Three SAILORS burst in. They find girls to dance with. FRAULEIN KOST stops one of them)* Otto . . .

SAILOR: *(Correcting her)* Rudy.

FRAULEIN KOST: Rudy—it's Fraulein Schneider's party. If you want to dance—dance with her!

FRAULEIN SCHNEIDER: No—no.

FRAULEIN KOST: Dance with her, Otto!

SAILOR: Rudy! *(He comes up to FRAULEIN SCHNEIDER)* It is my pleasure, Fraulein.

FRAULEIN SCHNEIDER: But I do not . . . And you are so young . . . It is out of the question. Unthinkable—absolutely unthinkable. Absolutely.

(And she begins to dance with him—the fruit-shop dance. At the end of the dance, ERNST LUDWIG enters. He has a swastika armband on his overcoat)

ERNST: Clifford—Sally.

SALLY: Ernst!

ERNST: You have the briefcase? *(CLIFF points to the swastika armband)* Oh—I come direct from the meeting. *(ERNST takes his overcoat off. He is wearing a business suit)* I am sorry, Clifford—since you did not wish to know my politics. However—the briefcase, please. You have it?

(CLIFF hesitates. SALLY hands it to ERNST)

SALLY: Here it is.

CLIFF: *(To ERNST)* You said it was a good cause—if I remember correctly.

ERNST: And so it is! Our party will be the builders of the new Germany. And you are helping! So—for you— *(ERNST extends an envelope to CLIFF. CLIFF doesn't take it)* Something is wrong?

(SALLY takes the envelope)

SALLY: No. Of course not. Thank you, Ernst.

CLIFF: *(To ERNST)* I've been reading your leader's book . . .

ERNST: Ah, yes. *Mein Kampf.*

CLIFF: Have you read it?

ERNST: Certainly!

CLIFF: Then I don't understand. I mean—that man is out of his mind. It's right there on every page . . .

ERNST: Clifford—this is not the time nor the place for such a discussion. Perhaps you would never understand. At any rate—now I find myself a flapper—I enjoy the party. *(ERNST leaves CLIFF and SALLY. He goes up to FRAULEIN SCHNEIDER)* Fraulein Schneider—I wish you much happiness!

FRAULEIN SCHNEIDER: Thank you.

ERNST: I am sorry to be late, but there was a meeting. An important business meeting.

FRAULEIN SCHNEIDER: One does what one must.

ERNST: But now I look forward to a most delightful evening.

(ERNST wanders off—looking for a flapper. HERR SCHULTZ, carrying a bottle of schnapps and some glasses, comes up to FRAULEIN SCHNEIDER)

SCHULTZ: Schnapps?

FRAULEIN SCHNEIDER: You've had enough.

(HERR SCHULTZ watches the dancing couples admiringly)

SCHULTZ: Beautiful dancing! Beautiful! *(He suddenly notes two boys dancing together. He looks around to see if anyone else has noticed.)* All right! Enough dancing! Enough! No more dancing!

FRAULEIN SCHNEIDER: But why?

SCHULTZ: No more dancing! *(The music stops. The dancers stop)* Sit down, every-one! We do something else.

FRAULEIN SCHNEIDER: Something else? What else?

SCHULTZ: What else? What? *(Suddenly inspired)* I will entertain!

FRAULEIN SCHNEIDER: *(To the guests, apologetically)* He has had too much schnapps . . .

SCHULTZ: But I insist! So you will not think my only talent is fruit. *(HERR SCHULTZ sees to it that everyone is seated and ready)* Now—the only word you have to know in order to understand my little song is the Yiddish word: *"meeskite." "Meeskite"* means ugly, funny-looking. *"Meeskite"* means . . . *(He sings)*

Meeskite, Meeskite,
Once upon a time there was a meeskite, meeskite,
Looking in the mirror he would say, "What an awful shock,
I got a face that could stop a clock."

Meeskite, meeskite,
Such a pity on him, he's a meeskite, meeskite,
God up in his heaven left him out on a shaky limb,
He put a meeskite on him.

But listen, he grew up. Even meeskites grow up. *(He sings again)*

And soon in the Chader (that means Hebrew school)
He sat beside this little girl
And when he asked her her name she replied,
"I'm Pearl."
He ran to the Zayda (that means grandfather)
And said in that screechy voice of his,
"You told me I was the homeliest!
Well, Gramps, you're wrong. Pearl is!

"Meeskite, meeskite,
No one ever saw a bigger meeskite, meeskite,

Everywhere a flaw and maybe that is the reason why
I'm going to love her until I die.

"Meeskite, meeskite,
Oh, is it a pleasure she's a meeskite, meeskite,
She's the one I'll treasure, for I thought there could never be
A bigger meeskite than me."

So, they were married,
And in a year she turned and smiled:
"I'm afraid I am going to have . . . a child."
Nine months she carried,
Worrying how that child would look,
And all the cousins were worried too.
But what a turn fate took!

Gorgeous, gorgeous,
They produced a baby that was gorgeous, gorgeous,
Crowding round the cradle all the relatives aahed and oohed,
"He ought to pose for a baby food.

"Gorgeous, gorgeous,
Would I tell a lie? He's simply gorgeous, gorgeous,
Who'd have ever thought that we would see such a flawless gem
Out of two meeskites like them?"

Sing with me, somebody? Fraulein Schneider? Herr Ludwig—we make a duet?
Sally?
(SALLY comes forward and sings with HERR SCHULTZ)

SCHULTZ and SALLY:
Meeskite, meeskite,
Once upon a time there was a meeskite, meeskite,
Looking in the mirror he would say, "What an awful shock,
I got a face that could stop a clock."

Meeskite, meeskite,
What's the good denying I'm a meeskite, meeskite,
God up in his heaven made a joke for the world to see . . .

(SALLY kisses SCHULTZ and sits)

SCHULTZ:
He made a meeskite of me.

Now, wait! The story has a moral! All my stories have morals!

Moral, moral,
Yes indeed, the story has a moral, moral,
Though you're not a beauty it is nevertheless quite true,
There may be beautiful things in you.

Meeskite, meeskite,
Listen to the fable of the meeskite, meeskite,
Anyone responsible for loveliness, large or small,

Is not a meeskite
At all!

(All applaud except ERNST, who puts on his coat)

ERNST: Fraulein Schneider—Clifford—I wish to say good evening.

FRAULEIN SCHNEIDER: But why so early?

ERNST: I find that I do not belong here. I cannot stay.

FRAULEIN SCHNEIDER: As you wish.

ERNST: Fraulein—you and I are old acquaintances. I have sent you many new
   lodgers . . . So let me urge you—think what you are doing. This marriage is
   not advisable. I cannot put it too strongly. For your own welfare.

CLIFF: What about Herr Schultz's welfare?

ERNST: He is not a German.

FRAULEIN SCHNEIDER: But he was born here!

ERNST: He is not a German. Good evening.

   (ERNST goes to the door. As he reaches it, FRAULEIN KOST runs up to him)

FRAULEIN KOST: Herr Ludwig—wait! You are not leaving so early?

ERNST: I do not find the party amusing.

FRAULEIN KOST: Oh—but it is just beginning! Come—we will make it amusing
   —you and I, ja? (She pulls ERNST back into the center of the shop) Ladies and
   gentlemen—quiet please! Quiet! (To ERNST) Herr Ludwig—this is for you. (She
   sings)

The sun on the meadow is summery warm,
The stag in the forest runs free.
But gather together to greet the storm,
Tomorrow belongs to me.

Ja?
The branch of the linden is leafy and green,
The Rhine gives its gold to the sea.
But somewhere a glory awaits unseen,
Tomorrow belongs to me.

Herr Ludwig! Sing with me!

   (ERNST, wearing the coat with the swastika armband, goes to her side. The guests
form a circle around them, as if magnetically attracted)

FRAULEIN KOST and ERNST: (Singing)
The babe in his cradle is closing his eyes,
The blossom embraces the bee.
But soon, says a whisper, arise, arise,
Tomorrow belongs to me.

FRAULEIN KOST: And now—everyone!

   (The guests join in the singing—their voices growing louder and louder, even rather
frightening. Only FRAULEIN SCHNEIDER, HERR SCHULTZ, CLIFF and SALLY remain
outside the circle)

FRAULEIN KOST, ERNST and GUESTS: (Singing)
Oh, Fatherland, Fatherland, show us the sign
Your children have waited to see.

The morning will come when the world is mine,
Tomorrow belongs to me.

(As the song ends amid cheers and applause, the EMCEE *appears at the top of the spiral stairs—puffing on a cigar. He takes in the scene:* FRAULEIN SCHNEIDER *and* CLIFF *watching the singers with great concern—*HERR SCHULTZ *and* SALLY *laughing, unaware of what is happening. As the* EMCEE *descends the stairs the fruit shop vanishes. The people on stage freeze against a black background. The* EMCEE *slowly crosses the stage—looking at everyone. Then he turns to the audience. He shrugs, he smiles, and exits)*

Blackout

ACT TWO

SCENE I

Eight girls dance out on stage—obviously the Kit Kat Klub chorus. They do a spirited dance of high kicks. Suddenly we are aware that one of the girls is the EMCEE. *As the dance begins to fall apart, we hear the ominous sound of military drums; the music changes to a martial version of "Tomorrow Belongs to Me" as the* EMCEE *and* GIRLS *goose-step offstage.*

Blackout

SCENE 2

Inside HERR SCHULTZ'S *shop,* HERR SCHULTZ *is taking down some of the remaining party decorations. Passers-by can be seen through the windows.* FRAULEIN SCHNEIDER *enters. She is obviously troubled.*

SCHULTZ: Fraulein Schneider—good morning!

FRAULEIN SCHNEIDER: Good morning, Herr Schultz.

SCHULTZ: New apples. Fresh off the tree. Perfection! *(He wipes one off and hands it to her)* Please . . .

FRAULEIN SCHNEIDER: *(Refusing it)* Perhaps later.

SCHULTZ: Such a party last evening! I have never been to a finer party! Such food! Such music! *(Suddenly very contrite)* Can you ever forgive me?

FRAULEIN SCHNEIDER: For what? A few glasses of schnapps?

SCHULTZ: I promise you—on our wedding day—no drinking—you will be proud of me.

FRAULEIN SCHNEIDER: I am already proud of you. But—as concerns the wedding . . .

SCHULTZ: Yes?

FRAULEIN SCHNEIDER: There are problems. New problems.

SCHULTZ: If it is my drunkenness—I swear to you, Fraulein: I am not an alcoholic.

FRAULEIN SCHNEIDER: There is a thing—far more serious.

SCHULTZ: A *new* problem . . . ?

FRAULEIN SCHNEIDER: New to *me*—because I have not thought about it. But at the party my eyes were opened.

SCHULTZ: And?

FRAULEIN SCHNEIDER: I saw that one can no longer dismiss the Nazis. Because suddenly they are my friends and neighbors. And how many others? And—if so—is it possible they will come to power?

SCHULTZ: And you will be married to a Jew.

FRAULEIN SCHNEIDER: *(Frightened)* I need my license to rent my rooms! If they take it away . . .

SCHULTZ: They will take nothing away. I promise you. *(Softly)* I feel such tenderness for you. It is difficult to express. Are we too old for words like "love"?

FRAULEIN SCHNEIDER: Far too old. I am no Juliet. You are no Romeo. We must be sensible.

SCHULTZ: And live alone. How many meals have you eaten alone? A thousand? Ten thousand?

FRAULEIN SCHNEIDER: Fifty thousand.

SCHULTZ: Then *be* sensible. Governments come. Governments go. How much longer can we wait? *(FRAULEIN SCHNEIDER says nothing)* Let me peel you an orange . . .

(HERR SCHULTZ takes a knife and starts peeling an orange rather clumsily. The underscoring of the music to "Married" is heard. FRAULEIN SCHNEIDER reaches for the orange)

FRAULEIN SCHNEIDER: *I* will do it.

(She peels the orange. For a moment, we are back to the mood of their scenes in the first act)

SCHULTZ: *(Singing)*
And the old despair
That was often there
Suddenly ceases to be.

For you wake one day,
Look around and say,
Somebody wonderful
Married me.

(A brick crashes through the window. FRAULEIN SCHNEIDER and HERR SCHULTZ jump up)

FRAULEIN SCHNEIDER: You see? You see!

SCHULTZ: It is nothing! Children on their way to school! Mischievous children! Nothing more! I assure you! *(HERR SCHULTZ runs out. We see him outside the broken window, looking for the culprit and questioning the onlookers. No one seems to have seen anything. HERR SCHULTZ comes back in)* Schoolchildren. Young—full of mischief. You understand?

FRAULEIN SCHNEIDER: *(Slowly—thoughtfully)* I understand.

    Lights fade

SCENE 3

The EMCEE enters, walking hand-in-hand with a gorilla. The gorilla is really rather attractive—as gorillas go. She wears a chic little skirt and carries a handbag.

EMCEE: *(Singing)*

I know what you're thinking—
You wonder why I chose her
Out of all the ladies in the world.
That's just a first impression—
What good's a first impression?
If you knew her like I do,
It would change your point of view.

If you could see her through my eyes,
You wouldn't wonder at all.
If you could see her through my eyes,
I guarantee you would fall like I did.

When we're in public together,
I hear society groan.
But if they could see her through my eyes,
Maybe they'd leave us alone.

How can I speak of her virtues?
I don't know where to begin:
She's clever, she's smart, she reads music,
She doesn't smoke or drink gin like I do.

Yet when we're walking together,
They sneer if I'm holding her hand.
But if they could see her through my eyes,
Maybe they'd all understand.

(They waltz)

I understand your objection,
I grant you the problem's not small.
But if you could see her through my eyes,
She isn't a meeskite at all!
Alternate: *She wouldn't look Jewish at all!*

Blackout

SCENE 4

CLIFF'S *room.* SALLY *is dressing to go out.* CLIFF *enters, wearing a coat.*
SALLY: Cliff! I've been waiting so anxiously! Did you get a job?
CLIFF: I'll try again tomorrow.
(They kiss)
SALLY: And you'll find something! I'm sure of it! President of a bank!
CLIFF: They're closed.
SALLY: Guess who visited me today! Bobby and Victor! From the Kit Kat! You remember them?
CLIFF: How could I forget them?
SALLY: They say business at the Klub's way off since I left. And Lulu—one of the girls—had her teeth knocked out by a Lithuanian. Oh—and Max . . . you remember Max? He's fallen madly in love. And it turns out she's a dedicated Communist *and* a dedicated virgin. Isn't that heaven!

CLIFF: Heaven.

SALLY: Would you simply *hate* it if I went back to work at the Klub?

CLIFF: I sure would.

SALLY: But we need the money so badly!

CLIFF: Not *that* badly.

SALLY: I don't understand you. Really I don't. First you tell me you're not going to Paris for Ernst any more—even though it does seem the very easiest way in the world to make money . . .

CLIFF: Or the hardest. *(SALLY looks at him blankly)* Someday I've simply got to sit you down and read you a newspaper. You'll be amazed at what's going on.

SALLY: You mean—politics? But what has *that* to do with us?

CLIFF: You're right. *Nothing* has anything to do with us. Sally, can't you see—if you're not against all this, you're for it—or you might as well be.

SALLY: At any rate, the Kit Kat Klub is the most *un*political place in Berlin. Even *you*'ve got to admit *that*.

CLIFF: Sally—do me a favor? Let *me* earn the money for this family. At least give me the chance. If I can't even get something—washing beer glasses—then we'll talk about you working in some cabaret. And after you've tried every other club in Berlin, we might even talk about the Kit Kat Klub. And I imagine I'll still say no. But—who knows? By that time I may be almost ready to listen to reason. Okay? *(There is a knock at the door)* Come in!

(The door opens. FRAULEIN SCHNEIDER is there. She carries a large gift-wrapped package)

FRAULEIN SCHNEIDER: I intrude?

SALLY: No. No. Come in, Fraulein Schneider.

CLIFF: *(To FRAULEIN SCHNEIDER)* Have you seen Herr Schultz this morning? *(FRAULEIN SCHNEIDER nods)* How is he? A little hung-over? *(She nods again)*

SALLY: Fraulein Schneider—is that the fruit bowl? Is something wrong with it? *(She indicates the package FRAULEIN SCHNEIDER is carrying)*

FRAULEIN SCHNEIDER: *(Shaking her head)* I cannot keep it.

SALLY: But why?

FRAULEIN SCHNEIDER: An engagement present. But there is no engagement.

SALLY: What do you mean?

FRAULEIN SCHNEIDER: We have—reconsidered—Herr Schultz and I.

CLIFF: Fraulein, you can't give up that way!

FRAULEIN SCHNEIDER: Oh, yes! I can. That is easy to say! Easy for you. Fight! And—if you fail—what does it matter? You pack your belongings. You move to Paris. And if you do not like Paris—where? It is easy for *you*. But if you were *me* . . . *(She sings)*

With time rushing by,
What would you do?

With the clock running down,
What would you do?
The young always have the cure—
Being brave, being sure
And free,
But imagine if you were me.

Alone like me,
And this is the only world you know.
Some rooms to let—
The sum of a lifetime, even so.

I'll take your advice.
What would you do?

Would you pay the price?
What would you do?

Suppose simply keeping still
Means you manage until the end?
What would you do,
My brave young friend?

Grown old like me,
With neither the will nor wish to run;
Grown tired like me,
Who hurries for bed when day is done;
Grown wise like me,
Who isn't at war with anyone—
Not anyone!
With a storm in the wind,
What would you do?

Suppose you're one frightened voice
Being told what the choice must be.

Go on, tell me,
I will listen.

What would you do
If you were me?

CLIFF: Aren't you forgetting something? If you marry Herr Schultz—whatever problems come up—you'll still have each other.

FRAULEIN SCHNEIDER: All my life I have managed for myself—and it is too old a habit to change. I have battled alone, and I have survived. There was a war —and I survived. There was a revolution—and I survived. There was an inflation—billions of marks for one loaf of bread—but I survived! And if the Nazis come—I will survive. And if the Communists come—I will still be here— renting these rooms! For, in the end, what other choice have I? This—is my world! *(Softly)* I regret—very much—returning the fruit bowl. It is truly magnificent. I regret—everything. *(She exits)*

SALLY: Oh, Cliff—how terrible. Should I speak to her?

CLIFF: What could you say?

SALLY: Oh—that it will all work itself out.

CLIFF: I don't think she'd believe you.

SALLY: It seems *nobody* believes me today. It's quite obvious *you* don't—about Max. If he wants me back at the Klub, it's not for the reason you think. Did it ever occur to you I just might be a tremendous asset to that Klub? The fact is, they're waiting there this very minute—to rehearse *my* numbers. So I really must go.

(CLIFF has gone to his typewriter, opened it, and started to dust it with his handkerchief)

CLIFF: The fact is, you're going a lot farther than the Kit Kat Klub.

SALLY: I *am?*

CLIFF: Home. *(SALLY looks at him blankly)* America—since you won't go to England.

SALLY: You're joking!

(CLIFF indicates the typewriter)

CLIFF: I'm going to sell this. The money should get us as far as Paris. And I'll cable home for steamship fare.

SALLY: What are you talking about?

CLIFF: Leaving Berlin—as soon as possible. Tomorrow!

SALLY: But we love it here!

CLIFF: Sally—wake up! The party in Berlin is *over!* It was lots of fun, but it's over. And what is Berlin doing *now?* Vomiting in the street.

SALLY: How ugly, Cliff!

CLIFF: You're damn right it's ugly! And it's going to get a lot worse. So how could we live here? How could we raise a family?

SALLY: But is America the answer? Running away to America?

CLIFF: We're *not* running away. There's no place to run to. We are going home.

SALLY: Oh, certainly—that's fine for *you.* But what about *me?* My career?

CLIFF: You've got a new career.

SALLY: But I can work at the Klub for several months at least. And then—in November—oh, Cliff, I want the world for our baby—all the most elegant, expensive things.

CLIFF: We'll talk about it tomorrow—on the train. *(He finishes preening the typewriter. He closes it and starts for the door with it)*

SALLY: Cliff—wait! We can't just—uproot our lives—that quickly!

CLIFF: Oh, no? You give me one hour! And don't move! *(He pushes her into a chair)* Sit down! Or—better yet—start packing! *(He puts a suitcase on the bed)* There's plenty to do! *(CLIFF goes toward the door. Then he reaches into a pocket, takes out a coin and gives it to SALLY in a gesture of reconciliation)* Here. *Call* the Klub. Tell them goodbye.

(CLIFF exits. SALLY looks at the coin. Then she makes up her mind. She springs up, grabs her fur coat and rushes out the door)

Blackout

SCENE 5

A crowded evening at the Kit Kat Klub. CLIFF *enters.*

WAITER: Good evening, sir.

(CLIFF sees SALLY at the bar and goes to her)

CLIFF: What the hell are you doing here? I—

SALLY: May I speak for a moment?

CLIFF: Get your coat! I'm taking you home!

SALLY: *(Pulling CLIFF to a table)* Please, Cliff! If we go to America, there's no assurance you can get a job. There *is* a great deal of unemployment there. You've said so yourself.

CLIFF: I'll find *something.*

SALLY: Maybe, but *this* is sure!

CLIFF: This! What the hell is *this?* You keep talking about *this* as if it really existed. When are you going to realize, the only way you got this job is by sleeping with somebody!

SALLY: That's not true!

CLIFF: And the only way you'll get a job in New York or Paris or London is by sleeping with someone else! But you're sleeping with *me* these days!

SALLY: Shut up, Cliff!

CLIFF: Sally, face it. Say goodbye to Berlin, Max, this dump, everybody. Believe me, they'll never even know you've left.

SALLY: I've got to change for my next number. *(She runs off)*

CLIFF: Sally!

(But she is gone. CLIFF is trembling with anger. The phone on his table lights up. He answers it)

CLIFF: Hello.

(A spotlight picks up ERNST LUDWIG, who is sitting at a table with an attractive girl)

ERNST: *(Into his phone)* Clifford—this is Ernst Ludwig. I am at table nine. Will you join me for a drink?

CLIFF: Not now, Ernst.

ERNST: I have been trying to reach you at Fraulein Schneider's—but you do not answer. I have another urgent errand for you.

CLIFF: Sorry.

ERNST: This time I pay—one hundred and fifty marks.

CLIFF: The answer is no.

ERNST: But what is wrong, Clifford? You are angry with me?

CLIFF: I am?

ERNST: It is because of the party last evening? If you were a German, you would understand these things.

CLIFF: Goodbye, Ernst.

(CLIFF hangs up. ERNST stands and comes toward CLIFF, who is anxious to follow SALLY)

ERNST: Wait! It is very important—this errand. I pay—two hundred marks.

CLIFF: Go to hell!

(CLIFF tries to leave. ERNST grabs him)

ERNST: But what is wrong with you? I don't understand!

CLIFF: Take your hands off me—

(ERNST does)

ERNST: Clifford—I know you need the money. So why won't you go? It is because of that Jew at the party?

(CLIFF socks ERNST, knocking him down. Immediately two men wearing Nazi armbands jump on CLIFF—beating him unconscious. They drag him out of the Klub as the patrons watch. ERNST rises and goes back to his table. The EMCEE appears—laughing rather hysterically—as if the fight were part of the floor show)

EMCEE: And now—once again—Fraulein Sally Bowles!

(SALLY enters and sings)

SALLY:

What good is sitting alone in your room?
Come hear the music play.
Life is a cabaret, old chum,
Come to the cabaret.

Put down the knitting, the book and the broom,
Time for a holiday.
Life is a cabaret, old chum,
Come to the cabaret.

Come taste the wine,
Come hear the band,
Come blow a horn, start celebrating.
Right this way, your table's waiting.

No use permitting some prophet of doom
To wipe every smile away.
Life is a cabaret, old chum,
Come to the cabaret.

I used to have a girl friend known as Elsie
With whom I shared four sordid rooms in Chelsea.
She wasn't what you'd call a blushing flower;
As a matter of fact, she rented by the hour.

The day she died the neighbors came to snicker,
"Well, that's what comes of too much pills and liquor."
But when I saw her laid out like a queen,
She was the happiest corpse I'd ever seen.

I think of Elsie to this very day.
I remember how she'd turn to me and say . . .

(SALLY *has walked off the Kit Kat Klub stage. She heads directly downstage as the Kit Kat Klub disappears.* SALLY *stands alone*)

What good is sitting alone in your room?
Come hear the music play.
Life is a cabaret, old chum,
Come to the cabaret.

Put down the knitting, the book and the broom,
Time for a holiday.
Life is a cabaret, old chum,
Come to the cabaret.

And as for me, as for me,
I made my mind up back in Chelsea.
When I go, I'm going like Elsie!

Start by admitting from cradle to tomb
Isn't that long a stay.
Life is a cabaret, old chum,

Only a cabaret, old chum,
And I love a cabaret!

Blackout

SCENE 6

CLIFF'S *room. It is late morning.* CLIFF *is busily packing. His face is bandaged and he moves a little stiffly.*

There is a knock at the door. CLIFF *rushes to the door and opens it.* HERR SCHULTZ *is there.*

CLIFF: *(Disappointed)* Good morning, Herr Schultz.

(HERR SCHULTZ enters. He has a suitcase in one hand and a brown paper bag in the other)

SCHULTZ: Excuse me—but I have come to say goodbye. *(He sees* CLIFF'S *bandages)*

CLIFF: It's nothing. A little accident. Where are you going?

SCHULTZ: I have taken a room on the other side of the Nollendorfplatz. I think it will be easier for *her. (He notes all the packing)* You are leaving also? You and Fraulein Bowles?

CLIFF: We're going home. To America.

SCHULTZ: America! I have sometimes thought of going there—

CLIFF: Why don't you? The way things look here—

SCHULTZ: But it will pass—I promise you!

CLIFF: I hope you're right.

SCHULTZ: I *know* I am right! Because I understand the Germans . . . After all, what am *I?* A German. *(The door opens and* SALLY *enters. She looks ill and exhausted. She wears a rather thin dress and is carrying her purse. She stands at the door.* HERR SCHULTZ *goes to her)* Ah—Fraulein Sally! I have come to say goodbye . . . all good fortune.

SALLY: Herr Schultz.

SCHULTZ: I have brought a small farewell gift. *(He gives* SALLY *the paper bag)* Seville oranges. Delicious.

(SALLY hugs him. Then CLIFF and HERR SCHULTZ shake hands)

CLIFF: Goodbye, Herr Schultz. And I wish you *mazel.*

SCHULTZ: *Mazel.* That is what we all need. *(He exits)*

CLIFF: *(Artificially cheerful)* I've finished your packing. You've got a lot of stuff, lady. You won't be able to find a thing. *(SALLY says nothing)* We're going to Paris today . . . remember?

SALLY: *(Looking at him)* Going . . . with *that* face? *(Her voice sounds very, very weary)*

CLIFF: I was in a little fight last night. Did you hear about it? *(SALLY nods)* You should see the other two guys. *(Pause)* Not a mark *on* them. *(He looks at his watch)* Do you realize how late it is? Almost time to go to the station . . .

SALLY: The fact *is,* Cliff—

CLIFF: Don't say it. Whatever it is. Let's just—forget the last twelve hours. Forget what I said at the Kit Kat Klub. Forget you've gotten even with me staying out all night . . . okay? *(He takes her hand)* You're so cold. Where's your coat? Your fur coat?

SALLY: You know what I'd love? A spot of gin! We've got some, don't we? I mean —I think one *must!*

CLIFF: First thing in the morning? How about a Prairie Oyster?

SALLY: Gin! *(She gets herself a drink)*

CLIFF: That can't be good for expectant mothers. We'll have to get some books on the subject. You know, I suddenly realize I don't know a damn thing about pregnancy. Where's your coat? Did you leave it at the Klub, or was it stolen?

SALLY: I left it at the doctor's office.

CLIFF: Were you sick last night? Is that why you didn't come home?

SALLY: Hals and beinbruch. It means neck and leg break. It's supposed to stop it from happening—though I doubt it does. I doubt you can stop *anything* happening. Any more than you can change people. I mean . . .

CLIFF: *What* do you mean?

SALLY: I mean—I'm not perfect. Far from it! I meet someone and I make all sorts of enormous promises. And then there's an argument—or something else ugly —and I suddenly realize I can't keep those promises—not possibly! Because I am still *me!*

CLIFF: Sally, what are you talking about?

SALLY: Oh, darling—you're such an innocent. Really! My one regret is I honestly believe you'd have been a wonderful father. And I'm sure someday you *will* be. Oh yes, and I've another regret: That greedy doctor! I'm going to miss my fur coat. *(CLIFF slaps her)* I'm glad you did that. Isn't it funny it always ends this way? Even when I finally *do* love someone terribly—for the first time. But it's still not—quite—enough. I'd spoil it, Cliff. I'd run away with the first exciting thing that came along. I guess I really am a rather strange and extraordinary person. *(CLIFF is packing his bag)* Cliff . . . I'm sorry. I'm so dreadfully, dreadfully sorry. Because . . . the truth is . . . I really would have liked . . .

(She can't go on. CLIFF finishes his preparations for leaving. Then he takes out his wallet. He removes one of the railroad tickets and puts it down on the table)

CLIFF: This is your ticket to Paris. You can cash it in . . . or tear it up . . . or do whatever you want with it. *(CLIFF takes his suitcase and goes to the door)* Sally . . . if . . . for any reason . . . you need to get in touch with me . . . in Paris . . . the American Express office. *(SALLY looks at him)* I'll be there at least a week.

(CLIFF obviously can't force himself to go out the door. SALLY wipes her eyes. She lights a cigarette in the long, long holder. She smiles—making a tremendous effort to be the old SALLY again for a moment)

SALLY: But—the truth is—Cliff: I've always rather *hated* Paris.

(She puffs on her cigarette. She smiles at CLIFF, as if telling him that she will be perfectly fine without him)

CLIFF: *(Sadly)* Oh, Sally. Goodbye.

SALLY: Goodbye, Cliff. Dedicate your book to me!

(CLIFF exits, closing the door behind him. SALLY takes the long cigarette holder out of her mouth. Her smile fades. She turns to the door as the lights dim very slowly)

SCENE 7

Before the lights come up we hear

LOUDSPEAKER VOICE: Letzte ansage! Berlin-Paris Express abfahrt vier uhr bahnsteig siebzehn. Alle einsteigen, bitte! *Letzte ansage!*

(The lights go up on a railroad compartment. CLIFF is alone in it. He has a writing

pad on his lap, a pencil in his hand. Two CUSTOMS OFFICERS *enter from the corridor)*

OFFICER: Deutsche grenzkontrolle. Ihren pass, bitte. *(CLIFF hands it to him. He hands it back to* CLIFF*)* I hope you have enjoyed your stay in Germany, Mr. Bradshaw. And you will return soon again?

CLIFF: It's not very likely.

OFFICER: You did not find our country beautiful?

CLIFF: *(Tonelessly)* Yes, I found it—beautiful.

OFFICER: A good journey, sir.

(The OFFICER *tips his cap and exits.* CLIFF *looks at his writing pad. He crosses out a few words, then adds a few. He reads what he has written)*

CLIFF: "There was a cabaret and there was a master of ceremonies and there was a city called Berlin in a country called Germany—and it was the end of the world and I was dancing with Sally Bowles—and we were both fast asleep . . ."

(Singing)
Willkommen, bienvenue, welcome,
Fremde, étranger, stranger.

(The EMCEE *has entered and come downstage. He moves his lips soundlessly as* CLIFF *sings. Then he begins singing along with* CLIFF*)*

CLIFF and EMCEE:
Glücklich zu seben,
Je suis enchanté,
Happy to see you.

(Then CLIFF *stops singing and the* EMCEE *finishes alone as the train moves upstage)*

EMCEE:
Bleibe, reste, stay,
Willkommen, bienvenue, welcome,
Im cabaret, au cabaret, to cabaret!

Meine Damen und Herren—Mesdames et Messieurs—Ladies and Gentlemen. Where are your troubles now? Forgotten? I told you so! We have no troubles here. Here life is beautiful—the girls are beautiful—even the orchestra is beautiful.

(The GIRL ORCHESTRA *appears onstage as do the characters from the opening scene, but this time the picture and the mood are much different. The girls are not as pretty, German uniforms and swastika armbands are apparent; it is not as bright, a dream-like quality that prevails. Dissonant strains of "Willkommen" are heard. Then from among the moving people, we see* HERR SCHULTZ*)*

SCHULTZ: Just children. Mischievous children on their way to school. You understand.

(The people move again and we see FRAULEIN SCHNEIDER*)*

FRAULEIN SCHNEIDER: I understand. One does what one must.

(Again the people move and we see SALLY*)*

SALLY: It'll all work out. It's only politics, and what's that got to do with us?

FRAULEIN SCHNEIDER: I must be sensible. If the Nazis come—what other choice have I?

SCHULTZ: I know I am right—because I understand the Germans. After all, what am I? A German.

(Suddenly SALLY *is lifted high on a chair)*

SALLY: *(Singing)*

I made my mind up back in Chelsea.
When I go I'm going like Elsie.

*(*SALLY *is lowered. The people gradually fade away)*

. . . from cradle to tomb
Isn't that long a stay.
Life is a cabaret, old chum,
Life is a cabaret, old chum,
Life is a cabaret.

*(*SALLY *disappears into the darkness—leaving the* EMCEE *alone on the stage)*

EMCEE:

Auf wiedersehen!
À bientôt!

(The EMCEE *bows, then suddenly vanishes. The stage is empty except for the street lamps, the mirror, and then, glowing in the darkness, the* Cabaret *sign)*

APPLAUSE

Book by Betty Comden and Adolph Green
Lyrics by Lee Adams
Music by Charles Strouse

(Based on the film *All About Eve* and the original story by Mary Orr)

Editor's Notes

A sparkling jewel in the Broadway diadem of 1970, *Applause* ran for 896 performances. Opening on March 30, 1970 with star Lauren Bacall giving a dazzling performance as Margo Channing, the press described it as "show business at its best . . . a driving, smart, entertaining show" that was "a whacking new hit." Clive Barnes reported in *The New York Times:* "This is a musical play that is bright, witty, direct and nicely punchy . . ." while his colleague on the same newspaper, Walter Kerr, pronounced it "a rock-solid success."

The musical won five Antoinette Perry (Tony) Awards, including one for the year's best musical, and three Drama Desk Awards. With Lauren Bacall once again heading the cast, it later was performed in London for almost a year, then was televised for network showing here and abroad.

Betty Comden and Adolph Green (coauthors of the book) are triply talented as authors, lyricists and performers. As a team, they occupy a unique place in stage and screen history. In *Applause,* for the first time they have focused on the writing of only the book, which received extraordinary acclaim for its characterizations, wit and pace. (NOTE: As lyricists, Comden and Green are represented in this same volume with *Wonderful Town.*)

The collaborators have a formidable record of achievement in both the theatre and in motion pictures. They've won Tony Awards for *Wonderful Town, Hallelujah, Baby!,* and *Applause.* They were recipients of Screen Writers Guild Awards for *The Bandwagon, On the Town, Singin' in the Rain,* and *It's Always Fair Weather,* as well as being honored with three Academy Award nominations.

Betty Comden was born in Brooklyn, New York, on May 3, 1919. She attended Brooklyn Ethical Culture School and Erasmus Hall High School, and received a Bachelor of Science Degree at New York University.

Adolph Green was born in the Bronx, New York, on December 2, 1915. He studied in New York public schools and first teamed with his future collaborator, Betty Comden, and the late Judy Holliday in a pioneering satirical act, *The Revuers,* which packed various nightclubs, including the Village Vanguard, in the 1940's. As performers, they made their Broadway debuts in their own musical, *On the Town* (with music by Leonard Bernstein, 1944). The show ran for 463 performances and established Comden and Green as topflight contributors to the American musical theatre. They returned to the Broadway stage on December 23, 1958, performing their own comedy and songs in a mini-revue entitled *A Party With Betty Comden and Adolph Green* for an engagement of 82 performances.

Best known, however, as writers, they have brightened Broadway stages as authors of the book and lyrics for such musicals as *Billion Dollar Baby, Two on the Aisle, Bells Are Ringing, Fade Out-Fade In,* and *Subways Are for Sleeping.*

They also wrote the lyrics for *Do Re Mi, Say, Darling,* Mary Martin's *Peter Pan* (additional lyrics only), *Wonderful Town,* and *Hallelujah, Baby!,* for which they shared with Jule Styne the 1968 Tony Award for best score of the season.

Their distinguished writing careers in the movies include the screenplays and lyrics for *Good News, On the Town, The Barkleys of Broadway, Take Me Out to the Ball Game, Singin' in the Rain, The Band Wagon, Auntie Mame, Bells Are Ringing, It's Always Fair Weather,* and *What a Way to Go.*

In private life, Miss Comden is the wife of Steven Kyle and they have two children, a girl and a boy. Mr. Green is married to actress Phyllis Newman and they, too, have a daughter and a son. Both families live in New York City.

Lee Adams (lyrics) was born in Mansfield, Ohio, in 1924 and attended the Columbia University Graduate School of Journalism. Before turning to lyric-writing, he worked on newspapers, magazines, television and radio. With Charles Strouse (music) he began writing for the theatre at Green Mansions, a resort in the Adirondacks.

Mr. Strouse was born in New York City on June 7, 1928. He studied at the Eastman School of Music and privately with David Diamond, Nadia Boulanger and Aaron Copland, among others. His first New York score was for *Shoestring Revue*, presented in 1955. After contributing music to several other revues, he and Mr. Adams burst upon the Broadway scene with *Bye Bye Birdie*, a leading success of 1960 that ran for 607 performances and won a Tony Award as the year's best musical. This was followed by *All American* (1962), *Golden Boy* (1964), and *It's a Bird . . . It's a Plane . . . It's Superman!* (1966).

Their partnership has lasted for more than two decades and during this period, in addition to their Broadway musicals, they have published more than three hundred popular songs. Among them: "Put on a Happy Face," "A Lot of Livin' to Do," "Once Upon a Time," "Kids," "Night Song," "I Want to Be With You" and "This Is the Life."

They also have written for motion pictures. Mr. Strouse did the scores for *Bonnie and Clyde* and *The Molly Maguires* and collaborated with Mr. Adams on *The Night They Raided Minsky's* and *There Was a Crooked Man*.

The genesis of *Applause* is somewhat unique, even in an industry where uniqueness abounds. The original story, *The Wisdom of Eve*, was written in four days by actress Mary Orr, whose only previous attempt at writing was the comedy, *Wallflower*, on which she collaborated with her husband, the playwright-director, Reginald Denham. Published as a novelette in *Cosmopolitan* magazine, her agent submitted it to various motion picture companies for a possible film sale. It was turned down. Then, Miss Orr converted it into a radio play and it was presented on NBC's Radio Guild Playhouse. Within days after the broadcast, she had a firm offer from Twentieth Century-Fox to do a movie version of the property. With a screenplay and direction by Joseph L. Mankiewicz, and now retitled *All About Eve*, the film won the Academy Award as the best motion picture of 1950. It also won five other major awards and has since become a cinematic classic. Encouraged by the extraordinary success of the movie, Miss Orr and Mr. Denham (who had retained the stage rights) set about dramatizing the story for the amateur play market, reverting to the original title *The Wisdom of Eve*. Meanwhile, they attempted to interest Broadway producers to musicalize the property but it never got off the ground until Joseph Kipness and Lawrence Kasha loomed onto the horizon; after protracted negotiations with the film company they secured the rights and the result, of course, became *Applause*.

Production Notes

Applause was first presented by Joseph Kipness and Lawrence Kasha, in association with Nederlander Productions and George M. Steinbrenner, III, at the Palace Theatre, New York, on March 30, 1970. The cast was as follows:

Tony Awards Announcer, *John Anania*   Peter, *John Anania*
Tony Host, *Alan King*   Bob, *Howard Kahl*
Margo Channing, *Lauren Bacall*   Piano Player, *Orrin Reiley*
Eve Harrington, *Penny Fuller*   Stan Harding, *Ray Becker*
Howard Benedict, *Robert Mandan*   Danny, *Bill Allsbrook*
Bert, *Tom Urich*   Bonnie, *Bonnie Franklin*
Buzz Richards, *Brandon Maggart*   Carol, *Carol Petri*
Bill Sampson, *Len Cariou*   Joey, *Mike Misita*
Duane Fox, *Lee Roy Reams*   Musicians, *Gene Kelton, Nat Horne, Da-*
Karen Richards, *Ann Williams*   *vid Anderson*
Bartender, *Jerry Wyatt*   TV Director, *Orrin Reiley*
Dancer in the Bar, *Sammy Williams*   Autograph Seeker, *Carol Petri*
Singers, *Sheilah Rae, Laurie Franks, Ernestine Jackson, Jeanette Seibert, Howard Kahl,*
    Orrin Reiley, Jerry Wyatt, Henrietta Valor. Dancers: *Renee Baughman, Joan Bell,*
    Debi Carpenter, Patti D'Beck, Marybeth Kurdock, Carol Petri, Bill Allsbrook, David
    Anderson, John Cashman, Nikolas Dante, Gene Foote, Gene Kelton, Nat Horne, Mike
    Misita, Ed Nolfi, Sammy Williams, Marilyn D'Honau, Jon Daenan.

The Singers and Dancers appear as the First-Nighters, the Boys, the Gypsies, the
    Guests, and in various minor roles throughout the play.

Directed and Choreographed by *Ron Field*
Scenery by *Robert Randolph*
Costumes by *Ray Aghayan*
Lighting by *Tharon Musser*
Musical Direction and Vocal Arrangements by *Donald Pippin*
Orchestrations by *Philip J. Lang*
Dance and Incidental Music Arranged by *Mel Marvin*

Act One

Scene 1: The Tony Awards.
Scene 2: Margo's dressing room, a year and a half earlier.
Scene 3: The Village bar, that night.
Scene 4: Margo's living room, later that night.
Scene 5: Margo's dressing room, four months later.
Scene 6: Joe Allen's.
Scene 7: Margo's bedroom.
Scene 8: Margo's living room, two weeks later.
Scene 9: Backstage, several days later.

Act Two

Scene 1: Buzz and Karen's Connecticut home, a few weeks later.
Scene 2: Margo's dressing room, the same night.
Scene 3: Joe Allen's.
Scene 4: Margo's living room, the following day.
Scene 5: Backstage, about two weeks later.
Scene 6: Margo's dressing room, a week later.
Scene 7: Backstage.

The entire action takes place in and around New York.

Musical Numbers

Act One

Overture	
Backstage Babble	First-Nighters
Think How It's Gonna Be	Bill
But Alive	Margo and the Boys
The Best Night of My Life	Eve
Who's That Girl?	Margo
Applause	Bonnie and the Gypsies
Hurry Back	Margo
Fasten Your Seat Belts	Buzz, Karen, Howard, Bill, Duane, Margo, and the Guests
Welcome to the Theater	Margo

Act Two

Inner Thoughts	Karen, Buzz, and Margo
Good Friends	Buzz, Margo, and Karen
The Best Night of My Life (Reprise)	Eve
She's No Longer a Gypsy	Duane, Bonnie, and the Gypsies
One of a Kind	Bill and Margo
One Hallowe'en	Eve
Something Greater	Margo and Bill

ACT ONE

SCENE 1

The Tony Awards.

The orchestra begins the overture, during which the TONY AWARDS AN-NOUNCER *says over a backstage microphone, "Ladies and gentlemen, tonight we bring you, live, from New York, the annual presentation of the Antoinette Perry Awards for outstanding achievement in the theater." While the orchestra continues playing, monitors on either side of the proscenium and elsewhere throughout the theater show silent filmed clips from a recent Tony Awards telecast, and the stage is set as if the live audience is attending this very event.*

At the center of the stage is a white podium. A Tony Awards seal forms its base, and behind it a large Tony medallion hangs in the middle of the curtain. At some point applause is heard, and the Tony Awards host, Alan King, appears filmed on the monitors.

ALAN KING: *(On the monitors)* From the applause, ladies and gentlemen, we gather that the award to Lou Pacelli for best actor in a supporting role was a popular one. And now, to present the award for best actress in a starring role, we proudly introduce two-time Tony winner, still playing in the long-run hit *The Friendly Arrangement,* that great lady of stage and screen, my good friend —Margo Channing.

(MARGO CHANNING enters on stage, acknowledges the audience, and goes to the podium. Her image appears at the same time on the monitors, in the same action, and from now till the end of the scene the action on the monitors is exactly the same as what is happening on stage. MARGO is the essence of the word "star"—arresting, elegant, and exuding that rare, fast-disappearing quality, glamour)

MARGO: Thank you, thank you, ladies and gentlemen. Well, here we are again, giving out the Tony Awards, and I just heard the theater's all washed up. Now where did I hear that? Oh, yes—from some big movie producer whose office is now a used-car lot . . . Well . . . The nominees for best actress in a starring role in a straight play are Maureen Parker in *The Computer Next Door,* Kelly Westbrook in *The Groupies,* Eve Harrington in *Somewhere to Love . . . (A page enters)* and Julie Sommers in *Figments.* And the winner is . . . *(The page hands her an envelope. She opens it and reads)* Eve Harrington!

(A spotlight hits EVE, sitting in an aisle seat down front in the theater. She springs up excitedly, looking startled and thrilled, and amidst applause, runs up the steps to the stage. She rushes across to MARGO, who graciously hands her the Tony and steps aside. She is young and pretty but under her breathless gratitude and humility, one can sense that she knows exactly what she is saying and doing. As she speaks, MARGO keeps looking at her with a fixed public smile)

EVE: Oh, thank you, thank you. Needless to say, this is the best night of my life! I have so many people to thank, I hardly know where to begin. There's my director, William Sampson; my author, Buzz Richards; my producer, Howard Benedict. But the one to whom I owe the most is . . . Margo Channing . . . not only a great actress, a legend in her own time, but the most generous, noble human being as well. I will never forget her. *(EVE'S voice begins to fade, and the lights dim, except for a strong spotlight on MARGO'S face)* As long as I live I will cherish the . . .

MARGO'S VOICE: *(Heard taped over the scene, as she stands unmoving, and with the same fixed smile on her face)* Goddamn it, Eve—I'm not dead yet! As a matter of fact, I feel more alive than ever. As I stand here, watching the audience drink you in, I am dumb-struck, filled with wonder and admiration. Can this dazzling vision be the same strange little mouse who pittered and pattered into my life on my opening night, just a year and a half ago? It can. It is. *(EVE has finished, takes a bow, and starts to move toward MARGO)* Oh, she's finished. What a lovely smile! Now kiss her on the cheek . . . *(EVE and MARGO are both in the spotlight. They kiss, EVE hiding MARGO from the audience)* Downstage cheek, dummy! You let her hide you! *(EVE passes in front of MARGO and goes off. The spotlight stays on MARGO)* Eve. Was it really less than two years ago that we met? *(MARGO exits, and the lights go out. Her voice is still heard)* That night was not only the beginning of the theatrical season, it was the beginning of open season for *me.*

(There is a close-up of her face, as if she were looking back into the past. The image ripples and fades as the curtain rises for the next scene)

SCENE 2

The scene is MARGO'S *dressing room, right after her opening-night performance,*
a year and a half earlier than the preceding scene. Her dressing room is filled with
telegrams, flowers and tumultuously babbling FIRST-NIGHTERS. *It is a comfortable*
room, with armchairs, a small couch and a small bar. It can be divided by pulling
a curtain across the center, leaving an area of privacy, stage left, with a dressing
table, mirror, and exit to a bathroom. Also visible is an area just outside the dressing
room door, stage right. The milling crowd fills the dressing room while others are
pressing against the door trying to get in. The focal characters in this crowd scene
are HOWARD BENEDICT, *the urbane and forceful producer of this play and many*
others; the playwright BUZZ RICHARDS, *eccentric and earthy-looking and a wild*
worrier; and MARGO'S *hairdresser, buddy, and confidante,* DUANE FOX. *The*
FIRST-NIGHTERS *are engaged in the kind of excited babble that is typical of all big*
opening nights.

FIRST-NIGHTERS: *(Sing "Backstage Babble")*
  Ba ba da, ba ba da,
  Ba ba da, ba ba da,
  Ba dom ba, da ba da,
  Ba dom ba, da ba da,
  Ba dom ba, da ba da.

  Ba ba da, ba da,
  Ba ba da, wonderful,
  Ba ba da, ba ba da,
  Margo was just da da!

  Ba ba da, she's lookin'
  Mighty ba ba da,
  Ba da ba, da ba wasn't she?

*(*BERT, *the stage manager, pushes through the crowd with a fresh batch of telegrams*
which he puts into DUANE'S *mouth, since both his hands are full, serving drinks.*
DUANE *hands the drinks out, and exits through the bathroom door)*

  La da da, ba da Mr. Benedict,
  Ba ba da, ba da ba,
  Ba ba da, producer,
  Ba ba da, ba da . . .

  La la la,
  Loved it, whoa whoa!

HOWARD: Bert, don't let any more people in. Too crowded already.
  *(*BERT *nods and exits)*
YOUNG WOMAN: *(Ga-ga and full-bosomed, chirping at* HOWARD, *who makes a*
  note of her for the future)

  Hee bee dee bee dee bee dee bee dee,
  Hee bee dee bee dee bee dee bee doo!

FIRST-NIGHTERS:
  Critics will certainly ba ba da,
  Ba da ba, da ba doo!

BUZZ: *(Approaching* HOWARD*)* What do you hear, Howard? Do you think they liked the play?

HOWARD: They seem to like it okay, but we won't get reviews for an hour or so.

(BILL SAMPSON, *the director, enters from the dressing room door)*

FIRST-NIGHTERS:
Didn't she ba ba da,
Bee buh dee, marvelous!
Ba da ba, da a bit!
Look who directed it!
Congratulations!

BILL: *(Trying to work his way toward* HOWARD*)* Thanks!

FIRST-NIGHTERS:
Ba ba da, ba da.

WOMAN: *(Stopping* BILL, *and gushing)*
Dyah dyah, da da da,
Dyah dyah, da da.

BILL: Yeah, she sure was!

MAN: *(Stopping* BILL *again)*
Dyah dyah, da da da,
Da da da dum!

BILL: You can say that again.

FIRST-NIGHTERS:
La la la la la la,
La la la la la la,
La da de da, just great!

(BILL *and* HOWARD *congratulate each other.* BUZZ *joins them, then they are again surrounded by the* FIRST-NIGHTERS*)*

Openings are really ba ba dah!
So exciting, ba ba da, ba da!
Lee bee dee bee doo bah dee bee,
Loved it very ba ba da!
Wasn't Margo ba ba da!
Thought the play was bee bee dee,
Sets and lights were bee bee dee,
What an uh-uh opening wow!

(After the number, MARGO *and* DUANE *enter from her bathroom where she has been changing. She is in her dressing gown. Everyone greets her; she and* BILL *try to get together, but* FIRST-NIGHTERS *surround her)*

MARGO: Bill!

WOMAN: Divine, Margo!

MARGO: How nice of you.

MAN: You're so witty.

MARGO: Thanks, but tell that to the author.

MAN: Miss Channing, I see everything you do.

MARGO: Oh, I hope not everything!

(BILL and MARGO finally get together and embrace. HOWARD comes over to them)

HOWARD: Nice work. Get yourself over to the party.

MARGO: I've just knocked myself out doing *this* show. Now I have to go over and do *that* one.

HOWARD: Get there.

MARGO: All right. But I want a minute with Bill before he leaves. Empty the room . . . diplomatically, of course.

HOWARD: Of course. Attention! *(They all listen to him)* Everybody—get the hell out! Margo will see you all at the party.

FIRST-NIGHTERS: *(Singing excitedly and exiting)*
 Ba ba da, marvelous!
 You were just ba ba da,
 Bee dee ba doo, sincere!
 Ra ba dee ba doo ba dee ba,
 Darling, get a cab . . .

YOUNG WOMAN: *(Again directing her charms at HOWARD)*
 Thank you, Mr. Benedict,
 I doo ba da ba dee!

FIRST-NIGHTERS:
 Ba ba da, terrific,
 Ba ba da, ba da ba,
 Da ba da ba, really,
 Ba ba da, ba da ba . . .

(The FIRST-NIGHTERS and HOWARD exit. BUZZ sits on the sofa, busy with his telegrams. DUANE is combing out a wig at the dressing table. BILL and MARGO are comparatively alone. The nature of their relationship becomes immediately apparent. They are in love, but he is somewhat younger than she, and despite her surface confidence and sharpness, she is uncertain and touchingly vulnerable. He is, in ways, more mature than she, and tries to understand her hangups and patiently kid her out of them)

BILL: Star, I have a few notes for you. *(She droops)* Absolute perfection! . . . *(She glows and goes to him)* Except you lost your biggest laugh in Act Two, dope, by moving on your own line, and—

MARGO: *(Cutting and defensive)* Listen, Herr Direktor, since you've elected to abandon us tonight, I don't have to take a goddamn thing from you. Who said you have to do that idiotic movie in Rome?

BILL: *I* said. You keep forgetting some men have careers just like women do. Expect me to give it all up? Slave over a hot stove all day?

MARGO: I never heard of such a thing! You know actors have to be watched like rotten kids. In a week the play will fall apart . . . and so will I. Oh, Bill! *(Collapsing, she runs to his arms as KAREN, BUZZ'S wife, enters)*

KAREN: *(Excited)* Bravo, Margo!

BUZZ: *(Gets up from the sofa)* Karen! I wish you'd sit next to me on opening nights!

KAREN: How can I? You spend the whole time in the men's room. *(Gives him his pills. KAREN is handsome, well-bred, involved in the theater only through marriage, and still full of girlish enthusiasms)*. Buzz, did you hear the laughs tonight?

I never can believe those funny lines are written by this undertaker I live with.

BUZZ: They come out of her mouth . . . *(Indicating* MARGO*)* That's what makes them funny. *(*MARGO *bows to this)* But there was one place in the second act—

*(*BILL *sits next to the dressing table)*

MARGO: Yes, yes, I know—I lost your biggest laugh. I'll tell you about that line. I choke on it! It reminds me, *and* the audience, I'm playing someone considerably younger than myself.

BILL: You're sick, Margo.

MARGO: No—I'm forty.

(She goes to the dressing table and sits. BERT *reenters)*

BERT: Sorry about that late curtain in Scene Three, Margo. *(He hands some telegrams to* KAREN *and exits)*

MARGO: Okay, Bert . . .

KAREN: *(Enthusiastically)* Listen, Margo . . . *(She goes over to* BILL *and hands him the wires)* I've been mingling. *The Friendly Arrangement* is a definite hit in the lobby, and the alley is full of fans just pouring love out at you.

MARGO: Love! Little beasts! All they care about is trading autographs. "I'll give you five Margo Channings for one Pearl Bailey." They've never even seen me on the stage.

KAREN: Well, one of them has. There's a girl out there who's seen every preview the whole three weeks. I brought her back here to meet you.

MARGO: What! Duane . . .

(She gestures to DUANE *to get rid of whoever it is. He moves toward the door, then stops as* KAREN *speaks)*

KAREN: *(Crossing to* MARGO*)* Wait! I've spotted her every night in the alley, half hidden in the shadows, and tonight she spoke up, and, Margo, this girl idolizes you! It's like something out of a book! You've *got* to—

BUZZ: Karen, on opening night!

KAREN: *(Seriously pleading)* She's spent her last penny to see you!

BILL: Make her happy, Margo. Receive her and let her kiss your ring.

MARGO: *(Gives in and gets up with a grand, satiric flourish)* Spent her last penny to see Margo Channing. The kid can't be all bad!

*(*KAREN *goes to the door and opens it. The men get up)*

KAREN: Come in, dear. *(It is* EVE, *looking quite different from the way she does in the Tony Awards scene. She is mousy and bedraggled, wearing a nondescript raincoat and pants)* Margo, this is Eve—Eve Harrington.

MARGO: How do you do.

EVE: *(Timid and awed, hanging back near the door)* How do you do.

MARGO: And this is Mr. Sampson, Mr. Richards, and Duane Fox.

EVE: Hello.

(The men murmur hellos)

MARGO: Won't you sit down?

EVE: No, thank you, really. I'm just glad I have this chance to congratulate you all, and to thank you, Miss Channing, for lighting up my life—saving it, really.

MARGO: *(Taken aback)* That's an extraordinary statement.

EVE: *(Sincerely)* I mean it—literally. Seeing you on the stage changed everything for me.

MARGO: Are you in the theater?

EVE: Oh, I love the theater passionately. For years I belonged to our local dramatic society. We did Pinter and Albee. But I never gave any thought to being in it professionally.

MARGO: *(Feeling she has done her duty, and moving back to the dressing table)* Oh.

BILL: *(Politely)* Where was all this?

EVE: Madison, Wisconsin. I grew up on a little farm near there. I used to try to escape from it into the world of my imagination—making up things, acting them out . . . Oh, what I'm saying is silly.

KAREN: Please go on.

EVE: Well, after school, I took a secretarial job. There I met someone wonderful who was also interested in theater. A dreamer, working in an office—like me. We got married. Soon enough the outside world woke us up. He was sent to Vietnam. I went to San Francisco to meet him on leave, then got the telegram that told me he was never coming back. Life was over for me. I went completely to pieces—dropped out, drifted aimlessly, half in a daze—hardly knowing who I was or what I was doing. I lost all contact with reality.

(They are all listening, spellbound. DUANE leaps up and breaks the mood)

DUANE: Wow! It's like being back in group therapy.

MARGO: Duane!

DUANE: Sorry.

EVE: *(Continuing)* I wound up in New York. One night, some kid I knew dragged me into a theater. I knew your movies, but it was the first time I'd ever seen you on the stage. I felt an energy and vitality . . . It was like suddenly walking into the sunlight again. I saw you every night until the play closed. I came back to life. *(Pauses)* I'm glad I've had this chance to tell you what you've meant to me. Good-bye.

MARGO: *(Touched, gets up and takes EVE's hand)* I think this is the nicest opening-night present I've ever had. Don't go, Eve. Stay around awhile.

BILL: *(Gets up, as do all the others)* Hey, I better get going.

MARGO: *(Turning to Bill)* Let me go to the airport with you!

BILL: We settled that already. I don't want to remember you in that neon light, with your mascara dripping into your shoes. Go to the party.

KAREN: We should be getting to that party. Come on, Buzz.

BUZZ: Wait for you, Margo?

MARGO: No, Duane'll drop me off.

KAREN: Good-bye, Bill. See you in three months. *Buona fortuna!*

BILL: *(Kissing her)* Grazie mille. *(Shaking hands with BUZZ)* Pretty sneaky of me ducking out before the notices.

BUZZ: *(To BILL)* Do you think they liked the play?

BILL: *(Shrugs)* I don't know, but I did get an opinion from Max, the guy who sells orange juice in the lobby.

BUZZ: Well?

BILL: *(Making a thumbs-down gesture and raspberry sound)* He said theater today is action, participation, mass rape!

BUZZ: I don't think much of his orange juice, either.

KAREN: Good-bye, Eve.

EVE: Mrs. Richards, I'll never forget you.

KAREN: Good luck.

BUZZ: Good-bye, Miss Harrington.

EVE: Good-bye.

(DUANE opens the door. BUZZ, KAREN, and DUANE leave. BILL and MARGO are in each others arms. EVE turns and sees them)

EVE: *(Uncomfortably)* I really should wait outside.

(BILL makes a little sound, indicating agreement. EVE leaves)

MARGO: Oh, Bill!

BILL: Marry me when I get back.

MARGO: *(Fencing)* I'll think about it.

BILL: You've been thinking about it for two years.

MARGO: I'm a slow thinker.

BILL: *(Turning to her, kidding, but trying to make a point)* Last chance to examine the merchandise! Classic profile, dazzling personality, talent, voted lover-of-the-year by his own high school. Aren't you afraid I'll be snapped up on the Via Veneto?

MARGO: Am I going to lose you?

BILL: Not a chance. I'll get you something beautiful in Rome.

MARGO: Just don't get *yourself* something beautiful in Rome.

BILL: *(He sings "Think How It's Gonna Be")*

> *Dry your pretty eyes,*
> *And let me have a smile,*
> *Think how it's gonna be*
> *When we're together again . . .*
>
> *I don't want to go,*
> *But planes come back, you know,*
> *Think how it's gonna be*
> *When we're together again . . .*
>
> *Oh, we'll take a long, long walk,*
> *Oh, we'll have a quiet talk,*
> *Then just when the fire's low,*
> *Honey, you know*
> *Where we'll go . . .*
>
> *So flash your famous smile,*
> *The one that gets 'em all,*
> *Think how it's gonna be,*
> *Nothing but you and me!*
> *Think how it's gonna be*
> *When we're together again.*

Hey, you know—I love you very much.

MARGO: I know. Hey, don't eat too much pasta. I want to be able to get my arms around you when you come back.

BILL: *(Singing)*

> *I don't want to go,*
> *But planes come back, you know,*
> *Think how it's gonna be,*
> *Nothing but you and me!*

Think how it's gonna be
When we're together again.

(*They stand looking at each other a moment and then* BILL *exits.* DUANE *and* EVE *re-enter.* MARGO *goes to the dressing table and slumps dejectedly*)

DUANE: Come on, Pagliacci, baby! Gotta get prettied up for the party!

EVE: And I should be getting back to my room.

MARGO: What! The girl who sat through this play twenty-four times? You're coming to the party!

EVE: Oh, I couldn't! I'd be so . . . uncomfortable!

MARGO: (*Getting up*) *You'd* be uncomfortable? How do you think I feel? Everyone glued to TV sets, huddled over advance copies of *The Times*, waiting for the poison gas to creep over the room . . . How'll I ever get through it without Bill? (*A sudden inspiration*) I know! I won't go!

DUANE: *What?*

MARGO: Well, I deserve a good time tonight! (*Filled with a new energy*) Duane, how'd you like to escort two lonely ladies out on the town?

DUANE: I've got a date.

MARGO: Bring him along.

(*She goes over to the closet to start changing.* DUANE *follows, and holds the dressing robe in front of her so she can dress behind it*)

DUANE: I was just going down to the Village—join some friends. I don't know if you'll like it.

MARGO: (*Taking a dress from the closet and getting into it*) We'll adore it. Eve, we're going to the Village!

EVE: But it's opening night. You must feel exhausted!

MARGO: I'm too exhausted to go to the party . . . but I'm much too excited to go home to sleep! (MARGO *is finished dressing. Revitalized and ready to take off, she sums up her feelings of that evening to* EVE *and* DUANE, *singing "But Alive"*)

I feel groggy and weary
And tragic,
Punchy and bleary
And fresh out of magic,
But alive,
But alive,
But alive!

I feel twitchy and bitchy
And manic,
Calm and collected
And choking with panic,
But alive,
But alive,
But alive!

I'm a thousand diff'rent people,
Ev'ry single one is real,
I've a million diff'rent feelings,
Okay, but at least I feel!

And I feel rotten
Yet covered with roses,
Younger than springtime
And older than Moses,
Frisky as a lamb,
Lazy as a clam,
Crazy, but I am
Alive!

(During this last verse, she links arms with EVE *and* DUANE *and they come downstage as the set changes behind them. The sound of discotheque music is heard)*

SCENE 3

The scene is a bar in Greenwich Village. A wall of colored, blinking lights descends downstage as the three dance off. As the wall is pulled up, it forms a ceiling; two side walls and a back wall fly in. The right wall is lined with bottles, as in a bar, and a rolling bar is then pushed on to the stage in front of the wall, while the rest of the bar set flies in. A large, lighted jukebox is rolled on.

The walls are covered with posters and large photographs of movie idols—mainly Paul Newman, Judy Garland and Marlon Brando.

The place is filled with people, all of them dancing, and it becomes apparent that all of them are male, dressed in varied flamboyant attire. MARGO, *followed by* EVE *and* DUANE, *enters. Suddenly the action freezes and, stunned, the* BOYS *stare at* MARGO.

BOYS: *(In one breath)* Margo Channing!

MARGO: Drat! I've been recognized!

BARTENDER: But I can't believe it. Here! I mean, didn't you open tonight? The Buzz Richards play?

MARGO: Guilty.

BARTENDER: *(Overcome)* This is a historic moment. We light candles in front of your picture!
(They are still frozen, gaping at her)

MARGO: Duane, I'm spoiling the fun.

DUANE: Shall I call the party and tell them you'll be there soon?

TWO BOYS: Don't go!

BARTENDER: Please stay!

MARGO: *(Making up her mind on the spot)* Silly boys . . . I'm here for the night!
(Without analyzing it, she feels relaxed and safe in this atmosphere of total adoration and no competition. She begins singing "But Alive" again)

I feel wicked and whacky
And mellow,
(Gives her cape to DUANE*)*
Firm as Gibraltar
And shaky as jello,
But alive,
But alive,
But alive!

I feel half Tijuana,
Half Boston,

Partly Jane Fonda
And partly Jane Austen,
But alive,
That's the thing!
But alive!

BOYS: *(Speaking at the same time)* Miss Channing! . . . Pleased to meet you!
. . . You're great! . . . Margo! . . . Love you . . .

MARGO:
This kaleidoscope of feelings
Whirls around inside my brain,
I admit I'm slightly coo-coo
But it's dull to be too sane . . .

And I feel brilliant and brash
And bombastic,
Limp as a puppet
And simply fantastic!
But alive,
But alive,
But alive!

*(*MARGO *dances with the* BOYS, *uninhibited, exuberant and free)*

BOYS:
She's here, my dear, can you believe it!
She's here, oh, God, I can't believe it!
She's here! It's just too groovy to believe!

MARGO, DUANE, EVE *and BOYS:*
This kaleidoscope of feelings
Whirls around inside my brain,
We admit we're slightly coo-coo,
But it's dull to be too sane!

Love, love . . . love, love, love . . .
(They clap)

MARGO: *(Leaping on top of the jukebox)*
I feel brilliant!
Bombastic!
Super!
Fantastic!

(Seven BOYS *leap up on the jukebox, surrounding her. When they jump off, she
has disappeared. She reappears from behind the jukebox)*

Alive . . .
Alive . . .
Alive!

BOYS: Margo!
(She dances more and more wildly with the BOYS. *They fling her back and forth,
and she winds up in a pose on* DUANE'S *shoulder. Then she kisses one of the* BOYS
(SAMMY) *good-bye and, as the music picks up and the wall of flashing lights descends,
she leaves with* DUANE *and* EVE*)*

BOYS: *(To* SAMMY*)* Let's go.

SAMMY: *(Pushing them away and starting to follow)* I love her. I mean I really love *her! (The* BOYS *pick him up and carry him off, while he protests, screaming)* Margo! Margo! Margo!

Blackout

SCENE 4

The scene is MARGO'S *living room, still later that evening.*

This set has four playing levels. It is an interesting, lived-in room, filled with theater memorabilia, pictures, etc. MARGO'S *Tony is set on a glass coffee table in the center of the stage, just in front of a light-colored sofa.*

There is a corridor on the right leading off to the kitchen. At the base of the right wall is a half-round cabinet on which sits a lamp and the phone. The wall is covered with pictures, and there is a set of double doors leading to the outside. There are some steps and a railed landing leading to MARGO'S *bedroom, the entrance to which is upstage and to the right.*

In the center of the back wall are double doors to the library. To the right of these doors is a table covered with pictures; to the left, an open bar with two backless barstools underneath.

The lowest playing level is in the central stage area. To the right of the sofa is a comfortable swivel chair. Upstage and to the left of the sofa are two steps to the terrace.

Five open perpendicular panels on the left wall are windows, the panels extending into the ceiling like an artist's skylight.

As the lights come up, DUANE *is at the bar pouring a drink.* EVE *is standing on the steps to the right, looking up at the pictures on the back-wall table.*

EVE: *(Excited)* Laurence Olivier! Noël Coward! *(Goes to the coffee table in front of the sofa and picks up the Tony Award)* And her Tony Award! I've never seen one close up!

(DUANE moves to the terrace and sits)

DUANE: *(Flatly)* Very few have.

(The phone rings. DUANE *"oh's" and gestures that he's too far away to get to it.* EVE *looks hesitant a moment, then goes and picks it up. She has the Tony with her and puts it down next to the phone)*

EVE: Oh! I'll get it. Uh . . . Miss Channing's residence.

BUZZ'S VOICE: Hello, Service, this is Buzz Richards again. She still . . . ?

EVE: Oh, it's Eve, Mr. Richards—Eve Harrington. We met backstage.

BUZZ'S VOICE: Oh, yeah. We've been calling everywhere. Where the hell's she been?

EVE: Well, she went out dancing with Duane and me.

BUZZ'S VOICE: We were ready to kill her till we read the notices.

EVE: The notices! Were they. . . ?

BUZZ'S VOICE: All terrific. She got two "glowings," three "brilliants," and one "incandescent."

EVE: *(Happily)* She's just changing. I'll call her and—

BUZZ'S VOICE: No, no! I'm in a street booth. Just tell her God has been good to us. By that I mean *The New York Times.*

EVE: Good night. *(As she hangs up,* MARGO *enters from the bedroom in pajamas and a robe, carrying her slippers.* DUANE *gets up)* That was Mr. Richards! They've been calling and calling. The reviews . . .

*(*DUANE *moves off the terrace as* MARGO *comes down the steps)*

MARGO: *(Apprehensively)* "The reviews"!

EVE: They said you were glowing, brilliant, incandescent!

MARGO: Lovely! What did they say about Bill?

EVE: It was great for everybody.

MARGO: We're a hit! *(She tosses her slippers gleefully in the air; they land behind the couch.* DUANE *and* MARGO *hug each other)*

DUANE: Good! Now I can buy that fun fur I've been laughing at! I'll put the water on for your Sanka. *(Starts to leave, then stops)* Put on your slippers! *(He goes for them, but* EVE *moves ahead of him)*

EVE: I'll get them!

*(*DUANE *looks at her a moment, a little uneasily then exits.* EVE *brings them over to* MARGO, *who is sitting on the terrace wall, next to the steps)*

MARGO: Thank you, dear. Tonight's been fun, hasn't it? *(She puts on the slippers)*

EVE: Fun? *(She sings "The Best Night of My Life" with great simplicity)*

The best night of my life
Is here, is now.
Knowing you has got to be
The greatest thing that ever happened to me.

If I could freeze this moment,
And take it home with me,
I would—I would,
But time goes by,
And, oh,
I know that I
Never can live
This moment again,
This moment again . . .

The best night of my life,
The best night of my life,
Don't go, don't go . . .

There's no way to say thank you,
It wouldn't come out right.
But . . . thank you
For the best night of my life.

*(*MARGO, *touched, gets up and goes to* EVE *to thank her.* DUANE *enters)*

DUANE: The water's boiling. We better cut out. Our go-go girl has got to get her rest. *(*MARGO *sits on the sofa)* Can I drop you someplace, Eve?

EVE: *(A little too eagerly)* I know! Instead of Sanka, I wish you'd let me fix you one of our hometown toddies. It'll help you sleep.

MARGO: That sounds nice, Eve.

EVE: It'll only take a minute. Good night, Duane. *(She exits to the kitchen)*

DUANE: *(Crossing to the TV set, turns it around, and on)* Okay, now watch the late movie, drink your "hometown toddy," and get to sleep. *(Kisses her on the head)*

Good night, sweetheart, you really were something tonight! I'm going to light a candle in front of your picture *myself! (He goes to the door)*

MARGO: Thanks, but let's not forget—without your magic fingers in my hair, I'd be nothing!

(DUANE blows a kiss and exits. MARGO is on the couch, relaxed. A voice from the TV set fills the room. It is MARGO'S voice, from an old movie)

MARGO'S VOICE: *(From the TV set)* Tomorrow I have to please General Von Schteichler. That's war. Tonight I just want to please you. That's—

MARGO: *(Leaping up, disgustedly)* Good God, another Margo Channing Festival! *(Takes off her robe and gets up to turn off the set)* There I am again! *(As MARGO is turning down the sound, EVE enters with the drink)*

EVE: *(In front of the sofa)* Oh, don't turn it off! *Victory at Dawn!* Leave the picture on, *please! (The sound is off. They both look at the picture)* I know just what Dana Andrews is saying! *(With a great deal of expression, as she stares at the set)* "Some day this war will be over, and the boys will come back home—Izzy, Pat, Sam, and Angelo—together again under a crazy blanket of red, white, and blue." And you say, "Oh, Terry, Terry," and then he says—

MARGO: Never mind what he says. I need that drink. *(Takes the toddy and sips it, looking unbelievingly at herself on the screen)* Look at her! *(Sits)* She was nineteen years old and a big blinding movie star. That year Bill Sampson fell in love with her. He was twelve. He worshipped her from afar . . . *(Gets up)* from a second balcony in Jersey City. In love with a shadow. *(She drinks)*

EVE: Now . . . I'm sure he loves you for what you are.

MARGO: Yes, but what *are* I? Hey! What's in this drink? And which one does he want to marry? Margo today? *(The refrain of "But Alive" is played lugubriously. She sinks down in the sofa in a schlumpfy pose)* Margo on stage? *(The refrain of "But Alive" is played glamorously. She takes a woman-of-the-world pose)* Or *that* one! *(She points to the set)* Miss Eternal Second Balcony! *(She sticks out her tongue at her image on the screen, then sings "Who's That Girl?")*

Who's that girl
With the permanent wave
And the dress below her knees?
Who's that doll
In the open-toed pumps,
Would you kindly tell me, please?

Look at her,
Miss Nineteen Forty-six!
Teen-age Margo,
Queen of the forties' flicks,
Mellowrooney!

Who's that girl
With the Maybelline eyes,
Acting like she knew the score?
Ixnay, Daddy-o,
I never saw that girl before!
Who's that girl with the
Permanent grin

And the stockings with the seams?
Did that kid with the caps on her teeth
Launch a million G.I.s' dreams?

Where is she,
That girl of yesterday?
With her falsies,
Leading Lew Ayres astray!
Boogie-woogie baby!

Who's that girl
With the chic shoulder pads,
Could it be that long ago?
Nosirreebob,
Fooryackasackee,
She isn't anyone I know!

(MARGO *begins to dance some mid-forties jitterbug steps and pulls up* EVE *to join her, spinning her around and back a few times till* EVE *falls back into a chair, laughing*)

Watch her dance,
You can tell that she's hep,
'Cause she digs that jumpin' jive!
Wind her up,
And she really can act,
You would swear that she's alive!

How she smokes
Those brand-new filter tips!
Watch her pucker
Those red-hot Tangee lips!
Hey-bob-a-ree-bob!

Who's that girl
In the platform heels,
Who could that tomato be?

That snazzy chick,
Floy doy, floy doy!
Truckin' on down
Tuxedo junction . . .

EVE: *(Singing)*
   In the pin-striped suit,

MARGO:
   And the upswept hair!
   Boogie-woogie bugle boy from Company B!
   Knock, knock . . .

EVE:
   Who's there?

MARGO:
   Me!
   Hubba hubba

(To finish the number, MARGO strikes a glamorous movie-star pose, then exits up the stairs and into her bedroom, popping out again for a last wave and then in again. EVE crosses to the TV to turn it off. As she does so, the phone rings. She rushes to get the phone on the first ring)

EVE: Hello? . . . A friend. Eve Harrington . . . Oh! Mr. Benedict . . . She's just gone up to her bedroom . . . I think she's going to sleep. Late reviews all good? . . . I'll tell her in the morning . . . *(With a secret smile)* Oh, yes—I'll be here.

(EVE hangs up. She sees the Tony standing there and picks it up. Holding it in front of her in both hands, she takes it and turns to face the audience. She sings as the light dims)

So thank you
For the best night of my life!

SCENE 5

The scene is Margo's dressing room, four months later. HOWARD, PETER, MAR-GO'S agent, and BOB, her lawyer, are engaged in a heated argument.

HOWARD: No, no, no. Tell your client, forget it!

PETER: But Howard . . . !

HOWARD: If she takes next week off, she can take off forever! I'll tear up her two-year contract!

BOB: Howard!

HOWARD: The play's running nearly four months, and I know what kind of hit I've got! I don't need her.

PETER: You're bluffing. Those benefit ladies bought *Margo.* Without her, they'll cancel!

(BUZZ bursts into the room, desperate, frantic. He hurries over to HOWARD)

BUZZ: Hey! What's this I hear—Margo wants to go to Rome! Close the show!

HOWARD: Christmas week!

BUZZ: I know Bill's stuck there doing that picture, but—

PETER: She's only human.

BUZZ: *I'm* only human! The bottom will fall out of the show . . . and out of my new country house! Japanese rock garden! Swimming pool! Cesspool!

HOWARD: *(To the group)* Look, is it my fault she insists on being faithful? *Tough.* Let her go jog around the reservoir till he comes back.

(DUANE enters)

DUANE: She'll be offstage in a minute, gentlemen.

(BOB goes to the bar for a drink and BUZZ joins him. PETER goes to the sofa)

HOWARD: *(Offhandedly)* Duane, when did the Empress first think up this brilliant plan?

DUANE: I'm in charge of what goes *on* her head, not what's in it.

HOWARD: Come on—you're her Prime Minister, you've got her ear.

DUANE: Someone else has her ear now. I'm just a simple peasant again, busy with my pin curls.

HOWARD: You know plenty. I'll take an option on your first play.

(MARGO sweeps in, wearing a glamorous pailletted evening gown, followed by EVE. EVE now looks less mousy, in a trim, simple dress)

MARGO: *(Over-heartily)* Hello, gentlemen!

HOWARD: Hello, Margo.

MARGO: Oh, Eve, were you watching? I got that laugh back in the last scene!

EVE: I know.

MARGO: She's terrific! She pointed out to me that Emerson has been upstaging me and—

HOWARD: *(Kisses her hand briskly and moves to leave)* Excuse me, Margo, but I must go.

MARGO: *(Looking around at all of them)* Oh. Then it's all settled?

HOWARD: *(Turning)* Margo, it's out of the question.

MARGO: *(Tightening)* Oh?

HOWARD: You're going mad.

MARGO: You're a mind reader. If I don't see Bill soon, I'm going to be a very . . . sick . . . lady

HOWARD: Don't threaten me with that nervous-breakdown crap. You're about as fragile as a moose!

MARGO: *(Suddenly very convincingly on the verge of tears and trembling)* It's . . . not a threat. I'm about to collapse. *(She looks very faint)*

HOWARD: *(Gently, with great sympathy)* Oh, Margo, I didn't realize. The public will understand. I'll just post a notice saying, "Show closed on account of a cold spell . . . *(Suddenly turning on her violently)* and hot pants!"
(MARGO is furious)

MARGO: Disgusting! I don't talk to you any more! I'm going to be on the plane next Sunday!

PETER: But sweetie, be realistic!

BOB: You've got a contract with Howard!

MARGO: *(To BOB)* And you represent both of us. I need someone on *my* side. Buzz?

BUZZ: *(Uncomfortably on the spot)* Geeeee, Margo . . .

MARGO: *(Mimicking him)* Geeeee, Buzz, you'd starve without those royalties for the week! Eve! Tell them I'm right.
(MARGO looks at them triumphantly, but EVE is silent. MARGO looks at her)

EVE: *(Quietly)* I can't. I'm really thinking of you. Mr. Sampson is so busy, you wouldn't have any time together, and you might feel you were just in the way. *(MARGO is taken aback, and stares at EVE)* And . . . all those people . . . coming in Christmas week, expecting to see Margo Channing . . .

MARGO: *(After a long pause)* As I said, it's a rotten idea, and how dare you try to talk me into it!

HOWARD: *(Relieved)* Margo, you're a pro. *(They kiss)* That's show business.

MARGO: *(Flatly, snapping her fingers)* Hey, I wish I'd said that.
(She exits into the bathroom, DUANE following. PETER and BOB exit)

EVE: *(Picking up her notebook and approaching HOWARD)* Oh, Mr. Benedict, now that you're here . . . *(Starts reading from her notes in a businesslike fashion)* Spotlight man's been drinking again. I've reported it to the union, but I'm afraid no one but you can do anything about it. Miss Channing's second-act shoes came back dyed the wrong color. She's very unhappy and must have another pair. We sent you a note about it a week ago.

HOWARD: *(Admiringly)* Well, I hope she's paying you plenty. You're certainly worth it.

EVE: Thank you.

BUZZ: *(Moves toward EVE as HOWARD goes to the door)* Would you tell Margo we hope she'll come up to the country this weekend? Karen told me you were something kind of special. Right, as usual.

EVE: And she told me at lunch your new play is kind of special. She says it's the best thing you've ever written.

BUZZ: She says that about everything I write—even my tax returns. *(Starts to leave)* Coming, Howard?

HOWARD: *(Who has been watching EVE, intrigued)* Yes. Good night.

(BUZZ and HOWARD exit. DUANE enters, holding the pailletted evening dress, followed by MARGO, who has changed into street clothes. He gives the dress to EVE, goes to the closet, puts on his coat, then takes out MARGO'S)

EVE: Mr. Richards hopes you'll come to Connecticut this weekend.

MARGO: *(Wistfully)* Instead of Rome—exotic Westport. Coming, Eve?

(MARGO walks toward the door. EVE examines the dress)

EVE: A couple of these paillettes are loose. I'll just stay a minute and tack them in place.

MARGO: Thank you, dear.

EVE: *(Stopping her)* Miss Channing, I'm sorry.

MARGO: You only said what you thought was right. Good night.

(DUANE looks at EVE, then he and MARGO go out, closing the door)

DUANE: *(Stopping MARGO, on the other side of the door)* Margo, ever hear of the union?

MARGO: Yes, we won the Civil War.

DUANE: I mean the *wardrobe* union. She's not supposed to do *that*, too.

(He points toward EVE. Inside the room, she is holding MARGO'S costume against her body, looking at herself in the mirror and bowing like a triumphant star)

MARGO: Oh, of course, I'll tell her. *(She opens the door, re-entering the dressing room, and sees what EVE is doing. She is taken aback, but recovers in a second)* Eve! *(EVE wheels around, whipping the dress aside)* I think you'd better let wardrobe take care of the wardrobe.

EVE: *(Composed)* Of course. I know how touchy they are. *(Moves toward the closet)* Don't forget. Two o'clock matinee, tomorrow.

MARGO: Thanks. Good night.

(She goes out and pauses, thoughtfully. EVE hangs up MARGO'S dress and takes her own coat from the closet)

DUANE: *(After a pause)* Anything wrong?

MARGO: *(Shaking it off)* No, no, nothing.

(They leave, and a moment later HOWARD comes into the dressing room)

HOWARD: Eve.

EVE: Oh, Mr. Benedict, I think you can just catch Miss Channing.

HOWARD: I've been hanging around to catch *you*, and thank you for taking my side.

EVE: I wouldn't have said it if I hadn't meant it.

HOWARD: Join me for a drink?

EVE: Well . . .

HOWARD: I must toast the new Prime Minister.

EVE: What?

HOWARD: The power behind Queen Margo.

EVE: *(With a little laugh)* I don't know what you're talking about.

HOWARD: I think you do. You're a very interesting girl. Come on. Joe Allen's. Just down the block. The gypsies go there after their shows.

(HOWARD *helps* EVE *into her coat. The* GYPSIES—*boy and girl dancers—enter as the dressing room set is being removed*)

GYPSIES: *(Singing another version of "Backstage Babble")*
Ba ba da, ba ba da,
Ba ba da, ba ba da,
Tryout for summer stock . . .

EVE: Gypsies?

HOWARD: Gypsy, my dear, is the name dancers affectionately give themselves as they go camping from show to show.

GYPSIES: *(Setting up tables)*
Ba da ba, da ba da,
And then I said to him . . .

PIANO PLAYER: *(At a piano being moved into place for the next scene)* Hi, Mr. Benedict! How's the new musical in Philly?

HOWARD: Lousy book, lousy score. Naturally everyone is blaming the costumes.

GYPSIES:
Ba ba da, résumé,
Ba ba da, ba ba da,
Agents are all ba da . . .

(HOWARD *motions* EVE *to an empty table. She sits, and he is about to, but he is stopped by a gypsy girl seated at the next table who sticks her leg out and blocks his path for the moment*)

GYPSY GIRL: *(Enthusiastically)* My ankle's okay. I'm back in the show.

HOWARD: *(Dismissing her)* Oh! Terrific. *(He joins* EVE *and sits at the table)*

GYPSIES:
Ba ba da, ba da, ba da ba,
Ba ba da, ba da . . .

(They repeat the refrain, to a fade-out finish)

SCENE 6

There has been no break in the action, but the set has now completely changed, and the scene is Joe Allen's, a bar and restaurant on West 46th Street in New York. The GYPSIES—*dancers and singers, patrons of Joe Allen's—have carried in the tables and chairs, the tables covered with bright red-checkered tablecloths.*

There are three large window arches and a door arch. The decor is of simulated red brick. A bar folds out from behind and to the right of the unit as it comes into position. A set of double doors swings on and locks into place.

The red-brick wall on the left is covered with pictures and with framed signs of Broadway shows. At the top of the wall are two blackboard menus, the daily specials prominent in chalk.

Waiters in shirt-sleeves are dashing between the kitchen door and the bar.

EVE: You have so many friends.

HOWARD: Friends! They're either in one of my shows or trying to get in.

(STAN HARDING, a columnist, approaches their table)

STAN: *(Joining them, speaking over* HOWARD'S *shoulder)* Howard!

HOWARD: *(Turning)* Oh, it's you, Stan. Eve, this is Stan Harding. I'm sure you read his nitwit chatter column religiously. Eve Harrington.

STAN: Hello.

HOWARD: This guy specializes in using all the old Leonard Lyons and Earl Wilson rejects. Miss Harrington is Margo's secretary.

STAN: *(Moving to* EVE'S *right)* Ah . . . If you want to do your boss a favor, tell Her Highness that a certain columnist thinks just once she ought to return his phone calls. Every other biggie does.

EVE: Don't blame her, she's an extraordinary woman. That must have been a terrible oversight on *my* part. It won't happen again.

STAN: Good quality, loyalty. Nice girl, Howard. See you.

(He moves to his own table. A waiter rushes by, before HOWARD *can hail him)*

HOWARD: That *was* our waiter who just flew by, wasn't it?

(A young woman across the room laughs)

EVE: Oh, there's Miss Channing's understudy.

HOWARD: *(Looking)* Oh, yes.

EVE: *(As if to herself)* Why does she keep doing it?

HOWARD: Doing what?

EVE: *(Casually)* You know, Bert is a very conscientious stage manager. He noticed that she has been standing in the wings right where Miss Channing can see her, mimicking everything she does. He's spoken to her a dozen times, but he's beginning to lose patience.

HOWARD: *(With a sigh)* Here we go again, looking for an understudy. Say, Karen told me *you* know every line of the play.

EVE: *(Glowing)* Every line, every move! I've watched it so many times, and Miss Channing still makes me laugh and cry every time!

HOWARD: Karen even suggested you if we should need a new understudy.

EVE: Me?

(BONNIE, one of the GYPSIES, enters and joins a nearby table)

HOWARD: Would you be interested in reading for it?

EVE: I don't think so. I'm happy behind the scenes or out in the audience.

HOWARD: You're a pretty cool character. There are kids in this place who'd *kill* for a chance like this! Danny!

DANNY: *(A GYPSY at another table)* Yes, Mr. Benedict.

HOWARD: Eve Harrington, Danny Burns.

EVE: How do you do.

HOWARD: Danny, if you were starving and had to sell something, which would you choose . . . your dancing shoes or your mother?

DANNY: My mother!

EVE: You really love what you're doing. You're very lucky.

GYPSY GIRL: Oh, we're *very* lucky.

BONNIE: *(Rising)* Sure. Do you know we make a hundred and sixty-four dollars and fifty cents a week?

DANNY: Every week we work, that is.

CAROL: *(A GYPSY)* And by statistics, we work an average of fourteen weeks a year.

BONNIE: So minus acting classes, singing and dancing lessons . . .

(This as well as the following dialogue is underscored by the PIANO PLAYER*)*

DANNY: Equity dues . . .

CAROL: Social security tax . . .

GYPSY GIRL: And cat food . . .

BONNIE: Leaves about twelve dollars and fifteen cents take-home pay. And it's so simple. You only have to study for ten years, and if you're lucky your career can last another ten . . . *(She does a step, and her knee hits the floor)* Unless you happen to smash your kneecap! But then you can always make eccentric jewelry at home and sell it to your friends . . . But it's all worth it—and why?

EVE: Why?

GYPSIES: *(Ad-libbing)* You tell 'em . . .

(BONNIE looks around. They all look puzzled. She gets an idea, does a warm-up, and goes over to HOWARD and EVE'S table, where she whips off the tablecloth without disturbing a thing. EVE spontaneously applauds. BONNIE nods at her)

BONNIE: *(She sings "Applause" and is joined by the GYPSIES)*

What is it that we're living for?
Applause, applause.
Nothing I know
Brings on the glow
Like sweet applause.

You're thinking you're through,
That nobody cares,
Then suddenly you
Hear it . . . starting . . .

And somehow you're in charge again,
And it's a ball!
Trumpets all sing,
Life seems to swing,
And you're the king
Of it all, 'cause . . .

You've had a taste of
The sound that says love,
Applause,
Applause,
Applause!

MALE GYPSY:
When I was eight
I was in a school play,
I'll never forget it,
I had one line to say!
My big moment came,
I said, "What, ho, the prince!"
My sister applauded,
I've been hooked ever since!

BONNIE:
It's better than pot!
It's better than booze!

A shot of applause
Will stamp out the blues.
You work till you're dead,
It ain't for the bread,
Call me out of my head!

Your bank account's bare,
Your cat has the flu,
You're losing your hair,
Then you . . . bear it . . .

(At this point the GYPSIES *begin to clap, starting with a low, distant sound, working their way up to a thunderous roar of applause)*

ALL:
That happy sound rolls over you,
And just like that,
Everything's bright,
This is the night,
Love hits you right where
You're at, 'cause . . .

You've had a taste of
The sound that says love,
Applause,
Applause,
There's wondr'ous applause,
Thund'rous applause,
Beautiful, soaring,
Magnificent, roaring!
It's better than pot!
It's better than booze!
A shot of applause
Will stamp out the blues.
Whatever you do you do better because
You're doing it to the beat of applause.
And nothing can beat the beat of applause.
When you hear it . . .

(Under BONNIE'S *direction, the* GYPSIES *put together a little stage made up of tables. Some pull up chairs and act as audience, while others go behind the archways, which become entrances to the improvised stage. They put on a rousing, satirical show, starting with quick take-offs of show-stopping moments in the annals of musical comedy history, ranging from a Rose-Marie duet à la Jeannette MacDonald/Nelson Eddy, through* Hello, Dolly! Fiddler on the Roof, Cabaret, West Side Story, *all using the word "applause" somewhere in the lyric, and finally winding up with a competition between three* GYPSIES *trying to do a wholesome rendition of* Oklahoma, *while, to their horror, three others are yelling "Oh! Calcutta!" and stripping down to their bare bottoms. The finale is pure vaudeville; tap dancers, ballet dancers, contortionists, baton-twirlers, jugglers, roller skaters, etc., all doing their individual routines at the same time, and ending with* BONNIE *popping up out of a huge serving dish. It is an all-out display of show-biz corn that begs the audience for that "big hand." Stepping forward at the end, with arms outstretched, they join together to sing)*

ALL:

> *Why do we work our asses off?*
> *What is it for?*
> *Cares disappear*
> *Soon as you hear*
> *That happy audience roar, 'cause*
> *You've had a taste of*
> *The sound that says love*
> *Applause!*
> *Applause!*
> *Applause!*

(The GYPSIES *excitedly receive their applause from the theater audience, then form a parade, led across by the flag-twirler. During this, the set is being struck behind them)*

ALL:

> *Wherever you are it's always the same*
> *Whenever applause is calling your name,*
> *No matter what kind,*
> *Never mind,*
> *You don't care*
> *As long as it's there . . .*
> *And somehow you're in charge again,*
> *And it's a ball.*
> *Trumpets all sing,*
> *Life seems to swing,*
> *And you're the king*
> *Of it all, 'cause*
> *You've had a taste of*
> *The sound that says love,*
> *Applause!*
> *Applause!*
> *Applause!*

*(*BONNIE *has led* HOWARD *and* EVE *over to watch the parade, and now pulls* EVE *in to dance with her on the last few bars. The* GYPSIES *carry off what remains of the set, and* HOWARD *and* EVE *wave good-bye to them, and exit together)*

SCENE 7

The scene is Margo's bedroom later that night. This set moves on from the right and is dominated by a large brass-framed bed. There is a door to the right of the stage, and next to it a hat rack. A yellow lamp with a purple shade sits on a table at the right side of the bed. On the left is an elephant-based table with a clock and a telephone.

A second door, upstage from the entrance door, leads to the bathroom. To its left is a bookcase with an oval mirror above. On the bureau is a blue vase filled with white and yellow roses.

On the other side of the stage, the left, is a bay window with three windows. The seats below are covered with pink cushions. Left of the seats is a desk which matches the bureau, and a chair pushed underneath. Next to one of the table legs on the left is a glass figure of a greyhound. The floor is covered with a plush white rug, and between the bed and the desk is a large pile of pillows of various colors.

The room is quite dark. MARGO *is asleep as the phone rings. She stirs. It rings again, and she fumbles for the light, switches it on, then picks up the phone.*

MARGO: *(Sleepily)* H'lo.

OPERATOR'S VOICE: We're ready with your call to Rome.

MARGO: Call? What call? *(She squints at her clock)* It's three A.M.

OPERATOR'S VOICE: Is this Templeton 0–8842? Miss Margo Channing?

MARGO: I think so . . .

OPERATOR'S VOICE: We're ready with the call you placed to Mr. William Sampson for eight A.M. Rome time.

MARGO: *I* placed?

ITALIAN OPERATOR'S VOICE: Pronto! . . . Meester Sampson . . . go ahead!

(BILL appears to the left of the stage, holding a phone)

BILL: Margo!

MARGO: Bill!

BILL: You stayed up so late just to talk to me!

MARGO: *(Fuzzily)* Yeah . . .

BILL: I'm not mad you're calling me on the set, but come on, say it . . . it's twelve thousand dollars a minute . . .

MARGO: *(Rising)* Well, sure . . . I love you.

BILL: We know all that . . . get to the point.

MARGO: Huh?

BILL: *(Laughing)* Come on, Margo. I'll be a year older before you get to it.

(MARGO gets out of the bed, suddenly wide awake)

MARGO: *(Guiltily)* Bill, it's your birthday—

BILL: And you remembered . . . you sweet thing.

MARGO: Happy Birthday, darling.

BILL: Thank you.

MARGO: *(Sinks to the pillows, lying on her back. The audience sees her face upside-down)* Oh, Bill, without you I'm beginning to climb walls . . . turning into a genuine crazy lady. I threatened Benedict with a breakdown if he didn't let me go to Rome for a week. Didn't work . . .

BILL: Aw, baby, I feel the same way . . . Listen, till I get back, use up your energy on things like hating Emerson for upstaging you and—

MARGO: Hey, how'd you know that?

BILL: Eve wrote me. She hasn't missed a week since I left. Keeps me filled in on all the backstage goings-on . . . everything you've been up to. You probably tell her what to write.

MARGO: *(Sits up)* Oh, sure.

BILL: I sent her a list of my addresses on location for the next couple of weeks, so if you want to get in touch with me, check with Eve.

MARGO: *(Stands up)* Right.

BILL: Do you love me?

MARGO: I'll check with Eve. I mean—of course I do.

BILL: *(Singing)*
  Hey, flash your famous smile . . .
  Are you smiling?

The one that gets 'em all,
Think how it's gonna be . . .

Arriverderci, cara mia.
MARGO: Good-bye Bill . . .
(They both hang up)

BILL:

Think how it's gonna be
When we're together again.

(The light blacks out on him. MARGO *paces around her room desperately)*
MARGO'S VOICE: *(On tape, singing "Hurry Back")*

Hurry back,
Hurry back,
It's no life at all
When you're not here to hold me.

Hurry back,
Hurry back,
What's the point of doing crazy things
When you're not here to scold me?
Honey . . .

(Walks over to the desk)
MARGO: *(Singing aloud, as her taped voice fades)*

Honey,
Hurry back,
Hurry back,
When I get you here
I'll give you so much love
You'll never leave me,
Believe me,
Hurry back.

(Goes over to the pillows and sinks down)

Come back home,
I'm so lonely.
There's so much to say
And so much love to make up.

Hurry back,
Hurry back,
I'll just die unless I see your face
Beside me when I wake up.

(Pulls herself up)

Honey . . .

Hurry back,
Make it fast,
Hurry back,
I can't last . . .
Hurry back.

(She sinks back on the pile of pillows on the floor. The lights go down. After a few moments they come on again. It is morning. MARGO is in bed. EVE knocks, enters, carrying a tray, crosses to the desk, and puts the tray down)

EVE: *(Businesslike)* 'Morning. Nothing fascinating in the mail.

MARGO: *(Groggily)* 'Morning.

EVE: *(Handing a glass of orange juice to MARGO)* Duane's here. He wants to pick up your fall . . .

MARGO: Sure.

(DUANE enters)

DUANE: Hi, Duchess.

MARGO: Hi, Duane. Want some coffee?

DUANE: Thanks.

(He goes to the desk to help himself. EVE walks back to the desk to get some bills in the drawer)

EVE: Hope you had a good night's sleep. I'll get started on the bills. Oh, and I've made up a list of tax deductions you haven't been taking.

MARGO: *(Faintly annoyed)* You think of everything.

EVE: *(Starts to leave)* That's my job.

MARGO: Eve, by any chance, did you place a call from me to Bill, eight A.M. Rome time?

EVE: *(Stops)* Oh, I forgot to tell you! That meeting in the dressing room knocked it out of my head completely.

MARGO: Don't worry about it. It was very thoughtful of you.

EVE: Mr. Sampson's birthday! I knew you'd never forgive me if I forgot that. *(Starts to exit)* As a matter of fact, I sent him a cable myself.

(She exits. MARGO and DUANE exchange a look)

DUANE: I saw her at Joe Allen's last night. She was table-for-twoing it with everybody's favorite producer.

MARGO: Out with Howard? How extraordinary. *(The phone rings. She picks it up)* Hello? . . . Rome? *(Stands up, grabs DUANE'S hand, worried)* Yes, yes, go ahead! Bill! Anything wrong? . . . *No! Two weeks!* . . . You bet you'll get a coming home party—pin-the-tail-on-the-donkey, paper hats . . . *(Turns DUANE around)* an orgy! . . . Right. Love you! *(She hangs up, ecstatic, and kicks a cushion. DUANE catches it)* Duane! Two weeks! He's coming home in two weeks! I told him how desperate I was; now they're letting him bring the film and cut it here! And all because Eve placed that call! *(DUANE drops the cushion)* You don't like her, do you? *(DUANE rolls his eyes heavenward in disgust)* But Duane, she's marvelous! She thinks only of me.

DUANE: *(Going over to the bed)* Let's say she thinks only *about* you. Studying you. The way you walk, the way you talk, the way you dress. *(He sings in a falsetto voice, imitating EVE)*

"The best night of my life . . ."

MARGO: *(Laughing and giving DUANE a push so he falls on the bed)* How do I look? I've got to look new! Different! Misty! Feminine! *Italian!* Duane, how do you say "Welcome home, Bill" in Italian?

DUANE: I don't know. See what happens if you try *"Vesti la giubba,* Bill!"

MARGO: Of course! *Vesti la giubba,* Bill!

(Laughing, she and DUANE start dancing a wild tarantella, which they continue as they move off with the bedroom set while the scene changes)

SCENE 8

The scene is Margo's living room, two weeks later. The bedroom set moves off to the right, and two waiters enter from the left, carrying a large banner reading "Vesti la Giubba, Bill." They are followed in by KAREN, in evening dress, who has a number of name-game signs over her shoulder and a pencil holder in her hand. BUZZ, in black tie, enters behind KAREN.

KAREN: *(Looking at the banner)* What does that mean?

BUZZ: *(Laughing confidently, then breaking off)* What does that mean? . . . I don't know. Isn't this an anti-climax? Bill's been home two days already.

KAREN: She promised him a party . . . *(The waiters go behind the sofa, where they place the banner. The omelet man, RUDY, crosses behind KAREN, pushing his cart. KAREN motions him to a position on the right. A bartender enters and walks up to the bar. On the terrace are three MUSICIANS, noisily setting up their instruments and tuning them. The bar has been set with several whiskey bottles and extra glasses. On the corner of the terrace is a candelabra, rigged so that the candles will appear to burn down to denote the passage of time. The MUSICIANS blare loudly. KAREN moves toward the sofa)* Hey, fellas! Cut! Cut! *(They stop)* Why don't you go to the kitchen and stuff yourselves until the guests start piling in? *(The MUSICIANS start collecting themselves, muttering hip phrases at her, like "Dig it baby," and exit. KAREN puts the pencil holder on the left arm of the sofa)* I've never seen Margo so nervous. You'd think it was her first prom. She's changing her outfit for the fourth time.

BUZZ: And she's had a martini for each change.

KAREN: Oh, no! *(EVE enters, wearing the dress MARGO wore to the village bar on opening night. She looks radiant and shapely, suddenly a woman)* Oh, Eve, don't you look smashing.

(BUZZ stares at EVE)

EVE: *(Moving to the center of the stage and turning around to flair the skirt)* Do I? Miss Channing gave it to me. It just needed a little alteration. You're sure I don't look foolish in it?

KAREN: I should look so foolish. Buzz, look at Eve.

BUZZ: You don't have to tell me. I'm looking.

KAREN: *(To EVE)* Now I'm really convinced. You know, that idea we talked about? Your reading for the understudy? You've *got* to.

EVE: Oh, no, it was a silly idea.

BUZZ: What do you mean? Karen's got good instincts. Try for it.

EVE: Well, we'll see.

KAREN: *(Hanging one of the signs around EVE'S neck)* Here, put this on. No, you mustn't look.

EVE: What is it?

BUZZ: It's a game. Bill's hooked on them.

KAREN: There's a famous name on it. Everyone gets one as he comes in the door. You have to guess who you are by the way people talk to you, and *you* talk to them the way you would if they really were those people. You'll catch on.

BUZZ: *(Indicating the signs)* C'mon Karen, let's put these out in the hall.

(BUZZ and KAREN exit. EVE turns, and on her back is the sign "Freud." She sits on the couch and accidentally knocks the pencil holder off the arm. She bends over the back to reach it. BILL enters, wearing a sign on his back, "Greta Garbo," and sees

just EVE*'s bottom and legs, and her back with the sign on it. Mistaking her for* MARGO, *because of the dress, he pats her lightly on the bottom)*

BILL: Your subconscious is showing, my darling!

(EVE *jumps up, startled.* BILL *jumps back, embarrassed)*

EVE: Oh, Bill . . . uh . . . Mr. Sampson!

BILL: Good God, I thought you were . . .

(He points at what she's wearing. They both talk at once)*

EVE: Miss Channing gave me this—

BILL: Eve . . . forgive me . . . I— *(They both break off, look at each other, and laugh)* Where *is* she?

EVE: She's dressing . . . a little behind schedule. Everyone will be here in a minute. (BILL *starts up the steps to the bedroom.* EVE *detains him by speaking)* Uh . . . what was that about my subconscious?

BILL: Oh. *(Instantly drawn into the game and coming back down toward her, by the sofa)* Uh . . . I would say you have a giant brain, my good man, but a smallish beard.

EVE: William Shakespeare!

BILL: *(Heavily Teutonic) Nein!*

EVE: *Nein.* Uh . . . Einstein? No, he only had that mustache. Let me see who you are. *(She looks at his sign and goes around the sofa. He sits on the right arm)* Oh. *(She sits in the swivel chair. With a terrible Swedish accent)* I'm surprised you came to the party. I thought you vould vant to be alone.

BILL: *(Laughing and pulling his sign around)* You're not supposed to make it so easy. I'm Garbo, who else?

EVE: I guess I'm not very good at games.

BILL: Of course you are. Now you're going to guess who you are if it takes all night. *(He takes her by the hands and seats her on the couch. He circles the sofa behind her. In a Viennese accent)* Imagine my running into you here. Are you still ze pride of Vienna?

EVE: Did Johann Strauss have a beard?

BILL: *Nein! Nein! (Impulsively takes the pillow and puts it in her lap, then lies with his head on it and his thumb in his mouth)* I vill simply have to lie down on zis couch und tell you all about it. You zee, ven I vas a little boy, my muzzer . . .

EVE: You mean if you tell me your dreams, I could maybe help you?

BILL: *(Encouragingly)* Aha! Aha!

EVE: I should have guessed it right away. Sigmund Freud!

BILL: No, Adolf Hitler! *(They both burst out laughing,* BILL *still with his head in her lap. At this point* MARGO *enters from the bedroom and takes in the scene.* BILL, *seeing her, gets up)* Margo!

EVE: *(Getting up and turning to* MARGO*)* Oh, Miss Channing, we were just playing the game.

MARGO: *(Menacingly flat)* One of the oldest.

BILL: *(Taking off the sign and putting it on the coffee table)* The kid, here, couldn't guess she was Freud till I—

MARGO: I wonder if the kid would mind checking to see why Rudy, the omelet man, isn't here.

EVE: I'd be glad to.

MARGO: Thank you so much. And just remember as you go through life that for every whole omelet there are two broken eggs. *(EVE exits)*

BILL: *(With enthusiasm, lovingly)* Margo, this looks like a party for a man who loves games, omelets, dancing—and crazy, beautiful stars. He's a pretty lucky guy. Thank you, my darling.

MARGO: *(Going up to the bar, moving away from him as he comes toward her)* I didn't even know you were here.

BILL: *(Casually)* I ran into Eve on my way up, and she said you were dressing.

MARGO: *(Going down the steps, avoiding him)* That never stopped you before.

BILL: Well, we started playing your sign game . . . the kid hasn't been around to these parties much . . .

MARGO: True. She's so innocent, so unspoiled.

BILL: Well, those are pretty rare qualities these days.

MARGO: She's a girl of so many rare qualities. So you've been telling me these last two days—warm, devoted, so young and fair.

BILL: *(With great control)* The kid's okay. Now darling—

MARGO: *(Cutting in)* Stop calling her a kid! Since you've been back, you two have had *so* much to talk over—in corners, here, at the theater, God knows where else . . .

BILL: *(Moving toward her)* Margo, you're hallucinating!

MARGO: *(Moving back)* So many things to chew over. Your trying to make films, her trying to make you . . .

BILL: *(Bursting out)* What the hell are you talking about?

MARGO: I'm talking about the departments of my life I want exclusively to myself—*you*, in particular! Hands off! No trespassing! Especially from the "warm," the "devoted," the "young," the "fair." *(She sits on the left side of the sofa)*

BILL: *(After a tense pause)* I suppose this is my cue to grab you in my arms and drown your silly doubts in an ocean of wet kisses, but I can't! I'm too damn mad!

MARGO: Guilty!

BILL: *(Moving to the right side of the sofa and around back)* No, *mad!* I turned a movie studio upside down to get back here to you. I missed you. I wanted you so much. But to come back to the same old fruit stand—this age obsession of yours . . . *(She gets up and goes to the omelet cart. He follows, but then turns away)* And now this ridiculous attempt to whip yourself up into a jealous froth because I spend ten minutes with a stage-struck kid who worships you. It shows a paranoiac insecurity you ought to be ashamed of!

MARGO: Paranoiac. A term you picked up, no doubt, from the vivacious Dr. Freud!

(During this exchange, EVE has entered and is behind MARGO)

EVE: *(Low-voiced, discreetly)* Excuse me, Miss Channing, the omelet man will be right in, the guests should be arriving, and I thought you might like another martini. *(She hands MARGO a martini, takes her glass, and goes up to the bar)*

MARGO: Isn't she a treasure? . . . I think I'll bury her! *(The MUSICIANS come back in. BILL goes to the sofa)* Ah, boys, music . . . music . . . music! *(Some GUESTS start arriving including HOWARD, KAREN, and BUZZ. The GUESTS are dressed in the high styles of the moment, ranging from the quietly chic to the wildly bizarre. Each one has a sign on his back with a famous name on it)* Ah, my guests! All my little friends from Madame Tussaud's Wax Works.

HOWARD: Hello, Margo!

MARGO: Ah! Howard. You all know the guest of honor—Greta Garbo! *(She presents* BILL*)*

KAREN: Margo, cut it out.

MARGO: *(As* HOWARD *moves to the center of the stage, she pulls his sign to the front; it reads "Al Capone")* Oh, Al Capone! Oh, Eve—Eve, you two must meet. You have so much in common. *(She turns and greets* PETER*)*

PETER: How are you, Margo?

MARGO: Don't ask. *(She moves to another guest, Bob, at the omelet table)* And Bill! Look who's here! The Great Lover—Rudolf Valentino! You could teach him a thing or two. Ha, ha, ha. *(She laughs;* BILL *imitates her laugh)*

HOWARD: *(Taking off his sign and handing it to* EVE*)* Well, there goes *that* game.

MARGO: Yes, Howard, but we can all still play the game of life—where some win, some lose, some cheat, some lie!

BUZZ: *(Joining* KAREN *on the sofa)* I can smell the sulphur in the air. What's going on?

MARGO: *(Fairly tight by now. On the terrace, with her back to the audience)* Step up, step up, folks. Continuous performance! Thrills, spills, chills! Watch the little lady do a back bend and pick up her heart with her teeth! Hurry, hurry, hurry!

KAREN: *(Sitting on the sofa)* Margo, is this the beginning or the end of something? *(*MARGO *is standing near the bass fiddle)*

MARGO: Fasten your seat belts . . . *(She plucks a bass-fiddle string, and there is a noisy twang. All eyes are on her)* It's going to be a bumpy night!

(She goes up to the bar. BUZZ, KAREN, HOWARD, BILL, *and* DUANE *sing "Fasten Your Seat Belts")*

BUZZ:
Fasten your seat belts,
It's gonna be a bumpy night,
(Makes a raspy S.O.S. sound)
Eh eh eh eh.

Batten the hatches,
We're gonna have a funsy flight!
Eh eh eh eh.

KAREN: *(Joining* BUZZ*)*
She's laughing a bit too loudly,
That's how the last one began . . .

HOWARD: *(Meeting* BILL *in the center of the stage)*
I figure she's two drinks from the spot
Where you-know-what
Hits the fan!

(Several new GUESTS *enter)*

BILL *and* HOWARD: *(To two* GUESTS*)*
Don't take off your coat,
You came the wrong night.
Get out while you can,
Mother is uptight!

KAREN, BUZZ, HOWARD, BILL, *and* DUANE:
> *Fasten your seat belts,*
> *It's gonna be, eh eh eh eh eh eh,*
> *A bumpy night!*

BUZZ: Let's get out of here.
KAREN: We can't. It's Bill's party.
BUZZ: Best party since the St. Valentine's Day Massacre.
(BILL and HOWARD sit on the sofa)

KAREN, BUZZ, HOWARD, BILL, *and* DUANE:
> *Fasten your seat belts,*
> *Say all your prayers and hold on tight,*
> *Drink and be merry,*
> *For the Titanic sails tonight,*
> *All aboard,*
> *It will be*
> *A bumpy night!*

(KAREN sits on the bench; BUZZ sits on the arm. EVE walks over to them, and the music continues to play in the background while they speak)
EVE: *(Unhappily)* I'm so puzzled. What did I do to offend Miss Channing?
BUZZ: It's beyond me.
KAREN: You've done nothing but wonders for Margo.
MARGO: *(Joining the group in time to hear to KAREN'S last line)* My dear, would you perform another of your wonders and bring me one of *my* hometown toddies—a double martini? And don't put your pretty little thumb in it, I don't want to die of sugar poisoning.
(EVE goes to a waiter standing near the steps, gets a martini and hands it to MARGO)

KAREN, BUZZ, HOWARD, BILL, and DUANE:
> *Fasten your seat belts,*
> *It's gonna be a bumpy night. Eh eh eh eh.*
> *Margo in action,*
> *Critics have called an awesome sight!*
> *Eh eh eh eh.*

(The music continues in the background as EVE calls HOWARD aside)
HOWARD: Don't worry about Margo. These lady stars—they suffer and suffer, but we're the ones that wind up with the ulcers. Has Margo Channing ever been sick? Which reminds me, Bert did fire the understudy. Too bad it's of no interest to you.
EVE: I tell you what. You set up your auditions, and that day . . . well, maybe, just for the hell of it—
(MARGO has wandered up near them, with her back to the audience, and catching EVE'S last words, she wheels around)
MARGO: Oh! "The hell of it"! Eve, such language! You go straight to your room —the one in Madison, Wisconsin!
(At this point a girl enters, wearing a revealing, black-beaded costume. She is followed by BILL, a girl in an East Indian outfit, DUANE, and a girl in a slave costume. They move toward MARGO)

BILL:
I've seen the Taj Mahal at dawn,

DUANE:
The Hanging Gardens of Babylon,

BILL and DUANE: *(With oriental head movements)*
But nothing compares with Miss Channing
When she's on,

BUZZ and KAREN:
And she's on!

HOWARD:
Yeah, she's on!

BILL:
Oh, she's on!

ALL:
And she's on,
Yeah, she's on!

(A dance number follows, with MARGO, a girl carrying a feather boa, and the girl in the beaded costume. There is stripper music, and the boa is utilized in the dance. MARGO executes some deft bumps and grinds and stripper walks, which convey a to-hell-with-you attitude to BILL)

It's going to be a bumpy night!

MARGO:
Here's a bump here,
There's a bump there,

GIRL WITH FEATHER BOA:
Here's a bump,

GIRL IN BEADED COSTUME:
There's a bump,

MARGO:
Everywhere a bump bump,
Turbulence ahead,
Turbulence behind,

Ready, girls?

(Turns to the girl in the beaded costume)
Silly dress!

(To a girl well-endowed)
Silicone!

(To a girl in a maternity dress)
Single girl!

(MARGO sees EVE standing in front of the omelet cart)
Eve! *(Everybody freezes. The music stops. MARGO circles in front of EVE)* You do look lovely in that dress. So smart! You had your eye on it from the begin-

ning. I'm glad I gave it to you. Anything else you have your eye on? *(EVE backs away from MARGO, not quite sure of MARGO'S intent.* Margo *then grabs* EVE, *and singing her own accompaniment of "Who's That Girl," does a few jitterbug steps with her as she did that first night* EVE *came along.* MARGO *spins* EVE *out and she bumps against* BILL, *coming toward them. The whole room is watching tensely. After a moment of silence)* You may all resume breathing. *(She circles around the bench and walks up to the bar)* On to the next game . . . Why don't you all choose up sides and go home!

GUESTS:
Thanks for the party!
Wow! What a blast!
Pick up the pieces,
Let's get out fast,
Get your coat,
Where's the door?
Man, it's been, eh eh eh eh eh,
A bumpy night, eh eh eh eh eh,
A bumpy night . . .

(The GUESTS *slip out as the music diminuendoes and the lights dim . . . The candles burn down and the room takes on an after-the-party view: used plates, cups, napkins, etc., are scattered here and there. At a bench which was placed earlier close to the omelet cart are* EVE, BILL, HOWARD, BUZZ, *and* KAREN*)*

BILL: Is it dawn yet? I can't believe it, but I've got to be in that cutting room at eight A.M.

(MARGO weaves over to them, carrying a saxophone. She blows it. EVE *jumps to her feet)*

MARGO: *(Moving between* BILL *and* EVE*)* Don't get up. You needn't act as if I were the Queen Mother.

EVE: I'm sorry, I— *(She runs out the door)*

BILL: Outside of a beehive, I wouldn't consider your behavior either queenly or motherly.

(MARGO blows on the sax again)

KAREN: Really, Margo, it's time you realized that what's attractive on stage is not necessarily attractive off.

MARGO: I haven't your unfailing good taste. I wish I had gone to "Radcliffee," too, but father needed my help at the fish market.

BILL: *(Wearily)* Cut it out!

MARGO: This is my house, not a theater. You're a guest here, not a *directawr!*

BUZZ: Then stop being a star.

HOWARD: And stop treating your friends as your supporting cast.

MARGO: Supporting! That's a joke. All of you . . . living off *my* hide! *My* charisma! *(She bursts into song and dance to "La Cucaracha."* BILL, BUZZ, HOWARD *and* KAREN *leave)*

La-ca-ca-risma!
La-ca-ca-risma!
Ca-ca-ca-ca-la-la-la!

(She hands the omelet man the saxophone)

Here, fry this! *(She gets up on the bench. In her deepest voice)* Now hear this
. . . hear this. This is your captain speaking!

(Singing drunkenly)
Fasten your seat belts,
It's really been a bumpy night,
I've got a secret,
I think I'm just a wee bit tight . . .

*(This breaks her up, and giggling, she collapses. A waiter catches her and puts her
behind the bench)*
Everybody bail out! Ooh, look at the star . . . The star is on her ass. Her
parachute wouldn't open. Eve must have packed it! *(With a little laugh, she lets
her head fall forward on the bench)*
DUANE: *(Moving from the bar to the terrace, surveying the wreckage of the room)*
Nothing will ever grow here again.
MARGO: *(Looking up)* Ah, the party's thinning out . . . down to my closest friends.
DUANE: *(Walking over to* MARGO, *pulling her up and moving toward the swivel
chair)* No, your closest friends have all left. Personally, I don't blame them. You
were the worst. Bill said he'd call you tomorrow.
MARGO: Was he mad?
DUANE: No, just hurt.
MARGO: I know that martyred look. Like St. Sebastian after the arrows hit.
*(*DUANE *helps her into the swivel chair. She keeps swiveling about)* I'll call *him*
. . . Maybe I *won't* . . Maybe I will. I'm sorry I behaved badly . . . No, I'm
not! My friends should know that's not the real me! . . . Yes, it *is*. I'm the worst.
(Brightening up) Not always! Sometimes I'm adorable! *(Gets up and goes up the
steps, shouting defiantly against the music of "But Alive")*

I'm a thousand diff'rent people,
Ev'ry single one is real.
I've a million diff'rent feelings,
Okay, but at least I feel,
At least I feel,
I feel . . .

(As the set moves up and off with EVE's *voice can still be heard,
overlapping with* EVE's *voice as the backstage set comes on)*

SCENE 9

*The scene takes place backstage, several days later. The set is the side view
of a bare stage, as if looking from the left wings. On the right is the proscenium.*
EVE *is auditioning, facing into the right wings.* BERT, *holding a script, is reading
with her.*
*There are footlights upstage and to the right. Against the back wall is a stage
manager's desk, with a clipboard hanging on the side and various papers atop. A
tormentor boom with five lights is next to the desk.*
*There is a sliding stage door right of center. It closes from left to right and has a
counterweight. To the left of the door are a fire extinguisher, a trunk with a chair
upside down on top, an old chair left of the trunk, a large mirror, and then a spiral
staircase, used from time to time during the show. It leads to a flyfloor approximately*

ten feet above the stage level, and ropes tied around pins are visible. The flyfloor is also used, so it must be strongly constructed.

The stage left wall is the stage right wall of MARGO'S *dressing-room set in its offstage storage position. A door is in the center of the wall. From the left has come a red chaise, followed by a gilded birdcage, a fern in a gold wicker basket, and an old dressing screen. The chaise stops left of center, the three trailing objects two feet behind.* EVE'S *voice is heard before the lights are fully up.*

EVE'S VOICE: I feel . . . I feel . . . fed up with being on display! An ornament! A Tiffany glass bottle with nothing inside. There *is* something inside!

(The lights go up as she is finishing. She is wearing a short, clinging dress, and for the first time she appears provocatively sexy)

BERT: *(Also reading from a script)* What do you want?

EVE: Nothing from you. I found someone who held that bottle up to the light, rubbed it in the right places, said some delicious magic words, and out popped the genie . . . me! And I'm never going back in! I like it out here!

(Applause is heard, and BUZZ, KAREN, HOWARD, *and* BILL *come out onto the stage.* BERT *congratulates* EVE *affectionately, then moves to the desk as the others join her. A stagehand enters, goes up the spiral staircase to the flyfloor, and lowers the overhead work light)*

BUZZ: *(Carried away, crossing to* EVE*)* Eve . . . I didn't want you to stop!

EVE: Oh, Mr. Richards!

BUZZ: It was like hearing my play for the first time . . . Please don't misunder-stand me. Margo acts the part marvelously . . . but hearing it read by someone who's *really* . . . the youth, the vitality . . . my words came alive!

KAREN: *(Glowing)* I'm supposed to butt out, but I just can't. I feel so proud.

EVE: Oh, thank you, Karen.

BILL: *(Crossing to* EVE *and shaking her hand)* That was a helluva first reading. After watching Margo all these months, it wasn't an imitation—you made it your own. I'm very impressed.

EVE: Oh, Mr. Sampson, I was so nervous, mainly because of you. By now we're almost friends, but *you*—I hardly know you at all. *(Tremulous giggle)* I was petrified!

HOWARD: Bert! How many waiting to read?

BERT: *(At the desk)* Five more.

HOWARD: No point in wasting their time. Miss Harrington's got the job. Thank them nicely and send them home.

BERT: Yes, sir!

HOWARD: Eve, welcome to the theater.

BUZZ: Welcome aboard!

(MARGO enters through the stage door)

MARGO: Who's welcoming who to what?

ALL: *(Ad-libbing)* Hello, Margo!

BILL: Margo, it's after three.

MARGO: Well?

BILL: The auditions began at two.

MARGO: *(Moving over to the chaise)* Well, how many stars turn up for these goddamn readings at all. I had a luncheon interview in connection with this very play we are all living on, and it ran late. I'm truly sorry. *(She takes off her coat)* Oh, come on, let's not stay mad at each other because of the other night. Now, shall we begin?

BUZZ: It's over.

MARGO: *(Going over to embrace BUZZ and KAREN warmly)* Oh? And who has the splendid job of standing by for the star who never misses a performance—knock on wood?

HOWARD: Eve.

MARGO: Eve? . . . *Eve?* *(She is taken aback and circles slowly behind EVE)* Well, I always knew you were interested in the theater, and in me, but I had no idea . . . Oh, yes, the Madison Dramatic Society . . . Pinter, Albee . . .

EVE: Miss Channing, I can't tell you how relieved I am that you arrived late . . . I would have dried up completely. I couldn't have gone on!

BUZZ: She gave a helluva reading.

KAREN: You would have been proud of her, too.

MARGO: *(Moving toward BILL)* Oh? And were you proud of her, Bill?

BILL: Yes. I must say she really is an actress. It was a pleasant surprise.

MARGO: Surprise? *I'm* the only one in this group who's had a surprise. Little surprises being planned behind my back. *(She moves toward HOWARD)*

HOWARD: Cut that, Margo! No one's kept anything from you. We asked you to be here.

MARGO: A pure formality. I'm sure it was all decided amongst you kiddies days and days ago . . . Or perhaps, Howard, during one of those magical evenings when you and Eve were dancing the night away!

HOWARD: *(Furious)* That's enough! Send me your objections in writing! You haven't got understudy approval in your contract in the first place! *(He storms out the stage door)*

MARGO: *(Crossing again toward BILL)* I can't get over it. It's just beginning to sink in. This little prairie flower has been standing in the wings, studying my every move—every line for five months—and I never saw what she was really up to! *(BILL exits to the dressing room)*

EVE: *(Walking toward MARGO, who is leaning against the chaise)* Miss Channing, I know I could never be more than adequate in covering the part, but if you . . . *(On the verge of tears)* have any objections, naturally I wouldn't dream . . .

KAREN: *(Holding EVE)* Wait . . . I'm taking you out for a drink. Come on, Buzz.

BUZZ: In a minute. Let's get this settled. I was surprised, too. She was a revelation.

MARGO: Well, naturally, it must have been a revelation to have a somewhat younger character played by a somewhat younger actress.

BUZZ: *(Guiltily)* What are you talking about?

MARGO: It must have sounded so new and fresh to you. You probably could hardly recognize your own play.

BUZZ: The play is actor-proof!

MARGO: Actor-proof! If you knew the bits, the schtick, I have to dredge out of the vaudeville trunk to give the illusion that something amusing is going on . . . *(She sits on the chaise)*

BUZZ: You empty-headed, conceited bass fiddle! You're just a body and a voice! Don't ever forget—I'm the brain!

(BUZZ starts to leave and is stopped by MARGO'S words)

MARGO: Till the autopsy, there's no proof!
(He stamps out)

KAREN: *(To MARGO)* Margo, you've been kicking us all around long enough. Someone ought to give *you* a good swift one for a change! *(She leaves)*

EVE: *(Moving slowly toward MARGO)* Miss Channing . . . if I ever dreamed that anything I did could possibly cause you any unhappiness, or come between you and your friends . . . please believe me.

MARGO: *(In a low, weary voice)* Oh, I do. And I'm full of admiration for you. *(Stands up and approaches EVE)* If you can handle yourself on the stage with the same artistry you display *off* the stage . . . well, my dear, you are in the right place. *(She speaks the following lines as the music of "Welcome to the Theater" begins)*

Welcome to the theater,
To the magic, to the fun!

(She sings)
Where painted trees and flowers grow,
And laughter rings fortissimo,
And treachery's sweetly done!

Now you've entered the asylum,
This profession unique,
Actors are children
Playing hide-and-ego-seek . . .

So welcome, Miss Eve Harrington,
To this business we call show,
You're on your way
To wealth and fame,
Unsheath your claws,
Enjoy the game!
You'll be a bitch
But they'll know your name
From New York to Kokomo . . .
Welcome to the theater,
My dear, you'll love it so!

(EVE exits, quietly defiant)
Welcome to the dirty concrete hallways,
Welcome to the friendly roaches, too,
Welcome to the pinches from the stagehands,
It's the only quiet thing they do . . .
Welcome to the Philadelphia critics,
Welcome, Librium and Nembutal,
Welcome to a life of laryngitis,
Welcome to dark toilets in the hall . . .
Welcome to the flop
You thought would run for years,
Welcome to the world
Of tears and cheers and fears . . .

Welcome to the theater,
With some luck you'll be a pro,
You'll work and slave
And scratch and bite,
You'll learn to kill
With sheer delight,
You'll only come
Alive at night
When you're in a show!
Welcome to the theater,
You fool, you'll love it so.

(BILL *enters from the dressing room and goes to her)*
BILL: *(In a kidding, comic tone, to cut through her mood)* Hellooo, Margo.
MARGO: *(Very down)* Margo. What's that? Just a body and a voice.
BILL: *(Puts his hands on her shoulders)* What a body. What a voice.
MARGO: Imagine, she turns up out of nowhere, and gives a performance!
BILL: A reading.
MARGO: *(Moving toward the chaise)* A performance!
BILL: *(Following* MARGO*)* Margo, you've got to stop hurting yourself and me, the two of us. I—
MARGO: *(Not listening, continuing her own line of thought, so that her speech and*
BILL'S *following speech are spoken at the same time)* I'm in a dream scene in one of those movies! I'm screaming down an empty tunnel . . . no one can hear me . . . no one will listen to me . . .
BILL: *(Continuing what he was saying)* I love you! You're a beautiful intelligent actress at the peak of her career, and—
MARGO: *(Interrupting)* And all the time she's coming at me with a knife!
BILL: Margo!
MARGO: Why can't you see it?
BILL: *(Takes her by the shoulders and sits her down at the end of the chaise)* Margo! There are always young, talented people coming along, but you're—you're unique! *(She struggles to get up, but he pushes her back on the chaise, pinning her down by the shoulders)* No one can possibly be a threat to you. It's beneath you to let an innocent girl like Eve turn you into a screaming harpy!
MARGO: She turns me into a heavy! *(He walks away)* She's Snow White, and you're all those cute little dwarfs, and I wind up as the Wicked Witch! Why can't *I* be Snow White for a change!
BILL: Ha! Anything! Bong! The fight's over. Calm down.
MARGO: I will not calm down!
BILL: Don't calm down.
MARGO: You're being very tolerant, aren't you?
BILL: Well, I'm trying.
MARGO: *(Standing up and moving toward him)* I don't want to be tolerated, or plotted against! Get her out of my life! You think she's talented? Fine. Help her. Get her a job in a touring company—a film in Lebanon! Let her run around naked off-Broadway someplace. Anyplace . . . Just away from *me* and away from *you!*
BILL: *(Going toward the chaise)* Are you still on that! You can't really believe—

MARGO: *(She follows, and they're now at opposite ends of the chaise)* What else am I going to believe! The girl turns up out of nowhere, inexperienced, amateur at best, and gives a performance that knocks everybody out—rehearsed, I have no doubt, over and over, day and night . . . full of those personal, unmistakable Bill Sampson touches!

(MARGO moves away)

BILL: *(Exploding, following MARGO)* Goddamn it! I've had it up to here! I'm sick to death of your paranoiac outbursts!

MARGO: Paranoiac—what a hangup on a word! I don't even know what it means!

BILL: Well, it's time you found out! Go to an analyst!

MARGO: Go to hell!

(There is tense silence)

BILL: *(Quietly)* We usually wind up screaming and throwing things as the curtain comes down, then it comes up again and everything's fine. But not this time. Good-bye, Margo. *(He goes to the stage door)*

MARGO: Where are you going, Bill? Mustn't keep the kid waiting.

BILL: Paranoia.

(He slams the door. MARGO stands alone on the empty stage)

MARGO: *(Singing)*
Where painted trees and flowers grow . . .
And laughter rings fortissimo,
And treachery's sweetly done.
Welcome to the theater,
You fool, you love it so.

Curtain

ACT TWO

SCENE 1

The scene is BUZZ *and* KAREN'S *Connecticut home, a few weeks later. The curtain goes up on the living room. The right wall is dominated by a large stone fireplace. Downstage of the fireplace is a cushioned chair with a small banjo on the wall behind the chair . . .*

In the middle of the set is a comfortable-looking built-in sofa. There is a railing above which guards the landing leading to the kitchen, off to the right. In front of the sofa is a large coffee table. To the left of the sofa is a section between the sofa and the steps to the landing. It has two levels, one with a yellow cushion for sitting and the other, higher, holding a large lamp, a phone, a Brandy decanter, three coffee mugs, and two plastic glasses.

Three steps on the left of the set lead to a landing. To the right of the landing is another step that goes to the kitchen landing. This landing is against the back wall, in the center of which is a window with floor-length drapes. The door to the outside is left of the window.

KAREN *is alone, looking out the window at the snow. She is highly excited, drinking, and slightly tipsy. The phone rings, and she rushes to answer it.*

KAREN: Hello? . . . Eve! Glad you called back. You're at the theater already?
. . . Good . . . No, nothing went wrong—you'll definitely go on tonight! I *told*
you I'd find a way! *(Sits)* Here's what I did. Buzz is driving Margo to the station,
but they'll never get there. No gas in the car . . . I emptied it! It can't go more
than a mile . . . Eve, there's no need to feel guilty. You simply said the most
direct way to show Margo is to have the curtain go up and the play to go on
just once without her. *(Gets up)* Well, tonight's the night! So keep calm, act
surprised. I'm just sick I have to miss it . . . Don't thank me, Eve. We *both*
thought of it. We're in it together! 'Bye. Good luck! *(KAREN hangs up and takes
a sip of her drink. She puts three cups out on the coffee table, realizes her error,
and quickly takes one away. She sings "Inner Thoughts")*

Just a prank, some harmless fun,
We'll laugh about it when it's done,
Won't we, Margo?
Sure we will!
Funny, I feel guilty now,
As if I'd been bad somehow,
Could it have a thing to do with Eve?
No, that's silly,
Really silly,
Eve's too sweet and too naïve.

(KAREN goes up the steps toward the kitchen area. The door opens, and in walks
BUZZ, *followed by* MARGO, *both bundled up and freezing)*
  Buzz? . . . Margo!
MARGO: *(At the top of the steps)* Any mail for me while I was gone?
KAREN: What happened?
BUZZ: *(Crossing to the fireplace)* Car ran out of gas. I was an idiot not to
  check it.
KAREN: It never happened before. But the train . . . did you miss it?
MARGO: *(Walking down the steps)* No, I'm on it. This is just a photograph of me.
  I can't believe it. *(Approaching the fireplace)* I can't believe this has happened
  to me. Karen, what a thing to do!
KAREN: *(Alarmed)* Wh—what do you mean?
MARGO: I know you come to the country for peace and quiet, but this is ridicu-
  lous! There isn't another human being for a thousand miles around. *(She warms
  herself by the fire)*
BUZZ: *(Crossing to the phone)* I'll call the theater . . . tell them what happened.
  What time is it?
KAREN: Twenty to eight. I'll get you some hot coffee. *(She exits to the kitchen)*
BUZZ: *(Sings "Inner Thoughts" to himself, moving downstage)*

It's a rotten thing to say,
But I'd love to see my play
Without Margo,
Just one time!

(MARGO takes off her coat and puts it on the sofa)

I'm an egocentric jerk,
But I wonder—would it work?

Would my words sound fresh and great and new?
Buzz, you're evil,
Evil, evil!
After all that Margo's done for you!

(KAREN *re-enters*)

MARGO: You mean we're stuck here?

KAREN: *(At the top of the steps)* Yes.

MARGO: You'd better stand back. At eight-thirty I start doing the play no matter where I am!

BUZZ: *(Crosses back to the phone and dials)* I'm sorry, Margo. I'm sorry for me. I'm such a stingy bastard, I'm thinking of all those refunds at the box office. *(KAREN walks over to MARGO and hands her a cup)*

KAREN: Here's your coffee.

(MARGO sits on the chair, and KAREN kneels next to the coffee table)

MARGO: Coffee! Hey, there's a coffee commercial I'm supposed to do tomorrow, and I've been counting on the loot. Damnit!

BUZZ: *(On the phone)* Hello, backstage? . . . Hello, Bert. Hold on. I've got some incredible news. Margo's stuck here with us in Connecticut. Car broke down. Blame me, I'm guilty! . . . Oh, good . . . *(To MARGO and KAREN)* Eve got there early tonight.

MARGO: *(Crossing to the phone)* Let me talk to her.

(KAREN reacts)

BUZZ: Bert, can she come to the phone? . . . Oh, good . . . *(Handing the phone to MARGO)* She's right there.

MARGO: *(Sits on the landing steps)* Hello, Eve? . . . Of course you're nervous. Who wouldn't be. But listen, if you can remember all of Dana Andrews' lines from my old movies, you can certainly remember these. Now look, that quick change in Act Three, it's a killer. Be sure to kick your shoes off *before* you step into the dress or you'll get all fouled up. Duane will help you. Okay? . . . good luck. *(She hangs up)*

BUZZ: Margo, that was nice.

MARGO: Was it? I thought it was minimally civilized. What's nice is your asking the body and the voice up for the weekend after all the rotten things she said about the brain.

(BUZZ goes over to KAREN)

BUZZ: We can't stay angry at each other. Sometimes I want to murder you, but only temporarily. We know you too well. *(He kisses KAREN on the forehead)*

MARGO: *(Sings "Inner Thoughts" to herself)*

So you know me, good for you,
How I wish that I did too,
Margo Channing,
Who is she?

(BUZZ goes to the sofa)

Now the play's about to start,
Eve is going to play my part!
Bill is there—I wonder what he thinks?
Wouldn't it be

Just terrific
If he thought she really stinks?

(KAREN *picks up* MARGO's *cup to hand it to her*)
KAREN: Drink your coffee, Margo. (MARGO *is silent*) It's only one performance.
MARGO: It isn't that.
KAREN: Bill? You two have had fights before.
MARGO: This one was special. I guess I got suspicious and jealous of Eve because of her age. And *his* age . . . And *my* age.
KAREN: Come on, Bill's not that much younger than you.
MARGO: He's thirty-three. He looked the same three years ago and he'll look the same thirty years from now. I hate men.
KAREN: *(Now at the sofa)* I'm sure he'll be back as usual.
BUZZ: Of course he will. *(To lighten the mood, he goes and pours a drink)* All right, we're here for the night, so let's enjoy it. All those who want to watch "Beat the Clock" raise hands! Monopoly? You wanna smoke some grass?
KAREN: Have you got some?
BUZZ: *(Moving toward the chair near the fireplace)* No, just seeing if you were paying attention.
MARGO: *(Going up to the top of the steps, laughing)* Well, if I finally had to miss a performance, it couldn't have happened in a nicer way . . . with a couple of people I love.
BUZZ: That really calls for a toast. *(Raising his brandy glass)* To friendship! *(He drains the glass and dashes it into the fireplace. It bounces back unbroken. They all stare at it)* I mean, to plastic., I mean, to the real things in life.
(BUZZ *takes his banjo off the wall. He sits on the arm of the chair. The three of them sing "Good Friends")*

BUZZ:
When you've got good friends,
You've got a good life,
Think about that.
When you've got good friends . . .

KAREN: Buzz, you're getting sentimental . . .

BUZZ:
You've got it all!

MARGO: Hold on, you're getting to me.

BUZZ:
For when life is cruel,
And they call you fool,
You're not alone,
If you've got good friends
On whom you can call!

Good friends, who couldn't care less,
If you're a failure, or a success,
They're there,
Whatever you do,
They like you for you!
Not your money or your gorgeousness!

Friendship is a ring,
A circular thing,
It never ends,
So kick off your shoes,
You're with good friends!
You're with good friends!

MARGO:
Life is full of frets,
Remorse and regrets,
Doors that are locked.
When you've got good friends,
You've got the key!

BUZZ and KAREN:
Good friends,
Good friends,
You're poor without
Good friends,
People you love,
People you trust,
You've got the key!

BUZZ:
As you go through life
There's three things you need,
Money is one,
Number two is sex,
You know number three!

KAREN and MARGO:
Do-do, do-do,
Do-do, do-do,
Do-do, do-do do.
All the way.

BUZZ, KAREN and MARGO:
Good friends,
Who really don't care,
If you're a swinger,
Or you're a square!

MARGO:
I know that you two,
You never could do
One mean thing to me!

KAREN: *(Moves away from* BUZZ *and* MARGO; *to herself)* Oh, I wish I'd never drained that tank . . .

BUZZ, KAREN, and MARGO:
Friendship is a ring,
A circular thing,
It never ends,
And we've got it good,
We've got good friends!

MARGO:
Without you life is empty!

KAREN: *(Guiltily, to herself)* Empty!

BUZZ:
Hey, baby, you're a gas!

MARGO: T'anks!

KAREN: *(With growing remorse)* Gas tanks!

MARGO:
It's just like New Year's Eve!

KAREN: Eve? Eve! Gas! Empty! Tanks! What have I done to my . . . ahh . . .

MARGO and BUZZ:
Good friends!

(KAREN sinks to the floor in a faint)
MARGO and BUZZ: *(Surprised)* Good God!

    Blackout

SCENE 2

    EVE, BERT, *and* STAN HARDING *enter as the dressing room set comes on behind them. EVE is wearing the pailletted evening dress that MARGO wore in Scene Five, and it seems made for her. She is heady with excitement, and though still under control, she is ready to get carried away with her instant success.*
BERT: The rest of the cast was twice as nervous as you were. You didn't even make a wrong move! It was like you'd been playing it forever.
EVE: Did you hear them! Did you hear that audience!
STAN: Terrific, Eve. Stardust time, believe me.
EVE: Oh, thank you, Mr. Harding . . .
STAN: I want to do a story on you for the column. Meet me at Joe Allen's later, will you? *(He starts to leave)*
EVE: I'll be there!
STAN: *(At the door)* And don't forget it, I discovered you first.
    (He exits. DUANE enters from the bathroom)
BERT: What else can I say? You're a young Margo.
EVE: *(Coldly)* Really?
DUANE: Well, I have to admit it . . . You wowed them.
EVE: *(Surprised, moving to the dressing table)* Thank you, Duane. Funny . . . tonight I was going to take a chance and just phone in. Good thing I changed my mind and turned up early.
DUANE: *(Picks up his coat from the chair)* Yeah. But how come the columnists and critics turned up? A little birdie must have told them . . . maybe a vulture. *(He exits)*
BERT: *(Adoringly)* It was one of those nights. I guess I had a little something to do with it . . . *(He moves toward her to embrace her)*
EVE: *(Sliding out of it coolly)* Oh, did you?
    (There is a knock, and BILL looks in)
BILL: Hello . . .
    (EVE looks thrilled at seeing BILL)
BERT: Terrific, wasn't she, Mr. Sampson?
BILL: Yeah!
BERT: Uh . . . I'll wait for you Eve.
EVE: *(Sweetly evasive)* Well, I don't think so . . . I feel so . . . well, you know . . .
BERT: *(Grimly)* Ohhh . . . G'night.
    (Exits looking at BILL's back, disgruntled. EVE turns to BILL)
BILL: Well, what I said after Act Two still goes. None of the earmarks of a one-shot performance. It's there.
EVE: *(Looking radiantly into his eyes)* Oh, Mr. Sampson . . .

BILL: You know, I've been spending all my time splicing strips of film together in a dark little room. Almost forgot what live theater can be—the excitement when someone up there makes contact with the audience! Have a good time tonight. You deserve it. *(Kisses her forehead)* Good night, Eve. *(He starts to go out)*

EVE: Bill . . .

BILL: *(Stopping)* Yes?

EVE: *(Walking toward him)* Thank you. *(Sings)*

> *The best night of my life*
> *Is here, is now . . .*

(Speaking)

I couldn't have done it without you.

BILL: *(Surprised)* Without *me?* Come *on* . . . I stopped by and gave you a five-minute pep talk before the curtain went up . . .

EVE: *(Sitting on the sofa)* Something you said made the whole difference. Without it, I might have been just plain embarrassing.

BILL: *(Sitting on the arm of the sofa)* Really? what was that?

EVE: You said, "The one thing that makes an audience uncomfortable is to see an actor pressing—sweating to make good." You said, "If you feel you're losing them, don't panic. Hold very still inside. Don't go after them; make them come to you."

BILL: *(Smiling)* And that's what did it?

EVE: I held on to that as if I were holding on to you. It meant everything to me —and so do you. *(She does just that, putting her hand on top of his)*

BILL: *(Gets up and moves away)* Well, that's a very comprehensive statement.

EVE: *(Gets up and slowly follows BILL. They face each other, very close)* Do you remember the night Greta Garbo met Sigmund Freud? I think it's time Bill Sampson met Eve Harrington.

(There is a slight pause)

BILL: You're quite a girl.

EVE: You think . . . ?

BILL: But I've *got* a girl. Remember Margo?

EVE: *(Confidently)* I'll never forget her. That's how I met *you.* Anyway, you're not together at the moment . . . Maybe this is *my* moment.

BILL: Do you mean *our* moment?

EVE: *(Starts to put her arms up around his neck)* Let's find out.

BILL: *(Evenly)* Only thing is . . . you're pressing . . . I think you've lost me. *(He steps back, out of her embrace)* Remember, Eve, offstage as well as on: don't go after them; make them come to you.

(He leaves. EVE, shocked and humiliated, recoils for a moment. Then, in a tearful rage, she hurls her shoes at the door, pulls the curtain across the room, and half pulls her dress off. HOWARD knocks on the door)

EVE: *(Shouting in anger)* Who is it?

HOWARD: *(Entering)* A flabbergasted and very lucky producer.

EVE: *(Pulling herself together, instantly)* Come in, Mr. Benedict.

HOWARD: *(Goes to closet and gets his coat)* I thought this only happened in those old Ruby Keeler movies. But tonight the understudy took over and turned a potential lynch mob into a cheering squad.

EVE: *(Getting her arms out of her dress and holding it up against her)* I'm so glad you came back. In all the confusion, I forgot to thank you for the flowers.

HOWARD: My pleasure. I just came back for my coat.

(EVE pulls open the curtain)

EVE: Are you still free? I've had a change of plans.

HOWARD: *(Looking her over)* Great, then we shall celebrate. My apartment. I've a bottle of Mumm's Cordon Rouge cooling on ice.

EVE: No, let's go to Joe Allen's. I feel like being with the gypsies.

HOWARD: *(Puts his coat on a chair)* Eve, you're a very clever girl. I came through for you, giving you the understudy part . . .

EVE: *(Quickly)* Haven't I come through for you by giving a good performance? We are friends, aren't we?

HOWARD: Yes, heaven knows, we're friends.

EVE: I have no illusions about tonight. It was just one performance. It could be forgotten tomorrow.

HOWARD: *(Moves in behind her)* Not necessarily. After Margo leaves, I could give you a crack at taking over the part.

EVE: *(Bursting out)* I don't want her hand-me-downs!

HOWARD: *(Preparing to leave, he picks up his coat)* Hm. You've gone up considerably in your esteem in the last—uh—three seconds.

EVE: *(Recovering herself)* I'm sorry to sound so unappreciative, but if I'm to go on with this, I want a part of my own—or nothing.

HOWARD: *(Turning and facing her)* Perhaps even something like that can be arranged. *(EVE, holding her dress up against her, crosses and takes her street dress from the closet, puts it down on the chair, and facing him, begins to unzip and take off the evening dress. Sings)*

So thank you
For the best night of my life.

(Slowly the dress slips to the floor)

SCENE 3

The scene is Joe Allen's. The GYPSIES have moved their chairs and tables into position. STAN enters. DANNY, BONNIE, and DUANE are down front on the right. They talk as the set comes on and the tables are arranged.

BONNIE: Well, did the audience just get up and leave when they announced Margo Channing wasn't going to appear?

DUANE: They groaned a lot, but most of them stayed.

DANNY: Really?

DUANE: Well, what are they gonna do? They wrote in September for their seats, finally got a pair in February. They've already paid the baby-sitter, made the trek in by dog sled, wolfed down a six-course dinner in twenty minutes. They can't leave—they're exhausted! Anyway, what's their choice? Go out on Eighth Avenue and get mugged? They'd stay to see *me* in the part. *(Starts to go and stops)* And I wouldn't be bad.

GYPSY GIRL: *(At another table)* But, Duane, how was she?

DUANE: *(Begrudgingly)* A sensation!

(EVE and HOWARD enter, and the GYPSIES applaud. STAN greets and leads them to a table. All three sit, EVE in the center)

STAN: Well, how do you feel?

EVE: *(Buoyantly)* Fantastic!

DANNY: *(Coming to their table)* Excuse me, Mr. Benedict. Eve, we're all so excited for you. Can you come over . . . We'd like to buy you a drink!

EVE: *(Sweetly, but distantly)* Not now, Danny. I'm busy. Maybe later.
(DANNY retreats)

DANNY: *(To the others at his table)* I just got the hello-but-don't-come-over bit.

STAN: They're all gonna want to meet you. Tonight, for my money, you had ten times as much heart as Miss Channing. And there wasn't a man who didn't have the hots for ya . . . That's a compliment. I'll put it more delicately in the column.

HOWARD: We rely on your good taste, Stan. *(A waiter dashes by)* Uh, waiter! Excuse me . . . I'll deal directly with the bar. *(He goes to the bar)*

STAN: *(Taking notes)* To continue, Miss Harrington, you're the right age for the part.

EVE: Mr. Harding, I do want to make one thing clear. I adore Margo Channing, and I only hope I'll have the energy and grace she has, when *I'm* her age. I mean, she represents an old theatrical tradition, when a star was a star! I do think today, however, in contemporary plays, that must be dropped, and young actresses given a chance to . . .

(Two GYPSIES come over)

FIRST GYPSY: Excuse us, Eve, we're dying to know what it . . .

SECOND GYPSY: *(His words overlapping)* How'd it feel? Were you nervous?

EVE: Hi, kids. I won't be very long. *(The boys withdraw)* Of course, mature actresses are sometimes also childlike, self-deluded people. They don't realize that they can be personally brilliant yet detrimental to the play, and—

BONNIE: *(Rushing over)* Eve! We heard you were sensational . . . !

EVE: *(Icily)* Please! Not now! Can't you see I'm busy . . . trying to answer a few questions!

(BONNIE bumps into HOWARD, returning with the drinks)

BONNIE: Excuse me! Oh, Mr. Benedict, I just wanted to—

EVE: *(Getting up)* Howard, you were right. We really should go someplace quieter. Do you mind, Mr. Harding?

STAN: *(Rising)* Not at all. Howard?
(They start toward the door. EVE and BONNIE come face to face. EVE haughtily walks around her and out, the GYPSIES watching)

BONNIE: *(Mimicking the grand manner EVE took on as she walks over to one of the tables)* Kids . . . she was *merely* trying to answer a few questions! *(The GYPSIES hoot)* Pull-ease, kids, not now. I'm *busy!*
(She sits. The music begins playing. DUANE grabs a pad and pencil and sits across from BONNIE)

DUANE: Hello, Miss Starshine. I'm from *Screw Magazine*, and our readers would like to know if success will change you.

BONNIE: No, I plan to be as obnoxious as I ever was!

DUANE: And you'll remember your old friends?

BONNIE: Of course. I'll never forget them. And I'll never see them either!

DUANE: *(Begins singing "She's No Longer a Gypsy)*

She's no longer a gypsy,
She'll be leaving us soon,
She did the understudy-to-the-rescue bit,
Now she's halfway to the moon!

She's no longer a gypsy,
No more Equity calls,
She's gonna get them crazy invitations now
To Truman Capote's balls . . .

GYPSIES:
Have a beer,
Your last one, dear,
From this night on it's all champagne!

BONNIE:
The star was late,
And I was great!

ALL:
You got up early

DUANE:
And pulled a Shirley MacLaine!

BONNIE:
I'm no longer a gypsy,
Put me on the marquee!
It's out-of-the-chorus-into-heaven time . . .

GYPSIES:
It should happen,
It should only happen,
God, let it happen to me!

ALL: *(To the sound of samba music)*
Aye yi yi yi,
Aye yi, aye yi . . .
She's no longer a gypsy!
It's the magic of Broadway,
Overnight you're a star.

DUANE:
Now ev'ry jerk who ever turned you down will claim
He made you what you are!

GIRLS:
No more automat coffee,

BONNIE:
It's the Plaza for tea.

GYPSIES:
You did the "Hey-world-now-you're-gonna-see-me" bit!

DUANE:
"I tell you, Manny, with this kid we got a hit!"

ALL:
> *It's that good old overnight sensation shit!*
> *It should happen,*
> *It should only happen,*
> *God, let it happen to me.*
>
> *She's no longer a gypsy,*
> *She'll be leaving the street.*
> *Hey, she's a regular Mitzi Gaynor now,*
> *Don't you love them dancing feet!*
>
> *(A wildly competitive dance number follows)*
> *Fame,*
> *Success,*
> *Autographs,*
> *Me . . . please God!*
>
> *Who?*
> *Broadway . . . Hollywood!*
> *Money, money!*
> *Thank you, thank you!*
> *Me!*
> *Me!*
> *Me!*
>
> *What is it that we're living for?*
> *Applause! Applause!*
> *Nothing I know*
> *Brings on the glow*
> *Like sweet applause.*

DUANE: *(In a hammy baritone)*
> *One alone to be my own.*

(BONNIE hits DUANE over the head with a sledgehammer. As the number progresses, the other dancers follow suit; every time one of them gets into the spotlight, he is quickly done away with. BONNIE has now acquired a blond wig, dark glasses, a fur stole, and a cigarette holder, and she sits in a glamorous pose away from the crowd)

ALL: *(Bowing modestly)* Thank you. Thank you. Thank you. Thank you. Thank you. Thank you.

> *Star me—*
> *To hell with you!*
>
> *Kill—*
> *For big chance!*
>
> *Hut, two, three, four!*
> *Enemy in sight!*
> *Ready, aim, fire!*

GYPSIES:
> *She's no longer a gypsy,*
> *It's good-bye to the bunch!*

BONNIE:

> *And if you ever get to Beverly Hills,*
> *Don't drop in for lunch!*

ALL:

> *Treat her nice,*
> *La, la, la!*
> *That's our advice,*
> *La, la, la!*
> *You take care of this dear girl!*

DUANE:

> *I'm telling you,*
> *She will come through,*
> *But if she doesn't,*
> *Why not give me a whirl?*

ALL:

> *She's no longer a gypsy,*
> *Put her on the marquee!*

BONNIE:

> *I'll get to meet George Jessel*
> *At a Friar's roast!*

DUANE:

> *You'll be a big fat star*
> *And have the world on toast,*

ALL:

> *But don't forget your friends*
> *Who love you most!*

(At this point all the dancers kill each other off with machine guns, daggers, dart guns, etc., and finally the stage is piled high with bodies, with BONNIE posing on top, triumphant)

> *It should happen,*
> *It should only happen,*
> *God, let it happen to me!*

(The number ends; then the music resumes as the dancers exit, chanting)

> *It should happen to me,*
> *It should happen to me,*
> *It should happen to me,*
> *It should happen to me.*

DUANE:

> *Ev'ry body's part gypsy,*
> *Ev'ry body I know,*
> *Oh, even I have dreamed*
> *That I could leap onstage,*
> *And really stop the show!*

(As the scene changes, a motion picture cameraman enters stage center and BON-NIE and DUANE vie for the most advantageous position in front of the lens, pushing each other aside. Finally DUANE carries her off, protesting all the way. As they exit, the living room set comes into position)

SCENE 4

MARGO*'S living room. It is mid-afternoon the following day; the place is set up for an El Dorado Coffee commercial. Present are the* TV DIRECTOR, *the cameraman, a script girl, and an assistant.*

MARGO, *wearing a simple yellow dress, looks tense and tired. She is seated on the sofa, holding a cup and saucer. On the coffee table are a jar of El Dorado Instant Coffee, a tin of El Dorado Regular, and a coffee server. TV lights are at each end of the sofa; the movie camera is directed at* MARGO.

Watching from the terrace are KAREN *and* PETER. KAREN*'S coat is draped over the brick wall. There are coffee cups in front of them, and* KAREN *is holding a folded newspaper. She shows her uneasiness throughout the scene. The script girl walks to the edge of the terrace and sits.*

DIRECTOR: *(To the right of the camera)* A little higher with the cup. Now raise it and take a sip. Now let's have that famous look over the rim of the cup . . . Good . . . Now put it down. That was perfect, Miss Channing, thank you. *(Walking over to the script girl by the terrace)* Just so you'll know, over that shot we hear the voice saying, "As an actress and star, Margo Channing is one-of-a-kind. So when she entertains at home, she always serves the one-of-a-kind coffee, El Dorado."

MARGO: *(Depressed)* All right. *(Gets up from the sofa)* Is that it?

DIRECTOR: *(Crosses to the sofa)* No, that was for El Dorado Regular Grind. We still have to do El Dorado Freeze-Dried and El Dorado Drip.

MARGO: I'm sorry, it's just that running in from the country, getting dressed in thirty seconds . . . I'm . . .

DIRECTOR: That's all right, Miss Channing, you're doing fine. Take a few minutes.

(The script girl rises, removes the cup and saucer from the coffee table, and goes off to the kitchen, returning with two cups and saucers which she places on the coffee table. Then she takes away the coffee and returns, walking behind the camera. MARGO *joins* PETER *and* KAREN*)*

MARGO: Couldn't we finish this tomorrow?

PETER: You know that's out of the question. They're here; get it over with. I don't want you to blow this. It's—

MARGO: *(Moving between KAREN and PETER)* Yes, I know—it's dignified, it's got residuals, it's security for my old age, which judging from this morning's paper I'm in the middle of right now.

PETER: Aw, Margo . . .

KAREN: I can't believe Eve would say those things.

MARGO: *(Reading from a newspaper taken from KAREN)* "Miss Harrington, while restating her admiration for Miss Channing, lamented the fact that mature actresses can be so self-deluded, they keep playing younger parts with detrimental results to the play." Detrimental, self-deluded. Does that sound like Stan Harding?

PETER: So someone bumraps you in a column. It stinks but . . .

MARGO: What gets me is how the papers and TV people happened to catch that particular performance.

PETER: Well, first performance you ever missed. That's instant news.

MARGO: So she got good notices. I hate it, but I can face it. But what about this from Stan . . . *(Reading)* "Miss Harrington was a radiant, natural young angel up there tonight. Quite a difference from Miss Channing, cleverly bundled up in her high-necked gowns, designed to conceal; and discreetly lit with all the pink gelatins in town, to create the illusion of youth." My God, she wore my costumes, and the lighting was exactly the same. It's so rotten—so unfair. *(She gives the paper to* PETER*)*

DIRECTOR: Can we go, Miss Channing?

MARGO: *(With a little laugh)* I guess I'd better, or it'll be all over town that I'm too feeble to work. *(*BILL *walks in and is standing at the side.* MARGO *doesn't see him and goes to sit on the couch again)* Okay, fellas! Let's get in there for that one-of-a-kind coffee! Get this one-of-a-kind profile before it crumbles. *(She lifts the cup, but she is trembling, and the cup falls and breaks)* I'm sorry.

(She gets up. The script girl picks up the pieces of broken cup and exits to the kitchen)

BILL: *(Going to her quickly)* Margo.

MARGO: Bill . . .

(She goes to him and he takes her in his arms. KAREN *takes her coat from the wall and puts it on)*

BILL: I read that piece of garbage. It's not even worth a tear. And you were right about that girl.

MARGO: Bill, I'm so tired.

DIRECTOR: Look, these things happen. We'll just leave everything here and pick up those two shots tomorrow.

PETER: Yes, do it tomorrow. That's *my* suggestion.

(The TV people and PETER *exit.* KAREN, *nervously working her way toward the door, bumps into the swivel chair)*

KAREN: *(Trying to hide her feelings of guilt)* Bill, I'm so glad you're here. She's had a terrible morning. *(*MARGO *sits on the sofa)* I had no idea . . . Well, now that you're here, I'll . . . Margo, call me later if there's anything . . . well, call me. So long.

BILL: So long, Karen. *(She exits.* BILL *tries to pull* MARGO *out of her depression)* I only dropped by because I wanted a cup of coffee. *(Takes his coat off and puts it on the small chair)* Come now, I want that coffee, and I want it poured by you, right now. *(Picks up the clapboard)* All right, we're rolling! Take one—Margo sad! *(Looks through the camera)* Cut! Perfect! Take two—Margo—glad! *(Looks through the camera again.* MARGO *has the same sad expression)* Cut! *(Like a wild foreign director)* Nothing! You're not doing it right. I want beeg smile! Plenty teeth! *(She grins)* More, more! *(She grins more and more)* No, not insanity! Cut! I got an easy one for you. Margo sexy! *(*MARGO *is lying down. He pans in on her)* Margo no feel sexy? Margo sad? *(She nods)* Sad Margo. *(She holds up her hands, witchlike, as if to scratch)* Evil Margo! Margo, the Wicked Witch! *(She does a funny witch's cackle, joining in his game, and snaps out of her depression)* Bravo! You're everything the slogan promises!

(He takes her hand and pulls her up on the back of the couch. He jumps over to sit beside her, and sings a gay, lilting waltz, "One of a Kind")

You're one of a kind,
A fabulous bird,
You're out of your mind
And 'way out of sight.
You're one of a kind,
Unique is the word,
And that's why I find
The others all trite . . .

(Puts his arm around her)

I like the weird things that happen
Inside of your skull,
Being with you may be hard on the nerves,

(Her head is on his shoulder)

But it's never dull,
No, sir, never dull . . .

(He stands up on the sofa)

You walk in a room,
The people all stare,

(She stands up on the sofa)

'Cause, baby, you bloom.
They'd have to be blind

(He jumps down)

To not recognize
The rarest of rare
Right under their eyes,
You're one of a kind!

(Goes to the light on the right, turns it on, and indicates a model's pose. She rejects the idea)

If there were two of you,
Or, God forbid, a few of you,

(Circles the camera and looks through it)

Too much is what it would be,
But you're one of a kind,

(MARGO gets off the sofa, and BILL goes to join her)

One of a kind,
One of a kind,
One of a kind,
And you're the kind of a woman for me!

Who else would take a swim completely dressed
In Central Park at three A.M.
The night she won the Tony?

MARGO: *(Turning)* I didn't do that . . .

BILL:
Well, you did!

MARGO:
Who grabbed a flaming cherries jubilee
And burned a movie script at Chasen's,
Yelling it was phony!

BILL: Was that me?
MARGO: Um hmmmm . . .

BILL and MARGO: *(Singing side by side)*
You always were a crazy kid!

(Now with their backs together)

I shudder at the things you did!!

BILL:
Your ego seems to suit my id . . .

MARGO:
So kiss me!

BILL: You mad fool! *(Picking up* MARGO*)*
You know you grind your teeth at night.

MARGO:
Your snoring is a real delight.

BILL and MARGO:
It's noisy, but we sleep all right!

(Bill puts her down and fakes a hurt back)

You . . .
Are . . .
One of a kind,
A fabulous bird,
You're out of your mind,
And 'way out of sight!
You're one of a kind,
Unique is the word,
And that's why I find
The others all trite . . .

MARGO: *(Waltzes across the stage)*
At times you're selfish and stubborn
And blind as a mole,
(Turns)
But even so, you're a kick to be with,
You're good for my soul,
So good for my soul . . .

BILL and MARGO: *(Doing a two-step)*
You walk in a room,
The people all stare,

'Cause, baby, you bloom.
They'd have to be blind
To not recognize
The rarest of rare
Right under their eyes,
You're one of a kind!

MARGO:

If there were two of you,
Or, God forbid, a few of you,
Too much is what it would be!

BILL and MARGO:

But you're one of a kind,
One of a kind,
One of a kind,
One of a kind,

(They strike a dance pose)

And you're the kind of a nut

(They kiss)

For me!

(They do an eccentric little waltz clog and finish it by striking a Ballet Russe pose. They kiss happily for a long time)

MARGO: *(As if in a dream)* Bill?

BILL: Mmmmmmmmmm . . . ? *(He is kissing her face and neck)*

MARGO: Bill . . . tell me one thing?

BILL: *(Still kissing her)* Yes?

MARGO: Was she good?

BILL: Who?

MARGO: You were there last night. Eve . . . was she that good?

BILL: Forget it. *(He kisses her)*

MARGO: *(Through the kiss)* Well, *was* she?

BILL: *(Breaking from her and moving a couple of steps away)* Yes, she was good. So *that's* what you're thinking about.

MARGO: I can't very well help it, can I?

BILL: I'm kissing you, thinking of nothing but you, and *that's* what's racing around in your mind!

MARGO: You and me—that's on my mind, too.
(They go toward the sofa. She sits)

BILL: Yeah! In the bottom drawer someplace. You certainly know how to make a fella feel wanted and loved. What the hell's the matter with me! Why do I keep coming back and getting kicked in the teeth? Because I keep thinking each time things are going to be different! That you're going to change!

MARGO: But I don't want you to change, Bill. I want you just as you are. I've missed you so. *(She pulls him down next to her)* Who else is going to catch me every time I fall off the high wire? *(She puts his arm around her and her head on his shoulder)* Do me a favor, Bill . . . marry me?

BILL: *(After a pause)* No. You don't need me, my love . . . you need a safety net. The answer is no.

MARGO: *(Sitting up)* I knew you'd get cold feet if I ever really—

BILL: It's just that for the first time I'm facing it honestly. Why should you change? How can you? A lifetime of conditioning since you were nineteen, defending your own little place up on top. It's a full-time job. *(Gets up and moves away)* Marrying you would be bigamy. You're already married. You're a star . . . *that* comes first.

MARGO: *(Gets up)* Well, what do you want? A little wifey-poo waiting for you in the kitchen, knee-deep in lasagna?

BILL: Yeah, I guess I do. *(Suddenly very unhappy)* No, I don't. Because then it wouldn't be you, and you're the one I love. I'd be miserable. Damn it! There isn't any solution . . . *(Walks toward her)* Go take a nap, you must be exhausted. You do have to face your public in a couple of hours.

MARGO: You're right. And I'd better look particularly dazzling tonight. Will you pick me up afterward? *(There is a brief silence)*

BILL: I'm working late.

MARGO: When will I see you?

BILL: I don't know.

MARGO: *(Pleading)* Bill, I love you. *(She starts going toward her bedroom)*

BILL: I wish you could realize what a rival a fellow has in you.

MARGO: *(Partway up the steps)* I just don't understand.

(She exits. BILL looks after her, thoughtfully)

BILL: *(Singing)*
> We were doing fine,
> I thought we'd be okay.
> Once it was you and me . . .
> Now where the hell are we?
> Two people who can't be . . .
> Together.

   Blackout

SCENE 5

The scene takes place backstage, two weeks later. As the lights come up, EVE enters between the proscenium and the backstage wall. She is wearing an attractive red dress, and radiates total confidence. She walks toward the center of the stage, and looks around possessively. BERT, who is standing next to the spiral staircase, sees her and approaches her from behind.

BERT: Eve?

EVE: *(Startled by his voice, turns to face him)* Oh, hello, Bert! I just came by to pick up my things.

BERT: At midnight?

EVE: I wanted to be sure everyone had gone. My make-up box is in Margo's room someplace. I left it there the night I went on.

BERT: The two weeks since then have been pretty tense.

EVE: *(Goes toward the chaise)* Well, you should be glad I'm leaving.

BERT: *(Grimly)* You were pretty nice to me for a while. As long as it took to get rid of the understudy. I've served my purpose.

EVE: *(Turning to face him)* I've got to get my things.

BERT: Then you struck out with Bill Sampson . . . moved in fast on Buzz Richards.

EVE: That's foolish, dangerous gossip. You could hurt a lot of people with lies like that. *(Puts her coat down on the chaise)* Good-bye, Bert.

BERT: Good luck.

EVE: Don't worry. I'll be back in this theater, or another—and with my own understudy. *(She exits to the dressing room)*

BERT: You're quite a girl. *(BUZZ enters through the stage door and heads for the dressing room, not seeing BERT)* Hello, Mr. Richards!

BUZZ: *(Spinning around, guiltily)* Hello, Bert.

BERT: Looking for someone?

BUZZ: No . . . I . . . I was just . . . How's the show going?

BERT: We should sell tickets to what goes on *after* the show.

(He exits through the stage door. EVE comes out of the dressing room with her bag)

BUZZ: Eve! *(She runs into his arms and they kiss eagerly)* I got delayed finishing those rewrites in Act One—the ones we talked about last night. God! I couldn't sleep, thinking about the way you read Leslie. The more I work on it, the more I know the girl is you.

EVE: I know! I feel it, too!

BUZZ: The play's ready to go; Howard doesn't want Margo to leave this one. What can stand in the way? And listen . . . no more meeting like this. Starting tomorrow night we've got the Reeves' apartment. *(Holds up two keys)* Matching keys, his and hers. *(Hands her one)* You may not like the paintings—lots of little orphans with big eyes. But we won't be looking at them much. *(Gives her a long hug and kiss)* I can't figure out what the hell you see in me.

(He exits through the stage door, and she lifts her hand to wave good-bye)

EVE: *(Sighing happily, she looks around at the theater and then begins to sing "One Hallowe'en")*

Remember that Hallowe'en
When you were nine?
You wore a fairy-queen costume of your own design . . .

Well, look at you now . . .

And you put on rouge and lipstick
Though it wasn't allowed,
You were so proud!
And Daddy said, "Wash your face,
You look like a whore,"
That's what he said,
No more.

And so you went upstairs,
Washed your face,
Took off the dress,
Threw it away,
Got into bed,
As though it were the end
Of an ordinary day . . .
And outside,

The moon continued to shine.
Remember that Hallowe'en
When you were nine?

Well, screw you, Daddy. Look at your little girl now!
(Turns, puts the key on the chaise, then runs up the spiral steps and stops to look down on the stage—the world she is about to conquer)

She feels twitchy and bitchy
And manic,
Calm and collected
And no sign of panic,
She's alive,
She's alive,
So alive!

(Starts moving down the steps)

I'm wound up like a spring
That's been tightened,
Dreamy and dizzy
But not a bit frightened,
I'm alive,
I'm alive,
So alive!

(Leaves the steps and walks toward the wings)

Ev'rybody loves a winner,
But nobody loves a flop!
No one worries how you got there
Once you're standing on the top!

(Now faces forward)

So I feel up and together
And steady,
Eager, excited,
So come on, I'm ready!
Ready for the climb,
Baby, it's my time!
You believe it, I'm
Alive! Alive!

(She turns and picks up her bag, coat, and key. HOWARD *enters from the right)*
Howard!
HOWARD: *(Casually)* Hello!
EVE: *(Taken aback)* How long have you . . . ?
HOWARD: *(Moving slowly toward her)* Long enough. I came in through the front. Bert told me I might find you here. I've never seen you caught off guard before.
EVE: *(Standing at the end of the chaise, composed)* Howard, there's nothing to hide. Something wonderful has happened to me. We've fallen in love! He's rewriting Leslie for me . . . and, well . . . it's getting pretty serious. Of course I feel awful about Karen . . .

HOWARD: Yes, yes, of course—that makes it tough.

EVE: *(Goes toward the stage door)* Well, I've got to go . . .

HOWARD: If there's a wedding license, don't forget to write Evelyn Hinkle. That's your name, isn't it?

EVE: *(Stopping)* Yes, what about it?

HOWARD: I've done a bit of research on you. That whole pathetic-lost-soul autobiography. Very touching, but a complete lie, from beginning to end.

(EVE puts down her case and coat, and walks quickly back toward HOWARD)

EVE: I just *had* to get in to see Margo. I had to make them like me.

HOWARD: They liked you all right. And what have you done for them in return? The bodies are piling up. I don't want mine among them.

EVE: *(Defiantly)* Howard, Buzz and I—

HOWARD: *(Taking her key)* Forget about "Buzz and I." It's "you and I."

EVE: It *was* you and I, Howard . . . for one night. But with Buzz . . . I really love him.

HOWARD: Don't you think your future with Buzz could be complicated by his hearing about your current activities? Hopscotch to the top, from bed to bed —Bert, Stan Harding, me.

EVE: Buzz loves me. I can explain all that.

HOWARD: Really. Can you explain this simple fact: your husband wasn't killed in Vietnam. He's still there—alive!

(She looks at him coldly)

EVE: What do you want?

HOWARD: *(Circling behind her, then moving back)* You, until I start yawning. I want you to let Buzz down gently. Take a week or so—I want a playwright, not a blubbering wreck. And then, if you're a very good girl, we'll see about the part in the play. Come here. *(She doesn't budge)* Come here. *(She walks over to him slowly. He takes her chin in his hand and kisses her)* Don't clench your teeth when I kiss you.

(He kisses her again, this time pulling back quickly and touching his lip. There is blood. He slaps her)

EVE: *(Under her breath)* Goddamn you! Goddamn you!

HOWARD: Eve, we both know what you want. And you know I can get it for you, don't you? . . . Don't you? *(Defeated, she nods)* Well, then. Here . . . *(He puts some money in her hand)* Take a taxi, get your things, and be at my place in an hour. And if I'm not there—wait.

(He exits. EVE stands there, stunned, unable to move)

SCENE 6

It is a week later. The dressing room set comes on, and MARGO, in her dressing gown, is seen pacing. PETER is seated next to the dressing table, and DUANE is sitting on the sofa.

PETER: *(Soothingly)* C'mon, sweetie, it's not the only part ever written . . . or the greatest. Now you just play out this run, take it on the road . . .

MARGO: *(Still pacing, helplessly)* Where *is* everybody? I asked for a meeting here after the matinee, not just you, but the whole office. *(She goes to the bar)*

PETER: Well, the boss is in L.A., Bob's in London, and . . .

MARGO: And what's the point of it without Howard here?

PETER: He wouldn't return my call.

MARGO: *(Moving to her chair, then pacing again, urgently)* You're not going to let Howard get away with this! It all comes from him. This is *my* part. It was written for me. It's always been understood.

PETER: *(Following* MARGO *unhappily)* The play's ready. They're anxious to get it on, and we have no written contract . . .

MARGO: Buzz certainly couldn't have agreed to this. *(*PETER *shrugs)* And Bill? Is he directing it? . . . With her?

PETER: You'd know better than anyone.

MARGO: Would I? Haven't seen him in weeks. That part was the only thing in my future. *(Looking lost)* Now where am I?

PETER: But, sweetie, it's not the end of the world.

MARGO: Maybe not for you. *(Looking around the dressing room, encompassing it with a gesture)* Get it straight, Peter. This is it. This is my whole life. *(Imploring)* Do something about it! *(He shrugs helplessly. She is resigned)* Go home and have a good dinner. You look awful.

PETER: *(Touched)* Thanks, Margo. G'night.

(He leaves. DUANE *walks over to her, gives her a light kiss, and puts his arm around her shoulder)*

MARGO: *(To* DUANE, *trying to smile)* Hey, you're not going to be her hairdresser, are you?

DUANE: Only when she's laid out.

MARGO: *(Overwhelmed again)* How am I going to stop her?

DUANE: How can you when she's got the author in her pocket?

MARGO: Hm?

DUANE: Well . . . in her bed.

MARGO: *(Stunned)* Buzz . . . and Eve?

DUANE: It's practically been a headline in *Variety*.

(The door opens. KAREN *looks in)*

KAREN: Margo?

MARGO: Karen!

KAREN: I'm glad you're still here. I'll tell the doorman to let the cab go. *(She ducks out)*

DUANE: Hey, look. I better cut out. See you at half-hour. And make sure you eat something. *(To* KAREN, *as she comes in and he is leaving)* Oh, hi, Mrs. Richards.

KAREN: Hi, Duane.

MARGO: *(Nervously trying to be offhand)* Hello . . . what's the good word? Uh . . . who said that? I never say things like that. Uh . . . you want a shrimp? Some steak? Can I get you a drink?

*(*KAREN *has the intense look of someone who has been drinking. She takes off her coat and puts the coat and her pocketbook on the sofa)*

KAREN: Yeah! Jack Daniels . . . cooking sherry . . . anything. Margo, justice is not dead!

MARGO: *(Pouring a drink and taking it to* KAREN*)* Oh, good.

KAREN: Retribution. Punishment for sins. I've been doing a lot of thinking.

MARGO: You mean *drinking*.

KAREN: I wish I could get plotzed. All the time. Can't live with myself. Your little Radcliffee girl emptied that gas tank, loused up her friend, and now she's getting what she deserves . . . Didn't you hear me?

MARGO: I heard. You and the gas tank. It took me a whole day to figure that out.

(Puts her hands on KAREN'S *shoulders)* I knew it was Eve pulling the strings.

KAREN: Margo, you were so right about—

MARGO: Yes, I win a lot of medals for being on to that girl. They're pinned right to my skin. I . . . just heard about Buzz.

KAREN: *(Moving away)* You marry a funny-looking, lovable little playwright, put him through college, sharpen his pencils, pretend to like his early plays, and then . . . suddenly . . . *(Stamping her foot, then breaking down)* I'll kill him! I'll kill them both! *(Weeping, she slumps into the chair near the dressing table)* Margo, help me!

*(*MARGO *goes over to* KAREN *and holds her)*

MARGO: You've certainly come to an expert. I've lost every man who ever came into my life, including the only one I really loved.

KAREN: What do we do?

MARGO: I know exactly what *you* have to do. Nothing.

KAREN: Huh?

MARGO: Eve doesn't want your playwright husband. She wants his play.

KAREN: She'd do all this for a part in a play?

MARGO: Right. Sit still and wait.

KAREN: Wait! *(Gets up)* That's no way to fight a woman like that!

MARGO: *(Sitting* KAREN *back down)* Listen to me! On *this* subject, I really *am* an expert. Buzz is just one step up for her. Those dainty claws are already dug in for the next jump, and jump she will, no matter whose body is in the way. If she's talented, she'll get there. But *staying* up there—that's the backbreaker, the full-time job. I almost feel sorry for Eve, because in the end she'll wind up empty and alone, married to herself, fighting for parts she's no longer right for . . . and . . . and no *wonder* I'm such an expert on this subject. It's *me!*

KAREN: *(Getting up and running to* MARGO*)* No!

MARGO: You must admit there's a faint resemblance. And I don't like it. Karen, I've got to do something about it.

(They kiss. KAREN *picks up her coat and pocketbook from the sofa)*

KAREN: *(Excitedly)* And I've got to go right home and . . . and . . . do nothing!

(They are at the door. KAREN *goes, and* MARGO *follows her into the area outside the door)*

MARGO: *(Stopping* KAREN*)* Karen, got a good recipe for lasagna?

KAREN: What?

MARGO: I'll call you. *(*KAREN *exits.* MARGO *steps forward and with a growing sense of realization and urgency sings "Something Greater")*

A scrapbook full of clippings
Of things long forgotten,
There's something greater!

A picture in the paper
That makes you look rotten,
There's something greater!

The meaningless attention,
The bowing and the smirking
Of some headwaiter . . .

That lost and empty feeling
The nights that you're not working,
I know there's something better,
I know there's something greater!

A theater full of strangers
Adoring you blindly,
There's something greater,
There's something greater!

The friends who know you're lonely
And treat you too kindly,
There's something greater,
There's something greater!

There's needing to be where he is,
Waking up and there he is,
Being to your man what a woman should be!
That's something greater,
Something greater!
And, finally, that's for me!

(The music continues to play as MARGO *paces up and down excitedly. The dressing room set goes off, revealing the backstage set)*

SCENE 7

Backstage. As MARGO *paces, the lights dim. At the opposite side of the stage, a spotlight picks up* BILL. MARGO *turns and sees him.*

BILL: *(Moving toward* MARGO, *singing)*
There's needing to be where she is,
Waking up and there she is . . .

MARGO: *(Moving toward him, singing)*
Being to your man what a woman should be!

(The music continues in the background)
Bill, I'm sorry.

BILL: *I'm* sorry. I should have protected you from that girl. She's a—

MARGO: *(Putting her hand over his mouth)* Don't say a word against her. And let the kid have the part. If it weren't for her, I would have lost you. *(Looking out to the front with a happy grin, and calling)* Eve! You four-star bitch! Thank you!

BILL and MARGO: *(Singing)*
That's something greater!
Something greater!
And, finally, that's for me!

(They turn, walk upstage, and embrace)

Curtain

A LITTLE NIGHT MUSIC

Book by Hugh Wheeler
Music and Lyrics by Stephen Sondheim

(Suggested by a Film by Ingmar Bergman)

Editor's Notes

A Little Night Music burst upon the Broadway scene with a magic that was enthusiastically acclaimed by audiences and critics. Clive Barnes of *The New York Times* rapturously exclaimed: "Good God!—an adult musical! Heady, civilized, sophisticated and enchanting . . . Hugh Wheeler's book is uncommonly urbane and witty. The jokes are funny, and the very real sophistication has considerable surface depth . . . Then, of course, there are Stephen Sondheim's breathtaking lyrics" and his "music is a celebration of ¾ time, an orgy of plaintively memorable waltzes, all talking of past loves and lost worlds."

Others found it: "Witty, saucy, classy, stylish . . . a beautiful, daring, innovative musical. It is a sparkling gem" that is "thoroughly delightful, fresh and beautiful." Brendan Gill of *The New Yorker* wrote: "Throwing caution to the winds, I assert that *A Little Night Music* comes as close as possible to being the perfect romantic musical comedy."

Otis Guernsey, Jr., in his coverage of the Broadway season in *The Best Plays of 1972–1973* stated: "Leading the season's parade of thirteen Broadway musicals was—as usual—a Harold Prince show, *A Little Night Music*, with Stephen Sondheim at the top of his virtuosity, and with a beguiling book by Hugh Wheeler based on Ingmar Bergman's film *Smiles of a Summer Night* (it was about the ways of love on a Swedish country estate on Midsummer's Eve, when the sun never sets and the characters from both drawing room and scullery wander in pairs among the birch trees throughout the long, warm twilight). This show took an operetta form, not as a pastiche but in a very high style" and "ranks among the best that the Broadway theatre has to offer."

Opening on February 25, 1973, the show ran for 601 performances, won a parcel of awards, notably, the New York Drama Critics' Circle Award as the season's best musical, six Antoinette Perry (Tony) Awards (including one for best musical), and three Drama Desk Awards for best lyricist, composer and author of a musical book.

Accolades for *A Little Night Music* were not confined to New York. The national road company (headed by Jean Simmons and Margaret Hamilton) toured for a year and received three major awards from the Los Angeles Drama Critics' Circle.

The musical opened in London on April 15, 1975, to generally ecstatic notices and undoubtedly will duplicate the success it had in the American theatre.

Shortly after *West Side Story* had opened in 1957, Harold Prince and Stephen Sondheim first came up with the notion of collaborating on a musical with a score made up entirely of waltzes. But unable to find a suitable property, they put the notion aside to work on other projects. After their prize-winning *Follies* had opened in 1971, they resumed their search for a basis for their "waltz" musical. They asked Hugh Wheeler to aid them in their search, but it was Sondheim who recalled Ingmar Bergman's 1956 film, *Smiles of a Summer Night*, one of the film maker's few comedies. The three men screened the film and immediately knew they had found the right property. Mr. Bergman was approached and sold the rights when he was assured that the producer did not intend "a rigid adaptation" of his film, but rather a musical freely suggested by it. Thus, *A Little Night Music* was born, "a stylish celebration of romantic love, set in the enchanted birch groves of Sweden at the turn of the century."

Hugh Wheeler was born in London on March 19, 1916, the son of a civil servant. He was educated at Clayesmore School and the University of London, graduating in 1936. A naturalized American citizen, he has resided in this country for more than thirty years. It was shortly after coming here that he began a vastly successful career as a mystery writer under the pseudonyms Patrick Quentin and Q. Patrick, and four of his novels—*Black Widow, Man in the Net, The Green-Eyed Monster,* and *The Man With Two Wives*—were made into motion pictures.

Mr. Wheeler emerged under his true by-line as a playwright of exceptional talent with the 1961 production of *Big Fish, Little Fish* which co-starred Jason Robards, Jr. and Hume Cronyn. His next Broadway venture was *Look, We've Come Through* (1965), followed by an adaptation of Shirley Jackson's *We Have Always Lived in the Castle* (1966).

His other writings have included screenplays for *Something for Everyone* (starring Angela Lansbury), *Cabaret,* and *Travels With My Aunt* with Maggie Smith in the title role.

During the 1973 season, Mr. Wheeler had the distinction of being represented on Broadway with two musical successes, for in addition to *A Little Night Music,* he also coauthored (with Joseph Stein) the book for *Irene* in which Debbie Reynolds made her New York stage debut.

The author's most recent work for the theatre is the new book for the widely-acclaimed revival of Leonard Bernstein's *Candide* which, as of this writing, is well into its second Broadway year.

Stephen Sondheim is, indisputably, the reigning composer-lyricist of the contemporary American musical theatre. (T. E. Kalem described him in *Time* magazine as: "Literate, ironic, playful, enviably clever, altogether professional, Sondheim is a quicksilver wordsmith in the grand tradition of Cole Porter, Noël Coward and Lorenz Hart.")

Beginning the decade with the prize-winning *Company,* his musicals have since won two additional New York Drama Critics' Circle Awards—for *Follies* (book by James Goldman, 1971) and, of course, *A Little Night Music.* Personally, he also has garnered several Tony Awards as well as won every recent poll that has a "best lyricist/composer" category.

Mr. Sondheim was born in New York City on March 22, 1930. He attended Williams College, where he majored in music, and as an undergraduate gained a certain celebrity on campus by writing the book, lyrics and music for two college shows. Winner of the Hutchinson Prize for Musical Composition, after graduation he studied theory and composition with Milton Babbitt.

His first professional writing was done in 1953 when he authored scripts for the *Topper* television series. In 1956, he came to the Broadway theatre with the incidental music for *Girls of Summer,* but it was in the following year that he first commanded major attention with the lyrics for *West Side Story* and, after that, *Gypsy.*

It was in 1962, however, that Stephen Sondheim came full sail into the theatre as both composer and lyricist for *A Funny Thing Happened on the Way to the Forum.* Subsequent productions that were highlighted by Sondheim scores and lyrics include *Anyone Can Whistle* (1964), *Company* (1970), *Follies* (1971), and *A Little Night Music.*

In addition to the aforementioned, Mr. Sondheim (who is the incumbent president of The Dramatists Guild) served as lyricist for *Do I Hear a Waltz?* (book by Arthur Laurents, music by Richard Rodgers, 1965), and as the composer of incidental music for Mr. Laurents' 1960 comedy, *Invitation to a March*.

Most recently, he provided additional lyrics for the new version of *Candide* and his next musical, *Pacific Overtures* (with a book by John Weidman) is scheduled to open in January, 1976, once again under the production auspices of Harold Prince.

In March, 1973, *Sondheim*, a musical tribute, was presented at the Shubert Theatre, New York. It was an impressive celebration of the talents of the composer-lyricist, and an equally impressive demonstration of the way Broadway feels about him. During the gala evening at least two dozen stars performed Sondheim songs from all of his musicals and at the conclusion of the program, Mr. Sondheim thanked the director of the event, "Burt Shevelove, without whom tonight would not have been possible," and "Hal Prince, without whom *I* would not have been possible."

(NOTE: *West Side Story, Gypsy,* and *Company* are included in this editor's previous volume.)

Production Notes

A Little Night Music was first presented by Harold Prince, in association with Ruth Mitchell, at the Shubert Theatre, New York, on February 25, 1973. The cast was as follows:

Mr. Lindquist, *Benjamin Rayson*
Mrs. Nordstrom, *Teri Ralston*
Mrs. Anderssen, *Barbara Lang*
Mr. Erlansen, *Gene Varrone*
Mrs. Segstrom, *Beth Fowler*
Fredrika Armfeldt, *Judy Kahan*
Madame Armfeldt, *Hermione Gingold*
Frid, *her butler, George Lee Andrews*
Henrik Egerman, *Mark Lambert*
Anne Egerman, *Victoria Mallory*

Fredrik Egerman, *Len Cariou*
Petra, *D. Jamin-Bartlett*
Desirée Armfeldt, *Glynis Johns*
Malla, *her maid, Despo*
Bertrand, *a page, Will Sharpe Marshall*
Count Carl-Magnus Malcolm, *Laurence Guittard*
Countess Charlotte Malcolm, *Patricia Elliott*
Osa, *Sherry Mathis*

Production Directed by *Harold Prince*
Choreography by *Patricia Birch*
Scenic Production Designed by *Boris Aronson*
Costumes Designed by *Florence Klotz*
Lighting Designed by *Tharon Musser*
Orchestrations by *Jonathan Tunick*
Musical Direction by *Harold Hastings*

> *Time:* Turn of the Century.
> *Place:* Sweden.

Musical Numbers

Overture	Mr. Lindquist, Mrs. Nordstrom, Mrs. Anderssen, Mr. Erlansen, Mrs. Segstrom

Act One

Night Waltz	Company
Now	Fredrik
Later	Henrik
Soon	Anne, Henrik, Fredrik
The Glamorous Life	Fredrika, Desirée, Malla, Madame Armfeldt, Mrs. Nordstrom, Mrs. Segstrom, Mrs. Anderssen, Mr. Lindquist, Mr. Erlansen
Remember?	Mr. Lindquist, Mrs. Nordstrom, Mrs. Segstrom, Mr. Erlansen, Mrs. Anderssen
You Must Meet My Wife	Desirée, Fredrik
Liaisons	Madame Armfeldt
In Praise of Women	Carl-Magnus
Every Day A Little Death	Charlotte, Anne
A Weekend In The Country	Company

Act Two

The Sun Won't Set	Mrs. Anderssen, Mrs. Segstrom, Mrs. Nordstrom, Mr. Lindquist, Mr. Erlansen
It Would Have Been Wonderful	Fredrik, Carl-Magnus
Perpetual Anticipation	Mrs. Nordstrom, Mrs. Segstrom, Mrs. Anderssen
Send In The Clowns	Desirée
The Miller's Son	Petra
Finale	Company

&

Before the houselights are down, MR. LINDQUIST *appears and sits at the piano. He removes his gloves, plunks a key, and begins to vocalize.* MRS. NORDSTROM *enters, hits a key on the piano, and vocalizes with him.* MRS. ANDERSSEN, MR. ERLANSEN *and* MRS. SEGSTROM *come out and join the vocalizing.*

MEN:
　La, La La La
　La, La La La

GIRLS:
　La, La La La
　La, La La La

MRS. NORDSTROM:
　The old deserted beach that we walked—
　Remember?

MR. ERLANSEN:
Remember?
The cafe in the park where we talked—
Remember?

MRS. ANDERSSEN:
Remember?
The tenor on the boat that we chartered,
Belching "The Bartered Bride"—

ALL:
Ah, how we laughed,
Ah, how we cried,

MR. LINDQUIST:
Ah, how you promised
And
Ah, how
I lied.

GIRLS and MEN:
La, La La La

Ah . . .
Lie . . . lie . . . lie . . .

MRS. SEGSTROM:
That dilapidated inn—
Remember, darling?

MR. ERLANSEN:
The proprietress' grin,
Also her glare.

MRS. NORDSTROM:
Yellow gingham on the bed—
Remember, darling?

MR. LINDQUIST:
And the canopy in red,
Needing repair.

ALL:
Soon, I promise.
Soon I won't shy away,
Dear old—
Soon. I want to.
Soon, whatever you say.
Even

GIRLS:
Now
When we're close and
We
Touch
And you're kissing my
Brow,
I don't mind it
Too much.
And you'll have to

MEN:
Now, when we touch,

Touching my brow,

Ahhhh . . .

ALL:

Admit I'm endearing,
I help keep things humming,
I'm not domineering,
What's one small shortcoming?

And

Unpack the luggage, La La La
Pack up the luggage, La La La
Unpack the luggage, La La La
Hi-ho, the glamorous life!
Unpack the luggage, La La La
Pack up the luggage, La La La
Unpack the luggage, La La La
Hi-ho, the glamorous life!

MR. LINDQUIST:
Ahhhh . . .

OTHER MEMBERS OF QUINTET:
Unpack the luggage, La La La
Pack up the luggage, La La La

MRS. NORDSTROM:
Ahhhh . . .

OTHER MEMBERS OF THE QUINTET:
Unpack the luggage, La La La
Hi-ho, the glamorous life!

ALL:

Bring up the curtain, La La La
Bring down the curtain, La La La
Bring up the curtain, La La La

ALL:

Hi-ho, hi-ho
For the glamorous life!

(After the applause, the QUINTET *starts to waltz. The show curtain flies out, revealing the* MAIN CHARACTERS *doing a strangely surreal waltz of their own, in which partners change partners and recouple with others. The* QUINTET *drifts up into the waltzing* COUPLES, *and reappears to hum accompaniment for the last section of the dance.* FREDRIKA *wanders through the waltz, too, watching)*

ACT ONE

PROLOGUE

At the end of the Opening Waltz, MADAME ARMFELDT *is brought on in her wheelchair by her butler,* FRID. *In her lap is a tray containing a silver cigarette box, a small vase with four yellow bud-roses, and the cards with which she is playing solitaire. She is watched by* FREDRIKA ARMFELDT, *thirteen—a grave, very self-contained and formal girl with the precise diction of the convent-trained.*

FREDRIKA: If you cheated a little, it would come out.

MADAME ARMFELDT: *(Continuing to play)* Solitaire is the only thing in life that demands absolute honesty. As a woman who has numbered kings among her lovers, I think my word can be taken on that point. *(She motions to* FRID, *who crosses down and lights her cigarette)* What was I talking about?

FREDRIKA: You said I should watch.

MADAME ARMFELDT: Watch—what?

FREDRIKA: It sounds very unlikely to me, but you said I should watch for the night to smile.

MADAME ARMFELDT: Everything is unlikely, dear, so don't let that deter you. Of course the summer night smiles. Three times.

FREDRIKA: But how does it smile?

MADAME ARMFELDT: Good heavens, what sort of a nanny did you have?

FREDRIKA: None, really. Except Mother, and the other actresses in the company —and the stage manager.

MADAME ARMFELDT: Stage managers are not nannies. They don't have the talent.

FREDRIKA: But if it happens—how does it happen?

MADAME ARMFELDT: You get a feeling. Suddenly the jasmine starts to smell stronger, then a frog croaks—then all the stars in Orion wink. Don't squeeze your bosoms against the chair, dear. It'll stunt their growth. And then where would you be?

FREDRIKA: But why does it smile, Grandmother?

MADAME ARMFELDT: At the follies of human beings, of course. The first smile smiles at the young, who know nothing. *(She looks pointedly at* FREDRIKA*)* The second, at the fools who know too little, like Desirée.

FREDRIKA: Mother isn't a fool.

MADAME ARMFELDT: *(Going right on)* Um hum. And the third at the old who know too much—like me. *(The game is over without coming out. Annoyed at the cards,* MADAME ARMFELDT *scatters them at random, and barks at* FRID*)* Frid, time for my nap.

FREDRIKA: *(Intrigued in spite of herself, gazes out at the summer night)* Grand- mother, might it really smile tonight?

MADAME ARMFELDT: Why not? Now, practice your piano, dear, preferably with the soft pedal down. And as a treat tonight at dinner, I shall tell you amusing stories about my liaison with the Baron de Signac, who was, to put it mildly, peculiar.

(FRID wheels her off and FREDRIKA *goes to sit at the piano)*

SCENE 1

The Egerman rooms.

Two rooms: the parlor and the master bedroom, indicated on different levels. ANNE EGERMAN, *a ravishingly pretty girl of eighteen, is on the bed. She goes to the vanity table, toys with her hair, and then enters the parlor.* HENRIK EGERMAN, *her stepson, a brooding young man of nineteen, is seated on the sofa, playing his cello. Beside him on the sofa is a book with a ribbon marker.* ANNE *looks at* HENRIK, *then leans over the sofa to get his attention.*

ANNE: Oh Henrik, dear, don't you have anything less gloomy to practice?

HENRIK: It isn't gloomy, it's profound.

ANNE: *(Reaches down, takes* HENRIK'S *book, and begins reading from it)* ". . . in discussing temptation, Martin Luther says: 'You cannot prevent the birds from flying over your head, but you can prevent them from nesting in your hair.'"

Oh dear, that's gloomy too! Don't they teach you anything at the seminary a little more cheerful?

HENRIK: *(Grand)* A man who's going to serve in God's Army must learn all the ruses and stratagems of the Enemy.

ANNE: *(Giggling)* And which of your professors made that historic statement?

HENRIK: *(Caught out)* Pastor Ericson, as a matter of fact. He says we're like generals learning to win battles against the devil.
(Her ball of silk falls off her lap)

ANNE: Oh dear, my ball! *(HENRIK bends down to pick up the ball. He stands beside her, obviously overwhelmed by her nearness. ANNE pats her lap)* You can put it there, you know. My lap isn't one of the Devil's snares.
(Flushing, HENRIK drops the ball into her lap and moves away from her)

HENRIK: Anne, I was wondering—could we go for a walk?

ANNE: Now?

HENRIK: I've so much to tell you. What I've been thinking, and everything.

ANNE: Silly Henrik, don't you realize it's almost tea-time? And I think I hear your father. *(She rises, puts down the ball of silk)* I'm sure you've made the most wonderful discoveries about life, and I long to talk, but—later. *(FREDRIK enters, followed by PETRA)* Fredrik dear!

HENRIK: *(Mutters to himself)* Later.

ANNE: Look who's come home to us—holier than ever.

FREDRIK: Hello, son. How was the examination?

HENRIK: Well, as a matter of fact . . .

FREDRIK: *(Breaking in)* You passed with flying colors, of course.

ANNE: First on the list.

HENRIK: *(Trying again)* And Pastor Ericson said . . .

FREDRIK: *(Breaking in)* Splendid—you must give us a full report. Later.

ANNE: He'd better be careful or he'll go straight to heaven before he has a chance to save any sinners.

FREDRIK: Don't tease him, dear.

ANNE: Oh, Henrik likes to be teased, don't you, Henrik? Fredrik, do you want your tea now?

FREDRIK: Not now, I think. It's been rather an exhausting day in Court and as we have a long evening ahead of us, I feel a little nap is indicated. *(He produces theater tickets from his pocket)*

ANNE: *(Grabbing at them, delighted as a child)* Tickets for the theater!

FREDRIK: It's a French comedy. I thought it might entertain you.

ANNE: It's "Woman Of The World," isn't it? With Desireé Armfeldt! She's on all the posters! Oh, Fredrik, how delicious! *(To HENRIK, teasing)* What shall I wear? My blue with the feathers— *(FREDRIK pours water)* genuine angel's feathers—? Or the yellow? Ah, I know. My pink, with the bosom. And Henrik, you can do me up in the back. *(She goes into the bedroom)*

FREDRIK: I'm sorry, son. I should have remembered you were coming home and got a third ticket. But then perhaps a French comedy is hardly suitable. *(He takes a pill)*

HENRIK: *(Outburst)* Why does everyone laugh at me? Is it so ridiculous to want to do some good in this world?

FREDRIK: I'm afraid being young in itself can be a trifle ridiculous. Good has to be so good, bad so bad. Such superlatives!

HENRIK: But to be old, I suppose, is not ridiculous.

FREDRIK: *(Sigh)* Ah, let's not get into that. I love you very much, you know. So does Anne—in her way. But you can't expect her to take your mother's place. She's young, too; she has not yet learned . . .

HENRIK: . . . to suffer fools gladly?

FREDRIK: *(Gentle)* You said that, son. Not I.

ANNE: Fredrik! *(As FREDRIK moves into the bedroom, HENRIK picks up his book and reads. ANNE is buffing her nails)* You were sweet to think of the theater for me.

FREDRIK: I'll enjoy it, too.

ANNE: Who wouldn't—when all the posters call her The One And Only Desirée Armfeldt? *(FREDRIK begins to try to kiss her. She rattles on)* I wonder what it would feel like to be a One and Only! The One and Only—Anne Egerman! *(She leaves FREDRIK on the bed and moves to the vanity table. As aware as he is of her rejection)* Poor Fredrik! Do I still make you happy? After eleven months? I know I'm foolish to be so afraid—and you've been so patient, but, soon—I promise. Oh, I know you think I'm too silly to worry, but I do . . . *(As FREDRIK looks up to answer, she gives a little cry)* Oh no! For heaven's sakes, can that be a pimple coming?

(FREDRIK, deflated, begins to sing)

FREDRIK: *(Singing)*
> *Now, as the sweet imbecilities*
> *Tumble so lavishly*
> *Onto her lap . . .*

ANNE: Oh Fredrik, what a day it's been! Unending drama! While Petra was brushing my hair, the doorbell . . .

FREDRIK:
> *Now, there are two possibilities:*
> *A, I could ravish her,*
> *B, I could nap.*

ANNE: . . . that grumpy old Mrs. Nordstrom from next door. Her sister's coming for a visit.

FREDRIK:
> *Say it's the ravishment, then we see*
> *The option*
> *That follows, of course:*

ANNE: . . . do hope I'm imperious enough with the servants. I try to be. But half the time I think they're laughing at me.

FREDRIK:
> *A, the deployment of charm, or B,*
> *The adoption*
> *Of physical force.*

(Music)

> *Now B might arouse her,*
> *But if I assume*

I trip on my trouser
Leg crossing the room . . .

(Music)

Her hair getting tangled,
Her stays getting snapped,
My nerves will be jangled,
My energy sapped . . .

(Music)

Removing her clothing
Would take me all day
And her subsequent loathing
Would turn me away—
Which eliminates B
And which leaves us with A.

ANNE: Could you ever be jealous of me?

FREDRIK:
Now, insofar as approaching it,
What would be festive
But have its effect?

ANNE: Shall I learn Italian? I think it would be amusing, if the verbs aren't too irregular.

FREDRIK:
Now, there are two ways of broaching it:
A, the suggestive
And B, the direct.

ANNE: . . . but then French is a much chic-er language. Everyone says so. *Parlez-vous Français?*

FREDRIK:
Say that I settle on B, to wit,
A charmingly
Lecherous mood . . .

(Music)

A, I could put on my nightshirt or sit
Disarmingly,
B, in the nude . . .

(Music)

That might be effective,
My body's all right—
But not in perspective
And not in the light . . .

(Music)

I'm bound to be chilly
And feel a buffoon,

But nightshirts are silly
In midafternoon . . .

(Music)

Which leaves the suggestive,
But how to proceed?
Although she gets restive,
Perhaps I could read . . .

(Music)

In view of her penchant
For something romantic,
De Sade is too trenchant
And Dickens too frantic,
And Stendhal would ruin
The plan of attack,
As there isn't much blue in
"The Red and the Black."

(Music)

De Maupassant's candor
Would cause her dismay.
The Brontës are grander
But not very gay.
Her taste is much blander,
I'm sorry to say,
But is Hans Christian Ander-
Sen ever risque?
Which eliminates A.

(Exits upstage)

ANNE: And he said, "You're such a pretty lady!" Wasn't that silly?

FREDRIK: *(As he walks back on)*

Now, with my mental facilities
Partially muddied
And ready to snap . . .

ANNE: *(At the jewel box now)* . . . I'm sure about the bracelet. But earrings, earrings! *Which* earrings?

FREDRIK:
Now, though there are possibilities
Still to be studied,
I might as well nap . . .

ANNE: Mother's rubies? . . . Oh, the diamonds are—Agony! I know . . .

FREDRIK:
Bow though I must
To adjust
My original plan . . .

ANNE: Desirée Armfeldt—I just know she'll wear the most glamorous gowns!

FREDRIK:

How shall I sleep
Half as deep
As I usually can? . . .

ANNE: Dear, distinguished old Fredrik!

FREDRIK:

When now I still want and/or love you,
Now, as always,
Now,
Anne?

(FREDRIK turns over and goes to sleep. They remain frozen. PETRA, twenty-one, the charming, easy-going maid, enters the parlor)

PETRA: Nobody rang. Doesn't he want his tea?

HENRIK: *(Still deep in book)* They're taking a nap.

PETRA: *(Coming up behind him, teasingly ruffling his hair)* You smell of soap.

HENRIK: *(Pulling his head away)* I'm reading.

PETRA: *(Caressing his head)* Do those old teachers take a scrubbing brush to you every morning and scrub you down like a dray horse? *(Strokes his ear)*

HENRIK: *(Fierce)* Get away from me!

PETRA: *(Jumping up in mock alarm)* Oh, what a wicked woman I am! I'll go straight to hell! *(Starting away, she goes toward the door, deliberately wiggling her hips)*

HENRIK: *(Looking up, even fiercer)* And don't walk like that!

PETRA: *(Innocent)* Like—what? *(Wiggles even more)* Like this?

HENRIK: *(Pleadingly)* Stop it. Stop it?

(He rises, goes after her, clutches her, and starts savagely, clumsily, to kiss her and fumble at her breasts. She slaps his hand)

PETRA: Careful! *(Breaks away)* That's a new blouse! A whole week's wages and the lace extra! *(Looks at him)* Poor little Henrik! *(Then affectionately pats his cheek)* Later! You'll soon get the knack of it!

(She exits. HENRIK puts down the book, gets his cello and begins to sing, accompanying himself on the cello)

HENRIK:

Later . . .
When is later? . . .
All you ever hear is "Later, Henrik! Henrik, later . . ."
"Yes, we know, Henrik.
Oh, Henrik—
Everyone agrees, Henrik—
Please, Henrik!"
You have a thought you're fairly bursting with,
A personal discovery or problem, and it's
"What's your rush, Henrik?
Shush, Henrik—
Goodness, how you gush, Henrik—
Hush, Henrik!"

You murmur,
"I only . . .
It's just that . . .
For God's sake!"
"Later, Henrik . . ."

"Henrik" . . .
Who is "Henrik?" . . .
Oh, that lawyer's son, the one who mumbles—
Short and boring,
Yes, he's hardly worth ignoring
And who cares if he's all dammed—

(Looks up)

—I beg your pardon—
Up inside?
As I've
Often stated,
It's intolerable
Being tolerated.
"Reassure Henrik,
Poor Henrik."
"Henrik, you'll endure
Being pure, Henrik."

Though I've been born, I've never been!
How can I wait around for later?
I'll be ninety on my deathbed
And the late, or rather later,
Henrik Egerman!

Doesn't anything begin?

(ANNE, in the bedroom, gets up from the vanity table and stands near the bed, singing to FREDRIK)

ANNE:
Soon, I promise.
Soon I won't shy away,
Dear old—

(She bites her lip)

Soon. I want to.
Soon, whatever you say.
Even now,
When you're close and we touch,
And you're kissing my brow,
I don't mind it too much.
And you'll have to admit
I'm endearing,
I help keep things humming,
I'm not domineering,

What's one small shortcoming?
And think of how I adore you,
Think of how much you love me.
If I were perfect for you,
Wouldn't you tire of me
Soon,
All too soon?
Dear old—

(The sound of HENRIK'S *cello.* FREDRIK *stirs noisily in bed.* ANNE *goes into the parlor)*

Henrik! That racket! Your father's sleeping!

(She remains, half-innocent, half-coquettish, in her negligee. For a second, ANNE *watches him. She closes her nightgown at the neck and goes back into the bedroom)*

ANNE: *(Back at the bed)*
   Soon—

HENRIK:
   "Later" . . .

ANNE:
   I promise.

HENRIK:
   When is "later?"

(Simultaneously)

ANNE:	HENRIK:
Soon	*"Later, Henrik, later."*
I won't shy	*All you ever hear is,*
Away,	*"Yes, we know, Henrik, oh, Henrik,*
Dear old—	*Everyone agrees, Henrik, please, Henrik!"*

*(*FREDRIK *stirs. Simultaneously)*

ANNE:	HENRIK:	FREDRIK:
Soon.	*"Later"* . . .	*Now,*
I want to.	*When is "later?"*	*As the sweet*
Soon,	*All you ever*	*imbecilities*
	Hear is	*Trip on my trouser leg,*
Whatever you	*"Later, Henrik,*	
Say.		
		Stendahl
		eliminates
	Later."	*A,*
	As I've often	
	Stated	*But*
	When?	*When?*

ANNE:	HENRIK:	FREDRIK:
Even	*Maybe*	*Maybe*
Now,		
When you're close	*Soon, soon*	*Later,*
And we touch	*I'll be ninety*	
	And	
And you're kissing	*Dead.*	*When I'm kissing*
My brow		
I don't mind it		*Your brow*
Too much,	*I don't mind it*	*And I'm stroking*
	Too much,	*your head,*
		You'll come into
		my bed.
And you'll have	*Since I have to*	*And you have to*
To admit	*Admit*	*Admit*
I'm endearing,	*I find peering*	*I've been bearing*
I help	*Through life's*	*All those*
Keep things	*Gray windows*	*tremulous cries*
Humming, I'm	*Impatiently*	*Patiently.*
Not domineering,	*Not very cheering.*	*Not interfering*
What's one small	*Do I fear death?*	*With those*
		tremulous thighs.
Shortcoming?	*Let it*	
And	*Come to me*	*Come to me*
Think of how	*Now,*	*Soon,*
I adore you		
Think of how	*Now,*	*Soon,*
Much you love me.		
If I were perfect	*Now,*	*Soon,*
For you,		
Wouldn't you tire	*Now.*	*Soon.*
Of me		
Later?	*Come to me*	*Come to me*
	Soon. If I'm	*Soon,*
	Dead,	
We will,	*I can*	
Later.	*Wait.*	*Straight to me,*
		never mind
	How can I	*How.*
We will . . .	*Live until*	*Darling,*
Soon.	*Later?*	*Now—*
		I still want and/or
	Later . . .	*Love*
		You,
Soon.		
		Now, as
	Later . . .	*Always,*

ANNE:
 Soon.

FREDRIK:
 Now,
  (He does a kiss)
 Desirée

(ANNE stares out, astonished, as the lights go down. FREDRIKA, still at the piano, is playing scales)

FREDRIKA: *(Singing)*
 Ordinary mothers lead ordinary lives:
 Keep the house and sweep the parlor,
 Cook the meals and look exhausted.
 Ordinary mothers, like ordinary wives,
 Fry the eggs and dry the sheets and
 Try to deal with facts.

 Mine acts.

(DESIRÉE sweeps on with MALLA in tow. MALLA carries a wig box, suitcase, and parasol)

DESIRÉE: *(Singing)*
 Darling, I miss you a lot
 But, darling, this has to be short
 As mother is getting a plaque
 From the Halsingborg Arts Council
 Amateur Theatre Group.
 Whether it's funny or not,
 I'll give you a fuller report
 The minute they carry me back
 From the Halsingborg Arts Council
 Amateur Theatre Group . . .
 Love you . . .

(THE QUINTET appears)

QUINTET:
 Unpack the luggage, La La La
 Pack up the luggage, La La La
 Unpack the luggage, La La La
 Hi-ho, the glamorous life!

MRS. SEGSTROM:
 Ice in the basin, La La La

MR. ERLANSEN:
 Cracks in the plaster, La La La

MRS. ANDERSSEN:
 Mice in the hallway, La La La

THE QUINTET:
 Hi-ho, the glamorous life!

MEN:
 Run for the carriage, La La La

WOMEN:
Wolf down the sandwich, La La La

THE QUINTET:
Which town is this one? La, La, La
Hi-ho, the glamorous life!

(FRID *wheels* MADAM ARMFELDT *onstage*)

MADAME ARMFELDT: *(Singing)*
Ordinary daughters ameliorate their lot,
Use their charms and choose their futures,
Breed their children, heed their mothers.
Ordinary daughters, which mine, I fear, is not,
Tend each asset, spend it wisely
While it still endures . . .

Mine tours.

DESIRÉE: *(Singing)*
Mother, forgive the delay,
My schedule is driving me wild.
But, mother, I really must run,
I'm performing in Rottvik
And don't ask where is it, please.
How are you feeling today
And are you corrupting the child?
Don't. Mother, the minute I'm done
With performing in Rottvik,
I'll come for a visit
And argue.

MEN:
Mayors with speeches, La La La

WOMEN:
Children with posies, La La La

MEN:
Half-empty houses, La La La

ALL THE QUINTET:
Hi-ho, the glamorous life!

MRS. NORDSTROM:
Cultural lunches,

ALL THE QUINTET:
La La La

MRS. ANDERSSEN:
Dead floral tributes,

ALL THE QUINTET:
La La La

MR. LINDQUIST:
Ancient admirers,

ALL THE QUINTET:
La La La
Hi-ho, the glamorous life!

DESIRÉE:
Pack up the luggage, La La La!
Unpack the luggage, La La La
Mother's surviving, La La La
Leading the glamorous life!

(Holds up a mirror)

Cracks in the plaster, La La La
Youngish admirers, La La La
Which one was that one? La La La
Hi-ho, the glamorous life!

DESIRÉE and THE QUINTET:
Bring up the curtain, La La La
Bring down the curtain, La La La
Bring up the curtain, La La La
Hi-ho, the glamorous . . .
Life.

SCENE 2

Stage of local theater.
The show curtain is down. Two stage boxes are visible. Sitting in one are MR.
LINDQUIST, MRS. NORDSTROM, *and* MR. ERLANSEN. ANNE *and* FREDRIK *enter,*
and speak as they walk to their box.
ANNE: Does she look like her pictures?
FREDRIK: Who, dear?
ANNE: Desirée Armfeldt, of course.
FREDRIK: How would I know, dear?
ANNE: *(Pause)* I only thought . . .
FREDRIK: You only thought—what?
ANNE: Desirée is not a common name. I mean, none of your typists and things
   are called Desirée, are they?
FREDRIK: My typists and things in descending order of importance are Miss Osa
   Svensen, Miss Ona Nilsson, Miss Gerda Bjornson, *and* Mrs. Amalia Lindquist.
   (A PAGE enters, and knocks three times with the staff he is carrying. The show
   curtain rises revealing the stage behind it, a tatty Louis XIV "salon." For a moment
   it is empty. Then TWO LADIES, in rather shabby court costumes, enter)
FIRST LADY: (MRS. SEGSTROM) Tell me something about this remarkable Count-
   ess, Madame.
SECOND LADY: (MRS. ANDERSSEN) I shall try as best I can to depict the personality of the Countess, Madame, although it is too rich in mysterious contra-
   dictions to be described in a few short moments.
FIRST LADY: It is said that her power over men is most extraordinary.
SECOND LADY: There is a great deal of truth in that, Madame, and her lovers
   are as many as the pearls in the necklace which she always wears.
FIRST LADY: Your own husband, Madame, is supposed to be one of the handsomest pearls, is he not?

SECOND LADY: He fell in love with the Countess on sight. She took him as a lover for three months and after that I had him back.

FIRST LADY: And your marriage was crushed?

SECOND LADY: On the contrary, Madame! My husband had become a tender, devoted, admirable lover, a faithful husband and an exemplary father. The Countess' lack of decency is most moral.

(THE PAGE re-enters)

PAGE: The Countess Célimène de Francen de la Tour de Casa.

(The COUNTESS—DESIRÉE—*makes her sensational entrance. A storm of applause greets her.* FREDRIK *claps.* ANNE *does* not *as she glares at the stage.*

During the applause, DESIRÉE *makes a deep curtsey, during which, old pro that she is, she cases the house. Her eye falls on* FREDRIK. *She does a take and instantly* all action *freezes)*

MR. LINDQUIST: *(Sings)*
Remember?

MRS. NORDSTROM: *(Sings)*
Remember?

(MR. LINDQUIST and MRS. NORDSTROM leave the stage box)

MRS. NORDSTROM:
The old deserted beach that we walked—
Remember?

MR. LINDQUIST:
Remember?
The cafe in the park where we talked—
Remember?

MRS. NORDSTROM:
Remember?

MR. LINDQUIST:
The tenor on the boat that we chartered,
Belching "The Bartered Bride"—

BOTH:
Ah, how we laughed,
Ah, how we cried.

MR. LINDQUIST:
Ah, how you promised and
Ah, how I lied.

MRS. NORDSTROM:
That dilapidated inn—
Remember, darling?

MR. LINDQUIST:
The proprietress' grin,
Also her glare . . .

MRS. NORDSTROM:
Yellow gingham on the bed—
Remember, darling?

MR. LINDQUIST:
> *And the canopy in red,*
> *Needing repair?*

BOTH:
> *I think you were there.*

(They return to the stage box and the action continues)

ANNE: *(Fierce, to* FREDRIK*)* She looked at us. Why did she look at us?

DESIRÉE: *(To* SECOND LADY*)* Dear Madame Merville, what a charming mischance to find you here this evening.

FREDRIK: I don't think she looked especially at us.

ANNE: She did! She peered, then she smiled.	SECOND LADY: Charming, indeed, dear Celimène.

SECOND LADY: May I be permitted to present my school friend from the provinces? Madame Vilmorac—whose husband, I'm sure, is in dire need of a little expert polishing.

FIRST LADY: Oh, dear Countess, you are all but a legend to me. I implore you to reveal to me the secret of your success with the hardier sex!

ANNE: She smiled at us! *(Grabs* FREDRIK'S *opera glasses and studies the stage)*

DESIRÉE: Dear Madame, that can be summed up in a single word—

ANNE: She's ravishingly beautiful.

FREDRIK: Make-up.

DESIRÉE: —dignity.

TWO LADIES: Dignity?

ANNE: *(Turning on* FREDRIK*)* How can you be sure—if you've never seen her?

FREDRIK: Hush!

DESIRÉE: *(Playing her first-act set speech)* Dignity. We women have a right to commit any crime toward our husbands, our lovers, our sons, as long as we do not hurt their dignity. We should make men's dignity our best ally and caress it, cradle it, speak tenderly to it, and handle it as our most delightful toy. Then a man is in our hands, at our feet, or anywhere else we momentarily wish him to be.

ANNE: *(Sobbing)* I want to go home!	FREDRIK: Anne!

ANNE: I want to go home!

FREDRIK: Anne!

(They run off)

SCENE 3

The Egerman rooms.

In the parlor, PETRA, *lying on the couch, is calmly rearranging her blouse.* HENRIK, *in a storm of tension, is pulling on his trousers. On the floor beside them is a bottle of champagne and two glasses.*

HENRIK: We have sinned, and it was a complete failure! *(Struggling with his fly buttons)* These buttons, these insufferable buttons!

PETRA: Here dear, let me. *(She crosses, kneels in front of him, and starts to do up the fly buttons)* Don't you worry, little Henrik. Just let it rest a while. *(She pats his fly)* There. Now you put on your sweater and do a nice little quiet bit of reading. *(She gets his sweater from the back of a chair and helps him into it.* ANNE *enters, still crying. She sees* HENRIK *and* PETRA, *lets out a sob, and runs into the bedroom.* FREDRIK *enters)*

PETRA: *(Perfectly calm, to* FREDRIK*)* My, that was a short play.

FREDRIK: My wife became ill; I had to bring her home. *(He gives* HENRIK *a look, sizing up the situation approvingly, before following* ANNE *into the bedroom)* Anne!

(HENRIK starts again toward PETRA, *who avoids him)*

PETRA: No, lamb. I told you. Give it a nice rest and you'll be surprised how perky it'll be by morning.

(She wriggles her way out. FREDRIK *has now entered the bedroom,* ANNE *is no longer visible—as if she had moved into an inner room. In the parlor,* HENRIK *picks up the champagne bottle and glasses and puts them on the table)*

ANNE: *(Off. Calling)* Fredrik!

FREDRIK: Yes, dear.

ANNE: *(Off)* Did you have many women between your first wife and me? Sometimes when I think of what memories you have, I vanish inside.

FREDRIK: Before I met you I was quite a different man. Many things were different. Better? *(ANNE comes back into the bedroom)* Worse? Different, anyway.

ANNE: Do you remember when I was a little girl and you came to my father's house for dinner and told me fairy tales? Do you remember?

FREDRIK: Yes, I remember.

ANNE: *(Sitting on* FREDRIK'S *lap)* Then you were "Uncle Fredrik" and now you're my husband. Isn't that amusing? You were so lonely and sad that summer. I felt terribly sorry for you, so I said: Poor thing, I'll marry him. Are you coming to bed yet?

FREDRIK: Not just yet. I think I'll go out for a breath of fresh air.

ANNE: That wasn't an amusing play, was it?

FREDRIK: We didn't see that much of it.

ANNE: I wonder how old that Armfeldt woman can be. At least fifty—don't you think?

FREDRIK: I wouldn't say that old.

ANNE: Well, goodnight.

FREDRIK: Goodnight.

(As FREDRIK *moves into the parlor,* MR. LINDQUIST *and* MRS. NORDSTROM *appear. There is a musical sting and* FREDRIK *[and* HENRIK*] freeze)*

MRS. NORDSTROM: *(Sings)*
Remember?

MR. LINDQUIST: *(Sings)*
Remember?

BOTH:
Remember?
Remember?

(FREDRIK unfreezes, clasps his hands together and goes into the parlor. HENRIK *looks anxiously at his* FATHER*)*

HENRIK: Is she all right now?

FREDRIK: Oh yes, she's all right.

HENRIK: It wasn't anything serious?

FREDRIK: No, nothing serious.

HENRIK: You don't think—a doctor? I mean, it would be terrible if it was some-thing—serious.

FREDRIK: Pray for her, son. Correction—pray for me. Goodnight.

HENRIK: Goodnight, father.

(FREDRIK *exits, and* MRS. NORDSTROM *and* MR. LINDQUIST *sweep down-stage)*

MRS. NORDSTROM: *(Sings)*
The local village dance on the green—
Remember?

MR. LINDQUIST: *(Sings)*
Remember?
The lady with the large tambourine—
Remember?

MRS. NORDSTROM:
Remember?
The one who played the harp in her boa
Thought she was so a-
Dept.

BOTH:
Ah, how we laughed,
Ah, how we wept.
Ah, how we polka'd

MRS. NORDSTROM:
And ah, how we slept.
How we kissed and how we clung—
Remember, darling?

MR. LINDQUIST:
We were foolish, we were young—

BOTH:
More than we knew.

MRS. NORDSTROM:
Yellow gingham on the bed,
Remember, darling?
And the canopy in red,

MR. LINDQUIST:
Or was it blue?

(MRS. NORDSTROM *and* MR. LINDQUIST *are joined by* MRS. SEGSTROM, MRS. ANDERSSEN *and* MR. ERLANSEN, *who appear downstage)*

MRS. SEGSTROM:
The funny little games that we played—
Remember?

MR. ERLANSEN:
Remember?
The unexpected knock of the maid—
Remember?

MRS. ANDERSSEN:
Remember?
The wine that made us both rather merry
And, oh, so very
Frank.

ALL:
Ah, how we laughed.
Ah, how we drank.

MR. ERLANSEN:
You acquiesced

MRS. ANDERSSEN:
And the rest is a blank.

MR. LINDQUIST:
What we did with your perfume—

MR. ERLANSEN:
Remember, darling?

MRS. SEGSTROM:
The condition of the room
When we were through . . .

MRS. NORDSTROM:
Our inventions were unique—
Remember, darling?

MR. LINDQUIST:
I was limping for a week,
You caught the flu . . .

ALL:
I'm sure *it was—*
You.

(They drift off as DESIRÉE'S *digs come on)*

SCENE 4

Desirée's digs.
FREDRIK *walks on, as* DESIRÉE, *in a robe, enters, munching a sandwich and carrying a glass of beer.*
FREDRIK: They told me where to find you at the theater.
DESIRÉE: Fredrik!
FREDRIK: Hello, Desirée.
(For a moment they gaze at each other)
DESIRÉE: So it *was* you! I peered and peered and said: "Is it . . . ? Can it be . . . ? Is it possible?" And then, of course, when you walked out after five minutes, I was sure.

FREDRIK: Was my record that bad?

DESIRÉE: Terrible. You walked out on my Hedda in Helsingborg. And on my sensational Phaedra in Ekilstuna.

FREDRIK: *(Standing, looking at her)* Fourteen years!

DESIRÉE: Fourteen years!

FREDRIK: No rancor?

DESIRÉE: Rancor? For a while, a little. But now—no rancor, not a trace. *(Indicating a plate of sandwiches)* Sandwich?

FREDRIK: *(Declining)* Hungry as ever after a performance, I see.

DESIRÉE: Worse. I'm a wolf. Sit down. *(Pouring him a glass of schnapps)* Here. You never said no to schnapps.

(FREDRIK sits down on the love seat. She stands, looking at him)

FREDRIK: About *this* walking out! I'd like to explain.

DESIRÉE: The girl in the pink dress, I imagine.

FREDRIK: You still don't miss a thing, do you?

DESIRÉE: Your wife.

FREDRIK: For the past eleven months. She was so looking forward to the play, she got a little overexcited. She's only eighteen, still almost a child. *(A pause)* I'm waiting.

DESIRÉE: For what?

FREDRIK: For you to tell me what an old fool I've become to have fallen under the spell of youth, beginnings, the blank page.

(Very coolly, DESIRÉE opens the robe, revealing her naked body to him)

DESIRÉE: The page that has been written on—*and* rewritten.

FREDRIK: *(Looking, admiring)* With great style. Some things—schnapps, for example—improve with age.

DESIRÉE: Let us hope that proves true of your little bride. *(She closes the wrapper and stands, still very cool, looking at him)* So you took her home and tucked her up in her cot with her rattle and her woolly penguin.

FREDRIK: Figuratively speaking.

DESIRÉE: And then you came to me.

FREDRIK: I wish you'd ask me why.

DESIRÉE: *(Deadpan)* Why did you come to me?

FREDRIK: For old times' sake? For curiosity? To boast about my wife? To complain about her? Perhaps—Hell, why am I being such a lawyer about it? *(Pause)* This afternoon when I was taking my nap . . .

DESIRÉE: So you take afternoon naps now!

FREDRIK: Hush! . . . I had the most delightful dream.

DESIRÉE: About . . . ?

FREDRIK: . . . you.

DESIRÉE: Ah! What did we do?

FREDRIK: Well, as a matter of fact, we were in that little hotel in Malmo. We'd been basking in the sun all day.

DESIRÉE: *(Suddenly picking it up)* When my back got so burned it was an agony to lie down so you . . . ?

FREDRIK: As vivid as . . . Well, *very* vivid! So you see. My motives for coming here are what might be called—mixed.

(DESIRÉE suddenly bursts into laughter)

FREDRIK: *(Tentative)* Funny?

DESIRÉE: *(Suddenly controlling the laughter, very mock solemn)* No. Not at all.

(There is a pause, distinctly charged with unadmitted sex)

FREDRIK: *(Looking around, slightly uncomfortable)* How familiar all this is.

DESIRÉE: Oh yes, nothing's changed. Uppsala one week. Orebroe the next. The same old inevitable routine.

FREDRIK: But it still has its compensations?

DESIRÉE: Yes—no—no—yes.

FREDRIK: That's a rather ambiguous answer. *(Pause)* You must, at least at times, be lonely.

DESIRÉE: *(Smiling)* Dear Fredrik, if you're inquiring about my love life, rest assured. It's quite satisfactory.

FREDRIK: I see. And—if I may ask—at the moment?

DESIRÉE: A dragoon. A very handsome, very married dragoon with, I'm afraid, the vanity of a peacock, the brain of a pea, but the physical proportions . . .

FREDRIK: Don't specify the vegetable, please. I am easily deflated. *(They both burst into spontaneous laughter)* Oh, Desirée!

DESIRÉE: Fredrik!

(Another charged pause. FREDRIK tries again)

FREDRIK: Desirée, I . . .

DESIRÉE: Yes, dear?

FREDRIK: I—er . . . That is . . . *(Loses his nerve again)* Perhaps a little more schnapps?

DESIRÉE: Help yourself.

(FREDRIK crosses to the writing desk, where, next to the schnapps, is a framed photograph of FREDRIKA. He notices it)

FREDRIK: Who's this?

DESIRÉE: *(Suddenly rather awkward)* That? Oh—my daughter.

FREDRIK: Your daughter? I had no idea . . .

DESIRÉE: She happened.

FREDRIK: She's charming. Where is she now?

DESIRÉE: She's with my mother in the country. She used to tour with me, and then one day Mother swept up like the Wrath of God and saved her from me —You never knew my mother! She always wins *our* battles. *(Wanting to get off the subject)* I think perhaps a little schnapps for me, too.

FREDRIK: Oh yes, of course.

(FREDRIK pours a second schnapps. The charged pause again)

DESIRÉE: *(Indicating the room)* I apologize for all this squalor!

FREDRIK: On the contrary, I have always associated you—very happily—with chaos. *(Pause)* So.

DESIRÉE: So.

FREDRIK: *(Artificially bright)* Well, I think it's time to talk about my wife, don't you?

DESIRÉE: Boast or complain?

FREDRIK: Both, I expect.

(Singing)
She lightens my sadness,
She livens my days,

She bursts with a kind of madness
My well-ordered ways.
My happiest mistake,
The ache of my life:
You must meet my wife.

She bubbles with pleasure,
She glows with surprise,
Disrupts my accustomed leisure
And ruffles my ties.
I don't know even now
Quite how it began.
You must meet my wife, my Anne.

One thousand whims to which I give in,
Since her smallest tear turns me ashen.
I never dreamed that I could live in
So completely demented,
Contented
A fashion.

So unlike, so winning,
So unlike a wife.
I do think that I'm beginning
To show signs of life.
Don't ask me how at my age
One still can grow—
If you met my wife,
You'd know.

DESIRÉE: Dear Fredrik, I'm just longing to meet her. Sometime.

FREDRIK: *(Singing)*
She sparkles.

DESIRÉE: *(Singing)*
How pleasant.

FREDRIK:
She twinkles.

DESIRÉE:
How nice.

FREDRIK:
Her youth is a sort of present—

DESIRÉE:
Whatever the price.

FREDRIK:
The incandescent—what?—the—

DESIRÉE: *(Proffering a cigarette)*
Light?

FREDRIK:
—of my life!
You must meet my wife.

DESIRÉE:
Yes, I must, I really must. Now—

FREDRIK:
She flutters.

DESIRÉE:
How charming.

FREDRIK:
She twitters.

DESIRÉE:
My word!

FREDRIK:
She floats.

DESIRÉE:
Isn't that alarming?
What is she, a bird?

FREDRIK:
She makes me feel I'm—what?—

DESIRÉE:
A very old man?

FREDRIK:
Yes—no!

DESIRÉE:
No.

FREDRIK:
But—

DESIRÉE:
I must meet your Gertrude.

FREDRIK:
My Anne.

DESIRÉE:
Sorry—Anne.

FREDRIK:
She loves my voice, my walk, my mustache,
The cigar, in fact, that I'm smoking.
She'll watch me puff until it's just ash,
Then she'll save the cigar butt.

DESIRÉE:
Bizarre, but
You're joking.

FREDRIK:
She dotes on—

DESIRÉE:
Your dimple.

FREDRIK:
My snoring.

DESIRÉE:
How dear.

FREDRIK:
The point is, she's really simple.

DESIRÉE: *(Smiling)*
Yes, that much seems clear.

FREDRIK:
She gives me funny names.

DESIRÉE:
Like—?

FREDRIK:
"Old dry-as-dust."

DESIRÉE:
Wouldn't she just?

FREDRIK:
You must meet my wife.

DESIRÉE:
If I must—

(Looks over her shoulder at him and smiles)

Yes, I must.

FREDRIK:
A sea of whims that I submerge in,
Yet so lovable in repentance.
Unfortunately, still a virgin,
But you can't force a flower—

DESIRÉE: *(Rises)*
Don't finish that sentence!
She's monstrous!

FREDRIK:
She's frightened.

DESIRÉE:
Unfeeling!

FREDRIK:
Unversed.
She'd strike you as unenlightened.

DESIRÉE:
No, I'd strike her first.

FREDRIK:
Her reticence, her apprehension—

DESIRÉE:
Her crust!

FREDRIK:
No!

DESIRÉE:
Yes!

FREDRIK:
No!

DESIRÉE:
Fredrik . . .

FREDRIK:
You must meet my wife.

DESIRÉE:
Let me get my hat and my knife.

FREDRIK:
What was that?

DESIRÉE:
I must meet your wife.

FREDRIK: DESIRÉE:
Yes, you must.   *Yes, I must.*

DESIRÉE: *(Speaks)* A virgin.
FREDRIK: A virgin.
DESIRÉE: Eleven months?
FREDRIK: Eleven months.
DESIRÉE: No wonder you dreamed of me!
FREDRIK: At least it was you I dreamed of, which indicates a kind of retroactive fidelity, doesn't it?
DESIRÉE: At least.
FREDRIK: *(Suddenly very shy)* Desirée, I—
DESIRÉE: Yes?
FREDRIK: Would it seem insensitive if I were to ask you—I can't say it!
DESIRÉE: Say it, darling.
FREDRIK: Would you . . . *(He can't)*
DESIRÉE: Of course. What are old friends for? *(She rises, holds out her hand to him. He takes her hand, rises, too)* Wait till you see the bedroom! Stockings all over the place, a rather rusty hip-bath—and the Virgin Mary over the headboard.
(They exit, laughing, into the bedroom. MADAME ARMFELDT appears and sings with one eye on the room)

MADAME ARMFELDT:

At the villa of the Baron de Signac,
Where I spent a somewhat infamous year,
At the villa of the Baron de Signac
I had ladies in attendance,
Fire-opal pendants . . .

Liaisons! What's happened to them?
Liaisons today.
Disgraceful! What's become of them?
Some of them
Hardly pay their shoddy way.

What once was a rare champagne
Is now just an amiable hock,
What once was a villa at least
Is "digs."

What was once a gown with train
Is now just a simple little frock,
What once was a sumptuous feast
Is figs.
No, not even figs—raisins.
Ah, liaisons!

Now let me see . . . Where was I? Oh yes . . .

At the palace of the Duke of Ferrara,
Who was prematurely deaf but a dear,
At the palace of the Duke of Ferrara
I acquired some position
Plus a tiny Titian . . .

Liaisons! What's happened to them?
Liaisons today.
To see them—indiscriminate
Women, it
Pains me more than I can say,
The lack of taste that they display.

Where is style?
Where is skill?
Where is forethought?
Where's discretion of the heart,
Where's passion in the art,
Where's craft?
With a smile
And a will,
But with more thought,
I acquired a chateau
Extravagantly o-
Verstaffed.

Too many people muddle sex with mere desire,
And when emotion intervenes,
The nets descend.
It should on no account perplex, or worse, inspire.
It's but a pleasurable means
To a measurable end.
Why does no one comprehend?
Let us hope this lunacy is just a trend.

Now let me see . . . Where was I? Oh, yes . . .

In the castle of the King of the Belgians,
We would visit through a false chiffonier.
In the castle of the King of the Belgians
Who, when things got rather touchy,
Deeded me a duchy . . .

Liaisons! What's happened to them?
Liaisons today.
Untidy—take my daughter, I
Taught her, I
Tried my best to point the way.
I even named her Desirée.

In a world where the kings are employers,
Where the amateur prevails and delicacy fails to pay,
In a world where the princes are lawyers,
What can anyone expect except to recollect
Liai . . .

(She falls asleep. FRID *appears and carries her off. A beat)*
CARL-MAGNUS: *(Offstage)* All right, all right. It's broken down. So *do* something! Crank it up—or whatever it is!
*(*FREDRIK *and* DESIRÉE *appear at the bedroom door,* FREDRIK *in a bathrobe,* DESIRÉE *in a negligee)*
FREDRIK: What can it be?
DESIRÉE: It can't!
FREDRIK: The dragoon?
DESIRÉE: Impossible. He's on maneuvers. Eighty miles away. He couldn't . . .
CARL-MAGNUS: *(Offstage, bellowing)* A garage, idiot! That's what they're called.
DESIRÉE: He could.
FREDRIK: Is he jealous?
DESIRÉE: Tremendously. *(Suppresses a giggle)* This shouldn't be funny, should it?
FREDRIK: Let him in.
DESIRÉE: Fredrik . . .
FREDRIK: I am not a lawyer—nor are you an actress—for nothing. Let him in.
*(*DESIRÉE *goes to open the door.* CARL-MAGNUS *enters, immaculate but brushing imaginary dust from his uniform. He is carrying a bunch of daisies)*
DESIRÉE: *(With tremendous poise)* Carl-Magnus! What a delightful surprise!
(Totally ignoring FREDRIK, CARL-MAGNUS *bows stiffly and kisses her hand)*
CARL-MAGNUS: Excuse my appearance. My new motorcar broke down. *(Hand kiss. Presents the daisies)* From a neighboring garden.

DESIRÉE: *(Taking them)* How lovely! Will you be staying—long?

CARL-MAGNUS: I have twenty hours leave. Three hours coming here, nine hours with you, five hours with my wife and three hours back. *(Still ignoring FREDRIK)* Do you mind if I take off my uniform and put on my robe?

DESIRÉE: Well—at the moment it's occupied.

CARL-MANGUS: *(Not looking at FREDRIK)* So I see.

DESIRÉE: Mr. Egerman—Count Malcolm.

FREDRIK: Sir.

CARL-MAGNUS: *(Still ignoring FREDRIK)* Sir.

FREDRIK: I feel I should give you an explanation for what may seem to be a rather unusual situation. *(With tremulous aplomb)* For many years, I have been Miss Armfeldt's mother's lawyer and devoted friend. A small lawsuit of hers—nothing major, I'm happy to say—comes up in Court tomorrow morning and at the last minute I realized that some legal papers required her daughter's signature. Although it was late and she had already retired . . .

DESIRÉE: I let him in, of course.

CARL-MAGNUS: *(Turning the icy gaze on her)* And then?

DESIRÉE: Ah, yes, the—the robe. Well, you see . . .

FREDRIK: Unfortunately, sir, on my way to the water-closet—through Miss Armfeldt's darkened bedroom—I inadvertently tripped over her hip-bath and fell in. Miss Armfeldt generously loaned me this garment while waiting for my clothes to dry in the bedroom.

CARL-MAGNUS: In that case, Miss Armfeldt, I suggest you return to the bedroom and see whether this gentleman's clothes are dry by now.

DESIRÉE: Yes. Of course.

(She crosses between FREDRIK and CARL-MAGNUS and exits. Pacing, CARL-MAGNUS begins to whistle a military march. FREDRIK counters by whistling a bit of Mozart)

CARL-MAGNUS: Are you fond of duels, sir?

FREDRIK: I don't really know. I haven't ever tried.

CARL-MAGNUS: I have duelled seven times. Pistol, rapier, foil. I've been wounded five times. Otherwise fortune has been kind to me.

FREDRIK: I must say I'm impressed.

CARL-MAGNUS: *(Picking up fruit knife)* You see this fruit knife? The target will be that picture. The old lady. Her face. Her eye. *(Throws knife, which hits target)*

FREDRIK: *(Clapping)* Bravo.

CARL-MAGNUS: Are you being insolent, sir?

FREDRIK: Of course—sir.

(DESIRÉE returns from the bedroom. She is carrying FREDRIK'S clothes in a soaking wet bundle. She has dipped them in the hip-bath)

DESIRÉE: They're not *very* dry.

FREDRIK: Oh, dear me, they're certainly not, are they?

CARL-MAGNUS: A predicament.

FREDRIK: Indeed.

CARL-MAGNUS: I imagine, Miss Armfeldt, you could find this gentleman one of my nightshirts.

FREDRIK: Thank you, thank you. But I think I'd prefer to put on my own—er —garments. *(He takes the wet bundle from DESIRÉE)*

CARL-MAGNUS: Unfortunately, sir, you will not have the time for that. *(To* DESIRÉE*)* Perhaps you could tell him where to look.

DESIRÉE: Oh yes, yes. The left hand—no, the right hand bottom draw of the— er— *(Indicating a chest of drawers)* . . . thing.

*(*FREDRIK *gives her the wet clothes)*

FREDRIK: *(Hesitating, then:)* Thank you.

(He goes into the bedroom. While he is away, DESIRÉE *and* CARL-MAGNUS *confront each other in near-silence:* CARL-MAGNUS *only whistles a bit of the march that he whistled at* FREDRIK *earlier)*

FREDRIK: *(Returns in a nightshirt, carrying the robe, which he holds out to* CARL-MAGNUS*)* Your robe, sir. *(*CARL-MAGNUS *receives it in silence.* FREDRIK *puts on the nightcap that goes with the nightshirt)* Well—er—goodnight. Miss Armfeldt, thank you for your cooperation. *(*FREDRIK *takes the wet bundle from* DESIRÉE *and exits)*

CARL-MAGNUS: *(Singing, to himself)*
>She wouldn't . . .
>Therefore they didn't . . .
>So then it wasn't . . .
>Not unless it . . .
>Would she?
>She doesn't . . .
>God knows she needn't . . .
>Therefore it's not.
>
>He'd never . . .
>Therefore they haven't . . .
>Which makes the question absolutely . . .
>Could she?
>She daren't . . .
>Therefore I mustn't . . .
>What utter rot!
>
>Fidelity is more than mere display,
>It's what a man expects from life.

(The unit that DESIRÉE *is sitting on starts to ride off as* CHARLOTTE, *seated at her breakfast table, rides on)*

>Fidelity like mine to Desirée
>And Charlotte, my devoted wife.

SCENE 5

Breakfast room in Malcolm country house.

*Breakfast for one (*CHARLOTTE'S*)—and an extra coffee cup—stands on an elegant little table. Music under.*

CHARLOTTE: How was Miss Desirée Armfeldt? In good health, I trust?

CARL-MAGNUS: Charlotte, my dear. I have exactly five hours.

CHARLOTTE: *(Deadpan)* Five hours this time? Last time it was four. I'm gaining ground.

CARL-MAGNUS: *(Preoccupied)* She had a visitor. A lawyer in a nightshirt.

CHARLOTTE: Now, *that* I find interesting. What did you do?

CARL-MAGNUS: Threw him out.

CHARLOTTE: In a nightshirt?

CARL-MAGNUS: In *my* nightshirt.

CHARLOTTE: What sort of lawyer? Corporation, Maritime, Criminal—Testamentary?

CARL-MAGNUS: Didn't your sister's little school friend Anne Sorensen marry a Fredrik Egerman?

CHARLOTTE: Yes, she did.

CARL-MAGNUS: Fredrik Egerman.

(He sings)
The papers,
He mentioned papers,
Some legal papers
Which I didn't see there . . .
Where were they,
The goddamn papers
She had to sign?

What nonsense . . .
He brought her papers,
They were important
So he had to be there . . .
I'll kill him . . .
Why should I bother?
The woman's mine!

Besides, no matter what one might infer,
One must have faith to some degree.
The least that I can do is trust in her
The way that Charlotte trusts in me.

(Speaks)
What are you planning to do today?

CHARLOTTE: *After* the five hours?

CARL-MAGNUS: Right now. I need a little sleep.

CHARLOTTE: Ah! I see. In that case, my plans will have to be changed. What will I do? *(Sudden mock radiance)* I know! Nothing!

CARL-MAGNUS: Why don't you pay a visit to Marta's little school friend?

CHARLOTTE: Ah ha!

CARL-MAGNUS: She probably has no idea what *her* husband's up to.

CHARLOTTE: And I could enlighten her. Poor Carl-Magnus, are you *that* jealous?

CARL-MAGNUS: A civilized man can tolerate his wife's infidelity, but when it comes to his mistress, a man becomes a tiger.

CHARLOTTE: As opposed, of course, to a goat in a rut. Ah, well, if I'm back in two hours, that still leaves us three hours. Right?

CARL-MAGNUS: *(Unexpectedly smiling)* You're a good wife, Charlotte. The best.

CHARLOTTE: That's a comforting thought to take with me to town, dear. It just may keep me from cutting my throat on the tram. *(She exits)*

CARL-MAGNUS: *(Sings)*

Capable, pliable . . .
Women, women . . .
Undemanding and reliable,
Knowing their place.
Insufferable, yes, but gentle,
Their weaknesses are incidental,
A functional but ornamental

(Sips coffee)

Race.
Durable, sensible . . .
Women, women . . .
Very nearly indispensable
Creatures of grace.
God knows the foolishness about them,
But if one had to live without them,
The world would surely be a poorer,
If purer, place.
The hip-bath . . .
About that hip-bath . . .
How can you slip and trip into a hip-bath?
The papers . . .
Where were the papers?
Of course, he might have taken back the papers . . .
She wouldn't . . .
Therefore they didn't . . .
The woman's mine!

(He strides off)

SCENE 6

The Egerman rooms.
In the bedroom, ANNE, *in a negligee, sits on the bed while* PETRA *combs her hair.*

ANNE: Oh, that's delicious. I could purr. Having your hair brushed is gloriously sensual, isn't it?

PETRA: I can think of more sensual things.

ANNE: *(Giggles, then suddenly serious)* Are you a virgin, Petra?

PETRA: God forbid.

ANNE: *(Sudden impulse)* I am.

PETRA: I know.

ANNE: *(Astonished and flustered)* How on earth can you tell?

PETRA: Your skin, something in your eyes.

ANNE: Can everyone see it?

PETRA: I wouldn't think so.

ANNE: Well, that's a relief. *(Giggles)* How old were you when—

PETRA: Sixteen.

ANNE: It must have been terrifying, wasn't it? *And* disgusting.

PETRA: Disgusting? It was more fun than the rolly-coaster at the fair.

ANNE: Henrik says that almost everything that's fun is automatically vicious. It's so depressing.

PETRA: Oh him! Poor little puppy dog!

ANNE: *(Suddenly imperious)* Don't you dare talk about your employer's son that way.

PETRA: Sorry, Ma'am.

ANNE: I forbid anyone in this house to tease Henrik. *(Giggles again)* Except me. *(ANNE goes to the vanity, sits, opens the top of her robe, studies her reflection in the table-mirror)* It's quite a good body, isn't it?

PETRA: Nothing wrong there.

ANNE: Is it as good as yours? *(Laughing, she turns and pulls PETRA onto the bed, trying to undo PETRA'S uniform)* Let me see! *(For a moment, PETRA is shocked. Laughing, ANNE continues, PETRA starts laughing too. They begin struggling playfully together)* If I was a boy, would I prefer you or me? Tell me, tell me! *(Still laughing and struggling they stumble across the room and collapse in a heap on the bed)* You're a boy! You're a boy!

PETRA: *(Laughing)* God forbid!

(As they struggle, the front doorbell rings)

ANNE: *(Sits up)* Run, Petra, run. Answer it.

(PETRA climbs over ANNE to get off of the bed. As PETRA hurries into the parlor and exits to answer the door, ANNE peers at herself in the mirror)

Oh dear, oh dear, my hair! My—everything!

(PETRA returns to the Parlor with CHARLOTTE)

PETRA: Please have a seat, Countess. Madame will be with you in a minute. *(CHARLOTTE looks around the room—particularly at FREDRIK'S picture—PETRA hurries in the bedroom. Hissing)* It's a Countess!

ANNE: A Countess?

PETRA: Very grand.

ANNE: How thrilling! Who on earth can she be? *(After a final touch at the mirror, she draws herself up with great dignity and, with PETRA behind her, sweeps into the living room. At the door, she stops and stares. Then delighted, runs to CHARLOTTE)* Charlotte Olafsson! It is, isn't it? Marta's big sister who married that magnificent Count Something or other—and I was a flower girl at the wedding.

CHARLOTTE: Unhappily without a time-bomb in your lily of the valley bouquet.

ANNE: *(Laughing)* Oh, Charlotte, you always did say the most amusing things.

CHARLOTTE: I still do. I frequently laugh myself to sleep contemplating my own future.

ANNE: Petra, ice, lemonade, cookies.

(PETRA leaves. Pause)

CHARLOTTE: Well, dear, how are you? And how is your marriage working out?

ANNE: I'm in bliss. I have all the dresses in the world and a maid to take care of me and this charming house and a husband who spoils me shamelessly.

CHARLOTTE: That list, I trust, is in diminishing order of priority.

ANNE: How dreadful you are! Of course it isn't. And how's dear Marta?

CHARLOTTE: Ecstatic. Dear Marta has renounced men and is teaching gymnastics in a school for retarded girls in Beetleheim. Which brings me or . . . *(Glancing at a little watch on her bosom)* . . . rather should bring me, as my time is strictly limited—to the subject of men. How do you rate your husband as a man?

ANNE: I—don't quite know what you mean.

CHARLOTTE: I will give you an example. As a man, my husband could be rated as a louse, a bastard, a conceited, puffed-up, adulterous egomaniac. He constantly makes me do the most degrading, the most humiliating things like . . . like . . . *(Her composure starts to crumble. She opens a little pocketbook and fumbles)*

ANNE: Like?

CHARLOTTE: Like . . . *(Finding tiny handkerchief from purse, dabbing at her nose and bursting into tears)* Oh, why do I put up with it? Why do I let him treat me like—like an intimidated corporal in his regiment? Why? Why? Why? I'll tell you why. I despise him! I hate him! I *love* him! Oh, damn that woman! May she rot forever in some infernal dressing room with lipstick of fire and scalding mascara! Let every billboard in hell eternally announce: Desirée Armfeldt in —in—in *The Wild Duck!* *(Abandons herself to tears)*

ANNE: Desirée Armfeldt? But what has she done to you?

CHARLOTTE: What has she *not* done? Enslaved my husband—enslaved yours . . .

ANNE: Fredrik!

CHARLOTTE: He was there last night in her bedroom—in a nightshirt. My husband threw him out into the street and he's insanely jealous. He told me to come here and tell you . . . and I'm actually *telling* you! Oh, what a monster I've become!

ANNE: Charlotte, is that the truth? Fredrik was there—in a nightshirt?

(CHARLOTTE sobs)

CHARLOTTE: My husband's nightshirt!

ANNE: Oh, I knew it! I was sure he'd met her before. And when she *smiled* at us in the theater . . . *(She begins to weep)*

CHARLOTTE: Poor Anne!

(PETRA enters with the tray of lemonade and cookies and stands gazing at the two women in astonishment)

PETRA: The lemonade, Ma'am.

ANNE: *(Looking up, controlling herself with a great effort, to the weeping* CHARLOTTE*)* Lemonade, Charlotte?

CHARLOTTE: *(Looking up too, seeing the lemonade)* Lemonade! It would choke me!

(Sings)
Every day a little death
In the parlor, in the bed,
In the curtains, in the silver,
In the buttons, in the bread.
Every day a little sting
In the heart and in the head.
Every move and every breath,
And you hardly feel a thing,
Brings a perfect little death.

He smiles sweetly, strokes my hair,
Says he misses me.
I would murder him right there
But first I die.

He talks softly of his wars,
And his horses
And his whores,
I think love's a dirty business!

ANNE: *So do I!*

CHARLOTTE:
  I'm before him
  On my knees
  And he kisses me.

ANNE:
  So do I . . .

CHARLOTTE:
  He assumes I'll lose my reason,
  And I do.
  Men are stupid, men are vain,
  Love's disgusting, love's insane,
  A humiliating business!

ANNE:
  Oh, how true!

CHARLOTTE:
  Ah, well . . .

ANNE:
  Every day a little death,

CHARLOTTE:
  Every day a little death,

ANNE:
  On the lips and in the eyes,

CHARLOTTE:
  In the parlor, in the bed,

CHARLOTTE:
  In the curtains,
  In the silver,
  In the buttons,
  In the bread.

ANNE:
In the murmurs,
In the pauses,
In the gestures,
In the sighs.

Every day a little dies,

  Every day a little sting.

In the looks and in
The lies.

In the heart
And in the head.

Every move and
Every breath,
And you hardly feel a
Thing,
Brings a perfect little
Death.

And you hardly feel a
Thing,
Brings a perfect little
Death.

(After the number, HENRIK *enters, taking off his hat and scarf)*

HENRIK: Oh, excuse me.

ANNE: *(Trying to rise to the occasion)* Charlotte, this is Henrik Egerman.

HENRIK: *(Bows and offers his hand)* I am happy to make your acquaintance, Madam.

CHARLOTTE: Happy! Who could ever be happy to meet *me?*

(Holding HENRIK'S *hand, she rises and then drifts out.* ANNE *falls back sobbing on the couch.* HENRIK *stands, gazing at her)*

HENRIK: Anne, what is it?

ANNE: Nothing.

HENRIK: But what did that woman say to you?

ANNE: Nothing, nothing at all.

HENRIK: That can't be true.

ANNE: It is! It is! She—she merely told me that Marta Olafsson, my dearest friend from school is—teaching gymnastics . . .

(Bursts into tears again, falls into HENRIK*'s arms.* HENRIK *puts his arms around her slowly, cautiously)*

HENRIK: Anne! Poor Anne! If you knew how it destroys me to see you unhappy.

ANNE: I am not unhappy!

HENRIK: You know. You must know. Ever since you married Father, you've been more precious to me than . . .

ANNE: *(Pulls back, suddenly giggling through her tears)* . . . Martin Luther?

*(*HENRIK, *cut to the quick, jumps up)*

HENRIK: Can you laugh at me even now?

ANNE: *(Rises)* Oh dear, I'm sorry. Perhaps, after all, I am a totally frivolous woman with ice for a heart. Am I, Henrik? *Am I?*

*(*PETRA *enters)*

MADAME ARMFELDT'S VOICE: *(Off. Pushed in chair by* FRID*)* Seven of hearts on the eight of spades.

ANNE: *(Laughing again)* Silly Henrik, get your book, quick, and denounce the wickedness of the world to me for at least a half an hour.

*(*ANNE *runs off as the bedroom and parlor go.* HENRIK *follows her, as does* PETRA, *carrying the lemonade tray)*

MADAME ARMFELDT'S VOICE: The Ten of Hearts! Who needs the Ten of Hearts! !

SCENE 7

Armfeldt terrace.

MADAME ARMFELDT *is playing solitaire with* FRID *standing behind her.* FREDRIKA *sits at the piano, playing scales.*

MADAME ARMFELDT: Child, I am about to give you your advice for the day.

FREDRIKA: Yes, Grandmother.

MADAM ARMFELDT: Never marry—or even dally with—a Scandinavian.

FREDRIKA: Why not, Grandmother?

MADAME ARMFELDT: They are all insane.

FREDRIKA: All of them?

MADAME ARMFELDT: Uh-hum. It's the latitude. A winter when the sun never rises, a summer when the sun never sets, are more than enough to addle the brain of any man. Further off, further off. You practically inhaled the Queen of Diamonds.

DESIRÉE: *(Off)* Who's home?

FREDRIKA: *(Jumps up, thrilled)* Mother!

(DESIRÉE enters and FREDRIKA rushes to her, throwing herself into DESIRÉE's arms)

DESIRÉE: Darling, you've grown a mile; you're much prettier, you're irresistible! Hello, Mother.

MADAME ARMFELDT: *(Continuing to play, unfriendly)* And to what do I owe the honor of this visit?

DESIRÉE: I just thought I'd pop out and see you both. Is that so surprising?

MADAME ARMFELDT: Yes.

DESIRÉE: You're in one of your bitchy moods, I see.

MADAME ARMFELDT: If you've come to take Fredrika back, the answer is no. I do not object to the immorality of your life, merely to its sloppiness. Since I have been tidy enough to have acquired a sizeable mansion with a fleet of servants, it is only common sense that my granddaughter should reap the advantages of it. *(To FREDRIKA)* Isn't that so, child?

FREDRIKA: I really don't know, Grandmother.

MADAME ARMFELDT: Oh, yes, you do, dear. Well, Desirée, there must be something you want or you wouldn't have "popped out." What is it?

DESIRÉE: All right. The tour's over for a while, and I was wondering if you'd invite some people here next weekend.

MADAME ARMFELDT: If they're actors, they'll have to sleep in the stables.

DESIRÉE: Not actors, Mother. Just a lawyer from town and his family—Fredrik Egerman.

MADAME ARMFELDT: In my day, one went to lawyers' offices but never consorted with their *families.*

DESIRÉE: Then it'll make a nice change dear, won't it?

MADAME ARMFELDT: I am deeply suspicious, but very well.

DESIRÉE: *(Producing a piece of paper)* Here's the address.

MADAME ARMFELDT: *(Taking it)* I shall send 'round a formal invitation by hand. *(She snaps her fingers for FRID. As he wheels her off:)* Needless to say, I shall be polite to your guests. However, they will not be served my best champagne. I am saving that for my funeral.

(FREDRIKA runs to DESIRÉE; they embrace, and freeze in that pose. The screens divide the stage so that we see, in another area, PETRA bringing ANNE an invitation on a small silver tray)

PETRA: *(Sings)*
   Look, ma'am,
   An invitation.
   Here, ma'am,
   Delivered by hand.
   And, ma'am,
   I notice the station-
   Ery's engraved and very grand.

ANNE:

Petra, how too exciting!
Just when I need it!
Petra, such elegant writing,
So chic you hardly can read it.
What do you think?
Who can it be?
Even the ink—
No, here, let me . . .
"Your presence . . ."
Just think of it, Petra . . .
"Is kindly . . ."
It's at a chateau!
"Requested . . ."
Et cet'ra, et cet'ra,
". . . Madame Leonora Armf—"
Oh, no!
A weekend in the country!

PETRA:

We're invited?

ANNE:

What a horrible plot!
A weekend in the country!

PETRA:

I'm excited.

ANNE:

No, you're not!

PETRA:

A weekend in the country!
Just imagine!

ANNE:

It's completely depraved.

PETRA:

A weekend in the country!

ANNE:

It's insulting!

PETRA:

It's engraved.

ANNE:

It's that woman,
It's that Armfeldt . . .

PETRA:

Oh, the actress . . .

ANNE:

> *No, the ghoul,*
> *She may hope to*
> *Make her charm felt,*
> *But she's mad if she thinks*
> *I would be such a fool*
> *As to weekend in the country!*

PETRA:

> *How insulting!*

ANNE:

> *And I've nothing to wear!*

ANNE and PETRA:

> *A weekend in the country!*

ANNE:

> *Here!*

> (ANNE *gives the invitation back to* PETRA)

> *The last place I'm going is there!*

(ANNE *and* PETRA *exit behind a screen.* DESIRÉE *and* FREDRIKA *unfreeze and begin to move downstage*)

DESIRÉE: *(Speaks)* Well, dear, are you happy here?

FREDRIKA: Yes. I think so. But I miss us.

DESIRÉE: Oh, so do I! *(Pause)* Darling, how would you feel if we had a home of our very own with me only acting when I felt like it—and a man who would make you a spectacular father?

FREDRIKA: Oh, I see. The lawyer! Mr. Egerman!

DESIRÉE: Dear child, you're uncanny.

(DESIRÉE *and* FREDRIKA *freeze once again, and the screens close in to provide a stagette for the appearance of* FREDRIK, ANNE, *and* PETRA)

PETRA: *(Sings)*

> *Guess what, an invitation!*

ANNE:

> *Guess who, begins with an "A" . . .*
> *Armfeldt—*
> *Is that a relation*
> *To the decrepit Desirée?*

PETRA:

> *Guess when we're asked to go, sir—*
> *See, sir, the date there?*
> *Guess where—a fancy chateau, sir!*

ANNE:

> *Guess, too, who's lying in wait there,*
> *Setting her traps,*
> *Fixing her face—*

FREDRIK:
Darling,
Perhaps a change of pace . . .

ANNE:
Oh, no!

FREDRIK:
A
Weekend in the country
Would be charming,
And the air would be fresh.

ANNE:
A weekend
With that woman . . .

FREDRIK:
In the country . . .

ANNE:
In the flesh!

FREDRIK:
I've some business
With her mother.

PETRA:
See, it's business!

ANNE:
. . . Oh, no doubt!
But the business
With her mother
Would be hardly the business I'd worry about.

FREDRIK and PETRA:
Just a weekend in the country,

FREDRIK:
Smelling jasmine . . .

ANNE:
Watching little things grow.

FREDRIK and PETRA:
A weekend in the country . . .

ANNE:
Go!

FREDRIK:
My darling,
We'll simply say no.

ANNE:
Oh!

(They exit. FREDRIKA *and* DESIRÉE *unfreeze)*
FREDRIKA: *(Speaks)* Oh Mother, I know it's none of my business, but . . . that dragoon you wrote me about—with the mustache?

DESIRÉE: Oh, him! What I ever saw in him astounds me. He's a tin soldier—arms, legs, brain—tin, tin, tin!

(They freeze *on the downstage bench. The screens close in, providing a new playing area for* ANNE *and* CHARLOTTE*)*

ANNE: *(Sings)*
    A weekend!

CHARLOTTE:
    How very amusing.

ANNE:
    A weekend!

CHARLOTTE:
    But also inept.

ANNE:
    A weekend!
    Of course, we're refusing.

CHARLOTTE:
    Au contraire,
    You must accept.

ANNE:
    Oh, no!

CHARLOTTE:
    A weekend in the country . . .

ANNE:
    But it's frightful!

CHARLOTTE:
    No, you don't understand.
    A weekend in the country
    Is delightful
    If it's planned.
    Wear your hair down
    And a flower,
    Don't use make-up,
    Dress in white.
    She'll grow older
    By the hour
    And be hopelessly shattered by
    Saturday night.
    Spend a weekend in the country.

ANNE:
    We'll accept it!

CHARLOTTE:
    I'd a feeling
    You would.

BOTH:
    A weekend in the country!

ANNE:
Yes, it's only polite that we should.

CHARLOTTE:
Good.

(ANNE and CHARLOTTE both disappear behind the screens. DESIRÉE and FRE-DRIKA unfreeze)

FREDRIKA: Count Malcolm's insanely jealous, isn't he? You don't suppose he'll come galloping up on a black stallion, brandishing a sword?

DESIRÉE: Oh dear, I hadn't thought of that. But no, no, thank heavens. It's his wife's birthday this weekend—sacred to domesticity. At least we're safe from him.

(They freeze. CARL-MAGNUS enters from behind a screen; CHARLOTTE follows opposite to meet him)

CARL-MAGNUS: *(Sings)*
Well?

CHARLOTTE:
I've an intriguing little social item.

CARL-MAGNUS:
What?

CHARLOTTE:
Out at the Armfeldt family manse.

CARL-MAGNUS:
Well, what?

CHARLOTTE:
Merely a weekend,
Still I thought it might am-
Use you to know who's invited to go,
This time with his pants.

CARL-MAGNUS:
You don't mean—?

CHARLOTTE:
I'll give you three guesses.

CARL-MAGNUS:
She wouldn't!

CHARLOTTE:
Reduce it to two.

CARL-MAGNUS:
It can't be . . .

CHARLOTTE:
It nevertheless is . . .

CARL-MAGNUS:
Egerman!

CHARLOTTE:
Right! Score one for you.

CARL-MAGNUS: *(Triumphantly)*
Aha!

CHARLOTTE: *(Triumphantly)*
Aha!

CARL-MAGNUS: *(Thoughtfully)*
Aha!

CHARLOTTE: *(Worriedly)*
Aha?

CARL-MAGNUS:
A weekend in the country . . .
We should try it—

CHARLOTTE:
How I wish we'd been asked.

CARL-MAGNUS:
A weekend in the country . . .
Peace and quiet—

CHARLOTTE:
We'll go masked.

CARL-MAGNUS:
A weekend in the country . . .

CHARLOTTE:
Uninvited—
They'll consider it odd.

CARL-MAGNUS:
A weekend in the country—
I'm delighted!

CHARLOTTE:
Oh, my God.

CARL-MAGNUS:
And the shooting should be pleasant
If the weather's not too rough.
Happy Birthday,
It's your present.

CHARLOTTE:
But . . .

CARL-MAGNUS:
You haven't been getting out nearly enough,
And a weekend in the country . . .

CHARLOTTE:
It's perverted!

CARL-MAGNUS:
Pack my quiver and bow.

CHARLOTTE and CARL-MAGNUS:
A weekend in the country—

CARL-MAGNUS:
At exactly 2:30, we go.

CHARLOTTE:
We can't.

CARL-MAGNUS:
We shall.

CHARLOTTE:
We shan't.

CARL-MAGNUS:
*I'm getting the car
And we're motoring down.*

CHARLOTTE:
*Yes, I'm certain you are
And I'm staying in town.*

(The screens open to reveal ANNE, FREDRIK, *and* PETRA*)*

CARL-MAGNUS: *Go and pack my suits!*	ANNE: *We'll go.*
CHARLOTTE: *I won't!*	PETRA: *Oh, good!*
CARL-MAGNUS: *My boots!* *Pack everything I own* *That shoots.*	FREDRIK: *We will?*
CHARLOTTE: *No!*	ANNE: *We should.* *Pack everything white.*
CARL-MAGNUS: *Charlotte?*	PETRA: *Ma'am, it's wonderful news!*
CHARLOTTE: *I'm thinking it out.*	FREDRIK: *Are you sure it's all right?*
CARL-MAGNUS: *Charlotte!*	ANNE: *We'd be rude to refuse.*
CHARLOTTE: *There's no need to shout.*	FREDRIK: *Then we're off!*
CARL-MAGNUS: *Charlotte!*	PETRA: *We are?*

CHARLOTTE:
All right, then,

BOTH:
We're off on our way,
What a beautiful day
For

FREDRIK:
We'll take the car.

ALL THREE:
We'll bring champagne
And caviar!
We're off on our way,
What a beautiful day
For

ALL:
A weekend in the country,
How amusing,
How delightfully droll,
A weekend in the country
While we're losing our control.
A weekend in the country,
How enchanting
On the manicured lawns.
A weekend in the country,
With the panting and the yawns.
With the crickets and the pheasants
And the orchards and the hay,
With the servants and the peasants,
We'll be laying our plans
While we're playing croquet
For a weekend in the country,
So inactive that one has to lie down.
A weekend in the country
Where . . .

(HENRIK *enters*)

HENRIK:
A weekend in the country,
The bees in their hives,
The shallow worldly figures,
The frivolous lives.
The devil's companions
Know not whom they serve.
It might be instructive
To observe.

(DESIRÉE *and* FREDRIKA *unfreeze*)
DESIRÉE: However, there is one tiny snag.
FREDRIKA: A snag?
DESIRÉE: Lawyer Egerman is married.
FREDRIKA: That could be considered a snag.
DESIRÉE: Don't worry, my darling. I was not raised by your Grandmother for nothing.
(DESIRÉE *holds out her arm, and* FREDRIKA *runs to her. Together, they walk upstage as the screens open, revealing, for the first time, the facade of the Armfeldt*

Mansion. FRID *stands at the door, and once* DESIRÉE *and* FREDRIKA *have entered, he closes it behind them)*

CARL-MAGNUS:
Charlotte!

CHARLOTTE:
I'm thinking it out.

CARL-MAGNUS:
Charlotte!

CHARLOTTE:
There's no need
To shout.

MRS. NORDSTROM
and MR. ERLANSEN:
A weekend of
   playing
Croquet,

A weekend of
   strolling
The lawns,

CARL-MAGNUS, CHAR-
LOTTE,
FREDRIK, ANNE and PE-
TRA:
We're off and away,
What a beautiful day!

ALL:
With riotous laughter
We quietly suffer
The season in town,
Which is reason enough for
A weekend in the country,
How amusing,
How delightfully droll!
A weekend in the country,
While we're losing our control.
A weekend in the country,
How enchanting
On the manicured lawns.
A weekend in the country,
With the panting and the yawns.
With the crickets and the pheasants
And the orchards and the hay,
With the servants and the peasants

FREDRIK:
We're off!

PETRA:
We are?

FREDRIK and ANNE:
We'll take the car.

FREDRIK, ANNE, and
PETRA:
We'll bring
Champagne and
Caviar!

MR. LINDQUIST:
Confiding our
   motives
And hiding our
   yawns,

HENRIK:
A weekend in the
Country,
The bees in their
Hives . . .

MRS. SEGSTROM and
MRS. ANDERSSEN:
We're off! We are?
We'll take the car.

We'll
Bring
Champagne
And caviar!

ALL THE QUINTET:
The weather is spectacular!

We'll be laying our plans
While we're playing croquet
For a weekend in the country,
So inactive
That one has to lie down.
A weekend in the country
Where
We're twice as upset as in,
Twice as upset as in,
Twice as upset as in,
Twice as upset as in . . .

(ALL, *simultaneously*)

CARL-MAGNUS:

Charlotte, we're going!
Charlotte, we're going!
Charlotte, we're going!
Charlotte, we're going!

CHARLOTTE:

We're uninvited!
We're uninvited!
We're uninvited!
We should stay in . . .

ANNE:

A weekend!
A weekend!
A weekend!
A weekend!
A weekend!
A weekend!
A weekend!
A weekend
In

FREDRIK:

Are you sure you want
to go?
Are you sure you want
to go?
Are you sure you want
to go
Away and leave,
Go and leave

PETRA:

A weekend!
A weekend!
A weekend!
A weekend!
A weekend!
A weekend!
A weekend!
A weekend
In

HENRIK:

World's shallow people going,
Shallow world's people going
To

THE QUINTET:

Twice as upset as in
Twice as upset as in
Twice as upset as in
Twice as upset as in
Twice as upset as in
Twice as upset as in
Twice as upset as in
Twice as upset as in

ALL:

Town!

Curtain

After a musical Entr'Acte, THE QUINTET *enters.*

MRS. ANDERSSEN:

The sun sits low,
Diffusing its usual glow.
Five o'clock . . .
Twilight . . .
Vespers sound,
And it's six o'clock . . .

Twilight
All around,

ALL:
But the sun sits low,
As low as it's going to go.

MR. ERLANSEN:
Eight o'clock . . .

MR. LINDQUIST:
Twilight . . .

GIRLS:
How enthralling!

MR. ERLANSEN:
It's nine o'clock . . .

MR. LINDQUIST:
Twilight . . .

GIRLS:
Slowly crawling towards

MR. ERLANSEN:
Ten o'clock . . .

MR. LINDQUIST:
Twilight . . .

GIRLS:
Crickets calling,

ALL:
The vespers ring,
The nightingale's waiting to sing.
The rest of us wait on a string.
Perpetual sunset
Is rather an unset-
Tling thing.

(The show curtain rises on Act Two, Scene 1)

ACT TWO

SCENE 1

The Armfeldt lawn.
FRID *is serving champagne to* DESIRÉE *and* MALLA. FREDRIKA, *upstage, is playing croquet with the help of* BERTRAND, MADAME ARMFELDT'S *page.* FRID *returns to* MADAME ARMFELDT. OSA *passes with a tray of cookies, and* FREDRIKA *takes one.* DESIRÉE *gets a mallet and begins to play croquet.*
MADAME ARMFELDT: To lose a lover or even a husband or two during the course of one's life can be vexing. But to lose one's teeth is a catastrophe.

Bear that in mind, child, as you chomp so recklessly into that ginger snap.

FREDRIKA: Very well, Grandmother.

MADAME ARMFELDT: *(Holding up her glass to* FRID*)* More champagne, Frid. *(*FRID *gets a fresh bottle)* One bottle the less of the Mumms '87 will not, I hope, diminish the hilarity at my wake.

*(*DESIRÉE *sits on the rise.* FRID *opens the bottle with a loud* POP!*)*

THE QUINTET:
The sun won't set.
It's fruitless to hope or to fret.
It's dark as it's going to get.
The hands on the clock turn,
But don't sing a nocturne
Just yet.

(Off, we hear a car-horn)

DESIRÉE: They're coming!

MADAME ARMFELDT: Nonsense!

DESIRÉE: But they are!

MADAME ARMFELDT: Impossible. No guest with the slightest grasp of what is seemly would arrive before five-fifteen on a Friday afternoon. *(We hear the car-horn again, and this time it's louder)* Good God, you're right!

DESIRÉE: Malla!

*(*DESIRÉE *runs up into the house, followed closely by* MALLA, *and* OSA. BERTRAND *exits with the croquet set)*

MADAME ARMFELDT: Frid! We cannot be caught squatting on the ground like Bohemians!

*(*FRID *scoops her up and carries her into the house.* FREDRIKA *follows.* THE QUINTET *runs on to collect the furniture and props left on stage:* MR. ERLANSEN *gets the champagne buckets,* MRS. NORDSTROM *the fur rug,* MRS. ANDERSSEN *the cookie stand,* MR. LINDQUIST *the wickets and croquet pole,* MRS. SEGSTROM MADAME 'S wicker stool. They* freeze *for a moment at the sound of the car-horn, and then all run off.*

A beat later, CARL-MAGNUS' *sports car drives on.* CARL-MAGNUS *is driving;* CHARLOTTE *sits beside him.* CARL-MAGNUS *stops the car and gets out)*

CHARLOTTE: *(Looking around)* Happy birthday to me!

CARL-MAGNUS: *(Inspecting a wheel)* What was that?

CHARLOTTE: I merely said . . . oh, never mind.

CARL-MAGNUS: If that damn lawyer thinks he's going to get away with something—Haha!

CHARLOTTE: Haha! indeed, dear.

*(*CARL-MAGNUS *helps* CHARLOTTE *out of the car)*

CARL-MAGNUS: Watch him, Charlotte. Watch them both like a . . .

CHARLOTTE: Hawk, I know, dear. You're a tiger, I'm a hawk. We're our own zoo.

(As she speaks, a touring car sweeps on from the opposite side. It is driven rather erratically by FREDRIK *with* ANNE *beside him.* HENRIK *and* PETRA *are in the back seat with a pile of luggage. The car only just misses* CARL-MAGNUS' *car as it comes to a stop. Recognition comes.* FREDRIK *gets out of his car)*

FREDRIK: Good day, sir. I was not aware that you were to be a fellow guest.

(FREDRIK *opens the car and helps* ANNE *out.* HENRIK *helps* PETRA *out of the back seat)*

CARL-MAGNUS: Neither is Miss Armfeldt. I hope our arrival will in no way inconvenience you.

FREDRIK: Not at all, not at all. I am happy to see that you have gotten through yet another week without any serious wounds.

CARL-MAGNUS: What's that? Wounds, sir?

FREDRIK: Rapier? Bow and arrow? Blow dart?

(At this point, ANNE *and* CHARLOTTE *see each other. They run together. On the way,* ANNE *drops her handkerchief)*

ANNE: *(Hissing)* So you did come? *(Pause)* Talk later.	CHARLOTTE: *(Hissing)* So you did come? *(Pause)* Talk later.

*(*HENRIK, *tremendously solicitous, holds out the handkerchief to* ANNE*)*

HENRIK: Your handkerchief, Anne.

ANNE: *(Taking it, moving away)* Thank you.

HENRIK: You must have dropped it.

*(*PETRA *taps* HENRIK *on the shoulder)*

PETRA: Your book, Master Henrik.

HENRIK: *(Taking it)* Thank you.

PETRA: *(With soupy mock-solicitousness)* You must have dropped it.

*(*PETRA *moves to get the luggage.* FRID, *seeing and immediately appreciating* PETRA, *goes to her)*

FRID: Here. Let me.

PETRA: *(Handing him two suitcases)* Let you—*what?*

*(*PETRA, *with one suitcase, enters the house, followed by* FRID, *who is carrying two.* HENRIK *is moodily drifting away as* DESIRÉE *emerges from the house. She is followed by* FREDRIKA, *and smiling dazzingly for the* EGERMANS*)*

DESIRÉE: Ah, here you all are . . . (CARL-MAGNUS *clears his throat noisily. The smile dies)* Count Malcolm!

CARL-MAGNUS: *(Bowing frigidly over her hand)* My wife and I were in the neighborhood to visit her cousin. Unhappily, on arrival, we discovered the chateau was quarantined for . . . *(Flicks his fingers at* CHARLOTTE*)*

CHARLOTTE: Plague.

CARL-MAGNUS: Since I am due back to maneuvers by dawn, we venture to propose ourselves for the night.

DESIRÉE: *(Concealing no little fluster)* Well, yes. Indeed. Why not? Mother will be honored!—surprised, but honored. (DESIRÉE *crosses to* CHARLOTTE, *and sweeps past her, barely touching her hand)* Countess Malcolm, I presume?

CHARLOTTE: *(As* DESIRÉE *sweeps past her)* You do indeed, Miss Armfeldt.

DESIRÉE: And Mr. Egerman! How kind of you all to come. Mother will be overjoyed.

FREDRIK: *(Bending over her hand)* It is your mother who is kind in inviting us. Allow me to present my rather antisocial son, Henrik. *(Points to the drifting away* HENRIK, *who turns to acknowledge her)* And this is my wife. *(He presents* ANNE*)*

DESIRÉE: How do you do?

ANNE: *(Icy)* How do you do?

DESIRÉE: *(Indicating* FREDRIKA*)* And this is *my* daughter. *(Pause)* You must all be exhausted after your journeys; my daughter will show you to your rooms. Mother likes dinner at nine.

(FREDRIKA leads them into the house: CHARLOTTE, then ANNE, then HENRIK, then OSA. FREDRIKA then stays on the terrace. Simultaneously, both FREDRIK and CARL-MAGNUS turn, both with the same idea: to get DESIRÉE alone)

CARL-MAGNUS and FREDRIK: Where shall I put the car?

(They exchange a hostile glare)

DESIRÉE: *(Even more flustered)* Ah, the cars, the cars! Now let me see.

CARL-MAGNUS: *(Hissing)* I must speak to you at once!

DESIRÉE: *(Hissing)* Later. *(Out loud)* How about the stables? They're straight ahead.

FREDRIK: *(Hissing)* I must speak to you at once!

DESIRÉE: *(Hissing)* Later. *(Reassured, CARL-MAGNUS and FREDRIK return to their cars. Calling after FREDRIK)* You can't miss them, Mr. Egerman. Just look for the weather vane. A huge tin cockerel. *(Spinning to FREDRIKA, pulling her downstage)* Disaster, darling!

FREDRIKA: But what are you going to do? The way he glared at Mr. Egerman! He'll kill him!

DESIRÉE: Let us keep calm.

(FREDRIK and CARL-MAGNUS, both with auto-cranks in hand, start back toward DESIRÉE)

FREDRIKA: *(Noticing)* They're coming back!

DESIRÉE: *(Totally losing her calm)* Oh, no! Oh, God! *(She starts to run up to the house)*

FREDRIKA: *(Calling after her)* But what should I say?

DESIRÉE: Anything!

(She runs into the house, as FREDRIK and CARL-MAGNUS, gazing after DESIRÉE in astonishment, come up to FREDRIKA)

FREDRIKA: *(On the spot but gracious, seemingly composed)* Mr. Egerman—Count Malcolm . . . Mother told me to tell you that she suddenly . . . *(She breaks)* . . . oh, dear, oh, dear. *(She scurries up into the house. The two men react, then, ignoring each other, return to their cars. They each crank their cars and get into them. The screens close in as the cars back out offstage. MR. ERLANSEN and MRS. NORDSTROM enter)*

MRS. NORDSTROM: *(Sings)*
The sun sits low
And the vespers ring,

MR. ERLANSEN:
And the shadows grow
And the crickets sing,
And it's . . .

MRS. NORDSTROM:
Look! Is that the moon?

MR. ERLANSEN:
Yes.
What a lovely afternoon!

MRS. NORDSTROM:
Yes.

MR. ERLANSEN:
The evening air
Doesn't feel quite right

MRS. NORDSTROM:
In the not-quite glare
Of the not-quite night,
And it's . . .
Wait! Is that a star?

MR. ERLANSEN:
No.
Just the glow of a cigar.

MRS. NORDSTROM:
Oh.

(They exit)

SCENE 2

The other part of the garden.
ANNE *leads* CHARLOTTE *on. Both women carry parasols.*
ANNE: . . . After I spoke to you, I thought: I will go! I won't! Then I thought: Why not? We'll go to that awful woman's house and I'll say to her: "How dare you try to steal my husband? At your age you should have acquired at least some moral sense." And then—then in the motorcar coming here, I thought: "Oh dear, I'll never have the courage and maybe it's all my fault." And oh, I want to go home. *(Bursts into sobs)*
CHARLOTTE: Have no fears. Miss Armfeldt has met her match.
ANNE: *(Astonished, even through tears)* She has? Who?
CHARLOTTE: Me. When I told my husband, he instantly became a tiger—his word, of course—and then, as if from heaven, a plan flashed into my mind. *(Pause)* Do you feel up to hearing my plan, dear? *(ANNE gives a little nod)* I shall make love to your husband.
ANNE: *(Aghast)* You, too?
CHARLOTTE: Confident of my own charms, I shall throw myself into your husband's arms. He will succumb. Why not? Carl-Magnus, in a storm of jealousy, will beg my forgiveness and swear eternal fidelity. And as for Miss Desirée Armfeldt, she will be back peddling her dubious commodities elsewhere. At least, that is the plan.
ANNE: *(Suddenly forgetful of her tears)* Oh, how amusing. How extremely amusing. Poor old Fredrik. And it serves him right, too.
CHARLOTTE: I am not sure I appreciate that remark, dear.
(FREDRIK appears, walking toward them)
FREDRIK: Ah, here you are, ladies.
CHARLOTTE: *(Sudden devastating smile at* FREDRIK*)* Oh, Mr. Egerman! If you'll pardon my saying so, that's a simply ravishing cravat.
FREDRIK: *(Slightly bewildered)* It is?
CHARLOTTE: *(Taking* FREDRIK'S *left arm;* ANNE *takes his right arm)* I can't remember when I have seen so seductive a cravat.
(As ANNE suppresses giggles, they all walk off together. As ANNE, CHARLOTTE, and FREDRIK exit, MR. LINDQUIST and MRS. SEGSTROM appear)

MR. LINDQUIST: *(Sings)*
> *The atmosphere's becoming heady,*
> *The ambiance thrilling,*

MRS. SEGSTROM:
> *The spirit unsteady,*
> *The flesh far too willing.*

MR. LINDQUIST:
> *To be perpetually ready*
> *Is far from fulfilling . . .*

MRS. SEGSTROM:
> *But wait—*
> *The sun*
> *Is dipping.*

MR. LINDQUIST:
> *Where?*
> *You're right.*
> *It's dropping.*
> *Look—!*
> *At last!*
> *It's slipping.*

MRS. SEGSTROM:
> *Sorry,*
> *My mistake,*
> *It's stopping.*

(They exit)

SCENE 2A

> *The other part of the garden.*
> FREDRIKA *enters.*

FREDRIKA: Oh, I do agree that life at times can seem complicated.
> *(*HENRIK *enters behind her)*

HENRIK: Complicated! If only you knew! Oh, Miss . . . Miss . . .

FREDRIKA: Armfeldt. I am not legitimate.

HENRIK: I see. Oh, Miss Armfeldt, all my life, I've made a fiasco of everything. If you knew how poor an opinion I have of myself! If you knew how many times I wish I had been one of the spermatazoa that never reached the womb. *(He breaks from her)* There, there! You see? I've done it again!

FREDRIKA: Mr. Egerman, I have toured with mother, you know. I'm broad-minded.

HENRIK: You are? Then in that case, might I make a confession to you?

FREDRIKA: Of course.

HENRIK: I hate to burden you on so slight an acquaintance, but bottling it up inside of me is driving me insane. *(Pause. With great effort)* Oh, Miss Armfeldt, for the past eleven months, although I am preparing to enter the Ministry, I — *(He can't get it out)*

FREDRIKA: What, Mr. Egerman?

HENRIK: I have been madly, hopelessly in love with my stepmother. Do you realize how many mortal sins that involves? Oh, damn everything to hell! I beg your pardon.

(They link arms and walk off. MR. LINDQUIST, MRS. SEGSTROM, MR. ER-LANSEN, MRS. ANDERSSEN *and* MRS. NORDSTROM *enter and sing)*

ALL:
The light is pink
And the air is still
And the sun is slinking
Behind the hill.
And when finally it sets,
As finally it must,
When finally it lets
The moon and stars adjust,
When finally we greet the dark
And we're breathing amen,

MRS. ANDERSSEN:
Surprise of surprises,
It instantly rises
Again.

*(*THE QUINTET *exits)*

SCENE 3

Armfeldt terrace.
Both dressed for dinner, FREDRIK *and* CARL-MAGNUS *are discovered;* FREDRIK *downstage,* CARL-MAGNUS *pacing on the porch.* FREDRIK *has a cigar and a small liqueur glass;* CARL-MAGNUS *carries a champagne glass.*

FREDRIK: *(Sings)*
I should never have
Gone to the theater.
Then I'd never have come
To the country.
If I never had come
To the country,
Matters might have stayed
As they were.

CARL-MAGNUS: *(Nods)*
Sir . . .

FREDRIK: *(Nods)*
Sir . . .

If she'd only been faded,
If she'd only been fat,
If she'd only been jaded
And bursting with chat,
If she'd only been perfectly awful,
It would have been wonderful.
If . . . if . . .

If she'd been all a-twitter
Or elusively cold,
If she'd only been bitter,
Or better,
Looked passably old,
If she'd been covered with glitter
Or even been covered with mold,
It would have been wonderful.

But the woman was perfection,
To my deepest dismay.
Well, not quite perfection,
I'm sorry to say.
If the woman were perfection,
She would go away,
And that would be wonderful.

Sir . . .

CARL-MAGNUS:
Sir . . .

If she'd only looked flustered
Or admitted the worst,
If she only had blustered
Or simpered or cursed,
If she weren't so awfully perfect,
It would have been wonderful.
If . . .
If . . .
If she'd tried to be clever,
If she'd started to flinch,
If she'd cried or whatever
A woman would do in a pinch,
If I'd been certain she never
Again could be trusted an inch,
It would have been wonderful.

But the woman was perfection,
Not an action denied,
The kind of perfection
I cannot abide.
If the woman were perfection,
She'd have simply lied,
Which would have been wonderful.

FREDRIK:
If she'd only been vicious . . .

CARL-MAGNUS:
If she'd acted abused . . .

FREDRIK:
Or a bit too delicious . . .

CARL-MAGNUS:
Or been even slightly confused . . .

FREDRIK:
If she had only been sulky . . .

CARL-MAGNUS:
Or bristling . . .

FREDRIK:
Or bulky . . .

CARL-MAGNUS:
Or bruised . . .

BOTH:
It would have been wonderful.

CARL-MAGNUS:
If . . .

BOTH:
If . . .

FREDRIK:
If she'd only been willful . . .

CARL-MAGNUS:
If she only had fled . . .

FREDRIK:
Or a little less skillful . . .

CARL-MAGNUS:
Insulted, insisting . . .

FREDRIK:
In bed . . .

CARL-MAGNUS:
If she had only been fearful . . .

FREDRIK:
Or married . . .

CARL-MAGNUS:
Or tearful . . .

FREDRIK:
Or dead . . .

BOTH:
It would have been wonderful.
But the woman was perfection,
And the prospects are grim.
That lovely perfection
That nothing can dim.
Yes, the woman was perfection,
So I'm here with him . . .

CARL-MAGNUS:

Sir . . .

FREDRIK:

Sir . . .

BOTH:

It would have been wonderful.

*(*FREDRIKA *enters from the house)*

FREDRIKA: Excuse me, Count Malcolm, but Mother says she would like a word with you in the green salon.

*(*CARL-MAGNUS, *glaring triumphantly at* FREDRIK, *jumps up and strides into the house.* FREDRIKA *stands and grins shyly at* FREDRIK, *then follows* CARL-MAGNUS *into the house.* DESIRÉE *enters)*

DESIRÉE: Fredrik, you wanted a moment alone with me, I believe. Here it is.

FREDRIK: *(Puzzled)* But that child said . . .

DESIRÉE: Oh, that was just Fredrika's little stratagem.

FREDRIK: Fredrika? Your child is called Fredrika?

DESIRÉE: Yes.

FREDRIK: Ah!

DESIRÉE: Really Fredrik, what vanity. As if you were the only Fredrik in the world. *(Brisk)* Now, what is it you want to tell me?

FREDRIK: As a matter of fact, I thought you should know that my wife has no inkling of the nightshirt episode. So we should be discreet.

DESIRÉE: Dear Fredrik, of course. I wouldn't dream of giving that enchanting child a moment's anxiety.

FREDRIK: Then you do see her charm?

DESIRÉE: How could anyone miss it? How lovely to see you, Fredrik.

FREDRIK: In spite of Count Malcolm's invasion? You're sure we're not complicating . . .

CARL-MAGNUS: *(Off)* Desirée!

FREDRIK: Oh, God! Something tells me I should make myself scarce.

CARL-MAGNUS: *(Off)* Desirée!

FREDRIK: Later, perhaps?

DESIRÉE: Any time.

FREDRIK: In your room?

DESIRÉE: In my room.

*(*FREDRIK *looks around for a place to hide. He finds the statue, puts his glass on it, and hides behind it. He douses his cigar in another glass resting on the statue)*

CARL-MAGNUS: *(Comes out of the house)* Desirée!

DESIRÉE: *(Calling, excessively sweet)* Here, dear!

CARL-MAGNUS: That child said the green salon.

DESIRÉE: She did? How extraordinary.

CARL-MAGNUS: Where's that goddamn lawyer?

DESIRÉE: *(Airy)* Mr. Egerman? Oh, somewhere about, no doubt.

CARL-MAGNUS: What's he doing here anyway?

DESIRÉE: He's visiting my mother, of course. He told you. They're the most devoted old friends.

CARL-MAGNUS: That had better be the truth. If I catch him so much as touching you, I'll call him out—with rapiers! *(Glares)* Where is your bedroom? Readily accessible, I trust.

DESIRÉE: *(Aghast)* But, Carl-Magnus! *(FRID enters from the house, crosses down-stage)* With your *wife* here . . . !

CARL-MAGNUS: Charlotte is irrelevant. I shall visit your bedroom at the earliest opportunity tonight.

FRID: Madame, Count Malcolm! Dinner is served. *(As he moves past them to pick up FREDRIK'S glass, he sees FREDRIK behind the statue. Totally unaware of complications)* Dinner is served, Mr. Egerman. *(FRID exits up into the house)*

DESIRÉE: *(Rising to it)* Ah, there you are, Mr. Egerman! *(FREDRIK comes out from behind the statue, laughing)* Gentlemen, shall we proceed?
(Gives one arm to each as they start up into the house and freeze *in place)*

SCENE 4

The dining room.
As the dining room table and GUESTS *come on,* MRS. NORDSTROM, MRS. SEGSTROM *and* MRS. ANDERSSEN *sing.*

MRS. NORDSTROM:
Perpetual anticipation
      is
Good for the soul
But it's bad for the
    heart.
It's very good for prac-
    ticing

Self-control.
It's very good for
Morals,
But bad for morale.
It's very bad.
It can lead to

Going quite mad.

It's very good for

Reserve and

Learning to do

What one should.
It's very good.

Perpetual
Anticipation's
A delicate art,

MRS. SEGSTROM:
Perpetual antici-
Pation is good for

The
Soul, but it's bad
For the
Heart.
It's very good for
Practicing self-
Control. It's
Very good for
Morals but bad

For morale. It's

Too unnerving.

It's very good,

Though, to have
Things to contem-

Plate.

Perpetual
Anticipation's

MRS. ANDERSSEN:
Per-
Petual antici-
Pation is good
For
The soul, but
It's
Bad for the
Heart.
It's
Very good,
Though,
To learn to
Wait.

Perpetual

Playing a role,	*A* *Delicate art,*	*Anticipation's* *A* *Delicate art,*
Aching to start,	*Aching to start,*	
Keeping control *While falling* *Apart.*	*Keeping control* *While falling* *Apart.*	*Keeping control* *While falling* *Apart.*
Perpetual *Anticipation is* *Good for the soul* *But it's bad for the* *Heart.*	*Perpetual* *Anticipation is* *Good* *But it's bad for the* *Heart.*	*Perpetual* *Anticipation is* *Bad for the* *Heart.*

(The dining room table has moved onstage with MADAME ARMFELDT *already seated in place, facing the audience in solitary splendor. The table is elaborately dressed with fruit and floral pieces and expensive dinnerware. There are also two large candelabra, one at each end of the table. Parallel to the table and upstage of it, the line of* SERVANTS *has come on:* BERTRAND, OSA, PETRA, *and* FRID. OSA *and* PETRA *stand with trays as* FRID *and* BERTRAND *light the candelabra.*

Once the table is in place, FREDRIK *and* CARL-MAGNUS *move up to it with* DESIRÉE. FREDRIK *pulls out a chair for* DESIRÉE *and she sits.* FREDRIK *gets* ANNE *and seats her.* CHARLOTTE *enters,* CARL-MAGNUS *seats her on the extreme right end of the table. He then moves to the extreme left, and sits down next to* DESIRÉE. HENRIK *sits between* DESIRÉE *and* ANNE, FREDRIK *between* ANNE *and* CHARLOTTE. *The* GUESTS *all sit facing upstage.* FRID *and* BERTRAND *pour, and* MADAME ARMFELDT *raises her glass. The* OTHERS *follow her. When the glasses come down, there is a burst of laughter and noise from the* GUESTS.

FREDRIKA, *seated at the piano, "accompanies" the scene)*

DESIRÉE: . . . So you won the case after all, Mr. Egerman! How splendid!

FREDRIK: I was rather proud of myself.

DESIRÉE: And I'm sure you were tremendously proud of him too, Mrs. Egerman.

ANNE: I beg your pardon? Oh, I expect so, although I don't seem to remember much about it.

(CHARLOTTE extends her glass; BERTRAND fills it)

FREDRIK: I try not to bore my wife with my dubious victories in the courtroom.

DESIRÉE: How wise you are. I remember when I was her age, anything less than a new dress, or a ball, or a thrilling piece of gossip bored me to tears.

FREDRIK: That is the charm of youth.

CHARLOTTE: Dearest Miss Armfeldt, do regale us with more fascinating reminiscences from your remote youth.

CARL-MAGNUS: Charlotte, that is an idiotic remark.

FREDRIK: A man's youth may be as remote as a dinosaur, Countess, but with a beautiful woman, youth merely accompanies her through the years.

CHARLOTTE: Oh, Mr. Egerman, that is too enchanting! *(Leaning over her chair)*

Anne, dear, where on earth did you find this simply adorable husband?

ANNE: *(Leans. In on the "plan," of course, giggling)* I'm glad you approve of him.

CHARLOTTE: *(To* HENRIK*)* Your father *(*HENRIK *leans)* is irresistible. *(*CARL-MAGNUS *leans)* I shall monopolize him for the entire weekend. *(*DESIRÉE *leans. Then, to* ANNE*)* Will you lease him to me, dear?

ANNE: *(Giggling)* Freely. He's all yours. *(*FREDRIK *looks at* ANNE, *then at* CHARLOTTE, *then leans)* . . . unless, of course, our hostess has other plans for him.

DESIRÉE: *(Smooth, getting out of her seat)* I had thought of seducing him into rolling the croquet lawn tomorrow, but I'm sure he'd find the Countess less exhausting.

CHARLOTTE: *(Rising)* I wouldn't guarantee that! *(Clapping her hand over her mouth)* Oh, how could those wicked words have passed these lips!

CARL-MAGNUS: *(Astonished. Rising)* Charlotte!

CHARLOTTE: Oh, Carl-Magnus, dear, don't say you're bristling! *(To* FREDRIK *who has also risen. From here the two of them move to the music in a stylized fashion)* My husband, Mr. Egerman, is a veritable porcupine. At the least provocation he is all spines—or is it quills? Beware. I am leading you down dangerous paths!

CARL-MAGNUS: *(Frigid)* I apologize for my wife, sir. She is not herself tonight.

FREDRIK: *(Both amused and gracious)* If she is this charming when she is *not* herself, sir, I would be fascinated to meet her when she *is.*

CHARLOTTE: Bravo, bravo! My champion! *(*HENRIK *and* ANNE *get up from the table and join the stylized dance)* May tomorrow find us thigh to thigh pushing the garden roller in tandem.

FREDRIK: *(Turning it into a joke)* That would depend on the width of the rollers. *(To* DESIRÉE*)* Miss Armfeldt, as a stranger in this house, may I ask if your roller . . .

CARL-MAGNUS: *(Instantly picking this up)* Stranger, sir? How can you call yourself a stranger in *this* house?

FREDRIK: *(Momentarily bewildered)* I beg your pardon?

CARL-MAGNUS: *(Triumphantly sure he has found* FREDRIK *and* DESIRÉE *out, to* MADAME ARMFELDT*)* I understand from your daughter, Madame, that Mr. Egerman is an old friend of yours and consequently a frequent visitor to this house.

MADAME ARMFELDT: *(Vaguely aware of him, peering through a lorgnette)* Are you addressing me, sir? Whoever you may be.

CARL-MAGNUS: I am, Madame.

MADAME ARMFELDT: Then be so kind as to repeat yourself.

DESIRÉE: *(Breaking in)* Mother, Count Malcolm—

MADAME ARMFELDT: *(Overriding this, ignoring her, to* CARL-MAGNUS*)* Judging from the level of the conversation so far, young man, you can hardly expect me to have been paying attention.

*(*CARL-MAGNUS *is taken aback)*

CHARLOTTE: Splendid! The thrust direct! I shall commandeer that remark and wreak havoc with it at all my husband's regimental dinner parties!

(Dance section. Finally MADAME ARMFELDT *tings on a glass with her fork for silence)*

MADAME ARMFELDT: *(As* FRID *and* BERTRAND *serve)* Ladies and gentlemen, tonight I am serving you a very special dessert wine. It is from the cellars of the King of the Belgians who—during a period of intense intimacy—presented me with all the bottles then in existence. The secret of its unique quality is unknown, but it is said to possess the power to open the eyes—even of the blindest among us . . . *(Raising her glass)* To Life!

(The GUESTS *all raise their glasses)*

THE OTHERS: To Life!

MADAME ARMFELDT: And to the only other reality—Death!

(Only MADAME ARMFELDT *and* CHARLOTTE *drink.*

A sudden chilly silence descends on the party as if a huge shadow had passed over it. The GUESTS *slowly drift back to the table in silence.*

At length the silence is broken by a little tipsy giggle from CHARLOTTE*)*

CHARLOTTE: Oh I *am* enjoying myself! What an unusual sensation! *(Raises her glass to* DESIRÉE*)* Dearest Miss Armfeldt, at this awe-inspiring moment—let me drink to *you* who have made this evening possible. The One and Only Desirée Armfeldt, beloved of hundreds—regardless of course of their matrimonial obligations! *(Hiccups)*

CARL-MAGNUS: Charlotte, you will go to your room immediately!

(There is general consternation)

FREDRIK: Miss Armfeldt, I'm sure the Countess—

ANNE: Oh, dear, oh, dear, I am beside myself.

HENRIK: *(Suddenly jumping up, shouting, smashing his glass on the table)* Stop it! All of you! Stop it!

(There is instantly silence)

FREDRIK: Henrik!

HENRIK: *(Swinging to glare at him)* Are *you* reproving *me?*

FREDRIK: I think, if I were you, I would sit down.

HENRIK: Sit, Henrik. Stand, Henrik. Am I to spend the rest of my life at your command, like a lapdog? Am I to respect a man who can permit such filthy pigs' talk in front of the purest, the most innocent, the most wonderful . . . ? I despise you all!

ANNE: *(Giggling nervously)* Oh, Henrik! How comical you look!

DESIRÉE: *(Smiling, holding out her glass to him)* Smash this too. Smash every glass in the house if you feel like it.

HENRIK: *(Bewildered and indignant)* And you! You're an artist! You play Ibsen and —and Racine! Don't any of the great truths of the artists, come through to you at all? Are you no better than the others?

DESIRÉE: Why don't you just laugh at us all, my dear? Wouldn't that be a solution?

HENRIK: How can I laugh, when life makes me want to vomit? *(He runs out of the room)*

ANNE: Poor silly Henrik. Someone should go after him. *(She gets up from the table, starts away)*

FREDRIK: *(Very authoritative)* Anne. Come back.

(Meekly, ANNE *obeys, sitting down again at the table. Total silence.* FREDRIK *sits. Then, after a beat: A hiccup from* CHARLOTTE*)*

DESIRÉE: Dear Countess, may I suggest that you try holding your breath—for a very long time?

(The screens close in on the scene, and the table moves off)

SCENE 5

Armfeldt garden.
HENRIK, *who has run from the dining room, runs and stands near the bench in despair.* FREDRIKA, *at the piano sees him.*
FREDRIKA: *(Stops playing)* Mr. Egerman! *(*HENRIK *ignores her)* Mr. Egerman?
*(*HENRIK *looks up)*
HENRIK: I have disgraced myself—acting like a madman, breaking an expensive glass, humiliating myself in front of them all.
FREDRIKA: Poor, Mr. Egerman!
HENRIK: *(Defending himself in spite of himself)* They laughed at me. Even Anne. She said, "Silly Henrik, how comical you look!" Laughter! How I detest it! Your mother—everyone—says, "Laugh at it all." If all you can do is laugh at the cynicism, the frivolity, the lack of heart—then I'd rather be dead.
ANNE: *(Off)* Henrik!
HENRIK: Oh, God! There she is! *(He runs off)*
ANNE: *(Off)* Henrik dear!
FREDRIKA: *(Calls after him)* Mr. Egerman! Please don't do anything rash! *(*ANNE *runs on)* Oh, Mrs. Egerman, I'm so terribly worried.
ANNE: You poor dear. What about?
FREDRIKA: About Mr. Egerman—Junior, that is.
ANNE: Silly Henrik! I was just coming out to scold him.
FREDRIKA: I am so afraid he may do himself an injury.
ANNE: How delightful to be talking to someone younger than myself. No doubt he has been denouncing the wickedness of the world—and quoting Martin Luther? Dearest Fredrika, all you were witnessing was the latest crisis in his love affair with God.
FREDRIKA: Not with God, Mrs. Egerman—with you!
ANNE: *(Totally surprised)* Me!
FREDRIKA: You may not have noticed, but he is madly, hopelessly in love with you.
ANNE: Is that really the truth?
FREDRIKA: Yes, he told me so himself.
ANNE: *(Thrilled, flattered, perhaps more)* The poor dear boy! How ridiculous of him—and yet how charming. Dear friend, if you knew how insecure I constantly feel, how complicated the marriage state seems to be. I adore old Fredrik, of course, but . . .
FREDRIKA: *(Interrupting)* But Mrs. Egerman, he ran down towards the lake!
ANNE: *(Laughing)* To gaze over the ornamental waters! How touching! Let us go and find him. *(*ANNE *takes* FREDRIKA*'s arm and starts walking off with her)* Such a good-looking boy, isn't he? Such long, long lashes . . .
(They exit giggling, arm-in-arm)

SCENE 5A

Another part of the garden.
FRID *runs on from behind a screen, followed by a more leisurely* PETRA. *They have a bottle of wine and a small bundle of food with them.*
PETRA: Who needs a haystack? Anything you've got to show, you can show me right here—that is, if you're in the mood.

FRID: *(Taking her into his arms)* When am I not in the mood?

PETRA: *(Laughing)* I wouldn't know, would I? I'm just passing through.

FRID: I'm in the mood. *(Kiss)* I'm in it twenty-four hours a day. *(Kiss)*

(FREDRIKA runs across stage)

FREDRIKA: Mr. Egerman!

PETRA: Private here, isn't it?

(ANNE runs across stage)

ANNE: Henrik! Henrik!

PETRA: What *are* they up to?

FRID: Oh, them! What are they ever up to?

(ANNE runs back across)

ANNE: Henrik!

(FREDRIKA runs back across)

FREDRIKA: Mr. Egerman!

FRID: You saw them all at dinner, dressed up like waxworks, jabbering away to prove how clever they are. And never knowing what they miss. *(Kiss)*

ANNE'S VOICE: Henrik!

FRID: Catch one of them having the sense to grab the first pretty girl that comes along—and do her on the soft grass, with the summer night just smiling down. *(Kiss)* Any complaints yet?

PETRA: Give me time.

FRID: You've a sweet mouth—sweet as honey.

(The screen moves, wiping out FRID and PETRA. It reveals HENRIK, who has been watching them make love. After an anguished moment, he runs straight up into the house, slamming the doors behind him)

SCENE 6

Desirée's bedroom.

DESIRÉE sits on the bed, her long skirt drawn up over her knees, expertly sewing up a hem. FREDRIK enters and clears his throat.

FREDRIK: Your dragoon and his wife are glowering at each other in the Green Salon, and all the children appear to have vanished, so when I saw you sneaking up the stairs . . .

DESIRÉE: I ripped my hem on the dining room table in all that furore.

FREDRIK: *(Hovering)* Is this all right?

DESIRÉE: Of course. Sit down. *(Patting the bed beside her, on which tumbled stockings are strewn)*

FREDRIK: *On* the stockings?

DESIRÉE: I don't see why not. *(There is a long pause)* Well, we're back at the point where we were so rudely interrupted last week, aren't we?

FREDRIK: Not quite. If you'll remember, we'd progressed a step further.

DESIRÉE: How true.

FREDRIK: I imagine neither of us is contemplating a repeat performance.

DESIRÉE: Good heavens, with your wife in the house, and my lover and his wife and my daughter . . .

FREDRIK: . . . and my devoted old friend, your mother.

(They both laugh)

DESIRÉE: *(During it, like a naughty girl)* Isn't my dragoon awful?

FREDRIK: *(Laughs)* When you told me he had the brain of a pea, I think you were being generous.

(They laugh more uproariously)

DESIRÉE: What in God's name are we laughing about? Your son was right at dinner. We don't fool that boy, not for a moment. The One and Only Desirée Armfeldt, dragging around the country in shoddy tours, carrying on with someone else's dim-witted husband. And the Great Lawyer Egerman, busy renewing his unrenewable youth.

FREDRIK: Bravo! Probably that's an accurate description of us both.

DESIRÉE: Shall I tell you why I really invited you here? When we met again and we made love, I thought: Maybe here it is at last—a chance to turn back, to find some sort of coherent existence after so many years of muddle. *(Pause)* Of course, there's your wife. But I thought: perhaps—just perhaps—you might be in need of rescue, too.

FREDRIK: From renewing my unrenewable youth?

DESIRÉE: *(Suddenly tentative)* It was only a thought.

FREDRIK: When my eyes are open and I look at you, I see a woman that I have loved for a long time, who entranced me all over again when I came to her rooms . . . who gives me such genuine pleasure that, in spite of myself, I came here for the sheer delight of being with her again. The woman who could rescue me? Of course. *(Pause)* But when my eyes are not open—which is most of the time—all I see is a girl in a pink dress teasing a canary, running through a sunlit garden to hug me at the gate, as if I'd come home from Timbuctu instead of the Municipal Courthouse three blocks away . . .

DESIRÉE: *(Sings)*
Isn't it rich?
Are we a pair?
Me here at last on the ground,
You in mid-air.
Send in the clowns.
Isn't it bliss?
Don't you approve?
One who keeps tearing around,
One who can't move.
Where are the clowns?
Send in the clowns.

Just when I'd stopped
Opening doors,
Finally knowing
The one that I wanted was yours,
Making my entrance again
With my usual flair,
Sure of my lines,
No one is there.

(FREDRIK rises)

Don't you love farce?
My fault, I fear.

I thought that you'd want what I want—
Sorry, my dear.
But where are the clowns?
Quick, send in the clowns.
Don't bother, they're here.

FREDRIK: Desirée, I'm sorry. I should never have come. To flirt with rescue when one has no intention of being saved . . . Do try to forgive me.
(He exits)

DESIRÉE:

Isn't it rich?
Isn't it queer?
Losing my timing this late
In my career?
And where are the clowns?
There ought to be clowns.
Well, maybe next year . . .

(The lights iris out on DESIRÉE*)*

SCENE 7

The trees.
As DESIRÉE*'s bedroom goes off,* HENRIK *emerges from the house, carrying a rope. He runs downstage with it.*
ANNE *and* FREDRIKA *run on; when* HENRIK *hears them, he runs behind the screens to hide.*
ANNE: *(As she runs on)* Henrik! *(To* FREDRIKA*)* Oh, I'm quite puffed! Where can he be? *(Noticing* FREDRIKA*'s solemn face)* Poor child, that face! Don't look so solemn. Where would you go if you were he?
FREDRIKA: Well, the summer pavilion? And then, of course, there's the stables.
ANNE: Then you go to the stables and I'll take the summer pavilion. *(Laughing)* Run! *(She starts off)* Isn't this exciting after that stodgy old dinner!
(They run off, and HENRIK *runs back on. He stops at the tree, stands on the marble bench, and, after circling his noose around his neck, throws the other end of the rope up to the tree limb)*
ANNE'S VOICE: Henrik!
*(*HENRIK *falls with a loud thud, as* ANNE *enters)*
ANNE: What an extraordinary . . . ! Oh, Henrik—how comical you look! *(Pulling him up by the noose still around his neck)* Oh, no! You didn't! *(Pause)* For me? *(She gently removes the noose from his neck)* Oh, my poor darling Henrik. *(She throws herself into his arms)* Oh, my poor boy! Oh, those eyes, gazing at me like a lost Saint Bernard . . .
(They start to kiss passionately)
HENRIK: I love you! I've actually *said* it!
ANNE: *(Returning his kisses passionately)* Oh, how scatter-brained I was never to have realized. Not Fredrik . . . not poor old Fredrik . . . not Fredrik at all!
(They drop down onto the ground and start to make passionate love.
The trees wipe them out, revealing PETRA *and* FRID. FRID *is still asleep)*

PETRA: *(Sings)*

> *I shall marry the miller's son,*
> *Pin my hat on a nice piece of property.*
> *Friday nights, for a bit of fun,*
> *We'll go dancing.*
> *Meanwhile . . .*
> *It's a wink and a wiggle*
> *And a giggle in the grass*
> *And I'll trip the light fandango,*
> *A pinch and a diddle*
> *In the middle of what passes by.*
> *It's a very short road*
> *From the pinch and the punch*
> *To the paunch and the pouch and the pension.*
> *It's a very short road*
> *To the ten thousandth lunch*
> *And the belch and the grouch and the sigh.*
> *In the meanwhile,*
> *There are mouths to be kissed*
> *Before mouths to be fed,*
> *And a lot in between*
> *In the meanwhile.*
> *And a girl ought to celebrate what passes by.*
>
> *Or I shall marry the businessman,*
> *Five fat babies and lots of security.*
> *Friday nights, if we think we can,*
> *We'll go dancing.*
> *Meanwhile . . .*
> *It's a push and a fumble*
> *And a tumble in the sheets*
> *And I'll foot the highland fancy,*
> *A dip in the butter*
> *And a flutter with what meets my eye.*
> *It's a very short fetch*
> *From the push and the whoop*
> *To the squint and the stoop and the mumble.*
> *It's not much of a stretch*
> *To the cribs and the croup*
> *And the bosoms that droop and go dry.*
> *In the meanwhile,*
> *There are mouths to be kissed*
> *Before mouths to be fed,*
> *And there's many a tryst*
> *And there's many a bed*
> *To be sampled and seen*
> *In the meanwhile.*
> *And a girl has to celebrate what passes by.*

Or I shall marry the Prince of Wales—
Pearls and servants and dressing for festivals.
Friday nights, with him all in tails,
We'll have dancing.
Meanwhile . . .
It's a rip in the bustle
And a rustle in the hay
And I'll pitch the quick fantastic,
With flings of confetti
And my petticoats away up high.
It's a very short way
From the fling that's for fun
To the thigh pressing under the table.
It's a very short day
Till you're stuck with just one
Or it has to be done on the sly.
In the meanwhile,
There are mouths to be kissed
Before mouths to be fed,
And there's many a tryst
And there's many a bed.
There's a lot I'll have missed
But I'll not have been dead when I die!
And a person should celebrate everything
Passing by.

And I shall marry the miller's son.

(She smiles, as the lights fade on her)

SCENE 8

Armfeldt house and garden.
FREDRIKA *is lying on the grass reading.* MADAME ARMFELDT, *seated in a huge wingchair upstage.* DESIRÉE, *on the bed, is writing in her diary.* CARL-MAGNUS *paces on the terrace and then goes into the house.* MRS. SEGSTROM *and* MR. LINDQUIST *are behind trees,* MR. ERLANSEN *and* MRS. ANDERSSEN *are behind opposite trees.* CHARLOTTE *sits downstage on a bench.*
After a beat, FREDRIK *enters, sees the* FIGURE *on the bench. Is it* ANNE? *He hurries toward her.*
FREDRIK: Anne?—Oh, forgive me, Countess. I was looking for my wife.
CHARLOTTE: *(Looking up, through sobs)* Oh Mr. Egerman, how can I face you after that exhibition at dinner? Throwing myself at your head!
FREDRIK: On the contrary, I found it most morale-building. *(Sits down next to her)* It's not often these days that a beautiful woman does me that honor.
CHARLOTTE: I didn't.
FREDRIK: I beg your pardon?
CHARLOTTE: I didn't do you that honor. It was just a charade. A *failed* charade! In my madness I thought I could make my husband jealous.
FREDRIK: I'm afraid marriage isn't one of the easier relationships, is it?

CHARLOTTE: Mr. Egerman, for a woman it's impossible!

FREDRIK: It's not all that possible for men.

CHARLOTTE: Men! Look at you—a man of an age when a woman is lucky if a drunken alderman pinches her derierre at a village fete! And yet, you have managed to acquire the youngest, prettiest . . . I hate you being happy. I hate *anyone* being happy!

(HENRIK and ANNE emerge from the house, carrying suitcases. They start stealthily downstage)

HENRIK: The gig should be ready at the stables.

ANNE: *(Giggling)* Oh, Henrik darling, I do hope the horses will be smart. I do detest riding in a gig when the horses are not smart.

(HENRIK stops, pulls her to him. They kiss)

MRS. SEGSTROM: *(Turns, looking onstage, sings)*
Think of how I adore you,
Think of how much you love me,
If I were perfect for you,
Wouldn't you tire of me
Soon . . . ?

HENRIK: Let all the birds nest in my hair!

ANNE: Silly Henrik! Quick, or we'll miss the train!

(THEY are now downstage. Unaware of FREDRIK and CHARLOTTE, they move past them. For a long moment, FREDRIK and CHARLOTTE sit, while FREDRIK'S world tumbles around his ears)

CHARLOTTE: It was, wasn't it?

FREDRIK: It was.

CHARLOTTE: Run after them. Quick. You can catch them at the stables.

FREDRIK: *(Even more quiet)* After the horse has gone? *(Pause)* How strange that one's life should end sitting on a bench in a garden.

MR. ERLANSEN: *(Leans, looking onstage, sings)*
She lightens my sadness,
She livens my days,
She bursts with a kind of madness
My well-ordered ways.
My happiest mistake,
The ache of my life . . .

(As they sit, the lights come up on DESIRÉE'S BEDROOM, as CARL-MAGNUS enters)

DESIRÉE: Carl-Magnus, go away!

CARL-MAGNUS: *(Ignoring her, beginning to unbutton his tunic)* I'd have been here half an hour ago if I hadn't had to knock a little sense into my wife.

DESIRÉE: Carl-Magnus, do not take off your tunic!

CARL-MAGNUS: *(Still ignoring her)* Poor girl. She was somewhat the worse for wine, of course. Trying to make me believe that she was attracted to that asinine lawyer fellow.

DESIRÉE: Carl-Magnus, listen to me! It's over. It was never anything in the first place, but now it's OVER!

CARL-MAGNUS: *(Ignoring this, totally self-absorbed)* Of all people—that lawyer!

Scrawny as a scarecrow and without a hair on his body, probably. *(He starts removing his braces)*

DESIRÉE: *(Shouting)* Don't take off your trousers!

CARL-MAGNUS: *(Getting out of his trousers)* Poor girl, she'd slash her wrists before she'd let any other man touch her. And even if, under the influence of wine, she did stray a bit, how ridiculous to imagine I would so much as turn a hair! *(As he starts to get out of his trouser leg, he stumbles so that he happens to be facing the "window." He stops dead, peering out)* Good God!

DESIRÉE: What is it?

CARL-MAGNUS: *(Peering)* It's her! And him! Sitting on a bench! She's touching him! The scoundrel! The conniving swine! Any man who thinks he can lay a finger on *my* wife! *(Pulling up his pants and grabbing his tunic as he hobbles out)*

DESIRÉE: Carl-Magnus, what are you doing?

CARL-MAGNUS: My duelling pistols! *(And he rushes out)*

(DESIRÉE runs after him)

DESIRÉE: Carl-Magnus!

(The bed rolls off)

MADAME ARMFELDT: A great deal seems to be going on in this house tonight. *(Pause)* Child, will you do me a favor?

FREDRIKA: Of course, Grandmother.

MADAME ARMFELDT: Will you tell me what it's all for? Having outlived my own illusions by centuries, it would be soothing at least to pretend to share some of yours.

FREDRIKA: *(After thought)* Well, I think it must be worth it.

MADAME ARMFELDT: Why?

FREDRIKA: It's all there is, isn't it? Oh, I know it's often discouraging, and to hope for something too much is childish, because what you want so rarely happens.

MADAME ARMFELDT: Astounding! When I was your age I wanted everything— the moon—jewels, yachts, villas on the Riviera. And I got 'em, too,—for all the good they did me. *(Music. Her mind starts to wander)* There was a Croatian Count. He was my first lover. I can see his face now—such eyes, and a mustache like a brigand. He gave me a wooden ring.

FREDRIKA: A wooden ring?

MADAME ARMFELDT: It had been in his family for centuries, it seemed, but I said to myself: a wooden ring? What sort of man would give you a wooden ring, so I tossed him out right there and then. And now—who knows? He might have been the love of my life.

(In the GARDEN, FREDRIK and CHARLOTTE pause)

CHARLOTTE: To think I was actually saying: How I hate you being happy! It's —as if I carry around some terrible curse. *(CARL-MAGNUS enters from house, runs down steps)* Oh, Mr. Egerman . . . I'm sorry.

(CHARLOTTE breaks from FREDRIK with a little cry. FREDRIK, still dazed, merely turns, gazing vaguely at CARL-MAGNUS)

CARL-MAGNUS: *(Glaring, clicks his heels)* Sir, you will accompany me to the Pavilion.

(CHARLOTTE looks at the pistol. Slowly the wonderful truth begins to dawn on her. He really cares! Her face breaks into a radiant smile)

CHARLOTTE: Carl-Magnus!

CARL-MAGNUS: *(Ignoring her)* I think the situation speaks for itself.

CHARLOTTE: *(Her ecstatic smile broadening)* Carl-Magnus, dear, you won't be *too* impulsive, will you?

CARL-MAGNUS: Whatever the provocation, I remain a civilized man. *(Flourishing the pistol)* The lawyer and I are merely going to play a little Russian Roulette.

CHARLOTTE: Russian Roulette?

CARL-MAGNUS: *(To FREDRIK)* Well, sir? Are you ready, sir??

FREDRIK: *(Still only half aware)* I beg your pardon. Ready for what??

CHARLOTTE: *(Thrilled)* Russian Roulette!

FREDRIK: Oh, Russian Roulette. That's with a pistol, isn't it? And you spin the . . . *(Indicating)* Well, why not? *(Very polite, to CHARLOTTE)* Excuse me, Madame.

(CARL-MAGNUS clicks his heels and struts off. FREDRIK follows him off slowly)

MR. LINDQUIST: *(Sings)*
A weekend in the country . . .

MR. LINDQUIST and MRS. ANDERSSEN:
So inactive

MR. LINDQUIST, MRS. ANDERSSEN and MR. ERLANSEN:
That one has to lie down.

MR. LINDQUIST, MRS. ANDERSSEN, MR. ERLANSEN, MRS. SEGSTROM, MRS. NORDSTROM:
A weekend in the country
Where . . .

(FRID and PETRA enter, unobserved, and lean against a tree. Gunshot)

We're twice as upset as in town!

(THE QUINTET scatters and runs off, except for MRS. ANDERSSEN who stands behind a tree. DESIRÉE runs out of the house and down to CHARLOTTE)

DESIRÉE: What is it? What's happened?

CHARLOTTE: Oh, dear Miss Armfeldt, my husband and Mr. Egerman are duelling in the pavilion!

DESIRÉE: Are you insane? You let them do it?

(She starts to run to the PAVILION. CARL-MAGNUS enters, carrying FREDRIK over one shoulder. Quite roughly, he tosses him down on the grass, where FREDRIK remains motionless)

DESIRÉE: You lunatic! You've killed him! Fredrik!

CHARLOTTE: Carl-Magnus!

CARL-MAGNUS: My dear Miss Armfeldt, he merely grazed his ear. I trust his performance in the Law Courts is a trifle more professional. *(He clears his throat. To CHARLOTTE)* I am prepared to forgive you, dear. But I feel this house is no longer a suitable place for us.

CHARLOTTE: Oh yes, my darling, I agree!

CARL-MAGNUS: You will pack my things and meet me in the stables. I will have the car ready.

CHARLOTTE: Yes, dear. Oh, Carl-Magnus! You became a tiger for me!
(They kiss)

MRS. ANDERSSEN: *(Sings)*
> *Men are stupid, men are vain,*
> *Love's disgusting, love's insane,*
> *A humiliating business . . .*

MRS. SEGSTROM:
> *Oh, how true!*

(CARL-MAGNUS and CHARLOTTE break the kiss. CARL-MAGNUS exits. CHARLOTTE runs up to the house)

MRS. ANDERSSEN:
> *Aaaah,*

(When CHARLOTTE closes the house doors)

> *Well . . .*

DESIRÉE: Fredrik? Fredrik!

FREDRIK: *(Stirs, opens his eyes, looks dazedly around)* I don't suppose this is my heavenly reward, is it?

DESIRÉE: Hardly, dear, with *me* here.

FREDRIK: *(Trying to sit up, failing, remembering)* Extraordinary, isn't it? To hold a muzzle to one's temple—and yet to miss! A shaky hand, perhaps, is an asset after all.

DESIRÉE: Does it hurt?

FREDRIK: It hurts—spiritually. You've heard, I imagine, about the evening's other event?

DESIRÉE: No, what?

FREDRIK: Henrik and Anne—ran off together.

DESIRÉE: Fredrik!

FREDRIK: Well, I think I should get up and confront the world, don't you?

DESIRÉE: *(Sings)*
> *Isn't it rich?*

FREDRIK: *(Sings)*
> *Are we a pair?*
> *You here at last on the ground.*

DESIRÉE:
> *You in mid-air.*

> *(Speaks)*
> Knees wobbly?

FREDRIK: No, no, it seems not. In fact, it's hardly possible, but . . .

DESIRÉE: *(Sings)*
> *Was that a farce?*

FREDRIK: *(Sings)*
> *My fault, I fear.*

DESIRÉE:
> *Me as a merry-go-round.*

FREDRIK:
Me as King Lear.

(Speaks)
How unlikely life is! To lose one's son, one's wife, and practically one's life within an hour and yet to feel—relieved. Relieved, and, what's more, considerably less ancient. *(He jumps up on the bench)* Aha! Desirée!

DESIRÉE: Poor Fredrik!

FREDRIK: No, no, no. We will banish "poor" from our vocabulary and replace it with "coherent."

DESIRÉE: *(Blank)* Coherent?

FREDRIK: Don't you remember your manifesto in the bedroom? A coherent existence after so many years of muddle? You and me, and of course, Fredrika?

(They kiss. The music swells)

FREDRIK: *(Sings)*
Make way for the clowns.

DESIRÉE: *(Sings)*
Applause for the clowns.

BOTH:
They're finally here.

(The music continues)

FREDRIK: *(Speaks)* How does Malmo appeal to you? It'll be high sunburn season.

DESIRÉE: Why not?

FREDRIK: Why not?

DESIRÉE: Oh, God!

FREDRIK: What is it?

DESIRÉE: I've got to do Hedda for a week in Halsingborg.

FREDRIK: Well, what's wrong with Purgatory before Paradise? I shall sit through all eight performances.

(They go slowly upstage. FREDRIKA wakes up)

FREDRIKA: Don't you think you should go to bed, Grandmother?

MADAME ARMFELDT: No, I shall stay awake all night for fear of missing the first cock-crow of morning. It has come to be my only dependable friend.

FREDRIKA: Grandmother—

MADAME ARMFELDT: What, dear?

FREDRIKA: I've watched and watched, but I haven't noticed the night smiling.

MADAME ARMFELDT: Young eyes are not ideal for watching. They stray too much. It has already smiled. Twice.

FREDRIKA: It has? Twice? For the young—and the fools?

MADAME ARMFELDT: The smile for the fools was particularly broad tonight.

FREDRIKA: So there's only the last to come.

MADAME ARMFELDT: Only the last.

(MADAME ARMFELDT dies.

We become more aware of the underscoring, the same used under the opening waltz.

HENRIK *and* ANNE *suddenly waltz on, and then all of the* OTHER COUPLES, *at last with their proper partners, waltz through the scene.*

The screens close, and MR. LINDQUIST *appears at the piano. He hits one key of the piano, just as he did at the opening.*

And the play is over)

STANLEY RICHARDS

Since the publication of his first collection in 1968, Stanley Richards has become one of our leading editors and play anthologists, earning rare encomiums from the nation's press (the *Writers Guild of America News* described him as "Easily the Best Anthologist of Plays in America"), and the admiration of a multitude of devoted readers.

In addition to *Great Musicals of the American Theatre, Volume 2*, Mr. Richards has edited the following anthologies and series: *The Best Short Plays 1976; The Best Short Plays 1975; The Best Short Plays 1974; The Best Short Plays 1973; The Best Short Plays 1972; The Best Short Plays 1971; The Best Short Plays 1970; The Best Short Plays 1969; The Best Short Plays 1968; Ten Great Musicals of the American Theatre; Best Plays of the Sixties; Best Mystery and Suspense Plays of the Modern Theatre; 10 Classic Mystery and Suspense Plays of the Modern Theatre* (the latter four, *The Fireside Theatre-Literary Guild* selections); *America on Stage: Ten Great Plays of American History; Best Short Plays of the World Theatre: 1958–1967; Best Short Plays of the World Theatre: 1968–1973; Modern Short Comedies from Broadway and London;* and *Canada on Stage.*

An established playwright as well, he has written 25 plays, 12 of which (including *Through a Glass, Darkly; Tunnel of Love; August Heat; Sun Deck; O Distant Land;* and *District of Columbia*) were originally published in earlier volumes of *The Best One-Act Plays* and *The Best Short Plays* annuals.

Journey to Bahia, which he adapted from a prize-winning Brazilian play and film, *O Pagador de Promessas*, premiered at The Berkshire Playhouse, Massachusetts, and later was produced in Washington, D. C., under the auspices of the Brazilian Ambassador and the Brazilian American Cultural Institute. The play also had a successful engagement Off-Broadway during the 1970–1971 season; and in September, 1972, it was performed in a Spanish translation at Lincoln Center. During the summer of 1975, the play was presented at the Edinburgh International Festival in Scotland, after a tour of several British cities.

Mr. Richards' plays have been translated for production and publication abroad into Portuguese, Afrikaans, Dutch, Tagalog, French, German, Korean, Italian and Spanish.

He also has been the New York theatre critic for *Players Magazine* and a frequent contributor to *Playbill, Theatre Arts, The Theatre* and *Actors' Equity Magazine*, among other periodicals.

As an American Theatre Specialist, Mr. Richards was awarded three successive grants by the U. S. Department of State's International Cultural Exchange Program to teach playwriting and directing in Chile and Brazil. He taught playwriting in Canada for over ten years and in 1966 was appointed Visiting Professor of Drama at the University of Guelph, Ontario. He has produced and directed plays and has lectured extensively on theatre at universities in the United States, Canada and South America.

Mr. Richards, a New York City resident, is now at work on *The Best Short Plays 1977* and a collection of Antoinette Perry (Tony) Award plays.